Just Methods
An Interdisciplinary Feminist Reader

EDITED BY ALISON M. JAGGAR

Paradigm Publishers
Boulder • London

Copyright © 2008 Paradigm Publishers

Published in the United States by Paradigm Publishers, 2845 Wilderness Place, Boulder, CO 80301 USA.

Paradigm Publishers is the trade name of Birkenkamp & Company, LLC, Dean Birkenkamp, President and Publisher.

Library of Congress Cataloging-in-Publication Data

Just methods : an interdisciplinary feminist reader / edited by Alison M. Jaggar.
    p. cm.
  Includes bibliographical references and index.
  ISBN 978-1-59451-204-9 (alk. paper)
  1. Women's studies—Methodology.   2. Women—Research—Methodology.   3.
Research—Methodology.   4. Research—Moral and ethical aspects.   5. Feminist theory.
I. Jaggar, Alison M.
  HQ1180.J87 2007
  305.42072—dc22

                                                                        2007014974

Printed and bound in the United States of America on acid free paper that meets the standards of the American National Standard for Permanence of Paper for Printed Library Materials.

Designed and Typeset by Straight Creek Bookmakers.

12 11 10 09 08 2 3 4 5

Contents

PART II. FEMINISTS RETHINKING METHODOLOGY

Acknowledgments

This reader evolved from several years of teaching WMST 5190, a course in feminist methodology required for the University of Colorado Graduate Certificate in Women's Studies (now Women and Gender Studies). Teaching this class was a wonderful learning experience for me and I am extremely grateful to all the lively and engaged graduate students who helped me to figure out which readings did and did not work and also made suggestions for readings that would work better.

I am also grateful to many friends and colleagues who made innumerable valuable suggestions. Some of them were anonymous reviewers of the initial proposal but Dr. Jackie Colby and Dr. Annette Dula were especially generous in helping me think about feminist methodology in the health sciences.

I have been delighted by the opportunity to work with Paradigm Publishers, whose staff members bring personal as well as professional enthusiasm to the books they publish. I am especially appreciative of the support provided by Publisher Dean Birkenkamp, Director of Production and Philosophy Editor Jason Potter, and Managing Editor Melanie Stafford.

This book would never have been completed without the dedicated work of Audra King, currently a Ph.D candidate in the Philosophy Department at the University of Colorado. Audra was involved at every stage of preparing this book, suggesting selections, searching for alternative selections, editing the selections we chose, and pursuing sources and permissions. I hardly know how to express my appreciation for Audra's vision, resourcefulness, and generosity.

Finally, my children and partner David continued to provide encouragement and David also provided much appreciated culinary support.

Introduction: The Project of Feminist Methodology

Feminist methodology seeks to assess knowledge-generating strategies in terms of their suitability for feminist research. The readings in this book present a variety of views regarding such strategies, their strengths, and their weaknesses. The introduction offers some preliminary comments about the project of feminist methodology and its relationship to feminist research.

WHAT IS FEMINISM?

I myself have never been able to find out precisely what feminism is: I only know that people call me a feminist whenever I express sentiments that differentiate me from a doormat.
—Rebecca West, *The Clarion*, November 14, 1913

Feminism is a cluster of social and political ideals that continuously evolve and change. As with other large social values, such as freedom, justice, equality, and democracy, feminism's meanings are constantly in dispute. Many alternative visions of a feminist world exist, as do alternative histories of feminism. Some visions are incompatible with each other and some histories find feminist activism among people to whom the word and perhaps the concept were unknown. The ongoing and often passionate disputes about feminism's meaning and history reveal the continuing importance of feminist ideals in a world where women and those categorized as feminine are disproportionately subjected to violence, impoverishment, and marginalization; they also indicate the vitality of the countless varied struggles worldwide to put an end to these forms of domination.

Since feminism's meanings and boundaries are so contested, no definition of feminism is uncontroversial or authoritative. For the purposes of this book, however, I take feminism to refer to activity directed toward transforming social arrangements and systems of thought that accord disproportionate honor, authority, and power to men and to whatever is categorized as masculine—and that simultaneously degrade and subordinate women and whatever is defined culturally as feminine, including many groups of men. Since women and men are always located within various systems of social power, and since culturally defined constructions of sex and gender are always interwoven with other constructions of inequality, such as class, caste, religion, sexuality, and nation, feminist activism is typically continuous with other activity directed toward promoting justice and equality.

WHAT IS FEMINIST RESEARCH?

When a self-identified feminist research movement first surfaced in North America and Western Europe in the late 1960s and early 1970s, feminist research was often equated with the study of women and the symbolically feminine. This is hardly surprising, since much research of the period did indeed focus on women and the feminine. Some of this research revealed previously unacknowledged violence and discrimination against women; the hitherto well-kept secrets of systematic domestic abuse, rape, and incest were made public at this time. Some research challenged accepted theories that portrayed women as deficient or inferior to men; some offered new accounts of women's previously unrecognized or devalued capacities or achievements; some research did all of these at once. Scholarly literatures burgeoned in areas such as "women in society," "women in literature" and "women's" history, psychology, and art. Scholars engaged in this research often viewed their work as remedying the Western tradition's neglect or devaluation of women and women's achievements, so the belief that feminist research consisted in the study of women and the symbolically feminine became institutionalized in many programs of "women's studies" that were founded in the 1970s.

Equating feminist research with the study of women and the culturally feminine was soon seen to be simplistic. One obvious reason was that these objects of study were not new; on the contrary, women have been studied for centuries and ideas of the feminine have been long been explored in the arts and humanities, social sciences, and even physical sciences. Rather than addressing material different from that pursued in traditional fields of study, the new feminist research often focused on the same material but interpreted it differently. These new interpretations sometimes challenged basic assumptions in existing disciplines and made it impossible simply to "add women and stir" them into established systems of disciplinary knowledge. For instance, a focus on women's history revealed the limits of widely accepted ways of categorizing historical periods; a focus on women's psychology revealed the male bias in prevailing conceptions of "human" psychology; a focus on women's art and literature revealed that standards of artistic excellence were tilted toward masculine sensibilities.

It quickly became evident that equating feminist research with the study of women and the symbolically feminine was misguided also for a second reason, namely that women and men—and masculinities and femininities—are always constructed in relation to each other. Feminist scholars recognized that incorporating feminist insights about women and the feminine into existing systems of knowledge requires simultaneously reexamining prevailing understandings of men and the masculine. Indeed, they argued, incorporating these insights ultimately requires rethinking much that hitherto had been taken as human but that feminist research revealed to be overtly or covertly masculine.

Feminist research cannot be identified primarily by its objects of study. Although it often focuses on women, women's productions, and the symbolically feminine, it also often addresses men and men's productions, the symbolically masculine, animals, and other aspects of the nonhuman world. It cannot even be identified by its focus on gender disparities, since these too may be studied from perspectives that are not feminist. In principle, the subject matter of feminist scholarship has no limits; anything, from anthropology to zoology, may be studied from a feminist perspective. To date, most feminist research has occurred in the humanities, arts, social sciences, and biological sciences, but no field of study is exempt in principle from feminist scrutiny.

Just as feminist research is not to be identified with any particular objects of study, neither is it identical with any specific set of theories, doctrines, or knowledge claims. Although feminist research has produced a body of scholarship and counterscholarship that often challenges prevailing views in various disciplines, the research itself is defined by no orthodox substantive content. For instance, it would be a mistake to identify feminist psychology with a commitment to the relational self or feminist ethics with the ethics of care. Although bodies of work certainly exist that many feminist scholars regard as canonical, the feminist canon is diverse and undergoes continual transformation. Many developments regarded as groundbreaking discoveries by the feminist scholars of yesteryear are seen by today's feminists as naïve, incomplete, biased, or downright wrong. Feminist research cannot be equated with any specific set, or sets, of knowledge claims.

Rather than being identified in terms of either its substantive content or its objects of study, feminist research is distinguished by its commitment to producing knowledge useful in opposing the many varieties of gender injustice. Feminist research pursues knowledge that is free from gender and related biases and so does not lend itself to rationalizing the subordination of women and others subjected to oppressive constructions of sex and gender, including many men. Instead of being a specific product, feminist research is a tradition of inquiry that seeks knowledge for emancipation.

That feminist research has social commitments does not make it unique. Most research traditions are motivated by larger social purposes and their products are rarely if ever value-free. However, feminist inquiry is unusual in being explicit about its ethical and political stance, which motivates feminists to seek out and challenge the social biases lurking often unnoticed in existing knowledge claims. In the end, the tradition of feminist research is uniquely distinguished by its dedication to the value of gender justice in knowledge and in the world, a dedication that carries with it a commitment to oppose all those other injustices that are inseparable from gender divisions.

The social commitments of feminist inquiry are manifested both critically and constructively. Feminist research confronts scholarship that rationalizes some men's dominance over other men and most women, as well as the dominance of the culturally masculine over the culturally feminine. It challenges asymmetric and inequitable constructions of masculinities and femininities, systematically related and gendered sets of norms and symbols that seem always to be interwoven with other oppressive constructions, such as class, ethnicity, and nation. These complex constructions rationalize unequal and exploitative divisions of labor by assigning different tasks and values to individuals categorized as biologically male and female, as well as to those categorized as racially, religiously, or otherwise superior and inferior. Feminist researchers seek to rethink the related ways in which the symbolically masculine is overvalued in specific cultures and the symbolically feminine is undervalued, and they pursue new knowledge likely to be valuable in the quest for gender equity. At its heart, therefore, feminist research is a socially engaged tradition of intellectual work; it is scholarship that seeks epistemic truth and social justice.

WHO PRACTICES FEMINIST RESEARCH?

As an enterprise that frequently challenges established knowledge, feminist research has a long history outside the academy. Feminist activists and scholars with no academic affiliation have long produced works that sometimes have become classics. In the late 1960s and early 1970s, however, a self-identified feminist research movement emerged in North America. Groundbreaking work was done by graduate students and junior academics but they often faced hostility because their ideas collided with established scholarship. Women's studies programs were founded both to provide an academic home for embattled feminist scholars and also to encourage interdisciplinary work. Many scholars hoped that these programs would be transitional and that the products of feminist research would eventually be incorporated into the mainstreams of the various existing disciplines.

Today, almost four decades later, feminist work has had considerable influence on several disciplines, but feminist ideas are still widely controversial; for instance, a conservative website recently included *The Second Sex* by Simone de Beauvoir and *The Feminine Mystique* by Betty Friedan on its list of the ten most dangerous books. Independent institutional bases of feminist scholarship are still needed, though many erstwhile women's studies programs now include the word gender in their names and a very few proclaim themselves to be programs in feminist studies—which would be a courageous move in today's political climate. Much feminist research emerges from these programs and from related programs such as ethnic studies and sexuality studies, but groups of feminist scholars are also active in most traditional disciplines. Some feminist research is still done by activists and other research is done under the auspices of organizations such as Oxfam and the United Nations, as well as at think tanks such as the Institute for Women's Policy Research and the Women's Research and Education Institute.

Most feminist scholars to date have been women but many male scholars have also carried out valuable feminist research. Often but certainly not always male scholars have studied constructions of masculinities.

WHAT IS GOOD FEMINIST RESEARCH?

We have seen that feminist research resembles other research traditions in being infused by social values but that it is distinguished primarily by its commitment to the specific values of gender equity and empowerment. Advancing these social values requires that inquiry be guided by additional epistemic and ethical values.

First, it is unlikely that gender equity will be promoted in the long run by research that is biased or partial or that pleads for narrow interests. Thus, feminist research in every discipline must aspire to that discipline's highest standards of soundness, credibility, and trustworthiness. It must aim to meet discipline-appropriate standards of empirical adequacy, reliability, transferability, accountability, validity, and objectivity. Second, any research process that can plausibly claim to be feminist must be guided by feminist ethical principles; these must inform the selection and design of its research programs, its strategies for gathering and interpreting evidence, and its approaches to publicizing its results.

Happily, it appears that these various conditions may often be mutually supporting. For instance, not only does gender equity require knowledge that is trustworthy and produced by means that are compatible with feminist ethical/political principles; in addition, and as we shall see, many feminist scholars have argued that trustworthiness is likely to be increased when inquiry is motivated by emancipatory aims and utilizes methods that are just. Thus, epistemic truth and social justice often promote each other.

The value of self-styled feminist research is not guaranteed by the good intentions of the researchers; in any field of endeavor, gaps exist between intention and execution. In practice, research proclaimed as feminist may incorporate dominant social values, rely on inadequate evidence, draw flawed inferences, or violate feminist ethical principles. The best feminist research comes as close as possible to meeting its sociopolitical, epistemic, and ethical commitments, but success is always a matter of degree.

WHAT IS FEMINIST METHODOLOGY?

Almost two decades ago, Sandra Harding helpfully distinguished among the terms *method*, *methodology*, and *epistemology* (1987:2–3). She noted that research methods are techniques for gathering evidence. Since evidence is typically discipline-specific, so are the methods for gathering it; they may involve investigating archives, looking into cloud chambers, taking surveys, analyzing samples, or reading texts. Methodologies, as Harding explained them, are theories and analyses of how research should proceed and how evidence should be gathered. Finally, epistemologies raise questions on a higher level of abstraction about the possibility and nature of knowledge. They explore how knowledge claims are justified and what the grounds are for according authority to knowers.

The discussions in this book occur on the level of methodology, though they inevitably intersect with questions of both epistemology and method. Because techniques of inquiry are typically discipline-specific, the volume is in no way intended as a handbook providing detailed instruction in the specific practices used to acquire knowledge in various disciplines. Instead, it is designed to help researchers think critically and constructively about methodology in a broad sense, which includes not only techniques for gathering evidence but also processes of selecting and designing research projects and publicizing their results. The readings reflect on the epistemic, political, and ethical assumptions and implications of these processes as they have been used or abused in several disciplines. Feminist methodology is itself one type of feminist research.

One main theme of the readings, as suggested by the title of the book, is the complex interrelationship between social power and inequality, on the one hand, and the production of knowledge on the other. Many readings illustrate how the production of knowledge in many disciplines has been shaped by inegalitarian assumptions and priorities and how the knowledge produced has then been used to rationalize, reinforce, normalize, and naturalize social inequalities.

A second and related theme is the inseparability of research projects and methods from social and ethical values. Since no research can be value-free, readings expose the social and ethical values that have been incorporated into past research projects at various levels. They encourage researchers to be aware of the value commitments that inevitably inform their projects and help them reflect on how these commitments can be maintained at all levels of their research processes.

STRUCTURE OF THE VOLUME

The volume is divided into two main parts, each with several chapters.

Part I presents feminist critiques (several now classic) of various research strategies used in the humanities and the social and biological sciences. The readings reveal how this research has often devalued the authority of women (or marginalized groups of women or men) as knowers, generated knowledge biased against women (or other marginalized groups), and/or violated feminist ethical principles.

Part II develops a variety of approaches to remedying problems identified in mainstream research methodology. Many of these approaches are naturalized, in the sense of taking their inspiration from practices of producing knowledge utilized by women or by feminists. For instance, feminist empiricism seeks to ground feminist research in the specific experiences of women; feminist standpoint theory contends that different social locations make possible different views on social reality, some of which are more illuminating than others; feminist postmodernism rejects the view that knowledge has foundations and presents epistemic concepts such as reason, truth, and objectivity as value-laden and contested. The final sections of the book focus on topics related to feminists' search for more epistemically reliable and ethically responsible strategies for producing knowledge. They consider how feminists should think about objectivity, how research might be democratized, and how it may be informed by feminist ethics.

REFERENCES

Harding, Sandra, ed. 1987. *Feminism and Methodology.* Bloomington: Indiana University Press.
West, Rebecca, 1911–1917. "Selections of Rebecca West's Writings," in *The Young Rebecca,* edited by Jane Marcus. London: Macmillan, 1982.

Part I

FEMINIST CRITIQUES OF METHODOLOGY

1

The Humanities

The humanities are a cluster of disciplines dedicated to studying the human condition and the meanings of human life. In an influential 1959 lecture and subsequent book, *The Two Cultures,* British scientist and novelist C. P. Snow drew a sharp contrast between the humanities and the sciences based on their respective methodologies. He contended that the humanities and the sciences comprised two distinct cultures in modern society and that the breakdown of communication between them was a major obstacle to solving the problems of the world. Snow's work was widely read and discussed in Great Britain and North America, where the expression "two cultures" became popular shorthand for the supposed contrasts between two methodological approaches to understanding the world. Scientific methods were understood as designed to screen out the influence of emotion and value; they were seen as quantitative, precise, systematic, and reliant on observations that could be replicated by any properly situated observer. They produced knowledge regarded as objective in the sense of invariant across time and culture. By contrast, the knowledge produced in the humanities was seen as expressing the distinctive insight and vision of a unique human consciousness, and the methods of the humanities were recognized as purposely utilizing emotion and value. Although the knowledge produced in the humanities is often valued for its universal meaning, it is infused simultaneously with the subjectivity of specific individuals and with the values of specific times and places.

These widely accepted accounts of the contrasts between methodology in the humanities, on the one hand, and the sciences, on the other, are embodied in the administrative structure of contemporary knowledge-producing institutions and funding agencies. Today, humanities disciplines include philosophy, the classics, literature, literary criticism, comparative literature, art, art history, art criticism, art theory, music, and musicology. Cultural and area studies of regional interdisciplinary fields such as American Studies, East Asian Studies, and Middle Eastern Studies are also often categorized as humanities disciplines, although they include methods characteristic of the social sciences. Another borderline discipline is history, traditionally regarded as central to the humanities but moving increasingly in the direction of social science. It should also be noted that several disciplines categorized administratively as social sciences, such as cultural anthropology, sociology, political science, archaeology, and parts of economics, in fact often include qualitative descriptions and analyses of the types regarded as characteristic of the humanities.

Administrative distinctions among disciplines do not reflect natural divisions among kinds of knowledge; instead, they are historically and culturally contingent artifacts, which inevitably incorporate a degree of arbitrariness and stereotyping. One theme running through this book is that the supposed contrasts between methodologies in the sciences and the humanities are often overdrawn; in particular, that the methods used in the social sciences include more humanistic and evaluative elements than is commonly supposed. However, the present chapter includes methodological reflections from disciplines of philosophy, history, and literature, generally categorized as humanities. These disciplines are quite diverse but reflection on their methods reveals some parallels across the disciplines as they have evolved over the past four decades in response to feminist challenges.

FEMINIST METHODOLOGY AS CRITIQUE OF ANDROCENTRISM

Western feminist scholarship in the humanities at first took the form of a revolt against the exclusion of women and the culturally feminine from traditional Western ideals of what it means to be human. In the late 1960s and early 1970s, feminist historians challenged the presentation of Western history as a narrative of men's achievements, an unending parade of kings, generals, and statesmen. Similarly, feminist literary critics pointed to overwhelmingly male literary representations of heroes, facing distinctively masculine predicaments and coming of age or proving themselves through distinctively masculine adventures; if women in literature had adventures, the critics noted, they were typically sexual adventures. Feminist philosophers pointed out that Western philosophy imagined the ideal human as male; the ideal knower was a man of reason; the ideal citizen was a male property-owning warrior. If philosophers discussed women as knowers, it was generally to derogate their reasoning capacities by portraying them as emotional and intuitive; if they noticed women's work, which made possible the leisure and wealth of the ideal male citizen, they represented it as closer to nature than men's and less than fully human.

Feminists responded to these exclusions by revising the humanities to include women and the culturally feminine. Feminist critics began to focus on portrayals of women and gender in literature and also to study the work of women writers. Feminist philosophers began to challenge philosophical construction of the feminine as inferior to the masculine and to recuperate the work of long-forgotten women philosophers. A few women had always been present in traditional histories, mostly warriors and queens (or warrior queens) such as Joan of Arc, Catherine the Great, Cleopatra, and Boadicea; however, feminist historians began to focus also on more ordinary women in those spheres of life culturally defined as feminine. They supplemented diplomatic and military histories with social and family histories.

Feminist work in the humanities was conceived originally as a project of inclusion and balance. Its values were those of equality and androgyny, and it insisted that women were as fully human as men, including being as capable of participating in humanities scholarship. However, the feminist project of expanding the humanities canon provoked queries about why male-dominant ideals of humanity had been presented and accepted for so long. Could it be because most artists and humanities scholars had been male, producing art and knowledge for overwhelmingly masculine audiences? Methodological questions began to be raised about the "male gaze" of artists and audiences and about what it might mean to "read as a woman." Philosopher Janice Moulton argues that philosophy's dominant method, the adversary paradigm, reflects values that are culturally masculine; she points out some limitations of this method, which facilitates silencing people with less social power and confidence, including many women. Feminist concerns about exclusion developed into concerns about bias and misrepresentation.

GYNOCENTRIC METHODOLOGY

Feminist scholars of the 1970s and early 1980s quickly discovered that expanding the canon required more than simply inserting materials dealing with or authored by women. In an often-quoted phrase, feminist scholarship is not just a matter of adding women and stirring. As Joan Kelly-Gadol points out, women's lives cannot always be understood through categories developed to make sense of men's lives; for instance, periods traditionally categorized as times of progress in Western history were often times when the status of women declined. Declaring that women are fully human means more than insisting that women are capable of performing men's activities and living up to male standards; this simply pushes women into a masculine mold. Some argued that the male-biased ideals that have pervaded the Western humanities must be challenged and supplemented or even replaced by more gynocentric ideals.

Gynocentric feminist scholarship sought to transfer women from the margins to the center of the humanities. Its methodology called for rebuilding the humanities from women's perspective. The new canon would be informed not only by feminist critiques of androcentrism but also by distinctively feminine perspectives, methods, and values. Thus, in the 1980s the ethics of care was promoted as a distinctively feminine way of doing ethics. A classic example of the gynocentric approach is artist Judy Chicago's heroic-scale installation, *The Dinner Party*, which features an enormous triangular table set for thirty-nine women. The installation utilizes media that are culturally associated with the feminine, porcelain plates and intricate textiles, and each plate features an image based on the butterfly, symbolizing the central core of a vagina.

Gynocentric feminist methodology was also known as "difference feminism." It recognized that gender differences are also inequalities, so that men and whatever is categorized as masculine receive disproportionate honor, authority, and power, and women and whatever is culturally defined as feminine are degraded and subordinated. Gynocentric feminist methodology inverted traditional gender valuations, seeking to replace the ideal man of the Western humanities tradition with an ideal woman. However, the emphasis on supposed differences between men and women and between the culturally masculine and the culturally feminine obscured many other differences among them.

DIFFERENCE AS METHODOLOGY IN THE HUMANITIES

Feminist methodological debates of the 1980s were dominated by concerns about what came to be called essentialism. In the context of feminist methodology, essentialism is the assumption that it is possible to identify a generic woman and a generic man, whose characteristics represent women's and men's real natures and whose situations represent the universal condition of each sex. Critics of essentialism pointed out that the supposedly universal woman at the center of gynocentric feminist theory has often been privileged along a number of dimensions; for instance, like most of the guests at *The Dinner Party*, she was often imagined as white, Western, and upper- or middle-class. The supposedly universal man was imagined as similarly privileged. When the situation of privileged women and men is taken as the model for understanding the situation of all women and men, those who are less privileged—who are the large majority—either become invisible or are "othered," that is, treated as exceptions to the norm. Political strategies recommended on the basis of these models are likely to disregard the interests of those seen as "other."

Feminist challenges to essentialist methodologies were continuous with the challenges to universal theorizing posed by other new disciplines such as queer theory and ethnic and postcolonial studies. Work in these disciplines revealed that supposedly universal representations of humanity typically incorporated historically contingent values and reflected specific political interests. They brought into question the Western humanities' traditional aspiration to present a view of the human condition *sub specie aeternitatis*.

The category of difference began to be used in a new way to explore the production of social identities through the interplay of historical forces and individual agency. Differences were regarded as contested and identities as only temporarily stable. Lines between disciplines were blurred as scholars in one discipline borrowed methods from others. For instance, the so-called new historicist approach in literary criticism encouraged reading sociological, medical, legal, and political documents alongside literary texts.

CONTEMPORARY CHALLENGES FOR FEMINIST
METHODOLOGY IN THE HUMANITIES

The humanities are often regarded as illuminating universal values, but for feminists they have political as well as ethical significance. The Western humanities tradition frequently glorifies "the" human individual, who is simultaneously unique and representative of all humanity. Over the past thirty years, feminist studies, together with other disciplines such as queer theory and ethnic and postcolonial studies, have not only revealed the specific, partial, and local values often used to characterize the universal human; they have also questioned when any individual can ever stand for all. Yet reflection on the value and meaning of human life still seems indispensable. One challenge for feminist methodology in the humanities is to consider how to construct salient categories between the individual and the universal, and how to recognize systematic forms of domination while finding humanity in diversity.

A second challenge may be to contest the cultural categorization of the humanities as feminine. Whether the division between "two cultures" of the sciences and the humanities was gender neutral when it was drawn a half century ago, today it is interpreted in deeply gendered terms. For instance, many regard the sciences as providing objectivity while the humanities offer only insight. Both the sciences and the humanities aspire to universality, but conclusions of the sciences are presented with mathematical precision in which the only aesthetic quality is a spare elegance; by contrast, the value of the humanities lies in their form as much as their content. The sciences are technical and professionalized, whereas the humanities are broad, interdisciplinary, and allow intervention by amateurs. The sciences are directed toward the pragmatic masculine goal of controlling the world, whereas the humanities are thought to beautify, enrich, and add ethical value to life. The sciences are thought to serve the public interest. The interests served by the humanities are those of the private, feminine sphere. Finally, the sciences have become increasingly wealthy in comparison with the humanities.

These factors as well as the influence of feminism may help to explain why women scholars are clustered disproportionately in the humanities rather than the sciences. One of the few humanities disciplines in which men still far outnumber women is philosophy, perhaps because many philosophers struggle to promote an image of their discipline that resembles the sciences in being technical, precise, and objective; it may not be accidental that philosophy is also the humanities discipline in which feminist work remains the most marginal. Feminist scholars are especially well placed to challenge the gendered methodological stereotypes that rationalize the devaluation of the humanities in the academic hierarchy and in the public mind.

Joan Kelly-Gadol

The Social Relation of the Sexes: Methodological Implications of Women's History

. . .

Women's history has a dual goal: to restore women to history and to restore our history to women. . . . In seeking to add women to the fund of historical knowledge, women's history has revitalized theory, for it has shaken the conceptual foundations of historical study. It has done this by making problematical three of the basic concerns of historical thought: (1) periodization, (2) the categories of social analysis, and (3) theories of social change.

. . . I should also like to show how the conception of these problems expresses a notion which is basic to feminist consciousness, namely, that the relation between the sexes is a social and not a natural one. This perception forms the core idea that upsets traditional thinking in all three cases.

PERIODIZATION

Once we look to history for an understanding of woman's situation, we are, of course, already assuming that woman's situation is a social matter. But history, as we first came to it, did not seem to confirm this awareness. Throughout historical time, women have been largely excluded from making war, wealth, laws, governments, art, and science. Men, functioning in their capacity as historians, considered exactly those activities constitutive of civilization.... Women figured chiefly as exceptions, those who were said to be as ruthless as, or wrote like, or had the brains of men. In redressing this neglect, ... compensatory history is not enough.... Nor could it be another subgroup of historical thought, a history of women to place alongside the list of diplomatic history, economic history, and so forth, for all these developments impinged upon the history of women. Hence feminist scholarship in history ... came to focus primarily on the issue of women's status. I use "status" ... throughout ... to refer to ... the roles and positions women hold in society by comparison with those of men.

In historical terms, this means to look at ages or movements of great social change in terms of their liberation or repression of woman's potential, their import for the advancement of her humanity as well as "his." The moment ... one assumes that women are a part of humanity in the fullest sense—the period or set of events with which we deal takes on a wholly different character or meaning from the normally accepted one. Indeed, what emerges is a fairly regular pattern of relative loss of status for women precisely in those periods of so-called progressive change.[2] ... [I]f we apply Fourier's famous dictum—that the emancipation of women is an index of the general emancipation of an age—our notions of so-called progressive developments, such as classical Athenian civilization, the Renaissance, and the French Revolution, undergo a startling reevaluation. For women, "progress" in Athens meant concubinage and confinement of citizen wives in the gynecaeum. In Renaissance Europe it meant domestication of the bourgeois wife and escalation of witchcraft persecution, which crossed class lines. And the Revolution expressly excluded women from its liberty, equality, and "fraternity." Suddenly we see these ages with a new, double vision—and each eye sees a different picture.

... Only one of these views has been represented by history up to now. Regardless of how these periods have been assessed, they have been assessed from the vantage point of men. Liberal historiography in particular, which considers all three periods as stages in the progressive realization of an individualistic social and cultural order, expressly maintains—albeit without considering the evidence—that women shared these advances with men. In Renaissance scholarship, for example, almost all historians have been content to situate women exactly where Jacob Burckhardt placed them in 1890: "on a footing of perfect equality with men." For a period that rejected the hierarchy of social class and the hierarchy of religious values in its restoration of a classical, secular culture, there was also, they claim, "no question of 'woman's rights' or female emancipation, simply because the thing itself was a matter of course."[3] Now while it is true that a couple of dozen women can be assimilated to the humanistic standard of culture which the Renaissance imposed upon itself, what is remarkable is that *only* a couple of dozen women can. To pursue this problem is to become aware of the fact that there was no "renaissance" for women—at least not during the Renaissance. There was, on the contrary, a marked restriction of the scope and powers of women. Moreover, this restriction is a consequence of the very developments for which the age is noted.

What feminist historiography has done is to unsettle such accepted evaluations of historical periods. It has disabused us of the notion that the history of women is the same as the history of men and that significant turning points in history have the same impact for one sex as for the other. Indeed, some historians now go so far as to maintain that, because of woman's particular connection with the function of reproduction, history could, and women's history should, be rewritten and periodized from this point of view, according to major turning points affecting childbirth, sexuality, family structure, and so forth.[5] ... [A]lthough the logic of [my] thought ... protests against a periodization that is primarily geared to changes in reproduction. Such criteria threaten to detach psychosexual development and family patterns from changes in the general social order....

To my mind, what is more promising about the way periodization has begun to function in women's history is that it has become *relational*. It relates the history of women to that of men, as Engels did in *The Origin of the Family, Private Property and the State,* by seeing in common social developments institutional reasons for the advance of one sex and oppression of the other. Handled this way, traditional periodizing concepts may well be retained—and ought to be insofar as they refer to major structural changes in society. But in the evaluation of such changes we need to consider their effects upon women as distinct from men.... When women are excluded from the benefits of the economic, political, and cultural advances made in certain periods, a situation which gives women a different historical experience from men, it is to those "advances" we must look to find the reasons for that separation of the sexes.

SEX AS A SOCIAL CATEGORY

Two convictions are implicit in this more complete and more complex sense of periodization: one, that women do form a distinctive social group and, second, that the invisibility of this group in traditional history is not to be ascribed to female nature. These notions ... affect another, related change in the conceptual foundations of history by introducing sex as a category of social thought.

Feminism has made it evident that the mere fact of being a woman meant having a particular kind of social and hence historical experience, but the exact meaning of "woman" in this historical or social sense has not been so clear. What accounts for woman's situation as "other," and what perpetuates it historically? The "Redstockings Manifesto" of 1969 maintained that "women are an oppressed class" and suggested that the relations between men and women are class relations, that "sexual politics" are the politics of class domination. The most fruitful consequence of this conception of women as a social class has been the extension of class analysis to women by Marxist feminists such as Margaret Benston and Sheila Rowbotham.[6] They have traced the roots of woman's secondary status in history to economics inasmuch as women as a group have had a distinctive relation to production and property in almost all societies. The personal and psychological consequences of secondary status can be seen to flow from this special relation to work. As Rowbotham and Benston themselves make clear, however, it is one thing to extend the tools of class analysis to women and quite another to maintain that women *are* a class. Women belong to social classes, and the new women's history and histories of feminism have borne this out.[7]...

On the other hand, ... women as a group cut through male class systems. Although I would quarrel with the notion that women of all classes, in all cultures, and at all times are accorded secondary status, there is certainly sufficient evidence that this is generally, if not universally, the case. From the advent of civilization, and hence of history proper as distinct from prehistorical societies, the social order has been patriarchal. Does that then make women a caste, a hereditary inferior order? This notion has its uses, too, as does the related one drawn chiefly from American black experience, which regards women as a minority group.[8] The sense of "otherness" which both these ideas convey is essential to our historical awareness of women as an oppressed social group. They help us appreciate the social formation of "femininity" as an internalization of ascribed inferiority which serves, at the same time, to manipulate those who have the authority women lack. As explanatory concepts, however, notions of caste and minority group are not productive when applied to women. Why should this majority be a minority? And why is it that the members of this particular caste, unlike all other castes, are not of the same rank throughout society? Clearly the minority psychology of women, like their caste status and quasi-class oppression, has to be traced to the universally distinguishing feature of all women, namely their sex.... In short, women have to be defined as women. We are the social opposite ... of a sex: men. We are a sex, and categorization by gender no longer implies a mothering role and subordination to men, except as social role and relation recognized as such, as socially constructed and socially imposed.

A good part of the initial excitement in women's studies consisted of this discovery, that what had been taken as "natural" was in fact manmade, both as social order and as description of that order as natural and physically determined. Examples of such ideological reasoning go back to the story of Eve, but the social sciences have been functioning the same way, as myth reinforcing patriarchy....

Historians could not lay claim to special knowledge about the "natural" roles and relation of the sexes, but they knew what that order was, or ought to be. History simply tended to confirm it. *Bryan's Dictionary of Painters and Engravers* of 1904 says of the Renaissance artist, Propertia Rossi: "a lady of Bologna, best known as a sculptor and carver, but who also engraved upon copper, and learnt drawing and design from Marc Antonio. She is said to have been remarkable for her beauty, virtues, and talents, and to have died at an early age in 1530, in consequence of unrequited love. Her last work was a bas-relief of Joseph and Potiphar's wife!"[12] An exclamation mark ends the entry, ... signifying that the "lady," ... who was beautiful and unhappy in love, was naturally absorbed by just that. Historians really *knew* why there were no great women artists. That is why it was not a historical problem until the feminist art historian, Linda Nochlin, posed it as such—by inquiring into the institutional factors, rather than the native gifts, that sustain artistic activity.[13]

When the issue of woman's place did appear openly, and male historians such as H. D. Kitto rose to defend "their" society, the Greek in his case, the natural order of things again came to the rescue.[14] ... Kitto's major argument was reserved for the family: its religious and social importance in Athenian society.... He rightly points out that extinction of a family or dissipation of its property was regarded as a disaster. But for him, this fact is an argument, for his position is that it is woman's "natural" place to serve that family and continue it by raising legitimate heirs through whom to pass on its property and its rites. If, under the conditions of Greek society, that task should require confinement to the household and its rounds, that justifies the legal disabilities of wives. As for the other orders of women Athenian society demanded and regulated by law, concubines are not mentioned and hetaerae are "adventuresses who had said No to the serious business of life. Of course they amused men—'But, my dear fellow, one doesn't *marry a* woman like that.'"

Kitto wrote his history in 1951.

If our understanding of the Greek contribution to social life and consciousness now demands an adequate representation of the life experience of women, so too the sexual order, as shaped by the institutions of family and state, is a matter we now regard as not merely worthy of historical inquiry but central to it. This, I think, is a second major contribution women's history has made to the theory and practice of history in general. We have made of sex a category as fundamental to our analysis of the social order as other classifications, such as class and race. And we consider the relation of the sexes, as those of class and race, to be socially rather than naturally constituted, to have its own development, varying with changes in social organization.... Our new sense of periodization reflects an assessment of historical change from the vantage point of women as well as men. Our use of sex as a social category means that our conception of historical change itself, as change in the social order, is broadened to include changes in the relation of the sexes....

The activity, power, and cultural evaluation of women simply cannot be assessed except in relational terms: by comparison and contrast with the activity, power, and cultural evaluation of men, and in relation to the institutions and social developments that shape the sexual order....

THEORIES OF SOCIAL CHANGE

If the relationship of the sexes is as necessary to an understanding of human history as the social relationship of classes, what now needs to be worked out are the connections between changes in class and sex relations.[18] For this task, I suggest that we consider significant changes in the respective roles of men and women in the light of fundamental changes in the mode of production. I am not here proposing a simple socioeconomic scheme. A theory of social change that incorporates the relation of the sexes has to consider how general changes in production affect and shape production in the family and, thereby, the respective roles of men and women. And it has to consider, as well, the flow in the other direction: the impact of family life and the relation of the sexes upon psychic and social formations.

    … Engels in particular solidly established the social character of woman's relation to man, although it was only one change in that relation—albeit the major one—that concerned him: the transition to patriarchy with the advance from kin society to civilization, and the overthrow of patriarchy with the advent of socialism. His analysis of the subordination of women in terms of the emergence of private property and class inequality is basic to much of feminist scholarship today.… Certain conclusions, which in turn open new directions for historical and anthropological research, can already be drawn from this recent work. One is that "woman's social position has not always, everywhere, or in most respects been subordinate to that of men."[19] … The dominant causal feature that emerges from anthropological studies of the sexual order (in the Rosaldo and Lamphere collection I have mentioned) is whether, and to what extent, the domestic and the public spheres of activity are separated from each other. Although what constitutes "domestic" and what "public" varies from culture to culture, and the lines of demarcation are differently drawn, a consistent pattern emerges when societies are placed on a scale where, at one end, familial and public activities are fairly merged, and, at the other, domestic and public activities are sharply differentiated.

    Where familial activities coincide with public or social ones, the status of women is comparable or even superior to that of men. This pattern is very much in agreement with Engels's ideas, because in such situations the means of subsistence and production are commonly held and a communal household is the focal point of both domestic and social life. Hence it is in societies where production for exchange is slight and where private property and class inequality are not developed that sex inequalities are least evident. Women's roles are as varied as men's, although there are sex-role differences; authority and power are shared by women and men rather than vested in a hierarchy of males; women are highly evaluated by the culture; and women and men have comparable sexual rights.

    The most one can say about the sexual division of labor in societies at this end of the scale is that there is a tendency toward mother/child or women/children grouping and toward male hunting and warfare. This "natural" division of labor, if such it is, is not yet socially determined. That is, men as well as women care for children and perform household tasks, and women as well as men hunt. The social organization of work, and the rituals and values that grow out of it, do not serve to separate out the sexes and place one under the authority of the other. They do just that at the opposite end of the scale where the domestic and public orders are clearly distinguished from each other. Women continue to be active producers all the way up the scale, … but they steadily lose control over property, products, and themselves as surplus increases, private property develops, and the communal household becomes a private economic unit, a family (extended or nuclear) represented by a man. The family itself, the sphere of women's activities, is in turn subordinated to a broader social or public order—governed by a state—which tends to be the domain of men. This is the general pattern presented by historical or civilized societies.

    As we move in this direction on the scale, it becomes evident that sexual inequalities are bound to the control of property.…

    How does this attachment of women to domestic work develop, and what forms does it take? This process is one of the central problems confronting feminist anthropology and history. By definition, this query rejects the traditional, simple biological "reasons" for the definition of woman-as-domestic. The privatizing of child rearing and domestic work and the sex typing of that work are social, not natural, matters. I suggest, therefore, that in treating this problem, we continue to look at *property relations* as the basic determinant of the sexual division of labor and of the sexual order. The more the domestic and the public domains are differentiated, the more work, and hence property, are of two clearly distinguishable kinds. There is production for subsistence and production for exchange. However the productive system of a society is organized, it operates, as Marx pointed out, as a continuous process which reproduces itself: that is, its material means and instruments, its people, and the social relations among them. Looked at as a continuous process (what Marx meant by reproduction), the productive work of society thus includes procreation and the socialization of children who must find their places within the social order.[22] I suggest that what shapes the relation of the sexes is the way this work of procreation and socialization is organized in relation to the organization of work that results in articles for subsistence and/or exchange. In sum, what patriarchy means as a general social order is that women function as the property of men in the maintenance and production of new members of the social order; that these relations of production are worked out in the organization of kin and family; and that other forms of work, such as production of goods and services for immediate use, are generally, although not always, attached to these procreative and socializing functions.[23]

Inequalities of sex as well as class are traced to property relations and forms of work in this scheme, but there are certain evident differences between the two. In the public domain, by which I mean the social order that springs from the organization of the general wealth and labor of society, class inequalities are paramount. For the relation of the sexes, control or lack of control of the property that separates people into owners and workers is not significant. What is significant is whether women *of either class* have equal relations to work or property with men of their class.

In the household or family, on the other hand, where ownership of all property resides in historic societies characterized by private property, sex inequalities are paramount and they cut through class lines. What is significant for the domestic relation is that women in the family, like serfs in feudal Europe, can both have and *be* property....

Regardless of class, and regardless of ownership (although these modify the situation in interesting ways), women have generally functioned as the property of men in the procreative and socializing aspect of the productive work of their society. Women constitute part of the means of production of the private family's mode of work.

Patriarchy, in short, is at home at home. The private family is its proper domain. But the historic forms that patriarchy takes, like its very origin, are to be traced to the society's mode of production. The sexual order varies with the general organization of property and work because this shapes both family and public domains and determines how they approach or recede from each other.

These relations between the domestic and the public orders, in turn, account for many of the unexpected oppositions and juxtapositions expressed by our new sense of historical periods.[25] ... [T]oday, the two domains approach each other as private household functions—child rearing, production of food and clothing, nursing, and so forth—become socially organized. Women can again work and associate with each other outside the household, and the sexual division of labor, although far from overcome, appears increasingly irrational.

Where domestic and public realms pulled apart, however, sexual inequalities became pronounced as did the simultaneous demand for female chastity and prostitution. This was the case with Athens of the classical period, where the private household economy was the basic form of production and the social or public order of the polis consisted of many such households which were subordinated to and governed by it. Wives of the citizenry were confined to the order of the household.... Although necessary to the public order, wives did not directly belong to or participate in it, and free women who fell outside the domestic order and its property arrangements fell outside the public order as well.... The family in modern society has served as the domain for the production and training of the working class. It has been the alleged reason for women having to function as underpaid, irregular laborers whose wages generally had to be supplemented by sexual attachment to a man, inside or outside family arrangements. And it has served to compensate the worker whose means of subsistence were alienated from him but who could have private property in his wife.

Such has been the institutionally determined role of the family under capitalism, and women of both the owning and the working classes, women both in and outside the family, have had their outer and inner lives shaped by the structure of its social relations.

Surely a dominant reason for studying the social relation of the sexes is political. To understand the interests, aside from the personal interests of individual men, that are served by the retention of an unequal sexual order is in itself liberating. It detaches an age-old injustice from the blind operation of social forces and places it in the realm of choice....

But women's history also opens up the other half of history, viewing women as agents and the family as a productive and social force. The most novel and exciting task of the study of the social relation of the sexes is still before us: to appreciate how we are all, women and men, initially humanized, turned into social creatures by the work of that domestic order to which women have been primarily attached. Its character and the structure of its relations order our consciousness, and it is through this consciousness that we first view and construe our world.[26] To understand the historical impact of women, family, and the relation of the sexes upon society serves a less evident political end, but perhaps a more strictly feminist one. For if the historical conception of civilization can be shown to include the psychosocial functions of the family, then with that understanding we can insist that any reconstruction of society along just lines incorporates reconstruction of the family—all kinds of collective and private families, and all of them functioning, not as property relations, but as personal relations among freely associating people.

NOTES

. . .

2. Conference of New England Association of Women Historians, Yale University (October 1973): Marilyn Arthur, Renate Bridenthal, Joan Kelly-Gadol; Second Berkshire Conference on the History of Women, Radcliffe (October 1974): panel on "The Effects of Women's History upon Traditional Historiography," Renate Bridenthal, Joan Kelly-Gadol, Gerda Lerner, Richard Vann (papers deposited at Schlesinger Library); Sarah Lawrence symposium (March 1975): Marilyn Arthur, Renate Bridenthal, Gerda Lerner, Joan Kelly-Gadol (papers available as *Conceptual Frameworks in Women's History* [Bronxville, N.Y.: Sarah Lawrence Publications, 1976]). For some recent comments along some of these same lines, see Carl N. Degler, *Is There a History of Women?* (Oxford: Clarendon Press, 1975)....

3. *The Civilization of the Renaissance in Italy* (London: Phaidon Press, 1950), p. 241. With the exception of Ruth Kelso, *Doctrine for the Lady of the Renaissance* (Urbana: University of Illinois Press, 1956), this view is shared by every work I know of on Renaissance women except for contemporary feminist historians....

. . .

5. Vann (n. 2 above).

6. "Redstockings Manifesto," in *Sisterhood Is Powerful,* ed. Robin Morgan (New York: Random House, 1970), pp. 533–36. Margaret Benston, *The Political Economy of Women's Liberation* (New York: Monthly Review reprint, 1970). Sheila Rowbotham, *Woman's Consciousness, Man's World* (Middlesex: Pelican Books, 1973), with bibliography of the periodical literature....

7. Eleanor Flexner, *Century of Struggle* (New York: Atheneum, 1970); Sheila Rowbotham, *Women, Resistance and Revolution* (New York: Random House, 1974); panel at the Second Berkshire Conference on the History of Women, Radcliffe (n. 2 above), on "Clara Zetkin and Adelheid Popp: The Development of Feminist Awareness in the Socialist Women's Movement—Germany and Austria, 1890–1914," with Karen Honeycutt, Ingurn LaFleur, and Jean Quataert. Karen Honeycutt's paper on Clara Zetkin is in *Feminist Studies* (Winter 1975/76).

8. Helen Mayer Hacker did interesting work along these lines in the 1950s, "Women as a Minority Group," *Social Forces* 30 (October 1951–May 1952): 60–69, and subsequently, "Women as a Minority Group: Twenty Years Later" (Pittsburgh: Know, Inc., 1972). Degler has recently taken up these classifications and also finds he must reject them (see n. 2 above).

. . .

12. *Bryan's Dictionary of Painters and Engravers* (London: Geo. Bell, 1904), 4:285.

13. "Why Have There Been No Great Women Artists?" *Art News* 69, no. 9 (January 1971): 22–39, 67–71.

14. H. D. Kitto, *The Greeks* (Baltimore: Penguin Books, 1962), pp. 219–36.

...

18. See panel papers, *Conceptual Frameworks in Women's History* (n. 2 above).

19. Karen Sacks, "Engels Revisited," in Rosaldo and Lamphere, p. 207. See also Eleanor Leacock's introduction to Engels, *The Origin of the Family, Private Property and the State* (New York: International Publishers, 1972); also Leacock's paper delivered at Columbia University Seminar on Women in Society, April 1975.

...

22. In *Woman's Estate* (New York: Random House, 1973), Juliet Mitchell (developing an earlier essay) offered the categories of reproduction/production within which to consider the history of women.... See my review of Rowbotham in *Science and Society* 39, no. 4 (Winter 1975/76): 471–74, and Lise Vogel's review essay on Juliet Mitchell, "The Earthly Family," *Radical America* 7 (Fall 1973): 9–50.

23. Ideas along these lines have been developed by Rowbotham, *Woman's Consciousness, Man's World;* Bridget O'Laughlin, "Mediation of Contradiction: Why Mbum Women Do Not Eat Chicken," in Rosaldo and Lamphere, pp. 301–20.

...

25. For examples given here, see the articles on the periods in question in Bridenthal and Koonz, *Becoming Visible.*

26. This is one of Rowbotham's points in *Woman's Consciousness, Man's World.* I believe it should lead to development of the genre of psychohistorical studies and studies in family history exemplified by Philippe Aries, *Centuries of Childhood: A Social History of Family Life* (New York: Alfred A. Knopf, 1965); Nancy Chodorow, "Family Structure and Feminine Personality," in Rosaldo and Lamphere, pp. 43–67; David Hunt, *Parents and Children in History* (New York: Harper & Row, 1972); the Frankfurt school in *Autorität und Emilie,* ed. Max Horkheimer (Paris: Alcan, 1936); Wilhelm Reich, *The Mass Psychology of Fascism* (New York: Farrar, Straus & Giroux, 1970); and Eli Zaretsky, "Capitalism, the Family and Personal Life," *Socialist Revolution* nos. 13, 14, 16 (1973). See the excellent article on this mode of historical inquiry by Lawrence Stone, in the *New York Review of Books* 21 (November 14, 1974): 25.

Janice Moulton

A Paradigm of Philosophy: The Adversary Method

THE UNHAPPY CONFLATION OF AGGRESSION WITH SUCCESS

It is frequently thought that there are attributes, or kinds of behavior, that it is good for one sex to have and bad for the other sex to have. Aggression is a particularly interesting example of such an attribute. This paper investigates and criticizes a model of philosophic methodology that accepts a positive view of aggressive behavior and uses it as a paradigm of philosophic reasoning. But before I turn to this paradigm, I want to challenge the broader view of aggression that permits it positive connotations.

Defined as "an offensive action or procedure, especially a culpable unprovoked overt hostile attack," aggression normally has well-deserved negative connotations. In human contexts, aggression often invokes anger, uncontrolled rage, and belligerence....

However, this negative concept, when it is specifically connected to males qua males or to workers in certain professions (sales, management, law, philosophy, politics) often takes on positive associations.... [M]ales and workers in certain professions are not required to physically attack or eat their customers and co-workers to be considered aggressive. In these contexts, aggression is thought to be related to more positive concepts such as power, activity, ambition, authority, competence, and effectiveness, concepts that are related to success in these professions. And exhibition of these positive concepts is considered evidence that one is, or has been, aggressive.

Aggression may have no causal bearing on competence, superiority, power, etc., but if many people believe aggressive behavior is a sign of these properties, then one may have to learn to behave aggressively in order to appear competent, to seem superior, and to gain or maintain power. This poses a dilemma for anyone who wants to have those positive qualities, but does not wish to engage in "culpable unprovoked overt hostile attacks."

Of reluctant aggressors, males have an advantage over females. For as members of the masculine gender, their aggression is thought to be "natural." Even if they do not engage in aggressive behavior, they can still be perceived as possessing that trait, inherently, as a disposition. And if they do behave aggressively, their behavior can be excused, after all, it's natural.... On the other hand, since women are not expected to be aggressive, we are much more likely to notice the slightest aggressive behavior on the part of a woman ... because it seems unnatural.... Since, as I shall argue, aggressive behavior is unlikely to win friends and influence people in the way that one would like, this presents a special problem for women.

... I am going to ... question the assumption that aggression deserves association with more positive qualities. I think it is a mistake to suppose that an aggressive person is more likely to be energetic, effective, competent, powerful or successful and also a mistake to suppose that an energetic, effective, etc. person is therefore aggressive.

Even those who object to sex-roles stereotyping seldom balk specifically at the assumption that more aggressive people are better suited to "be the breadwinners and play the active role in the production of commodities of society," but only at the assumption that aggression is more natural to one sex than the other. Robin Lakoff assumes that more aggressive speech is both more effective and typical of males, and objects to the socialization that forbids direct questions and assertions, devoid of polite phrases, in women's speech.[2] ... She does not see that polite, nonabrupt speech, full of hesitations and qualifiers can be a sign of great power and very effective in giving the impression of great thought and deliberation, or in getting one's listeners on one's side. Although polite, nonabrupt speech can be more effective and have more power than aggressive speech, the conceptual conflation of aggression with positive concepts has made this hard to remember.

Consider some professional occasions where aggression might be thought an asset. Aggression is often equated with energy, but one can be energetic and work hard without being hostile. It may seem that aggression is essential where there is competition, but people who just try to do their best, without deliberately trying to do in the other guy may do equally well or even better.... Even those who think it is a dog-eat-dog world can see that there is a difference between acting to defeat or undermine competition and acting aggressively towards that competition. Especially if one's success depends on other parties, it is likely to be far wiser to *appear* friendly than to engage in aggressive behavior.... So if aggression is likely to make enemies, as it seems designed to do, it is a bad strategy in these professions. What about other professional activities? A friendly, warm, nonadversarial manner surely does not interfere with persuading customers to buy, getting employees to carry out directions conscientiously, convincing juries, teaching students, getting help and cooperation from coworkers, and promotions from the boss. An aggressive manner is more likely to be a hindrance in these activities.

If these considerations make us more able to distinguish aggression from professional competence, then they will have served as a useful introduction to the main object of this essay: an inquiry into a paradigm of philosophy that, perhaps tricked by the conflation of aggression and competence, incorporates aggression into its methodology.

SCIENTIFIC REASONING

Once upon a time it was thought that scientific claims were, or ought to be, objective and value-free; that expressions of value were distinguishable from expressions of fact; and that science ought to confine itself to the latter. This view was forsaken, reluctantly by some, when it was recognized that theories incorporate values, because they advocate one way of describing the world over others, and that even observations of facts are made from some viewpoint or theory about the world already presupposed.[3]

Still devoted to a fact-value distinction, Popper recognized that scientific *statements* invoked values, but believed that the *reasoning* in science was objective and value-free.[4] Popper argued that the primary reasoning in science is deductive. Theories in science propose laws of the form "All A's are B's" and the job of scientific research is to find, or set up, instances of *A* and see if they fail to produce or correlate with instances of *B*. The test of a theory was that it could withstand attempts to falsify it. A good theory encouraged such attempts by making unexpected and broad claims rather than narrow and expected claims. If instances of *B* failed to occur given instances of *A,* then the theory was falsified. A new theory that could account for the failure of *B* to occur in the same deductive manner would replace the old theory. The reasoning used to discover theories, the way a theory related to physical or mathematical models or other beliefs, was not considered essential to the scientific enterprise. On this view, only the thinking that was exact and certain, objective and value-free was essential to science.

However, Kuhn then argued that even the reasoning used in science is not value-free or certain.[5] Science involves more than a set of independent generalizations about the world waiting to be falsified by a single counterinstance. It involves a system, or paradigm, of not only generalizations and concepts, but beliefs about the methodology and evaluation of research: about what are good questions to ask, what are proper developments of the theory, what are acceptable research methods. One theory replaces another, not because it functions successfully as a major premise in a greater number of deductions, but because it answers some questions that the other theory does not.... Theory changes occur because one theory is more *satisfying* than the other, because the questions it answers are considered more *important*. Research under a paradigm is not done to falsify the theory, but to fill in and develop the knowledge that the paradigm provides a framework for. The reasoning involved in developing or replacing a paradigm is not simply deductive, and there is probably no adequate single characterization of how it proceeds. This does not mean that it is irrational or not worth studying, but that there is no simple universal characterization of good scientific reasoning.

This view of science, or one like it, is widely held by philosophers now. It has been suggested that philosophy too is governed by paradigms.

PHILOSOPHY REASONING—THE ADVERSARY PARADIGM

I am going to criticize a paradigm or part of a paradigm in philosophy.[6] It is the view that applies the now-rejected view of value-free reasoning in science to reasoning in philosophy. On this view all philosophic reasoning is, or ought to be, deductive. General claims are made and the job of philosophic research is to find counterexamples to the claims. And most important, the philosophic enterprise is seen as an unimpassioned debate between *adversaries* who try to defend their own views against counterexamples and produce counterexamples to opposing views. The reasoning used to discover the claims, and the way the claims relate to other beliefs and systems of ideas are not considered relevant to philosophic reasoning if they are not deductive. I will call this the Adversary Paradigm.

Under the Adversary Paradigm, it is assumed that the only, or at any rate, the best, way of evaluating work in philosophy is to subject it to the strongest or most extreme opposition. And it is assumed that the best way of presenting work in philosophy is to address it to an imagined opponent and muster all the evidence one can to support it. The justification for this method is that a position ought to be defended from, and subjected to, the criticism of the strongest opposition; that this method is the only way to get the best of both sides; that a thesis that survives this method of evaluation is more likely to be correct than one that does not; and that a thesis subjected to the Adversary Method will have passed an "objective" test.... Of course, it will be admitted that the Adversary Method does not *guarantee* that all and only sound philosophical claims will survive, but that is only because even an adversary does not always think of all the things that ought to be criticized about a position, and even a proponent does not always think of all the possible responses to criticism. However ... if one wants philosophy to be objective, one should prefer the Adversary Method to other, more subjective, forms of evaluation that would give preferential treatment to some claims by not submitting them to extreme adversarial tests. Philosophers who accept the Adversary Paradigm in philosophy may recognize that scientific reasoning is different, but think "So much the worse for science. At least philosophy can be objective and value-free."

I am going to criticize this paradigm in philosophy. My objection to the Adversary Method is to its role as a paradigm. If it were merely one procedure among many for philosophers to employ, there might be nothing worth objecting to except that conditions of hostility are not likely to elicit the best reasoning. But when it dominates the methodology and evaluation of philosophy, it restricts and misrepresents what philosophic reasoning is.

It has been said about science that criticism of a paradigm, however warranted, will not be successful unless there is an alternative paradigm available to replace it.[7] But the situation in philosophy is different. It is not that we have to wait for an alternative form of reasoning to be developed. Nonadversarial reasoning exists both outside and within philosophy but our present paradigm does not recognize it.

DEFECTS OF THE ADVERSARY PARADIGM

The defense of the Adversary Method identified adversary criticism with severe evaluation. If the evaluation is not adversarial it is assumed it must be weaker and less effective. I am going to argue that this picture is mistaken.

As far back as Plato it was recognized that in order for a debate or discussion to take place, assumptions must be shared by the parties involved.[8] A debate is not possible among people who disagree about everything. Not only must they agree about what counts as a good argument, what will be acceptable as relevant data, and how to decide on the winner, but they must share some premises in order for the debate to get started.

The Adversary Method works best if the disagreements are isolated ones, about a particular claim or argument. But claims and arguments about particular things rarely exist in isolation. They are usually part of an interrelated system of ideas.

Under the Adversary Paradigm we find ourselves trying to disagree with a system of ideas by taking each claim or argument, one at a time. Premises which might otherwise be rejected must be accepted, if only temporarily, for the sake of the argument.... Such a method can distort the presentation of an opponent's position, and produce an artificially slow development of thought.

When a whole system of ideas is involved, as it frequently is, a debate that ends in defeat for one argument, without changing the whole system of ideas of which that argument was a part, will only provoke stronger support for other arguments with the same conclusion, or inspire attempts to amend the argument to avoid the objections.... In order to alter a *conclusion,* it could be more effective to ignore confrontation on the particular points, not provide counterexamples, however easy they may be to find, and instead show how other premises and other data support an alternative system of ideas. If we are restricted to the Adversary Method we may have to withhold evaluation for a system of ideas in order to find a common ground for debate. And the adversarial criticism of some arguments may merely strengthen support for other ideas in the system, or inspire makeshift revisions and adjustments.

Moreover, the Adversary Paradigm allows exemption from criticism of claims in philosophy that are not well worked out, that are "programmatic." Now any thesis in philosophy worth its salt will be programmatic in that there will be implications which go beyond the thesis itself. But the claims that have become popular in philosophy are particularly sketchy, and secure their immunity from criticism under the Adversary Paradigm *because* their details are not worked out. A programmatic claim will offer a few examples that fit the claim along with a prediction that, with some modification (of course), a theory can be developed along these lines to cover all cases. Counterexamples cannot refute these claims because objections will be routinely dismissed as merely things to be considered later, when all the details are worked out. Some programmatic claims that were once quite popular are now in disrepute, such as sense-data theories, but not because they were disproved, perhaps more because they failed to succeed[,] no one ever worked out the details and/or people gave up hope of ever doing so. The Adversary Method allows programmatic claims to remain viable in philosophy, however sketchy or implausible, as long as they are unrefuted.

MISINTERPRETING THE HISTORY OF PHILOSOPHY

Under any paradigm we are likely to reinterpret history and recast the positions of earlier philosophers. With the Adversary Paradigm we understand earlier philosophers as if they were addressing adversaries instead of trying to build a foundation for scientific reasoning or to explain human nature. Philosophers who cannot be recast into an adversarial mold are likely to be ignored. But our reinterpretations may be misinterpretations and our choice of great philosophers may be based not so much on what they said as on how we think they said it.

One victim of the Adversary Paradigm is usually thought to be a model of adversarial reasoning: the Socratic Method. The Socratic Method is frequently identified with the *elenchus*, a method of discussion designed to lead the other person into admitting that her/his views were wrong, to get them to feel what is sometimes translated as "shame" and sometimes as "humility." *Elenchus* is usually translated as "refutation," but this is misleading.... Unlike the Adversary Method, the justification of the *elenchus* is not that it subjects claims to the most extreme opposition, but that it shakes people up about their cherished convictions so they can begin philosophical inquiries with a more open mind. The aim of the Adversary Method, in contrast, is to show that the other party is wrong, challenging them on any possible point, regardless of whether the other person agrees. In fact, many contemporary philosophers avoid considerations of how to convince, supposing it to be related to trickery and bad reasoning.

In general the inability to win a public debate is not a good reason for giving up a belief. One can usually attribute the loss to one's own performance instead of to inadequacies in one's thesis. A public loss may even make one feel more strongly toward the position that wasn't done justice by the opposition. Thus the Adversary Method is not a good way to convince someone who does not agree with you.

The *elenchus*, on the other hand, is designed just for that purpose. One looks for premises that the other person will accept and that will show that the original belief was false. The discussion requires an acceptance by both parties of premises and reasoning.

Of course, one could use the *elenchus* in the service of the Adversary Paradigm to win a point rather than convince. And it has been assumed by many that that is what Socrates was doing.[10] ... But in fact Socrates's method is contrasted with that of an antagonist or hostile questioner in the dialogues.[11] Socrates jokes frequently at the beginning of a dialogue or when the other party is resisting the discussion, and the jokes encourage the discussion, which would not be the case if they were made at the expense of the speaker.[12] ... His aim is not to rebut, it is to show people how to think for themselves.... I suspect that the reason we have taken Socrates's method to be the Adversary Method ... is that under the influence of the Adversary Paradigm we have not been able to conceive of philosophy being done any other way.

RESTRICTIONS OF PHILOSOPHICAL ISSUES

The Adversary Paradigm affects the kinds of questions asked and determines the answers that are thought to be acceptable. This is evident in nearly every area of philosophy. The only problems recognized are those between opponents, and the only kind of reasoning considered is the certainty of deduction, directed to opposition. The paradigm has a strong and obvious influence on the way problems are addressed.

For example in philosophy of language the properties investigated are analyzed when possible in terms of properties that can be subjected to deductive reasoning. Semantic theory has detoured questions of meaning into questions of truth. Meaning is discussed in terms of the deductive consequences of sentences. We ask not what a sentence says, but what it guarantees, what we can deduce from it. Relations among ideas that affect the meaning are either assimilated to the deductive model or ignored.[14]

In philosophy of science, the claim that scientific reasoning is not essentially deductive has led to "charges of irrationality, relativism, and the defense of mob rule."[15] Nondeductive reasoning is thought to be no reasoning at all....

In ethics, a consequence of this paradigm is that it has been assumed that there must be a single supreme moral principle. Because moral reasoning may be the result of different moral principles that may make conflicting claims about the right thing to do, a supreme moral principle is needed to "adjudicate rationally [that is, deductively] among different competing moralities."[16] The relation between moral principles and moral decision is thought to be deductive.... The possibilities that one could adjudicate between conflicting moral precepts without using deduction, that there might be moral problems that are not the result of conflicts in moral principles, and that there might be moral dilemmas for which there are no guaranteed solutions, are not considered.

... It is assumed that only systems of ideas that can be openly proclaimed and debated are to count as theories, or as philosophy. Again this is the Adversary Paradigm at work, allowing only systems of ideas that can be advocated and defended, and denying that philosophy might examine a system of ideas for its own sake, or for its connections with other systems.[17]

... With the Adversary Paradigm we do not try to assess positions or theories on their plausibility or worthiness or even popularity. Instead we are expected to consider, and therefore honor, positions that are most *unlike* our own in order to show that we can meet their objections.... Since the most extreme opposition may be a denial of the existence of something, much philosophic energy is expended arguing for the existence of some things, and no theory about the nature of those things ever gets formulated. We find an abundance of arguments trying to prove that determinism is false because free will exists, but no positive accounts giving an explanation, in terms of chance and indeterminism, of what free will would be....

Philosophy, by attention to extreme positions because they are extreme, presents a distorted picture about what sorts of positions are worthy of attention, giving undo attention and publicity to positions merely because they are those of a hypothetical adversary's and possibly ignoring positions that make more valuable or interesting claims.

THE PARADIGM LEADS TO BAD REASONING

It has mistakenly been assumed that whatever reasoning an adversary would accept would be adequate reasoning for all other circumstances as well.[20] The Adversary Paradigm accepts only the kind of reasoning whose goal is to convince an opponent, and ignores reasoning that might be used in other circumstances: to figure something out for oneself, to discuss something with like-minded thinkers, to convince the indifferent or the uncommitted....

In illustration, let us consider the counterexample reasoning that is so effective in defending one's conclusions against an adversary. When an adversary focuses on certain features of a problem, one can use those features to construct a counterexample. To construct a counterexample, one needs to abstract the essential features of the problem and find another example, an analogy, that has those features but that is different enough and clear enough to be considered dispassionately apart from the issue in question. The analogy must be able to show that the alleged effect of the essential features does not follow.

But in order to reach a conclusion about moral issues or scientific theories or aesthetic judgments, one may have to consider all the important features and their interactions. And to construct an analogy with all the features and their interactions, which is *not* part of the issue in question, may well be impossible. Any example with all the features that are important may just be another example of the problem at issue. If we construct an analogy using only some of the important features, or ignoring their interactions, a decision based on this could be bad reasoning. It would ignore important aspects of the problem.

Consider a work in the Adversary Paradigm, Judith Thomson's excellent "A Defense of Abortion."[21] Thomson says: All right, let's give the "right-to-lifers" all their premises. Let's suppose, for the sake of argument, that a fetus is a person, and even that it is a talented person. And then she shows by counterexample that it does not follow that the fetus has a right to life. Suppose that you woke up one morning and found that you were connected to a talented violinist (because he had a rare kidney disease and only you had the right blood type) and the Music Lover's Society had plugged you together. When you protested, they said, "Don't worry, it's only for nine months, and then he'll be cured. And you can't unplug him because now that the connection has been made, he will die if you do." Now, Thomson says to the right-to-lifers, surely you have the *right* to unplug yourself. If the time were shorter than nine months, say only nine minutes, you might be an awful person if you did not stay plugged in, but even then you have the *right* to do what you want with your body.

The violinist analogy makes the main point, and Thomson explains it by comparing the right to one's own body to the right to property (a right that the right-to-lifers are unlikely to deny). One's right to property does not stop because some other person needs it, even if they need it to stay alive.

The argument using a counterexample is as effective against adversaries as any argument could be, and therefore a good method for arguing within the adversary tradition.... In general, in order to handle adversaries one may abstract the features they claim to be important, and construct a counterexample which has those same features but in which the conclusion they claim does not hold.

All Thomson tried to show was that abortion would not be wrong just because the fetus was a person.[22] She did not show that abortion would, or would not, be wrong. There are many features besides personhood that are important to the people making a decision about abortion: That it is the result of sexual intercourse so that guilt, atonement or loyalty about the consequences may be appropriate; that the effects only occur to women, helping to keep a power-minority in a powerless position ... [etc.]. There are many questions connected to whole systems of ideas that need answers when abortion is a personal issue: What responsibility does one have to prevent shame and hardship to others—parents, friends, other children, future friends and future children? When do duties toward friends override duties of other sorts? ... There is a lot of very serious moral reasoning that goes on when an individual has to make a decision about abortion, and the decisions made are enormously varied. But this moral reasoning has largely been ignored by philosophers because it is different from the reasoning used to address an adversary and it is too complex and interrelated to be evaluated by counterexamples.

... Counterexample reasoning can be used to rule out certain alternatives, or at least to show that the current arguments supporting them are inadequate, but not to construct alternatives or to figure out what principles *do* apply in certain situations....

If counterexample reasoning is not a good way to reach conclusions about complex issues, and it is a good way to construct arguments to defeat adversaries, then we should be careful when we do philosophy to bear this in mind. Instead, most of the time we present adversary arguments as if they were the only way to reason. The Adversary Paradigm prevents us from seeing that systems of ideas that are *not* directed to an adversary may be worth studying and developing, and that adversarial reasoning may be incorrect for nonadversarial contexts.

How would discarding the Adversary Paradigm affect philosophy? Any paradigm in philosophy will restrict the way reasoning is evaluated. I have argued that the Adversary Paradigm not only ignores some forms of good reasoning, but fails to evaluate and even encourages some forms of bad reasoning. However, criticism of the Adversary Paradigm is not enough; we need alternatives.

One of the problems with a paradigm that becomes really entrenched is that it is hard to conceive of how the field would operate without it. What other method of evaluating philosophy is there but the Adversary Method?

An alternative way of evaluating reasoning, already used in the history of philosophy and history of science, is to consider how the reasoning relates to a larger system of ideas. The questions to be asked are not just "Must the argument as it stands now be accepted as valid?" but also "What are the most plausible premises that would make this argument a good one?" "Why is this argument important?" "How do its form and its conclusion fit in with other beliefs and patterns of reasoning?" For example, one can consider not only whether Descartes's proofs of the existence of God are valid, but what good reasons there are for proving the existence of God; how Descartes's concept of God is related to his concept of causation and of matter. One can examine the influence of methodology and instrumentation in one scientific field on the development of a related field.[23] Such an approach to relations of ideas that are not deductive can also be evaluated. We can look at how world-views relate to different philosophical positions about free will and determinism, about rationality and ethical values, about distinctions claimed between mind and body, self and other, order and chaos.

A second way of treating systems of ideas involves a greater shift from the Adversary Paradigm. It may even require a shift in our concept of reasoning for it to be accepted. It is that experience may be a necessary element in certain reasoning processes. While many philosophers recognize that different factual beliefs, and hence basic premises, may arise from different experiences, it is believed that philosophical discussions ought to proceed as if experience plays no essential role in the philosophical positions one holds. Experience may be necessary to resolve factual disputes but aside from errors about the facts, any differences in experience that might account for differences in philosophical beliefs are ignored or denied. It is thought that all genuine philosophical differences can be resolved through language. This belief supports the Adversary Paradigm, for adversarial arguments could be pointless if it was experience rather than argument that determined philosophical beliefs. Yet might it not be possible, for example, that belief in a supreme deity is correlated with perceived ability to control one's future? . . . Belief in a deity would benefit, would be rational for the *very* young, the very old, the poor and the helpless. But for others, with the experience of being able to control their own lives and surroundings, the difference in experience would give rise to a different belief.

I am not arguing for this account, but suggesting it as an illustration for how different experiences could determine different philosophical positions that are not resolvable by argument. . . .

These alternatives to the Adversary Paradigm may be objected to by philosophers who are under the delusion that philosophy is different from science, that unlike science, its evaluation procedures are exact and value-free. But for those who accept that what philosophers have said about science (that scientific evaluation is not free from uncertainty and values, because it is dependent on paradigms) is also true of philosophy, other means of evaluation besides the Adversary Method will not be so objectionable.

I have been criticizing the use of the Adversary Method as a paradigm. And I think one of the best ways to reduce its paradigm status is to point out that it is a paradigm, that there are other ways of evaluating, reasoning about and discussing philosophy.

NOTES

. . .

2. Robin Lakoff, *Language and Woman's Place* (New York: Harper & Row, 1975).

3. Logical positivism.

4. Sir Karl Popper, *The Logic of Scientific Discovery* (New York: Harper & Row, 1958).

5. Thomas Kuhn, *The Structure of Scientific Revolutions,* 2nd edition (Chicago: University of Chicago Press, 1962).

6. It may be that the Adversary Method is only part of the larger paradigm that distinguishes reason from emotion, and segregates philosophy from literature, aligning it with science (dichotomies that Martha Nussbaum [*Philosophy and Literature* 1, 1978] attributes to Plato).... I consciously employ the kinship philosophy claims with science in this paper, arguing that truths we have learned about scientific reasoning ought to hold for philosophic reasoning as well.

7. Thomas Kuhn, "Reflections on My Critics," in *Criticism and the Growth of Knowledge,* ed. Imre Lakatos and Alan Musgrave (Cambridge: Cambridge University Press, 1970), 231–278.

8. See the *Meno* 75d-e.

. . .

10. See Richard Robinson, *Plato's Earlier Dialectic* (Oxford: Clarendon Press, 1953) for this view of Socrates's style. I don't mean to single out Robinson for what seems to be the usual interpretation of Socrates. Robinson at least thought irony and insincerity objectionable....

11. See *Euthydemus* 227d, 288d, 295d, where Socrates's method contrasted with Euthydemus's jeering and belligerent style, and *Meno* 75c-d where Socrates contrasts the present friendly conversation with that of a disputatious and quarrelsome kind. Socrates disapproved of ridicule (*Lathes* 1959, *Gorgias* 473d-e, *Euthydemus* 278d, and *Protagoras* 333e).

12. Socrates teases Polus to get him to change his style (*Gorgias* 461c-462a) and responds to Callicles's insults with praise to get him to agree to a dialogue. Socrates flirts with Meno when he resists questioning (*Meno* 76b-c) and draws out Lysis by getting him to laugh at his questions (*Lysis* 207c and ff.).

. . .

14. For example, Donald Davidson, "Truth and Meaning," *Synthese* 17 (1967): 304–323.

15. T. Kuhn, "Reflections on My Critics," 234. See Feyerabend, Watkins etc. in that volume and Dudley Shapere's review of *Structure of Scientific Revolutions,* in *Philosophical Review.*

16. For example, Alan Gewirth, *Reason and Morality* (Chicago: University of Chicago Press, 1978).

17. See particularly Brian Medlin, "Ultimate Principles and Ethical Egoism," *Australasian Journal of Philosophy* 39 (1957): 111–118.

. . .

20. See John Rawls, *A Theory of Justice* (Cambridge, MA: Belknap Press, 1971), 191.

21. Judith Jarvis Thomson, "A Defense of Abortion," *Philosophy and Public Affairs* 1 (1971): 47–66.

22. Thomson, in general, makes it very clear that she is addressing an adversary. Nevertheless, she does claim to reach some conclusion about the morality of abortion, although the central issues for people making the decision are barely discussed—the consequences. See her section 8.

23. Lindley Darden and Nancy Maul, "Interfield Theories," *Philosophy of Science* 44 (1977): 43–64.

Paula Gunn Allen

Kochinnenako in Academe: Three Approaches to Interpreting a Keres Indian Tale

. . .

A feminist approach to the study and teaching of American Indian life and thought is essential because the area has been dominated by paternalistic, male-dominant modes of consciousness since the first writings about American Indians in the fifteenth century. This male bias has seriously skewed our understanding of tribal life and philosophy, distorting it in ways that are sometimes obvious but are most often invisible.

Often what appears to be a misinterpretation caused by racial differences is a distortion based on sexual politics. When the patriarchal paradigm that characterizes western thinking is applied to gynecentric tribal modes, it transforms the ideas, significances, and raw data into something that is not only unrecognizable to the tribes but entirely incongruent with their philosophies and theories....

To demonstrate the interconnections between tribal and feminist approaches as I use them in my work, I have developed an analysis of a traditional Kochinnenako, or Yellow Woman, story of the Laguna-Acoma Keres, as recast by my mother's uncle John M. Gunn in his book *Schat Chen.*[1] My analysis utilizes three approaches and demonstrates the relationship of context to meaning, illuminating three consciousness styles and providing students with a traditionally tribal, nonracist, feminist understanding of traditional and contemporary American Indian life.

SOME THEORETICAL CONSIDERATIONS

Analyzing tribal cultural systems from a mainstream feminist point of view allows an otherwise overlooked insight into the complex interplay of factors that have led to the systematic loosening of tribal ties, the disruption of tribal cohesion and complexity, and the growing disequilibrium of cultures that were anciently based on a belief in balance, relationship, and the centrality of women, particularly elder women. A feminist approach reveals not only the exploitation and oppression of the tribes by whites and white government but also areas of oppression within the tribes and the sources and nature of that oppression. To a large extent, such an analysis can provide strategies for ameliorating the effects of patriarchal colonialism, enabling many of the tribes to reclaim their ancient gynarchical,[2] egalitarian, and sacred traditions.

At the present time, American Indians in general are not comfortable with feminist analysis or action within the reservation or urban Indian enclaves. Many Indian women are uncomfortable with feminism because they perceive it (correctly) as white-dominated. They (not so correctly) believe it is concerned with issues that have little bearing on their own lives, ... and because they have been reared in an Anglophobic world that views white society with fear and hostility. But because of their fear ... and bitterness ... American Indian women often overlook the central areas of damage done to tribal tradition by white Christian and secular patriarchal dominance. Militant and "progressive" American Indian men are even more likely to quarrel with feminism; they have benefitted in certain ways from white male-centeredness....

It is within the context of growing violence against women and the concomitant lowering of our status among Native Americans that I teach and write. Certainly ... feminist theory applied to my literary studies clarifies a number of issues for me, including the patriarchal bias that has been systematically imposed on traditional literary materials and the mechanism by which that bias has affected contemporary American Indian life, thought, and culture.

The oral tradition is more than a record of a people's culture. It is the creative source of their collective and individual selves. When that wellspring of identity is tampered with, the sense of self is also tampered with; and when that tampering includes the sexist and classist assumptions of the white world within the body of an Indian tradition, serious consequences necessarily ensue.

The oral tradition is a living body. It is in continuous flux, which enables it to accommodate itself to the real circumstances of a people's lives. That is its strength, but it is also its weakness, for when a people finds itself living within a racist, classist, and sexist reality, the oral tradition will reflect those values and will thus shape the people's consciousness to include and accept racism, classism, and sexism, and they will incorporate that change, hardly noticing the shift. If the oral tradition is altered in certain subtle, fundamental ways, if elements alien to it are introduced so that its internal coherence is disturbed, it becomes the major instrument of colonization and oppression.

Such alterations have occurred and are still occurring. Those who translate or "render" narratives make certain crucial changes, many unconscious.... Culture is fundamentally a shaper of perception, after all, and perception is shaped by culture in many subtle ways. In short, it's hard to see the forest when you're a tree. To a great extent, changes in materials translated from a tribal to a western language are a result of the vast difference in languages.... Language embodies the unspoken assumptions and orientations of the culture it belongs to. So while the problem is one of translation, it is not simply one of word equivalence. The differences are perceptual and contextual as much as verbal.

... When shifts of language and context are coupled with the almost infinite changes occasioned by Christianization, secularization, economic dislocation from subsistence to industrial modes, destruction of the wilderness and associated damage to the biota, much that is changed goes unnoticed or unremarked by the people being changed. This is not to suggest that Native Americans are unaware of the enormity of the change they have been forced to undergo by the several centuries of white presence, but much of that change is at deep and subtle levels that are not easily noted or resisted.

John Gunn received the story I am using here from a Keres-speaking informant and translated it himself. The story, which he titles "Sh-ah-cock and Miochin or the Battle of the Seasons," is in reality a narrative version of a ritual. The ritual brings about the change of season and of moiety among the Keres. Gunn doesn't mention this, perhaps because he was interested in stories and not in religion or perhaps because his informant did not mention the connection to him.

What is interesting about his rendering is his use of European, classist, conflict-centered patriarchal assumptions as plotting devices. These interpolations dislocate the significance of the tale and subtly alter the ideational context of woman-centered, largely pacifist people whose ritual story this is. I have developed three critiques of the tale as it appears in his book, using feminist and tribal understandings to discuss the various meanings of the story when it is read from three different perspectives.

... Each analysis is somewhat less detailed than it might be; but as I am interested in describing modes of perception and their impact on our understanding of cultural artifacts (and by extension our understanding of people who come from different cultural contexts than our own) rather than critiquing a story, they are adequate.

YELLOW WOMAN STORIES

The Keres of Laguna and Acoma Pueblos in New Mexico have stories that are called Yellow Woman stories. The themes and to a large extent the motifs of these stories are always female-centered, always told from Yellow Woman's point of view. Some older recorded versions of Yellow Woman tales (as in Gunn) make Yellow Woman the daughter of the hocheni. Gunn translates hocheni as "ruler." But Keres notions of the hocheni's function and position are as cacique or Mother Chief, which differ greatly from Anglo-European ideas of rulership. However, for Gunn to render hocheni as "ruler" is congruent with the European folktale tradition.[3]

Kochinnenako, Yellow Woman, is in some sense a name that means Woman-Woman because among the Keres, yellow is the color for women (as pink and red are among Anglo-European Americans), and it is the color ascribed to the Northwest. Keres women paint their faces yellow on certain ceremonial occasions and are so painted at death so that the guardian at the gate of the spirit world, Naiya Iyatiku (Mother Corn Woman), will recognize that the newly arrived person is a woman. It is also the name of a particular Irriaku, Corn Mother (sacred corn-ear bundle)....

Yellow Woman stories are about all sorts of things—abduction, meeting with happy powerful spirits, birth of twins, getting power from the spirit worlds and returning it to the people.... Yellow Woman's sisters are often in the stories (Blue, White, and Red Corn)....

Many Yellow Woman tales highlight her alienation from the people: she lives with her grandmother at the edge of the village, for example, or she is in some way atypical.... In many ways Kochinnenako is a role model, though she possesses some behaviors that are not likely to occur in many of the women who hear her stories. She is, one might say, the Spirit of Woman.

The stories do not necessarily imply that difference is punishable; on the contrary, it is often her very difference that makes her special adventures possible, and these adventures often have happy outcomes for Kochinnenako and for her people. This is significant among a people who value conformity and propriety above almost anything. It suggests that the behavior of women, at least at certain times or under certain circumstances, must be improper or nonconformist for the greater good of the whole....

Other Kochinnenako stories are about her centrality to the harmony, balance, and prosperity of the tribe. "Sh-ah-cock and Miochin" is one of these stories. John Gunn prefaces the narrative with the comment that while the story is about a battle, war stories are rarely told by the Keres because they are not "a war like people" and "very rarely refer to their exploits in war."

SH-AH-COCK AND MIOCHIN OR THE BATTLE OF THE SEASONS

In the Kush-kut-ret-u-nah-tit (white village of the north) was once a ruler by the name of Hut-cha-mun Ki-uk (the broken prayer stick), one of whose daughters, Ko-chin-ne-nako, became the bride of Sh-ah-cock (the spirit of winter), a person of very violent temper. He always manifested his presence by blizzards of snow or sleet or by freezing cold, and on account of his alliance with the ruler's daughter, he was most of the time in the vicinity of Kush-kut-ret, and as these manifestations continued from month to month and year to year, the people of Kush-kut-ret found that their crops would not mature, and finally they were compelled to subsist on the leaves of the cactus.

On one occasion Ko-chin-ne-nako had wandered a long way from home in search of the cactus and had gathered quite a bundle and was preparing to carry them home by singeing off the thorns, when on looking up she found herself confronted by a very bold but handsome young man. His attire attracted her gaze at once. He wore a shirt of yellow woven from the silks of corn, a belt made from the broad green blades of the same plant, a tall pointed hat made from the same kind of material and from the top which waved a yellow corn tassel. He wore green leggings woven from kow-a-nuh, the green stringy moss that forms in springs and ponds. His moccasins were beautifully embroidered with flowers and butterflies. In his hand he carried an ear of green corn.

His whole appearance proclaimed him a stranger and as Ko-chin-ne-nako gaped in wonder, he spoke to her in a very pleasing voice asking her what she was doing. She told him that on account of the cold and drouth [sic], the people of Kush-kut-ret were forced to eat the leaves of the cactus to keep from starving.

"Here," said the young man, handing her the ear of green corn. "Eat this and I will go and bring more that you may take home with you."

He left her and soon disappeared going towards the south. In a short time he returned bringing with him a big load of green corn. Ko-chin-ne-nako asked him where he had gathered corn and if it grew nearby. "No," he replied, "it is from my home far away to the south, where the corn grows and the flowers bloom all the year around. Would you not like to accompany me back to my country?" Ko-chin-ne-nako replied that ... she could not go with him because she was the wife of Sh-ah-cock. And then she told him of her alliance with the Spirit of Winter, and admitted that her husband was very cold and disagreeable and that she did not love him. The strange young man urged her to go with him to the warm land of the south, saying that he did not fear Sh-ah-cock. But Ko-chin-ne-nako would not consent. So the stranger directed her to return to her home with the corn he had brought and cautioned her not to throw away any of the husks out of the door. Upon leaving he said to her, "you must meet me at this place tomorrow. I will bring more corn for you."

Ko-chin-ne-nako had not proceeded far on her homeward way ere she met her sisters who, having become uneasy because of her long absence, had come in search of her. They were greatly surprised at seeing her with an armful of corn instead of cactus. Ko-chin-ne-nako told them the whole story of how she had obtained it, and thereby only added wonderment to their surprise.

They helped her to carry the corn home; and there she again had to tell her story to her father and mother.

When she had described the stranger even from his peaked hat to his butterfly moccasins, and had told them that she was to meet him again on the day following, Hut-cha-mun Ki-uk, the father, exclaimed:

"It is Mi-o-chin!"

"It is Mi-o-chin! It is Mi-o-chin!" echoed the mother. "Tomorrow you must bring him home with you."

The next day Ko-chin-ne-nako went again to the spot where she had met Mi-o-chin, for it was indeed Mi-o-chin, the Spirit of Summer. He was already there, awaiting her coming. With him he had brought a huge bundle of corn.

Ko-chin-ne-nako pressed upon him the invitation of her parents to accompany her home, so together they carried the corn to Kush-kut-ret. When it had been distributed there was sufficient to feed all the people of the city. Amid great rejoicing and thanksgiving, Mi-o-chin was welcomed at the Hotchin's (ruler's) house.

In the evening, as was his custom, Sh-ah-cock, the Spirit of the Winter, returned to his home. He came in a blinding storm of snow and hail and sleet, for he was in a boisterous mood. On approaching the city, he felt within his bones that Mi-o-chin was there, so he called in a loud and blustering voice:

"Ha! Mi-o-chin, are you here?"

For answer, Mi-o-chin advanced to meet him.

Then Sh-ah-cock, beholding him, called again,

"Ha! Mi-o-chin, I will destroy you."

"Ha! Sh-ah-cock, I will destroy you," replied Mi-o-chin, still advancing.

Sh-ah-cock ... was covered from head to foot with frost (skah). Icicles (ya-pet-to-ne) draped him round. The fierce, cold wind proceeded from his nostrils.

As Mi-o-chin drew near, the wintry wind changed to a warm summer breeze. The frost and icicles melted and displayed beneath them, the dry, bleached bulrushes (ska-ra-ru-ka) in which Sh-ah-cock was clad.

Seeing that he was doomed to defeat, Sh-ah-cock cried out:

"I will not fight you now, for we cannot try our powers. We will make ready, and in four days from this time, we will meet here and fight for supremacy. The victor shall claim Ko-chin-ne-nako for his wife."

With this, Sh-ah-cock withdrew in rage. The wind again roared and shook the very houses; but the people were warm within them, for Mi-o-chin was with them.

The next day Mi-o-chin left Kush-kut-ret for his home in the south. Arriving there, he began to make his preparations to meet Sh-ah-cock in battle.

First he sent an eagle as a messenger to his friend, Ya-chun-ne-ne-moot (kind of shaley rock that becomes very hot in the fire), who lived in the west, requesting him to come and help to battle Sh-ah-cock. Then he called together the birds and the four legged animals—all those that live in sunny climes....

Meantime Sh-ah-cock had gone to his home in the north to make his preparations for battle. To his aid he called all the winter birds and all of the four legged animals of the wintry climates....

When these formidable forces had been mustered by the rivals, they advanced, Mi-o-chin from the south and Sh-ah-cock from the north, in battle array.

Ya-chun-ne-ne-moot kindled his fires and piled great heaps of resinous fuel upon them until volumes of steam and smoke ascended, forming enormous clouds that hurried forward toward Kush-kut-ret and the battle ground. Upon these clouds rode Mi-o-chin, the Spirit of Summer, and his vast army. All the animals of the army, encountering the smoke from Ya-chun-ne-ne-moot's fires, were colored by the smoke so that, from that day, the animals from the south have been black or brown in color.

Sh-ah-cock and his army came out of the north in a howling blizzard and borne forward on black storm clouds driven by a freezing wintry wind. As he came on, the lakes and rivers over which he passed were frozen and the air was filled with blinding sleet.

When the combatants drew near to Kush-kut-ret, they advanced with fearful rapidity. Their arrival upon the field was marked by fierce and terrific strife.

Flashes of lightning darted from Mi-o-chin's clouds. Striking the animals of Sh-ah-cock, they singed the hair upon them, and turned it white, so that, from that day, the animals from the north have worn a covering of white or have white markings upon them.

From the south, the black clouds still rolled upward, the thunder spoke again and again. Clouds of smoke and vapor rushed onward, melting the snow and ice weapons of Sh-ah-cock and compelling him, at length, to retire from the field. Mi-o-chin, assured of victory, pursued him. To save himself from total defeat and destruction, Sh-ah-cock called for armistice.

This being granted on the part of Mi-o-chin, the rivals met at Kush-kut-ret to arrange the terms of the treaty. Sh-ah-cock acknowledged himself defeated. He consented to give up Ko-chin-ne-nako to Mi-o-chin. . . .

It was then agreed between the late combatants that, for all time thereafter, Mi-o-chin was to rule at Kush-kut-ret during one-half of the year, and Sh-ah-cock was to rule during the remaining half, and that neither should molest the other.[4]

John Gunn's version has a formal plot structure that makes the account seem to be a narrative. But had he translated it directly from the Keres, even in "narrative" form, as in a storytelling session, its ritual nature would have been clearer. I can only surmise about how the account might go if it were done that way, basing my ideas on renderings of Keres rituals in narrative forms I am acquainted with. But a direct translation from the Keres would have sounded more like the following than like Gunn's rendition of it:

Long ago. Eh. There in the North. Yellow Woman. Up northward she went. Then she picked burrs and cactus. Then here went Summer. From the south he came. Above there he arrived. Thus spoke Summer. "Are you here? How is it going?" said Summer. "Did you come here?" thus said Yellow Woman. Then answered Yellow Woman, "I pick these poor things because I am hungry." "Why do you not eat corn and melons?" asked Summer. Then he gave her some corn and melons. "Take it!" Then thus spoke Yellow Woman, "It is good. Let us go. To my house I take you." "Is not your husband there?" "No. He went hunting deer. Today at night he will come back."

Then in the north they arrived. In the west they went down. Arrived then they in the east. "Are you here?" Remembering Prayer Sticks said. "Yes," Summer said. "How is it going?" Summer said. Then he said, "Your daughter Yellow Woman, she brought me here." "Eh. That is good." Thus spoke Remembering Prayer Sticks.

The story would continue, with many of the elements contained in Gunn's version but organized along the axis of directions, movement of the participants, their maternal relationships to each other (daughter, mother, mother chief, etc.), and events sketched in only as they pertained to directions and the division of the year into its ritual/ceremonial segments, one belonging to the Kurena (summer supernaturals or powers who are connected to the summer people or clans) and the other belonging to the Kashare, perhaps in conjunction with the Kopishtaya, the Spirits. . . .

A KERES INTERPRETATION

When a traditional Keres reads the tale of Kochinnenako, she listens with certain information about her people in mind: she knows, for example, that Hutchamun Kiuk (properly it means Remembering Prayer Sticks, though Gunn translates it as Broken Prayer Sticks)[6] refers to the ritual (sacred) identity of the cacique and that the story is a narrative version of a ceremony related to the planting of corn. She knows that Lagunas and Acomas don't have rulers in the Anglo-European sense of monarchs, lords, and such (though they do, in recent times, have elected governors, but that's another matter), and that a person's social status is determined by her mother's clan and position in it rather than by her relationship to the cacique as his daughter. . . .

In any case, our hypothetical Keres reader also knows that the story is about a ritual that takes place every year and that the battle imagery refers to events that take place during the ritual; she is also aware that Kochinnenako's will, as expressed in her attraction to Miochin, is a central element of the ritual. She knows further that the ritual is partly about the coming of summer and partly about the ritual relationship and exchange of primacy between the two divisions of the tribe ... and that Yellow Woman in her Corn Mother aspect is the center of this and other sacred rites of the Kurena....

The presence of Kochinnenako and Hutchamun Kiuk and the Shiwana Miochin and Sh-ah-cock means something sacred is going on for the Keres.

The ritual transfers the focus of power, or the ritual axis, held in turn by two moieties whose constitution reflects the earth's bilateral division between summer and winter, from the winter to the summer people. Each moiety's right to power is confirmed by and reflective of the seasons, as it is reflective of and supported by the equinoxes. The power is achieved through the Iyani (ritual empowerment) of female Power,[7] embodied in Kochinnenako as mask dancer and/or Irriaku. Without her empowering mediatorship among the south and north Shiwana, the cacique, and the village, the season and the moiety cannot change, and balance cannot be maintained.

Unchanging supremacy of one moiety/season over the other is unnatural and therefore undesirable because unilateral dominance of one aspect of existence and of society over another is not reflective of or supported by reality at meteorological or spiritual levels. Sh-ah-cock is the Winter Spirit or Winter Cloud, a *Shiwana* (one of several categories of supernaturals), and as such is cold and connected to sleet, snow, ice, and hunger. He is not portrayed as cold because he is a source of unmitigated evil (or of evil at all, for that matter).

Half of the people (not numerically but mystically, so to speak) are Winter, and in that sense are Sh-ah-cock; and while this aspect of the group psyche may seem unlovely when its time is over, that same half is lovely indeed in the proper season. Similarly, Miochin will also age—that is, pass his time—and will then give way for his "rival," which is also his complement. Thus balance and harmony are preserved for the village through exchange of dominance, and thus each portion of the community takes responsibility in turn for the prosperity and well-being of the people.

A Keres is of course aware that balance and harmony are two primary assumptions of Keres society and will not approach the narrative wondering whether the handsome Miochin will win the hand of the unhappy wife and triumph over the enemy, thereby heroically saving the people from disaster. The triumph of handsome youth over ugly age or of virile liberality over withered tyranny doesn't make sense in a Keres context because such views contradict central Keres values.

A traditional Keres is satisfied by the story because it reaffirms a Keres sense of rightness, of propriety.... Such a reader is likely to be puzzled by the references of rulers and by the tone of heroic romance but will be reasonably satisfied by the account because in spite of its westernized changes, it still ends happily with the orderly transfer of focality between the moieties and seasons accomplished in seasonal splendor.... In the end, the primary Keres values of harmony, balance, and the centrality of woman to maintain them have been validated, and the fundamental Keres principle of proper order is celebrated and affirmed once again.

A MODERN FEMINIST INTERPRETATION

A non-Keres feminist, reading this tale, is likely to wrongly suppose that this narrative is about the importance of men and the use of a passive female figure as a pawn in their bid for power. And, given the way Gunn renders the story, a modern feminist would have good reason to make such an inference. As Gunn recounts it, the story opens in classic patriarchal style and implies certain patriarchal complications: that Kochinnenako has married a man who is violent and destructive. She is the ruler's daughter, which might suggest that the traditional Keres are concerned with the abuses of power of the wealthy. This in turn suggests that the traditional Keres social system, like the traditional Anglo-European ones, suffer from oppressive class structures in which the rich and powerful bring misery to the people, who in the tale are reduced to bare subsistence seemingly as a result of Kochinnenako's unfortunate alliance....

Given the usual assumptions that underlie European folktales, the Western romantic view of the Indian, and the usual antipatriarchal bias that characterizes feminist analysis, a feminist reader might assume that Kochinnenako has been compelled to make an unhappy match by her father the ruler, who must be gaining some power from the alliance....

Gunn's tale does not clarify these issues. Instead it proceeds in a way best calculated to confirm a feminist's interpretation of the tale as only another example of the low status of women in tribal cultures. In accordance with this entrenched American myth, Gunn makes it clear that Kochinnenako is not happy in her marriage; she thinks Sh-ah-cock is "cold and disagreeable, and she cannot love him." Certainly, contemporary American women will read that to mean that Sh-ah-cock is an emotionally uncaring, perhaps cruel husband and that Kochinnenako is forced to accept a life bereft of warmth and love. A feminist reader might imagine that Kochinnenako, like many women, has been socialized into submission.... As it turns out (in Gunn's tale), Kochinnenako is delivered from the clutches of her violent and unwanted mate by the timely intervention of a much more pleasant man, the hero.

A radical feminist is likely to read the story for its content vis à vis racism and resistance to oppression. From a radical perspective, it seems politically significant that Sh-ah-cock is white.... Clearly, while the story does not give much support to concepts of a people's struggles, it could be construed to mean that the oppressor is designated white in the story because the Keres are engaged in serious combat with white colonial power and, given the significance of storytelling in tribal cultures, are chronicling that struggle in this tale. Read this way, it would seem to acknowledge the right and duty of the people in overthrowing the hated white dictator....

Briefly, in this context, the story can be read as a tale about the nature of white oppression of Indian people, and Kochinnenako then becomes something of a revolutionary fighter through her collusion with the rebel Miochin in the overthrow of the tyrant Sh-ah-cock. In this reading, the tale becomes a cry for liberation and a direct command to women to aid in the people's struggle to overthrow the colonial powers that drain them of life and strength, deprive them of their rightful prosperity, and threaten them with extinction....

When read as a battle narrative, the story as Gunn renders it makes clear that the superiority of Miochin rests as much in his commitment to the welfare of the people as in his military prowess and that because his attempt to free the people is backed up by their invitation to him to come and liberate them, he is successful. Because of his success he is entitled to the hand of the ruler's daughter, Kochinnenako, one of the traditional Old World spoils of victory. Similarly, Sh-ah-cock is defeated not only because he is violent and oppressive but because the people, like Kochinnenako, find that they cannot love him.

A radical lesbian separatist might find herself uncomfortable with the story even though it is so clearly correct in identifying the enemy as white and violent. But the overthrow of the tyrant is placed squarely in the hands of another male figure, Miochin.... No one asks Kochinnenako what she wants to do; the reader is informed that her marriage is not to her liking when she admits to Miochin that she is unhappy....

Some readers (like myself) might find themselves wondering hopefully whether Miochin isn't really female, disguised by males as one of them in order to buttress their position of relative power. After all, this figure is dressed in yellow and green, the colors of corn, a plant always associated with Woman. Kochinnenako and her sisters are all Corn Women and her mother is, presumably, the head of the Corn Clan; and the Earth Mother of the Keres, Iyatiku, is Corn Woman herself. Alas, I haven't yet found evidence to support such a wishful notion, except that the mask dancer who impersonates Kochinnenako is male, dressed female, which is sort of the obverse side of the wish.

A FEMINIST-TRIBAL INTERPRETATION

The feminist interpretation I have sketched—which is a fair representation of one of my early readings from what I took to be a feminist perspective—proceeds from two unspoken assumptions: that women are essentially powerless and that conflict is basic to human existence. The first is a fundamental feminist position, while the second is basic to Anglo-European thought; neither, however, is characteristic of Keres thought. To a modern feminist, marriage is an institution developed to establish and maintain male supremacy; because she is the ruler's daughter, Kochinnenako's choice of a husband determines which male will hold power over the people and who will inherit the throne.[8]

... Western assumptions about the nature of human society (and thus of literature) when contextualizing a tribal story or ritual must necessarily leave certain elements unclear....

The contexts of Anglo-European and Keres Indian life differ so greatly in virtually every assumption about the nature of reality, society, ethics, female roles, and the sacred importance of seasonal change that simply telling a Keres tale within an Anglo-European narrative context creates a dizzying series of false impressions and unanswerable (perhaps even unposable) questions.

For instance, marriage among traditional Keres is not particularly related to marriage among Anglo-European Americans.... [A] child belongs to its mother's clan, not in the sense that she or he is owned by the clan, but in the sense that she or he belongs within it. Another basic difference is the attitude toward conflict; the Keres can best be described as a conflict-phobic people, while Euro-American culture is conflict-centered. So while the orderly and proper annual transference of power from Winter to Summer people through the agency of the Keres central female figure is the major theme of the narrative from a Keres perspective, the triumph of good over evil becomes its major theme when it is retold by a white man.

Essentially what happens is that Summer (a mask dancer dressed as Miochin) asks Kochinnenako permission, in a ritual manner, to enter the village. She ... follows a ritual order of responses and actions that enable Summer to enter....

Agency is Kochinnenako's ritual role here; it is through her ritual agency that the orderly, harmonious transfer of primacy between the Summer and Winter people is accomplished. This transfer takes place at the time of the year that Winter goes north and Summer comes to the pueblo from the south.... Thus, in the proper time, Kochinnenako empowers Summer to enter the village....

A feminist who is conscious of tribal thought and practice will know that the real story of Sh-ah-cock and Miochin underscores the central role that woman plays in the orderly life of the people. Reading Gunn's version, she will be aware of the vast gulf between the Lagunas and John Gunn in their understanding of the role of women in a traditional gynecentric society such as that of the western Keres. Knowing that the central role of woman is harmonizing spiritual relationships between the people and the rest of the universe by empowering ritual activities, she will be able to read the story for its western colonial content, aware that Gunn's version reveals more about American consciousness when it meets tribal thought than it reveals about the tribe. When the story is analyzed within the context to which it rightly belongs, its feminist content becomes clear, as do the various purposes to which industrialized patriarchal people can put a tribal story.

If she is familiar with the ritual color code of this particular group of Native Americans, a feminist will know that white is the color of Shipap, the place where the four rivers of life come together and where our Mother Iyatiku lives. Thus she will know that it is appropriate that the Spirit of Woman's Power/Being (Yellow Woman) be "married" (that is, ritually connected in energy-transferring gestalts) first with Winter who is the power signified by the color white ... and then with Summer, whose color powers are yellow and green....

A feminist will know that the story is about how the Mother Corn Iyatiku's "daughter" ... comes to live as Remembering Prayer Sticks' daughter first with the Winter people and then with the Summer people, and so on.

The net effect of Gunn's rendition of the story is the unhappy wedding of the woman-centered tradition of the western Keres to patriarchal Anglo-European tradition and thus the dislocation of the central position of Keres women by their assumption under the rule of the men. When one understands that the hocheni is the person who tells the time and prays for all the people, even the white people, and that the Hutchamun Kiuk is the ruler only in the sense that the Constitution of the United States is the ruler of the citizens and government of the United States, then the Keres organization of women, men, spirit folk, equinoxes, seasons, and clouds into a balanced and integral dynamic will be seen reflected in the narrative. Knowing this, a feminist will also be able to see how the interpolations of patriarchal thinking distort all the relationships in the story and, by extension, how such impositions of patriarchy on gynocracy disorder harmonious social and spiritual relationships.

A careful feminist-tribal analysis of Gunn's rendition of a story that would be better titled "The Transfer of Ianyi (ritual power, sacred power) from Winter to Summer" will provide a tribally conscious feminist with an interesting example of how colonization works, however consciously or unconsciously to misinform both the colonized and the colonizer. She will be able to note the process by which the victim of the translation process, the Keres woman who reads the tale, is misinformed because she reads Gunn's book. Even though she knows that something odd is happening in the tale, she is not likely to apply sophisticated feminist analysis to the rendition; in the absence of real knowledge of the colonizing process of story-changing, she is all too likely to find bits of the Gunn tale sticking in her mind and subtly altering her perception of herself, her role in her society, and her relationship to the larger world.

The hazard to male Keres readers is, of course, equally great. They are likely to imagine that the proper relationship of women to men is subservience. And it is because of such a shockingly untraditional modern interpretation, brought on as much by reading Gunn as by other, perhaps more obvious societal mechanisms, that the relationships between men and women are so severely disordered at Laguna that wife-abuse, rape, and battery of women there have reached frightening levels in recent years.

POLITICAL IMPLICATIONS OF NARRATIVE STRUCTURE

The changes Gunn has made in the narrative are not only changes in content; they are structural as well. One useful social function of traditional tribal literature is its tendency to distribute value evenly among various elements, providing a model or pattern for egalitarian structuring of society as well as literature. However, egalitarian structures in either literature or society are not easily "read" by hierarchically inclined westerners.

Still, the tendency to equal distribution of value among all elements in a field, whether the field is social, spiritual, or aesthetic (and the distinction is moot when tribal materials are under discussion), is an integral part of tribal consciousness and is reflected in tribal social and aesthetic systems all over the Americas. In this structural framework, no single element is foregrounded, leaving the others to supply "background." Thus, properly speaking, there are no heroes, no villains, no chorus, no setting (in the sense of inert ground against which dramas are played out)....

In tribal literatures, the timing of the foregrounding of various elements is dependent on the purpose the narrative is intended to serve. Tribal art functions something like a forest in which all elements coexist, where each is integral to the being of the others.... For example, when tribal women on the eastern seaboard went out to gather sassafras, what they noticed, what stood out sharply in their attention, were the sassafras plants. But when they went out to get maple sugar, maples became foregrounded. But the foregrounding of sassafras or maple in no way lessens the value of the other plants or other features of the forest. When a woman goes after maple syrup, she is aware of the other plant forms that are also present.

In the same way, a story that is intended to convey the importance of the Grandmother Spirits will focus on grandmothers in their interaction with grandchildren and will convey little information about uncles. Traditional tales will make a number of points, and a number of elements will be present, all of which will bear some relationship to the subject of the story. Within the time the storyteller has allotted to the story, and depending on the interests and needs of her audience at the time of the storytelling, each of these elements will receive its proper due.

Traditional American Indian stories work dynamically among clusters of loosely interconnected circles.... There is no "point of view" as the term is generally understood, unless the action itself, the story's purpose, can be termed "point of view." But as the old tales are translated and rendered in English, the western notion of proper fictional form takes over the tribal narrative. Soon there appear to be heroes, point of view, conflict, crisis, and resolution, and as western tastes in story crafting are imposed on the narrative structure of the ritual story, the result is a western story with Indian characters. Mournfully, the new form often becomes confused with the archaic form by the very people whose tradition has been re-formed.

The story Gunn calls "Sh-ah-cock and Mi-o-chin or the Battle of the Seasons" might be better termed "How Kochinnenako Balanced the World," though even then the title would be misleading to American readers, for they would see Kochinnenako as the heroine, the foreground of the story.... There is no central figure in the tale, though there is a central point. The point is concerned with the proper process of a shift in focus, not the resolution of a conflict. Kochinnenako's part in the process is agency, not heroics; even in Gunn's version, she does nothing heroic. A situation presents itself in the proper time, and Yellow Woman acts in accordance with the dictates of timing, using proper ritual as her mode. But the people cannot go from Winter into Summer without conscious acceptance of Miochin, and Yellow Woman's invitation to him, an acceptance that is encouraged and supported by all involved, constitutes a tribal act.

The "battle" between Summer and Winter is an accurate description of seasonal change in central New Mexico during the spring. This comes through in the Gunn rendition, but because the story is focused on conflict rather than on balance, the meteorological facts and their intrinsic relationship to human ritual are obscured. Only a non-Indian mind, accustomed to interpreting events in terms of battle, struggle, and conflict, would assume that the process of transfer had to occur through a battle replete with protagonist, antagonist, a cast of thousands, and a pretty girl as the prize. For who but an industrialized patriarch would think that winter can be vanquished? Winter and Summer enjoy a relationship based on complementarity, mutuality, and this is the moral significance of the tale.

TRIBAL NARRATIVES AND WOMEN'S LIVES

Reading American Indian traditional stories and songs is not an easy task. Adequate comprehension requires that the reader be aware that Indians never think like whites and that any typeset version of traditional materials is distorting.

In many ways, literary conventions, as well as the conventions of literacy, militate against an understanding of traditional tribal materials. Western technological-industrialized minds cannot adequately interpret tribal materials because they are generally trained to perceive their entire world in ways that are alien to tribal understandings.

This problem is not exclusive to tribal literature. It is one that all ethnic writers who write out of a tribal or folk tradition face, and one that is also shared by women writers, who, after all, inhabit a separate folk tradition. Much of women's culture bears marked resemblance to tribal culture. The perceptual modes that women, even those of us who are literate, industrialized, and reared within masculinist academic traditions, habitually engage in more closely resemble inclusive-field perception than excluding foreground-background perceptions.

Women's traditional occupations, their arts and crafts, and their literature and philosophies are more often accretive than linear, more achronological than chronological, and more dependent on harmonious relationships of all elements within a field of perception than western culture in general is thought to be. Indeed, the patchwork quilt is the best material example I can think of to describe the plot and process of a traditional tribal narrative, and quilting is a non-Indian woman's art, one that Indian women have taken to avidly and that they display in their ceremonies, rituals, and social gatherings as well as in their homes.

It is the nature of woman's existence to be and to create background. This fact, viewed with unhappiness by many feminists, is of ultimate importance in a tribal context. Certainly no art object is bereft of background. Certainly the contents and tone of one's background will largely determine the direction and meaning of one's life and, therefore, the meaning and effect of one's performance in any given sphere of activity.

Westerners have for a long time discounted the importance of background. The earth herself, which is our most inclusive background, is dealt with summarily as a source of food, metals, water, and profit, while the fact that she is the fundamental agent of all planetary life is blithely ignored. Similarly, women's activities—cooking, planting, harvesting, preservation, storage, homebuilding, decorating, maintaining, doctoring, nursing, soothing, and healing, along with the bearing, nurturing, and rearing of children—are devalued as blithely. An antibackground bias is bound to have social costs that have so far remained unexplored, but elite attitudes toward workers, nonwhite races, and women are all part of the price we pay for overvaluing the foreground.

In the western mind, shadows highlight the foreground. In contrast, in the tribal view the mutual relationships among shadows and light in all their varying degrees of intensity create a living web of definition and depth, and significance arises from their interplay. Traditional and contemporary tribal arts and crafts testify powerfully to the importance of balance among all elements in tribal perception, aesthetics, and social systems.

Traditional peoples perceive their world in a unified-field fashion that is very different from the single-focus perception that generally characterizes western masculinist, monotheistic modes of perception. Because of this, tribal cultures are consistently misperceived and misrepresented by nontribal folklorists, ethnographers, artists, writers, and social workers.... The one is unidimensional, monolithic, excluding, and chronological while the other is multidimensional, achronological, and including.

How one teaches or writes about the one perspective in terms of the other is problematic. This essay itself is a pale representation of a tribal understanding of the Kochinnenako tale. I am acutely aware that much of what I have said is likely to be understood in ways I did not intend, and I am also aware of how much I did not say that probably needed to be said if the real story of the transfer of responsibility from one segment of the tribe to the other is to be made clear.

In the end, the tale I have analyzed is not about Kochinnenako or Sh-ah-cock and Mio-chin. It is about the change of seasons and it is about the centrality of woman as agent and empowerer of that change. It is about how a people engage themselves as a people within the spiritual cosmos and in an ordered and proper way that bestows the dignity of each upon all with careful respect, folkish humor, and ceremonial delight. It is about how everyone is part of the background that shapes the meaning and value of each person's life. It is about propriety, mutuality, and the dynamics of socioenvironmental change.

NOTES

1. John M. Gunn, *Schat Chen: History, Traditions and Narratives of the Queres Indians of Laguna and Acoma* (Albuquerque, N. Mex.: Albright and Anderson, 1917; reprint, New York: AMS, 1977). Gunn, my mother's uncle, lived among the Lagunas all his adult life. He spoke Laguna (Keres) and gathered information in somewhat informal ways while sitting in the sun visiting with older people. He married Meta Atseye, my great-grandmother, years after her husband (John Gunn's brother) died and may have taken much of his information from her stories or explanations of Laguna ceremonial

events. She had a way of "translating" terms and concepts from Keres into English and from a Laguna conceptual framework into an American one, as she understood it. For example, she used to refer to the Navajo people as "gypsies," probably because they traveled in covered wagons and the women wear long, full skirts and head scarves and both men and women wear a great deal of jewelry.

2. In a system where all persons in power are called Mother Chief and where the supreme deity is female, and social organization is matrilocal, matrifocal, and matrilineal, gynarchy is happening. However, it does not imply domination of men by women as patriarchy implies domination by ruling class males of all aspects of a society.

3. His use of the term may reflect the use by his informants, who were often educated in Carlisle or Menaul Indian schools, in their attempt to find an equivalent term that Gunn could understand to signify the deep respect and reverence accorded the hocheni tyi'a'muni. Or he might have selected the term because he was writing a book for an anonymous non-Keres audience, which included himself. Since he spoke Laguna Keres, I think he was doing the translations himself, and his rendering of words (and contexts) was likely influenced by the way Lagunas themselves rendered local terms into English. I doubt, however, that he was conscious of the extent to which his renderings reflected European traditions and simultaneously distorted Laguna-Acoma ones. Gunn was deeply aware of the importance and intelligence of the Keresan tradition, but he was also unable to grant it independent existence. His major impulse was to link the western Keres with the Sumerians, to in some strange way demonstrate the justice of his assessment of their intelligence. An unpublished manuscript in my possession written by John Gunn after *Schat Chen* is devoted to his researches and speculations into this idea.

4. Gunn, *Schat Chen,* pp. 217–222.

. . .

6. Boas, *Keresan Texts,* p. 288. Boas says he made the same mistake at first, having misheard the word they used.

7. … The kind of cultural chauvinism that has been promulgated by well-intentioned but culturally entranced feminists can lead to serious misunderstandings such as this and in the process become a new racism based on what becomes the feminist canon. Not that feminists can be faulted entirely on this—they are, after all, reflecting the research and interpretation done in a patriarchal context, by male-biased researchers and scholars, most of whom would avidly support the young radical feminist's strenuous position. It's too bad, though, that feminists fall into the patriarchal trap!

8. For a detailed exposition of what this dynamic consists of, see Adrienne Rich, "Compulsory Heterosexuality and Lesbian Existence," *Signs: Journal of Women in Culture and Society,* vol. 5, no. 4 (Summer 1980). Reprinted in 1982 as a pamphlet with an updated foreword, Antelope Publications, 1612 St. Paul, Denver, CO 80206.

. . .

2
The Social Sciences

Like the humanities, the social sciences study the human rather than the nonhuman aspects of the world; more specifically, they study human beings in their social contexts. They are distinguished from the humanities not so much by the objects of their study as by their practitioners' efforts to study these objects in a way that is "scientific." Scholars in the social science disciplines wish their work to attain the privileged epistemic status of science, which is often regarded as the most dependable kind of knowledge. In pursuit of this status, they have often sought to study humans in society with methods similar to those credited with enabling the spectacular successes of the physical sciences.

The boundaries of various disciplines in the social sciences are drawn on the basis of both subject matter and method. Because of overlap among these subject matters and methods, the boundaries sometimes may appear to have an element of arbitrariness. As we have seen, some disciplines usually categorized as falling within the humanities, such as history and "area" studies, frequently use methods associated with the social sciences. For instance, the distinction between political philosophy and political science is drawn according to the latter's supposed use of the scientific method; however, political theory, a part of political science, depends heavily on conceptual analysis, and political philosophers frequently make use of extensive empirical material. Given this overlap, how can we identify a distinctively scientific approach to studying human beings in society?

POSITIVISM IN THE SOCIAL SCIENCES

The methodological foundations of contemporary social science were laid in the late nineteenth century by theorists such as Auguste Comte and Karl Marx. These authors and their followers envisioned that the social sciences would formulate universal laws of human society, parallel to the seemingly universal laws of nature presented in Newtonian theory, and they believed that, to achieve this, the social sciences must emulate the methods attributed to the physical sciences. Such methods were thought to require the theoretical elaboration of empirical observations, often in the form of mathematically precise measurements. An important methodological requirement was that the observations and measurements should be repeatable by multiple observers, a requirement intended to maximize objectivity by eliminating the possibility of idiosyncrasies, errors, and biases on the part of observers. The origins of C. P. Snow's distinction between two cultures can be seen already in late nineteenth- and early twentieth-century social scientists' aspiration for knowledge of human societies that would be universal, secular, and value-free.

MASCULINE BIAS IN THE SOCIAL SCIENCES

In the late 1960s and early 1970s, North American feminist scholars began arguing that several social science disciplines had realized these aspirations only partially, at best. The critics contended that much work in the social sciences was not only inaccurate but also biased systematically against women and other subordinated populations. The landmark 1970 collection *Sisterhood Is Powerful* included an article, "'Kinder, Küche, Kirche as Scientific Law': Psychology Constructs the Female" (Weisstein 1970). Its author, Naomi Weisstein, argued that clinical psychology and psychiatry portrayed women as innately servile and childishly dependent, portrayals that were "worse than useless in contributing to a vision which could truly liberate—men as well as women." Weisstein attributed these errors to methodological flaws, including disregard of evidence and failure to "look to the social context within which individuals live." In 1974, Dorothy Smith published her groundbreaking article, "Women's Perspective as a Radical Critique of Sociology." This raised several themes developed over the following decades by other feminist critics of the social sciences.

One theme was simply the exclusion of women and the culturally feminine, a theme paralleled in feminist criticism of the humanities. Dorothy Smith argued that sociology focused on what she called a "male social universe," a conceptual world that included not only a recognized set of issues ("industrial sociology, political sociology, social stratification, etc."), but also an acceptance of the fundamental social and political structures within which these particular issues have meaning. This focus marginalized the universe of women, which Smith identified as a world centered on, though not limited to, the domestic. She described it as the "natural," concrete, and immediate world of particular human bodies and the work needed to care for them. Feminist scholars in other social science disciplines noted similarly gendered omissions; for instance, they observed that anthropology had focused on men's rather than women's subsistence activities and on practices of war rather than practices of child rearing; thus mainstream anthropology had identified the tools of hunting rather than of gathering as crucial to human evolution. Feminist scholars in psychology noted that the project of understanding the human mind was pursued largely through studying the mental states and activities of men.

As feminist critics observed, the emphasis on men's minds and activities meant that women and the culturally feminine appeared only in the background shadows. When the social sciences did address women and the feminine, their perceptions and interpretations were often biased by masculinist stereotypes and assumptions. Psychologist Lawrence Kohlberg produced a framework for measuring moral development that was based exclusively on studies of boys and men; women's relatively low scores on this measure were interpreted as evidence of female deficiency rather than taken to indicate that the measure might be male biased (see Chapter 7 of this volume). In the third reading of Chapter 2, Linda Tuhiwai Smith argues that European scholars researched Maori life "through imperial eyes," imposing Western categories of gender as well as of space and time.

Both Dorothy Smith and Linda Tuhiwai Smith assert that the social sciences are linked with the practice of ruling. They produce knowledge for the elites who administer social life, elites that Dorothy Smith identifies as male and that Linda Tuhiwai Smith identifies additionally as European colonial. Social scientific studies generate representations of social life that justify an oppressive status quo. European women are presented as auxiliaries to civilization; Maori women are presented as indolent and needing the discipline of training as domestic servants.

According to many feminist critics, the methods through which much social scientific knowledge has been produced are not only epistemically unreliable; they have also often been unethical. In the second selection in this chapter, Toby Epstein Jayaratne and Abigail J. Stewart cite the example of Stanley Milgram's famous studies of "obedience," in the course of which research subjects were deceived and manipulated. Feminists also expressed concern about social scientists using their information in exploitative ways, harming the research subjects even as they enhanced their own reputations.

Dorothy Smith argues that women scholars find themselves estranged from the standard operating procedures of sociology. Their consciousness is bifurcated, so that they recognize the gap between their professional and conceptual activities of research, teaching, and administration and the concrete work of cleaning and caring for bodies that makes the former activities possible. Smith's reflections on the more inclusive perspective attainable by women scholars inspired standpoint theorists, such as Patricia Hill Collins and Sandra Harding, whose work appears later in this volume.

Elaborating these criticisms of the social sciences, feminist scholars argued that many disciplines' pretensions to precision, accuracy, and value-neutrality were exaggerated and often simply wrong. Instead, the social science disciplines were riddled with biased observations skewed by unexamined assumptions and unacknowledged values. The requirement that observations be repeatable was sufficient to eliminate idiosyncratic biases among social scientists but was unable to challenge pervasive and typically unacknowledged assumptions, such as masculinist and Eurocentric assumptions, shared by the discipline as a whole. Feminists disagreed over whether these recurrent problems were a result of social scientists' misuse of the scientific method or whether this method as a whole needed to be reconceptualized. Some feminists thought that the problem lay in the neopositivist approach to methodology and sought to develop a "women's" alternative to this. The alternative approach would feature new objects of study, new methods, new goals, new ethical standards, and new authors of knowledge.

FEMINIZING THE SOCIAL SCIENCES

In the feminized alternative to neopositivism developed in the late 1970s and early 1980s, the new objects of study would, of course, be women and the culturally feminine. This new focus would remedy the omissions of mainstream theory, enabling hitherto untold stories to be told and heard. The importance of the culturally feminine would be recognized and women's agency acknowledged.

The new methods would be primarily phenomenological, aiming to reveal women's lives as experienced by those who lived them (Stanley and Wise 1983). Early feminist critics of the social sciences often advocated the use of qualitative rather than quantitative methods, which typically took the form of in-depth interviewing. Researchers were often urged to develop personal relationships with their research subjects, to identify with them rather than objectify them, and to rely on their hearts as well as their heads (Rose 1983). The resulting interactions would be personal rather than impersonal and should be reported in the active rather than the passive voice. Thus researchers would appear not as neutral observers occupying a universal perspective beyond space and time but rather as particular situated individuals participating in and shaping specific processes of research. This conception of social scientific method, in which each research encounter would be unique, obviously required abandoning the requirement that observations be repeatable.

The goals of the new social sciences would be explicitly political. As Dorothy Smith put it, they would be social sciences "for" women, providing the knowledge necessary for women's liberation. Telling the hitherto untold stories of women's lives would contribute to this goal by "validating" women's experiences. Social scientists would not impose their own interpretations but instead test their theories against women's experience.

The methods of the new social sciences would be nonexploitative and nonobjectifying, embodying women's values of compassion and inclusion. The hierarchical relationship between researchers and their subjects would be eliminated. Researchers would often become friends with their subjects, sometimes intervening to assist them with their life problems. Research subjects would collaborate with researchers not only by providing information but also by reflecting on the researchers' presentations and interpretations of that information. In many ways, the research process would resemble consciousness-raising; Catharine MacKinnon (1982) even stated, "consciousness-raising *is* feminist method."

Finally, early work on feminist methodology was often characterized by the assumption that social science produced "for" women would also be produced *by* women. Again, Dorothy Smith's early works were influential. In her view, socially constructed worlds can be known only from within. Because women's lives differ systematically from men's, women sociologists are able not only to perceive and problematize a culturally feminine world that male sociologists ignore but also to see men's world differently and to recognize mainstream sociology as a practice of domination.

PROBLEMS WITH FEMINIZING THE SOCIAL SCIENCES

This radical vision of feminized social science provided a stark challenge to the scientistic pretensions of much existing scholarship. Not surprisingly, it was met with other strong challenges. Antifeminist critics drew on prevailing stereotypes of both traditional femininity and feminism to ridicule the vision as "soft" and overly idealistic, as well as being antiscience and even antireason. In the view of these critics, the proponents of this feminine vision had abandoned the aspiration to scientific objectivity in favor of a "feel-good" process that was based on feminist ideological prejudices and therefore merely confirmed them. Some feminist critics shared some of these fears, though they did not express them so harshly. In addition, they presented some distinctively feminist criticisms of the vision, which paralleled ideas current in other areas of feminist scholarship.

One set of criticisms revolved around "essentialist" notions of "women's" experience. The critics pointed out that women are not a unified social group; instead, they are separated by vast social divisions, such as class, race, and ethnicity. Norms of femininity and patterns of experience vary enormously among these social groups, none of which typifies "women." In addition, critics pointed out that women and femininity are relational categories, which can be understood only in the context of correlative and also varying conceptions of men and masculinities. For these reasons, the project of researching "women's" experience leaves unanswered crucial questions not only about identifying female research subjects but also about the possibility of understanding their experiences without comparing them with those of men.

A second set of problems revolved around the notion of "experience." Could this be reported without also being interpreted? Were the subjects of experience the final authorities on how to interpret it? How should researchers deal with changes in the subjects' stories? By the late 1980s, considerable feminist criticism of "experientialism" was emerging, as well as criticism of the rejection of quantitative work. Many feminist social scientists were reluctant to abandon traditional aspirations to large-scale studies, precision, and objectivity.

These concerns obviously raised questions regarding the idea of a social science *for* women. Some feminists asked not only *which* women would be served by the new social sciences but also *how* these sciences would serve them. Providing more information about the diversity of women's lives would certainly be of feminist interest, but how would this information be presented and theorized? Dorothy Smith, who advocates a focus on women's experience, also notes that the determinants of this experience lie outside it. How could these determinants be identified? And what would be the criteria of theoretical adequacy? Finally, some feminists were concerned that the idea of a social science constructed especially for women suggested that it might not be relevant to or even believable by men, raising the specter of relativism.

The idea of feminist research as a collaboration between researchers and subjects also raised practical and theoretical questions. What if subjects did not have time or inclination to provide feedback on feminist scholarship? Should they be paid for their collaboration? What if the subjects were not feminists or if they disagreed with the researchers? Were not problems raised by researchers' and research subjects' inevitably differing investments in the results of the research process? Did not the vision of egalitarian collaboration collapse the distinction between researchers and their subjects, resulting in the conclusion that researchers should study only themselves? What about scholarly expertise, authority, and responsibility?

Finally, the assumption that feminist social scientists should be women seemed questionable. After all, feminism is a moral/political commitment and those so committed cannot be identified by their sex/gender identities. Not all women social scientists are feminist, perhaps only a minority, and many men have been feminists.

Overall, feminist critics of the idea of feminizing the social sciences worried that this approach to methodology relied on and reinforced gendered stereotypes of women as both objects and authors of knowledge. Some feminists began seeking methodological approaches to social science that would be feminist as opposed to feminine.

FROM FEMININE TO FEMINIST METHODOLOGY

Feminist approaches to methodology in the social sciences build on the insights of earlier theorists dedicated to valorizing the culturally feminine, but they also seek to go beyond them. These approaches will be explored more fully in the remainder of this book, but all are characterized by certain epistemic and ethical commitments.

First, contemporary feminist methodology in the social sciences rejects the idea that women are a natural kind. Instead, it recognizes that considerable arbitrariness and coercion characterize social processes of sex assignment, that the meaning of sexual identity varies according to social context, and that norms of feminine gendering are mediated by many other social categories. In addition, this methodology recognizes that women and femininities are relational categories indicating not only difference but also dominance, differential status, and power. Therefore, contemporary feminist methodology recommends that feminist research focus not on "women" *simpliciter* but rather on the gendered experiences of those variously constructed as masculine and feminine, as these experiences are simultaneously shaped by other categories of inequality.

Second, feminist approaches to methodology are not restricted to the use of "qualitative" methods. Instead, as Jayaratne and Stewart argue, feminist methodological approaches to the social sciences may and should utilize both qualitative and quantitative methods. "Women's (and men's) experience" is taken as the starting point rather than the terminus of feminist research in the social sciences.

Contemporary feminist methodology has not abandoned the idea of a social science *for* women, but it has become considerably more sophisticated in considering what this might mean. For instance, it recognizes that women may be agents as well as objects of oppression, indeed that they are often simultaneously agents and objects, and it explores human agency within the context of complex structures of inequality. It is also concerned with accountability: To whom are feminist social scientists accountable and how might they carry out this responsibility?

Feminist methodology in the social sciences retains a concern for the ethical as well as the political dimensions of social science research. It is sensitive to the power relations between researchers and their subjects and questions how researchers can be respectful of and responsive to their subjects but still retain a commitment to their own conception of truth. It insists that researchers must always reflect on the ways in which their research is influenced by their own social positioning, their gender, race, class, and so on. How does this positioning affect the questions they ask, the interactions they have with their subjects, the ways they interpret their data, and the consequences of publication for their own lives? This insistence on reflexivity is motivated by concerns that are both epistemic and ethical.

Finally, contemporary feminist social science has abandoned the assumption that feminist social scientists must be women, an assumption that no longer seemed plausible once the focus of feminist social science shifted from women's experience to gendered lives. Many well-respected feminist social scientists are male, often studying masculinities and their implications for gender justice.

This sketch of contemporary feminist approaches to methodology leaves many questions unanswered. In the remainder of this volume, we shall see that the implications of feminist reflections on this topic are not simply to "soften" the social sciences but instead to make them more inclusive, objective, and just.

REFERENCES

MacKinnon, Catharine. 1982. "Feminism, Marxism, Method, and the State: An Agenda for Theory." *Signs: Journal of Women in Culture and Society* 7(3): 515–544.

Rose, Hilary. 1983. "Hand, Brain, and Heart: Towards a Feminist Epistemology for the Natural Sciences." *Signs: Journal of Women in Culture and Society* 19(1): 73–96.

Stanley, Liz, and Sue Wise. 1983. *Breaking Out: Feminist Consciousness and Feminist Research.* Boston: Routledge and Kegan Paul.

Weisstein, Naomi. 1970. "'Kinder, Küche, Kirche' as Scientific Law: Psychology Constructs the Female," in *Sisterhood Is Powerful: An Anthology of Writings from the Women's Liberation Movement,* ed. Robin Morgan. New York: Random House.

Dorothy E. Smith
Women's Perspective as a Radical Critique of Sociology

The women's movement has given us a sense of our right to have women's interests represented in sociology, rather than just receiving as authoritative the interests traditionally represented in a sociology put together by men.... [This] bring[s] us to ask first how a sociology might look if it began from the point of view of women's traditional place in it and what happens to a sociology which attempts to deal seriously with that. Following this line of thought, I have found, has consequences larger than they seem at first.

From the point of view of "women's place" the values assigned to different aspects of the world are changed.... We might take as a model the world as it appears from the point of view of the afternoon soap opera. This is defined by (though not restricted to) domestic events, interests, and activities. Men appear in this world as necessary and vital presences. It is not a woman's world in the sense of excluding men. But it is a women's world in the sense that it is the relevances of the women's place that govern. Men appear only in their domestic or private aspects or at points of intersection between public and private.... Their occupational and political world is barely present. They are posited here as complete persons, and they are but partial—as women appear in a sociology predicated on the universe occupied by men.

But it is not enough to supplement an established sociology by addressing ourselves to what has been left out, overlooked, or by making sociological issues of the relevances of the world of women. That merely extends the authority of the existing sociological procedures and makes of a women's sociology an addendum. We cannot rest at that because it does not account for the separation between the two worlds and it does not account for or analyze for us the relation between them....

The first difficulty is that how sociology is thought—its methods, conceptual schemes, and theories—has been based on and built up within the male social universe (even when women have participated in its doing). It has taken for granted not just that scheme of relevances as an itemized inventory of issues or subject matters (industrial sociology, political sociology, social stratification, etc.) but the fundamental social and political structures under which these become relevant and are ordered. There is a difficulty first then of a disjunction between how women find and experience the world beginning (though not necessarily ending up) from their place and the concepts and theoretical schemes available to think about it in....

A second difficulty is that the two worlds and the two bases of knowledge and experience don't stand in an equal relation. The world as it is constituted by men stands in authority over that of women. It is that part of the world from which our kind of society is governed and from which what happens to us begins....

The two difficulties are related to one another in a special way. The effect of the second interacting with the first is to impose the concepts and terms in which the world of men is thought as the concepts and terms in which women must think their world. Hence in these terms women are alienated from their experience.

The profession of sociology is predicated on a universe which is occupied by men and it is itself still largely appropriated by men as their "territory."... Thus the institutions which lock sociology into the structures occupied by men are the same institutions which lock women into the situations in which they find themselves oppressed. To unlock the latter leads logically to an unlocking of the former. What follows then, or rather what then becomes possible—for it is of course by no means inevitable—is less a shift in the subject matter than a different conception of how it is or might become relevant as a means to understand our experience and the conditions of our experience (both women's and men's) in corporate capitalist society.

When I speak here of governing or ruling I mean something more general than the notion of government as political organization. I refer rather to that total complex of activities differentiated into many spheres, by which our kind of society is ruled, managed, administered. It includes that whole section which in the business world is called "management,"... government more conventionally defined and also the activities of those who are selecting, training, and indoctrinating those who will be its governors. The last includes those who provide and elaborate the procedures in which it is governed and develop methods for accounting for how it is done and predicting and analyzing its characteristic consequences and sequences of events, namely the business schools, the sociologists, the economists, etc. These are the institutions through which we are ruled and through which we, and I emphasize this we, participate in ruling.

Sociology then I conceive as much more than ideology, much more than a gloss on the enterprise which justifies and rationalizes it and at the same time as much less than "science": The governing of our kind of society is done in concepts and symbols. The contribution of sociology to this is that of working up the conceptual procedures, models, and methods by which the immediate and concrete features of experience can be read into the conceptual mode in which the governing is done. What is actually observed or what is systematically recovered by the sociologist from the actualities of what people say and do, must be transposed into the abstract mode. Sociology thus participates in and contributes to the formation and facilitation of this mode of action and plays a distinctive part in the work of transposing the actualities of people's lives and experience into the conceptual currency in which it is and can be governed.

Thus the relevances of sociology are organized in terms of a perspective on the world which is a view from the top and which takes for granted the pragmatic procedures of governing as those which frame and identify its subject matter. Issues are formulated as issues which have become administratively relevant not as they are significant first in the experience of those who live them.

...

The governing processes of our society are organized as social entities constituted externally to those persons who participate in and perform them. The managers, the bureaucrats, the administrators, are employees, are people who are *used*. They do not own the enterprises or otherwise appropriate them. Sociologists study these entities under the heading of formal organization.... The academic professions are also set up in a mode which externalizes them as entities vis-à-vis their practitioners. The body of knowledge which its members accumulate is appropriated by the discipline as its body....

...

An important set of procedures which serve to constitute the body of knowledge of the discipline as something which is separated from its practitioners are those known as "objectivity." The ethic of objectivity and the methods used in its practice are concerned primarily with the separation of the knower from what he knows and in particular with the separation of what is known from any interests, "biases," etc., which he may have which are not the interests and concerns authorized by the discipline.... What they feel and think about society can be taken apart from and kept out of what they are professionally or academically interested in.

The sociologist enters the conceptually ordered society when he goes to work.... He observes, analyses, explains, and examines as if there were no problem in how that world becomes observable to him. He moves among the doings of organizations, governmental processes, bureaucracies, etc., as a person who is at home in that medium. The nature of that world itself, how it is known to him and the conditions of its existence or his relation to it are not called into question. His methods of observation and inquiry extend into it as procedures which are essentially of the same order as those which bring about the phenomena with which he is concerned, or which he is concerned to bring under the jurisdiction of that order. His perspectives and interests may differ, but the substance is the same. He works with facts and information which have been worked up from actualities.... He fits that information back into a framework of entities and organizational processes which he takes for granted as known.... He passes beyond the particular and immediate setting in which he is always located in the body (the office he writes in, the libraries he consults, the streets he travels, the home he returns to) without any sense of having made a transition. He works in the same medium as he studies.

But like everyone else he also exists in the body in the place in which it is. This is also then the place of his sensory organization of immediate experience, the place where his coordinates of here and now before and after are organized around himself as centre; the place where he confronts people face to face in the physical mode in which he expresses himself to them and they to him as more and other than either can speak.... Into this space must come as actual material events, whether as the sounds of speech, the scratchings on the surface of paper which he constitutes as document, or directly anything he knows of the world. It has to happen here somehow if he is to experience it at all.

...

Women are outside and subservient to this structure. They have a very specific relation to it which anchors them into the local and particular phase of the bifurcated world. For both traditionally and as a matter of occupational practices in our society, the governing conceptual mode is appropriated by men and the world organized in the natural attitude, the home, is appropriated by (or assigned to) women (Smith 1973).

It is a condition of a man's being able to enter and become absorbed in the conceptual mode that he does not have to focus his own relation to its conditions because the sociologist as actual person in an actual concrete setting has been cancelled in the procedures which objectify and separate him from his knowledge. Thus the linkage which points back to its conditions is lacking.

For women those conditions are central as a direct practical matter, to be somehow solved in the decision to take up a sociological career. The relation between ourselves as practicing sociologists and ourselves as working women is continually visible to us, a central feature of experience of the world, so that the bifurcation of consciousness becomes for us a daily chasm which is to be crossed, on the one side of which is this special conceptual activity of thought ... and on the other the world of concrete practical activities in keeping things clean, managing somehow the house and household and the children, a world in which the particularities of persons in their full organic immediacy (cleaning up the vomit, changing the diapers, as well as feeding) are inescapable. Even if we don't have that as a direct contingency in our lives, we are aware of that as something that our becoming may be inserted into as a possible predicate.

It is also present for us to discover that the discipline is not one which we enter and occupy on the same terms as men enter and occupy it. We do not fully appropriate its authority, i.e. the right to author and authorize the acts and knowing and thinking which are the acts and knowing and thinking of the discipline as it is thought. We cannot therefore command the inner principles of our action. That remains lodged outside us. The frames of reference which order the terms upon which inquiry and discussion are conducted originate with men. The subjects of sociological sentences (if they have a subject) are male. The sociologist is "he." And even before we become conscious of our sex as the basis of an exclusion *(they* are not talking about us), we none the less do not fully enter ourselves as the subjects of its statements, since we must suspend our sex, and suspend our knowledge of who we are as well as who it is that in fact is speaking and of whom. Therefore we do not fully participate in the declarations and formulations of its mode of consciousness. The externalization of sociology as a profession which I have described above becomes for women a double estrangement.

There is then for women a basic organization of their experience which displays for them the structure of the bifurcated consciousness. At the same time it attenuates their commitment to a sociology which aims at an externalized body of knowledge based on an organization of experience which excludes theirs and excludes them except in a subordinate relation.

An alternative approach must somehow transcend this contradiction without reentering Bierstedt's "transcendental realm" (1966). Women's perspective, as I have analyzed it here, discredits sociology's claim to constitute an objective knowledge independent of the sociologist's situation. Its conceptual procedures, methods, and relevances are seen to organize its subject matter from a determinate position in society. This critical disclosure becomes then the basis for an alternative way of thinking sociology.

. . .

We would reject, it seems to me, a sociology aimed primarily at itself. We would not be interested in contributing to a body of knowledge the uses of which are not ours and the knowers of whom are who knows whom, but generally male—particularly when it is not at all clear what it is that is constituted as knowledge in that relation. The professional sociologist's practice of thinking it as it is thought would have to be discarded. She would be constrained by the actualities of how it happens in her direct experience. Sociology would aim at offering to anyone a knowledge of the social organization and determinations of the properties and events of their directly experienced world. Its analyses would become part of our ordinary interpretations of the experienced world, just as our experience of the sun's sinking below the horizon is transformed by our knowledge that the world turns. (Yet from where we are it seems to sink and that must be accounted for.)

The only way of knowing a socially constructed world is knowing it from within. We can never stand outside it. A relation in which sociological phenomena are objectified and presented as external to and independent of the observer is itself a special social practice also known from within. The relation of observer and object of observation, of sociologist to "subject," is a specialized social relationship. Even to be a stranger is to enter a world constituted from within as strange. The strangeness itself is the mode in which it is experienced.

. . .

To begin from direct experience and to return to it as a constraint or "test" of the adequacy of a systematic knowledge is to begin from where we are located bodily. The actualities of our everyday world are already socially organized. Settings, equipment, "environment," schedules, occasions, etc., as well as the enterprises and routines of actors are socially produced and concretely and symbolically organized prior to our practice. By beginning from her original and immediate knowledge of her world, sociology offers a way of making its socially organized properties first observable and then problematic.

Let me make it clear that when I speak of "experience" I do not use the term as a synonym for "perspective." ... Such subjectivist interpretations of "experience" are themselves an aspect of that organization of consciousness which bifurcates it and transports us into mind country while stashing away the concrete conditions and practices upon which it depends.... Rather the sociologist's investigation of our directly experienced world as a problem is a mode of discovering or rediscovering the society from within. She begins from her own original but tacit knowledge and from within the acts by which she brings it into her grasp in making it observable and in understanding how it works. She aims not at a reiteration of what she already (tacitly) knows, but at an exploration through that of what passes beyond it and is deeply implicated in how it is.

. . .

If we address the problem of the conditions as well as the perceived forms and organization of immediate experience, we should include it in the events as they actually happen or the ordinary material world which we encounter as a matter of fact—the urban renewal project which uproots 400 families; how it is to live on welfare as an ordinary daily practice.... When we examine them, we find that there are many aspects of how these things come about of which we have little as sociologists to say. We have a sense that the events which enter our experience originate somewhere in a human intention, but we are unable to track back to find it and to find out how it got from there to here. Or take this room in which I work or that room in which you are reading and treat that as a problem. If we think about the conditions of our activity here, we could track back to how it is that there are chairs, table, walls, our clothing, our presence; how these places (yours and mine) are cleaned and maintained, etc. There are human activities, intentions, and relations which are not apparent as such in the actual material conditions of our work.... We bypass in the immediacy of the specific practical activity, a complex division of labor which is an essential precondition to it.

> ...

Women's situation in sociology discloses to her a typical bifurcate structure with the abstracted conceptual practices on the one hand and the concrete realizations, the maintenance routines, etc., on the other. Taking each for granted depends upon being fully situated in one or the other so that the other does not appear in contradiction to it. Women's direct experience places her a step back where we can recognize the uneasiness that comes in sociology from its claim to be about the world we live in and its failure to account for or even describe its actual features as we find them in living them. The aim of an alternative sociology would be to develop precisely that capacity from that beginning so that it might be a means to anyone of understanding how the world comes about for her and how it is organized so that it happens to her as it does in her experience.

Though such a sociology would not be exclusively for or done by women it does begin from the analysis and critique originating in their situation. Its elaboration therefore depends upon a grasp of that which is prior to and fuller than its formulation. It is a little like the problem of making a formal description of the grammar of a language. The linguist depends and always refers back to the competent speakers' sense of what is correct usage, what makes sense, etc. In her own language she depends to a large extent upon her own competence. Women are native speakers of this situation and in explicating it or its implications and realizing them conceptually, they have that relation to it of knowing it before it has been said.

The incomprehensibility of the determinations of our immediate local world is for women a particularly striking metaphor. It recovers an inner organization in common with their typical relation to the world. For women's activities and existence are determined outside them and beyond the world which is their "place." ... As a sociologist then the grasp and exploration of her own experience as a method of discovering society restores to her a centre which in this enterprise at least is wholly hers.

REFERENCES

Bierstedt, Robert (1966), "Sociology and General Education," in Charles H. Page (ed.), *Sociology and Contemporary Education* (New York: Random House).

Gouldner, Alvin (1971), *The Coming Crisis in Western Sociology* (London: Heinemann Educational Books).

Smith, Dorothy E. (1973), "Women, the Family and Corporate Capitalism," in M. L. Stephenson (ed.), *Women in Canada* (Toronto: Newpress).

Toby Epstein Jayaratne and Abigail J. Stewart

Quantitative and Qualitative Methods in the Social Sciences: Current Feminist Issues and Practical Strategies

Within the last decade, the feminist research community has engaged in a dialogue concerning the use of quantitative versus qualitative methods in social research. Much of this debate has concerned the claim that quantitative research techniques—involving the translation of individuals' experience into categories predefined by researchers—distort women's experience and result in a silencing of women's own voices. Advocates of qualitative methods have argued that individual women's understandings, emotions, and actions in the world must be explored in those women's own terms. Defenders of quantitative methods in turn have worried that qualitative methods often include few safeguards against the operation of researcher biases and that abandonment of all aspects of traditional methodology may carry political and scholarly costs. In addition, some have pointed out that although quantitative methods can be and have been used to distort women's experience, they need not be....

We believe that much of the feminist debate about qualitative and quantitative research has been sterile and based on a false polarization. Moreover, as we will show below, solutions offered for methodological problems have frequently been either too general or too constraining to be realistically incorporated into research activity. Finally, much of the discussion of feminist methodology is really a discussion of basic epistemological issues (for example, the validity of various forms of knowledge); the dialogue is, therefore, fundamental but relatively esoteric and inaccessible....

THE FEMINIST METHODOLOGY DIALOGUE

Feminist Criticism

The initial dialogue on feminist methodology originated from feminist criticism of traditional quantitative research.... DuBois (1983) succinctly defined the basic issue by stating, "we literally cannot see women through traditional science and theory" (p. 110).

Specific criticisms of this research have included

1. The selection of sexist and elitist research topics (Cook and Fonow, 1984; Frieze, Parsons, Johnson, Ruble, and Zellman, 1978; Grady, 1981; Jayaratne, 1983; Scheuneman, 1986) and the absence of research on questions of central importance to women (see Parlee, 1975; Roberts, 1981)

2. Biased research designs, including selection of only male subjects (Grady, 1981; Lykes and Stewart, 1986)
3. An exploitative relationship between the researcher and the subject (Jayaratne, 1983; Mies, 1983; Oakley, 1981; Reinharz, 1979; Stanley and Wise, 1983) and within research teams (Birke, 1986; Harding, 1987)
4. The illusion of objectivity, especially associated with the positivist approach (Bleier, 1984; Jayaratne, 1983; Lykes and Stewart, 1986; Stanley and Wise, 1983; Wallston, 1981)
5. The simplistic and superficial nature of quantitative data (Jayaratne, 1983)
6. Improper interpretation and overgeneralization of findings (Jayaratne and Kaczala, 1983; Lykes and Stewart, 1986; Westkott, 1979), including the use of person-blame explanations and application to women of theory tested on exclusively male subjects
7. Inadequate data dissemination and utilization (Jayaratne, 1983; Tangri and Strasburg, 1979)....

Many classic studies in social science may be analyzed now in terms of these criticisms. For example, Milgram's (1974) famous studies of "obedience," in which participants were led to believe they were administering painful shocks to another person (actually a "stooge" of the experimenter) in the name of "teaching," may be considered in light of these issues.

First, Milgram's definition of "obedience" (following the experimenter's instructions) relied on the rather abstract authority of the "scientist" and ignored both economic and personal safety factors which may in fact motivate "obedience" among those without power. In addition, if participants generally assumed that the experimental situation was one in which nothing dangerous or harmful could "really" happen, the relevance of that situation to real-world "obedience" contexts (e.g., war) is unclear. Second, *all* of Milgram's studies involved a male victim or "learner" and a male experimenter.... [M]ost of his studies included only white, male, well-educated subjects in New Haven, Connecticut (although one study was conducted with 40 female subjects of unknown age, occupation, social class, or other characteristics, and some experiments apparently included industrial workers and unemployed persons).

Third, the entire research design depended on maximizing the hierarchical distance between experimenter and research participants; in addition, the experimenter actually deceived the participants throughout the experiment. At the end, a "debriefing" was held, in which "at the very least every subject was told that the victim had not received dangerous electric shocks" (p. 24)....

Fourth, the "indicators" selected for analysis were thoroughly "objective," for example, the actual voltage of the current, apparently administered to the stooge "learner" by the research participant. Similarly, fifth, analysis of the data was conducted in the most quantitative terms; thus, the participants' beliefs about their actions, and their feelings in the situation, were often not assessed at all. When such attitudes were measured, they too were assessed in highly quantitative terms: "the experimental subjects were asked to indicate on a 14-point scale just how nervous or tense they felt at the point of maximum tension" (p. 41).

Sixth, despite the rather narrow definition of "obedience" and the limited range of people included as research participants, Milgram believed that

the essence of obedience consists in the fact that a person comes to view himself [sic] as the instrument for carrying out another person's wishes, and he therefore no longer regards himself as responsible for his actions. Once this critical shift of viewpoint has occurred in the persons, all of the essential features of obedience follow.... The question of generality, therefore, is not resolved by enumerating all the manifest differences between the psychological laboratory and other situations but by carefully constructing a situation that *captures the essence of obedience.* (Milgram, 1974, p. xii; italics added)

The critical question, of course, is how we know that the "essence of obedience" has indeed been captured. Although Milgram invokes an internal, self-definitional process as accounting for "obedience," he does not in fact assess directly any aspect of that process. Moreover, although he explores a number of contextual factors affecting rates of obedience, he concludes—without proof—that the "essence" of it is captured in all variants of the experimental paradigm. Hornstein (1988), in a completely different context, has argued that in general shifts toward quantification in psychology have accompanied burial of the question of the link between the measure and what is being measured. Thus, just as intelligence came to be thought of as that which intelligence tests measure, so too obedience comes to be defined as that which the obedience paradigm assesses.

Clearly, then, the feminist criticisms of traditional research practice are relevant not only to some social science research, but to many of the most respected and significant "landmark" studies.

Sources of Feminist Criticism

The specific feminist criticisms of traditional methodology derive from at least three sources. First, criticism has resulted from negative personal experiences with traditional research (for example, see Weisstein, 1977)....

A second source of criticism is political, stemming from a concern that existing methodologies support sexist, racist, and elitist attitudes and practices and therefore negatively affect people's lives. For example, Unger (1981) states that "it is time to reexamine our methodologies. We need to know not only how many significant differences between the sexes exist, but the extent to which psychological studies contribute to the sexual reality with which we deal" (p. 652). Research which only documents differences between the sexes offers no understanding of why those differences exist or how such differences may be attenuated and therefore may reinforce (or create) the public's preconceived and sexist attitudes.

Thus, for example, ... Yllo (1988) documents the damage done by research reporting that husbands and wives are equally likely to engage in "violent acts," when that research was used as an excuse not to provide services to battered women. Later "clarifications" revealed the nontrivial fact that there were large sex differences in the tendency to resort to violence in self-defense and in the amount of physical harm inflicted by the violence....

A third source of feminist criticism is philosophical and is based on a general rejection of positivism, its claim that science is value neutral, and that the scientific method protects against contamination of findings by "subjectivity" (see Wittig, 1985). Thus, for example, Unger (1983) argues that "The logic of [positivist empiricist] methods (and even their language) prescribes prediction and control. It is difficult for one who is trained in such a conceptual framework to step beyond it and ask what kind of person such a methodology presupposes" (p. 11). Many feminist critics have argued that the person "presupposed" is a male scientist trained to ignore or mistrust feelings and subjectivity (see, for example, Keller, 1985).

Partly because the accepted methods of research in the social sciences have been quantitative, the focus of all three kinds of feminist criticism has been on quantitative research.[1] Some feminists have argued that the issue of quantitative versus qualitative methods reflects the relationship between gender and science (Keller, 1978). Keller, along with many others, such as Oakley (1981) and Bernard (1973), has suggested that most scientists are men and that, as a result, the masculine values of autonomy, separation, distance, and control are embodied in traditional quantitative research.

Feminist Support for Qualitative Methods

In response to these criticisms, some feminist researchers recognized the need to discover or develop research methodologies consistent with feminist values (Mies, 1983) that could be advocated for general use in the social sciences.... A deep suspicion of quantitative methods as having concealed women's real experience has motivated much preoccupation with, and advocacy of, qualitative methods as methods which permit women to express their experience fully and in their own terms. Thus, for example, Smith (1974/1987) argues that social scientists' methods must permit respondents to describe the world as they experience it.

One frequent source of enthusiasm for qualitative methods stems from their potential to offer a more human, less mechanical relationship between the researcher and "the researched." For example, Oakley (1981) suggests that "the goal of finding out about people through interviewing is best achieved when the relationship of interviewer and interviewee is nonhierarchical and when the interviewer is prepared to invest his or her own personal identity in the relationship" (p. 41). For Oakley, the process of "collecting data" which will, according to traditional social science ideals, be transformed into numbers should be replaced by a process of "interviewing women," in which "personal involvement is more than dangerous bias—it is the condition under which people come to know each other and to admit others into their lives" (p. 58).

... Despite the argument that qualitative methods provide more accurate and valid information about respondents' experience, use of qualitative methods, and especially qualitative feminist research, often produces strong negative reactions in the mainstream academic community (Cook and Fonow, 1984; DuBois, 1983; Healy and Stewart, in press; Reinharz, 1979), primarily because it is thought to be "unscientific" or politically motivated, and therefore overtly biased.... Penalties for the use of these methods have ranged from publication rejections and the consequent development of alternative, lower-prestige publication outlets (see Lykes and Stewart, 1986) to difficulty getting tenure.

An Inclusive Feminist Perspective

Over time, though, feminist theorists and researchers have increasingly distinguished between qualitative methods and a feminist approach to social science research, thus deemphasizing the critical focus on quantification. For example, Stanley and Wise (1983) have argued that "methods in themselves aren't innately anything" (p. 159). They point out that although "positivist methods and world views are objectionable, sexist even, ... what should be objected to about them isn't quantification or their use of statistical techniques" (p. 159). Instead, the ways in which research participants are treated and the care with which researchers attempt to represent the lived experience of research participants are of more central concern. In fact, in reviewing recent discussions of feminist methods, Harding (1987) argues that "feminist researchers use just about any and all of the methods, in this concrete sense of the term, that traditional androcentric researchers have used. Of course, precisely how they carry out these methods of evidence gathering is often strikingly different" (p. 2)....

An inclusive viewpoint on methods ... takes the form of promoting the value and appropriate use of both qualitative and quantitative methods as feminist research tools. The emphasis here is on using methods which can best answer particular research questions, but always using them in *ways* which are consistent with broad feminist goals and ideology.... Thus, Jayaratne (1983) and Wittig (1985) have argued that both types of methods can be effectively utilized by feminists and can be implemented in ways which are consistent with feminist values. Procedures commonly used in quantitative research which are inconsistent with feminist values can be altered without abandoning the quantitative strategies which can be beneficial to feminists. Moreover, combining methods, sometimes termed "triangulation" (see Denzin, 1978; Jick, 1979) permits researchers to "capture a more complete, holistic, and contextual portrayal" (Jick, p. 603). As Jick points out, "the effectiveness of triangulation rests on the premise that the weaknesses in each single method will be compensated by the counterbalancing strengths of another" (p. 604).

Yllo (1988) is most persuasive in making this case with respect to research on marital rape. As she points out, the true nature of marital rape cannot be captured in statistics; the experience of violent victimization at the hands of a loved one in an act grotesquely similar to and totally different from an act of love cannot be conveyed in traditional questionnaire or survey format. Thus, Yllo conducted (along with her colleague; see Finkelhor and Yllo, 1985) extensive qualitative interviews with a sample of women who volunteered to be in a study of marital rape. She points out that this analysis yielded a new typology of marital rape (p. 32). "I learned a great deal about wife abuse from those 50 women that the quantitative data on over 2,000 couples could not begin to reveal. My talks with battered women made clear to me that I am a part of what I am studying.... Being aware of this makes a difference in how I understand the problem" (p. 34). On the other hand, Yllo points out that associations which are powerfully significant to an individual woman cannot be understood in terms of their generality without careful survey research. "For example, we found that a large portion of the marital rape victims had also been sexually abused as children. We cannot discover the extent of the relationship between child sexual abuse and marital rape unless we construct a controlled study using a representative sample" (p. 35)....

CURRENT ISSUES IN THE FEMINIST METHODOLOGY LITERATURE

Although there seems to be increasing consensus in the feminist community that quantitative methods are legitimate research tools and that methods should be chosen based on an appropriate fit with the research question, there remain at least three conceptual areas in discussions of feminist methodology where the dialogue remains problematic. First are definitional difficulties with the terms "quantitative," "qualitative," "method" and "methodology." Second is the tendency of many authors to take an essentialist position, which assumes that female researchers feel comfortable, and are competent using only certain "female" methods. The third problem concerns the epistemological issue of objectivity/subjectivity, a continuing central focus for debate.

Definitional Issues

A number of terms used in the feminist methodology dialogue have different implicit or explicit definitions, resulting in some confusion. This difficulty is particularly apparent with regard to the distinction between "methods" and "methodology" and between "quantitative" and "qualitative" processes. Researchers considering the merits of an argument must, therefore, be careful to assess the precise definitions being proposed or implied. Harding (1987) has recently suggested one set of distinctions among terms. She identifies "methods" as particular procedures used in the course of research (e.g., interviews), "methodology" as a theory of how research is carried out or the broad principles about how to conduct research and how theory is applied (e.g., survey research methodology or experimental methodology), and "epistemology" as a theory of knowledge (e.g., the "scientific method" which aims to establish the truth-value of various propositions). It follows from these definitions that first, quantitative and qualitative "methods" are simply specific research procedures; second, "feminist methodology" or a "feminist perspective on methodology" must be taken to refer to a much broader theory of how to do feminist research. There may, then, be a "feminist methodology" without any particular feminist "methods." ...

   Besides distinguishing methods and methodology, we also distinguish historical from logical associations between specific procedures and specific ideologies. For example, quantitative methods have been associated historically with sexist and antifeminist attitudes. We propose that although quantitative research may have been used in the past to obscure the experience of women, it need not always be used in that way. That is, the association is an historical one but not a logical one. Similarly, we propose that although some feminist researchers use qualitative methods to reveal important aspects of women's experience, there is no guarantee that they always will be used to do so.

However, despite the prevalence of these historical associations, there may be some absolute constraints or limitations associated with each type of method. Thus, for example, quantitative methods may never provide the kind of richly textured "feeling for the data" that qualitative methods can permit. As Healy and Stewart (in press) indicate, "Kotre (1984) argues that *only* qualitative analysis can accurately capture the complex pattern of an individual life without violating the integrity of the life or dehumanizing the individual" (p. 3)…. However, it can also be argued that multivariate statistical analyses of large data sets may provide the most truly "contextual" analyses of people's experience. This is because certain multivariate statistical procedures allow the incorporation of a large number of contextual variables, permitting the simultaneous testing of elaborate and complex theoretical models. It has been argued that such analysis is more "ecologically valid" (Bronfenbrenner, 1977).

One common stereotype of qualitative methods is that they are unsystematic and thus unscientific. Clearly such methods can be unsystematic, but they need not be. Hornstein (in press) is able to spell out detailed procedures for a "phenomenological approach to the study of lives." She describes three stages in the researchers' analysis of a phenomenological account. In the first stage the researcher is "attempting to uncover the structure of an experience," and therefore "takes each bit of the subject's report and scrutinizes it to uncover its meaning." She points out that "crucial to this process is a way of thinking termed *imaginal variation,* in which a given feeling, thought, or outcome is compared with other possibilities" (pp. 6–7). The second stage of analysis involves construction of "analytic categories" that emerge from the themes identified in the first stage. "To the greatest extent possible, one strives to allow the categories to emerge from the data themselves, rather than from a preconceived theoretical or empirical framework" (p. 7). Finally, the researcher attempts to describe the relationships among the various categories in order to identify the "pattern" or "structure" of the experience—the ways in which the elements combine to create a unified whole (p. 8). This approach is wholly qualitative and rigorously systematic. Similarly, Gerson (1985) applies Glaser and Strauss's (1967) "constant comparative method" to interviews with a relatively small sample of women in a way which is qualitative, aimed at theory development, and systematic.

Thus, we would distinguish between methods which are systematic and methods which are quantitative. Quantification, in a strict sense, only refers to the transformation of observations (by a researcher or participant) into numbers…. Thus, while historical associations between quantitative and systematic methods can be documented, logical associations between them are debatable, suggesting that a feminist methodology cannot ultimately be tied to either qualitative or quantitative methods.

An additional difficulty with the terms "quantitative" and "qualitative" is that they have frequently been used to refer to an absolute methodological dichotomy (Healy and Stewart, in press), so that the entire research process or methodology is characterized as discretely quantitative or qualitative. However, if we think of a research project as involving a group of separate procedures or methods, it is useful to reconceptualize each procedure as located on a qualitative to quantitative continuum (Healy and Stewart). Thus, not only can specific research procedures be more or less quantitative or qualitative, but the entire research approach, made up of these separate procedures, may also be characterized in these relative terms.

"Essentializing" the Issue: What Is "Women's Research"?

… [M]any authors incorrectly base their criticisms [of quantitative methods] on what we term "the different voice" perspective. This perspective, represented in Gilligan's *In a Different Voice* (1982), emphasizes the difference between the male voice, which defines the self in terms of distinctness and separation from others, and the female voice, which defines the self in terms of connections and relationships. Numerous discussions of feminist methodology have applied this essentialist view to the quantitative and qualitative dialogue (for example, see Davis, 1985, and Sheuneman, 1986) concluding that the female voice is, in fact, qualitative. Furthermore, this view has emphasized the differences between qualitative and quantitative research, regarding the former as subjective, relevant, and descriptive and the latter as objective, irrelevant, and superficial.

In general, those who take an essentialist position believe that women are more able than men to study issues of importance to women. According to Mies (1983), because of women's personal experience with oppression they "are better equipped than their male counterparts to make a comprehensive study of the exploited groups" (p. 121). While we generally agree that women, on the average, *should* have a better understanding of issues important to feminists, it is unclear whether this is, in fact the case, and, if it is true in general, under what circumstances it is true. Overall, evidence in support of the essentialist position is lacking, and thus a more cautious approach to evaluating this belief is appropriate. Moreover, differences among women are ignored and rendered invisible by this exclusive focus on intersex differences.

The essentialist view is exemplified by two beliefs found in the literature or raised as issues for discussion in the feminist community. One belief about women researchers is that they take a more "contextual" approach. Thus, for example, Gilligan (1982) suggests that where men see individuals arranged in hierarchies, women see a web of interconnected relationships. Scheuneman (1986) argues that this tendency toward a contextual perspective ... will lead women to use multivariate research designs. However, no evidence for this belief is presented, and it runs counter to the stereotype of women as fearful and avoidant of complex statistics (see below).

A second essentialist belief expressed in some feminist literature is that women researchers are more likely to study issues important to feminists. Interestingly, in an analysis of articles published in personality and social psychology between 1963 and 1983, Lykes and Stewart (1986) found that "female authorship was uncorrelated with the sex-typing of research topics, age of subjects, analysis of sexes separately, inclusion of gender as an aspect of the research question, discussion of sex roles, or interpretation of gender differences" (p. 400). Thus, there is no automatic association between gender of researcher and research methods used.

We suggest several problems with the essentialist position, in addition to the lack of empirical support. First, it amounts to wishful thinking by confusing an ideal with reality. In other words, although essentialist beliefs appear consistent with feminist values, they may have no basis in fact. The underlying values expressed in this literature could, however, function more usefully as ideals. For example, DuBois's (1983) call for a wholistic (contextual and nonlinear) approach is clearly stated as an ideal we must develop and use. Second, these beliefs about women's use of research methods confuse *women's* and *feminists'* beliefs. Although there is no evidence that either women or feminists might conduct research in this way, it is certainly more likely that feminists, rather than women in general, would do this, since it is consistent with feminist values. To hold essentialist views about all women is to stereotype all women as feminists. It is too easy to forget that most women researchers (including feminist researchers) are primarily trained and socialized as traditional quantitative methodologists and, despite any interest in alternative procedures, it is far more likely than not that they will carry out their research largely using traditional methods and methodologies (Lykes and Stewart, 1986).

... [A]dvanced mathematical or statistical skills ... are advantageous to feminist researchers for a number of reasons. First, ... they are used consistently and effectively as research tools. Furthermore, whether or not one intends to use these skills in one's own research, it is important that feminist researchers obtain adequate statistical or mathematical knowledge in order to evaluate and critique research which does use such tools. Given the abundance of research with an antifeminist message, it is absolutely critical that feminist researchers understand the methods behind such research, so that their critiques will be cogent.

A second reason ... is in their application to both qualitative and quantitative research. Without a basic understanding of the functioning of these principles in research procedures such as design, sample selection, data interpretation, and generalization, both qualitative and quantitative research can result in erroneous and misleading findings. However, more damaging than inaccurate results is the potential for others to generalize from one example of inferior research motivated by feminist values and to stereotype all feminist research as being politically motivated and biased, exactly the charge feminists make of traditional research. When feminist research is poorly done, it is not only difficult to defend the charge of bias, but it makes it increasingly difficult to defend quality feminist research as well.

Perhaps the clearest example of research claiming to be "qualitative" which has been problematic for feminists is Hite's study on women's sexuality and love relationships, which resulted in two well-publicized books (Hite, 1976, 1987). Her work—not associated with any traditional academic discipline or setting—has been prominently identified as feminist, both by her and by some of the media; it thereby reflects on all research by feminists. One difficulty with this work is that, while it strongly supports the feminist call for more qualitative, in-depth study of women's lives, it violates some very basic methodological principles, thus jeopardizing the validity of its conclusions. Although there are numerous examples which could be targeted for criticism, one stands out in particular. In *Women and Love* (Hite, 1987) Hite distributed approximately 100,000 questionnaires, 4,500 being returned. In spite of her attempt to justify the representativeness of her sample, it is clear that it is a highly self-selected sample[4] and not representative of the U.S. female population, which she implies it is. Because of the unknown nature of the sample, it is inaccurate to draw *any* conclusions about what U.S. women in general may believe. Nevertheless, such conclusions are intended in this volume....

The negative press which this type of research received, primarily for its shoddy methodology (see, for example, Tavris, 1987, and Ferguson, 1987), detracts from its message and contributes to the stereotype of feminists as incapable of sophisticated and valid research. If Hite had used proper methodological procedures (even just better sampling methods), and the book were still attacked for its feminist message (which undoubtedly it would have been), at least it could have been defended. Instead, we are faced with guilt by association....

Detailed consideration of the signs which distinguish excellent qualitative research may help make this point clearer. Gerson (1985) conducted a qualitative study of different patterns of work and family life among contemporary young women. In a thoughtful appendix to the monograph describing her findings, Gerson explained that "the research questions called for an exploratory study" (p. 240), which was based on "open-ended, in-depth interviews with a carefully targeted sample of women" (p. 241). She explained her sampling procedure in detail, spelling out the biases and limitations of the sample (pp. 241–45). She concluded that "the insights and conclusions of this analysis can and, I hope will be applied to and tested among other groups of women in different social environments and of other races and age cohorts" (p. 243). Perhaps most important, in the body of the text itself, Gerson pointed to the proper use of her findings: "They should be considered in the context of corroborative findings from larger, more representative samples" (p. 217)....

The Issue of Objectivity: What Is the Issue?

A frequent theme in feminist criticism of social science research is the negative consequences of professional obsessiveness with "scientific objectivity," which is in turn associated (historically, though not logically) with quantification. Feminist criticisms have focused on several important points: (1) apparently "objective" science has often been sexist (hence, not "objective") in its purposes and/or its effects (see, for example, DuBois, 1983; Sherif, 1979/1987); (2) glorification of "objectivity" has imposed a hierarchical and controlling relationship upon the researcher-researched dyad (Keller, 1978; Fee, 1983; Arditti, 1980); and (3) idealization of objectivity has excluded from science significant personal subjectively based knowledge and has left that knowledge outside of "science" (Unger, 1983; Wallston, 1981). This last point makes it clear that leaving the subjective outside of science also leaves it unexamined. Thus, Harding (1987), has recently concluded that "the best feminist analysis ... insists that the inquirer her/himself be placed in the same critical place as the overt subject matter, thereby recovering the entire research process for scrutiny in the results of research" (p. 9). It may be, then, that an important source of the sexist (and racist and classist) bias in traditional "objective" research is the fact that the personal and subjective—which inevitably influences many aspects of the research process—were exempt from analysis (see Hubbard, 1978; Unger, 1983).

For some feminists a "truly feminist social science" originates "from women's experience of women's reality" (Stanley and Wise, 1983, p. 165; see also Smith, 1974/1987). Some believe that this perspective implies the exclusion of the concept of objectivity in the research process. It is clear, nevertheless, that most contemporary feminists reject any notion that objectivity should be renounced as a goal altogether. Although absolute objectivity is not possible (even if it were desirable), the pursuit of some types of objectivity, as a goal, does have potential to protect against several forms of bias. For example, a researcher who has an investment in a particular theory may tend to use methods that are likely to produce supportive findings. However, the use of certain research procedures generally accepted in the social sciences mitigates against such biased results. An illustration of this safeguard is representative sampling techniques. Such techniques do not permit a researcher to generalize from a sample of selected respondents who are likely to exhibit the researcher's pet hypothesis. Thus, while many feminists wish to incorporate subjective elements into the research process, they also reject the notion that the process must be entirely subjective. As Rose (1982) states, "feminist methodology seeks to bring together subjective and objective ways of knowing the world" (p. 368). Furthermore, Birke (1986) notes that "the association of objectivity with masculinity has sometimes led feminists to reject objectivity and to glorify subjectivity in opposition to it. While it is necessary to revalue the subjective ... we do ourselves a disservice if we remove ourselves from objectivity and rationality; we then simply leave the terrain of rational thought ... to men, thus perpetuating the system which excluded us in the first place" (p. 157).

There is, then, increasing recognition that the use of particular methods and procedures does not automatically confer objectivity, just as inclusion of analysis of one's personal subjective experience does not preclude it. With no necessary connection between (qualitative and quantitative) methods and (objective vs. subjective) outcomes, there is no substitute for a reflexive social science conducted by reflective social scientists (Harding, 1987; Unger, 1983).

Dangers of Apparent Objectivity

Despite our recognition of the legitimate use of objective methods, there are realistic dangers of poor quality antifeminist research disguised as good, quantitative and, thus, "objective" research. An example of such research which required a strong feminist critique and reinterpretation is work by Benbow and Stanley on math achievement (1980, 1983). This study, which made headlines in major newspapers[5] throughout the country, supported the view that girls were innately less capable of math achievement than boys. A study assessing the negative impact of this research (Jacobs and Eccles, 1985) concluded that "one of the major effects of popular media coverage of the research report was that it changed the 'social desirability' climate. Before the media coverage, it was popular to espouse a belief in equal math abilities of males and females. After the media coverage it was 'okay' to say that males are better than females in math" (p. 24).

Numerous problems with this research have been pointed out (for example, see Eccles and Jacobs, 1986; Fennema, 1981), and many are violations of basic principles for conducting quantitative research. Most important, the research failed adequately to examine the roles of values and attitudes in girls' math performance (see Eccles and Jacobs, 1986), which reasonably may have explained the sex difference in performance. Although these critiques did not receive as much press coverage as the original Benbow and Stanley article, such critical analysis of traditional objective research is essential in the feminist and academic community and requires a thorough knowledge of basic research and statistical procedures. Thus, there is a very practical need for feminists to acquire such knowledge if we are even to attempt to counter the effects of such harmful, "objective" work.

Benefits and Uses of Traditional Research Methods

Although this example illustrates the damage which this kind of research can do, as feminists we must also consider any potential benefits which our own use of "objectivity" can bring. The greatest benefit of apparent objectivity lies in its power to change political opinion. Thus, traditional research methods can be used to our advantage to change sexist belief systems or to support progressive legislation. Two examples of the uses of statistics attest to its power. First, as noted in Jayaratne (1983), prior to the court decision of *Griggs v. Duke Power Company* (1971), which was argued under Title VII of the Civil Rights Act of 1964, sex discrimination could be substantiated in court only if one could prove intent on the part of the defendant. The decision resulting from this case, however, was that discrimination could be demonstrated by presenting statistics which show a different and unfair impact on a racial, sex, or other group covered by Title VII. This decision set a new course for discrimination suits....

An additional benefit derived from the use of "objective" methods in research lies in their ability to provide tests of theories. Thus, statistics can be a practical tool in the evaluation of feminist theories, since such analysis can identify the most effective strategies for implementing feminist goals. This remains an imperative task if feminists are going to correctly target problem areas for change or effectively direct our energies toward change.

A FEMINIST PERSPECTIVE ON METHODOLOGY

In much of the feminist methodology literature the critical questions ask for the definition of the "feminist perspective" on research. We believe that there is now some consensus on the answer to this question. Thus, there is general concurrence in recent writing on feminist methodology that there can be no single, prescribed method or set of research methods consistent with feminist values, although there are methods antithetical to such values. "The idea that there is only 'one road' to the feminist revolution, and only one type of 'truly feminist' research, is as limiting and as offensive as male-biased accounts of research that have gone before" (Stanley and Wise, 1983, p. 26). There is, then, no substitute for each researcher making independent assessments about the appropriateness of a given method for a given research question and purpose, as well as about the competence of the execution of the research method used....

We believe that the focus of feminist dialogue on "methods," and particularly on qualitative versus quantitative methods, obscures the more fundamental challenge of feminism to the traditional "scientific method" (see also DuBois, 1983). That challenge really questions the epistemology, or theory of knowledge, underlying traditional science and social science, including the notion that science is, or can be, value free. It is appropriate and timely now to move the focus of the feminist methodology dialogue from definition to implementation....

STRATEGIES FOR PRACTICAL IMPLEMENTATION OF A FEMINIST PERSPECTIVE IN SOCIAL SCIENCE RESEARCH

... Feminist researchers must develop realistic and pragmatic strategies which allow for implementation of the feminist perspective. The following specific procedures are examples of such strategies. They derive both from the above discussions of qualitative and quantitative methods, and from those research values explicitly found in the feminist methodology literature. We would like to emphasize, parenthetically, the importance of researchers selecting or developing other procedures which they can effectively implement. Thus, researchers need to consider practical issues such as the time, effort, money and other resources available to the research staff. It is our belief that *any,* even a limited, attempt at increasing the feminist value of research is worthwhile.

1. *When selecting a research topic or problem, we should ask how that research has potential to help women's lives and what information is necessary to have such impact.* The desire to conduct research can either stem from a general theoretical interest in a subject matter (e.g., beliefs about rape), or from a specific political perspective (e.g., how can research help to decrease the incidence of rape). Although ultimately the goal should always be political, theoretical research can also be important to feminists (Jayaratne, 1983). Whatever the origins of the research topic, it is important to determine, specifically, the kind of information which will be most useful and will have the most positive impact on women's lives. One research goal is not always better or more appropriate for a given problem. For example, if a researcher is interested in helping battered women, legitimate research goals might vary from increasing public understanding of their plight to influencing legislation.

2. *When designing the study, we should propose methods that are both appropriate for the kind of question asked and the information needed and which permit answers persuasive to a particular audience.* Once a researcher knows the research goal or question and what information is necessary, the types of methods needed in the research should be clear. This view has been stated frequently in the feminist literature (DuBois, 1983; Jayaratne, 1983; Healy and Stewart, in press; Scheuneman, 1986; Wallston, 1981). As a general guideline, if the research goal is descriptive of individual lives and designed to promote understanding of a particular viewpoint of the subjects, more qualitative methods may be appropriate. If the goal is to document the operation of particular relationships between variables (e.g. how a government policy affects women), more quantitative methods may be useful. For example, if a researcher is interested in investigating the lives of homeless women, there are numerous approaches she can take. If her goal is to influence legislation to offer employment training to these women, the most persuasive case may involve gathering statistics on women whose job training led to employment and permanent housing. However, if the goal is to help the public to understand these women, in-depth interviews and narrative accounts might be most appropriate.

3. *In every instance of use of either qualitative and quantitative methods or both, we should address the problems associated with each approach.* Thus, if using qualitative methods, we must be aware of methodological problems of poor representation and overgeneralization. Alternatively, if using quantitative methods, we must consciously and actively incorporate feminist values into the procedures. Because quantitative methods have historically exploited women and excluded feminist values, those using such methods should be particularly aware of these problems. (Examples can be found above, in the section on feminist criticism.)

4. *Whenever possible, we should use research designs which combine quantitative and qualitative methods.* This approach, termed a "mixed method," has been advocated by numerous authors as a way to offset the disadvantages of one method with the strengths of the other (Denzin, 1978; Healy and Stewart, in press; Jick, 1979). This strategy suggests the value of acquiring knowledge of both methods. Although this combination of methods is not always possible or even practical, it should result in a more powerful research product, that is, one which not only effectively tests theory but also is convincing.

5. *Whether the research methods are quantitative or qualitative, it is critical that procedures be bias free or sex fair.* Not only will such research better test theory or more accurately communicate the research goal, but such research should be more influential on policymakers and the public. In fact, because feminist research tends to be suspect already, it is especially critical that procedures be free from apparent contaminating bias. (See Grady, 1981, for examples of methods to minimize bias.)

6. *We should take the time and effort to do quality research.* This means learning and

using a variety of appropriate research skills, rather than taking short cuts which are more expedient. (See Jayaratne, 1983, p. 151, for a discussion of the abundance of "quick and dirty research" in social science.)

7. *When interpreting results, we should ask what different interpretations, always consistent with the findings, might imply for change in women's lives.* We should consider interpretations that imply the most effective interventions for improving women's lives. For example, victim-blaming interpretations tend to result in individual intervention strategies, whereas situational/environmental interpretations can often yield more effective political strategies for change.

8. *We should always attempt some political analysis of the findings.* We should make an effort to explore how policy change suggested by research results might positively affect women's lives. This goal is not always clear from the findings and must be made explicit, when possible.

9. *Finally, as much as possible (given a realistic assessment of the frantic pace of academic life), we should actively participate in the dissemination of research results.* The importance of dissemination cannot be overstressed, since it is the goal of feminist research to make a difference in women's lives. If research is not "advertised" it will not have an impact, either on policymakers or on the public.

In conclusion, we would like to reemphasize that we view these strategies, combined with others discussed in the feminist literature, as a contribution to dialogue focusing on the practical application of feminist theory in social research. Such dialogue can best advance feminist goals by producing research which not only positively affects women's lives, but also makes the research endeavor itself an exciting, relevant, and profitable experience for the researcher.

NOTES

1. It should be pointed out that criticism of quantitative methods has a long history which extends beyond the feminist community (Healy and Stewart, in press; Hornstein 1988; Mies, 1983).

...

4. Not only is her return rate profoundly low, but the highly personal and lengthy nature of the questionnaire would result in a sample of women to whom this subject is unusually salient, such as women who are unhappy in their love relationships.

5. Popular media coverage of this research included headlines such as "Do Males Have a Math Gene?" in *Newsweek* (Williams and King, 1980) and in "The Gender Factor in Math: A New Study Says Males May Be Naturally Abler Than Females" in *Time* (The Gender Factor, 1980).

REFERENCES

Arditti, R. (1980). Feminism and science. In R. Anditti, P. Brennan, and S. Cavrale, eds., *Science and liberation.* Boston: South End.

Benbow, C. P., and J. Stanley (1980). Sex differences in mathematical ability: Fact or artifact? *Science,* 210, 1262–64.

———. (1983). Sex differences in mathematical reasoning ability: More facts. *Science* 222, 1029–31.

Bernard, J. (1973). My four revolutions: An autobiographical history of the ASA. In J. Huber, ed., *Changing women in a changing society.* Chicago: University of Chicago Press.

Birke, L. (1986). *Women, feminism and biology.* New York: Methuen.

Bleier, R. (1984). *Science and gender.* New York: Pergamon.

Bronfenbrenner, U. (1977). Toward an experimental ecology of human development. *American Psychologist,* 32, 513–29.

Cook, J. A., and M. M. Fonow (1984). Am I my sister's gatekeeper? Cautionary tales from the academic hierarchy. *Humanity and Society* 8, 442–52.

Davis, L. V. (1985). Female and male voices in social work. *Social Work* 32, 106–113.

Denzin, N. K. (1978). *The research act.* New York: McGraw Hill.

DuBois, B. (1983). Passionate scholarship: Notes on values, knowing and method in social science. In G. Bowles and R. D. Klein, eds., *Theories of women's studies,* pp. 105–116. Boston: Routledge & Kegan Paul.

Eccles, J. (1984). Sex differences in mathematics participation. In M. Steinkam and M. Maehr, eds., *Advances in motivation and achievement,* pp. 93–137, vol. 2. Greenwich, Conn: JAI Press.

Eccles, J. S., and J. E. Jacobs (1986). Social forces shape math attitudes and performance. *Signs* 11, 367–89.

Fee, E. (1983). Women's nature and scientific objectivity. In M. Lowe and R. Hubbard, eds., *Women's nature: Rationalizations of inequality,* pp. 9–28. New York: Pergamon.

Fennema, E. (1981). Women and mathematics: Does research matter? *Journal for Research in Mathematics Education,* 12, 380–85.

Ferguson, A. (1987). She says it's a dog's life in a man's world. *Wall Street Journal,* Nov. 13, p. 13.

Finkelhor, D., and K. Yllo (1985). *License to rape: Sexual abuse of wives.* New York: Free Press.

Frieze, I. H., J. E. Parsons, P. B. Johnson, D. N. Ruble, and G. L. Zellman (1978). *Women and sex roles: A social psychological perspective.* New York: W. W. Norton.

The gender factor in math: A new study says males may be naturally abler than females. (1980). *Time,* Dec. 15, p. 57.

Gerson, K. (1985). *Hard choices.* Berkeley: University of California Press.

Gilligan, C. (1982). *In a different voice.* Cambridge, Mass.: Harvard University Press.

Glaser, B., and A. Strauss (1976). *The discovery of grounded theory.* Chicago: Aldine.

Grady, K. E. (1981). Sex bias in research design. *Psychology of Women Quarterly* 5, 628–36.

Griggs v. Duke Power Company (1971), 401 US 424.

Hacker, S. (1983). Mathematization of engineering: Limits on women and the field. In T. Rothschild, *Machina ex dea: Feminist perspectives on technology.* New York: Elsevier.

Harding, S. (1987). Introduction. Is there a feminist method? In S. Harding, ed., *Feminism and methodology,* pp. 1–14. Bloomington: Indiana University Press.

Healy, J. M., Jr., and A. J. Stewart (in press). On the compatibility of quantitative and qualitative methods for studying individual lives. In A. J. Stewart, J. M. Healy, Jr., and D. Ozer, eds., *Perspectives on personality: Theory, research, and interpersonal dynamics,* vol. 3. Greenwich, Conn.: JAI Press.

Hite, S. (1976). *The Hite report.* New York: Macmillan.

———. (1987). *Women and love.* New York: Alfred Knopf.

Hornstein, G. A. (1988). Quantifying psychological phenomena: Debates, dilemmas, and implications. In J. G. Morawski, ed., *The rise of experimentation in American psychology.* New Haven: Yale University Press.

———. (In press). Painting a portrait of experience: The phenomenological approach to the study of lives. In A. J. Stewart, J. M. Healy, Jr., and D. J. Ozer, eds., *Perspectives in personality: Approaches to studying lives.* Greenwich, Conn.: JAI Press.

Hubbard, R. (1978). Have only men evolved? In R. Hubbard, M. S. Henifin, and B. Fried, eds., *Women look at biology looking at women.* Cambridge: Schenkman.

Jacobs, J., and J. S. Eccles (1985). Gender differences in math ability: The impact of media reports on parents. *Educational Researcher,* 14, 20–25.

Jayaratne, T. E. (1983). The value of quantitative methodology for feminist research. In G. Bowles and R. Duelli Klein, eds., *Theories of women's studies,* pp. 140–61. Boston: Routledge & Kegan Paul.

Jayaratne, T. E., and C. M. Kaczala (1983). Social responsibility in sex difference research. *Journal of Educational Equity and Leadership* 3, 305–316.

Jick, T. D. (1979). Mixing qualitative and quantitative methods: Triangulation in action. *Administrative Science Quarterly* 24, 602–610.

Keller, E. F. (1978). Gender and science. *Psychoanalysis and contemporary thought,* 1, 409–433.

———. (1982). Feminism and science. *Signs* 7, 589–602.

———. (1985). *Reflections on gender and science.* New Haven, Conn.: Yale University Press.

Kelly, A. (1978). Feminism and research. *Women's Studies International Quarterly* 1, 225–32.

Kotre, J. (1984). *Outliving the self.* Baltimore: Johns Hopkins University.

Lott, B. (1981). A feminist critique of androgyny: Toward the elimination of gender attributions of learned behavior. In C. Mayo and N. Henley, eds., *Gender and nonverbal behavior,* pp. 171–80. New York: Springer-Verlag.

Lykes, M. B., and A. J. Stewart (1986). Evaluating the feminist challenge to research in personality and social psychology: 1963–1983. *Psychology of Women Quarterly* 10, 393–412.

Mies, M. (1983). Towards a methodology for feminist research. In G. Bowles and R. Duelli Klein, *Theories of women's studies,* pp. 117–39. Boston: Routledge and Kegan Paul.

Milgram, S. (1974). *Obedience to authority.* New York: Harper.

Morawski, J. (1985). The measurement of masculinity and femininity: Engendering categorical realities. *Journal of Personality* 53, 196–223.

Oakley, A. (1981). Interviewing women: A contradiction in terms. In H. Roberts, ed., *Doing feminist research,* pp. 30–61. Boston: Routledge & Kegan Paul.

Parlee, M. B. (1975). Psychology: Review essay. *Signs* 1, 119–38.

Reinharz, S. (1979). *On becoming a social scientist.* San Francisco: Jossey-Bass.

Roberts, H., ed. (1981). *Doing feminist research.* Boston: Routledge & Kegan Paul.

Rose, H. (1982). Making science feminist. In E. Whitelegg et al., eds., *The changing experience of women.* Oxford: Martin Robinson.

Scheuneman, J. D. (1986). The female perspective on methodology and statistics. *Educational Researcher* 15, 22–23.

Sherif, C. W. (1987). Bias in psychology. In S. Harding, ed., *Feminism and methodology,* pp. 37–56. Bloomington: Indiana University Press. (Reprinted from J. A. Sherman and E. T. Beck, eds. [1979]). *The prism of sex.* Madison: University of Wisconsin Press.)

Siefert, K., and L. D. Martin (1988). Preventing black maternal mortality: A challenge for the 90s. *Journal of Primary Prevention* 9, 57–65.

Smith, D. E. (1987). Women's perspective as a radical critique of sociology. In S. Harding, ed., *Feminism and methodology,* pp. 84–96. Bloomington: Indiana University Press. (Reprinted from *Sociological Inquiry,* 1974, 44, 7–13.)

Stanley, L., and S. Wise (1983). *Breaking out: Feminist consciousness and feminist research.* London: Routledge and Kegan Paul.

Stasz Stoll, C. (1974). *Female and male: Socialization, social roles and social structure.* New York: Brown.

Tangri, S. S., and G. L. Strasburg (1979). Can research on women be more effective in shaping policy? *Psychology of Women Quarterly* 3, 321–43.

Tavris, C. (1987). Method is all but lost in the imagery of social-science fiction. *Los Angeles Times,* Nov. 1, p. V5.

Unger, R. K. (1981). Sex as a social reality: Field and laboratory research. *Psychology of Women Quarterly* 5, 645–53.

———. (1983). Through the looking glass: No wonderland yet! (The reciprocal relationship between methodology and models of reality). *Psychology of Women Quarterly* 8, 9–32.

Wallston, B. (1981). What are the questions in psychology of women? A feminist approach to research. *Psychology of Women Quarterly* 5, 597–617.

Weisstein, N. (1977). How can a little girl like you teach a great big class of men? the chairman said, and other adventures of a woman in science. In S. Ruddick and P. Daniels, eds., *Working it out,* pp. 241–50. New York: Pantheon.

Westkott, M. (1979). Feminist criticism of the social sciences. *Harvard Educational Review* 49, 4220.

Williams, D. A., and P. King (1980). Do males have a math gene? *Newsweek,* Dec. 15, p. 73.

Wittig, M. (1985). Metatheoretical dilemmas in the psychology of gender. *American Psychologist* 40, 800–812.

Wolinsky, H. (1986). Program targets maternal deaths. *Chicago Sun-Times,* Aug. 11, p. 22.

Wolinsky, H., and P. Franchine (1986). Black maternal deaths here 4 times U.S. level. *Chicago Sun-Times,* Aug. 8, p. 3.

Yllo, K. (1988). Political and methodological debates in wife abuse research. In K. Yllo, ed., *Feminist perspectives on wife abuse,* pp. 28–50. Newbury Park, N.J.: Sage.

LINDA TUHIWAI SMITH
Research through Imperial Eyes

Many critiques of research have centered around the theory of knowledge known as empiricism and the scientific paradigm of positivism which is derived from empiricism. Positivism takes a position that applies views about how the natural world can be examined and understood to the social world of human beings and human societies. Understanding is viewed as being akin to measuring. As the ways we try to understand the world are reduced to issues of measurement, the focus of understanding becomes more concerned with procedural problems. The challenge then for understanding the social world becomes one of developing operational definitions of phenomena which are reliable and valid. The analysis in this chapter begins with a much broader brushstroke. Most indigenous criticisms of research are expressed within the single terms of "white research," "academic research," or "outsider research." The finer details of how Western scientists might name themselves are irrelevant to indigenous peoples who have experienced unrelenting research of a profoundly exploitative nature. From an indigenous perspective Western research is more than just research that is located in a positivist tradition. It is research which brings to bear, on any study of indigenous peoples, a cultural orientation, a set of values, a different conceptualization of such things as time, space and subjectivity, different and competing theories of knowledge, highly specialized forms of language, and structures of power.

In this chapter I argue that what counts as Western research draws from an "archive" of knowledge and systems, rules and values which stretch beyond the boundaries of Western science to the system now referred to as the West. Stuart Hall makes the point that the West is an idea or concept, a language for imagining a set of complex stories, ideas, historical events and social relationships. Hall suggests that the concept of the West functions in ways which (1) allow "us" to characterize and *classify* societies into categories, (2) condense complex images of other societies through *a system of representation,* (3) provide a standard *model of comparison,* and (4) provide *criteria of evaluation* against which other societies can be ranked.[1] These are the procedures by which indigenous peoples and their societies were coded into the Western system of knowledge.

Research contributed to, and drew from, these systems of classification, representation and evaluation. The cultural archive did not embody a unitary system of knowledge but should be conceived of as containing multiple traditions of knowledge and ways of knowing. Some knowledges are more dominant than others, some are submerged and outdated. Some knowledges are actively in competition with each other and some can only be formed in association with others. Whilst there may not be a unitary system there are "rules" which help make sense of what is contained within the archive and enable "knowledge" to be recognized. These rules can be conceived of as rules of classification, rules of framing and rules of practice.[2] Although the term "rules" may sound like a set of fixed items which are articulated in explicit ways as regulations, it also means rules which are masked in some way and which tend to be articulated through implicit understandings of how the world works. Power is expressed at both the explicit and implicit levels. Dissent, or challenges to the rules, is manageable because it also conforms to these rules, particularly at the implicit level. Scientific and academic debate in the West takes place within these rules. Two major examples of how this works can be found in Marxism and Western feminism. Arguably, Western feminism has provided a more radical challenge to knowledge than Marxism because of its challenge to epistemology: not just the body of knowledge and world view, but the science of how knowledge can be understood. Even Western feminism, however, has been challenged, particularly by women of color, for conforming to some very fundamental Western European world views, value systems and attitudes towards the Other.

Indigenous peoples would probably claim to know much of this implicitly but in this chapter some fundamental ideas related to understandings of being human, of how humans relate to the world, are examined. Differences between Western and indigenous conceptions of the world have always provided stark contrasts. Indigenous beliefs were considered shocking, abhorrent and barbaric and were prime targets for the efforts of missionaries. Many of those beliefs still persist; they are embedded in indigenous languages and stories and etched in memories.

THE CULTURAL FORMATIONS OF WESTERN RESEARCH

Forms of imperialism and colonialism, notions of the Other, and theories about human nature existed long before the Enlightenment in Western philosophy. Some scholars have argued that the key tenets of what is now seen as Western civilization are based on black experiences and a black tradition of scholarship, and have simply been appropriated by Western philosophy and redefined as Western epistemology.[3] Western knowledges, philosophies and definitions of human nature form what Foucault has referred to as a cultural archive and what some people might refer to as a "storehouse" of histories, artefacts, ideas, texts and/or images, which are classified, preserved, arranged and represented back to the West. This storehouse contains the fragments, the regions and levels of knowledge traditions, and the "systems" which allow different and differentiated forms of knowledge to be retrieved, enunciated and represented in new contexts.[4] Although many colonized peoples refer to the West, usually with a term of their own, as a cohesive system of people, practices, values and languages, the cultural archive of the West represents multiple traditions of knowledge....

Foucault also suggests that the archive reveals "rules of practice" which the West itself cannot necessarily describe because it operates within the rules and they are taken for granted. Various indigenous peoples would claim, indeed do claim, to be able to describe many of those rules of practice as they have been "revealed" and/or perpetrated on indigenous communities. Hall has suggested that the Western cultural archive functions in ways which allow shifts and transformations to happen, quite radically at times, without the archive itself, and the modes of classifications and systems of representation contained within it, being destroyed. This sense of what the idea of the West represents is important here because to a large extent theories about research are underpinned by a cultural system of classification and representation, by views about human nature, human morality and virtue, by conceptions of space and time, by conceptions of gender and race. Ideas about these things help determine what counts as real. Systems of classification and representation enable different traditions or fragments of traditions to be retrieved and reformulated in different contexts as discourses, and then to be played out in systems of power and domination, with real material consequences for colonized peoples. Nandy, for example, discusses the different phases of colonization, from "rapacious bandit-kings" intent on exploitation, to "well-meaning middle class liberals" intent on salvation as a legitimation of different forms of colonization.[5] These phases of colonization, driven by different economic needs and differing ideologies of legitimation, still had real consequences for the nations, communities and groups of indigenous people being colonized. These consequences have led Nandy to describe colonization as a "shared culture" for those who have been colonized and for those who have colonized. This means, for example, that colonized peoples share a language of colonization, share knowledge about their colonizers, and, in terms of a political project, share the same struggle for decolonization. It also means that colonizers, too, share a language and knowledge of colonization.

THE INTERSECTIONS OF RACE AND GENDER

David Theo Goldberg argues that one of the consequences of Western experiences under imperialism is that Western ways of viewing, talking about and interacting with the world at large are intricately embedded in racialized discourses.[6] Notions of difference are discussed in Greek philosophy, for example, as ways of rationalizing the essential characteristics and obligations of slaves.[7] Medieval literature and art represent fabulous monsters and half-human, half-animal creatures from far-off places. According to Goldberg, concern about these images led to "observers [being] overcome by awe, repulsion and fear of the implied threat to spiritual life and the political state."[8] Goldberg argues that whilst these early beliefs and images "furnished models that modern racism would assume and transform according to its own lights," there was no explicit category or space in medieval thought for racial differentiation.[9] What did happen, according to Goldberg, was that the "savage" was internalized as a psychological and moral space within the individual that required "repression, denial, and disciplinary restraint."[10] In Goldberg's analysis, modernity and the philosophy of liberalism (which underpins modernist discourses) transformed these fragments of culture into an explicit racialized discourse. Race, as a category, was linked to human reason and morality, to science, to colonialism and to the rights of citizenship in ways that produced the racialized discourse and racist practices of modernity.[11]

Western concepts of race intersect in complex ways with concepts of gender. Gender refers not just to the roles of women and how those roles are constituted but to the roles of men and of the relations between men and women. Ideas about gender difference and what that means for a society can similarly be traced back to the fragmented artefacts and representations of Western culture, and to different and differentiated traditions of knowledge. The desired and undesired qualities of women for example, as mothers, daughters and wives, were inscribed in the texts of the Greeks and Romans, sculptured, painted and woven into medieval wall hangings, and performed through oral poetry. Different historical ideas about men and women were enacted through social institutions such as marriage, family life, the class system and ecclesiastic orders.[12] These institutions were underpinned by economic systems, notions of property and wealth, and were increasingly legitimated in the West through Judeo-Christian beliefs. Economic changes from feudal to capitalist modes of production influenced the construction of the "family" and the relations of women and men in Western societies. Gender distinctions and hierarchies are also deeply encoded in Western languages. It is impossible to speak without using this language, and, more significantly for indigenous peoples, it is impossible to translate or interpret our societies into English, French or Castilian, for example, without making gendered distinctions.

The process of engendering descriptions of the Other has had very real consequences for indigenous women in that the ways in which indigenous women were described, objectified and represented by Europeans in the nineteenth century have left a legacy of marginalization within indigenous societies as much as within the colonizing society. In New Zealand many of these issues are the subject of a claim brought by a group of prominent Maori women to the Waitangi Tribunal. The Waitangi Tribunal was established to hear the claims by Maori relating to contraventions of the Treaty of Waitangi.[13] Before this Tribunal, the Maori women taking the claim are having to establish and argue, using historical texts, research and oral testimonies, that the Crown has ignored the *rangatiratanga,* or chiefly and sovereign status, of Maori women. To argue this, the claimants are compelled to prove that Maori women were as much *rangatira* (chiefs) as Maori men. At a very simple level the "problem" is a problem of translation. *Rangatiratanga* has generally been interpreted in English as meaning chieftainship and sovereignty, which in colonialism was a "male thing."

This claim illustrates the complexities which Stuart Hall raised. Several different and differentiated sets of ideas and representations are to be "retrieved" and "enunciated" in the historically specific context of this claim. In summary these may be classified as: (1) a legal framework inherited from Britain, which includes views about what constitutes admissible evidence and valid research; (2) a "textual" orientation, which will privilege the written text (seen as expert and research-based) over oral testimonies (a concession to indigenous "elders"); (3) views about science, which will allow for the efficient selection and arrangement of "facts"; (4) "rules of practice" such as "values" and "morals," which all parties to the process are assumed to know and to have given their "consent" to abide by, for example, notions of "good will" and "truth telling"; (5) ideas about subjectivity and objectivity which have already determined the constitution of the Tribunal and its "neutral" legal framework, but which will continue to frame the way the case is heard; (6) ideas about time and space, views related to history, what constitutes the appropriate length of a hearing, "shape" of a claim, size of the panel; (7) views about human nature, individual accountability and culpability; (8) the selection of speakers and experts, who speaks for whom, whose knowledge is presumed to be the "best fit" in relation to a set of proven "facts"; and (9) the politics of the Treaty of Waitangi and the way those politics are managed by politicians and other agencies such as the media. Within each set of ideas are systems of classification and representation; epistemological, ontological, juridical, anthropological and ethical, which are coded in such ways as to "recognize" each other and either mesh together, or create a cultural "force field" which can screen out competing and oppositional discourses. Taken as a whole system, these ideas determine the wider rules of practice which ensure that Western interests remain dominant.

CONCEPTUALIZATIONS OF THE INDIVIDUAL AND SOCIETY

Social science research is based upon ideas, beliefs and theories about the social world. While it is acknowledged that people always live in some form of social organization (for example, a family unit, an efficient hunting and gathering unit, a pastoral unit, and increasingly larger and more effective and sophisticated variations of those basic units), Western forms of research also draw on cultural ideas about the human "self and the relationship between the individual and the groups to which he or she may belong. Such ideas explore both the internal workings of an individual and the relationships between what an individual is and how an individual behaves. These ideas suggest that relationships between or among groups of people are basically causal and can be observed and predicted. Some earlier accounts of how and why individuals behave as they do were based on ideas which often began with a creation story to explain the presence of people in their specific environment and on understandings of human behavior as being connected to some form of external force, such as spiritually powerful beings, "gods" or sacred objects. Human activity was seen to be caused by factors outside the control of the individual. Early European societies would not have made much distinction between human beings and their natural environment. Classical Greek philosophy is regarded as the point at which ideas about these relationships changed from "naturalistic" explanations to humanistic explanations. Naturalistic explanations linked nature and life as one and humanistic explanations separate people out from the world around them, and place humanity on a higher plane (than animals and plants) because of such characteristics as language and reason.[14] Socrates, Plato and Aristotle are regarded as the founders of this humanistic tradition of knowledge.

Human nature, that is, the essential characteristics of an individual person, is an overarching concern of Western philosophy even though "human" and "nature" are also seen to be in opposition to each other. Education, research and other scholarly traditions have emerged from or been framed by debates relating to human nature. The separation between mind and body, the investing of a human person with a soul, a psyche and a consciousness, the distinction between sense and reason, definitions of human virtue and morality, are cultural constructs. These ideas have been transformed as philosophers have incorporated new insights and discoveries, but the underlying categories have remained in place. From Aristotle and Plato, in Greek philosophy, the mind-body distinction was heavily Christianized by Aquinas. French philosopher Descartes developed this dualism further, making distinctions which would relate to the separate disciplines required to study the body (physiology) and the mind (psychology). His distinctions are now referred to as the Cartesian dualism. Hegel reasoned that the split was dialectical, meaning that there was a contradictory interplay between the two ideas and the form of debate required to develop these ideas. It must be remembered, however, that concepts such as the mind or the intellect, the soul, reason, virtue and morality are not in themselves "real" or biological parts of a human body. Whilst the workings of a mind may be associated in Western thinking primarily with the human brain, the mind itself is a concept or an idea. In Maori world views, for example, the closest equivalent to the idea of a "mind" or intellect is associated with the entrails and other parts of the body. The head was considered *tapu* for other reasons.

What makes ideas "real" is the system of knowledge, the formations of culture, and the relations of power in which these concepts are located. What an individual is—and the implications this has for the way researchers or teachers, therapists or social workers, economists or journalists, might approach their work—is based on centuries of philosophical debate, principles of debate and systems for organizing whole societies predicated on these ideas. These ideas constitute reality. Reality cannot be constituted without them. When confronted by the alternative conceptions of other societies, Western reality became reified as representing something "better," reflecting "higher orders" of thinking, and being less prone to the dogma, witchcraft and immediacy of people and societies which were so "primitive." Ideological appeals to such things as literacy, democracy and the development of complex social structures, make this way of thinking appear to be a universal truth and a necessary criterion of civilized society. Although eighteenth- and nineteenth-century forms of colonization brought Christian beliefs about the soul and human morality to indigenous peoples, these concepts were discussed in Western traditions prior to Christianity. Christianity, when organized into a system of power, brought to bear on these basic concepts a focus of systematic study and debate which could then be used to regulate all aspects of social and spiritual life.

The individual, as the basic social unit from which other social organizations and social relations form, is another system of ideas which needs to be understood as part of the West's cultural archive. Western philosophies and religions place the individual as the basic building block of society. The transition from feudal to capitalist modes of production simply emphasized the role of the individual. Concepts of social development were seen as the natural progression and replication of human development. The relationship between the individual and the group, however, was a major theoretical problem for philosophy. This problem tended to be posed as a dialectic or tension between two irreconcilable notions. Hegel's dialectic on the self and society has become the most significant model for thinking about this relationship. His master-slave construct has served as a form of analysis which is both psychological and sociological, and in the colonial context highly political.

Rousseau has a particular influence over the way indigenous peoples in the South Pacific came to be regarded.... It is to Rousseau that the idea of the "noble savage" is attributed. This view linked the natural world to an idea of innocence and purity, and the developed world to corruption and decay.... This romanticized view was particularly relevant to the way South Pacific women were represented, especially the women of Tahiti and Polynesia. The view soon lost favor, or was turned around into the "ignoble savage," when it was found that these idealized humans actually indulged in "barbaric" and "savage" customs and were capable of what were viewed as acts of grave injustice and "despicability."

Just as in the psychological traditions the individual has been central, so within sociological traditions the individual is assumed to be the basic unit of a society. A major sociological concern becomes a struggle over the extent to which individual consciousness and reality shapes, or is shaped by, social structure. During the nineteenth century this view of the individual and society became heavily influenced by social Darwinism. This meant, for example, that a society could be viewed as a "species" of people with biological traits.[15] "Primitive" societies could be ranked according to these traits, predictions could be made about their survival and ideological justifications could be made about their treatment. Early sociology came to focus on the belief systems of these "primitive" people and the extent to which they were capable of thought and of developing "simple" ideas about religion. This focus was intended to enhance the understandings of Western society by showing how simple societies developed the building blocks of classification systems and modes of thought. These systems, it was believed, would demonstrate how such social phenomena as language developed. This in turn would enable distinctions to be made between categories which were fixed—that is, the structural underpinnings of society—and categories which people could create, that is, the cultural aspects of the life-world. It also reinforced, through contrasting associations or oppositional categories, how superior the West was.

CONCEPTIONS OF SPACE

Similar claims can be made about other concepts, such as time and space. These concepts are particularly significant for some indigenous languages because the language makes no clear or absolute distinction between the two: for example, the Maori word for time or space is the same. Other indigenous languages have no related word for either space or time, having instead a series of very precise terms for parts of these ideas, or for relationships between the idea and something else in the environment. There are positions within time and space in which people and events are located, but these cannot necessarily be described as distinct categories of thought. Western ideas about time and space are encoded in language, philosophy and science. Philosophical conceptions of time and space have been concerned with: (1) the relationships between the two ideas, that is, whether space and time are absolute categories or whether they exist relationally; and (2) the measurement of time and space.[16] Space came to be seen as consisting of lines which were either parallel or elliptical. From these ideas, ways of thinking which related to disciplines of study emerged (for example, mapping and geography, measurement and geometry, motion and physics). These distinctions are generally part of a taken-for-granted view of the world. Spatialized language is frequently used in both everyday and academic discourses.

Henri Lefebvre argues that the notion of space has been "appropriated by mathematics" which has claimed an ideological position of dominance over what space means.[17] Mathematics has constructed a language which attempts to define with absolute exactness the parameters, dimensions, qualities and possibilities of space. This language of space influences the way the West thinks about the world beyond earth (cosmology), the ways in which society is viewed (public/private space, city/country space), the ways in which gender roles were defined (public/domestic, home/work) and the ways in which the social world of people could be determined (the market place, the theatre).[18] Compartmentalized, space can be better defined and measured.

Conceptions of space were articulated through the ways in which people arranged their homes and towns, collected and displayed objects of significance, organized warfare, set out agricultural fields and arranged gardens, conducted business, displayed art and performed drama, separated out one form of human activity from another. Spatial arrangements are an important part of social life. Western classifications of space include such notions as architectural space, physical space, psychological space, theoretical space and so forth. Foucault's metaphor of the cultural archive is an architectural image. The archive not only contains artefacts of culture, but is itself an artefact and a construct of culture. For the indigenous world, Western conceptions of space, of arrangements and display, of the relationship between people and the landscape, of culture as an object of study, have meant that not only has the indigenous world been represented in particular ways back to the West, but the indigenous world view, the land and the people, have been radically transformed in the spatial image of the West. In other words, indigenous space has been colonized. Land, for example, was viewed as something to be tamed and brought under control. The landscape, the arrangement of nature, could be altered by "Man": swamps could be drained, waterways diverted, inshore areas filled, not simply for physical survival, but for further exploitation of the environment or making it "more pleasing" aesthetically. Renaming the land was probably as powerful ideologically as changing the land. Indigenous children in schools, for example, were taught the new names for places that they and their parents had lived in for generations. These were the names which appeared on maps and which were used in official communications. This newly named land became increasingly disconnected from the songs and chants used by indigenous peoples to trace their histories, to bring forth spiritual elements or to carry out the simplest of ceremonies. More significantly, however, space was appropriated from indigenous cultures and then "gifted back" as reservations, reserved pockets of land for indigenous people who once possessed all of it.

Other artefacts and images of indigenous cultures were also classified, stored and displayed in museum cases and boxes, framed by the display cases as well as by the categories of artefacts with which they were grouped. Some images became part of the postcard trade and the advertising market or were the subject of Western artistic interpretations of indigenous peoples. Still other "live" and performing examples were put "on stage" as concert parties to entertain Europeans. Indigenous cultures became framed within a language and a set of spatialized representations.[19]

A specific example of the colonization of an indigenous architectural space and of indigenous spatial concepts can be found in the story of the Mataatua, a carved Maori house built in 1875 as a wedding gift from one tribal group to another. The New Zealand government negotiated and gained agreement to send the Mataatua to the British Empire Exhibition at Sydney in 1879. The house was displayed according to the aesthetic and economic sense of the exhibition's curators: "Finding that it would cost at least 700 pounds to erect it in the ordinary manner as a Maori house, the walls were reversed so that the carvings showed on the outside; and the total cost, including painting and roofing with Chinese matting was reduced to 165 pounds."[20] A "Maori House," displayed inside-out and lined with Chinese matting was seen as an important contribution by New Zealand to the Sydney Exhibition. As argued by its original owners, "the house itself had undergone a transformation as a result of being assimilated into a British Empire Exhibition. It changed from being a 'living' meeting house which the people used and had become an ethnological curiosity for strange people to look at the wrong way and in the wrong place."[21]

Having gained agreement for this single purpose, the New Zealand government then appropriated the house and sent it to England, where it was displayed at the South Kensington Museum, stored for forty years at the Victoria and Albert Museum, displayed again at the Wembley British Empire Exhibition in 1924, shipped back to New Zealand for a South Seas Exhibition in Dunedin in 1925, and then "given," by the government, to the Otago Museum. Ngati Awa, the owners of this house, have been negotiating for its return since 1983. This has now been agreed upon by the New Zealand government after a case put to the Waitangi Tribunal, and the "door lintel" of the Mataatua has been returned as a symbolic gesture prior to the return of the entire house over the next two years.

Space is often viewed in Western thinking as being static or divorced from time. This view generates ways of making sense of the world as a "realm of stasis," well-defined, fixed and without politics.[22] This is particularly relevant in relation to colonialism. The establishment of military, missionary or trading stations, the building of roads, ports and bridges, the clearing of bush and the mining of minerals all involved processes of marking, defining and controlling space. There is a very specific spatial vocabulary of colonialism which can be assembled around three concepts: (1) the line, (2) the centre, and (3) the outside. The "line" is important because it was used to map territory, to survey land, to establish boundaries and to mark the limits of colonial power. The "centre" is important because orientation to the centre was an orientation to the system of power. The "outside" is important because it positioned territory and people in an oppositional relation to the colonial centre; for indigenous Australians to be in an "empty space" was to "not exist." That vocabulary in New Zealand is depicted in Table 2.1.

CONCEPTIONS OF TIME

Time is associated with social activity, and how other people organized their daily lives fascinated and horrified Western observers. The links between the industrial revolution, the Protestant ethic, imperialism and science can be discussed in terms of time and the organization of social life. Changes in the mode of production brought about by the industrial revolution, an emerg-

Table 2.1   *The spatial vocabulary of colonialism in nineteenth-century* **Aotearoa**

The Line	The Centre	The Outside
maps	mother country	empty land
charts	London	*terra nullius*
roads	magistrate's residence	uninhabited
boundaries	redoubt, stockade, barracks	unoccupied
pegs	prison	uncharted
surveys	mission station	reserves
claims	Parliament	*Maori pa*
fences	store	*Kainga*
hedges	Church	*Marae*
stone walls	Europe	burial grounds
tracks	port	background
genealogies	foreground	hinterland
perimeters	flagpole	

ing middle class able to generate wealth and make distinctions in their lives between work, leisure, education and religion, and a working-class evangelical movement which linked work to salvation contributed to a potent cultural mix. In Africa, the Americas and the Pacific, Western observers were struck by the contrast in the way time was used (or rather, not used or organized) by indigenous peoples. Representations of "native life" as being devoid of work habits, and of native people being lazy, indolent, with low attention spans, are part of a colonial discourse that continues to this day. There were various explanations advanced for such indolence; a hot climate, for example, was viewed as a factor. Often it was a simple association between race and indolence, darker skin peoples being considered more "naturally" indolent.

An example of how integral time is to social life can be found in the journals of Joseph Banks. Banks accompanied Cook on his first voyages to the South Pacific. The Royal Society supervised the Greenwich Observatory which eventually set the worldwide standard of time measurement (Greenwich mean time) and was instrumental in organizing Cook's voyage to Tahiti in 1769 to observe the transit of Venus. Throughout this journey Banks kept a detailed diary which documents his observations and reflections upon what he saw. The diary was a precise organization of his life on board ship, not only a day by day account, but an account which included weather reports, lists of plants and birds collected, and details on the people he encountered. Life on board the *Endeavour* was organized according to the rules and regulations of the British Admiralty, an adaptation of British time. Not only did the diary measure time, but there were scientific instruments on board which also measured time and place. As an observer, Banks saw the Pacific world through his own sense of time, his observations were prefaced by phrases such as, "at daybreak," "in the evening," "by 8 o'clock," "about noon," "a little before sunset."[23] He confessed, however—after describing in detail such things as dress, ornaments, tattooing, house construction and layout, clothing, gardens, net making, the women, food, religion and language, and after describing visits he and a companion made at particular times to observe the people eating, carrying out their daily activities and sleeping—that he was unable to get a "complete idea" of how the people divided time.

The connection between time and "work" became more important after the arrival of missionaries and the development of more systematic colonization. The belief that "natives" did not value work or have a sense of time provided ideological justification for exclusionary practices which reached across such areas as education, land development and employment. The evangelical missionaries who arrived in the Pacific had a view of salvation in which were embedded either lower middle-class English or puritanical New England work practices and values. It was hard work to get to heaven and "savages" were expected to work extra hard to qualify to get into the queue. This also meant wearing "decent" clothes designed more for hard labor in cold climates, eating "properly" at "proper" meal times (before and after work) and reorganizing family patterns to enable men to work at some things and women to support them.

Lineal views of both time and space are important when examining Western ideas about history. Here, the Enlightenment is a crucial point in time. Prior to this period of Western development was an era likened to a period of "darkness" (the "Age of Darkness") which "coincided" with the rise of power to the east. This era was followed by reformation within the Church of Rome. During these periods of time, which are social "constructions" of time, society was said to be feudal, belief systems were based on dogma, monarchs ruled by divine authority, and literacy was confined to the very few. People lived according to myths and stories which hid the "truth" or were simply not truths. These stories were kept alive by memory. The Enlightenment has also been referred to as the "Age of Reason." During this period history came to be viewed as a more reasoned or scientific understanding of the past. History could be recorded systematically and then retrieved through recourse to written texts. It was based on a lineal view of time and was linked closely to notions of progress. Progress could be "measured" in terms of technological advancement and spiritual salvation. Progress is evolutionary and teleological and is present in both liberal and Marxist ideas about history.

Different orientations towards time and space, different positioning within time and space, and different systems of language for making space and time "real" underpin notions of past and present, of place and of relationships to the land. Ideas about progress are grounded within ideas and orientations towards time and space. What has come to count as history in contemporary society is a contentious issue for many indigenous communities because it is not only the story of domination; it is also a story which assumes that there was a "point in time" which was "prehistoric." The point at which society moves from prehistoric to historic is also the point at which tradition breaks with modernism. Traditional indigenous knowledge ceased, in this view, when it came into contact with "modern" societies, that is the West. What occurred at this point of culture contact was the beginning of the end for "primitive" societies. Deeply embedded in these constructs are systems of classification and representation which lend themselves easily to binary oppositions, dualisms, and hierarchical orderings of the world.

One of the concepts through which Western ideas about the individual and community, about time and space, knowledge and research, imperialism and colonialism can be drawn together is the concept of distance. The individual can be distanced, or separated, from the physical environment, the community. Through the controls over time and space the individual can also operate at a distance from the universe. Both imperial and colonial rule were systems of rule which stretched from the centre outwards to places which were far and distant. Distance again separated the individuals in power from the subjects they governed. It was all so impersonal, rational and extremely effective. In research the concept of distance is most important as it implies a neutrality and objectivity on behalf of the researcher. Distance is measurable. What it has come to stand for is objectivity, which is not measurable to quite the same extent.

Research "through imperial eyes" describes an approach which assumes that Western ideas about the most fundamental things are the only ideas possible to hold, certainly the only rational ideas, and the only ideas which can make sense of the world, of reality, of social life and of human beings. It is an approach to indigenous peoples which still conveys a sense of innate superiority and an overabundance of desire to bring progress into the lives of indigenous peoples—spiritually, intellectually, socially and economically. It is research which from indigenous perspectives "steals" knowledge from others and then uses it to benefit the people who "stole" it. Some indigenous and minority group researchers would call this approach simply racist. It is research which is imbued with an "attitude" and a "spirit" which assumes a certain ownership of the entire world, and which has established systems and forms of governance which embed that attitude in institutional practices. These practices determine what counts as legitimate research and who count as legitimate researchers. Before assuming that such an attitude has long since disappeared, it is often worth reflecting on who would make such a claim, researchers or indigenous peoples? A recent attempt (fortunately unsuccessful) to patent an indigenous person in the New Guinea Highlands might suggest that there are many groups of indigenous peoples who are still without protection when it comes to the activities of research.[24]

Although in this particular case the attempt was unsuccessful, what it demonstrated yet again is that there are people out there who in the name of science and progress still consider indigenous peoples as specimens, not as humans.

NOTES

1. Hall, S. (1992), "The West and the Rest: Discourse and Power," Chapter 6 of *Formations of Modernity,* eds. S. Hall and B. Gielben, Polity Press and Open University, Cambridge, pp. 276–320.

2. Bernstein, B. (1971), "On the Classification and Framing of Knowledge," in *Knowledge and Control. New Directions for the Sociology of Education,* ed. M. F. D. Young, Collier Macmillan, London, pp. 47–69.

3. See for example, Bernal, M. (1991), *Black Athena: The Afroasiatic Roots of Civilisation,* Vintage, London.

4. Foucault, M. (1972), *The Archaeology of Knowledge,* trans. A. Sheridan Smith, Pantheon, New York.

5. Nandy, A. (1989), *The Intimate Enemy: Loss and Recovery of Self under Colonialism,* Oxford University Press, Delhi, p. xi.

6. Goldberg, D. T. (1993), *Racist Culture, Philosophy, and the Politics of Meaning,* Blackwell, Oxford.

7. Ibid., p. 23.

8. Ibid., p. 23.

9. Ibid., p. 23.

10. Ibid., p. 23.

11. Ibid., pp. 41–60.

12. Erler, M. and M. Kowaleski (1988), *Women and Power in the Middle Ages,* University of Georgia Press, Athens.

13. The Treaty of Waitangi was signed between Maori chiefs and the British Crown in 1840. The Waitangi Tribunal was established by Parliament under The Treaty of Waitangi Act 1975. This Act established the Tribunal with the brief of hearing claims by Maori that the Crown had contravened the principles of the Treaty of Waitangi. This applied to recent grievances. The Tribunal was given powers to recommend actions to the Crown. The Act was amended in 1985 in order to extend the scope of claims back to 1840.

14. Brennan, J. F. (1991), *Racist Culture: The History and Systems of Psychology,* third edition, Prentice Hall International, New Jersey.

15. Goldberg, *Racist Culture,* pp. 62–9.

16. In the fifth century Zeno, for example, posited a series of paradoxes which centered around two ideas, one which suggests that space and time are continuous, and one which suggests that they are made up of divisible parts. Others have argued since Zeno that there can be no such thing as "empty" space because, if it is empty, it does not exist.

17. Lefebvre, H. (1991), *The Production of Space,* Blackwell, USA.

18. See for example, Williams, R. (1973), *The Country and the City,* Paladin, London. See also Fanon, Frantz (1967), *The Wretched of the Earth,* Penguin, London, p. 30. Fanon talks about "zones" where natives live and "zones" where settlers live. For him, the border between the two [is] clear and there is no possibility of reconciliation.

19. See also, Gidley, M., ed. (1994), *Representing Others: White Views of Indigenous Peoples,* University of Exeter Press.

20. Appendices to the Journals of the New Zealand House of Representatives, 1880, H5: 2.

21. Te Runanga o Ngati Awa (1990), *Nga Karoretanga o Mataatua Whare: The Wanderings of the Carved House, Mataatua,* Ngati Awa Research Report 2, Whakatane, New Zealand.

22. Massey, D. (1993), "Politics and Space/Time," in *Place and the Politics of Identity,* eds. M. Keith and S. Pile, Routledge, London, pp. 141–61.

23. Beaglehole, J. C. (1962), *The Endeavour Journal of Joseph Banks,* Angus and Robertson, Sydney.

24. See account of this attempt in *Third World Resurgence,* no. 63, p. 30.

3
Economics

FEMINISM AND ECONOMICS

Economic practices and systems are sets of social arrangements through which humans organize the production, distribution, and consumption of the material goods and services that are necessary for human life. The discipline of economics studies how these systems and practices work, and feminist economics investigates their gendered dimensions; that is to say, feminist economics studies the gendered aspects of economic life. Feminist methodology in economics investigates how the discipline produces economic "facts" and theories.

At the level of daily life, feminist economists are concerned with how divisions of labor and distributions of products and services are influenced by social norms of gender. Gender is often central in social decisions about who should do which work and who is entitled to the benefits of that work. Feminist economists study the ways in which systems of production, distribution, and consumption are shaped by social expectations for people in various classes and social groups who are identified respectively as masculine and feminine and by presumptions regarding how such people should be treated. Feminist economics also studies how various alternative economic policies and systems are likely to affect the members of these gendered groups. It is especially concerned with gendered disparities embedded in various economic arrangements, questioning the rationales for these arrangements and asking whether they impose disproportionate economic burdens on members of groups categorized respectively as feminine or masculine or award disproportionate economic benefits to them.

At the level of methodology, feminist economists scrutinize the discipline of economics, its representations of economic life, and its prescriptions concerning economic arrangements. Feminist methodologists focus especially on economic theory's tendency to obscure gendered inequities or to bring them to light.

SOME GENDER BIASES IN ECONOMIC THEORY

The word *economics* derives etymologically from two Greek terms: *oikos,* meaning "house, home, or dwelling place"; and *nomos,* meaning "custom, regulation, or human law." The combination of these two terms, *oikonomeo,* refers to the administration or management of the household and all of domestic life. Xenophon's book, *Oikonomikos,* may be the single best example of all the things that *oikonomos* includes. It is sometimes translated as "estate management," and it deals with all types of care for property.

With the advent of industrialization, much production moved outside the household and most products were no longer intended for immediate use within the family; instead, within capitalism, most goods are produced for sale on the market. Today, the discipline of economics focuses primarily on the production and distribution of goods and services through markets; it tends to ignore forms of production and distribution that do not involve buying or selling. Thus it tends to exclude subsistence hunting, gathering, and agriculture as well as the production and distribution of goods and services that occur within households. Many feminists consider that economic theory's preoccupation with markets to the exclusion of nonmarket systems of production and distribution reflects gender and other biases.

When economic life is represented within a market framework, value is equated with price; thus, costs and benefits can be expressed only as monetary losses and gains. For example, damage to health must be measured in terms such as lost hours of paid work or costs to health insurers, rather than in terms of individual suffering; it may even appear as income to medical professionals. Similarly, damage to the environment must be measured in terms such as dollar costs to health services, agriculture, or tourism, and it may also appear as income, for instance, to those who clean up oil spills. Price is a useful measure of costs and benefits insofar as it allows the relative value of things that seem otherwise incommensurable to be compared, but it also has disadvantages because it can express their value only in limited, partial ways. Price cannot represent the costs and benefits of things that are not bought or sold; within the framework of market economics, types of human suffering or enjoyment that have no price appear to have no disvalue or value.

A considerable feminist literature argues that contemporary economic theory provides only a partial and distorted representation of economic life, particularly of many economic transactions shaped by gender. Definitions of economic activity that exclude activities performed outside the market fail to recognize how much recipients gain from goods and services they do not have to buy; these definitions also fail to recognize the costs of unpaid work to those who perform it. In some societies, much food and clothing is still produced at home for direct family consumption, and in virtually all societies many vital services, such as food preparation, household maintenance, and care of children, elders, and the sick, are performed at home without pay.

Household work, which is performed disproportionately by women, is a prime example of unpaid work, and the goods and services that household work produces are excellent examples of value produced outside the market. These goods and services are enjoyed disproportionately by children and male family members, and if they were sold on the market they would have enormous monetary value—up to one-third of gross national product (GNP), by some estimates. However, that value is not recognized by an economic theory that relies exclusively on market measures. Similarly, market economics can recognize the cost of household work to those women who perform it only in terms such as foregone opportunities for paid work; it cannot recognize the value or disvalue of long hours and emotional energy that are not sold on the market.

Markets are only one possible way of organizing the production and distribution of life's necessities; however, contemporary economic theory typically presents them as the *most* efficient, free, and fair way of organizing economic life.

1. Markets are said to be efficient in ensuring that the economy produces what most people want at the lowest cost.
2. They are said to be free in the senses that people can choose their purchases from a wide array of products and that no one is coerced into working.
3. Finally, they are said to be fair in rewarding talent and hard work, disregarding rank or caste, and democratic in reflecting everyone's preferences.

However, *efficiency, freedom,* and *fairness* are all evaluative terms capable of multiple interpretations, and markets are not efficient, free, or fair from every perspective. For instance:

1. Markets are efficient at producing goods and services for which there is a market demand, but they are not efficient in producing goods and services for which people cannot afford to pay; thus they encourage the production of whatever is wanted by those with economic resources but not by those who lack such resources.
2. Markets are free in contrast with various forms of physically forced labor, such as

slavery, but economic need still forces many people to work long hours in dangerous conditions for low pay.

3. Finally, markets are democratic and fair in the sense that they are not controlled directly by particular individuals, but they do not reflect the preferences of all members of society equally; instead, supposedly impersonal "market forces" mediate those preferences, giving weight only to those that appear as effective market demand.

Thus, production organized through markets responds primarily to the interests of those whose financial resources enable them to translate their preferences into effective market demand. They do not respond to those whose resources are insufficient to purchase the means of meeting their preferences. Thus markets are not efficient, free, and fair from the perspective of all members of society equally. Women especially often find them inefficient, costly, and unfair.

Many feminist economists have observed that in societies where most social necessities are provided through the market, women tend to fare worse than men who are otherwise similarly situated. It is true that markets provide opportunities for many women to support themselves, thus reducing their economic dependence on men. However, many labor markets are gender segregated, forcing women to accept work that is lower paid and more menial than most men's, and often sexualized as well. Even when labor markets are not gender segregated, women often find it harder than men to compete in such markets because they are culturally assigned a heavier burden of family caretaking responsibility. Moreover, women's culturally assigned needs for family services are often unmet in market societies, even though sexual services for men are typically readily available. When economic theory presents markets as efficient, free, and fair, it obscures their systematic bias against people who have greater needs or fewer resources. Disproportionately though certainly not exclusively, these people are women.

Feminists have argued that the key concepts used in market economic theory are often interpreted in ways that incorporate gender and other biases. For example, the environment is viewed as valuable only insofar as it provides a resource for human economic exploitation; development is equated with growth in the GNP regardless of whether it is accompanied by increasing inequality or deteriorating quality of life. By market standards, many women appear economically inactive, unproductive, or dependent rather than engaged in skilled and hard labor that makes a vital social contribution; women who choose not to sell their services on the market appear to be economically irrational.

Because the discipline of economics carries the prestige of science, the technical meanings that it assigns to commonly used words often shape their generally accepted meanings. Thus, broader noneconomic interpretations of terms such as *rationality, value, cost, benefit, work, contribution, productivity, efficiency, development, resources,* and so on, appear fuzzy or utopian. When these terms are used in political debate, the prestige of economics influences their meanings and creates a systematic bias toward market values, discouraging consideration of other ethical concerns. Critics charge that the discipline of economics tends to naturalize, normalize, and justify market economic systems and foreclose needed political debate about the ethical problems associated with them. These ethical problems include markets' unresponsiveness to many human needs, their tendency to undermine community by promoting competition and inequality, and their potential to exploit the environment, animals, and workers. The almost exclusive focus of economic theory on the market tends to occlude the possibility of other economic systems that might embody the values of efficiency, freedom, and fairness in ways that are more responsive to the needs of the majority of the population and especially to the needs of many women.

FEMINIST METHODOLOGY AND ECONOMIC THEORY

Webster's dictionary defines economics as "the science that deals with the production, distribution, and consumption of goods and services, or the material welfare of humankind." The idea that economics is a science may be thought to imply that its theoretical models offer only value-neutral descriptions and explanations of economic phenomena, envisioned as natural objects whose properties await discovery. The extensive use of formal models in economics may also encourage the impression that this discipline is value-neutral as well as mathematically precise. However, feminists find these suggestions misleading. They observe that economic theory inevitably relies on value-laden presuppositions about human welfare and social contribution and so in fact is not at all value-free. Feminists point out not only that economic practices and systems incorporate specific social values but also that the economic theories that aim to represent these practices and systems tacitly incorporate values too (like all systems of knowledge).

One concern of feminist methodology is the empirical adequacy of theoretical descriptions of economic arrangements. Like all conceptual models, economic theories place some phenomena in the foreground and others in the background, highlighting some features of their object of study and obscuring others. Feminist methodology studies the values implicit in those theoretical models, arguing that what they obscure is too often the economic activity and contributions of women and other marginalized groups. For instance, Strassman points out that the descriptions of economic life provided by economic theory often rely on myths that obscure the realities of many women's economic lives: the myth that economic agents are mutually disinterested and self-aggrandizing, the myth of the benevolent patriarch, the myth of the woman of leisure, the myth of free choice. Feminist methodology asks in whose interest it is that these omissions and myths are perpetuated. Many feminists contend that the discipline of economics frequently obscures the interests of less powerful social groups, especially women.

In addition to its concern with the empirical adequacy of representations of economic life in economic theory, feminist methodology investigates the value judgments lurking in the way such theory is focused, the questions it selects to address, and those that it omits. Feminist methodologists ask who is interested in raising these questions and whose interests are promoted by the answers offered. They study the values and priorities implicit in various conceptual models of economic life and ask whether these are the values and priorities of some groups rather than others. They are especially concerned with revealing any gender biases built into economic theory and method.

Feminist methodology seeks to develop knowledge-generating strategies for economic research that are capable of addressing not only questions that are primarily of concern to the privileged classes but also questions of interest to a broad range of people, including many women. For instance, feminist economists are currently developing methods for assigning a monetary value to nonmarket work. Feminist research methods are unlikely to abandon quantification, transforming economics into qualitative sociology; as we saw in Chapter 2, quantification is not inherently masculine, despite its cultural associations. However, feminist methodology does reflect critically on how values are assigned to variables and, as Benería and Waring argue, it tends toward developing richer interpretations of central methodological concepts such as rationality and more inclusive interpretations of central economic concepts such as human welfare, progress, sustainability, and development.

Feminist methodology itself is not a value-neutral enterprise. In the area of economics, it is committed to developing research methods that enable theorists to address those questions in which women tend to have a special interest and to represent economic life more fully and fairly. It examines the definitions, questions, and methods of economic theory, and assesses the strengths and weaknesses of various theoretical approaches to studying economic life with reference to feminism's defining commitment to opposing gender injustice.

Diana Strassmann
Not a Free Market: The Rhetoric of Disciplinary Authority in Economics

In recent years, mainstream American economics has increasingly been built around core ideas of self-interested individualism and contractual exchange. The central character of economic analysis is the autonomous agent who trades with other agents in order to maximize a utility or profit function. Both microeconomists and macroeconomists explain the economy in ways that are consistent with this microfoundations core. Modern mainstream economics therefore may be identified as an explanatory approach rather than as a domain of facts to be explained. An explanatory approach is unusual, however, for disciplines oriented toward explaining empirical phenomena. Most other empirical disciplines, such as the physical and biological sciences, define themselves in terms of the empirical domain to be explained (Shapere 1984).

How has the identification of economics as an approach rather than as an empirical domain become predominant? What voices have been included and represented in this construction of economics? How has this construction shaped economic research? My thesis is that the tendency of mainstream economics to be identified with an approach rather than with a set of empirical phenomena limits the kinds of explanations that the discipline can provide.[1] ... I shall argue that the resulting theories reflect a distinctly androcentric and Western perspective on selfhood and individual agency.

CORE IDEAS AND THE SHAPING OF ECONOMIC RESEARCH

A popular view among mainstream practitioners is that explanations based on self-interested individualism and contractual exchange merit their high status in economics because of their obvious logic or superior power. The conceptual structure of economics indeed appears natural and obvious to most practitioners in the discipline, and this is no accident. The selection and socialization process for becoming an economist ensures that those to whom this structure might be less obvious learn how to do proper economics or be screened out. Those who remain economists easily forget that the organization of the discipline, based on the core assumptions of self-interested individualism and contractual exchange, means that the construction of economic knowledge is partial.

Economists' typical description of a good model as focusing on the most "important" elements of some phenomenon displays an implicit recognition of the nature of models. Models, like maps, highlight certain aspects of a situation while suppressing others. Since a model can never completely capture the phenomenon in its entirety, questions of the "truth" or "falsity" of a model are less relevant to judgments about its quality than are questions of its appropriateness, aptness, and helpfulness in a given context. Our models can help us to understand those aspects of the world we choose to emphasize, but the principles or laws we derive from our models are "true" only in the model, not literally true in the world (Cartwright 1983).

Well-socialized economists, however, in practice tend to view their simplifications—especially those required by the core assumptions of self-interested individualism and contractual exchange—as relatively innocent.... The microfoundations of economic theory are seen as being approximately true rather than as only partially true. The notion of modeling as approximation, however, disguises the value judgments hidden behind the decision to count some phenomena as more important than others. These judgments need to be understood in the context of the model-makers' own experience, and hence their partial views of the world.

Rather than encouraging a search for the most appropriate simplifications for a given context of application, the discipline requires that explanatory accounts be built on the foundational assumptions of self-interested individualism and contractual exchange, thereby insulating itself against accounts built on alternative assumptions. Four case studies of the partial nature of mainstream economics stories will illustrate the problems created, in theory and in policy, by the narrowness of the range of explanatory accounts in the discipline. I use the term "story" to highlight the nature of economic knowledge and the restrictions the discipline places on the acceptable structure of economic accounts.[3] Like any model, the story model is a partial description of accounts of the world.[4]

THE STORY OF THE MARKETPLACE OF IDEAS

The story of the marketplace of ideas is a classical example of economic imperialism—the application of economic explanations to domains viewed as being outside the traditional purview of economics, in this case the philosophy of science and anthropology. In the marketplace of ideas the "best" ideas bubble to the top, rising in value according to merit. Ideas are exchanged as in a marketplace, their worth ascertained in a competitive process of bidding and exchange. This story implies that predominant economic theories are valued because of their worthiness, with no role for cultural values or institutional configurations. In Deirdre McCloskey's (1985) version of this story, the success of a theory depends on its inherent quality as well as on the quality of the rhetoric used to support it: the community of "honest" scholars is the judge (28).

But who are these judges in the "economy of intellect," those select and worthy scholars who have become economists? They have not been produced in a vacuum. The persuasiveness of any particular argument does not lie wholly in the argument itself; the success of an argument depends in part on the composition of the judging audience. The arguments that appeal to economists need to be understood in the context of the complex processes by which economists have been selected and socialized, and the processes by which other potential economists have been excluded.[5]

To the extent that the marketplace metaphor does indeed apply to the exchange of ideas, perfect competition does not predominate. The marketplace of academia lacks, for example, both free entry and perfect knowledge—essentials for perfect competition. So what happens if there is *imperfect* competition in the marketplace of ideas? Helen Longino (1990a) claims that objectivity within a discipline is enhanced when qualified practitioners share intellectual authority.[6] Her arguments translate easily to the language of economics. The absence of free entry into the marketplace of economic ideas distorts the relative valuations of ideas in this arena, giving market power to dominant practitioners.... As any economist would agree, barriers to entry create price distortions. Exclusionary practices lead to a divergence between the social and private value of ideas. The private value is determined by the reward structure within the discipline and the subtle processes of selection, socialization, and exclusion.

But even this story of imperfect competition in the marketplace of ideas obscures the influence of social and cultural values. When entry into the discipline is filtered by the requirement that members adhere to a core conceptual structure, dissenting voices are screened out.... The inability of economics to give much credence to issues of values, power, and social construction may be due to the way practitioners have been selected and socialized to discount the role of such factors, and to give excessive credence to stories based on core assumptions and models.

One example is the story of the benevolent patriarch.

THE STORY OF THE BENEVOLENT PATRIARCH

The standard economic model of the family is a story of a benevolent patriarch.[7] In this story, the patriarch makes choices in the best interests of the family. A patriarch is necessarily male; as head of the prototypical family, he has a wife and one or more children dependent upon him for providing for their needs.[8] Although family members may have conflicting needs, the good provider dispassionately and rationally makes decisions that are in the best interests of the family. In particular, the patriarch participates in markets, making choices that link market values to his own assessment of family needs.

This story is useful for economic theory because it allows the family to be treated as an individual agent. The metaphor of the invisible hand and its modern expression in general equilibrium theory rest critically on this foundational story by linking decision-making with individual well-being. The link implicitly assumes that family decisions (made by the patriarch) give equal weight to the needs of all family members....

An individual patriarch may indeed take individual family members' preferences into account, perhaps far better than a distant bureaucrat would. However, the linking of decision-making with individual well-being need not necessarily hold for the dominant decision-makers in families, who are overwhelmingly male (Sen 1984). Widespread wife and child abuse as well as the substantial evidence for unequal food distribution within the family, which again harms women and children, clearly undermines the notion that family members necessarily behave altruistically (Sen 1984). Rather, the distribution of power among family members, often directly related to their individual resources, appears to play a major role in family decisions and the intrafamily distribution of resources.

The story of the benevolent patriarch, like all stories, is partial. The problem is not the partiality of the story per se but its inappropriate use, which leads to numerous misguided policy judgments. In an early response to Milton Friedman's (1953) claim that the realism of assumptions does not matter, Robert Solow suggests that when theoretical results stem directly from a "crucial" assumption, that assumption should be reasonably realistic (1956, 65). I would like to call attention to the possibility that an assumption may be "crucial" for some application areas but not for others.

For example, the story of the benevolent patriarch serves as a background to theories of income distribution, taxation, welfare, and economic development. Although Amartya Sen's work shows that the linking of decision-making with individual well-being is a crucial assumption underlying many of these theories, such theories are not generally understood to be crucially dependent upon this linkage.[9] Children and women in particular get shortchanged by some economic policies based on the story of the benevolent patriarch. Sen calls attention to "the grave tragedy of the disproportionate undernourishment of children," "the sharper undernourishment of the female children in distress situations," and the "unusual morbidity of women" in India and in poverty more generally. Sen attributes these phenomena to the selfish behavior of family patriarchs and concludes that the failure of family decision-makers to behave altruistically calls into question the reliability of many of the economic analyses based upon this premise, including the traditional efficiency or optimality results related to the market mechanism (1984, 363, 364).... I suggest that the problem with the story of the benevolent patriarch is that economists fail to recognize the limited scope of application of models built on this story, a failure that has led to inadequate and inappropriate theories and policies in a wide variety of contexts.

THE STORY OF THE WOMAN OF LEISURE

Another old economic fable is that women do not work. The woman of leisure stays at home tending to the domestic needs of her family. Although she may perform many activities, these activities are limited to her family and have no value because they are not traded in the market-place. Dependent on her husband, the benevolent patriarch, she relies on him and the money he earns from his productive and marketed activities to provide for her needs.

Unlike the story of the benevolent patriarch, however, the story that women do not work is slowly giving way to other stories, many of them told by the women who have become economists in recent decades.[10] Although labor economists have begun to recognize the concept of nonmarket production, the very term "household production" represents a borrowing from a category formed to describe male activity. While economists have given lip service to women's work in the home as *one* of those "unfortunate" exclusions from the national income accounts, gendered conceptualizations of what counts as work matter greatly for public policy. The exclusion of women's work from national income accounts, for example, has had particularly pernicious effects for women in developing nations (Waring 1988). That finding a way to measure and include nonmarket production has remained a low priority activity in the discipline attests to the small degree of concern over this exclusion.[11] ...

THE STORY OF FREE CHOICE

Another partial story, related to the previous two, is the story of free choice. The agent in economic theory is a creature with wishes and desires as well as with various resources at his disposal.... Because his resources are always inadequate to attain all his wishes and desires, economic man must make choices. Faced with the available array of goods and services, each with an attached price, he dispassionately considers his various possibilities for satisfaction and carefully weighs their costs against their respective degrees of potential satisfaction. Eventually, he will conclude that he prefers one of these options, and that option becomes his choice. The agent in economic theory is a self-contained individual—an adult able to choose from an array of options, limited only by "constraints."

But by focusing on choice, the theory contains a number of ancillary, more hidden assumptions: (1) people are independent agents and unique selves, taking only their own needs and wishes into account; (2) people are able and responsible for taking care of their own needs.

Such assumptions are not actually intended by the theory, ... but are implicit in actual use. Economists do not universally deny that these assumptions are problematic, but, like the exclusion of women from national income accounts, these assumptions are viewed as fairly benign. Such assumptions indeed may be typical of the perceived experiences of adult, white, male, middle-class American economists, but they fail to capture economic reality for many others.[13] Economic theory's conception of selfhood and individual agency is located in Western cultural traditions as well as being distinctly androcentric.[14] Economic man is the Western romantic hero, a transcendent individual able to make choices and attain goals.

Are these assumptions really benign? Consider the case of infants and children, who do not make choices in a process of rational optimization. They are not calculating machines; their needs are met by others. The nursing relationship between mother and child, far more ancient than market relationships, is the natural mainstay of sustenance for infants. In this relationship, and in the other connective bonds between child and parent, one finds an interdependence that belies separative conceptions of the self.... The choices that influence [infants'] welfare are made by adults. Because economic theory examines adult behavior, parents' gifts of time, love, and money to infants and children are reconceptualized as "natural endowments," and thus are hidden by a theory that focuses on how people get what they choose. These lost gifts, forgotten or ignored by economic theory, are yet another manifestation of the invisibility of women's work.[15]

Some economic theorists have attempted to explain gifts to children in the context of parents receiving some form of expected return. Such accounts reflect a general tautological tendency in economic theory, that is, defining any choices, including any form of giving, as being in an individual's self-interest—reconceptualizing any form of giving as self-interest. Virginia Held (1990) describes an alternative view of parent-child relations. She defines a "mothering person" as someone, male or female, who is engaged in the practice of "mothering,"[16] and suggests that any element of a bargain between mothering person and child is very different from the bargain supposedly characteristic of the marketplace:

> If a parent thinks "I'll take care of you now so you'll take care of me when I'm old," it must be based, unlike the contracts of political and economic bargains, on enormous trust and on a virtual absence of enforcement.... At least the bargain would only be resorted to when the callousness or poverty of the society made the plight of the old person desperate.... [T]he intention and goal of mothering is to give of one's care without obtaining a return of a self-interested kind. The emotional satisfaction of a mothering person is a satisfaction in the well-being and happiness of another human being, and a satisfaction in the health of the relation between the two persons, not the gain that results from an egoistic bargain. (1990, 297–98)

A number of alternative conceptions of economic relations focus on giving and the satisfaction of human needs, concepts obscured by the standard economic metaphors tied to separative conceptions of selfhood (Nancy Folbre and Heidi Harmann 1983, 1988; Dorinne Kondo 1990; Julie A. Nelson 1990)....

The lack of emphasis on constraints and interdependence stems from the way economic models focus on individual rational choice processes, a focus that deemphasizes (if not ignores) the fact that human beings begin (and often end) life in a state of helplessness and unchosen dependency. Although the dependency of infancy lessens, our lives are always a mix of connectedness and separation.

Economists *are* aware that constraints will theoretically influence outcomes. A theory that focuses on the choices people make assumes that individual outcomes are a consequence of those choices.... One may ask whether certain contemporary policy failures, particularly the undue suffering of infants and children, may be partially attributable to the current thinking, of economics, which coheres with the American story of resources going to those who work for and deserve them.

CAN MAINSTREAM THEORIES BE FIXED?

Economists would like to believe that most difficulties and problems in standard theories can be resolved within the mainstream framework. They have worked hard to develop stories that reconcile the major "anomalies" with the standard economic approach.[19] For example, by fixing economic theory to provide better explanations of women's behavior, many such deficiencies in the theory have (in some sense) been resolved.[20] The likelihood of a mainstream "fix," however, depends upon the nature of the difficulty in the standard story. Difficulties linked to core assumptions (such as self-interested individualism) will be extremely hard to change because of the identification of economics as an approach that uses those assumptions. Because any account of the world is constructed on the basis of a partial perspective, standard economic accounts do more than just leave out other voices. They create a conceptual framework for organizing an understanding of the world in which some features are prioritized over others. Therefore, problems less linked to core assumptions can be more easily changed within a mainstream framework. Consequently, women's activities in the home have been more easily reconceptualized as useful and productive (instead of as leisure) because nonmarketed exchanges are not inconsistent with foundational metaphors (although less prototypical than marketed exchanges).

Even where mainstream fixes are possible, however, such modifications often will remain peripheral to the theoretical core of the discipline. For example, the influence and centrality of game-theoretic reconceptualizations of the family, which extend self-interest into the family, are limited by the central role of the benevolent patriarch story with which they conflict. As long as adherence to central stories determines theoretical importance, modifications that do not adhere to these stories will be marginalized and known in detail almost exclusively by those who specialize in them. Furthermore, specialists are unlikely to be aware of the full extent to which the prototype fails over a broad range of economic contexts. Because few economists learn much about research on the "fringes," modifications to core theories cannot be easily coordinated to allow for the development of a unified conception of problems with core economic metaphors. Indeed, my discussion of impediments to alternative conceptualizations in economics conflicts with the popular story of the marketplace of ideas.

The conversation metaphor for knowledge construction used by Arjo Klamer (1984), Deirdre McCloskey (1985), and others has the potential to draw attention to questions obscured by the story of the marketplace of ideas (e.g., who gets to participate and who gets excluded? who listens and who gets listened to? who gets to decide which arguments are "good" and which are not?). McCloskey generally does not focus on these issues; she prefers to emphasize the protective aspects of the social character of science. She writes that "the social character of scientific knowledge does not make it arbitrary, touchie-feelie, mob-governed, or anything else likely to bring it into disrepute. It is still, for instance, 'objective,' if that is a worry" (1985, 152).[21]

But the social character of science protects it in a way that also "renders it vulnerable to social and political interests and values" (Longino 1990, 12). Helen Longino argues that reducing subjective preferences in science requires both that hypotheses and background assumptions be subjected to a variety of conceptual criticisms and that such criticisms can limit the acceptance of partial and idiosyncratic assumptions reflecting the views of a single same-minded group (1992, 21). Such a process cannot happen when "unreflective acceptance of assumptions" defines "what it is to be a member of such a community (thus making criticism impossible)" (1992, 17).

The entry of more women into the discipline may lead to theoretical changes that fit within the existing disciplinary framework of economics. But as long as dissent is labeled not economics and suppressed, critique of standard economic assumptions remains taboo.[22] Not surprisingly, neither anthropologists nor philosophers of science view the story of the marketplace of ideas as a fully credible or complete explanation of why some ideas or theories prevail over others. Their explanations include some features and questions that are left out of the story of the marketplace of ideas. A story that takes into account the incompleteness of models need not keep searching for the "best" model. Because models by their nature represent only a partial viewpoint, partiality or bias cannot be eliminated from theories. A greater openness to entertaining alternative perspectives is likely to lead to a multiplicity of perspectives that more adequately captures the complexity and diversity of economic activities.

NOTES

1.   ... I do not claim that the mainstream speaks with one voice; indeed the mainstream is beset with fierce and substantive internal debates....

3.   I owe a great intellectual debt to the anthropologist Sharon Traweek for directing me to think about the nature of storytelling in economics.... Also see McCloskey (1990) for a detailed discussion of narrative and storytelling in economics.

4.   Stories and metaphors, for example, are two different kinds of explanations: one static, the other dy-namic (McCloskey 1990). See Polanyi (1989) for a detailed discussion of different forms of explanatory accounts.

5.   Traweek (1988) describes these processes of socialization and exclusion in the high energy physics communities in the United States and Japan....

6.   See Seiz (1992) for a parallel discussion of knowledge construction in the economics community.

7.   See Folbre and Hartmann (1988) for a detailed discussion of the gender-related self-interest underlying the traditional acceptance of this model. See Adam Smith (1776) for a discussion of the dichotomous assumptions of perfect selfishness in the marketplace and perfect altruism in the home, and Gary S. Becker (1981) for a more contemporary elaboration.

8. Families are, of course, more complex and diverse than this simple story indicates, but that is obscured when this background story is hidden from analysis. Recent game-theoretic accounts of family behavior challenge the story of the benevolent patriarch and explore a variety of issues related to decisionmaking in the family. See, for example, Manser and Brown (1980), McElroy and Homey (1981), Pollak (1985), and Lundberg and Pollak (1990). Although such accounts are mainstream in the sense of maintaining consistency with assumptions of individual optimization, they have been treated as relatively peripheral and have not been incorporated into economic theory more generally. See Cooper (1990) for an analysis of mainstream resistance to game-theoretic accounts of the family.

9. Samuels (1992) makes a related point in criticizing analyses that purport to reach "optimal" solutions on the basis of implicit normative premises.

10. Differences in the stories people with different experiences tell illustrate how experiences may influence the way people construct accounts of the world. Brown (1989), for example, shows how economists' "discovery" of women workers coincides with the entry of the wives of these male economists into the marketplace.

11. The *American Economic Review* has not published a single article on this topic for at least the past ten years; details of such work elsewhere remain largely unknown to most economists....

13. Developments in a variety of disciplines have shown how the social construction of gender has created a tendency for men and women to differ in how they conceptualize their experiences, moral choices, and epistemological views as well as in their orientation toward separation and connection. See, for example, Chodorow (1978); England (1989); Gilligan (1982); Harding (1986); and Belenky et al. (1986).

14. See Kondo (1990) for a discussion of the relation between cultural traditions and conceptions of selfhood.

15. Although there is a growing literature on intergenerational transfers, much of this literature focuses on bequests and other pecuniary (male-identified) gifts rather than on gifts of time and attention.

16. She adds that "if men feel uncomfortable being referred to as, or even more so in being, 'mothering persons,' this may possibly mirror the discomfort many mothers feel adapting to the norms and practices, and language, of 'economic man'" (Held 1990, 290)....

19. Such modifications include some of the recent research on the family, symmetrical research programs on the theory of the firm, and research on the economic behavior of women and minorities.

20. However, theoretical changes regarding the treatment of women have often proceeded on a selective basis, resulting in ad hoc rather than theory-driven explanations for women's behavior. Brown describes how "explanations" of racial differences in women's labor force participation range from "matriarchal family structure" in black families to variations in the fear of losing husbands (1989, 9).

21. Both McCloskey (1985, 152) and Longino (1990) give objectivity a social definition.

22. See Strassmann and Polanyi (1992) for further discussion of the status of critique in economic analysis and the relationship between critique and disciplinary membership.

REFERENCES

Becker, Gary. 1981. A *Treatise on the Family*. Cambridge, Mass.: Harvard University Press.

Belenky, Mary, et al. 1986. *Women's Ways of Knowing*. New York: Basic Books.

Brown, Lisa Jo. 1989. "Gender and Economic Analysis: A Feminist Perspective." Paper presented at the American Economic Association annual meeting, December.

Cartwright, Nancy. 1983. *How the Laws of Physics Lie*. Oxford: Clarendon Press.

Chodorow, Nancy. 1978. *The Reproduction of Mothering: Psychoanalysis and the Sociology of Gender*. Berkeley: University of California Press.

Cooper, Brian. 1990. "Marital Problems: A Reconsideration of Neoclassical Bargaining Models of Household Decision-Making." Manuscript, Economics Department, Harvard University.

David, Lester, and Irene David. 1987. "How We Can Save Our Babies." *Health* (August), 29–31, 61–66.

England, Paula. 1989. "A Feminist Critique of Rational-Choice Theories: Implications for Sociology." *American Sociologist* 20(1): 14–28.

Folbre, Nancy. 1991. "The Unproductive Housewife: Her Evolution in Nineteenth-Century Economic Thought." *Signs* 16(3): 463–84.

————, and Heidi Hartmann. 1988. "The Rhetoric of Self-Interest: Ideology and Gender in Economic Theory," in *The Consequences of Economic Rhetoric,* ed. Arjo Klamer, Deirdre N. McCloskey and Robert M. Solow, 184–203. New York: Cambridge University Press.

Friedman, Milton. 1953. "The Methodology of Positive Economics," in *Essays in Positive Economics,* 3–43. Chicago: University of Chicago Press.

Gilligan, Carol. 1982. *In a Different Voice: Psychological Theory and Women's Development.* Cambridge, Mass.: Harvard University Press.

Harding, Sandra. 1986. *The Science Question in Feminism.* Ithaca, N.Y.: Cornell University Press.

Hartsock, Nancy. 1983. *Money, Sex, and Power: Toward a Feminist Historical Materialism.* New York: Longman.

Held, Virginia. 1990. "Mothering versus Contract," in *Beyond Self-Interest,* ed. Jane Mansbridge, 287–304. Chicago: University of Chicago Press.

Horton, Susan, and Diane Miller. 1991. "The Effect of Gender of Household Head on Food Expenditure: Evidence from Low Income Households in Jamaica." Manuscript, Economics Department, University of Toronto.

Klamer, Arjo. 1984. *Conversations with Economists.* Totowa, N.J.: Rowman & Allanheld.

————, Deirdre N. McCloskey, and Robert M. Solow, eds. 1988. *The Consequences of Economic Rhetoric.* New York: Cambridge University Press.

Kondo, Dorinne. 1990. *Crafting Selves: Power, Gender, and Discourses of Identity in a Japanese Workplace.* Chicago: University of Chicago Press.

Kumar, S. 1979. *Impact of Subsidized Rice on Food Consumption and Nutrition in Kerala.* Washington, D.C.: International Food Policy Research Institute.

Longino, Helen. 1990. *Science as Social Knowledge.* Princeton, N.J.: Princeton University Press.

————. 1992. "Essential Tensions—Phase Two: Feminist, Philosophical, and Social Studies of Science," in *Social Dimensions of Science,* ed. Ernan McMullin, 198–218. South Bend, Ind.: Notre Dame University Press.

Lundberg, Shelly, and Robert Pollak. 1990. "Gender Roles and Intrafamily Distribution." Manuscript, Economics Department, University of Washington.

Mansbridge, Jane, ed. 1990. *Beyond Self-Interest.* Chicago: University of Chicago Press.

Manser, Marilyn, and Murray Brown. 1980. "Marriage of Household Decisionmaking: A Bargaining Analysis." *International Economic Review* 21: 31–44.

McCloskey, Deirdre. 1985. *The Rhetoric of Economics.* Madison: University of Wisconsin Press.

————. 1988. "The Consequences of Rhetoric," in *The Consequences of Economic Rhetoric,* ed. Arjo Klamer, McCloskey, and Robert M. Solow, 280–93. New York: Cambridge University Press.

————. 1990. *If You're So Smart: The Narrative of Economic Expertise.* Chicago: University of Chicago Press.

McElroy, Marjorie B., and Mary Jean Homey. 1981. "Nash-Bargained Household Decisions: Toward a Generalization of the Theory of Demand." *International Economic Review* 22(2): 333–49.

Nelson, Julie. 1990. "Gender, Metaphor, and the Definition of Economics." Working Paper Series 350, University of California at Davis.

Pateman, Carole. 1988. *The Sexual Contract.* Stanford, Calif.: Stanford University Press.

Polanyi, Livia. 1989. *Telling the American Story: A Structural and Cultural Analysis of Conversational Storytelling.* Cambridge, Mass.: MIT Press.

Pollak, Robert A. 1985. "A Transaction Cost Approach to Families and Households." *Journal of Economic Literature* 23: 581–608.

Samuels, Warren. 1992. "Institutional Economics," in *Economics in Perspective,* ed. David Greenaway, Michael Bleaney, and Ian Stewart. London: Routledge.

Seiz, Janet. 1992. "Gender and Economic Research," in *Post-Popperian Methodology of Economics: Recovering Practice,* ed. Neil de Marchi, 273–319. Boston: Kluwer-Nijhoff.

Sen, Amartya. 1984. *Resources, Values and Development.* Cambridge, Mass.: Harvard University Press.

Shapere, Dudley. 1984. *Reason and the Search for Knowledge.* Dordrecht: D. Reidel.

Smith, Adam. 1937 [1776]. *An Inquiry into the Nature and Causes of the Wealth of Nations.* New York: Random House.

Solow, Robert. 1956. "A Contribution to the Theory of Economic Growth." *Quarterly Journal of Economics* (February): 65–94.

Strassmann, Diana, and Lyvia Polanyi. 1992. "Shifting the Paradigm: Value in Feminist Critiques of Economics." Paper presented at the First Annual Conference of the International Association for Feminist Economics, July 1992, Washington, D.C.

Traweek, Sharon. 1988. *Beamtimes and Lifetimes: The World of High Energy Physics.* Cambridge, Mass.: Harvard University Press.

———. 1992. "Border Crossings: Narrative Strategies in Science Studies among Physicists at Tsukuba Science City, Japan," in *Science as Practice and Culture,* ed. Andrew Pickering. Chicago: University of Chicago Press.

U.S. Department of Commerce. 1990. *Statistical Abstract of the U.S.* 110th ed., 460. Washington, D.C.: U.S. Government Printing *Office.*

Vaughan, Genevieve. 1990. "From Exchange to Gift Economy." Paper presented at the Other Economic Summit, July, Houston.

Waring, Marilyn. 1988. *If Women Counted: A New Feminist Economics.* San Francisco: Harper & Row.

Lourdes Benería
Paid and Unpaid Labor: Meanings and Debates

… This [reading] … is centered around what I have called the "accounting for women's work project." Its central theme is the analysis of how conceptual and theoretical conventions are at the root of statistical biases leading to the underestimation of women's work in labor force and national accounting statistics across countries. Initially viewed as a way of making women's work more visible, the project has gradually evolved to include all unpaid work, mostly performed by women but also by men, although to a smaller extent.…

Others had been concerned about this issue as well. Ester Boserup had pointed out that "the subsistence activities usually omitted in the statistics of production and income are largely women's work" (p. 163). Boserup was a pioneer in emphasizing the time-consuming character of these activities.… Earlier in the United States, Margaret Reid, in her book *Economics of Household Production* (1995), had been concerned about the exclusion of domestic production in national income accounts and had designed a method to estimate the value of housework.

… Many in the [women's] movement saw this issue as symbolic of society's undervaluation of women and of their contribution to social well-being.… Marylin Waring's book *If Women Counted* … [1988] made a significant contribution by making the analysis of this issue and of its implication for action more readily accessible to a larger audience. Finally, during the past two decades, an increasing number of governments and individual researchers and activist groups took up this project and prioritized it in their agendas.

… Its objective was officially sanctioned and summarized in the Platform of Action adopted in 1995 at the Fourth World Conference on Women in Beijing which called for the design and implementation of "suitable statistical means to recognize and make visible the full extent of the work of women and all their contributions to the national economy including their contribution in the unremunerated and domestic sectors, and to examine the relationship of women's unremunerated work to the incidence of vulnerability to poverty" (UN 2001: 93).

In the past and over the years, an important body of literature not necessarily imbued with feminist goals has developed, addressing time allocation data that includes unpaid work.… Since the 1960s, national and comparative studies of time use have been carried out for a variety of purposes, such as the expansion of national accounting statistics and the analysis of household behavior.… However, although useful and often with parallel objectives to those of the "accounting project," these studies do not contain a specific feminist concern regarding their implications for women and for gender equality.…

THE ACCOUNTING PROJECT

The underestimation of unpaid work in national and international statistics is reflected in labor force as well as GNP and national income data. Labor force statistics and national income accounts were designed primarily to gather information about the level of economic activity and changes over time, and to provide a basis for economic policy and planning. Given that, in capitalist economies, the market has been considered the core of economic activity, participation in the labor market was historically defined as engagement in work "for pay or profit" (as defined by the International Conference of Labor Force Statisticians in 1954). Likewise, the inclusion of production in national income accounts was defined by its connection to the market....

Thus, the problem of undercounting springs from the way "work" has been defined, in theory and in conventional statistics, as a paid economic activity linked to the market. Until World War II, statistics on the economically active population were gathered through population censuses, but ... [i]n 1938 the Committee of Statistical Experts of the League of Nations recommended a definition of the concepts "gainfully occupied" and "unemployed," and drew up proposals to standardize census data with the purpose of facilitating international comparisons. As a result, many countries expanded the collection of what, from then on, would be called "the labor force" (League of Nations 1938; ILO 1976). In 1966, the UN Statistical Commission updated the earlier definitions for the purpose of providing not only a measure of the unemployed but of labor availability. The adopted definition of "economically active population" referred to *all persons of either sex who furnish the supply of labor for the production of economic goods and services.* The objective of this definition was to facilitate not only estimates of employment and unemployment but of underemployment as well.[2]

Another aspect of this definition was the link assumed between the labor force and the national product—active labor being defined as that which contributes to the national product plus the unemployed. This definition leads to questionable measurements of work. Family members working part time can be classified as employed or underemployed when working in unremunerated agricultural activities but not when engaged in household production. A large proportion of unpaid work was therefore excluded from national product and income accounting as well as from labor force statistics under this definition. However, the problem of underestimation of unpaid work and the reasons behind it differ for each of the four sectors in which it predominates—namely, subsistence production, the household economy, the informal sector, and volunteer work.

The Subsistence Sector

Despite considerable efforts made since 1938 to improve labor force and national accounting statistics, the basic concepts remained essentially untouched until the past two decades. One important exception was the effort to include estimates of subsistence production in GNP accounts.... Methods to estimate the value of this type of production and the proportion of the population engaged in it were recommended in the UN system of national accounts during the 1950s, particularly for countries in which this sector had a relatively important weight.... By 1960 a working party of African statisticians recommended that estimates of rural household activities, such as the cultivation of backyard vegetables, could and should be added to those of subsistence production in agriculture, forestry, and fishing (Waring 1988). However, the recommendation was not accompanied with an implementation effort.

This process was consolidated with the 1966 definition of labor force recommended by the International Conference of Labor Statisticians, which referred to *all persons of either sex who furnish the supply of economic goods and services* (ILO 1976). Whether this supply was furnished through the market was irrelevant in this case. Thus, although what constituted "economic goods and services" was not clear, the new definition introduced an exception to the market criterion justified by the notion that subsistence production represents "marketable goods."

As a result, it seemed logical to view the labor engaged in the sector as part of the labor force, including "family labor." Thus, despite the practical difficulties in estimating the market value of subsistence production, it became an accepted practice without important theoretical or conceptual objections. The objective was to arrive at more accurate estimates of GNP and of economic growth. To quote Ester Boserup, "[T]he present system of underreporting subsistence activities not only makes the underdeveloped countries seem poorer than they really are in comparison with the more developed countries, but it also makes their rate of economic growth appear in a more favorable light than the facts warrant, since economic development entails a gradual replacement of the omitted subsistence activities by the creation of income in the nonsubsistence sector which is recorded more correctly" (Boserup 1970: 163).

In practice, however, the participation of women in subsistence production was not fully accounted for, given that the boundaries between agricultural and domestic work can be difficult to trace, particularly for women. To the extent that women's unpaid agricultural labor is highly integrated with domestic activities—such as with food cultivation, the fetching of wood, care of animals, and many others—the line between the conventional classifications of family labor (in agriculture) and domestic work becomes thin and difficult to draw unless some clearcut convention is established. The result has been a tendency to underestimate women's work in subsistence production, particularly whenever it is classified as domestic work.

The same problem appeared when censuses classified workers according to their "main occupation." In such cases, the tendency to underreport women family workers in agriculture or any other type of nondomestic production has been prevalent.... [T]here have been efforts to include this category of workers in many countries' labor force statistics. Even so, there are still reasons to believe that underreporting continues to be a problem; they range from the relative irregularity of women's work in agriculture ... to the deeply ingrained view, subject to multiple cultural and historical variations, that women's place is in the household. The result of these problems has been the nonexistence or the unreliability of national statistics regarding women's work and the difficulties in making meaningful comparisons across countries.[3]

The Informal Sector

A different type of problem is represented by the sparse statistical information on the informal sector at least until recently. This sector comprises a wide array of activities ranging from underground production of goods and services, to street vendors, to officially sanctioned microenterprises in all sorts of industries, including construction, garment, toys, and even shoes. In this case, the measurement problem is not one of conceptualization, given that it represents largely paid activities and therefore it falls within conventional definitions of work; the problem has to do with the difficulties of obtaining reliable statistics.

The absence of appropriate and systematic data collection on the informal sector becomes a significant problem given the large (and growing) proportion of its workforce in many countries. For women, the informal sector often provides a primary, even if precarious, source of income. Informal activities range from homework (industrial piecework) to preparing and selling street foods, to self-employment and work in microenterprises.... [R]ather than being gradually replaced by formal sector activities as the earlier literature had expected, ... the size of the informal sector has been growing, and it has absorbed the largest numbers of people who have remained marginal to the "modern economy" or expelled from it when unemployment has increased. To be sure, many case studies and efforts of data collection of informal activities have been undertaken, but the difficulties of gathering systematic, sectoral information are enormous; they derive from the invisible and even underground character of significant parts of this sector—illegal activities or at the borderline of illegality—and from its unstable, precarious, and unregulated nature.

Periodic and systematic country surveys, however, can be elaborated to provide estimates of the sector's weight in the labor force GNP estimates.... In the early 1990s, several branches within the UN prepared conceptual and methodological guidelines for the measurement of women's work in this sector—including industry, trade, and services—and carried out useful pilot studies, such as in Burkina Faso, Congo, the Gambia, and Zambia (UN Statistical Office/ECA/INSTRAW 1991a and 1991b; INSTRAW 1991). In each case, microeconomic survey data—for example for individuals and households—was combined with macroeconomic information, depending on data availability for each country.... This information-gathering effort is key to facilitate policy design and actions to improve the working conditions of those who participate in the sector.

Domestic Work

In the case of domestic production and related activities, the problem is not so much one of underestimation as of total exclusion because it has been conceptualized as falling outside of the conventional definition of work....

As mentioned earlier, with few exceptions such as Margaret Reid's, this exclusion of domestic work from labor force statistics was not much questioned until the late 1970s. Boserup argued strongly for the inclusion in national accounts "of food items obtained by collecting and hunting, of output of home crafts such as clothing, footwear, sleeping and sitting mats, baskets, clay pots, calabashes, fuel collected by women, funeral services, hair cuts, entertainment, and traditional administrative and medical services," together with "pounding, husking and grinding of foodstuffs and the slaughtering of animals" (pp. 162–63). However, she saw these activities as subsistence production—"marketable goods," not as domestic work.... Yet, she did emphasize the need to include production for own consumption, which she pointed out was larger in the economically less-developed and agricultural countries than in the more industrialized ones.

To some degree, a reversal in the historical trend for domestic work to shift from the household to the market as countries develop has been observed. As labor costs have increased in the high-income countries, self-help activities such as home construction, carpentry, and repairs, often performed by men, have also increased significantly. This has been added to the bulk of unpaid work at the household level, a trend reinforced by the decreasing tendency in the hiring of domestic workers as countries develop (Langfeldt 1987; Chadeau 1989; UNDP 1995).[5] In the United States, for example, some authors have estimated that the time allocated to unpaid work by men and women converged between the 1960s and 1980s (Bittman and Pixley 1997).... However, this convergence thesis ignores the extent to which multiple tasks are performed simultaneously. As Floro (1995) has argued, ... as women's participation in market work has increased, work intensification resulting from overlapping activities requires a revision of the convergence thesis.

To sum, production tends to shift out of the household at some stages in the development process while at least part of it might return at later stages, regardless of whether it is performed by women or men. If household production is not accounted for, growth rates are likely to be overestimated when this production shifts to the market; on the contrary, they are likely to be underestimated when paid activities are taken up by (unpaid) household members. Given the predominant division of labor and women's role in the domestic sphere, the exclusion affects mostly—but not exclusively—women's work. This takes into consideration the fact that some tasks are often carried out simultaneously—such as when a housewife is cooking, doing the wash, and caring for the children at the same time.

Volunteer Work

Like in the case of domestic work, the wide range of tasks in the volunteer sector creates both conceptual and methodological problems for measurement because it is not directly linked to the market. Conceptually, volunteer work refers to work whose beneficiaries must not be members of the immediate family. In addition, there cannot be any direct payment—it's unpaid work by definition, and the work must be part of an organized program. That is, volunteer work is clearly different from domestic work even though there are close connections between the two—as when volunteer work takes place in one's neighborhood or community—which can make the boundaries difficult to draw in some cases. In addition while some volunteer tasks can easily be defined as production, such as in the case of job training and home-building organizations, others are more difficult to classify, such as some of the activities associated with charitable or church-related work. Yet even in the later case, some accounting of these tasks seems important if they provide free substitutes for what otherwise would be paid market work....

Many factors influence the extent to which people engage in volunteer work—gender being one of them since gender asymmetries in this type of work are abundant. Thus, in the U.S., women are more likely than men to engage in volunteer activities, particularly women who are married and relatively well-educated with children under eighteen. These gendered disparities have many dimensions. For example, in 1984 New Zealand women mobilized around the notion that, while monetary contributions (often male) to charity are tax-deductible, time contributions (often female) are not. The result of this mobilization was the inclusion of a question about time dedicated to volunteer work in the 1986 Census of Population, a pioneer effort to New Zealand's credit (Waring 1988).

Similarly, volunteer work varies according to social characteristics. In the United States, a survey conducted in 1996 showed that volunteering correlated with income: the highest proportion (62 percent) of volunteering was among people with income above $75,000 and the lowest among those with income below $20,000 (AARP 1997). However, these differences might be misleading since much remains to be done to document volunteer work worldwide. Among the poor, volunteering can represent very significant individual and collective actions in times of crises.... It has been estimated that in Lima, Peru, 40,000 low-income women formally organized a federation of self-managed communal kitchens, located in 2,000 sites in Lima's poor neighborhoods, and pooled their resources to feed about 200,000 people as often as five times a week (Barrig 1996; Lind 1997). Managing such an impressive endeavor requires a wide range of skills, ... some of which were acquired by women as they engaged in survival work for their families and neighbors.

Collective food kitchens, in fact, raise questions about the conventional definition of volunteer work, since the beneficiaries often include both the immediate family *and* the community/neighborhood. Hence, these workers perform both domestic and volunteer work. Food kitchen volunteering also raises questions about the extent to which participation in volunteer work results from choice or lack of it; participation springs from the urgent needs of survival and from the inability of individual households to meet their needs on their own....

To sum, the project of accounting for women's work was twofold from its beginning. First, it required the refinement of categories and improvement of data collection in the areas of paid work that were, in theory at least, included in conventional statistics. Second, it resulted from the need to rethink and redefine the concept of work and to develop ways to measure unpaid activities involving mostly domestic and volunteer work. In what follows, I will concentrate largely on domestic work.

THE CONTRIBUTIONS OF TWO DECADES

Although questions and objections about the extent to which unpaid work should be measured still remain, much progress on the practical issues involved has been made since the 1980s. This progress has proceeded mainly on three fronts: conceptual, theoretical, and methodological. On the *conceptual* front and as a result of the initial Nairobi conference recommendation, the International Research and Training Institute for the Advancement of Women (INSTRAW) and the Statistical Office of the UN Secretariat took the lead to review and promote the revision of national accounts and other statistical information on women's work.... A significant consensus has been built on the need to measure unpaid domestic work on the basis that it makes an important contribution to welfare. Most recommendations have opted for the development of separate or supplementary accounts that would permit the generation of "augmented" estimates of GNP (UN Office of Vienna 1989).

The purpose of such "satellite accounts" is to measure unpaid production of goods and services by households and to provide indicators of their contribution to welfare. This can be done by using time as a form of measurement—as done in time-use surveys—or by imputing a monetary value to time inputs or to the goods and services produced. Given the numerous and varied tasks being performed in the home, the question of which tasks to include or exclude has been an important focus of the discussion. The most accepted operational criterion is still Margaret Reid's *third-person principle,* according to which domestic production should refer to unpaid activities that can also be performed by a third person in a paid form. While tasks such as shopping, cleaning, food preparation, and child care are included under this criterion, watching television and getting dressed are not. This still leaves some ambiguities (the very rich or the ill might have a paid person to help them dress) but as a whole it represents an important step in setting a standard of definition that can allow, for example, comparisons between countries.

The third-party principle has been criticized for assuming the market as the model of economic activity and therefore precluding "the existence of economic activity unique to the household, since anything that does not, or does not yet, have a commodity equivalent cannot be considered economic" (Wood 1997: 50). However, although the principle does assume market production as the point of reference, it does not follow that a domestic activity without a market equivalent cannot be included; it can, as long as a third person can perform it. Wood goes further in criticizing the principle for its exclusion of personal activities such as "emotional care-taking, sex and childbirth from definitions of economic activity" (Wood 1997: 52). This argument, however, takes up the discussion of what should be considered as "work" to a level of ambiguity that makes it difficult to define. In any case, what needs to be emphasized here is that, overall, a significant shift has taken place in the conceptualization of economic activity toward the inclusion of tasks that contribute to social reproduction and the maintenance of the labor force and which are not directly connected with the market.

At the *theoretical* front, significant changes preceded or were parallel to the conceptual and practical work of the last two decades, particularly in terms of a greater understanding of the nature of domestic production. Since the 1950s and even more so since the 1960s, economic analysis focused increasingly on the household—within the framework of different theoretical paradigms and with different objectives.... [T]he neoclassical literature ... analyzed household production as a way to understand the gender division of labor and the participation of men and women in the paid labor force. Feminist versions of this analysis have pointed out some of its shortcomings and have placed greater emphasis on the social construction of gender roles and the extent to which it results in gender discrimination (Blau and Ferber 1986). On the other hand, within the Mandan paradigm, the domestic labor debate of the 1970s emphasized the importance of domestic work for the daily maintenance and reproduction of the labor force. The emphasis was on understanding the nature of domestic work, its links to the market, and the economic and social power relations established between paid and unpaid domestic work and between men and women (Gardiner 1985; Molyneux 1979; Deere 1990)....

From a feminist perspective, neither of these two approaches placed enough attention to gender and power relations within the household. However, they were useful to enhance our understanding of the economic significance of domestic work and the need to develop methods to evaluate its contribution to production and welfare....

A different debate has centered around one of the main obstacles to measuring household production and volunteer work, namely the difficulty of comparing them with market production: can this comparison be made given that they take place under very different conditions and norms of behavior? In particular, domestic work is not subject to the competitive pressures of the market and therefore productivity levels might be very different in the two sectors. Likewise, the quality of outputs can differ substantially, according to whether these are performed at home or in the market.... Similar arguments can be applied to volunteer work. Could we then be comparing apples and oranges? ... [W]e should keep in mind that *there are several purposes to the project of measuring and documenting unpaid work.*

First, an important objective has been to make household work more visible and socially appreciated. Second, it facilitates the establishment of indicators to evaluate its contribution to social well-being and the reproduction of human resources, and it provides the basis for revising GNP and labor force statistics. Third, its measurement is crucial to analyzing the extent to which total work (paid and unpaid) is shared equally at the household and society level. Fourth, both at the micro and macro levels, measurement can provide information on how time is allocated between work (paid/unpaid) and leisure. Fifth, it is a crucial input for the project of "engendering budgets" in order to make explicit that they are not neutral tools of resource allocation (Bakker and Elson 1998). Sixth, measurement of unpaid domestic work has other practical uses such as in litigation and in estimating monetary compensation in divorce cases (Cassels 1993; Collins 1993). Seventh, even if productivity levels are not comparable, time-use indicators can be used to analyze tendencies and trends in the share of paid/unpaid work over time. Finally, this information can help governments and other entities to design policy and action more effectively.

At the *methodological* level, substantial progress has been made on two fronts. One is the revisions of data-gathering methods to capture with greater accuracy the contributions to GNP made by the various types of unpaid work. The other is the progress in dealing with the complex task of designing different methods to measure its value. Here, I will refer mostly to domestic work, differentiating between input- and output-related methods and showing the difficulties and advantages of each.... Two main approaches to measuring the value of domestic work have been introduced: one based on the imputation of value to labor time (i.e., an *input-related method*) and another based on the imputation of market prices to goods and services produced in the domestic sphere (i.e., an *output-related method*).

For each approach, different estimation methods have been used. For the input-related method, a key problem is which value to impute to labor time. Three main methods have been identified:

- The *global substitute* method uses the cost of a hired domestic worker, assumed to be paid to carry out all types of household tasks.
- The *specialized substitute* method uses the average wage of a specialist with skills for each specific household task.
- The *opportunity cost* method is based on the wage that the person performing domestic work could receive in the market.[12]

Each method has some advantages and disadvantages. The global substitute method tends to yield very low estimates given that domestic workers are at the lower end of the wage hierarchy. Also, a domestic worker is not likely to perform all of the work of the household. Therefore, unless the full contribution of all household members is estimated and added up, this approach will further reinforce the tendency toward low estimates. On the contrary, the specialized substitute method tends to generate high estimates, even though it is more indicative of the market value of household production. One practical problem associated with this method is the need to desegregate each task, with the corresponding problems, mentioned earlier, of comparing unpaid and paid work.

The opportunity cost method yields the widest range of estimates, depending on the skills and opportunity wage of the individual involved. This can result in rather absurd estimates since, for example, a meal produced by a doctor will be imputed a higher value than an identical meal prepared by an unskilled worker, even if the latter is a better cook. Another problem in this case has been pointed out repeatedly: the tautology suggested by the fact that, if the cook is a full-time housewife, her opportunity costs (i.e., the income she would get in the paid labor force) are, in turn, correlated to her condition as a full-time housewife. To quote Ferber and Birbaum (1980), "a person who has been out of the labor market, especially when it has been a long time, will not have reliable information about how much s/he could earn" (p. 389).

As for output-related estimates, they require methods of imputing value to domestic production and deducting the cost of inputs from it. The problem again is to determine which market goods and services are equivalent to those produced at home, and what price to impute to inputs such as labor and raw materials not purchased in the market (for example, wood gathered by family members or homemade utensils). A different problem, again, is the disparities in the quality of goods and services produced, which in the case of nonmarket work cannot be captured by an imputed price. At the empirical level, it is a tedious method requiring time-budgets data, hourly wages, and a relatively high number of input and output prices. While a proportion of such data can be obtained from existing censuses, most have to be generated through surveys. This is precisely the type of information that satellite accounts could provide periodically....

Input vs. output methods raise other issues with respect to their usefulness. For example, if the time needed to fetch water increases, input-related accounting will show an increase in time input while there is no increase in output. This suggests that, in terms of welfare, an output-related method is superior since it shows more accurately changes in welfare. Yet, from the perspective of documenting the time needed for domestic work, the input-related method is more explicit. In addition, the institutional and social dimensions of time complicate this issue. As Floro (1997) has argued, the notion of time and its uses is different across countries and cultures....

Although real, these difficulties are not insurmountable. The practical progress made so far and the guidelines provided by international organizations have laid a foundation from which to proceed. At the prate level, the efforts to measure unpaid work have been on the increase. [See table 3.1]....

At the international level, special mention should be made of the pioneer effort that UNDP undertook in preparing its annual *Human Development Report* in view of the 1995 UN Conference in Beijing. The report included estimates of the share of paid and unpaid work across a variety of countries. Based on time-use data for different years, it showed that, for both developing and industrial countries, on average women work more hours than men—their work representing 53 percent of total time in developing countries and 51 percent in industrial countries. In both groups of countries, only 34 percent of women's work was included in national income accounts; the corresponding figure for men was 76 percent for developing countries and 66 percent for industrial countries.

However, as tables 3.2 and 3.3 illustrate, country data vary widely and the rural-urban differences within countries are significant. Among selected developing countries, the urban difference between women's work burden and that of men's (table 3.2) ranges from 3 percent (Kenya) to 12 percent (Colombia); in the rural context, the range is between 10 percent (Bangladesh) and 35 percent (Kenya). Among selected industrial countries, table 3.3 shows that the corresponding figures for the country as a whole range between −2.0 percent (Denmark) and 21.1 percent (Italy). Although a good proportion of the data used for the report relied on the "third-person criterion" for its estimates, these figures were based on studies that varied in data collection methods—raising methodological questions about comparability.[13] Recognizing this problem, the report points out that, in the absence of better data, these estimates provide "a valuable glimpse of the general pattern of time use by women and men" across countries. Indeed, although these are rough estimates, they provide an indication upon which it is possible to construct more accurate measures.

Overall, these figures illustrate several basic facts. First, unpaid domestic work is important in relation to total work time. Second, women bear a larger burden of total work time. Third, a disproportionate amount of women's work is not included in national income accounts.

Table 3.1 Measuring Unpaid Work

Country	Scope of Measurement (and Agency Responsible)	Years Survey Undertaken	Measurement Methods Used	Some Highlights and Percentage of Child Care Time Provided by Women[a]
Australia	National (every 5 years) (Australian Bureau of Statistics)	1987 (pilot), 1992, 1997	time-use	78%
Austria	National (Vienna, Austrian Central Statistical Office)	1981, 1992	time-use	76%
Bangladesh	National	1989, 1992	time-use	Average hours per week of housework: Women = 31, Men = 5[a]
Bulgaria	Multinational Comparative (Bulgarian Academy of Science—1965) National (Sofia, Central Statistical Office—1988)	1965, 1988	time-use	81%
Canada	National (Ottawa, Statistics Canada)	1961, 1971, 1981, 1986, 1992	-time-use -input/output also for 1981, 1986[c]	71%
Denmark	National (Copenhagen, Danish National Institute of Social Research)	1987	time-use	64%
European Union	EUROSTAT (European Union, Statistical Office)	1996 (pilot), 1997	time-use	A harmonized time-use survey for countries in the EU is proposed for 1997 with the pilot in 1996[b]
Finland	National (Helsinki, Central Statistical Office of Finland)	1979, 1987, 1990	-time-use -input/output also for 1990[c]	75%
Former USSR	Multinational Comparative (1965—Academy of Sciences of the USSR) Join US-USSR Project (1986—Russian Academy of Sciences)	1965, 1986	time-use	75%
Germany, Federal Republic	National (Germany, Staticher Bundesamt)	1965, 1991, 1992	time-use	71%
Hungary	National Way of Life Survey (Budapest, Central Statistics Office)	1976, 1986	time-use	64%

Country	Source/Organization	Years	Method	Findings
India	National	1989, 1992	time-use	Average hours per week of housework: Women=34, Men=10[a] 75%
Israel	National Time-Budget Survey (Israel, Central Bureau of Statistics)	1991, 1992	time-use	
Italy	National (Rome, National Statistical Institute of Italy)	1988, 1989	time-use	
Japan	National (5 yearly) (Tokyo, Bureau of Statistics)	1976, 1981, 1986, 1991	time-use	-88% -Women work 9 times the amount of unpaid times as men do[a]
Korea, Republic of	National (Seoul, Korean Broadcasting System)	1987, 1990	time-use	80%
Latvia	National (Riga, Institute of Economics)	1972, 1987	time-use	69%
Lithuania	National (Helsinki, Central Statistical Office of Finland)	1974, 1988	time-use	75%
Nepal	National	1989, 1992	time-use	Average hours per week of housework: Women=42, Men=15[a] 71%
Norway	National (Oslo, Norwegian Central Bureau of Statistics)	1980, 1981, 1990	time-use	
Poland	Time Budget Survey of Working People (Warsaw, Cent. Stat. Office)	1984	time-use	69%
Spain	-National (Madrid, Instituto de Economia y Geografia) -Catalonia, Institute Catalá de la Dona	1991 2001	time-use time-use	86% % increase in GNP contributed by domestic production 66%[d]
Sweden	National (Stockholm, Statistics Sweden)	1990, 1991	time-use	72%
United Kingdom	Daily Life Survey	1984	time-use	76%
United States	National (Univ. of Michigan—1996) (Univ. of Maryland—1986)	1965, 1986	time-use	72%

Sources: [a]United Nations: The World's Women 1995: Trends and Statistics; [b]Luisella Goldschmidt-Clermont and Elisabetta Pagnossin-Aligisakis (1995), "Measures of Unrecorded Economic Activities in Fourteen Countries," Human Development Report Occasional Papers; [c]Duncan Ironmonger, "Counting outputs, capital inputs and caring labor: estimating gross household product"; [d]Comajuncosa et al. (2001).

Table 3.2   Burden of Work by Gender, Selected Developing Countries

Country	Year	Work Time (Minutes a Day) Average	Women	Men	Women's Work Burden Compared with Men's (% Difference)
Urban					
Colombia	1983	378	399	356	12
Indonesia	1992	382	398	366	9
Kenya	1986	581	590	572	3
Nepal	1978	567	579	554	5
Venezuela	1983	428	440	416	6
Average		471	481	453	6
Percentage share			51	49	
Rural					
Bangladesh	1990	521	545	496	10
Guatemala	1977	629	678	579	17
Kenya	1988	588	676	500	35
Nepal:	1978	594	651	547	17
–Highlands	1978	639	692	586	18
–Mountains	1978	592	649	534	12
–Rural hills	1978	552	583	520	12
Philippines	1975–77	499	546	452	21
Average		566	617	515	20
Percentage share			55	45	
National					
Korea, Republic of	1990	479	488	480	2
Average for sample countries		514	544	483	13
Percentage share			53	47	

Source: UNDP, Human Development Report, 1995, Table 4.1.

Table 3.3   Burden of Work by Gender, Selected Industrial Countries

Country	Year	Work Time (Minutes a Day) Average	Women	Men	Women's Work Burden Compared with Men's (% Difference)
Australia	1992	443	443	443	0
Austria	1992	416	438	393	11.5
Canada	1992	430	429	430	−0.2
Denmark	1987	454	449	458	−2
Finland	1987/88	420	430	410	4.9
France	1985/86	409	429	388	10.6
Germany	1991/92	441	440	441	−0.2
Israel	1991/92	376	375	377	−0.5
Italy	1988/89	419	470	367	28.1
Netherlands	1987	361	377	345	9.3
Norway	1990/91	429	445	412	8
United Kingdom	1985	412	413	411	0.5
USA	1985	441	453	428	5.8
Average for sample countries		419	430	408	5.8
Percentage share			51	49	

Source: UNDP, Human Development Report, 1995, Table 4.3.

There is much, however, that these figures cannot capture, given that they are based on averages. For example, working time for men and women var[ies] across social class. Likewise, there are areas of activity, such as shopping and driving the children to school—consumption and reproduction tasks—that could be considered "work" but conventionally are not. We will return to these issues below.

THE EMERGENCE OF NEW ISSUES

The accounting project continues to be important as current labor market trends have raised new questions about the links between paid and unpaid work and about their distribution and boundaries. We are witnessing a significant transition in the ways this distribution is affecting individuals, households, and communities across countries. Several developments are contributing to these trends.

First, the increasing participation of women in the paid labor force has reinforced the importance of how paid and unpaid work are shared among family members. Together with changing constructions of gender roles and of women's positioning in society, it is likely to decrease women's tolerance for gender inequality in the distribution of working time and to increase their autonomy and bargaining power.... Estimates of the extent and requirements of unpaid work will be necessary whether the solution to the crisis of care is worked through the market, the provision of public services, or equal sharing of those activities between men and women.

Second, in high-income countries those who are unemployed and marginalized from mainstream economic life have to negotiate survival strategies involving a shifting reliance on unpaid work, including forms of labor exchange that are not captured in conventional statistics.[14] The same can be said for developing countries undergoing structural adjustment or the consequences of financial policies leading to the intensification of unpaid work in the household and in communities; ... they tend to increase the number of activities that are not included in conventional statistics.

Third, high incidence of underemployment and of part-time work results in cyclical or fluid combinations of paid and unpaid activities related to changes in the economy and affecting women and men in different ways.... [M]easuring the extent of these changes is important in assessing variations in living standards and contributions to social well-being. Similarly, discussions about the thirty-five-hour week that have taken place, particularly in Western Europe, have many gender implications regarding the distribution of paid/unpaid work. These discussions are carried out under the assumption that a reduction in working time will be helpful in dealing with unemployment. But as Figart and Mutari (1998) have argued, the underlying assumption is that "full time, year-round employment is a social norm constructed around gendered assumptions," such as that "a full-time worker, presumably male, faces limited demands from unpaid work and family life" (p. 2). A different assumption, they argue, is that the concentration of women in part-time work will continue, regardless of their choice. This suggests that statistics documenting who performs unpaid work can be useful to understanding the distribution of working time. In the same way, households with multiple earners need to address this question if they are concerned about gender equality and about the fair distribution of caring work among household members.

Finally, given that unpaid work represents roughly 25 percent to 50 percent of economic activity, depending on the country and methods of estimation, its exclusion from national accounts is difficult to justify....

All of these factors explain why there has been an increasing awareness of the extent to which paid and unpaid work are unequally distributed among men and women.... [T]he 1996 report of the Independent Commission on Population and the Duality of Life, *Caring for the Future*, includes a call for the redefinition of work and for equality in the distribution of its output: "The Commission proposes ... to redefine work in a broad sense that encompasses both employment and unpaid activities benefitting society as a whole, families as well as individuals, and ensuring an equitable distribution of the wealth generated" (p. 147). To sum, the project of redefining and measuring unpaid work has gained much support in recent decades. However, and as expected given that we are dealing with a complex issue, there is also opposition to it. The following section discusses the various arguments casting doubts on the project.

THE CONTINUING DEBATE

At least three types of objections to the accounting for unpaid work project have emerged. Two of them actually derive from feminist circles, while the third springs out from the core of orthodox economics.

Useless Effort

We may call this objection "the waste-of-time argument." It results from the fear that the effort and use of resources necessary to generate statistics on unpaid work will not make any difference to those engaged in it, particularly women. To what extent, for example, can the information be used to decrease the burden of poor women who toil many hours a day or to empower the urban housewife with no income of her own? Could it be used to increase their bargaining power at some level? Can it really make a difference to those individuals engaged in unpaid activities? On the contrary, this argument goes, greater social recognition of the importance of domestic work might, in fact, reinforce a division of labor that relegates women to activities providing no financial autonomy and little control over the resources they need. This would therefore not contribute to gender equality; it would instead perpetuate women's dependence on men.

I call this type of argument "the post-Nairobi blues," reflecting the doubts some of us felt after the 1985 UN Conference on Women, which took place in Nairobi, Kenya. For the first time, the official report of the conference, *Forward-Looking Strategies for the Advancement of Women*, strongly recommended appropriate efforts to measure the contribution of women's paid and unpaid work "to all aspects and sectors of development." The report significantly moved the action forward and, in doing so, it also raised questions and doubts about whether setting this agenda would make any difference to women.

A similar version of this argument has been offered by Barbara Bergmann, who, although not objecting to the effort itself, thinks too much energy is spent on it. Feminists, she argues, should emphasize the need for women to engage in paid work in order to reduce their dependency on men and increase their bargaining power in and outside of the home. Thus, she believes that feminists should first place their efforts on the design and implementation of policies that facilitate the incorporation of women into the paid labor force, such as child care provision and maternity leave. Likewise, they should work on policy and action leading to the enforcement of gender equality in the labor market such as pay equity, affirmative action, and comparable worth. Bergmann is skeptical about the possibility that better information on unpaid work "can help a single woman," in the same way that "the inclusion in the GNP of food produced in the subsistence sector does not make any difference to farmers."[15] She also fears that statistics on housework are likely to be used by those who want "to glorify the housewife," as in the case of some right-wing groups in the United States, which "can argue that housework is irreplaceable because it performs crucial services to society." Hence, she concludes that "there is an anti-feminist implication in valorizing housework."

This type of objection ignores the fact that action, policy design, and implementation of projects affecting those engaged in unpaid work require as much systematic information as possible in order to make optimal estimates. We should remember the problems created by lack of information. In the words of Indian feminist Devaki Jain, "One of the greatest difficulties in assisting women has been the absence of any reliable data regarding their numbers, problems, and achievements" (Jain 1975). This applies not only to obvious problems requiring urgent solutions such as violence against women or wage discrimination; the weight and distribution of unpaid work can be important in many ways....

[I]t is important to know the extent to which an economic slowdown that increases unemployment and reduces household income results in unpaid labor picking up the slack, for example through the intensification of domestic work or subsistence production. We do know that the financial crises and adjustment policies of the past two decades led to coping strategies that required the intensification of unpaid work, with a disproportionate burden for women. In such cases, a decrease in real income may or may not result in a corresponding decline in family welfare—depending on the extent to which unpaid work makes up for the reduced income.... As Floro (1996) has argued, more precise information on people's daily activities helps us to assess the quality of their lives more accurately and develop indicators of work intensity, performance of multiple tasks, stress, individual health, and even of child neglect. This is because varied dimensions of work—such as work intensity and the length of the working day—have been shown to be related to stress and health of workers and their families (Floro 1996).

Thus, the accounting project must be viewed, on the one hand, not as an end in itself but as a means to understand who contributes to human welfare and human development—and to what extent.... On the other hand, these estimates can provide information for the design of policies to distribute the pains and pleasures of *work* in a more egalitarian fashion....

The Importance of "Difference"

A second objection, concerning mostly domestic and unpaid caring work, is perhaps more difficult to deal with since it springs from the notion that this type of activity includes personal and relational aspects that make it qualitatively very different from market work. Sue Himmelweit (1995) has argued that, although recognizing unpaid labor as "work" is an important way to make it visible and to validate women's contributions in the home, something is lost in the process. She questions "whether the best way for women's contribution to be appreciated [is] to force it into a preexisting category of 'work,' borrowed from an economics which inherently failed to value most of what made women's domestic contribution distinctive" (p. 2).

As an example, Himmelweit argues that "caring" is an ambiguous notion that can stretch from physical to emotional care; while the first "might to some extent be independent of the relation between the carer and the person cared for," the second requires that "the person doing the caring is inseparable from the care given" (p. 8). She points out a second characteristic of caring work—namely, its self-fulfilling quality. Hence, Himmelweit is reluctant to view as conventional "work" the time spent on activities that provide emotional care and support, which, in addition, are also very difficult to quantify.

Himmelweit concludes [that] ... "[b]y insisting that domestic activities gain recognition by conforming to an unchallenged category of work, the significance of caring and self-fulfilling activities remains unrecognized" (p. 14).

This argument, although interesting, seems problematic for different reasons. First, greater visibility and documentation of these unpaid activities is likely to increase the recognition of their significance for human welfare, particularly if their nature is well understood and emphasized. As we have seen, recent history demonstrates that this is exactly what the theoretical, methodological, and practical efforts of the last three decades have accomplished. The shift of a significant proportion of caring work from the unpaid reproductive sphere to the market has not always taken away some of its basic characteristics. For example, work motives associated with solidarity, altruism, and caring can be found in the market as well as in unpaid work. Second, many unpaid activities are not caring and self-fulfilling while some paid activities are. Hence, it is difficult to argue that there [are] no personal and relational aspects in some of the paid services offered through the market, even though the service is offered in exchange for a monetary reward.

To be sure, some market-oriented caring services are not likely to provide the same quality of care and emotional support that a loving family member can offer—whether or not the caring work might be based on motives such as love and affection, a sense of responsibility, respect, intrinsic enjoyment, altruism, or informal quid pro quo expectations. However, it is not difficult to find exceptions to these cases. To illustrate, there can be market-based care providing selfless emotional support beyond the exchange contract. On the other hand, there can be family care based on selfish expectations (an inheritance) or on some form of coercion.... As for Himmelweit's argument that something is lost in the process of evaluating unpaid caring work, it needs to be contrasted with the fact that something is also won.

Third, there is a dialectical relationship between market and nonmarket work, in such a way that, to some extent, the skills used in one sphere can be used in the other and vice versa.[16] Thus, a paid nanny or nurse might provide a high quality of personal care with skills learned at home; and managerial skills learned in the labor market might be used as a way to reduce unpaid working time in the household. This means that it is difficult to draw a clearly defined dividing line between the two.

Fourth, in addition to caring labor, unpaid work includes other types of activities that are only indirectly related to caring, such as gathering wood, taking care of domestic animals, cleaning the house, and participating in community activities. These tasks vary by country, cultural factors, and social background of participants. In this sense, Himmelweit's argument has a built-in bias—reflecting the activities of an urban nuclear family rather than those typical of rural settings.

Overall, this is not to dismiss Himmelweit's important arguments. They raise the question of the extent to which the selfless, caring work that is conventionally attributed to domestic labor can be projected onto other activities outside of the household, including market activity, a subject further discussed below.

Theoretically Misguided

The third type of objection to the project of measuring unpaid work is related to theoretical and methodological questions that spring from more conventional value theory in economics.... The discussion that follows is based on a paper by economist Sujai Shivakumar (1996), which represents a pioneering effort and in many ways captures many of the unwritten criticisms....

One of Shivakumar's objectives is to show that the *monetary imputation* of unpaid work "is not consistent with present conceptions of the theory of value in economics" and that this imputation is merely a "rhetorical effort" ... (p. 374).... First, he claims that the accounting project is a socialist-feminist effort in terms of its rhetoric, forms of analysis, and policy prescriptions—using gender as the central "tool of analysis," presenting alternative visions of economic processes, and centering economics around the notion of "provisioning of human life." Second, he argues that the project is based on Ricardian-Marxian notions of value based on the labor theory of value instead of the "modern" orthodox value theory based on subjective preferences and expressed through market prices; as such, he views the project as theoretically unacceptable.... In this sense, Shivakumar states that the money value estimates, such as those included in UNDP's 1995 *Human Development Report*, are meaningless because they are based on time-use data.

Third, Shivakumar criticizes the methods used to estimate the value of unpaid work. In doing so, he repeats many of the methodological objections that have previously been recognized and addressed by different authors.... However, rather than pointing out the ways in which methodologies might be improved, he does not see much redeeming value in the attempt to do so. Thus, comparing the accounting effort with that of the environmentalists who want to take environmental costs into consideration in national accounting statistics, he writes: "With no theoretical guideline on how to choose among alternative ways of conducting the valuation, the selection among alternative ways of imputation in environmental accounting then comes to reflect on the relative strengths of competing political interests" (p. 405). Hence, Shivakumar views the value estimates such as those of the 1995 *Human Development Report* as "meaning-less." Although the estimates present problems, as mentioned earlier, due to poor or insufficient data, a more constructive approach is to see them as a pioneering but nevertheless important effort in need of improvement....

Shivakumar's critique is more fundamentalist in his insistence on the issue that any monetary evaluation "displays an ignorance of the concept of value as *something realized through the exchange process*" (p. 27, emphasis added). That is, he views the exchange process as the only source of value, despite the fact that the value of nonmarket goods in subsistence production has been estimated for many years, and that many economists make use of "shadow prices" in their work. As argued above, this practice has been supported by the notion that subsistence production represents "marketable goods." Yet, a good proportion of domestic work is marketable and, with economic growth, increasing portions of it are taken up by paid work, including food production, cleaning services, and child care.

... Within neoclassical economics, the imputing of market prices to household production is a standard practice. Shivakumar does not make any reference to the fact that, in many ways, the New Household Economics pioneered the application of "modern" human capital theory to household production and decisionmaking and that other economists have also taken seriously the task of analyzing household production (Fraumeni 1998)....

In associating the effort to measure unpaid work to Ricardo and Marx, Shivakumar ignores the fact that orthodox Marxist theory would agree with his insistence on seeing value as originated only through the exchange process. In addition, it is far from clear that Marxian value theory is based on labor inputs without regard to the weight of demand to determine market value (Itoh and Yokokawa 1979; Elson 1979). Although he is right in affirming that gender as an analytical category and "the provisioning of human life" are central to feminist economics, this is not specific to any branch of feminism.... He also ignores that the actual work toward measuring unpaid labor includes a large number of feminists and professional men and women with diverse theoretical approaches and practical politics.

... What one reads in Shivakumar's paper is a strong irritation about the spoiling of a neatly defined, presumably "objective" economic paradigm by what he sees as the "normative" prescriptions of feminism....

CONCLUDING COMMENTS

... Ultimately, we are left with the basic question of how to measure and evaluate human wellbeing and how to recognize those who contribute to it. The point repeatedly being made is that current GNP statistics include what is bad for our health—such as the production of food with carcinogenic chemicals—or for the environment—such as the output of polluting factories. Yet, there has been resistance to the measuring of work and production of goods and services that sustain and enhance life. In Nancy Folbre's terms, societies and individuals need to know, among other things, "who pays for the kids?" This requires an effort to evaluate time spent and costs involved.

We also want to know, for example, who contributes to the survival strategies of the poor so that we can design gender-aware and social class–aware policies to overcome poverty. Unpaid work is not unevenly distributed across class and social groups.... There is a significant difference in the total number of hours that women from different income levels and social backgrounds dedicate to domestic work....

There is more to the challenge of measuring unpaid work since it calls for, in Elizabeth Minnich's terms, "transforming knowledge" or moving beyond the boundaries of conventional paradigms. This includes the rethinking of "mystified concepts," or "ideas, notions, categories, and the like that are so deeply familiar they are rarely questioned" and which result in "partial knowledge" (Minnich 1990).... Further, it leads us to question the assumptions behind received knowledge—in this case, those that conceptually link "work" to paid labor time and the market.

Finally, we have seen that the discussion about the difference between paid and unpaid work leads to questions about the extent to which economic rationality assumed to inform market-related behavior is the norm and to what extent human behavior is based on other motives and norms most commonly linked to unpaid work, such as love, compassion, altruism, empathy, individual and collective responsibility, and solidarity....

NOTES

. . .

2. UN Statistical Commission 1983. For a more detailed account, see Benería 1982.

3. For further detail, see Benería 1982.

. . .

5. There are, of course, exceptions to this trend, such as the phenomenon referred to as the "nanny bubble" since the late 1990s in the United States, representing an increase in employment of immigrant domestic workers among the very rich. If anything, this trend has accelerated in high-income countries ... particularly as the result of the crisis of care work.

. . .

12. A variation of the opportunity cost method is the *lifetime income approach* (Fraumeni 1998).

13. The sample of countries used was selected "on the basis of availability and reliability of time-use data" but with variations in the methods of data collection.

14. These strategies may consist of types of paid work outside of the mainstream monetary system, as with some cases in which the creation of a local currency facilitates exchanges. One such case has been developed in Ithaca, New York, where "Ithaca money" is issued locally and used to exchange labor services as well as to purchase from the local stores that accept it. Even though these cases have little weight for the economy as a whole, they can be important at the local level and they provide interesting examples of work not recorded in conventional statistics.

15. Based on my conversation with Barbara Bergmann on this topic, March 14, 1998.

16. I wish to thank a participant in a seminar I gave at Radcliffe's Public Policy Institute on this topic for this point. She mentioned her own experience in using managerial skills learned at home for her market work, and vice versa, to argue that it is often difficult to neatly differentiate between paid and unpaid work in terms of Himmelweit's analysis.

. . .

REFERENCES

AARP (American Association of Retired Persons). 1997. *The AARP Survey of Civic Involvement.* Washington, D.C.

Bittman, Michael, and Jocelyn Pixley. 1997. *The Double Life of the Family: Myth, Hope and Experience.* Sidney: Allen and Unwin.

Boserup, Ester. 1970. *The Conditions of Agricultural Growth: The Economics of Agrarian Change under Population Pressure.* Chicago: Aldine de Gruyter.

Cassels, Jamie. 1993. "User requirements and data needs." In *Summary of Proceedings,* International Conference on the Valuation and Measurement of Unpaid Work, sponsored by Statistics Canada and Status of Women Canada. Ottawa, Canada, April 18–30.

Chadeau, Ann. 1989. *Measuring Household Production: Conceptual Issues and Results for France.* Paper presented at the Second ECE/INSTRAW Joint Meeting on Statistics on Women. Geneva, November 13–16.

Collins, Mary. 1993. "Opening Remarks." *Summary of Proceedings,* International Conference on the Valuation and Measurement of Unpaid Work, sponsored by Statistics Canada and Status of Women Canada. Ottawa, Canada, April 18–30.

Ferber, Marianne, and Bonnie Birnbaum. 1980. "Housework: priceless or valueless?" *Review of Income and Wealth* 26(4), December: 387–400.

Figart, Deborah, and Ellen Mutari. 1998. "Degendering worktime in comparative perspective: alternative policy frameworks." Paper prepared for the Symposium on Work Time. *Review of Social Economy,* Winter: 460–80.

Floro, Maria Sagrario. 1994. "Work intensity and women's time use." In G. Young and B. Dickerson, eds. *Color, Class and Country: Experiences of Gender.* London: Zed Press, 162–81.

Gardiner, Jean. 1975. "Women's domestic labor." *New Left Review* 89, January/February: 47–58.

Himmelweit, Susan. 1995. "The discovery of unpaid work: the social consequences of the expansion of work." *Feminist Economics* 1(2) Summer: 1–19.

INSTRAW (United Nations International Research and Training Institute for the Advancement of Women). 1991. *Methods of Collecting and Analysing Statistics on Women in the Informal Sector and Their Contributions to National Product: Results of Regional Workshops.* INSTRAW/BT/CRP.1. Santo Domingo: United Nations.

International Labour Organization (ILO). 1976. *International Recommendations on Labour Statistics.* Geneva: ILO.

Itoh, Makoto, and Nobuharu Yokokawa. 1979. "Marx's theory of market-value?" In D. Elson, ed. *Value: The Representation of Labour in Capitalism.* London: CSE/Humanities Press, 102–14.

Langfeldt, Enno. 1987. "Trabajo no remunerado en el contexto familiar," in *Revista de Estudios Economicos* 1: 131–46.

League of Nations. 1938. *Statistics of the Gainfully Occupied Population: Definitions and Classifications Recommended by the Committees of Statistical Experts.* Studies and Reports on Statistical Methods, No. 1, Geneva.

Lind, Amy. 1997. "Gender, development, and urban social change: women's community action in global cities." *World Development* 25(8): 1205–23.

Minnich, Elizabeth Kamarck. 1990. *Transforming Knowledge.* Philadelphia: Temple University Press.

Molyneux, Maxine. 1979. "Beyond the domestic labour debate." *New Left Review* 115, July/August: 3–28.

Reid, Margaret. 1995 [1934]. *Economics of Household Production.* New York: John Wiley.

UNDP (United Nations Development Programme). *Human Development Report.* Various years. New York: Oxford University Press.

United Nations. 2001. *Engendering Development.* Washington, D.C.: The World Bank and Oxford University Press.

Waring, Marilyn. 1988. *If Women Counted: A New Feminist Economics.* New York: Harper and Row.

MARILYN WARING

Counting for Something! Recognizing Women's Contribution to the Global Economy through Alternative Accounting Systems

… Since the Second United Nations Women's Conference in Copenhagen in 1980,[2] feminists have strategized to force global and national accounting bodies to make women's economic contribution visible in their data. A main focus for attention has been the United Nations System of National Accounts (UNSNA). UNSNA was instigated in 1953, with the aim of enabling comparisons to be made between national economies, and serving as a guide to countries developing their own accounting systems. In the UNSNA, national economies are defined in terms of market transactions; consumption, investment, and saving measures are given in addition to income and production totals. A vast amount of work performed by women is for household consumption or unpaid work in the informal economy. This work is not counted in UNSNA. The lack of visibility of women's contribution to the economy results in policies which perpetuate economic, social and political inequality between women and men. There is a very simple equation operating here: if you are invisible as a producer in a nation's economy, you are invisible in the distribution of benefits (unless they label you a welfare "problem" or "burden").

In 1993, the rules of the UNSNA (United Nations 1993) were changed.... Paragraph 1.25 of the 1993 UNSNA establishes the "consumption boundary," enumerating the many domestic and personal services which do not "count" when they are produced and consumed within the same household. Women all over the planet perform the bulk of these tasks. They are the cleaning, decoration and maintenance of the dwelling occupied by the household; cleaning, servicing and repair of household goods; the preparation and serving of meals; the care, training and instruction of children; the care of the sick, infirm or old people; and the transportation members of the household or their goods. These services do count in the UNSNA when they are supplied by government or voluntary agencies, and when they are paid for. The "uncounted" tasks are termed "indicators of welfare."

Out of a breathtaking conceptual ignorance, and undoubted Western bias, the UNSNA fails to grasp there is no demarcation for women in the subsistence household between production inside and outside the consumption boundaries. Just picture the following. A woman wakes; she breastfeeds her four-month-old child (unproductive inactive primary production, consumed by a member of the household). There is no accurate way of ascribing value to this activity, even in the proposed "satellite accounts." (The satellite accounts are the "add-on" compromise that will include unpaid work. They have to be separate so as not to disturb what the experts call the "internal integrity and international comparability of the current accounting framework.") There is no market price for breast milk, so the satellite accounts will price that food at its nearest replacement equivalent. But infant formula, whatever cost is ascribed to it, cannot compete with the quality of breast milk, which means that its use will have a cost impact on the future health and education of the child.

Let's continue with the picture. The woman goes to collect water. She uses some to wash dishes from the family evening meal (unproductive work) and the pots in which she previously cooked a little food for sale (informal work). Next, she goes to the nearby grove to collect bark for dye for materials to be woven for sale (informal work), which she mixes with half a bucket of water (informal work). She also collects some roots and leaves to make a herbal medicine for her child (inactivity). She uses the other half of the bucket of water to make this concoction (inactivity). She will also collect some dry wood to build the fire to boil the water to make both the medicine and the dye (active and inactive labor). All this time she will carry the baby on her back (inactive work).

Of particular importance to feminists is paragraph 1.22 of the 1993 UNSNA, which describes the UNSNA as a "multipurpose system ... designed to meet a wide range of analytical and policy needs." It states that "a balance has to be struck between the desire for the accounts to be as comprehensive as possible," and their being swamped with nonmonetary values. The revised system excludes all "production of services for own final consumption within households.... The location of the production boundary ... *is a compromise, but a deliberate one that takes account of most users* [my emphasis—it is difficult to make extensive use of statistics in which you are invisible].... If the production boundary were extended to include production of personal and domestic services by members of households for their own final consumption, all persons engaged in such activities would become self-employed, making unemployment virtually impossible by definition." Rather than justifying leaving most of the work done by most women out of the equation, this statement surely demonstrates that the current definition of unemployment is inappropriate.

The International Labor Organization (ILO) specifies that the production of economic goods and services includes all production and processing of primary products, including that for home consumption, with the proviso that such production must be "an important contribution" to the total consumption of the household (ILO 1982). In a 1993 resolution concerning the international classification of status in employment, the International Conference of Labor

Statisticians defined subsistence workers as those "who hold a self-employment" job and in this capacity "produce goods and services which are predominantly consumed by their own household and constitute an important basis for its livelihood" (ILO 1993). Compare the concepts of "an important basis for livelihood," and "an important contribution" to the total consumption of the household, with the specific exclusions from production in the 1993 UNSNA.

    ... As the example above shows, women's lives are not so meaninglessly divided. All tasks of survival in such circumstances are related. The Statistical Commission reported: "As far as household production is concerned, the central framework includes for the first time all production of goods in households, whether sold or not, and services *if they are supplied to units other than their producers*" (my emphasis) (UN Statistical Commission, www.un.org/Depts/unsd/sna/sna2-en.html). As concerned as they have been with conceptual and measurement difficulties, and boundaries of consumption or production, the designers of the new UNSNA just miss the point, and in so doing fail to reflect the reality of the majority of women on the planet.

    The problem is systemic, and encompasses issues other than gender inequality. There are other significant measurement problems in the current UNSNA framework. Among the research topics of the Inter-Secretarial Working Group on national accounts, coordinated by the UN Statistical Commission, have been the indirect measurement of financial intermediation services; services in the informal sector; the classification of the purposes of nonprofit institutions serving households; a workshop on intangible assets; the issue of measuring e-commerce; and more on counting the hidden economy. All of these pose significant technical, measurement and valuation problems. Wild, speculative abstractions regarding these concerns have resulted in the figures produced being absolutely meaningless for the purposes of public policy, yet the framework of the UNSNA remains intact. However far removed from reality the UNSNA becomes, governments, business and multilaterals are committed to it, in the misguided conception that it accurately measures the thing which matters most: economic "growth."

    ...

INFORMATION ON REAL LIFE: ALTERNATIVE MODELS

In the past 12 years, some very fine work has resulted from the consideration of such issues. The figures feminists needed, to ensure that the realities of women's and children's lives are made visible to economists and politicians, are finally starting to be produced. Data on the ways in which we survive in a context of resource exploitation and environmental degradation are emerging. What alternative models have been developed which yield such material, and render it useful for public policy purposes? The new feminist challenge is to identify and use these models.

The Index of Sustainable [Economic] Welfare (ISEW)

The authors of this model, Herman Daly and John Cobb, share a concern that "what is needed is *a* new measure" (Daly and Cobb 1994, 378). They are particularly concerned that "costs" should be registered as deficits or depletions, not as "goods" or "benefits" in production and consumption, as in the UNSNA.

    Daly and Cobb propose the Index of Sustainable Economic Welfare (ISEW). In this method of data collection and analysis, growth is no longer God; the emphasis is now on sustainability. The characteristics used in the ISEW are personal consumption, distributional inequality, household labor services, consumer durables, services provided by highways and streets, improvement in health and education by way of public expenditures, expenditures on consumer durables and defensive private expenditures on health and education. Costs included are the costs of commuting, the costs of personal pollution control, costs of automobile accidents, costs of water pollution, air pollution, noise pollution, losses of wetlands, losses of farm land, depletion of nonrenewable resources, long-term environmental damage, cost of ozone depletion, net capital growth (that is, the growth in the stock of goods used to produce other goods) and a change in net international position (indebtedness).

Attempts to ascribe a value to leisure were omitted from the ISEW, because "the rather arbitrary assumptions upon which such a calculation is based ... are particularly problematic" (ibid., 455). However, Daly and Cobb include "a rather speculative estimate of long-term environmental damage, particularly from climate modification" (ibid.). They admit to being forced to make "heroic assumptions" in compiling the ISEW, such as the cost imposed on future generations by the depletion of natural resources (ibid.).

The ISEW falls down on the issue of unpaid work. While it shows evidence of new thinking, it remains patronizing. "Which of the activities within the household should be classified as work as opposed to leisure or an intrinsically satisfying activity?" (ibid., 457) they ask. There is an easy response to this point: members of the paid workforce also take time for leisure in paid time, and find elements of their employment intrinsically satisfying. We still count all their activities as work.

In addition, Daly and Cobb's valuations are based on old inequalities. In ascribing a value to unpaid work, they adopt Robert Eisner's method of estimating the value of time spent on unpaid household work on the basis of the average wage rate for household domestic workers (Eisner 1989). This, they say, avoids the problem of using differential market wage rates for men and women. However, this does not avoid the problems thrown up by using traditional low wage rates from a female occupation to estimate the value of the work of domestic workers, especially when much of that work is in the management of a small business, even if there is no market exchange!

... In retrospect, these studies can demonstrate that improvements in car safety and reductions in air pollution have made contributions to raising the level of economic welfare. So have social policies to reduce income inequality (ibid., 507). The categories included in the ISEW make this method of data collection yield a far more recognizable picture of reality. But the ISEW still remains one conglomerate, a single new measure, and the dollar is the measurement tool.

The Human Development Index (HDI)

Since its inception in 1990, the United Nations Human Development Report series has been dedicated to ending the mismeasurement of human progress by economic growth alone. "To be valuable and legitimate, development progress, both nationally and internationally, must be people-centered, equitably distributed and environmentally and socially sustainable.... If present trends continue economic disparities between the industrial and developing nations will move from inequitable to inhumane" (United Nations 1996, iii).

To make the HDI capture gender-related inequalities, life expectancy, adult literacy and education are disaggregated by sex, as are data on share of earned income. A "Gender Empowerment Measure" (GEM) includes data on the proportion of seats in parliament occupied by women, data on women as a percentage of administrators and managers, professional and technical workers, and women's percentage of earned income. The Human Development Reports are augmented with other data relevant to gender-based poverty and inequality. Despite the data limitations of timeliness and availability, the problems of currency conversions to the USD baseline, differing concepts, classifications and methods, and charges that there are too many data with too many different indicators, the HDI begins to approach approximate accurate input for the purpose of policy making.

Genuine Progress Indicators

One key indicator that is missing from the UN HDI is time-use. Time-use has figured prominently in the work to establish Genuine Progress Indicators (GPI) in Nova Scotia. Prepared by Dr Ronald Coleman, the Nova Scotia GPI project has been designated as a pilot with

Statistics Canada, which is providing ongoing assistance in data collection and analysis, and staff support. In addition to the national census, the GPI uses data from the Canadian System of Environmental and Resource Accounts. The index consists of twenty components with a sectoral approach and an emphasis on policy relevance.

The GPI indices distinguish direct contributions to economic welfare from defensive and intermediate expenditures, and from activities that produce an actual decline in well-being. Natural resource accounts include fisheries, soil and agriculture, forestry, wildlife, and greenhouse gas emissions. There are data on the costs of crime, income distribution, and transportation cost analysis. Monetary values are estimated where possible, but in the GPI it is not necessary that all components should have a financial value attributed to them.

The indicators of the GPI include statistics on unpaid work, divided into voluntary and community work, unpaid housework and parenting, and the value of unpaid overtime and underemployment. These figures can be gender-disaggregated. The monetary valuation method used in this study for calculating the economic value of unpaid work is the replacement cost (specialist) method. This reflects the hourly wage rate that would be paid in Nova Scotia to replace existing activities at market prices for the same kind of work. While this financial valuation is used to demonstrate linkages between the market and nonmarket sectors of the economy, a clear focus of the analysis is on time....

The GPI work in Nova Scotia is the most sophisticated measurement work for policy outcomes anywhere. I recommend it to you. Of particular use are the crosscutting sectoral work in the forestry accounts, the water accounts, and the unpaid work accounts in both the household and voluntary and community sectors....

KEY CHALLENGES REMAINING

The process in Nova Scotia partially solves two of the key problems that remained (at that point) with the GPI approach (which was originally Daly and Cobb's successor to the ISEW).

Asking People to Set Their Own Indicators of Well-Being

The first of these partial solutions is that while the indices seek to measure the well-being or development of a people or peoples, community, nation state or region, it is not usual for anyone to ask people themselves what indicators they would use to describe their well-being, and how they would measure outcomes of policies based on this data. Instead, the indicator sets are either what the authorities determine as being the figures they will collect (because the World Bank or IMF says so; because you can get a lot of software and hardware and vehicles if you collect particular data in a development assistance program; because they support a corrupt government and can be easily manipulated; or just because they are the ones that have always been collected and there is comparability over time), or the figures that can be collected, from a logistical and technical standpoint, with a so-called reasonable degree of accuracy. Sometimes the choice of what data to collect depends simply on what is on the UN agenda for that year.

Presenting and Interpreting Data in Nonmonetary Terms

The fine policy work in Nova Scotia also mitigates the second problem of data which cannot be presented and interpreted other than in monetary terms. This means that all sections of the population—not just academic statisticians and economists, can participate in debates about the research. It is expressed in the way that people might talk about it in a community meeting, in "real world" terms. It is also important that data can be debated in terms of its own integrity, instead of the somewhat farfetched abstractions that result when everything is given a monetary value. For example, if we think of gender inequality and the potential users and objectives of time-use data relating to women's and men's workloads, we know that it is not necessary for policy discussions to ascribe monetary values to that work. For example, awareness of unequal time-use may spark off discussions about the need for day nurseries to offer more flexible services so that women's need for child-care can be met. These discussions do not require information about the value of the work which women are undertaking for such long hours.... The need for monetary values to be ascribed occasionally is not a reason to abstract all time-use data to the economic model. Far more rigorous planning can be achieved by retaining the time-use framework, and it makes much more sense.

Ascribing monetary values to labor results in a loss of detail and specificity in policy analysis. Nowhere can the consequences of this be more starkly seen than in the case of children who work. Stories in the *State of the World's Children 1997* illustrate this. The ILO Minimum Age Convention allows light work at age 12 or 13, but prohibits hazardous work before 18. It also establishes a general minimum age of 15 years for paid work, provided 15 is not less than the age of completion of compulsory schooling. Yet, of the projected 190 million working children in the 10–14 age group in the developing world, three-quarters work six days a week or more, and one half work nine hours a day or more (UNICEF 1997, 25)....

Do we want to lose the detail of what we do to children by ascribing monetary values to their production? I certainly do not, but that would be the result of including their labor and its outcome under a generic "producer" category. Similarly, I do not want to lose the complexity of the impact of human activity on our ecosystem behind dollar signs. Yet that is the direction being pursued to give "visibility" to environmental issues. To establish the United Nations satellite system of integrated economic and environmental accounting, the first step for each country is to draw up a comprehensive balance sheet of natural resources, measured in physical quantities. That ought to be sufficient for effective policy planning. Different units yes, but with judgment exercised. But the economists want one baseline, so that depletion of capital could include not just depreciation of physical capital, but depletion of natural resources along with deterioration of environmental quality. The problem is, they say, that so much expenditure for environmental protection compensates for the negative impact of economic growth, so it should be a cost to be deducted from national income.

There's an attractive logic here, and it parallels the "costs" component of Daly and Cobb's ISEW system. The UN satellite system has been tested in several countries. For Mexico between 1986 and 1990, it was found that the environmentally adjusted domestic product was 13 per cent less than the conventionally measured net domestic product. The new accounting measures also showed that net investment, which conventional measures showed as positive at 4.6 billion pesos, was a negative 700 million pesos. Net savings, also assumed to be positives, were actually close to zero. A case study for Papua New Guinea over the same period produced similar results. There consumption exceeded output so net savings were negative (UN 1996, 63).

But there had to be a better way.

Alberta GPI

The latest work in which I have been involved as an adviser appears to have addressed both these major impediments to using the GPI in a major tool for policy planning. My challenge to the Alberta GPI Project Director, Mark Anielski at the Pembina Institute, was that the characteristics of well-being to be utilized in the Alberta GPI should reflect the values seen as indicative of well-being by Albertans themselves. The values held by Albertans should also determine how a characteristic in the GPI approach is treated. For example, in some communities, divorce is seen as a negative social cost. We know it usually leads to the economic downward mobility of women. Most governments focus on single-parent-headed households as a negative phenomenon. Yet we all know cases where the separation or divorce brings about an end to prolonged violence, and the well-being of children and mothers improves substantially. Divorce can therefore, in some contexts, be seen as positive. Similarly, some communities would see the rate of oil extraction in Alberta as a positive contribution to well-being; others might see such extraction as a cost, particularly in terms of intergenerational equity.

In the time available, the Alberta GPI team was not able to conduct new research, but it was able to undertake a meta-data analysis of the Canadian and Albertan research on community values as reflected in the past five to ten years. This had the immediate effect of increasing the characteristics to be included to over 50, as opposed to the 26 in the original GPI or the 20 used in Nova Scotia.

The next challenge was to find a way of presenting all the data without ascribing notional monetary values, in such a way that all characteristics were measured in terms of their own integrity. It would obviously be useful if the system or model could also make trade-offs visible, and could be accessible for communities to understand and to participate in the analysis and planning that flows from the presentation of data. It would also be a vast improvement if the system could have "open architecture"—that is, when a community or nation state demonstrated that a particular characteristic was no longer important to them, it could drop out of the system. Similarly, whenever a new measurement deemed important presented itself, it too could be introduced, without the tedium of "not disturbing the comparability of the model over time," which is the outdated approach of the UNSNA and its policy of satellites.

I believe there is now this model. It is based on the healing circle used by the First Nations People of North America. It requires no expensive software: it is a simple radar diagram in an Excel Program. The work can be downloaded from www.pembina.org.

I believe this approach offers enormous possibilities, but it must not be abused. (I dread to think of it as a tool in the hands of unethical postgraduate students who need a thesis.) In the first place, users should know the origins of opposition to the UNSNA approach, and how and why this alternative approach evolved. It must come as a whole piece of work, which is initiated by the communities whose well-being (or level of poverty, or development indicators) is or are being determined. These people themselves should determine the indicators to be included, and this list should be revisited with them every five to ten years. You can see immediately that the open architecture could deal with all the following: inflation rate, daily caloric intake, maternal mortality, the cost of a litre of water, last year's rainfall, notifiable and contagious disease levels, levels of education or literacy or school attendance, access to and use of family planning, agricultural extension programs, micro credit schemes, the retention of indigenous languages, natural disasters, pollution of air and water, deforestation—the list can be as long as a community determines. They should also be party to the interpretation of the radar diagram, which would determine the policy inputs required for desired outcomes, with trade-offs being very explicit.

I believe this model can be rigorous, ethical and accessible in our hands as a real break-through for policy work, with and for women and their communities.

CONCLUSION

The UNSNA is still the most influential model being used universally, but it is failing women miserably as a policy instrument, regardless of all its other problems. The feminist agenda in reinventing globalization sees the removal of this pathological arbiter of "well-being" as a critical focus. The satellite alternative is a co-option. The Alberta model is the most exciting alternative development in my lifetime—and one we can begin to use in our own nations and communities....

NOTES

...

2. The United Nations Decade for Women ran from 1975 to 1985.

...

REFERENCES

Daly, H. and John B. Cobb Jr. (1994) *For the Common Good: Redirecting the Economy Towards Community, the Environment and a Sustainable Future.* Boston: Beacon Press.

Eisner, R. (1989) *The Total Incomes System of Accounts.* Chicago: University of Chicago Press.

International Labour Organisation (1982) "Fifteenth International Conference of Labour Statisticians: Report II, Labour Force, Employment, Unemployment and Underemployment." Geneva: ILO.

International Labour Organisation (1993) "Fifteenth International Conference of Labour Statisticians: Report IV, Revision of the International Classification of Status in Employment." Geneva: ILO.

Ralston Saul, R. (1997) *The Unconscious Civilization.* Ringwood, Vic.: Penguin Books.

UNICEF (1997) *The State of the World's Children.* New York: UNICEF.

United Nations (1993) *A System of National Accounts.* New York: United Nations.

United Nations (1996) *Human Development Report.* New York: United Nations.

Waring, M. (1999) *Counting for Nothing—What Men Value and What Women Are Worth.* Toronto: University of Toronto Press.

4
Human Biology

Earlier readings have illustrated how sexist and other biases have affected several disciplines in the humanities and social sciences, and how the knowledge produced has then been used to justify various social inequalities. Readings in this section illustrate similar processes operating in the science of human biology.

SOCIAL VALUES INFLUENCE THE BIOLOGICAL SCIENCES

Social values have shaped biology in several ways. First, they have influenced the questions pursued by biologists, who have often sought biological causes of social differences and inequalities; for instance, a long tradition of biological research has sought biological causes of racial inequalities, from nineteenth-century medicine and anthropology (craniology) to contemporary IQ tests. Biological explanations have also been sought for male dominance as well as for ethnocentrism, slavery, warfare, laziness, drug addiction, competition, rape, poverty, violence, corruption, and political hierarchy. If a particular form of social organization can be linked with some feature of human biology, it is easy to argue that this form of organization is in some sense "natural." Thus, biological theories are often used to diagnose causes of human discontent or prescribe limits to social change. Such theories usually encourage fatalism, suggesting either that people must adapt their societies to take account of what are asserted to be unchangeable human propensities or that they must accept that a society with certain social ills is inevitable. Advocates of social change usually eschew theories that link forms of social organization with human biology, because they often encourage political fatalism; a rare exception is Peter Kropotkin's turn-of-the-twentieth-century classic, *Mutual Aid: A Factor of Evolution.*

Social values, including sexist ones, have also biased the assumptions guiding research in biology. For example, models of sexual reproduction have typically portrayed sperm as active, ova as passive. The readings by Jennifer Terry and Elisabeth Lloyd describe how biological research has been influenced by the assumption that homosexuals are somehow deficient or abnormal and that female sexuality is designed to facilitate reproduction and fertilization. The possibility of autonomous female sexuality has been ignored both by those studying lesbians and by those studying the evolutionary origin of human sexuality.

Finally, values have affected interpretations of biological data and the conclusions drawn from them. These values include such assumptions as the following: that differences among groups are more significant than differences within them, that persons of color or people of lower economic classes are less intelligent, that autonomous female sexuality is bad, and that women are inferior.

BIOLOGICAL DETERMINISM

When a link can be found between social and biological differences, social differences are often thought to be biologically determined. Biological determinist theories suggest that certain features of human social life are uniquely determined by the genetic constitution of human beings. Because such theories are often used to justify the subordination of women and other marginalized groups, proponents of social equality have sometimes responded by denying that human biology has any significant consequences for social organization. Instead, they have sometimes advocated environmental determinism, the view that culture is the primary determinant of human psychological characteristics and forms of social organization.

The distinction between sex and gender is often taken to provide a theoretical basis for denying that male dominance is determined biologically. Sex is presented as a universal and biologically fixed division among humans. It is defined by the division of functions in sexual reproduction, in which females produce eggs or young that have been fertilized by a male. Markers of sex include chromosomes, gonads, internal and external reproductive features, and hormones as well as "secondary" sex characteristics such as facial hair. Gender, by contrast, is presented as a set of social norms and expectations about the proper behavior of male and female persons, who are expected to behave in accordance with the respective norms of masculinity and femininity. Both sex and gender are frequently regarded as dimorphic.

Although "sex" and "gender" are often used interchangeably in contemporary discourse, the conceptualization of gender as a category of social analysis was a theoretical and political breakthrough of 1960s Western feminism. (Previously gender had been merely a category of grammar.) Making this distinction created a vocabulary for raising questions about the relationship between biology and society and especially for arguing that gender norms were not biologically determined and so not, presumably, inevitable.

Feminists of the 1960s and 1970s emphasized that gender norms varied not only cross-culturally but also across time, class, race, and ethnicity within the same society. They pointed out that in some societies more than two genders existed, that biological males were sometimes assigned a feminine gender and females a masculine gender, and that gender norms varied according to class and race in contemporary Western societies. In the late 1960s and early 1970s, the cross-cultural and historically variable nature of gender was frequently used as an argument against the idea that male dominance was biologically determined. It was taken to provide evidence against determinist claims that sex causes or necessitates gendered social divisions—or at least predisposes people toward certain types of gendered behavior or social institutions.

Many different theories have sought to establish a biological basis for male dominance, though sociobiology has been the most frequently used theoretical approach since the late 1970s. Feminist critics have challenged various aspects of these different accounts, including the alleged universality of male dominance among humans and claims of male dominance in those animal species most closely related to humans. However, criticizing specific aspects of any particular biological determinist theory always leaves open the possibility that some new theory will turn out to be valid. It is therefore helpful to understand the relation between human biology and social environment in terms that emphasize how each interacts with and mutually transforms the other.

AN ALTERNATIVE CONCEPTUALIZATION OF THE RELATION BETWEEN HUMAN BIOLOGY AND SOCIAL LIFE

An interactive or transformative understanding of human biology does not deny that biology plays a decisive role in human life, creating needs for food, air, sleep, and so on. Rather than seeing human biology as setting limits, however, it is better seen as opening up possibilities that may be infinite. Human genes make possible our distinctively human capacities, especially the capacities for intelligent thought and speech, which are the prerequisites for social problem solving and cultural development. However, genes "dictate" only at a very high level of generality; it is specific cultural contexts that determine how these potentials are actualized. For instance, our genes provide our ability to learn languages, engage in productive work, and develop social relations, but they do not determine that we learn English, build nuclear weapons, or act in selfish and competitive as opposed to altruistic and cooperative ways.

Human forms of social organization are determined by a complex interplay among our biological constitutions, the physical environments we inhabit, and our current levels of technological and cultural development. Thus, although it may be true that in a moderately harsh environment and with little technology, social survival depends on infant care by lactating women, it does not follow that infants must be cared for by women in situations where bottle feeding is available or where other kinds of productive work do not require heavy physical labor or long absences from home. We could say that the human biological constitution requires or determines a certain form of social organization within certain material circumstances, but it would be equally true to say that the material circumstances or the level of technological development determined a certain form of social organization, given certain features of the human biological constitution.

Human biology itself is at least in part a cultural product, not simply a presocial given. This is more obvious on the level of phenotype, where our physical structure results from interaction between our genetic inheritance and our social environment. Post–World War II British children were healthier and looked different from previous generations of children because of rationing, which distributed available food more equally, and policies that promoted social welfare. Second-generation Americans are typically larger than their parents. Even our genetic inheritance on the level of genotype is influenced by the social history of our species. Although human prehistory is highly speculative, it seems likely that some genetically heritable characteristics have been selected not only "naturally," as adaptations to such nonsocial circumstances as climate and food availability, but also socially, as adaptations to certain forms of social organization or even as the results of conscious social preferences. For instance, the average size difference between human males and females may have been a consequence as much as a cause of male dominance: if the dominant males fed first and most, only smaller-framed females could survive on the leftover food. Anne Fausto-Sterling has argued that sex distinction itself is not a fixed, universal, presocial given but that in fact social processes of sex assignment are characterized by considerable arbitrariness and coercion (1985, 1992, 1999).

The interactive or transformative conceptualization of the relation between human biology and social environment does not argue that biological determinism is false simply because it fails to give sufficient weight to the social determinants of human characteristics. Instead, this conceptualization brings into question the usefulness of the whole nature/culture distinction as an analytical framework for understanding human beings. Just as we cannot identify any cultural or social phenomena uninfluenced in some way by human biology, neither can we identify any human biological or "natural" features that are independent of social influence. The biological and the social are so intertwined in our history and in our present lives that it becomes impossible in principle to distinguish the natural from the social or cultural components in the constitution of human beings. As far as human beings are concerned, the relation between biology and culture is mutually constitutive: to oppose one to the other is incomprehensible. Biological determinism is not so much false as incoherent. Everything we are and do is simultaneously cultural and natural.

JUST METHODOLOGY IN BIOLOGICAL SCIENCES

How can feminists respond to the recognition that biology, like other disciplines, is saturated with social values? These not only have influenced biological theories on the levels of experimental design, data collection, predictions, hypothesis formulation, and evaluation of explanation; they also have been used to rationalize, reinforce, and normalize social inequalities. One possible response on the part of feminists would be to try to eradicate values, to construct a value-free biology. However, biological research, like all research, is designed to answer the questions that are important to the societies that support it. For this reason, it would be undesirable and indeed impossible to create biological theories that were completely value-free. A better response may be to develop biological theories based on more egalitarian values, including feminist ones.

One part of this project requires revealing and challenging sexist, racist, classist, and other inegalitarian assumptions incorporated into the design or interpretation of biological research. Another part requires undertaking research projects likely to be useful to women, people of color, and members of other underclass groups; such projects might include, for example, the impact of pollutants and toxins on human cells. Both of these projects would require more biologists from historically underrepresented groups, including women, men of color, and men from working-class backgrounds. People's politics are not determined by their social identities, but scholars are more likely to promote egalitarian values if they come from groups that historically have suffered disadvantage. Ultimately, a nonsexist and otherwise egalitarian biology can flourish only within a nonsexist and otherwise egalitarian society.

REFERENCES

Fausto-Sterling, Anne. 1992. *Myths of Gender: Biological Theories about Women and Men*, 2nd ed. New York: BasicBooks.
———. 1999. *Sexing the Body*. New York: BasicBooks.

Jennifer Terry
Lesbians under the Medical Gaze: Scientists Search for Remarkable Differences

... Ever since homosexuality was first cast as a problem for medicine in the late nineteenth century, scientists have been attempting to define its unique characteristics....

Two basic assumptions seem to underlie and structure much of the research on homosexuality carried out in the early decades of the twentieth century. First, it is clear that most research presumed a binary opposition between homosexuals and heterosexuals and tended to posit a generic, monolithic or stereotypical type ("*the* homosexual").... Second, much of the early research on homosexuality assumed that sexual behavior was linked to the individual's expression of masculinity or femininity. Scientists assumed that the male homosexual was always effeminate, and that the lesbian was always to some extent mannish.

This article discusses the efforts of a specific group of scientists in the 1930s who, operating with these assumptions, developed a wide array of techniques to probe the minds, bodies and experiences of "sex variants," their term for people who transgressed the conventions of heterosexuality. Although both men and women were scrutinized by doctors, this article focuses on their observations of female sex variants. Researchers saw lesbianism as a complex problem with psychological, somatic, social, and cultural dimensions. I will argue that the perspective guiding their research not only posed significant obstacles for explaining contradictory empirical evidence but had embedded within it theoretical limitations which placed a whole range of lesbian practices outside the researchers' comprehension. Specifically, given the assumed "masculinity" of lesbians, the researchers were confused when they found evidence of femininity in sex variant women and subsequently were unable to comprehend the complex expressions of lesbian desire.

...

SEX VARIANTS: A STUDY FROM THE 1930s

In the spring of 1936, the Committee for the Study of Sex Variants convened for the first time in New York City with the broad and ambitious aim "to undertake, support and promote investigations and scientific research touching upon and embracing the clinical, psychological and sociological aspects of variations from normal sex behavior ... through laboratory research and clinical study" (Henry, 1948, p. v). Members of the Committee included a panoply of medical specialists: psychiatrists, gynecologists, obstetricians, surgeons, radiologists, neurologists, as well as clinical psychologists, an urban sociologist, a criminal anthropologist, and a former commissioner of the New York City Department of Correction.... [T]he Committee's goal [was to learn] more about a homosexual population that appeared to be growing in size and significance specifically in the urban context of New York City.

After several years of collecting information, in 1941 Dr. George Henry, a psychiatrist who established the Committee and supervised the research, published the findings in a two volume report entitled *Sex Variants: A Study of Homosexual Patterns*. In his introduction to the report, Henry made clear that the aim of the multidisciplinary research went beyond a quest for knowledge. Rather, knowledge gained from the study was to assist doctors in identifying and treating patients who suffered from "sexual maladjustment." Moreover, this research would go toward preventing the spread of sex variance through the "general population." ...

In proclaiming its decidedly prophylactic purpose, the Committee distinguished its enlightened efforts from other explicitly punitive methods of dealing with homosexuality. Speaking for the Committee, Henry argued against what he considered to be sensationalist vice purges and public humiliation to homosexuals in favor of a new and arguably more benevolent approach to the study of homosexuality. From his point of view, medical and scientific research brought a modern and enlightened perspective to a problem that superstitious biases, vigilance campaigns and criminal punishment had exacerbated. This new thinking is reflected most obviously in the committee's decision to name homosexuality sexual *variance* rather than the pejorative term, sexual *deviance*, suggesting that homosexuals merely manifest or express variations from the normal gender traits of heterosexual men and women.

THE SUBJECTS

Subjects for the study were contacted through informal social networks in New York City by a "Miss Jan Gay," the pseudonym for an author of children's books and most likely a lesbian herself. Out of the hundreds of men and women who were contacted for the study, a total of eighty (forty men and forty women) were selected and agreed to submit to an extensive battery of physical and psychological examinations. These people were not prescreened nor is it clear from the study's report what, if any, specific criteria were used to select the subjects with one exception: they all admitted to preferring sexual relations with members of their own sex. There seems to have been no explicitly coercive force compelling the subjects to participate in the study. Indeed, it appears from the text of their psychiatric interviews that the subjects were as intrigued with understanding the origins of their sexuality as were the doctors. The women in the study ranged in age from twenty to forty and were predominantly white. Many of these "sex variant" women had been married or had sexual relations with men during various periods of their lives, and several had children. What they all had in common was that they were sexually attracted to women and had extensive sexual experience with other lesbians. In fact, what brought them into the study in the first place and earned them the label of "sex variant" was their own admission of engaging in lesbian sex. This self-selection process assured the researchers that since they wouldn't have to guess whether these women were heterosexual or homosexual, the subjects were like human specimens that could reveal any unique characteristics attributable to lesbianism.

Henry characterized study participants to be mostly "members of the professional classes"; however, among the female subjects, there were many women who made a living working occasional odd jobs which allowed them to pursue other interests in the arts and in radical politics. Drawn mostly from the dynamic neighborhoods of Harlem and Greenwich Village, many of the female subjects lived in a lively and cosmopolitan theatrical and artistic world, and some of them knew each other as friends or lovers....

A striking aspect of this study which sets it apart from many other published discussions of homosexuality of the time is the presence of the subject's own voices. The Sex Variant Study considered the subjects' verbal participation an important source of psychological and cultural data and included large excerpts from their psychiatric interviews in the final report.... While the doctors encouraged the testimonies of the subjects to aid in the diagnosis and treatment of variance (in the form of the "talking cure"), this method opened the possibility for women to express their own, sometimes contradictory views of their homosexuality, and even occasionally to advocate it as a positive alternative to heterosexuality.

METHODS

The Committee adopted a paradigm by which it understood various psychological and physical characteristics to be scattered across a gender spectrum, with masculine traits clustered on one side and feminine traits clustered on the other.

> [T]here is little scientific basis for precise classification of humans as male and female. Masculinity and femininity are quantitative and qualitative variations. These variations are registered in structural, physiological and psychological attributes which are peculiar to each individual. Regardless of the sex, a person gives expression to masculine or feminine traits in accordance with his [sic] innate tendencies to maleness or femaleness and in proportion to the opportunities for expression of these tendencies. (Henry, 1948. p. xii)

The traits of sex variants were believed to place them in the middle of this continuum, between the two ordinary genders of male and female.

Like earlier theories of sexual inversion (Ellie, 1915), this study assumed that the female sex variant would exhibit traits of the opposite sex. In other words, she would invert her proper gender role (Chauncey, 1983). Furthermore, her sexual desire for other women was seen as a consequence, rather than a cause, of this gender role inversion. Lesbianism was defined not simply by the object of the female sex variant's desire but by the masculine, aggressive form that desire took.

Generally speaking, any signs of "femininity" in female sex variants created confusion among the researchers. When these signs did appear, they were often discounted by researchers as elements of masquerade covering over more masculine essences. In fact, the notion of a "feminine" sex variant woman was practically and methodologically oxymoronic....

Since it was basically assumed that lesbian sexual desire was an effect produced by the female sex variant's masculinity, several significant questions remained unsolved. For example, researchers had difficulty explaining how and why a woman who appeared to be "feminine" could be sexually active in her pursuit of more "masculine" women. Since they assumed that sexual initiative was a sign of masculinity, how could a "feminine" sex variant initiate sex? ... Furthermore, while researchers tried to understand how a feminine woman might respond favorably to the sexual advances of a "masculine" woman, they had no way of understanding how she might welcome those of another "feminine" woman. For the most part, the "feminine" subjects were categorized as bisexual or narcissistic (rather than homosexual). They were either described as malingerers or weak-willed women seduced into lesbianism at the hands of a mannish woman. Or they were seen as so narcissistic and self-absorbed that any attention they got, whether from a man or a woman, was intoxicating and put them under the spell of masculine seduction. In any event, the notion of feminine lesbians having a sexual desire of their own was confounding to the doctors.

Conversely, explaining any sexual passivity of masculine women was something the researchers were at pains to do. It was seen as frustration resulting from the subject's sense of her own failure to approximate (heterosexual) male behavior sufficiently. In either the masculine or feminine subjects, the researchers could not account for those anomalous women who defied the study's gender-based sexual inversion paradigm. This was largely due to the fact that the doctors and scientists did not have a theory of sexual object choice which could operate independent of gender.

Their paradigm propelled these researchers to conduct elaborate searches for hidden or overt "masculine" and "feminine" traits in their subjects. In this way, the study was much more involved in establishing and maintaining gender boundaries than it was about understanding sexuality and homosexual object choice.

The researchers used techniques from their specialty areas to search for signs of masculinity and femininity. Psychiatrists used the psychoanalytic method of asking subjects to respond by free association to a number of questions about their families, cultural backgrounds, sexual experiences, and opinions on society's attitudes towards homosexuality. These transcribed and edited interviews were "supplemented" with findings from a regime of physical examinations. Pathologists looked at skin complexion, fat distribution, coarseness of hair, the condition of teeth, and commented on the overall facial and bodily structure of each subject. Radiologists took x-rays to determine cranial densities of the skull and "carrying angles" of the pelvis in order to identify anomalous gender characteristics. A dense skull was presumed to be masculine. "Graceful" and "delicate" pelvic bones were feminine.

Endocrinologists measured hormonal levels in some of the subjects, while urologists took semen samples from some of the men to measure their "fecundating properties." Interestingly, female subjects were not tested for fertility, suggesting that while the ability to produce fertile sperm was linked to masculinity, having viable ova and giving birth were not sufficient signs of femininity to preclude lesbianism, since some of the female subjects had already given birth.

Gynecologists and obstetricians examined all "but the most vigorous, assertive women" (i.e., those who refused to be examined) to look for indications of sex variance. Their focus was on evidence of "female-to-female sex-play." In this way, the gynecological exam differed from the other physical exams because it involved looking for the physical markings acquired through sexual activities, rather than simply identifying "innate" or "congenital" physical traits.

Sketches of genitals and breasts were drawn in order to document particular characteristics of sex variance which appeared on them....

In order to show graphic comparisons with "normal" women, Dickinson relied on sketches he drew of his own obstetrics patients who, because they were presumed to be heterosexual, acted as a control group. Dickinson emphasized the painstaking process of achieving a perfectly accurate image of sex variants at this level, as if neither he nor Dr. Moensch was engaged in an interpretive process. Dickinson's claim to scientific accuracy was reflected in the careful notation of specific measurements of genital parts and in reporting the duration of one subject's nipple erection.

One-third of the entire group of men and women allowed photographs to be taken of them in the nude. According to Henry, these photos served "to supplement morphological and other data useful in endocrinologic evaluation" (Henry, 1948. p. xiii) and to act as a diagnostic instrument "to facilitate the correlation of body form with behavior" (Henry, 1941, p. 1041)....
The photographs, in their stark presentation of the subjects, recall the photographs of diseased bodies which are commonly featured in medical textbooks. Although the images of these lesbians do not appear to be at all different from what one would expect heterosexual women to look like, the very composition of the photograph and the fact that it serves as an indicator of variant characteristics invites the viewer to look for and find pathology or difference.

A majority of the subjects participated in the Masculinity and Femininity Attitude and Interest Test devised by two clinical psychologists on the Committee, Catharine Cox Miles and Lewis Terman who was famous for his pioneering research on IQ testing (Terman, 1906, 1916). This test was divided into several exercises which were not explained but simply listed in the report: (1) word association; (2) ink-blot associations; (3) information; (4) emotional and ethical response; (5) interests; (6) personalities and opinions; and (7) introverted response. Overall, it was intended to locate each subject on a continuum that charted the psychological differences between men and women.

To ensure scientific objectivity, results of all physical examinations were reported by physicians who did not have access to the psychiatric histories and, according to Dr. Henry, by those who "had no particular interest in (any) subject" (Henry, 1948, p. xiv). After all the data were collected, Henry suggested that correlations between behavior and somatic characteristics would serve as proof of the difference between sex variants and normal heterosexual women, a difference that might be detectable *either* on the gynecological table or the psychiatric couch.

THE STRUCTURE OF THE CASE STUDY

The published report compiled the individual cases to emphasize the interconnections between psychoanalytic features of each subject and her physical characteristics, a format George Henry believed to be "accurately informative." For each subject, we find a long personal narrative, the results of various physical examinations, and the doctor's general comments on the subject's mannerisms and physical traits which, in his view, revealed something about the nature of sex variance. The particular way this information was organized for the reader underscores a tacit question of the study which is how behaviors, on one hand, and physical characteristics, on the other, might influence or determine each other.

. . .

The final report of the Committee placed each of the female subjects into one of three broad categories "according to the extent to which they deviate(d) from heterosexual adjustment": *narcissistics* and "those who show eccentricities in psychosexual behavior" (nine cases); *bisexuals,* "or those who approximate heterosexual adjustment" (seventeen cases); and *homosexuals* about which no qualifying remark is made (fourteen cases).

Each case study begins with a graphic genealogical tree locating the subject in relation to her kin. This chart indicates any unusual characteristics associated with family members, including alcoholism, tuberculosis, artistic ability, divorce, children born out of wedlock, promiscuity, or suicidal tendencies. The reason for including information about ancestors and other kin was to investigate two things about female sex variance: (1) the degree to which it might be an inherited condition; and (2) the degree to which it may emerge due to the presence of certain "opportunities" in some families for girls to express masculine tendencies.

Following the family tree the psychiatrist introduced the subject by giving his "General Impression" of her. This impression usually indicated the subject's age, race, ethnicity, profession, and any physical or behavioral features the doctor found significant in terms of masculinity and femininity. For example, in the case of Alberta I. (all the names given in the study were pseudonyms to protect true identities), Henry wrote: "Alberta is a small, tense woman of thirty. She has a pointed nose, small eyes, a well-formed forehead and thin, translucent skin. Her voice is sharp and rasping and her hands are delicate but strong. In her manner and bearing her homosexuality appears obvious although her sexual preference is not suggested in her dress or in her public attentions to women" (Henry, 1948, p. 866). Here Henry observed and delineated characteristics based on whether they were consonant or dissonant with what Alberta I., being a woman, should express. This particular quote also reveals Henry's attempt to deal with the complexities which arise when homosexual mannerisms cannot be concealed, even under the proper dress of femininity.

The subject's first-person narration of her family background and her personal history follows the doctor's cursory introduction. She speaks in streams of consciousness about her emotional and psychosexual development, prompted by Henry's questions. These sections offer rich and compelling accounts of lesbian lives, revealing joys as well as hardships and disappointments in love, sex and confrontations with heterosexuality and homophobia. These sections, Henry acknowledged, were composed "almost entirely" of statements made by the subject which he edited "to make a connected history" (Henry, 1948, p. xiii).

The . . . subject's spoken words are followed by general comments which sum up various physical examinations by noting significant findings, especially those related to masculinity and femininity. The stories told in the psychiatric interviews contrast sharply with the reduced form of the subject into a list of descriptive inventories such as "athletic-feminine type with rather boyish face," "fairly high cheek bones," "mouth medium," "pharynx normal," "voice low," "teeth regular," "skin thin and smooth," "feminine pubic hair," "fat, slight excess on buttocks," and "skeleton medium" (Henry, 1948, p. 852).

General comments on the gynecological exam follow this portion. . . . For example, results from Rose S.'s gynecological exam feature graphic adjectives suggesting the excesses and peculiarities of her genitals: "The labia majora are 10 cm. long and the minora pigmented in very pronounced fashion, notwithstanding the general coloration, and they protrude in pronounced, thick preputial curtains. The clitoris is 9 by 4 mm., and very erectile, the hymen worn and gone, admitting two or three fingers, the vagina with smooth lining of very high degree of distensibility, the pelvic floor relaxed, and while it is thick, showing no jump or throb during digital examination" (Henry, 1948, p. 933). This last sentence is a reference to the influence Dr. Mary Moensch's gender was presumed to have on the subjects being examined. The researchers asserted that because these women were lesbians, they exhibited an excited response to the female gynecologist's examination. A page showing clitorises indicates the difference between the subject's response to the male examiner and to the female examiner, noting the erection of the clitoris was larger in response to Dr. Moensch.

These data were compared with a group of women presumed to be heterosexual who, like the lesbians, showed no response to their male doctor's examination. However, since this heterosexual group was not examined by a female doctor to see if they would respond differently, using them as a control group was methodologically flawed. Regardless of this flaw, the study went on to argue that heterosexual women did not get excited when being examined by male physicians. Therefore, since female sex variants showed the presence of "glairy mucous" and nipple and clitoral erections during their examinations, these were the signs not only of (homo)sexual arousal but also evidence that lesbianism was a form of hypersexuality.

. . . After the reporting of physical observations, results of the Masculinity and Femininity test were presented. Then Dr. Henry's "Comment," in the style of Freudian psychoanalysis, gave a review of the most salient aspects of the psychiatric case history, often quoting or paraphrasing from the autobiographical account but interjecting authoritative comments about symptoms and possible causes of sexual maladjustment.

Finally, each case study ends with a section called "Resume," which is the most terse interpretation of the subject's condition, signified by the assignment of diagnostic labels such as neurotic, sadistic, or promiscuous. In a shorthand fashion, the psychiatrist summed up a vast and complex history into causal statements such as "(Birdie's) aversion to men (is) a defense because of insecurity over her small stature" (Henry, 1948, p. 908) or, in Marvel W.'s case, "homosexuality (is) an expression of craving for affection, especially from women, a craving which has persisted from infancy" (Henry, 1948, p. 898).

These case studies, together with several appendices containing photos, drawings and exam results made *Sex Variants* a desk reference text for the average physician. The volume also featured a "glossary of homosexuality" defining terms for homosexual practices and identities. Words and phrases used by sex variants within their subculture were delineated from those used (usually pejoratively) about homosexuality from outside the subculture. Most of the terms, however, referred to male homosexuality. Learning the native language of the subjects was, in Henry's mind, crucial to deciphering their spoken accounts and to understanding the social context in which homosexuals moved.

FINDINGS

The study's critical finding was that "it is scientifically inaccurate to classify persons as fully male or female. Instead, the attributes of persons should be studied to determine their relative masculinity and femininity" (Henry, 1948, p. 1026). Henry supported this conclusion in his summary, aptly called "Impressions," to acknowledge the tentative and sometimes contradictory findings of the study. There he broadly defined the sex variant as "a person who has failed to achieve and maintain adult heterosexual modes of sexual expression and who has resorted to other modes of sexual expression" (Henry, 1948, p. 1023). Focusing on the evolutionary and historical location of sex variance and implicitly echoing Freud's essay entitled "'Civilized' Sexual Morality and Modern Nervousness" (1908), Henry suggested that the sex variant is a type of person whose emergence is caused by the conditions of modern western culture which emphasizes parental responsibility in raising children properly.... Henry declared that, due to "an immature level of sexual adjustment," the sex variant evaded the cultural requirements of contributing to proper biological and social reproduction (Henry, 1948, p. 1023). However, this was not a matter of rational choice on the part of the sex variant but a result of three factors common to all sex variants: (a) constitutional deficiencies, (b) the influence of family patterns of sexual adjustment, and (c) lack of opportunities for psychosexual development (Henry, 1948, p. 1023).

In summarizing the results of the various methods of inquiry, Henry defined constitutional deficiencies as falling into three categories: structural, physiological and psychological. In the end, he concluded from the battery of tests that structural deficiencies were the least definitive (referring to data gathered from the physical studies of sex variants' bodies) while the psychological deficiencies (referring to data gathered from the psychiatric interviews) were most evident. This meant that physical markings previously attributed to female sex variants finally were not very reliable indicators of these subjects' gender inversion or sexually deviant practices. Instead, psychological, gestural and behavioral tendencies were much more reliable for indicating sex variance....

Reminiscent of theories of sexual inversion, the woman who transgressed her proper gender role of passivity in either the sexual or social realms was presumed to be masculine.

By agreeing to participate in the study the subjects admitted from the outset that they had sexual relations with other women. Therefore, the researchers knew they were looking at and talking to lesbians, and since they assumed a paradigm of sexual inversion, it is not surprising that they "found" masculinity everywhere in the bodies and experiences of these women....

In addition to masculine physical features and mannerisms, attitudes which challenged sexism were identified as evidence of sex variance. For example, the psychiatrist, in introducing Frieda's case states: "From the years of her first comprehension of the difference in standards and in the possibilities of achievement for men and women Frieda has fought constantly to equalize them. She is a thorough feminist with intense sex bitterness. She will take nothing from any man. She will give of herself to a man but only with a feeling of contempt for him" (Henry, 1948, p. 700).

Those tendencies which had greater cultural value—for example, character attributes of independence and assertiveness, as well as mannerisms and postures suggesting self-confidence and determination—were, of course, classified as masculine. By virtue of their association with masculinity, these tendencies were regarded affirmatively in men; however, when they appeared in women, they were considered signs of pathology: "Masculinity in a female may be manifested in aggressive occupations, aggressive attitudes towards society, and thorough intolerance of the personal relationships involved in being a wife and mother" (Henry, 1948, p. 1024).

Henry noted that while various constitutional deficiencies were present to some degree in all persons, they were more evident in the sex variant than in the adult heterosexual. As has often been true of studies of homosexuality, no heterosexual control group was constituted for comparative observation, making an assertion of this sort scientifically invalid. Beyond science, however, the cultural and social problem of homosexuality was complicated by the acknowledgement that adult heterosexuals may indeed be flawed, and for that reason, a somewhat slippery control group. The Sex Variant study aimed to recuperate sex variants from the reputation of willful criminals, but it did not give up the notion that heterosexuality as a system and heterosexuals as individuals would stand for "the normal," in spite of their constitutional deficiencies.

Henry acknowledged that … no single physical trait would definitively identify a sex variant woman. In fact, an individual lesbian might not differ substantially from a heterosexual woman. However, when taken as a group, sex variants displayed certain recognizable morphological patterns. Whenever possible, results of the tests were used to support "the general impression that the sex variant is intermediate between male and female" (Henry, 1948, p. 1034).

… Thus, for Henry, psychotics and sex variants belonged to a class of immature people who had not fully evolved. However, not every test suggested this; the torso-leg ratio measurements and fat distribution of sex variants appeared to be no different from those of the general (i.e., heterosexual) population. Furthermore, not every kind of exam was designed to investigate whether female sex variants had more in common with male sex variants than they did with other women. For example, the gynecological exams were focused specifically on distinguishing normal from abnormal female genitalia, making no comparison at all to male genitalia.

In analyzing the thirty pages of graphic sketches of breasts and genitals, Dr. Dickinson reported on the general genital differences recognizable in the female sex variant population. He identified ten characteristics which he argued set the sex variant apart from "normal women": (1) larger than average vulvas; (2) longer labia minora; (3) "labia minora protrude between the labia majora and are wrinkled, thickened or brawny"; (4) "the prepuce is large and wrinkled or in folds"; (5) the clitoris is "notably erectile" in many cases, with the glans distinctly larger than the average; (6) "eroticism is clearly in evidence on examination, as shown by dusky flush of the parts, with free flow of clear, glairy mucus, and with definite clitoris erection" (thanks to Dr. Moensch); (7) "the hymen is elastic and insensitive, worn or nicked"; (8) "the vagina is distensible"; (9) "the uterus tends to be small, menstruation normal, with cervix catarrh or inflammation absent, save in two cases"; and (10) "the nipple is erectile in two-thirds" (Henry, 1948, p. 1080). Fascinated by the possibility that these characteristics resulted from "sex play" between women but unsure of whether they were congenital or acquired, Dr. Dickinson concluded that

> "[a]ll these findings *can* be the result of strong sex urge [presumably an innate or congenital condition], plus:
>
> (a) Vulvar and vulvovaginal self-friction; or
>
> (b) Homosexual digital or oral play; or
>
> (c) Heterosexual manual or coital techniques, singly, or in any combination. (Henry, 1848, p. 1080)

In short, Dickinson acknowledged that he could not determine the cause of any of these "local findings." This uncertainty did not prevent him from attributing characteristics rather arbitrarily either to heredity or sexual practices.…

Race figured into the gynecological interpretation of sex variance in specific ways. For example, Susan, a black woman, described her "long" clitoris which made her capable of penetrating her female partners when it was "erect." This piece of information captured the imagination of the psychiatrist who focused on this point in his case notes and patient summary. Moensch and Dickinson were also compelled by this self-proclamation and noted the "distended" nature of Susan's clitoris.… Susan's name appeared next to the sketch along with exact measurements of her clitoris. The word "negress" appeared under the sketch. While not all the black subjects were described in this fashion, Pearl, one of the "bisexual cases" was also described as having a long clitoris. In the summaries of the various doctors, the black lesbians' elongated clitoris occupied an analogous position to the common representation of black men as having unusually long penises, signifying an ideological link between blackness and hypersexuality....

PREVENTIVE MEASURES

Since the prevention of sex variance was an express goal of the study, researchers were concerned about determining causation. They questioned the role heredity played in passing on the condition of sex variance. However, Henry concluded that neither heredity nor environmental causes of lesbianism could be determined with precision. Although the case histories included a lengthy portion on family background and Henry noted in his summary of each case how and why family characteristics may have contributed to the constitution of individual sex variants, he concluded that what he called *family patterns* of dominance and submission, of masculinity and femininity "were determined by the degree of masculinity and femininity of the members of the family, regardless of the genital sex of those members" (Henry, 1948, p. 1024).... In sum, the family served as a setting or apparatus for producing sex variants due either to hereditary or socioenvironmental degeneration of proper gender role behavior.

Clearly, in its own terms, the study worked within an evolutionary model like that of social Darwinism, emphasizing progressive evolution ("normal adult heterosexuality") and warning against retrogressive degeneration ("the maladjusted by-product of civilization"). Without being able to prove conclusively whether it was nature or nurture which caused sex variance, Henry asserted "[a] high proportion of masculinity in the females and of femininity in the males of a family is most likely to result in sex variants among the succeeding generations" (Henry, 1948, p. 1024)....

Henry noted that since human beings['] ... drive to reproduce is based on (hetero)sexual desire and not necessarily on what is best for civilization as a whole, we should not be surprised at the existence of "constitutionally predisposed sex variants." The Darwinian laws of natural selection did not exclude the possibility of the birth of a small number of sex variants....

Acknowledging the weakness of evidence used to prove that sex variants and heterosexuals were constitutionally different and that sex variance was clearly hereditary. Henry turned his attention to social strategies of proper parenting and mental hygiene intervention as the best ways to deal with the problem. Distancing himself from a eugenicist approach, he did not make a claim for sterilization of feminine men or masculine women who might contribute to the birth of these flawed creatures; nor did he encourage more biological reproduction by "normal" men and women. Instead, he emphasized the importance of parental influence and proper sex education which would encourage boys to be boys and girls to be girls.... In other words, she should prepare for her proper role as wife *and* mother in the social reproduction of the family....

Many of the female sex variant subjects mentioned that one or both of their parents really wanted a boy. In reporting this fact, both the subjects and the doctors suggest that the desire for a boy either caused the girl to display masculine characteristics to please her parents, or to develop as an "intermediate sex" or "congenital invert" in the womb of her mother who anticipated a son. To prevent these possible causes of sex variance, Henry recommended that parents not only accept but encourage the gender characteristics appropriate to the anatomical sex of their child.

Accordingly, parents were admonished to monitor their children to make sure they are acting properly in terms of their gender.... Since Henry believed that sex variance is caused by a crisis in gender, he saw sex variant sexual activity as merely an *effect* of this crisis. To do away with sex variance, parents and society as a whole must enforce proper gender roles.

The explicit focus of the Sex Variant Study was on homosexuality, but it is clear that this study was also concerned with heterosexuality, particularly its organization and enforcement. In fact, Henry suggested that information gathered about the affectionate relations of sex variants could contribute to the success of heterosexual unions.... In case after case, female sex variants commented on the pleasures of sex with other women that they never experienced with men. This raised the anxiety of the investigators who viewed female sexual autonomy as potentially dangerous and who saw, as a remedy for female sex variance, the development of "how-to" guides to female pleasure written for a male audience. By emphasizing the importance of proper sex education—by which he meant the learning of proper gender behavior—Dr. Henry cast heterosexuality not in terms of a system created and controlled by nature, but as a cultural or social institution that needed to be attended to in order to ensure civilized order....

Echoing many popular commentaries as well as other social scientific studies of homosexuality, Henry implied that sex variance carried a particular appeal or seductive quality. With a growing number of sex variants in society, Henry warned, more people (who would otherwise be heterosexual men and women) will be converted or seduced into homosexuality....

BEYOND THE SCOPE: LIMITS OF GENDER-BASED THEORIES OF HOMOSEXUALITY

The Committee's means of finding truth about the nature of sex variance involved the deployment of a variety of methods which constitute a complex and sometimes unstable apparatus for the production of truth. The research began with the acknowledgement that it was difficult, if not impossible, to determine the specific features of sex variants which distinguished them from the general population. However, the Committee believed that some inquiry into this urban subculture was necessary, so it set out to understand sex variance in terms of the gender categories of masculinity and femininity. Its findings, therefore, reflect a process of identifying and categorizing elements of the experiences and physical characteristics which, in the case of the female sex variants, the researchers took to be masculine.

The study represents a hybrid of approaches, located in a precarious historical and epistemological position between the psychoanalytic "talking cure" spoken first by the subject and then rephrased by the doctor, and a scopic regime which searched for markings of deviance on the body. In some respects, the study seems like a throwback to earlier anatomically based theories common in the latter half of the nineteenth century which were aimed at locating physical evidence of social and psychological deviance (Tardieu, 1857; Martineau, 1885; Lombroso, 1896). Even if ultimately it was unable to determine distinct and visible constitutional features of sex variants, the inclusion of nude photographs, pelvic x-rays, and detailed descriptions of bodies puts the study in the tradition of nineteenth century medicine and criminal anthropology which assumed that if deviance could be "seen," its existence was unquestionable and, therefore, it must be policed.

But the other great source of information in the study was gathered from the individual subjects' accounts of their families, motivations, fears, desires and opinions. Doctors used these stories as a way to look into the lesbian psyche and the homosexual subculture. Through their techniques of observation, these investigators selected and edited the words of the subjects from a perspective which presumed the pathological nature of sex variance. But in the end, the study's initial hypothesis—that one might be able to draw a definite correlation between the subjects' stories and their bodies—ultimately could not be demonstrated.

The very problem of the complex and multiple types of sex variants drove the inquiry in its ambitious undertakings to interpret the bodies and experiences of subjects in terms of the binary system of masculinity and femininity. This approach or paradigm raised particular problems in the research. Specifically it had great difficulty explaining cases where "feminine" women expressed active sexual desire for other women. The study's intense focus on visible evidence of gender inversion, either through describing gestures, postures, skeletons or genitals, followed from the original assumption that sex variance derived initially from the anomalous distribution of gender traits in each of the homosexuals the Committee studied. Lacking a separate analysis of lesbian or homosexual desire, the researchers instead searched minds and bodies for signs of gender.

What are the implications of remaining within a gender-based analytical framework? How can the sexual desire of women for women be understood, if it falls outside the assumptions of what is categorized as masculine or feminine? The search for lesbianism through signs of masculinity exposed the researchers' inability to imagine female sexuality not only separate from men, but also separate from masculinity. For lack of a better description, the researchers used the term "masculine" to describe most of what they saw of this emergent urban lesbian subculture. In elaborating the physical and social traits associated with femininity as well as masculinity, they took part in the construction of a newly reconstructed heterosexual female role for the time. She was a women who had a healthy and moderate sense of sexual passion, expressed normal signs of femininity, was sexually interested in men and would reproduce, together with her husband-companion, a mentally healthy and happy family where the girls were girls and the boys were boys. The lesbian remained and, in many ways still remains, a confounding character in a context where an autonomous female sexuality was literally unthinkable.

REFERENCES

Chauncey, G., Jr. (1983). From sexual inversion to homosexuality: Medicine and the changing conceptualization of female deviance. *Salmagundi* 58–59, 114–146.

Dickinson, R. L. (1932). *A thousand marriages: A medical study of sex adjustment.* Foreword by Havelock Ellis. Baltimore: William and Wilkins.

Ellis, H. (1915). Sexual inversion, 3rd rev. ed., *Studies in the psychology of sex,* vol. 2. Philadelphia: F. A. Davis.

Freud, S. (1908). "Civilized" sexual morality and modern nervousness. In P. Reiff, ed., *Sexuality and the psychology of love* (pp. 20–40). New York: Collier Books, 1963.

Henry, G. W. (1934). Constitutional factors in psychosexual development. *Proceedings of the Association for Research in Nervous and Mental Disease* 14, 287–300.

———. (1941). *Sex variants: A study of homosexual patterns,* vols. 1 and 2. New York: Paul B. Hoeber.

———. (1948). *Sex variants: A study of homosexual patterns* (one-volume ed.). New York: Paul B. Hoeber.

Krafft-Ebing, Richard von. (1908). *Psychopathic sexualis, with especial reference to antipathic sexual instinct.* Trans. F. J. Rebman. Brooklyn: Physicians and Surgeons Book Company.

Lombroso, C., and Ferreor, G. (1895). *The female offender,* ed. W. Douglas Morrison. London: T. Fisher Unwin.

Martineau, L. (1885). *La prostitution clandestine.* Paris.

Tardieu, Ambroise. (1857). *Etude medico-legale sur les attentats aux moeurs.* Paris.

Terman, L. M. (1906). *Genius and stupidity.* New York: Arno Press, 1975.

———. (1916). *The measurement of intelligence.* New York: Arno Press, 1975.

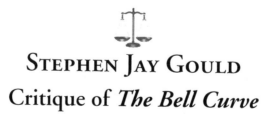

Stephen Jay Gould
Critique of *The Bell Curve*

THE BELL CURVE

The Bell Curve by Richard J. Herrnstein and Charles Murray provides a[n] ... opportunity for insight into the meaning of experiment as a method in science. Reduction of confusing variables is the primary desideratum in all experiments. We bring all the ... confusion of the external world into our laboratories and, holding all else constant, ... try to vary just one potential factor at a time. Often, however, we cannot use such an experimental method, particularly for most social phenomena when importation into the laboratory destroys the subject of our investigation.... If the external world therefore obliges and holds some crucial factors constant for us, then we can only offer thanks for such a natural boost to understanding.

When a book garners as much attention as *The Bell Curve* has received, we wish to know the causes. One might suspect content itself—a startling new idea, or an old suspicion now verified by persuasive data—but the reason might well be social acceptability, or just plain hype. *The Bell Curve* contains no new arguments and presents no compelling data to support its anachronistic social Darwinism. I must therefore conclude that its initial success in winning such attention must reflect the depressing temper of our time—a historical moment of unprecedented ungenerosity, when a mood for slashing social programs can be so abetted by an argument that beneficiaries cannot be aided due to inborn cognitive limits expressed as low IQ scores.

The Bell Curve rests upon two distinctly different but sequential arguments, which together encompass the classical corpus of biological determinism as a social philosophy. The first claim (Chapters 1–12) rehashes the tenets of social Darwinism as originally constituted. ("Social Darwinism" has often been used as a general term for any evolutionary argument about the biological basis of human differences, but the initial meaning referred to a specific theory of class stratification within industrial societies, particularly to the idea that a permanently poor underclass consisting of genetically inferior people had precipitated down into their inevitable fate.)

This social Darwinian half of *The Bell Curve* arises from a paradox of egalitarianism. So long as people remain on top of the social heap by accident of a noble name or parental wealth, and so long as members of despised castes cannot rise whatever their talents, social stratification will not reflect intellectual merit, and brilliance will be distributed across all classes. But if true equality of opportunity can be attained, then smart people rise and the lower classes rigidify by retaining only the intellectually incompetent.

This nineteenth-century argument has attracted a variety of twentieth-century champions, including Stanford psychologist Lewis M. Terman, who imported Binet's original test from France, developed the Stanford-Binet IQ test, and gave a hereditarian interpretation to the results (one that Binet had vigorously rejected); ... and Richard Herrnstein, coauthor of *The Bell Curve.* ... The general claim is neither uninteresting nor illogical, but does require the validity of four shaky premises, all asserted (but hardly discussed or defended) by Herrnstein and Murray. Intelligence, in their formulation, must be depictable as a single number, capable of ranking people in linear order, genetically based, and effectively immutable. If any of these premises are false, the entire argument collapses. For example, if all are true except immutability, then programs for early intervention in education might work to boost IQ permanently, just as a pair of eyeglasses may correct a genetic defect in vision. The central argument of *The Bell Curve* fails because most of the premises are false.

The second claim (Chapters 13–22), the lightning rod for most commentary, extends the argument for innate cognitive stratification by social class to a claim for inherited racial differences in IQ—small for Asian superiority over Caucasian, but large for Caucasians over people of African descent. This argument is as old as the study of race. The last generation's discussion centered upon the sophisticated work of Arthur Jensen (far more elaborate and varied than ... *The Bell Curve,* and therefore ... a better source for grasping the argument and its fallacies) and the cranky advocacy of William Shockley.

The central fallacy in using the substantial heritability of within-group IQ (among whites, for example) as an explanation for average differences between groups (whites vs. blacks, for example) is now well known and acknowledged by all, including Herrnstein and Murray, but deserves a restatement by example. Take a trait far more heritable than anyone has ever claimed for IQ, but politically uncontroversial—body height. Suppose that I measure adult male height in a poor Indian village beset with pervasive nutritional deprivation. Suppose the average height of adult males is 5 feet 6 inches, well below the current American mean of about 5 feet 9 inches. Heritability within the village will be high—meaning that tall fathers (they may average 5 feet 8 inches) tend to have tall sons, while short fathers (5 feet 4 inches on average) tend to have short sons. But high heritability within the village does not mean that better nutrition might not raise average height to 5 feet 10 inches (above the American mean) in a few generations. Similarly the well-documented 15-point average difference in IQ between blacks and whites in America, with substantial heritability of IQ in family lines within each group, permits no conclusion that truly equal opportunity might not raise the black average to equal or surpass the white mean.

Since Herrnstein and Murray know and acknowledge this critique, they must construct an admittedly circumstantial case for attributing most of the black-white mean difference to irrevocable genetics—while properly stressing that the average difference doesn't help at all in judging any particular person because so many individual blacks score above the white mean in IQ. Quite apart from the rhetorical dubriety of this old ploy in a shopworn genre—"some-of-my-best-friends-are-group-x"—Herrnstein and Murray violate fairness by converting a complex case that can only yield agnosticism into a biased brief for permanent and heritable difference. They impose this spin by turning every straw on their side into an oak, while mentioning but downplaying the strong circumstantial case for substantial malleability and little average genetic difference (impressive IQ gains for poor black children adopted into affluent and intellectual homes; average IQ increases in some nations since World War II equal to the entire 15-point difference now separating blacks and whites in America; failure to find any cognitive differences between two cohorts of children born out of wedlock to German women, and raised in Germany as Germans, but fathered by black and white American soldiers).

Disturbing as I find the anachronism of *The Bell Curve,* I am even more distressed by its pervasive disingenuousness. The authors omit facts, misuse statistical methods, and seem unwilling to admit the consequences of their own words.

DISINGENUOUSNESS OF CONTENT

The ocean of publicity that has engulfed *The Bell Curve* has a basis in what Murray and Herrnstein (*New Republic,* October 31, 1994) call "the flashpoint of intelligence as a public topic: the question of genetic differences between the races." And yet, since the day of publication, Murray has been temporizing and denying that race is an important subject in the book at all; instead, he blames the press for unfairly fanning these particular flames. He writes with Herrnstein (who died just a month before publication) in the *New Republic:* "Here is what we hope will be our contribution to the discussion. We put it in italics; if we could we would put it in neon lights: *The answer doesn't much matter.*"

Fair enough in the narrow sense that any individual may be a rarely brilliant member of an averagely dumb group (and therefore not subject to judgment by the group mean), but Murray cannot deny that *The Bell Curve* treats race as one of two major topics, with each given about equal space; nor can he pretend that strongly stated claims about group differences have no political impact in a society obsessed with the meanings and consequences of ethnicity. The very first sentence of *The Bell Curve*'s preface acknowledges equality of treatment for the two subjects of individual and group differences: "This book is about differences in intellectual capacity among people and groups and what these differences mean for America's future." And Murray and Herrnstein's *New Republic* article begins by identifying racial difference as the key subject of interest: "The private dialogue about race in America is far different from the public one."

DISINGENUOUSNESS OF ARGUMENT

The Bell Curve is a rhetorical masterpiece of scientism, and the particular kind of anxiety and obfuscation that numbers impose upon nonprofessional[s].... The book runs to 845 pages, including more than 100 pages of appendices filled with figures. So the text looks complicated, and reviewers shy away with a knee-jerk claim that, while they suspect fallacies of argument, they really cannot judge. So Mickey Kaus writes in the *New Republic* (October 31): "As a lay reader of *The Bell Curve,* I'm unable to judge fairly," as does Leon Wieseltier in the same issue: "Murray, too, is hiding the hardness of his politics behind the hardness of his science. And his science for all I know is soft.... Or so I imagine. I am not a scientist. I know nothing about psychometrics." Or Peter Passell in the *New York Times* (October 27, 1994): "But this reviewer is not a biologist, and will leave the argument to experts."

In fact, *The Bell Curve* is extraordinarily one-dimensional. The book makes no attempt to survey the range of available data, and pays astonishingly little attention to the rich and informative history of this contentious subject.... Virtually all the analysis rests upon a single technique applied to a single set of data—all probably done in one computer run....

The blatant errors and inadequacies of *The Bell Curve* could be picked up by lay reviewers if only they would not let themselves be frightened by numbers—for Herrnstein and Murray do write clearly and their mistakes are both patent and accessible. I would rank the fallacies in two categories: omissions and confusions, and content.

1. *Omissions and confusions:* While disclaiming on his own ability to judge, Mickey Kaus (in the *New Republic*) does correctly identify "the first two claims" that are absolutely essential "to make the pessimistic 'ethnic difference' argument work": "(1) that there is a single, general measure of mental ability; (2) that the IQ tests that purport to measure this ability ... aren't culturally biased."

Nothing in *The Bell Curve* angered me more than the authors' failure to supply any justification for their central claim, the *sine qua non,* of their entire argument: the reality of IQ as a number that measures a real property in the head, the celebrated "general factor" of intelligence (known as *g*) first identified by Charles Spearman in 1904. Murray and Herrnstein simply proclaim that the issue has been decided, as in this passage from their *New Republic* article: "Among the experts, it is by now beyond much technical dispute that there is such a thing as a general factor of cognitive ability on which human beings differ and that this general factor is measured reasonably well by a variety of standardized tests, best of all by IQ tests designed for that purpose."

Such a statement represents extraordinary obfuscation, achieved by defining "expert" as "that group of psychometricians working in the tradition of *g* and its avatar IQ." The authors even admit (pp. 14–19) that three major schools of psychometric interpretation now contend, and that only one supports their view of *g* and IQ—the classicists as championed in *The Bell Curve* ("intelligence as a structure"), the revisionists ("intelligence as information processing"), and the radicals ("the theory of multiple intelligences").

This vital issue cannot be decided, or even understood without discussing the key and only rationale that *g* has maintained since Spearman invented the concept in 1904—factor analysis. The fact that Herrnstein and Murray barely mention the factor analytic argument ... provides a central indictment and illustration of the vacuousness in *The Bell Curve.* How can authors base an eight-hundred-page book on a claim for the reality of IQ as measuring a genuine, and largely genetic, general cognitive ability—and then hardly mention, either pro or con, the theoretical basis for their certainty? Various clichés like "*Hamlet* without the Prince of Denmark" come immediately to mind.

Admittedly, factor analysis is a difficult subject, but it can be explained to lay readers with a geometrical formulation developed by L. L. Thurstone in the 1930s and used by me in Chapter 7 of *The Mismeasure of Man. A* few paragraphs cannot suffice for adequate explanation, so, although I offer some sketchy hints below, readers should not question their own IQ's if the topic still seems arcane.

In brief, a person's performances on various mental tests tend to be positively correlated—that is, if you do well on one kind of test, you tend to do well on the others. This result is scarcely surprising, and is subject to either purely genetic (the innate thing in the head that boosts all scores) or purely environmental interpretation (good books and good childhood nutrition to enhance all performances). Therefore, the positive correlations say nothing in themselves about causes.

Charles Spearman used factor analysis to identify a single axis—which he called *g*—that best identifies the common factor behind positive correlations among the tests. But Thurstone later showed that *g* could be made to disappear by simply rotating the factor axes to different positions. In one rotation, Thurstone placed the axes near the most widely separated of attributes among the tests—thus giving rise to the theory of multiple intelligences (verbal, mathematical, spatial, etc., with no overarching *g*). This theory (the "radical" view in Herrnstein and Murray's classification) has been supported by many prominent psychometricians, including J. P. Guilford in the 1950s, and most prominently today by Howard Gardner. In this perspective, *g* cannot have inherent reality, for *g* emerges in one form of mathematical representation for correlations among tests, and disappears (or at least greatly attenuates) in other forms that are entirely equivalent in amounts of information explained. In any case, one can't grasp the issue at all without a clear exposition of factor analysis—and *The Bell Curve* cops out completely on this central concept.

On Kaus's second theme of "cultural bias," *The Bell Curve*'s presentation matches Arthur Jensen's, and that of other hereditarians, in confusing a technical (and proper) meaning of bias (I call it "S-bias" for "statistical") with the entirely different vernacular concept (I call it "V-bias") that agitates popular debate. All these authors swear up and down (and I agree with them completely) that the tests are not biased—in the statistician's definition. Lack of S-bias means that the same score, when achieved by members of different groups, predicts the same consequence—that is, a black person and a white person with an identical IQ score of 100 will have the same probabilities for doing anything that IQ is supposed to predict....

But V-bias, the source of public concern, embodies an entirely different issue that, unfortunately, uses the same word. The public wants to know whether blacks average 85 and whites 100 because society treats blacks unfairly—that is, whether lower black scores record biases in this social sense. And this crucial question (to which we do not know the answer) cannot be addressed by a demonstration that S-bias doesn't exist (the only issue treated, however correctly, by *The Bell Curve*).

2. *Content:* As stated above, virtually all the data in *The Bell Curve* derive from one analysis—a plotting, by a technique called multiple regression, of the social behaviors that agitate us, such as crime, unemployment, and births out of wedlock (treated as dependent variables), against both IQ and parental socioeconomic status (treated as independent variables). The authors first hold IQ constant and consider the relationship of social behaviors to parental socioeconomic status. They then hold socioeconomic status constant and consider the relationship of the same social behaviors to IQ. In general, they find a higher correlation with IQ than with socioeconomic status; for example, people with low IQ are more likely to drop out of high school than people whose parents have low socioeconomic status.

But such analyses must engage two issues—form *and strength* of the relationship—and Herrnstein and Murray only discuss the issue that seems to support their viewpoint, while virtually ignoring (and in one key passage almost willfully and purposely hiding) the other factor that counts so profoundly against them. Their numerous graphs only present the *form* of the relationships—that is, they draw the regression curves of their variables against IQ and parental socioeconomic status. But, in violation of all statistical norms that I've ever learned, they plot *only* the regression curve and do not show the scatter of variation around the curve, so their graphs show nothing about the *strength* of the relationship—that is, the amount of variation in social factors explained by IQ and socioeconomic status.

Now why would Herrnstein and Murray focus on the form and ignore the strength? Almost all of their relationships are very weak—that is, very little of the variation in social factors can be explained by either IQ or socioeconomic status (even though the form of this small amount tends to lie in their favored direction). In short, IQ is not a major factor in determining variation in nearly all the social factors they study—and their vaunted conclusions thereby collapse, or become so strongly attenuated that their pessimism and conservative social agenda gain no significant support.

Herrnstein and Murray actually admit as much in one crucial passage on page 117, but then they hide the pattern. They write: "It almost always explains less than 20 percent of the variance, to use the statistician's term, usually less than 10 percent and often less than 5 percent. What this means in English is that you cannot predict what a given person will do from his IQ score.... On the other hand, despite the low association at the individual level, large differences in social behavior separate groups of people when the groups differ intellectually on the average." Despite this disclaimer, their remarkable next sentence makes a strong causal claim: "We will argue that intelligence itself, not just its correlation with socioeconomic status, is responsible for these group differences." But a few percent of statistical determination is not equivalent to causal explanation (and correlation does not imply cause in any case, even when correlations are strong—as in the powerful, perfect, positive correlation between my advancing age and the rise of the national debt). Moreover, their case is even worse for their key genetic claims—for they cite heritabilities of about 60 percent for IQ, so you must nearly halve the few percent explained if you want to isolate the strength of genetic determination by their own criteria!

My charge of disingenuousness receives its strongest affirmation in a sentence tucked away on the first page of Appendix 4, page 593, where the authors state: "In the text, we do not refer to the usual measure of goodness of fit for multiple regressions, R^2, but they are presented here for the cross-sectional analysis." Now why would they exclude from the text, and relegate to an appendix that very few people will read or even consult, a number that, by their own admission, is "the usual measure of goodness of fit." I can only conclude that they did not choose to admit in the main text the extreme weakness of their vaunted relationships.

Herrnstein and Murray's correlation coefficients are generally low enough by themselves to inspire lack of confidence. (Correlation coefficients measure the strength of linear relationships between variables; positive values run from 0.0 for no relationship to 1.0 for perfect linear relationship.) Although low figures are not atypical in the social sciences for large surveys involving many variables, most of Herrnstein and Murray's correlations are very weak—often in the 0.2 to 0.4 range. Now, 0.4 may sound respectably strong, but—and now we come to the key point—R^2 is the square of the correlation coefficient, and the square of a number between 0 and 1 is less than the number itself, so a 0.4 correlation yields an r-squared of only 0.16. In Appendix 4, then, we discover that the vast majority of measures for R^2, excluded from the main body of the text, have values less than 0.1. These very low values of R^2 expose the true weakness, in any meaningful vernacular sense, of nearly all the relationships that form the heart of *The Bell Curve*.

DISINGENUOUSNESS OF PROGRAM

Like so many conservative ideologues, ... Herrnstein and Murray claim that they only seek a hearing for unpopular views so that truth will out. And here, for once, I agree entirely. As a card-carrying First Amendment (near) absolutist, I applaud the publication of unpopular views that some people consider dangerous. I am delighted that *The Bell Curve* was written—so that its errors could be exposed, for Herrnstein and Murray are right in pointing out the difference between public and private agendas on race, and we must struggle to make an impact upon the private agendas as well.

But *The Bell Curve* can scarcely be called an academic treatise in social theory and population genetics. The book is a manifesto of conservative ideology, and its sorry and biased treatment of data records the primary purpose—advocacy above all. The text evokes the dreary and scary drumbeat of claims associated with conservative think tanks—reduction or elimination of welfare, ending of affirmative action in schools and workplaces, cessation of Head Start and other forms of preschool education, cutting of programs for slowest learners and application of funds to the gifted....

The penultimate chapter presents an apocalyptic vision of a society with a growing underclass permanently mired in the inevitable sloth of their low IQ's. They will take over our city centers, keep having illegitimate babies (for many are too stupid to practice birth control), commit more crimes, and ultimately require a kind of custodial state, more to keep them in check (and out of our high IQ neighborhoods) than with any hope for an amelioration that low IQ makes impossible in any case. Herrnstein and Murray actually write (p. 526): "In short, by custodial state, we have in mind a high-tech and more lavish version of the Indian reservation for some substantial minority of the nation's population, while the rest of America tries to go about its business."

The final chapter then tries to suggest an alternative, but I have never read anything so feeble.... They yearn romantically for the "good old days" of towns and neighborhoods where all people could be given tasks of value and self-esteem could be found for all steps in the IQ hierarchy (so Forrest Gump might collect the clothing for the church raffle, while Mr. Murray and the other bright folks do the planning and keep the accounts. Have they forgotten about the town Jew and the dwellers on the other side of the tracks in many of these idyllic villages?). I do believe in this concept of neighborhood, and I will fight for its return. I grew up in such a place within that mosaic known as Queens, New York City, but can anyone seriously find solutions (rather than important palliatives) to our social ills therein?

However, if Herrnstein and Murray are wrong about IQ as an immutable thing in the head, with humans graded in a single scale of general capacity, leaving large numbers of custodial incompetents at the bottom, then the model that generates their gloomy vision collapses, and the wonderful variousness of human abilities, properly nurtured, reemerges. We must fight the doctrine of *The Bell Curve* both because it is wrong and because it will, if activated, cut off all possibility of proper nurturance for everyone's intelligence. Of course we cannot all be ... the smartest of the smart, but those who can't might be rock musicians or professional athletes (and gain far more social prestige and salary thereby)—while others will indeed serve by standing and waiting.

I closed Chapter 7 in *The Mismeasure of Man* on the unreality of g and the fallacy of regarding intelligence as a single innate thing-in-the-head (rather than a rough vernacular term for a wondrous panoply of largely independent abilities) with a marvelous quote from John Stuart Mill, well worth repeating ...: "The tendency has always been strong to believe that whatever received a name must be an entity or being, having an independent existence of its own. And if no real entity answering to the name could be found, men did not for that reason suppose that none existed, but imagined that it was something particularly abstruse and mysterious."

How strange that we would let a single false number divide us, when evolution has united all people in the recency of our common ancestry—thus undergirding with a shared humanity that infinite variety which custom can never stale. *E pluribus unum.*

GHOSTS OF BELL CURVES PAST

I don't know whether or not most white men can jump (though I can attest, through long observation, that Larry Bird cannot—but, oh, Lord, could he play basketball). And I don't much care, though I suppose that the subject bears some interest and marginal legitimacy in an alternate framing that avoids such biologically meaningless categories as white and black. Yet I can never give a speech on the subject of human diversity without attracting some variant of this inquiry in the subsequent question period. I hear the "sports version," I suppose, as an acceptable surrogate for what really troubles people of good will (and bad, though for other reasons).

The old days of overt racism did not engender such squeamishness. When the grandfather of modern academic racism, Joseph-Arthur Comte de Gobineau (1816–1882), asked a similar question about the nature of supposedly inborn and unchangeable differences among racial groups, he laid it right on the line. The title of the concluding chapter to Volume 1 of his most influential work, *Essai sur l'inégalité des races humains (Essay on the Inequality of Human*

Races), reads: "Moral and Intellectual Characteristics of the Three Great Varieties." Our concerns have always centered upon smarts and decency, not jumping height and susceptibility to cardiovascular arrest.

And Gobineau left no doubt about his position:

> The idea of an innate and permanent difference in the moral and mental endowments of the various groups of the human species, is one of the most ancient, as well as universally adopted, opinions. With few exceptions, and these mostly in our own times, it has formed the basis of almost all political theories, and has been the fundamental maxim of government of every nation, great or small. The prejudices of country have no other cause; each nation believes in its own superiority over its neighbors, and very often different parts of the same nation regard each other with contempt.

Gobineau was undoubtedly the most influential academic racist of the nineteenth century. His writings strongly affected such intellectuals as Wagner and Nietzsche and inspired a social movement known as Gobinism. Largely through his impact on the English zealot Houston Stewart Chamberlain, Gobineau's ideas served as a foundation for the racial theories espoused by Adolf Hitler. Gobineau, an aristocratic royalist, ... authored several novels and works of historical nonfiction, ... but became most famous for his four-volume work on racial inequality, published between 1853 and 1855.

Gobineau's basic position can be easily summarized: the fate of civilizations is largely determined by racial composition, with decline and fall usually attributable to dilution of pure stocks by interbreeding. ... The white races ... might remain in command, Gobineau hoped, but only if they could be kept relatively free from miscegenation with intellectually and morally inferior stocks of yellows and blacks (Gobineau used these crude terms of color for his three major groups).

No one would doubt the political potency of such ideas, and no one would credit any claim that Gobineau wrote only in the interest of abstract truth, with no agenda of advocacy in mind. Nonetheless, it does no harm to point out that the American translation, published in Philadelphia in 1856, as Dred Scott's case came before the Supreme Court near the brink of our Civil War, surely touched a nerve in perilous times—for Gobineau's distinctive notion of racial purity, and the danger of intermixing, surely struck home in our nation of maximal racial diversity and pervasive inequality, with enslavement of blacks and decimation of Indians. J. C. Nott of Mobile, America's most active popularizer of anthropology in the racist mode, wrote a long appendix to the translation. ... Lest anyone miss the point of local relevance for this European treatise, the translator wrote in his preface:

> The aim [of studying racial differences] is certainly a noble one, and its pursuit cannot be otherwise than instructive to the statesman and historian, and no less so to the general reader. In this country, it is particularly interesting and important, for not only is our immense territory the abode of the three best defined varieties of the human species—the white, the negro, and the Indian—to which the extensive immigration of the Chinese on our Pacific coast is rapidly adding a fourth, but the fusion of diverse nationalities is nowhere more rapid and complete.

Yet Gobineau needed evidence for his claims. ... Therefore, in the last chapter of his work, Gobineau outlines an approach to securing the necessary data for his racism. He begins by telling us how we should *not* frame the argument. We should not, he claims, point to the poor accomplishments of individuals belonging to "inferior races," for such a strategy will backfire as egalitarians search for rare exemplars of high achievement within generally benighted groups. Gobineau begins his final chapter by writing (the quotation is long, and chilling, but well worth the space for its reminder about "certainties" of a not so distant past):

> In the preceding pages, I have endeavored to show that ... the various branches of the human family are distinguished by permanent and ineradicable differences, both mentally and physically. They

are unequal in intellectual capacity, in personal beauty, and in physical strength.... In coming to this conclusion, I have totally eschewed the method which is, unfortunately for the cause of science, too often resorted to by the ethnologists, and which, to say the least of it, is simply ridiculous. The discussion has not rested upon the moral and intellectual worth of isolated individuals.

I shall not even wait for the vindicators of the absolute equality of all races to adduce to me such and such a passage in some missionary's or navigator's journal, wherefrom it appears that some Yolof has become a skillful carpenter, that some Hottentot has made an excellent domestic, that some Caffre plays well on the violin, or that some Bambarra has made very respectable progress in arithmetic.

I am prepared to admit—and to admit without proof—anything of that sort, however remarkable, that may be related of the most degraded savages.... Nay, I go farther than my opponents, and am not in the least disposed to doubt that, among the chiefs of the rude negroes of Africa, there could be found a considerable number of active and vigorous minds, greatly surpassing in fertility of ideas and mental resources the average of our peasantry, and even of some of our middle classes.

... How, then, shall racial status be affirmed if arguments about individuals have no validity? Gobineau states that we must find a measure, preferably imbued with the prestige of mathematics, for average properties of groups: "Once [and] for all, such arguments [about individuals] seem to me unworthy of real science.... Let us leave such puerilities, and compare, not the individuals, but the masses.... This difficult and delicate task cannot be accomplished until the relative position of the whole mass of each race shall have been nicely, and, so to say, mathematically defined."

I was, I confess, prompted to reread Gobineau by the current brouhaha over *The Bell Curve* by Charles Murray and my late colleague Richard Herrnstein—for I recognized that they use exactly the same structure of argument about individuals and groups, though for quite a different purpose, and the disparity within the similarity struck me as eerie. Herrnstein and Murray also claim that average differences in intelligence between racial groups are real and salient (also largely innate and effectively immutable), and they also insist that such group disparities carry no implication for the judgment of individuals. In this way, they hope to avoid a charge of racism and secure a judgment as upholders of human rights—for no black individual, in their view, should be devalued because his group is innately less intelligent than whites; after all, this particular individual may be a rarely brilliant member of his averagely dumb race....

Gobineau wished to separate individual and group judgment because he didn't want the "reality" of group differences to be blurred by the uncharacteristic performance of rare individuals. Herrnstein and Murray make the distinction in a very different political climate; they emphasize the *reality* of individual achievement (rather than its annoying confusion) in order to avoid (fairly enough) the charge of racism while maintaining something quite close to Gobineau's differences in intelligence and the unlikelihood of their erasure. (Please understand that I am not trying to besmirch Herrnstein and Murray by name-calling from the past. I am not attempting to establish my indirect linkage to the Third Reich—and neither can we blame Gobineau for Hitler's extreme usages via Chamberlain. But I am fascinated that structures of ideas can be so similar across the centuries, while thinkers of basically consonant mind emphasize different parts of an entity in the climates of varying times.)

Gobineau, seeking a mathematical basis for group differences in intelligence and morality, was stuck with the crude and direct measures of nineteenth-century racist science—mainly shapes and sizes of skulls and other body parts (for no supposedly "direct" assessment by mental testing had yet been developed).... Gobineau located black destiny in external anatomy....

As measurement of bodies formed the crude and only marginally successful (even in their own terms) devices of scientific racism in the nineteenth century, so has the more sophisticated technology of mental testing—measuring the subtle inside, as it were, rather than the indirect outside—set the basis for most arguments about human inequality in the twentieth century.... (I am not opposed to all forms of mental testing and I certainly do not view the enterprise as inherently racist or devoted to arguing for immutable human differences—for exactly the opposite intention has often been promoted in using tests to measure the improvement that good education can supply.)

However, one particular philosophy of mental testing does undergird most arguments about intellectual differences among human groups made in our century. Moreover, this philosophy does emerge directly from the cruder techniques for measuring bodies that defined the subject in the nineteenth century. In this sense, we may trace continuity from Gobineau to the modern hereditarian theory of IQ. I thought that this philosophy had receded from influence as a joint result of well-exposed fallacies in the general argument and failure of data to validate the essential premises. But Herrnstein and Murray have revived this philosophy in its full and original form in *The Bell Curve*—and we must therefore return to the historical sources of fallacy.

The "Gobinist" version of mental testing—using the enterprise to argue for innate and ineradicable differences in general intelligence among human groups—relies upon four sequential and interrelated premises; each must be true individually (and all the linkages must hold as well), or else the entire edifice collapses:

1. The wonderfully multifarious and multidimensional set of human attributes that we call "intelligence" in the vernacular must all rest upon a single, overarching (or undergirding) factor of general intellectual capacity, usually called *g*, or the general factor of intelligence....

2. The general "amount" of intelligence in each person must be measurable as a single number (usually called "IQ"); a linear ranking of people by IQ must therefore establish a hierarchy of differential intelligence; and, finally (for the social factor in the argument), people's achievements in life, and their social ranks in hierarchies of worth and wealth, must be strongly correlated with their IQ scores.

3. This single number must measure an inborn quality of genetic constitution, highly heritable across generations.

4. A person's IQ score must be stable and permanent—subject to little change ... by any program of social and educational intervention.

In other words, to characterize each of the four arguments in a word or two, human intelligence must be abstractable (as a single number), rankable, highly heritable, and effectively immutable. If any of these assumptions fails, the entire argument and associated political agenda go belly up. For example, if only the fourth premise of immutability is false, then social programs of intense educational remediation may boost, substantially and permanently, an innate and highly heritable disadvantage in IQ just as I may purchase a pair of eyeglasses to correct an entirely inborn and fully heritable defect of vision. (The false equation of "heritable" with "permanent" or "unchangeable" has long acted as a cardinal misconception in this debate.)

I cannot, in this essay, present a full critique of *The Bell Curve*.... I only wish to trace some historical roots and to expose a stunning irony. *The Bell Curve*'s argument about average intelligence among racial groups is no different from and no more supportable than Gobineau's founding version. The major change in methodology and sophistication—from measuring bodies to measuring the content of heads in intelligence testing. But the IQ version relies upon assumptions (the four statements above) as unsupportable as those underpinning the old hierarchies of skull sizes proposed by nineteenth-century participants. In this light, we can gain great insight by revisiting the philosophy and intent of the man who first invented the modern style of mental testing during the first decade of our century—the French psychologist Alfred Binet (who later became the eponym of the test when Stanford professor Lewis M. Terman imported the apparatus to America, developed a local version, and called it the Stanford-Binet IQ test).

I shall show that Binet's intentions sharply contradicted the innatist version, for he believed strongly in educational remediation and explicitly rejected any hereditarian reading of his results.

Ironically, the hereditarian theory of IQ (the imposition of Binet's apparatus upon Gobineau's argument) arose in America, land of liberty and justice for all (but during our most jingoistic period during and following World War I). The exposure of Binet's original intent does not prove him right or the hereditarians wrong.... Rather, Binet is right because his arguments continue to have validity, and the distortion of his wise and humane effort must rank as one of the great tragedies of twentieth-century science.

In 1904, Binet was commissioned by the minister of public education in France to devise a way of identifying children in primary school whose difficulties in normal classrooms suggested some need for special education.... Binet decided on a purely practical approach. He devised a test based upon a hodgepodge of diverse tasks related to everyday problems of life (counting coins, for example) and supposedly involving basic processes of reasoning (logic, ordering, correction) rather than explicitly learned skills like reading. By mixing together enough tests of different attributes, Binet hoped to abstract a child's general potential with a single score. Binet emphasized the rough-and-ready, empirical nature of his test with a dictum: "It matters very little what the tests are so long as they are numerous."

Binet explicitly denied that his test—later called an intelligence quotient (or IQ) when the German psychologist W. Stern scored the results by dividing "mental age" (as ascertained on the test) by chronological age—could be measuring an internal biological property worthy of the name "general intelligence." First of all, Binet believed that the complex and multifarious property called intelligence could not, in principle, be captured by a single number capable of ranking children in a linear hierarchy. He wrote in 1905: "The scale, properly speaking, does not permit the measure of the intelligence because intellectual qualities are not superposable, and therefore cannot be measured as linear surfaces are measured."

Moreover, Binet feared that if teachers read the IQ number as an inflexible inborn quality, rather than (as he intended) a guide for identifying students in need of help, they would use the scores as a cynical excuse for expunging, rather than aiding, troublesome students. Binet wrote of such teachers: "They seem to reason in the following way: 'Here is an excellent opportunity for getting rid of all the children who trouble us,' and without the true critical spirit, they designate all who are unruly, or disinterested in the school." Binet also feared the powerful bias that has since been labeled "self-fulfilling prophecy" or the Pygmalion effect: if teachers are told that a student is inherently uneducable based on misinterpretation of low IQ scores, they will treat the student as unable, thereby encouraging poor performance by their inadequate nurture, rather than the student's inherent nature. Invoking the case then racking France, Binet wrote: "It is really too easy to discover signs of backwardness in an individual when one is forewarned. This would be to operate as the graphologists did who, when Dreyfus was believed to be guilty, discovered in his handwriting signs of a traitor or a spy."

Binet felt that this test could best be used to identify mild forms of retardation or learning disability. Yet even for such specific and serious difficulties, Binet firmly rejected the idea that his test could identify causes of educational problems, particularly their potential basis in biological inheritance. He only wished to identify children with special needs, so that help could be provided:

> Our purpose is to be able to measure the intellectual capacity of a child who is brought to us in order to know whether he is normal or retarded .... We shall neglect his etiology, and we shall make no attempt to distinguish between acquired and congenital [retardation].... We do not attempt to establish or prepare a prognosis, and we leave unanswered the question of whether this retardation is curable, or even improvable. We shall limit ourselves to ascertaining the truth in regard to his present mental state.

Binet avoided any claim about inborn biological limits because he knew that an innatist interpretation (which the test scores didn't warrant in any case) would perversely destroy his aim of helping children with educational problems....

Binet took pleasure in the successes of teachers who did use his tests to identify students and provide needed help. He defended remedial programs and insisted that gains so recorded must be read as genuine increases in intelligence: "It is in this practical sense, the *only* one accessible to us, that we say that the intelligence of these children has been increased. We have increased what constitutes the intelligence of a pupil: the capacity to learn and to assimilate instruction."

How tragic and how ironic! If IQ tests had been consistently used as Binet intended, their results would have been entirely beneficent. But the very innatist and antimeliorist spin that Binet had foreseen and decried did become the dominant interpretation, and Binet's intentions were overturned and inverted. And this reversal—the establishment of the hereditarian theory of IQ—occurred in America, not in elitist Europe. The major importers of Binet's method promoted the biodeterminist version that Binet had opposed—and the results continue to ring falsely in our time as *The Bell Curve.*

Consider the two leading initial promoters of Binet's scale in America. Psychologist H. H. Goddard, who translated Binet's articles into English . . . adopted both the hardline hereditarian view and the argument for intelligence as a single entity:

> Stated in its boldest form, our thesis is that the chief determiner of human conduct is a unitary mental process which we call intelligence: that this process is conditioned by a nervous mechanism which is inborn: that the degree of efficiency to be attained by that nervous mechanism and the consequent grade of intellectual or mental level for each individual is determined by the kind of chromosomes that come together with the union of the germ cells: that it is but little affected by any later influences except such serious accidents as may destroy part of the mechanism.

Lewis M. Terman, who codified IQ for America as the Stanford-Binet test, held the same opinion. . . .

But Binet had supplied all the right arguments in opposition—and his words, even today, can serve as a primer for the scientifically accurate and ethically principled refutation of Herrnstein and Murray's *Bell Curve,* . . . the hereditarian interpretation. Intelligence, Binet told us, cannot be abstracted as a single number. IQ is a helpful device for identifying children in need of aid, not a dictate of inevitable biology. . . .

Why must we follow the fallacious and dichotomous model of pitting a supposedly fixed and inborn biology against the flexibility of training—or nature vs. nurture in the mellifluous pairing of words that so fixes this false opposition in the public mind? . . . [O]ur extensive capacity for educational improvement records a genetic uniqueness vouchsafed only to humans among animals.

I was both heartened and distressed by a recent report in *Newsweek* (October 24, 1994) on a Bronx high school committed to high expectations for disadvantaged students. *Newsweek* reports:

> These 300 black and Latino students provide the basis for a strong retort to "The Bell Curve." Richard Herrnstein and Charles Murray argue that IQ is largely genetic and that low IQ means scant success in society. Therefore, they contend, neither effective schools nor a healthier environment can do much to alter a person's destiny. Yet, at Hostos, reading scores nearly doubled over two years. The dropout rate is low, and attendance is high. About 70 percent of the class of 1989 graduated on time, double the city's average.

Wonderful news, and a fine boost to Binet's original intentions. But I must object to the headline for this report: "In Defiance of Darwin," and to the initial statement: "Today, at 149th Street and the Grand Concourse, a public high school for at-risk children defies Darwin on a daily basis."

Why is Darwin the enemy and impediment? Perhaps *Newsweek* only intended the metaphorical meaning of Darwinism (also a serious misconception) as struggle in a tough world, with most combatants weeded out. But I think that the *Newsweek* editors used "Darwin" as a stand-in for a blinkered view of "biology" —in telling us that this school refutes the idea of fixed genetic limits. Biology is not the enemy of human flexibility, but the source and potentiator (while genetic determinism represents a false theory of biology). Darwinism is not a statement about fixed differences, but the central theory for a discipline—evolutionary biology—that has discovered the sources of human unity in minimal genetic distances among our races and in the geological yesterday of our common origin.

ELISABETH A. LLOYD
Bias in the Science of Evolution

I have reviewed and critiqued all of the evolutionary explanations for female orgasm that I could find. The goal of this [reading] is to draw some more general lessons from the material I've presented [elsewhere]. Are there common causes for the evidential failures I have documented? Is there an explanation for why Symons's hypothesis, with its supporting evidence, has been rejected in favor of hypotheses with fatal statistical problems? To address these questions, I undertake three levels of diagnosis. First, I review some ... evidential problems with evolutionary accounts of female orgasm. Second, I suggest four background assumptions that are playing crucial roles in the production of these evidential problems. Finally, I examine the commitments of ... evolutionary theorists involved in ... debates about female orgasm. I argue that using Helen Longino's account of how scientific communities produce objective scientific results can help us understand what went wrong in this community (and in its analysis of Symons and of Baker and Bellis). In addition, this case serves as a source of good fit for both Longino's and Elizabeth Anderson's models of scientific bias. In contrast, Philip Kitcher's more traditional account (1993) and Miriam Solomon's more psychologistic account (1995) fail to locate what is wrong with these adaptationist accounts. I conclude that the evolutionary community has failed to critically engage a key issue about adaptation because of the varying commitments of different theorists, but I suggest how the situation might be improved.

PROBLEMATIC ASSUMPTIONS

Using minimal standards for evolutionary explanations, I have emphasized that a number of the assumptions made by various practitioners in explaining female orgasm have been undermined or unsupported by readily available empirical evidence. Standard confirmatory evidence for adaptive accounts includes evidence showing that the different values of a trait (in our case, nonorgasm versus orgasm) are associated with fitness differences, evidence that different rates of orgasm have a genetic basis, and evidence showing that the selective regime postulated was really in effect, for instance, that selection pressures pushing the population in a particular direction really exist (Endler 1986; Lauder 1996). That evolutionary adaptive accounts require this evidence has been standard since Darwin (1964; Lloyd 1983). In addition, evidence regarding the description of the trait and how it behaves in various circumstances is relevant to the adequacy of a given account, as is information regarding ... whether evolutionary relatives show the trait ... (... Larson and Losos 1996; Novacek 1996).

Under normal circumstances, not all relevant sorts of evidence will be available, but the evolutionary account will be considered well confirmed to the extent that the various types of relevant evidence available or procurable support its various assumptions and explicit commitments (Lloyd 1988/1994, chap. 8). That the authors considered in this book accept these very general standards of evidence is suggested by their attempts to describe the trait of orgasm by appealing to the sexology literature, and by their efforts to postulate and support various selective pressures. Moreover, the studies I considered were pursued largely in the context of refereed scientific journals or collections.

In summary, evolutionary accounts of a trait must have scientifically defensible assumptions.... If the assumptions of the account are faulty, then the entire evolutionary explanation is threatened. I have documented ... cases in which assumptions that have been contradicted by or unsupported by evidence have been used in evolutionary explanations of female orgasm. Let me summarize the most important of these faulty assumptions here.

1. *The Assumption That Female Orgasm Is Tied to Reproductive Success, and Thus That It Is an Adaptation*

All authors discussed in this book except Symons and Gould make this assumption. It involves an approach to research that assumes that "behavior, even complex social behavior, has evolved and is adaptive" (Barash 1977, p. 8).... The bottom line ... is that no evidence has been offered that links female orgasm to either improved fertility or to increased birth rates or reproductive success. If such evidence were available, it would justify the search for an account of how exactly female orgasm does increase reproductive success. Without it, those who take an adaptationist line are relying on a future promise of such evidence being produced. One alternative is to take the available evidence of wide variability in the trait at face value, and to conclude ... that female orgasm is not an adaptation at all.... [T]his course of action is unlikely to uncover any links that *might* exist between female orgasm and reproductive success. Thus, [some] argue, assuming an adaptationist stance is a more fruitful research program. The problem we are presented with, though, is that 19 adaptive explanations for female orgasm have been advanced in the absence of the crucial evidence that the trait is an adaptation. Because of this lack of crucial evidence, all such adaptationist explanations should be interpreted as proceeding under an unsupported theoretical assumption, that female orgasm is an evolutionary adaptation....

2. *The Assumption That Female Orgasm Should Be Examined Only as It Appears with Intercourse*

This is a tacit assumption.... [R]esearchers treat ... female sexuality as if it is equivalent to reproductive sexuality. The reason that this assumption is a problem is the existence of the orgasm/intercourse discrepancy in women, along with the existence of frequent orgasm outside of intercourse. The alternative is to concentrate on the phenomenon of female orgasm per se, as it appears during intercourse, masturbation, and other sexual activities.

Explaining orgasm as it appears only with intercourse may be especially tempting to adaptationists, because such orgasms are thereby tied at least to the possibility of fertilization, since only intercourse is reproductive sex. But given the gaps orgasmic women show in having orgasm with intercourse, concentrating on orgasms with intercourse necessarily distorts the description of the trait to be explained: since there is no a priori reason to link female orgasm with intercourse, female orgasm *itself* (with or without intercourse) should be the target of evolutionary explanations.

It may look as though the recommendation is to treat female orgasm differently than male orgasm, because the existence of male orgasm is explained evolutionarily only as it relates to intercourse. But the cases are indeed different, which justifies their different treatment; male orgasm is known to be necessary for male reproductive success, while the same is not true for women.

3. *The Assumption That Sexual Intercourse Evokes the Same Response in Men and Women, Namely, Orgasm*

... [I]t is well established in the sexology literature that men and women do not necessarily have the same response to intercourse. There are very substantial numbers of women who do not have orgasm with intercourse on any given occasion, and also a substantial minority that *never* do, even though they are orgasmic. Nevertheless, [many] authors ... assume that sexual intercourse unproblematically yields orgasm for both men and women. What is most peculiar about these authors is their ritual citation of the sex literature, despite the fact that the very results cited show exactly the discrepancy they ignore.

Some authors recognize that there is a problem in treating both male and female orgasm as straightforward results of intercourse, but the situation is mischaracterized. Morris, for example, claims that women take longer to reach orgasm during intercourse—a phenomenon that he describes as "strange"—but claims that women generally have orgasm with a long enough period of intercourse. But the evidence from the sexology literature shows that this is not exactly so. Beyond a certain point, women are unlikely to have orgasm, no matter how much longer intercourse proceeds. Hrdy's account is subject to the same problem. Taken in combination with the evidence that men and women take equal amounts of time to reach orgasm during masturbation, this gives additional reason to treat the evolution of female orgasm itself as separate from orgasm with intercourse.

Allen and Lemmon take an entirely different approach to the fact that men and women often have different responses to intercourse. They acknowledge the orgasm/intercourse discrepancy, but claim that in the past women (with modern genitalia) *did* have frequent and reliable orgasm with intercourse. In doing so they go against all of the sexology literature that says that women's lack of orgasm during intercourse is due to inadequate stimulation because of the physiological mechanics of the situation. Rather than arguing against these findings, which contradict their claim, they simply ignore them.

Finally, I should mention one possible source of confusion regarding the reliability of female orgasm with intercourse. It seems possible that several authors, most prominently Morris and Sherfey, were misled by Masters and Johnson's account of *how* female orgasm occurs during intercourse, when it does, to a conclusion that female orgasm unproblematically occurs during intercourse. Such confusion, while understandable, still ignores the sizable amount of evidence, available at the time, that orgasm does not occur regularly during intercourse for nearly half of women surveyed, and occurred reliably in only 25 [percent].

4. *The Assumption That Female Sexual Response Is Like Male Sexual Response, More Generally*

In addition to the assumption that women routinely have orgasm with intercourse the way that men do, we find instances in which females are assumed to respond like males in other ways. For example, Morris claims that in females there is a rapid reversal of the physiological changes associated with sexual excitement. This is precisely what Masters and Johnson documented is not so. It is especially noteworthy that Morris bases much of his description of female sexual response exactly on Masters and Johnson's work, while failing to take their relevant evidence against his claim into account.

Similarly, Gallup and Suarez claim that there is a strong tendency to sleep following female orgasm. But the evidence they offer applies to male orgasm only, and they disregard or are unaware of prominent evidence that females often have tendencies to wakefulness and continued states of arousal after orgasm. In each of these cases, counterevidence to the authors' claims is ignored, although it was contained in the very sources they cite.

5. *The Assumption That Female Sexual Interest or Response Is Dictated by Hormones in Prehominids or Early Hominids*

There is an assumption shared by a number of authors ... that the loss of an estrus period in early hominids or prehominids necessitated the evolutionary construction of another motivation for the female to engage in intercourse, namely, female orgasm. These researchers all assume that there was a radical break between hominids and our more distant ancestors, that the hominid females were no longer subject to hormonal dictation of their sexual behavior. The evidential problem with this assumption is that it had already been shown that for nonhuman primates the hormonal cycle did not dictate sexual behavior....

Another related assumption made by Crook, Eibl-Eibesfeldt, and Barash is that "continuous receptivity" is linked to hominid monogamous pair bonding. Again, relevant evidence against this assumption comes from nonhuman primate data showing some continuous receptivity in species that are not monogamous. In each of these cases, relevant and available evidence from nonhuman primates was ignored.

6. *The Assumption That Female Nonhuman Primates Do Not Have Orgasm and Therefore That Orgasm Is a Uniquely Human Trait*

Morris, Barash, Campbell, and Hamburg all make this assumption, while Beach says that nonhuman primate female orgasms are rare and insignificant. Even Symons, although he reviews some of the evidence for nonhuman female orgasm, declares it unimportant. But there is good evidence that nonhuman female primates show the physiological manifestations of orgasm; some of the evidence comes from hard wiring, some from direct human manipulation, and some from close observation. Before 1970, only anecdotal accounts were available; thus Morris and Campbell should not be faulted for discounting the possibility of nonhuman female orgasm. The other authors, however, are vulnerable to criticism because they ignored or discounted such evidence. In fact, given the development of even better evidence in the 1980s and 1990s, current evaluation of any hypothesis must take this material into account. This turns out to be especially important with regard to recent evaluation of Symons's account, which is actually supported by this later evidence.

There is a persistent peculiarity in the evidence for nonhuman female orgasm: that most of the recorded and observed orgasms occurred in sexual contact with other females, and not during copulation. This leads me to the next problem.

7. *The Assumption That Evidence for Female Orgasm When One Female Mounts Another Counts as Evidence That Female Orgasm Occurs during Heterosexual Copulation*

... Several of the authors who originally documented cases of female orgasm in the stumptail macaque during female-female encounters went to great lengths to argue that it followed that orgasms also occurred during heterosexual copulation on a regular basis. Goldfoot and colleagues concluded that a minority of stumptail females had orgasm during heterosexual copulation, yet Chevalier-Skolnikoff and Slob and van der Werff ten Bosch argue for the existence of frequent orgasm during intercourse in contradiction to the evidence they offer. They seem to be committed to the prior view that females have the same response to intercourse that the males do.

In all of this work there is a blatant use of two different standards of evidence for female orgasm. Vague, incomplete, or unrepresentative evidence is used to show that most female responses to copulation are orgasmic, in contrast to the patent and straightforward evidence that orgasm occurs during female-female mounting. Slob and van der Werff ten Bosch, for example, present an especially egregious case of special pleading; they introduce a new standard of evidence for female orgasm in order to claim that "female sexual climax may occur during every copulation" (1991, p. 143). And the standard of evidence for female orgasm that Goldfoot and colleagues use is applied rigorously by Slob and van der Werff ten Bosch only in cases of female-female sexual encounters.

This evidential double standard involves a basic belief that the "natural" place for female orgasm is in heterosexual copulation; hence, any evidence for orgasm itself is also ipso facto evidence for orgasm in its "natural" place. This is related to assumption 2, above, that female orgasm should be explained primarily as it relates to intercourse. The problem is that the evidence does not justify this inference. Only direct evidence of female orgasm during intercourse should be used to infer that female nonhuman primates have orgasm during intercourse.

8. *The Assumption That Female Orgasm Induces a Sucking Motion of the Uterus*

Both the Baker and Bellis and the Thornhill and colleagues sperm-competition hypotheses for female orgasm explicitly motivate their views by appealing to evidence for uterine upsuck offered by Fox and colleagues (1970) and Singer (1973). … Evidence for the upsuck hypothesis is ambiguous at best. While Singer is often cited as offering evidence for the upsuck hypothesis, he offers an interpretation only, and no evidence. Thus the only evidence in favor of the upsuck hypothesis is the two trials done on one woman by Fox and colleagues. This is countered by evidence against upsuck from six subjects in research by Masters and Johnson (1966) and an unknown number of subjects in the study by Grafenberg (1950). Neither the Baker and Bellis nor the Thornhill and colleagues studies offers statistically sound evidence for the phenomenon of upsuck. Moreover, even if it actually exists, the existence of uterine upsuck, by itself, would be insufficient to establish a correlation between either fertility or reproductive success and female orgasm.

OPERATIVE BACKGROUND ASSUMPTIONS

Is there something that led these researchers to make such inappropriate assumptions, ones that have serious evidential problems, or is this merely a story about a scientific community working out a research problem over a period of 30-odd years? I think this is patently a story of scientific dysfunction, and I make my case in what follows. I would like to suggest that there are four basic background assumptions in operation that led most investigators either to neglect evidence that was there, to misinterpret evidence, to assume evidence correlating fitness with orgasm was adequate, or to assume that such evidence existed. These assumptions are: adaptationism, androcentrism, procreative focus, and human uniqueness.

Adaptationism

The most visible background assumption, operating in 20 of the 21 explanations of female orgasm that I have examined, is that of adaptationism. Here, adaptationism involves the presupposition that a trait that evolved served a particular adaptive function for the organism, and that is why it is present in the population. In other words, adaptationists assume that natural selection, rather than other evolutionary forces, directly shaped the trait into its present form, or that natural selection is currently maintaining the trait in the population, and that the explanatory challenge is to discover how. In the case of the female orgasm, the questions become: What selection pressures led to the current form of female orgasm? What is it an adaptation for? What contribution to reproductive success does orgasm make?

But there is a live alternative—Symons's—to the assumption that female orgasm is an adaptation, and thus orgasm's adaptive status cannot be taken for granted without evidence. As emphasized throughout the book, relevant evidence is lacking, which makes adaptationism about female orgasm an unsupported theoretical presupposition. Nevertheless, researchers routinely assume that female orgasm is in fact an adaptation, because they are operating within a theoretical framework in which most interesting traits are assumed to be adaptations. This sets their research agenda....

To fully appreciate what's going on here we need to examine the ideas [underlying] adaptationism in more detail. Let us consider first the research program of adaptationism. [It] involves starting an investigation into a trait by working under the ... assumption that female orgasm is an adaptation to some selection pressure. Investigation ... [measures] the differences in reproductive success owed to different values or manifestations of the trait, locating a genetic basis, or at least heritability, of the variants of the trait, pursuing an engineering analysis of the trait that shows that it is effective for coping with the selection pressure, and documenting that the selection pressure really did exist in the past and continues to do so today.... There are disagreements among researchers concerning which of these or other tasks are most important.... But all of these approaches begin with the working hypothesis that the trait is, indeed, a special adaptation to help its owner cope with selection pressures.

What happens, though, when the engineering analyses do not work out, or when the trait seems to be inefficient at doing its proposed job? This seems to be a matter of judgment. One alternative is to start over, with the assumption that the trait really is an adaptation, but one where we haven't figured out correctly what it is an adaptation for. This move runs the risk of turning the enterprise into one in which traits are always seen as adaptations, even when they may not be. But Williams defends the ad hoc reasons that adaptationists give for their failed predictions, and insists that it has been fruitful—he cites two vivid cases—to resist giving up on the thesis that a specific trait is, in fact, an adaptation (1985, p. 18). The problem is that this seems to lead in the direction of a methodological rule that *all* traits should be considered adaptations at the end of the analysis. It's a matter of not taking no for an answer. But this violates the larger commitment in evolutionary theory to the effect that factors other than natural selection can cause evolutionary change, and that there are important and live alternatives to thinking that all traits are adaptations (Ridley 1996, p. 341). The concern is that if one is doggedly following the thought that a trait is an adaptation, one might miss alternate explanations based on development or correlated characters that are, in some cases, correct. Even to the most careful of adaptationists, it is a judgment call when to countenance alternative explanations.

We can use this issue to sort out various kinds of adaptationists.... One type, which I have called the conservative adaptationists, pursues the various components of adaptationist research and, if an attractive and reasonable nonadaptationist explanation is proposed, is willing to consider it seriously as an alternative. The group that I've called the cavalier adaptationists differ from the conservative adaptationists by avoiding part of adaptationist research, the part in which the different values of a trait are demonstrated to go along with fitness differences. Nearly all of the adaptationist hypotheses [I consider here] are of this type.

The final type of adaptationists I identified was the ardent variety. They describe themselves as ardently pursuing the adaptationist program. This would suggest, correctly, that they attempt to find adaptive explanations for nearly all traits, and that they are generally unwilling to countenance nonadaptive alternative explanations. But this just seems to be a matter of degree; they are less willing than some adaptationists to consider alternative explanations. This formulation of their position is deceptive, however. I shall spell out exactly what the ardent adaptationists' position is in the next section.

For my purposes here, it is enough to note that the cavalier adaptationists avoid a crucial component of the adaptationist research program[;] ... they do not research whether or not the trait of female orgasm is significant for reproductive success; they simply assume that it is. Thus they become oblivious of evidence that it might not be, and are unconcerned about the lack of evidence that this trait makes any difference to reproductive success....

There is, however, also a slightly more dangerous element that arises with all sorts of adaptationism, and that is that grossly deficient evidence can be used to justify an adaptationist account. Thus we have Alcock and many others accepting the conclusions of Baker and Bellis and Thornhill and colleagues, evidently without having ever critically examined the papers in question.... The researchers were committed to orgasm's being an adaptation of some kind, and were apparently overeager to find a scenario that supported this view....

Androcentrism

Androcentrism involves looking at things from an exclusively male point of view, and subsequently neglecting a distinct treatment of a female point of view (Longino 1990, p. 129). With androcentrism, males are taken to be the normal type or the exemplar, while to the extent that they differ from the male type, females are invisible. In the present case androcentrism is implicated in the assumption that female sexuality is like male sexuality in all its essentials, and the result is the concomitant disappearance of an autonomous female sexuality. There are many ways in which female sexuality is, according to the best research, like male sexuality, and in these contexts androcentrism does no harm. But in the cases in which female sexuality differs from that of the male, the background assumption that the male is the normal type tends to obscure important evidence of differences.... [I]t turns out that these differences are significant for an accurate evolutionary account.

Androcentrism can be seen in the assumption that intercourse evokes the same response in males and females, namely orgasm. As a generalization, this is clearly false on all the available evidence, yet this assumption appears in numerous adaptive accounts of female orgasm. It amounts to a neglect of an autonomous female sexuality that is distinct from the male pattern. The same is true of the general assumption that females respond in the same ways as males to sexual activity, again an assumption easily shown to be false by the available evidence. In both of these cases, as soon as the evidence from sexological studies is examined, the differences between male and female responses become clear....

Procreative Focus

Procreative focus involves the assumption that all evolutionarily significant sex is procreative sex. This background assumption encourages looking at female sexuality exclusively by focusing on heterosexual intercourse. It is easy to see how this basic approach complements an adaptationist approach: if female orgasm is an adaptation, it must be correlated somehow with increased reproductive success for the female who possesses it. Reproductive success is naturally linked to reproductive sex (heterosexual intercourse); thus it seems natural to think that intercourse is the evolutionarily *important* kind of sex. There are elements of androcentrism and heterosexual bias operating in procreative focus as it applies to female orgasm, because procreative focus concentrates only on the kind of sex that is reliably associated with male reproductive success: intercourse. Thus both adaptationist and androcentric background assumptions contribute to a procreative focus. But heterosexist bias makes procreative focus distinct from a simple adaptationist bias.

Heterosexist bias may be particularly important in considering female orgasm. Both the macaques and the bonobo females have a fair amount of homosexual sex (around half of all female bonobo sexual encounters involve sex with other females). In the bonobos, this is considered to be a form of friendship or coalition building, which can have a profound effect on male behavior (Wrangham and Peterson 1996, pp. 208–210, 227). Thus there may be a fitness advantage in having homosexual sex, and if so, that would make the heterosexist bias a particularly pernicious bias.

Procreative focus promotes the presence of a couple of the evidentially problematic assumptions I have discussed. The assumption that female orgasm should be examined only as it appears with intercourse is a clear example of focusing only on procreative sex. The result is to treat female sexuality as if it is equivalent to reproductive sexuality, in the face of evidence to the contrary.... In addition, a procreative bias was certainly in play when the primatologists assumed, against their own evidence, that the incidence of female orgasm in nonhuman primates indicates widespread copulatory orgasms in these animals. The authors seem to find it difficult to imagine that female orgasm might be disengaged from the occurrence of reproductive sex. Thus they strain to produce arguments that female orgasm occurs during intercourse, even when it is not observed to do so.

Finally, some sort of procreative background assumption was at work when female orgasm was taken to induce a sucking motion of the uterus, despite the deficiencies of evidence adduced in its support. In this case, an adaptationist background assumption was also involved, since there seemed to be a certain desire to attach female orgasm to something that might affect reproductive success.

Human Uniqueness

The final background assumption consists in assuming that human beings are unique in the animal world. There is a strong tendency among some researchers to emphasize the gap between the human lineages and those of our closest relatives. This shows in the assumption of the human uniqueness of various traits, including aspects of female sexuality. For example, take the assumption that female sexual interest or response is dictated by hormones in prehominids or early hominids. Here, both our ancestors and nonhuman primates are taken to be significantly different from modern human beings, whose sexual activity may be affected but is not dictated by hormonal activity. There is a sharp line drawn between full-fledged hominids and others, based on the supposed differences in hormonal control of female sexuality. But the evidence indicates that the situation is much more fluid than this, and that, in fact, some nonhuman primates may be more like modern human beings in the lack of hormonal dictation of their sexual behavior.

The Deepest Problems

The background assumption of human uniqueness has tended recently to be out of play, and will not be discussed further. Procreative focus involves both adaptationism and androcentrism, and I shall proceed by exploring these latter two background assumptions. According to my analysis, some of the evidential problems in proposing and evaluating evolutionary explanations of female orgasm arise out of a background assumption of androcentrism. (Note that I am assuming throughout that commitment to a background assumption may not be the result of conscious deliberation.) In these cases, which involve not treating female sexuality as autonomous from either male sexuality or reproduction, it can seem sensible to focus on reproductive sexuality as the basis for understanding female sexuality. After all, the intuition goes, what is sexuality for beyond the fundamental function of reproduction? There is much intuitive support for the notion that evolutionary changes in female sexuality *must* be related to increases in the reproductive fitness of those females exhibiting the changes. The problem is that the evolutionary explanations created using this strong intuition have failed to track what is independently known about female sexuality. Female sexuality, particularly female orgasm, does not seem to follow this line of reasoning when taken from the intuitive standpoint that female sexuality evolved in tight concert with reproductive success. Once we add the sexology literature as a basis of evidence, it is easily seen that crucial aspects of female orgasm are being omitted from the androcentric evolutionary pictures. Such evidence demands an account of female orgasm that is autonomous and distinct from both male sexuality and reproductive sexuality.

Perversely, the only available explanation for female orgasm that does make it independent of both male sexuality and reproductive sexuality has been repudiated for being androcentric. Again, it is easy to see how this happened. The by-product account appears, at first glance, to preclude the possibility of an autonomous female sexuality because of its emphasis on the common embryological origins of human males and females and on the selection pressures on male orgasm. But interestingly, the by-product view severs the links between adult female sexuality and reproductive sex. It fully acknowledges and in fact accounts for the very features of female orgasm that the androcentric accounts ignore or attempt to explain away. Thus in my view this is the evolutionary account with the closest ties to the feminist value of separating definitions of women—including women's sexuality—from women's reproductive functions. It is also an evolutionary view that avoids the errors of assuming that female response is like male response both during intercourse and more generally. Thus it avoids all of the evidential problems produced by androcentric values that appear in many of the other available explanations.

It seems that, ultimately, the vision of female orgasm in the by-product view is considered androcentric precisely because a trait must be an adaptation itself in order to be considered genuinely culturally valuable. But this does not follow. Such a requirement would require accepting an extreme sort of adaptationism, and feminists have no independent reason—including any political reason—for buying the equation between adaptation and cultural significance. Feminists do maintain an interest, however, in continuing to fight for definitions of women that are not based on their reproductive roles. Hence, I conclude that in the feminist objections to the by-product theory a nonfeminist value placed on adaptation has superseded, without a good reason, a legitimate feminist value placed on separating women from their definition in terms of reproductive role.

Let me be very clear about this. I am not claiming that I prefer the by-product hypothesis on the basis of any social value, nor am I suggesting that anyone else do so. Nevertheless, Longino has emphasized that social values may, in particular cases, "have a positive role in grounding criticism of background assumptions and in fostering the development of empirical investigation in directions it would not otherwise go" (2002, p. 51). Hence, if—and I must emphasize the "if" here—social values do play a role in the full evaluation of the hypotheses and background assumptions under question, surely feminist values would be more in tune with the by-product account, given its separation of female orgasm from the function of reproduction. However, I prefer the by-product account primarily because it is supported by overwhelmingly better evidence....

The other major source of evidential problems in the evolutionary explanations I have examined is the background assumption of adaptationism. Thus two overarching and tightly interwoven kinds of background assumption have played the major roles in constructing and evaluating evolutionary explanations of female orgasm: androcentrism and adaptationism. The androcentric themes are intimately entwined with the adaptationist ones. Once we are looking for an explanation that ties female orgasm to reproductive success, we are ... inexorably driven into procreative and androcentric biases. The one explicitly feminist explanation, Hrdy's, still contains a procreative focus that leads her, it seems, into a misunderstanding of the sexology evidence about female orgasm. Of the other early accounts, only a few, such as Alcock's, Rancour-Laferriere's, and Bernds and Barash's, escape overt androcentrism, and these fail to provide the necessary supporting evidence for their hypotheses. In all of the other cases, adaptationism and androcentrism push the explanations toward an exclusive focus on female orgasm with intercourse, thus bypassing the very data that suggest that an explanation of female orgasm independent from intercourse may serve as the best evolutionary approach. The result is a shared set of androcentric and adaptationist background assumptions, which lead, I have argued, to the sorts of unacceptable treatment of evidence described here.

So, where are we now? I first reviewed assumptions in the evolutionary explanations that conflict with one or another body of evidence relevant to the evolution of female orgasm. I have now tried to isolate a set of overarching background assumptions that could be used to motivate, defend, or justify those faulty assumptions. I conclude that because they neglect or mistreat empirical evidence these four background assumptions are operating as pernicious or damaging biases in the pursuit of the explanation of female orgasm. A traditional approach to bias, as exemplified by the logical positivists, for example, poses bias as a systematic deviation from the normal methods for ensuring the objectivity of scientific results (Carnap 1962; Laudan 1984; Richardson 1984; Geertz 1990; Haack 1993; Sober 1993; Gross and Levitt 1994; Reichenbach 1966). Under this view, systematic deviations from objective rules are explained by thinking that scientific reasoning includes considerations that are irrelevant to the truth of theories or claims. This is hypothesized to occur especially because theories accord with preconceptions and special interests of human investigators.

One could argue that androcentrism embodies exactly the sort of bias rejected on this traditional account. But such a view turns a blind eye to how such biases are detected and corrected. Social values are involved in applying a corrective feminist view, which later helps eliminate androcentric bias. Thus it seems as if using social values in evaluating science is a good thing that contributes to the objectivity of scientific findings. But this conclusion is usually denied by those using the traditional approach, who separate the process by which bias is uncovered from the end result of reducing bias (Gross and Levitt 1994). Thus androcentrism could be accounted for by using this traditional approach to bias.

But the traditional approach would not be adequate for the present case study, in which adaptationism also plays a biasing role. Adaptationism does not embody the sort of social bias that is rejected on the traditional account. It is part of a legitimate research approach in evolutionary biology, and does not seem to incorporate social bias in the way that androcentrism does (Rose and Lauder 1996). In fact, the evidential standards for demonstrating that a trait is an adaptation are well worked out and quite strict.... The fact that adaptationism appears to be a problem in this case study suggests that the practices within evolutionary biology bear a closer look. This involves a contextual approach to science, a set of views developed to deal with the shortcomings of the traditional account.

So far, it looks as if background assumptions are themselves a bad thing for science. But philosophers of science have long argued that background assumptions are inevitable in science, and necessary to it. If this is right, then the real question becomes: How are we to adjudicate between background assumptions that are beneficial for scientific practice and those that are not?

No argument [here] is intended to establish that adaptationism and even androcentrism always lead by themselves to inadequate science. It is likely that much good science could be done with some of these background assumptions in the form of social or theoretical values in place. What I am considering is rather whether adaptationism and androcentrism have had a destructive effect on the discussion of the evolution of female orgasm, in particular. Judgments about whether particular background assumptions are damaging must be made on a case-by-case basis. What I have presented is a particular case in which both androcentrism and adaptationism have led to inadequate science judged at the most basic level of evidential support.

SCIENCE AND BACKGROUND ASSUMPTIONS

The operating assumption so far in this chapter has been that there is some neutral set of data to which a theory must be accountable. But this position is philosophically naive. Questions of adequacy to the data involve issues concerning which data a theory ought to be accountable to, which in turn involve a much larger vision of both how science actually works and how it should work (Longino 1995, p. 394). For the rest of this [reading] I shall make use of Helen Longino's well-developed framework for how science does and ought to work. According to Longino, "commitment to one or another model [theory] is strongly influenced by values or other contextual features. The models themselves determine the relevance and interpretation of data" (1990, p. 189). In this particular case, I would argue that the sexology literature is treated as a source of data to which all parties appeal in the debate about the evolution of female orgasm. Nevertheless, we need to explore further the relations between hypothesis and data. How, exactly, do background assumptions influence the choice of theories, and what effect does this have on the treatment of evidence? Can we glean any answers to such questions from the present case study?

According to Longino, the subjects of investigation are constructed, not simply given by nature. Any inquiry, she writes, "must characterize its subject matter at the outset in ways that make certain kinds of explanation appropriate and others inappropriate. This characterization occurs in the very framing of questions" (1990, p. 98). In the present case, inquiry into the evolutionary origins of female orgasm requires an evolutionary answer. But the situation is more complicated than that. Specification of the subject of investigation can depend in turn on the needs and interests of the questioners (Anderson 1995, pp. 44–46). For example, those following an adaptationist approach may frame the question: What is the evolutionary function of female orgasm? Or: What selection pressures led to the current form of female orgasm? Others, not following an adaptationist program, may ask a broader question: What accounts for the evolution of female orgasm? Thus background assumptions and values can play a role in specifying the very object of inquiry.

Longino offers a careful analysis of the role of background assumptions in evaluating evidence, and sees their role in science as inevitable. The most fundamental aspect of the relation between data and hypothesis is that it is flexible and changeable. The basic problem is that states of affairs (data and observations) do not tell us what they are evidence for. The same data can be thought of as evidence for two separate hypotheses, or for one hypothesis for two different reasons. This is a well-established result in philosophy of science, the underdetermination of hypotheses by evidence. In order to link particular data to a particular hypothesis, additional assumptions need to be brought in concerning the evidential relation between facts and hypotheses. Thus the evidential relevance of hypotheses to observations or experiments is a function of the background assumptions that help drive the inference. Thus, technically, we have only "data" until background assumptions make it "evidence" for or against a particular hypothesis.

Background assumptions can be of many sorts. Oftentimes they are simply assumptions about what there is in the world; sometimes they are simple inductive rules. But often they are more substantive than this, and they may bring in social and individual values, interests, and subjective preferences (Longino 1990, p. 48). Such preferences and values can be seen as a source of the biases that appear in the proposal of hypotheses and in their evaluation....

I want to approach my case study by couching the biases I've outlined in terms of their being background assumptions. I am still left, however, with the difficult task of discriminating background assumptions that are negative for science from those that are beneficial or neutral. Intuitively, the result here should be that androcentrism, adaptationism, procreative focus, and human uniqueness serve as pernicious background assumptions or biases, in these particular cases of scientific reasoning. Intuitively, an illustration of a beneficial background assumption will help. One higher-level background assumption important to this research is the assumption that not every biological character is adaptive—that there exist alternative evolutionary explanations available, such as evolutionary developmental accounts or accounts that cite correlations of growth.... This is a background assumption of evolutionary biology quite generally, and it is clearly relevant to the case of female orgasm. What we have to watch, though, is whether this assumption is actually engaged when researchers are arguing about whether female orgasm is an adaptation or not. There is an important difference between paying lip service to the view that there could be acceptable alternative explanations for a trait, and actually using this assumption when reasoning about a specific trait. As I shall argue below, there are adaptationists in the female orgasm debate who seem to find any explanation under which female orgasm is not considered an adaptation unacceptable, despite the fact that nonadaptive traits are one important possibility in evolutionary theory....

One approach to picking beneficial assumptions from those that are not has been offered by Elizabeth Anderson, in an expansion of Longino's work. Alvin Goldman and Philip Kitcher treat bias as a "kind of self-interested motivation that certain things be true rather than others" (Longino 2002, p. 166; see the citations to other traditional approaches). Longino's and Anderson's approach, in contrast, expands the role of biases to include background assumptions, which can be treated as potentially negative (but also potentially positive) biases. According to Anderson, pernicious bias is a failure of impartiality. Miriam Solomon treats bias as a descriptive concept. In her psychologistic view, a bias is anything that focuses attention or inclines belief in a certain direction. Biases, on Solomon's view, are productive; therefore there is no drive to eliminate bias (1995; 2001). The position taken [here] is normative rather than descriptive, and finds that certain biases can have a negative impact on scientific inquiry (see the discussion in Longino 2002, pp. 165–167). We can take Anderson to be defining when a background assumption has a damaging effect on the science.

When it comes to scientific inquiry, impartiality must be related to the specific goals of a particular inquiry, to the scientific question being asked: in my case, by what means did women evolve to be orgasmic? Like Longino, Anderson notes: "All inquiry begins with a question. Questions direct inquiry by defining what is to count as a significant fact and what is a complete or adequate account of a phenomenon" (1995, p. 42). She continues: "What counts as a significant truth is any truth that bears on the answer to the question being posed. The whole truth consists of all the truths that bear on the answer, or, more feasibly, it consists of a representative enough sample of such truths that the addition of the rest would not make the answer turn out differently" (1995, pp. 39–40).

According to Anderson, impartiality or lack of pernicious bias demands attention to all facets of available empirical data, including those that weigh background assumptions. In particular, impartiality requires taking into account data that support alternative hypotheses, or that are inconsistent with one's assumptions.... Anderson's view implies that both relevance and representativeness of data are legitimate criteria on the basis of which to choose theories.

What we have, in many of the explanations ... reviewed [here], is a failure of impartiality. Most frequently, data that bear on the question being posed have been either ignored or misrepresented in the suggested accounts of the evolution of female orgasm.... [T]his is partial science according to Anderson, and can be critiqued for being biased in a destructive way....

The discussion has so far been concerned with how to evaluate particular background assumptions in relation to a specific set of evidence. But I now turn to criteria of the capacity of a community to produce objective scientific inquiry that is based on how the community as a whole interacts. This community approach has the advantage of moving the focus away from individual idiosyncrasy, and instead focuses on communitywide standards of investigation. This will help formulate what has gone wrong within the community investigating the evolution of female orgasm.

According to Longino, community-level criteria can be used to discriminate among the products of scientific communities and, especially, to neutralize personal idiosyncrasy and challenge background assumptions. This approach requires that we consider all the people working on the evolution of female orgasm as a community of scientists, all aimed at solving a basic problem. The key to the process of arriving at a community with the capacity to produce objective scientific findings is the fulfillment of four criteria, which are seen as necessary to achieve a level of discussion where scientific mistakes that are made may be corrected through the critical interaction of the members of the community (1993b, pp. 112–113).

Longino's first criterion for objective inquiry is that there must be "publicly recognized forums for the criticism of evidence, of methods, and of assumptions of reasoning" (1993b, p. 112). This requirement would seem to have been fulfilled adequately for many of the explanations I have examined....

Longino's second criterion for objective knowledge production is that the community must change its beliefs and theories over time in response to the critical discourse among community members (1993b, p. 112). Again, this requirement would seem to be at least partly fulfilled in the female orgasm case, given the changes in favored explanations over the 37 years of research I have examined....

Longino's third criterion for objectivity is an especially demanding one: "There must be publicly recognized standards by reference to which theories, hypotheses, and observational practices are evaluated and by appeal to which criticism is made relevant to the goals of the inquiring community" (1993b, p. 112). The general family of standards can include "substantive content, criteria of evidence and reasoning, and methods of investigation" (2002, p. 148).

Here, there seem to be problems in my case study. Although the theorists advancing evolutionary hypotheses fully recognized the available sexology literature as providing evidence relevant to the theories in question, they used that evidence very selectively and sometimes misrepresented it. In addition, many theorists assumed that adaptationism was a publicly recognized and accepted background assumption, while others did not. Thus while there was, indeed, some response to criticism, as discussed above, it was far from complete and thoroughgoing....

The final criterion for effective inquiry is that communities must be characterized by tempered equality of intellectual authority. "What consensus exists must not be the result of the exercise of political or economic power or of the exclusion of dissenting perspectives; it must be the result of critical dialogue in which all relevant perspectives are represented" (1993b, pp. 112–113). Since there is, in fact, no deep consensus about the evolution of female orgasm, it might seem that this criterion does not apply to the female orgasm debate. Nevertheless, there has been a fairly clear dismissal of the by-product view on nonevidential grounds. For programmatic reasons favoring adaptationist explanations, the dissenting nonadaptationist view has been ridiculed and dismissed. Thus this view, although relevant, has failed to be fully represented in recent discussions. To the extent that there is now a consensus favoring the sperm-competition views that cannot, if my analysis is correct, be defended on evidential grounds, there might be a failure of equality of intellectual authority at work. In particular, it seems that the authority of an anthropologist (Symons) and a paleontologist (Gould) might not carry weight with those working in contemporary animal behavior, who are very much against the by-product account.

The effectiveness [and objectivity] of a given community of inquirers in producing objective scientific inquiry can be evaluated according to how well it fulfills the criteria listed above....

Longino requires that the community engage in critiques of its own background assumptions using publicly recognized standards. Anderson gives us one basis on which to evaluate background assumptions, in terms of their impartiality, which is a relation to a set of data. Once we examine the background assumptions of androcentrism, human uniqueness, and procreative focus, we can see that they are implicated in partial treatments of the data, in which relevant data are ignored. The same is true for adaptationism, though the situation here is more complicated. Thus Anderson's criteria can help us evaluate whether specific background assumptions are implicated in inadequate science. The standards for the background assumptions in the female orgasm story do seem to be shared for the most part, except for the case of ardent adaptationists.

I should note that even though evidence can be used to challenge background assumptions, there are yet further background assumptions required to link the challenged background assumption to this evidence. In general, background assumptions are challenged with relation to a particular set of other background assumptions and the public standards of a community (Longino 2002, pp. 127–129). The real benefit to the community lies in the effective critical interactions that are generated in challenging background assumptions. Following Mill and Feyerabend, Longino writes, "Criticism not only spurs evaluation and reevaluation of hypotheses, but also leads to better appreciation of their grounds and their consequences" (2002, p. 129).

One reading recent summaries of the situation with regard to female orgasm would come away with the impression that there is really only one live account being pursued, and that is the sperm-competition account.... Yet few ... seem to be examining the actual merits of this account. In particular, no one seems to have noticed the most fundamental flaws of all, which are that there is at best equivocal evidence that uterine upsuck actually occurs, and that there are fatal statistical problems with the Baker and Bellis data and interpretation. This is, indeed, a failure of basic critical examination, and seems to be affected by theoretical commitments to the idea that female orgasm must be an adaptation, at least among some of the theory's supporters.

Longino's criteria for community objectivity are quite general, and determining exactly how her criteria can be applied to the female orgasm case is nontrivial. Under my expanded analysis of Longino's third criterion, there are three major components of the evaluative standards that are not completely agreed upon by the practitioners I am considering. On my reading, evaluative standards include standards of which questions to ask; standards of which evidence is relevant, and appropriately established; and standards of which kinds of explanation are appropriate. Let us see how each of these types of evaluative standard differs between the adaptationists and those who support the by-product view.

In my case study, the object of inquiry seems to be defined differently for the two groups.... That is, for adaptationists the question is: What selection pressures led to the adaptation of female orgasm and what is its contribution to reproductive success? While for the by-product advocates, the question is: How did the trait of female orgasm appear and how is it maintained in the population? ...

Regarding standards of evidence, there has been plenty of critical dialogue concerning the merits of the by-product view and of various adaptationist accounts.... Nevertheless, the two groups seem to be adopting different standards of evidence. I [note elsewhere] that the adaptationists believed that recent data from Baker and Bellis established the elusive claim that there is a connection between female orgasm and reproductive success.... [H]owever, using completely customary standards of statistical evidence, this conclusion is simply unwarranted. Thus we ... lack ... evidence supporting the claim that female orgasm is a biological adaptation ... associated in some way with reproductive success. This is the basis of the claim, by those who support the by-product analysis, ... that adaptationist explanations of the trait are unnecessary. A closer look at what is at issue between the adaptationists and the by-product advocates makes it clearer that these two groups are using slightly different standards in evaluating their hypotheses—although they agree on the standards of evidence that I use in the first section of this [reading], to implicate the various assumptions.[10] In addition, they endorse different standards of explanation; in particular, the adaptationists rule out nonadaptationist explanations of female orgasm a priori.

As I note [elsewhere], ardent adaptationists and those supporting the by-product view use different standards of evidence.... In the case where there is a lack of evidence for a connection between female orgasm and reproductive success, the ardent adaptationists assert that there either is or must be such evidence, while the supporters of the by-product view take the lack of such evidence at face value. In addition, ardent adaptationists take a very negative view of the supporting evidence for the by-product approach, considering it either invisible or useless. They see the by-product view as a sort of "giving up" on evolutionary explanation (that is, on adaptive explanation). Evidence supporting the by-product view is never discussed in detail; however, the ardent adaptationists do accept a very limited version of the by-product view. Specifically, they accept as a fact that female and male orgasmic tissues arise from the same embryological roots. But they assert that this has nothing to do with why the trait of orgasm appears in the population of females over evolutionary time or why the trait is maintained today.

It is here we run into the different standards of explanation [in use by each group]. According to Alcock (1998), by-product explanations can never be evolutionary explanations ... because they highlight only the proximate (developmental or physiological) cause of the trait. Under this view, in order to be an evolutionary explanation at all, the account must give an adaptive explanation for female orgasm. Clearly, this is dogmatic....

A further example ... is the pragmatic argument put forth by ardent adaptationists. Here, the argument is that if we accept a by-product account of female orgasm, then that will prematurely stop the search for a viable adaptive account. This is deemed to be a bad thing.... Thus, given that an adaptive account may be just around the corner, we must not accept the by-product account. The ardent adaptationists' mistaken view that there is no supporting evidence for the by-product account comes in handy here. They treat the by-product account as ... akin to scientific surrender....

One very important background assumption is in play in these discussions.... Remember that one of the significant background assumptions for evolutionary biology is that there are a variety of mechanisms that can account for the evolution of an organism or a trait.... Selection, correlations of growth, drift, and developmental noise are various causes that can account for the manifestation of a particular trait. Lip service to this basic assumption is paid by all. However, in this case it seems that this assumption is being overridden; an adaptive explanation—one in which only selection is seen as an effective cause—is seen as the only really acceptable explanation for female orgasm.... Thus here we've got the denial of a basic background assumption of evolutionary biology.... [T]his puts the ardent adaptationists on a different page from the cavalier adaptationists, who are not committed to the denigration of alternative accounts. The cavalier adaptationists may share the basic standards of evidence and explanation with the supporters of the by-product view, while the ardent adaptationists seem to differ from both groups.

In other words, ... ardent adaptationists ... hold both standards of evidence and standards of explanation different from those of both more mainstream adaptationists and the supporters of the by-product view. This makes fulfillment of Longino's third criterion—that researchers accept shared standards of evaluation—unattainable in the case of the ardent adaptationists.... This makes it difficult for the types of challenges and responses that Longino says are required for the kind of community that is the best at producing objective inquiry.

If the two sides really do show a lack of agreement about standards of evaluation, then we have a violation of [the] third criterion, the demand for publicly recognized standards by reference to which hypotheses and observations are evaluated. According to Longino, there are two general types of criticism to which appeal can be made in this context. The first is "evidential" criticism, which "questions the degree to which a given hypothesis is supported by the evidence adduced for it, questions the accuracy, extent, and conditions of performance of the experiment and observations serving as evidence, and questions their analysis and reporting" (1990, p. 71). This ... covers the most basic types of empirical adequacy of hypotheses, and can be supported by appeal to widely shared standards, such as statistical practices.

A second type of criticism, "conceptual" criticism, cuts much more deeply into the assumptions underlying a theory. It can involve criticism of the conceptual soundness of a hypothesis, examination of the consistency of the hypothesis with accepted theory, and questions regarding the relevance of the evidence presented in support of a hypothesis (1990, p. 72). This type of criticism amounts to questioning the background assumptions in light of which the hypothesis is proposed and evaluated, and it is crucial for the achievement of objective inquiry. The present case, with the different treatments of the lack of evidence for orgasm being an adaptation, is ripe for conceptual criticism. I have illustrated what conceptual criticism of this case would look like[:] ... [n]either side accepts the other's standards for when evidence is crucially required for the endorsement of a hypothesis. They are at an impasse. Nevertheless, any adaptationists coming in and attempting to show a correlation between female orgasm and reproductive success could overcome the impasse. Then, at least, the nonardent adaptationists and the by-product supporters would be on the same page regarding basic evidence necessary for an adaptive explanation.

In fact, note that with all of the cavalier adaptationist accounts, they do not take a dogmatic stand like the ardent adaptationists, they simply make an assumption that female orgasm is an adaptation. Thus it seems to be unfair to group all of the adaptationists together. With most of them, there is simply a lack of evidence for a crucial assumption of their explanations, while in the case of the ardent adaptationists, there seem to be different standards of evidence and explanation operating altogether....

In summary, then, Longino gives an account of community objectivity in which background assumptions play a central role. As such, Longino's account, in combination with my expansion of it, is very helpful in pinpointing exactly where the ardent adaptationists part ways with others in the community of evolutionary biologists, at least on the issue of the evolution of female orgasm.... In the case of androcentrism, this background assumption ought to be rejected because it leads to missing a relevant chunk of evidence about autonomous female sexuality. And ardent adaptationism should be rejected for conflicting with a basic tenet of evolutionary biology, while cavalier adaptationism leads to a disregard of crucial evidence.

CONCLUSIONS

I have pinpointed a set of problematic background assumptions that appear in various explanations for the evolution of female orgasm.... I would propose jettisoning all four of the background assumptions I have considered—ardent and cavalier adaptationism, androcentrism, procreative focus, and the focus on human uniqueness—since they have all been implicated in badly reasoned or badly supported evolutionary explanations. There is a direct tie between making these background assumptions and making the specific evidential errors that I have detailed....

In summary, Longino's analysis of community objectivity in science commits us to the idea that background assumptions are always in operation in science. As noted before, this approach is in contrast to accounts of bias that view it as a personal preference for a particular outcome. Anderson's discussion of impartiality gives us a way to discriminate between harmful biases and beneficial ones. In particular, harmful biases lead to partiality in the treatment of data, which is exactly what I find in nearly all of the evolutionary explanations I examined. I can also use Longino's analysis of objective inquiry to [show] what went wrong in the ... ardent adaptationists' [account of female orgasm as a trait]. Specifically, these researchers seem to fail the requirement of having a shared set of standards with which to evaluate hypotheses....

I take myself to have demonstrated ... that there are serious evidential problems with all but one of the available evolutionary explanations for female orgasm ... [and] that certain background assumptions, especially adaptationism and androcentrism, are centrally implicated in the scientific failures so far....

The history of evolutionary explanations of female orgasm is a history of missteps, misuse of evidence, and missed references. The case is still open, and it is ripe for some good scientific work.

REFERENCES

Alcock, J. 1998. "Unpunctuated Equilibrium in the *Natural History* Essays of Stephen Jay Gould." *Evolution and Human Behavior* 19: 321–336.

Allen, J. L., and W. B. Lemmon. 1981. "Orgasm in Female Primates." *American Journal of Primatology* 1: 15–34.

Anderson, E. 1995. "Knowledge, Human Interests, and Objectivity in Feminist Epistemology." *Philosophical Topics* 23, no. 2: 27–58.

Baker, R. R., and M. A. Bellis. 1995. *Human Sperm Competition*. London: Chapman and Hall.

Barash, D. 1977. *Sociobiology and Behavior*. New York: Elsevier North-Holland.

Barrett, L., R. Dunbar, and J. Lycett. 2002. Human Evolutionary Psychology. Princeton, NJ: Princeton University Press.

Beach, F. A. 1976. "Sexual Attractivity, Proceptivity, and Receptivity in Female Primates." *Hormones and Behavior* 1, no. 7: 105–138.

Bernds, W. P., and D. Barash. 1979. "Early Termination of Parental Investment in Mammals, Including Humans." In *Evolutionary Biology and Human Social Behavior: An Anthropological Perspective*, ed. N. Chagnon and W. Irons, pp. 487–505.

Campbell, B. 1966. *Human Evolution: An Introduction to Man's Adaptations*. Chicago: Aldine.

Carnap, R. 1962. *Logical Foundations of Probability*. Chicago: University of Chicago Press.

Chevalier-Skolnikoff, S. 1974. "Male-Female, Female-Female, and Male-Male Sexual Behavior in the Stumptail Monkey." *Archives of Sexual Behavior* 3, no. 2: 95–116.

Crook, J. H. 1972. Sexual Selection, Dimorphism, and Social Organization in the Primates." In *Sexual Selection and the Descent of Man, 1871–1971*, ed. B. Campbell, pp. 231–281. Chicago: Aldine.

Darwin, C. 1964. *On the Origin of Species*. Cambridge, MA: Harvard University Press.

Eibl-Eibesfeldt, I. 1970. *Ethology: The Biology of Behavior*. New York: Holt, Rinehart, and Winston.

Endler, J. A. 1986. *Natural Selection in the Wild*. Princeton, NJ: Princeton University Press.

Fox, C. A., H. S. Wolff, and J. A. Baker. 1970. "Measurement of Intra-Vaginal and Intra-Uterine Pressures during Human Coitus by Radio-Telemetry." *Journal of Reproduction and Fertility* 22: 243–251.

Gallup, G. G., and S. D. Suarez. 1983. "Optimal Reproductive Strategies for Bipedalism." *Journal of Human Evolution* 12: 193–196.

Geertz, C. 1990. "A Lab of One's Own." New York Review of Books 37 (November 8): 19.

Goldfoot, D. A., H. Westerborg-van Loon, W. Groeneveld, and A. Koos Slob. 1980. "Behavioral and Physiological Evidence of Sexual Climax in the Female Stump-Tailed Macaque (*Macaca arctoides*)." *Science* 208: 1477–1478.

Gould, S. J. 1987. "Freudian Slip." *Natural History* 96, no. 2: 14–21.

Grafenberg, E. 1950. "The Role of the Urethra in Female Orgasm." *International Journal of Sexology* 3: 145–148.

Gross, P. R., and N. Levitt. 1994. *Higher Superstition: The Academic Left and Its Quarrels with Science.* Baltimore, MD: Johns Hopkins University Press.

Haack, S. 1993. *Evidence and Inquiry: Towards Reconstruction in Epistemology.* Oxford: Blackwell.

Hamburg, B. A. 1978a. "The Biosocial Bases of Sex Difference. In *Human Evolution: Biosocial Perspectives,* ed. S. L. Washburn and E. R. McCown, pp. 154–213. Menlo Park, CA: Benjamin/Cummings.

Hrdy, S. B. 1996. "The Evolution of Female Orgasms: Logic Please but No Atavism." *Animal Behaviour* 52: 851–852.

Kitcher, P. 1993. *The Advancement of Science: Science without Legend, Objectivity without Illusions.* Oxford: Oxford University Press.

Larson, A., and J. B. Losos. 1996. "Phylogenetic Systematics of Adaptation." In *Adaptation,* ed. M. R. Rose and G. V. Lauder, pp. 187–221. San Diego: Academic Press.

Laudan, L. 1984. *Science and Values: The Aims of Science and Their Role in Scientific Debate.* Berkeley: University of California Press.

Lloyd, E. A. 1983. "The Nature of Darwin's Support for the Theory of Natural Selection." *Philosophy of Science* 50: 112–129.

———. 1988/1994. The Structure and Confirmation of Evolutionary Theory. Westport, CT: Greenwood Press, 1988. (Reprinted in 1994, Princeton, NJ: Princeton University Press.)

Longino, H. E. 1990. *Science as Social Knowledge: Values and Objectivity in Scientific Inquiry.* Princeton, NJ: Princeton University Press.

———. 1993. "Subjects, Power, and Knowledge: Description and Prescription in Feminist Philosophies of Science." In *Feminist Epistemologies,* ed. L. Alcoff and E. Potter, pp. 101–120. London: Routledge.

———. 1995. "Gender, Politics, and the Theoretical Virtues." *Synthese* 104, no. 3: 383–397.

———. 2002. *The Fate of Knowledge.* Princeton, NJ: Princeton University Press.

Masters, W. H., and V. E. Johnson. 1966. *Human Sexual Response.* Boston, Little, Brown.

Morris, D. 1967. *The Naked Ape: a Zoologist's Study of the Human Animal.* New York: McGraw-Hill.

Novacek, M. J. 1996. "Paleontological Data and the Study of Adaptation." In *Adaptation,* ed. K. D. Rose and G. V. Lauder, pp. 311–363.

Rancour-Laferriere, D. 1983. "Four Adaptive Aspects of the Female Orgasm." *Journal of Social and Biological Structures* 6: 319–333.

Reichenbach, H. 1966. *The Rise of Scientific Philosophy.* Berkeley: University of California Press.

Richardson, R. 1984. "Biology and Ideology: The Interpretation of Science and Values." *Philosophy of Science* 51: 396–420.

Rose, M. R., and G. V. Lauder. 1996. *Adaptation.* San Diego: Academic Press.

Sherfey, M. J. 1973. *The Nature and Evolution of Female Sexuality.* New York: Random House.

Singer, I. 1973. *The Goals of Human Sexuality.* New York: W. W. Norton.

Slob, A. K., and J. J. van der Werff ten Bosch. 1991. "Orgasm in Nonhuman Species." In *Proceedings of the First International Conference on Orgasm,* pp. 135–149.

Sober, E. 1993. *Philosophy of Biology.* Boulder, CO: Westview Press.

Solomon, M. 1995. "Multivariate Models of Scientific Change." *Proceedings of the Biennial Meeting of the Philosophy of Science Association, 1994,* ed. R. Burian, M. Forbes, and D. Hull, pp. 287–297.

———. 2001. *Social Empiricism.* Cambridge: Massachusetts Institute of Technology Press.

Symons, D. 1979. *The Evolution of Human Sexuality.* New York: Oxford University Press.

Thornhill, R. 1990. "The Study of Adaptation." In *Interpretation and Explanation in the Study of Animal Behavior,* vol. 2: *Explanation, Evolution, and Adaptation,* ed. M. Bekoff and D. Jamieson, pp. 31–62. Boulder, CO: Westview Press.

Williams, G. C. 1985. "A Defense of Reductionism in evolutionary Biology." *Oxford Surveys in Evolutionary Biology* 2: 1–27.

Wrangham, R. W., and D. Peterson. 1996. *Demonic Males: Apes and the Origins of Human Violence.* Boston: Houghton Mifflin.

5
The Health Sciences

Research in the health sciences is directed toward the explicitly practical goal of acquiring knowledge useful in promoting human health and alleviating human injury and disease. Despite its seemingly universal humanist aims, feminists have noted that in practice health science research is often shaped by inegalitarian assumptions and practices.

THE WOMEN'S HEALTH MOVEMENT OF THE LATE 1960s AND 1970s

The emergence of the feminist women's health movement in the United States is often dated to 1970. In that year, a small activist group, the Boston Women's Health Collective, produced a pamphlet, *Women and Their Bodies,* initially as material for a course on women's health at a local college. Earlier than this, some feminists had organized to help women find providers of abortion, which was then illegal, and had sometimes provided underground abortions themselves. The provision of abortion was necessarily secret, but the Boston Women's Health Collective pamphlet quickly evolved into the best-selling book *Our Bodies, Ourselves.* This work inspired feminist health activism across the United States, with parallels in many other countries. Feminist activists addressed several issues central to research in the health sciences, including male-biased conceptualizations of health and disease and the use of medicine as a tool for the social control of women.

Feminist critics of the 1970s charged that the health sciences were androcentric in taking male bodies and bodily functions as the norm for humans. These sciences tended to regard bodily functions specific to women, such as menstruation, pregnancy, childbirth, and menopause, as anomalous to human health and thus to treat them as medical problems. This treatment contributed to stigmatizing these functions so that women often experienced them as shameful. Women's sexuality was considered mysterious, and sexual activity that was not directed toward heterosexual intercourse, such as masturbation and lesbianism, was pathologized and repressed.

Feminist critics also charged that the health sciences were used as tools for controlling women to serve male purposes. Women were often treated as passive objects for medical intervention; for instance, they were routinely strapped down for childbirth, electroshock treatment was administered to many lesbians, and there were many reports of health care providers sexually abusing their women patients. Some feminists saw the medical profession's promotion of contraceptive pills, cosmetic surgery, and hormone replacement therapy as collusion with the broader cultural treatment of women as "sex objects." Similarly, they saw the difficulty of obtaining abortions and the need for a (usually male) physician's agreement as limits on women's sexual autonomy.

The women's health movement of the 1960s and 1970s was dedicated to providing women with knowledge about their bodies, so that they would have more treatment options available and be able to make more informed decisions. Feminist health activists encouraged individual self-help practices, such as cervical self-examinations, menstrual extraction, unmedicated and home births, and peer therapy. They also aimed to include more women as research subjects in clinical trials. For many years, the normative medical model was a 160-pound white male; women were often excluded from trials partly because their menstrual cycles were thought to complicate the results and partly because of concern about potential harm to fetuses they might be carrying. As late as 1990 the U.S. Government Accounting Office reported that women were underrepresented in clinical trials. For instance, the Physicians' Health Study, which concluded in 1988 that an aspirin a day may help decrease risk of heart disease, studied 22,000 men and no women. Even some health problems that afflict far more women than men were studied through male subjects, a classic example being a study of breast cancer done exclusively on men. In addition to studying the implications of medical treatments for women as well as men, feminist health activists wished to promote more study of the health concerns specific to women's bodies. They believed that research and education would remove the shame surrounding many health issues and provide women with more control over their bodies, more autonomy, and more dignity. Masculine norms of health and disease would be replaced by human norms that would better reflect both the biological similarities and differences between males and females.

LIMITS OF THE EARLY WOMEN'S HEALTH MOVEMENT

The early women's health movement achieved great gains, especially for middle-class white women. However, its emphasis on generic "women's" health issues and on individual women's choice, autonomy, and control sometimes overlooked the health problems of most immediate concern to poor women and women of color. These women often confront health hazards different from those faced by white middle-class women. For instance, women of color have much higher morbidity and mortality than white women. They are one-and-a-half times more likely to have high blood pressure and to die of heart disease; two times more likely to die from strokes, diabetes, or obesity; and four times more likely to be murdered or die in childbirth. On average, women of color in the United States die six years before white women.

The reasons for these systematic health disparities are complex. Some result from differences in life circumstances; poorer people tend to have worse nutrition and face more occupational injuries. Some disparities result from differences in access to health care. Women of color receive less aggressive treatment for heart disease and AIDS; fewer mammograms, hip replacements, flu shots, and cholesterol screenings; and less monitoring and testing in ICU units, from which they are released sooner, even though they come in sicker. Women of color get fewer breast cancers than white women but have a higher death rate. Some health disparities between white women and women of color even result from an excess of so-called health care administered to women of color, since the treatment they receive is often more coercive and less respectful than that given to white women; for instance, women on welfare and on reservations have faced not only forced caesarean sections but also forced sterilization. By 1950, several states required the mothers of "illegitimate" children to be sterilized as a condition for receiving welfare, and by 1972 the U.S. government admitted to having sterilized 100,000–200,000 Native American women, a practice regarded by some as genocidal.

In addition to systematic disparities in access to health care and the delivery of services, health science research is marked by systematic biases with regard to gender, race, nation, sexuality, and ability.

GENDER, RACIST, AND OTHER BIASES IN HEALTH SCIENCE RESEARCH

Health science research is directed toward the human interest in reducing disease and promoting health, but often it has not been directed toward the health interests of all humans equally; instead, it has been conducted in the interests of certain groups. Not only have men's health concerns been prioritized over women's, but the health of wealthier people has been valued over that of lower-class people, the health of pale-skinned people over that of brown-skinned people, and the health of the able-bodied over that of people with disabilities.

One way in which inegalitarian social values have shaped research in the health sciences is by influencing which injuries and diseases have been selected as objects of study. In general, less research has been done on health problems suffered disproportionately by members of groups with less money to pay for health care and less political power to demand research. Health problems associated with female bodies have often been neglected, as well as diseases that occur more frequently among people of color, such as sarcoidosis, and tropical diseases such as malaria. Health problems attributable to social causes, including occupational injuries and environmental hazards, have also received less investigation, perhaps because such problems are more likely to affect lower-class than upper-class people. By contrast, extensive research has been devoted to such fields as cosmetic, bypass, and bariatric surgery and organ transplants, all of which are highly profitable and received more frequently by well-off people.

Sexist, racist, or otherwise inegalitarian values influence even definitions of health and illness. The ability to function in daily life has often been taken as a marker of mental health, but it may require abilities and character traits such as conformity and submission that are less than morally admirable; the slogan of the radical therapy movement of the 1960s and 1970s was "Therapy means change, not adjustment." Although social factors such as violence, racism, poverty, and war are significant health hazards, they are not generally recognized as areas for health science research. Geri L. Dickson's article on the metalanguage of menopause research clearly illustrates the influence of social values on the way menopause is conceptualized.

Value-laden assumptions about health and disease guide the approaches taken to health care research. If illness is regarded exclusively as a pathology of individual bodies, and bodies in turn are seen only as biological entities independent of their social identities and contexts, then research in the health sciences is likely to focus on the individual, biological, and genetic causes of ill health or pathology and to ignore the influence of social factors. This can be seen in research on the relationship between race and violence, which has tended to pursue genetic rather than social causes; for instance, studies have been done on African American boys and on the younger brothers of incarcerated young men, sometimes without the subjects' knowledge or consent. Research conducted on the assumption that illness is an individual pathology or a series of private events obscures the role played by social factors such as pollution that are influenced by systematic social inequalities.

One alternative to an exclusively biologistic model of research is study that investigates how people's health is influenced by their "lifestyles." On the basis of such studies, people are advised to know their bodies, eat better, refrain from smoking, get more exercise, and engage only in safe sex. This is usually good advice, but although the lifestyle model recognizes that bodily health and disease are affected by social factors, it still conceptualizes them primarily as matters of individual well-being or disorder. When lifestyles are seen as individual responsibilities, then eating disorders, obesity, and alcoholism become individual problems to be addressed primarily by self-help or patient-centered initiatives. Such a focus on individual autonomy and responsibility may blame the victim or personalize the political. It may ignore the social factors including the systematic inequalities that make it almost impossible for the members of some social groups to eat well, stop smoking, take exercise, insist that their sex partners use condoms, and live in pollution-free neighborhoods.

Health science research has a long history of testing treatments on members of disadvantaged social groups who have hardly been in positions to give informed consent. Some research has involved captives; for instance, in the nineteenth century Dr. Sims, "father of gynecology," did thirty agonizing operations in four years on Lucy and two other slaves, some bought expressly for his experiments (Barker-Benfield 1976:101). Other research has been conducted on prison populations. The U.S. government has sponsored some health science research that has been ethically disturbing. An especially notorious example was the Tuskegee syphilis study, conducted by the U.S. government on African American males in Macon County, Alabama, from 1932 to 1972. The research subjects were told they had "bad blood" and offered $25 to participate in the study, as well as $50 burial insurance; they did not receive penicillin, even when it became available in the 1950s as an effective treatment for syphilis. More recently, a survey published in 1984 found that 13,000 black women in Maryland were screened for sickle-cell anemia without their consent or the benefit of prescreening education and counseling. In other government-sponsored research, radiation was administered to research subjects who thought they were receiving therapy. Contraceptive pills were tested on brown women in Puerto Rico, and the Krieger Lead Paint Study, conducted in the mid-1990s, recruited healthy children and their parents to live in east Baltimore housing with varying degrees of lead paint contamination. The Kennedy Krieger Institute is an affiliate of the Johns Hopkins Medical School, and it is alleged that researchers withheld from parents test results that showed high levels of lead contamination in their children.

POLITICAL ECONOMY AND THE HEALTH SCIENCES

The biases affecting research in the health sciences result not only and perhaps not primarily from prejudice on the part of individual researchers; they are also profoundly influenced by the economics of health research. Funding sources shape the goals and sometimes even the findings of health science research. One important source of health science funding in the United States is the government, which has been extremely reluctant to investigate environmental toxins or side effects of weaponry such as Agent Orange or depleted uranium. Pharmaceutical companies are understandably reluctant to acknowledge that their products, such as hormone replacement therapy, involve possible health hazards, and the tobacco industry has sponsored extensive research designed to show that smoking is harmless (Diethelm, Rielle, and McKee 2004). The dairy industry promotes the supposed health benefits of dairy products, which are well tolerated by Americans of European descent, even though 90 percent of Asian Americans, 70 percent of African Americans, 70 percent of Native Americans, and 53 percent of Hispanics are lactose intolerant. Influenced by the dairy lobby, the U.S. Department of Agriculture has long recommended that everyone above age two should eat two or three servings of dairy products a day—even though this makes most nonwhite Americans sick.

JUST METHODOLOGY IN THE HEALTH SCIENCES

How can the epistemic and ethical biases of research in the health sciences be reduced so that knowledge is developed in ways that will address the health concerns of everyone? No simple answer to this question exists, but part of the answer is surely for researchers to become more aware of the ways in which health science methodology has been influenced by social inequalities. Such awareness might stimulate interest in researching the specific health concerns of people who are poor and marginalized, along with the health consequences of social divisions such as gender, race, and class. It might also promote more respect for the knowledge uniquely available to those whose health is impaired by injury or disease. In addition, such awareness might increase ethical sensitivity to the situation of research subjects in clinical trials, who not only may be uncertain about the risks they face but also may believe that they stand to gain health benefits, and whose agreement to participate may be influenced by poverty and desperation. Ethical assessment of health science research not only should consider the likely costs and benefits of proposed studies; in addition, it should ask specifically which individuals are likely to pay the costs of proposed research and which ones are likely to reap its benefits. Ethical research should consider whether those individuals tend to belong systematically to different social groups.

The epistemic and ethical biases of health science research are likely to be reduced when researchers gain greater awareness of the ways in which social inequalities affect health science methodology. Entirely eliminating these biases, however, would require large changes in public attitudes toward the resources used in health science research. Health science research is not a cottage industry; instead, it usually relies on vast coordinated efforts using expensive equipment and skilled personnel. Corporations control many of these resources, utilizing them to develop products that are profitable. Making the health sciences responsive to the health needs of all equally would require addressing difficult questions about the social responsibilities of corporations and the role of profit in health science research. It would also require questioning the responsibilities of government, which not only funds considerable research directly but also subsidizes the training of many health science researchers employed in private industry. In addition, government is responsible for regulating research in the health sciences as in other fields. Research in health care should not be driven by special-interest "disease" lobbies; instead, we need democratic pressure that reflects equitable priorities in the conduct of health science research. More extensive discussion of the role of democracy in health science research will be presented later in this book.

NOTE

My thinking in this area owes a great deal to the work of Dr. Annette Dula, who has taught me much about racism in the health sciences. Her comments on this introduction, as well as those of Dr. Jackie Colby, were extremely helpful. Unfortunately, I have been unable to respond to all of them.

REFERENCES

Barker-Benfield, G. J. 1976. *The Horrors of the Half-Known Life: Male Attitudes Toward Women and Their Sexuality in Nineteenth-Century America.* New York: Harper and Row.

Pascal A. Diethelm, Jean-Charles Rielle, and Martin McKee. "The Whole Truth and Nothing but the Truth: The Research That Philip Morris Did Not Want You to See." Available at www.thelancet.com (accessed November 11, 2004).

Geri L. Dickson

Metaphors of Menopause: The Metalanguage of Menopause Research

Our conceptual systems, in terms of thought, language, and action, are metaphoric in nature. Metaphors, according to Lakoff and Johnson, are related to facts and are capable of containing and transmitting knowledge; they have genuine meaning. Because metaphors are bits of language that imply a relationship of similarity between two things, they reflect beliefs and convey attitudes. The study of the metaphors used to describe or express a phenomenon in language is a way of shedding new light on that phenomenon.

The language of the scientific discourses and practices of the Western world have contributed to the evolution of a picture of the menopausal woman as irritable, frequently depressed, tired, asexual, and overwhelmed by hot flashes. These stereotypes of midlife women impose restricted positions on women as they are classified as products of their reproductive systems and their hormones. The available research on midlife women, most often conceptualized from a biomedical perspective, studies menopause as a "hormone deficiency disease": a cluster of symptoms, led by hot flashes and vaginal atrophy, including, also, many diffuse psychological problems....

Menopause, simply put, is the cessation of menses that without pathology or medical intervention occurs around the fiftieth birthday of women. The last menstrual flow represents a marker in the transition from a reproductive state to a nonreproductive state. Although menopause is a universal and definitive landmark of aging, knowledge generated from cross-cultural studies suggests that women of different cultures experience the menopausal transition in different ways (Beyene; Flint 1982; Lock).

The discourse of science, according to Popkewitz, can be viewed as having different layers of abstraction. These layers exist simultaneously and are superimposed one upon another. At one level, the language of science focuses on the question, the content, and the procedures of research. However, at a deeper, paradigmatic level we can view inquiry as metalanguage in which the narrative creates a particular style or form for thought. As Popkewitz explains, "The metalanguage maintains assumptions which are unconscious in the formal debates of science but by which the content and procedures of inquiry are made sensible and plausible" (33). Within the discourses, science's very language ... is filled with conscious and unconscious assumptions about both what the world is like and the nature of things. As an exemplar of the human construction of scientific inquiry, the study of women and menopause provides evidence to illuminate the social connection between science and societal values that combine to assign aging women to a maligned and marginal status in our society (McCrea).

The focus of study reported here was an exploration of the interrelationship among the underlying assumptions about science and about women, and the conceptualizations of menopause in the discourses of differing paradigms of research. Four scientific paradigms of menopausal research, with differing foundational assumptions, were identified: the biomedical, the sociocultural, a feminist, and a postmodern....

THE BIOMEDICAL PARADIGM

The groundwork for the current conceptualization of menopause as a disease began with hormone studies in the 1930s and 1940s. According to Bell, it was believed that the form, function, and behavior of females could be demonstrated in a dispassionately empirical way, thereby attributing the cause of women's behavior to biological processes. The traditional scientific method ... raised the possibility of treating, as a disease, the decrease in hormones in women at midlife (Bell).

Three crucial sets of assumptions can be teased from the metalanguage of biomedical menopause research using a Kuhnian paradigm analysis. They can be summarized as: (a) science is empirical validation that results in true knowledge; it is objective and value-free, and is based on a linear, causal model; (b) women are primarily products of their reproductive systems and hormones; and (c) there is something inherently pathological in the female's reproductive system (Dickson 1990a, 1990b). Based on these three sets of assumptions, overlaid one on top of another, menopause is studied as biomedical variables, treatments, and outcomes.

Underlying Assumptions about Science

The criteria for evaluating knowledge in the biomedical paradigm are based upon assumptions of science as an objective, precise, rigorous search for the relationship between facts of an ordered reality in which lawlike regularities can be identified, tested, and verified (Dickson 1989; Voda and George; H. S. Wilson). This worldview of science is based on empiricism and has been identified by some as the empirical/analytical paradigm of science (Allen et al.; Morgan; Popkewitz).

Cook described the basic assumptions of the empirical /analytical paradigm as "built on the supposition that an external world of objects exists, that these objects are lawfully interrelated, and that the relationships are mediated by a real force in objects that is called causation" (78). The basic aims of science have been identified by Kerlinger as explanation, prediction, and control; theory development is the ultimate aim. The adequacy of a theory can be judged by its predictive power ... (Kerlinger).

The purpose of scientific studies has been identified by Cook as the probing of "causal relations between manipulated independent variables (treatments) and measured outcomes" (74). To manipulate variables and measure outcomes, it is necessary to control such things as the environment, conditions, subjects, and treatment. In menopause studies, for example, a focus has developed on experimental studies that relate the effects of hormone replacement therapy (treatment) to the prevention of osteoporosis (outcome) (Genant et al.; Lindsay et al.; Riggs et al. 1986), and more recently to heart disease (Barrett-Connor).

Underlying Assumptions about Women

The assumptions about women arise from the Freudian belief that biology is destiny and women are assumed to be "the 'victims' of their changing bodies and fluctuating hormones" (Voda and George 56). The functions of women are determined biologically, and when reproduction is no longer possible, women are considered medically old and socially useless (Cohen). Accompanying this view is the belief that the physiological changes of menopause result in increased psychological distress (Lennon 1987).

... [A]n example of the biomedical view of women and menopause can be found in a report of work on hormone replacement therapy published in a peer-reviewed medical journal. Wilson and Wilson wrote: "The unpalatable truth must be faced that all postmenopausal women are castrates.... Our streets abound with them—walking stiffly in twos and threes, seeing little and observing less. It is not unusual to see an erect man of 75 vigorously striding along on a golf course, but never a woman of this age" (362). At first glance, this may appear to be an outdated view of women, but the male continues as the norm of the aging process. Therefore, the assumption of the "abnormal" nature of older women continues to be reinforced (Cohen; Fausto-Sterling).

Conceptualization of Menopause

The assumptions about the reality of menopause flow from the belief that the menopausal transition is a hormone deficiency disease, similar to diabetes, and treatable with hormone replacement therapy (Henig). The social and the scientific have coalesced to support the goal, advocated by physician-researcher Nachtigall, of preventing aging in women by returning women to their premenopausal physiological states with the use of hormones: the question is not raised as to who will benefit—women or the drug companies—if women return to their premenopausal physiological states.

Existing evidence indicates that the current state of the art of biomedical research is based on data from a relatively small proportion of self-selecting women who experience and report problems, utilize health facilities, and are, therefore, conveniently available as research subjects (McKinlay and McKinlay; Voda and George). The knowledge generated from these convenience-sample studies of predominantly patient populations is a clinical stereotype of the "typical" menopausal woman who presents a broad range of often diffuse symptoms and, consequently, consumes a disproportionate share of health resources (McKinlay et al.).

Further, very little data have been collected about the normal range of menopause experiences. In a comprehensive review of menopause studies, McKinlay and McKinlay reported that scarce data were available about the normal menopause....

Metaphors of Menopause in the Language of Biomedical Research

The specific historical base for the biomedical discourses and metaphors was laid in the nineteenth century with the medicalization of women's bodies: normal reproductive functions were treated as diseases. Foucault (1980), in his studies of sexuality, described how the female body was analyzed from the nineteenth century onward "as being thoroughly saturated with sexuality, whereby it was integrated into the sphere of medical practices, by reason of a pathology intrinsic to it" (104). The specter of the nineteenth-century science that was able to provide a plausible account of the sexual origins of the inferiority of women (Russett) was later found in the work of Deutsch.

Deutsch, a student of Freud, presented a view of motherhood and womanhood as one and the same in which the menopausal years became a struggle against the inevitable disaster of the physiological process of aging. Subsequent researchers built upon Deutsch's case studies of her psychiatric patients and carried forward her assumptions about women and menopause (McKinlay and McKinlay; Voda and George). In addition, there often is a strongly held belief in this kind of research that the individual woman is responsible for her own problematic experiences in menopause ... (Iatrakis et al., 117).

The language of the knowledge of menopause in the biomedical literature provides images of menopause as a breakdown of central control and failed production (Martin). Menopause is depicted by metaphors of disease or abnormal degeneration such as ... "sex-steroid deficiency" (Riggs and Melton) [and] "estrogen withdrawal symptoms" (Ravnikar).

Outcomes of this type of research indicate that the failure of female reproductive organs to produce estrogen after menopause is debilitating to health and leads to other diseases, such as osteoporosis (Martin) and, more recently, cardiovascular disease (Barrett-Connor). In addition, viewed from a different paradigmatic perspective, these experimental studies can be seen to limit and exclude the possibilities of alternative solutions for the prevention of osteoporosis or heart disease. The biomedical approach, with its paradigmatic assumptions and methodologies, lays "the ground work for hormone replacement therapy as a logical and 'scientific' choice to prevent and treat osteoporosis" (MacPherson 1985, 11) or heart disease.

THE SOCIOCULTURAL PARADIGM

In response to this ideology of the biomedical view and its negative implications for women, a second paradigm evolved in the 1970s, based on differing assumptions about science, about women, and about menopause. This literature remains a competing body of knowledge, but it contains a much smaller number of studies than that within the biomedical paradigm.

Underlying Assumptions about Science

Although the methods of research may vary, the epistemology of the sociocultural paradigm arises from assumptions about science that are similar to those in the empirical/analytical paradigm: here science also is based on a linear, causal model (Voda and George). However, the cause of any problem is social or cultural, rather than biological.

The assumptions about the world ... begin with a belief in the nature of the world as more dynamic than ... the assumptions underlying the biomedical approach. Experimental or quasi-experimental design studies are not usually conducted within this paradigm. The everyday-life world is important; research is conducted in field, not laboratory, studies. The actions of people are not considered the "facts" of science; rather, attention is given to the attitudes, relationships, roles, and interactions in a particular society and/or culture (Leininger; Wilson). The variables of interest are social and cultural in origin, and the assumption is embraced that it is the position of women and societal conditions that contribute to the reactions of women to menopause (McCrea; Posner; Voda and George).

Assumptions about the purpose of sociocultural menopause research, suggested by Lock, include: "investigat[ing] the meaning of the social transitions under study for the individual informant, in the context of her personal life history, social roles, and particular culture" (23). The roots and effects of knowledge and power, rather than being vested in the scientific discourse and clinical jurisprudence, as in the biomedical paradigm, are found in the everyday language of cultural, social, environmental, and philosophical phenomena.

Underlying Assumptions about Women

No longer are women viewed as being at the mercy of their fluctuating hormones or their biology. It is assumed, instead, that there is "no consistent relationship between the biochemical or physiological changes and behaviors" (Voda and George 61). By opting for the sociocultural approach, an attempt is made to discredit the assumption of the biomedical approach that women are physically and emotionally handicapped by menstruation and menopause.

Conceptualization of Menopause

Menopause is viewed as a natural process through which most women pass with minimum difficulty, not a disease process (McCrea). Kaufert (1982) stressed that menopause is a culturally constructed event to which people bring preconceived ideas about its nature. Contesting the biomedical assumption that menopause is a hormone deficiency disease, researchers within this paradigm often study cultures where women do not experience the same kinds of responses to menopause that women in the United States seem to experience. Their assumption is that true physiological variants of menopause are present in all women, not just in the modern Western population (Beyene).

Metaphors of Menopause in the Language of Sociocultural Research

The metaphors of menopause in the language of the sociocultural research differ from those in the biomedical studies. The "experience of menopause" or the "response to menopause" is the terminology used, rather than the distancing language referring to "the menopause," as often found in the biomedical paradigm. Metaphors of menopause include: "a developmental phase" (Hotchner); ... "a natural stage, a transitional phase in a woman's life" (Frey); ... and "alterations in wellness" (Engel). Other locutions from a cultural perspective include: "cultural construction" (Lock); "culturally constructed event" (Kaufert 1982); ... and "cultural context which shapes the pattern of a woman's roles" (Beyene). The conceptualization, images, and metaphors of menopause in the sociocultural approach are more varied than those found in the biomedical paradigm.

The historical basis for the sociocultural paradigm can be found in the work of Flint (1975). From her research, Flint concluded that the difference between the two million women in the United States with severe symptoms and the absence of incapacitation of Indian women during menopause could be attributed to differences in the attitudes the two cultures exhibit toward menopausal women. In the Indian culture, older women experience a heightened social prestige, whereas "in our culture, there is no reward for attaining menopause" (Flint 1975, 163). A comprehensive review of cultural menopausal research by Wilbush (1982) added support to the view of menopausal symptomatology as a phenomenon of Western cultural behavior.

In addition, ... social studies have been conducted in an attempt to link reactions to menopause with social roles. A foundational assumption of these studies is "that women experience reactions to the [menopausal transition] that are unpleasant and that these are rooted in the quantity and quality of social roles and relationships in their lives" (Voda and George 67). The childrearing role and the marital role (Dosey and Dosey; Uphold and Susman 1981), as well as the work role (Polit and LaRocco; Uphold and Susman 1985), were the emphasis of studies to determine the relationship between any unpleasant reactions to the transition and the various roles of women.

A FEMINIST PARADIGM

Underlying Assumptions

Feminist theory and research covers a broad spectrum of writings and feminist science presumes and utilizes a variety of assumptions and methods (Harding). Nevertheless, the underlying assumptions of feminist studies revolve around a view of the world as a place in which men have defined what being a woman means in the larger society. The studies presented are in the nature of a critique that exposes social conditions that hinder human communication and liberation (Bell; McCrea; MacPherson 1981, 1985). Feminists have sought to develop a new paradigm of social criticism that does not rely on traditional philosophical assumptions (Nicholson). Thus, feminist science often takes the form of an emancipatory sociocultural critique.

From this perspective, the entire tradition of Western science is challenged by exposing how the foundations of knowledge have been built on the assumptions of male domination and patriarchal power (Fee). The assumption is that "social life is structured by meaning, by rules, conventions, or habits adhered to by individuals as social beings" (Allen et al. 34). The aim of this research is the possibility of gaining an understanding of the patterns that structure human activity by exposing the relationship between the meanings of human activity and existing social structures. Feminists concentrate on the social and political forces found in the domination of women.

The number of feminist studies of menopause is small, and most of them are on the menstrual cycle. Posner speculated that the dearth of feminist literature on menopause resulted from a move away from doing research that focused on cyclical changes in women. However, Bleier and Harding have argued that cultural prejudices often have been disguised as scientific facts founded in a belief that women are physically and emotionally handicapped by the menstrual cycle and therefore are subordinate to men. In addition, as Whatley and others have indicated, traditional definitions of female bodies, health, and sexuality have been constructed and defined in male terms. Therefore, the uniqueness of "womanhood" often has been limited to menstruation and, of interest here, menopause....

Underlying Assumptions about Women

A foundational assumption in feminist menopause research is that women are not defined by their hormones. However, there is sometimes a tendency to develop essentialist assumptions about the nature of human beings (that there is an essential feminine or masculine nature) and the conditions for social life (Nicholson). Thus, in criticizing the feminist theories that underlie feminist research, Weedon points out that these theories often espouse the view that "there is an essential womanhood, common to all women, suppressed or repressed by patriarchy" (10). Not only does this drift toward essentialism undermine the feminist insight that conceptual construction accounts for the traditional, patriarchal conceptualization of the essential nature of women; it leads some theorists into a fault that is the mirror image of the patriarchal mistake. That is, in attempting to overcome the oppressive assumptions about women embedded in the traditional approaches, some feminist theorists have posited what they take to be (essentially) a feminine perspective, utilized that perspective to define "woman," and then taken woman so defined as the norm, with man as "the other." Building research on such universalist and normative assumptions leaves little room to explore and identify what may be the very different experiences of women of different cultures, classes, and colors.

Conceptualization of Menopause

The conceptualization of menopause in the feminist literature is as a natural female process with social and often class implications. Menopause is envisioned as a tabooed subject, veiled in secrecy and silence, in which women's rights are suppressed in the name of biology (Delaney et al.; MacPherson 1981, 1985; Weideger). The suppression of women's positions in the name of biology has led to the social control of women through the medicalization of menopause.

MacPherson (1981) clearly documented how the medical community has responded with "treatments" for women that helped to create the submissive female patient.... With the transformation of menopause into a disease classification, women can continue to be controlled politically, economically, and sexually. This opens the door for definitions of femininity and sexuality that are constructed by medical experts, rather than by women themselves.... Yet, ironically, when it comes to the feminist research on menopause, the experiences of women themselves are generally left out of the endeavor.

METAPHORS OF MENOPAUSE IN THE LANGUAGE OF FEMINIST LITERATURE

The metaphors found in the feminist studies of menopause are concerned with the need to offset the metaphor of menopause as breakdown and disease promoted in the dominant scientific discourses. From the historical, cultural study of Delaney et al. metaphors have arisen, such as in ... Mary Winfrey's "At Menopause," in which "the poet compares her body to a fruitless grapevine. Although the grapes are gone, the vine continues to grow strong and to give shelter.... the change of life can be an affirmation of our uniquely female experience and an opportunity for new directions" (Delaney et al. 237, 239)....

Nurses, as health professionals, are challenged by MacPherson (1981) to contribute to a growing body of literature that discusses menopause positively and which may present the menopausal woman as a "hero." In further writings, MacPherson (1985) has described how menopause changed from a disease to a syndrome, which allowed for menopause to become a treatable disorder. These feminist descriptions can be viewed as in opposition to the powerful images in the scientific or biomedical discourses about women and menopause in our society. But in the realm of "power discourses" about menopause, their effects are weak compared to the effects of the dominant biomedical views of science, women, and menopause.

A POSTMODERN PARADIGM

Postmodernism ... deals with the question of knowledge and social power in a postindustrial society (Lyotard). Scientific knowledge is viewed as a kind of discourse. However, scientific knowledge does not represent the totality of knowledge; it has always existed in addition to, in competition and conflict with, another kind of knowledge that Lyotard calls "narrative" knowledge. This knowledge includes notions of "knowing-how" ... (18).

Language assumes a new importance in postmodernism. Language is important, not because of its syntax and rules of grammar or the specifics of actual speaking, but insofar as it allows people to think, speak, and give meaning to the world around them. Discourse can be seen as a particular area of language use that may be identified by the institutions to which it relates, by the social position from which it comes, and by that position (such as scientist or expert) which it marks out for the speaker (Macdonnell). Discourses, simply put, are language put into practice.

Basic to postmodernism is the tenet of context. The plurality of discourses and the impossibility of fixing meaning, once and for all, place any interpretation of language within the context of, at best, being specific to the discourses within which it is produced. Yet, language is the site of historically and socially specific discourses; this is where we perceive possibilities of social change through the range of discourses available to us. As Weedon suggests, it may be possible to transform the meaning of experience by bringing to bear a different set of assumptions on the language of the competing discourses.

Underlying Assumptions about Science

In postmodernism, assumptions about science flow from certain fundamental beliefs. First is the assumption that knowledge is fallible. It merely represents the best explanation available in which we trust enough to act. Second, knowledge is developed in a historical and cultural context. Historical knowledge helps to elucidate the unacknowledged conditions of research. Third, it recognized that the values of the researcher have an impact on the choice of questions to study, as well as how to go about the study.

Fourth, the presumption is accepted that language is knowledge and that it is through the powerful discourses of a society that the subjectivity of an individual is formed in a way that is governed by specific social and historical factors. From the postmodern perspective, knowledge and power are viewed as opposite sides of the same coin; even the least of us is not powerless (Foucault 1977; Lyotard). Lastly, it is acknowledged that the scientific and medical literature is a reflection of the social and cultural conditions of a society and provides an insightful view of the larger society.

These assumptions allow for a study of language that encompasses both discursive and social fields, rather than that of individual men and women. Within this paradigm, "the rational individual is seen not as a proposition to be defended (or refuted), but as the consequence of social-historical processes" … (Poster 27).

Underlying Assumptions about Women

Differences between men and women are acknowledged in this paradigm. These differences are neither a means to explain nor a way to form behavior with a physiological base. Rather, the physiological differences are positive and mutually generative, not denied. "Different" does not mean unequal…. A concern with difference can explore physiological differences, as well as those socially imposed upon women. The menstrual cycle is acknowledged and studied as women experience it and are concerned with it.

The historical and social discourses that are specific to women and menopause have helped to shape the experiences of women today. In this paradigm, women are assumed (a) to be equal to, but different from men; (b) to have experienced gender power imbalances in society as a result of unacknowledged conditions; and (c) to be capable of playing an active role in research addressing questions of concern to women (Dickson 1989).

Underlying Assumptions about Menopause

Menopause, in this paradigm, is assumed to be a physiological transition that all women will experience. It may occur naturally during midlife or be medically imposed at any time in a woman's life. Women experiencing the menopausal transition are assumed to do so with a great deal of individual variation. What the experience is like is unknown, since normalcy of the transition has not been adequately addressed in research…. However, the assumption also is made that some women may have physiological changes that are problematic for them in maintaining their desired lifestyles.

A woman's response to this transition is a complex one, incorporating not only physiological dimensions, but social, historical, cultural, political, and economic dimensions as well. Therefore, any research designed to gain insight into the impact and scope of the menopausal transition should attend to physiological, social, historical, and cultural dimensions of knowledge and power. The postmodern paradigm provides the opportunity to develop a kind of research on menopause that (a) takes into account the historical and the sociocultural, as well as the biological, and (b) generates knowledge that represents *a* truth, not *"the* Truth," about menopause.

A Postmodern Study of Menopause

Exemplars of postmodern studies of menopause (and the only ones I am aware of) are in the work of Dickson (1989, 1990a, 1990b). In these studies, emerging from a postmodern paradigm, I explored the interrelation between the concept of knowledge in the scientific discourses and the concept of knowledge in the everyday discourses of midlife women regarding the closure of menstrual life. The data for analysis were twofold: the language of menopause in the scientific or biomedical literature of menopause, both present and past, and the language of a select group of midlife women.

Twenty interviews were conducted with eleven healthy, white, middle-class women, ranging in age from forty-seven to fifty-five years. The interrelation of the effects of professional "knowledge" upon midlife women was investigated through a discourse analysis comparing the scientific conceptualizations of menopause with the experiences described by the sample of midlife women. The outcomes of the research were identified as metaphors of menopause from the historical horizon and the everyday discourses, as well as those presented earlier from the biomedical, sociocultural, and feminist paradigms.

Metaphors of Menopause in the Language of Postmodern Research: The Historical Horizon

... The dominant conceptualization of menopause during the Victorian period was that of moral fault (Dickson 1989). The scientific view of womanhood that evolved was one in which the physician's would-be scientific views reflected and helped shape the social definition of the appropriate bounds of woman's role and identity. The scientific was called into play because women had become an issue, a social problem—something to be investigated, analyzed, and solved. Victorian society demanded that a woman be chaste, delicate, and loving. But, inside this discreet exterior and hidden deep within her lay her reproductive organs, which exercised a controlling influence on her whole body. Her reproductive organs were seen as "the source of her peculiarities, the center of her sympathies, and the seat of her disease" (Smith-Rosenberg 1973, 59). Yet, with a life expectancy of forty-seven years, many women did not live through menopause (Ehrenreich and English).

The first medical writings about menopause were by Tilt and appeared in France in 1851 (Wilbush 1980). By 1882 an edition had been translated into English for American audiences (Tilt). He used several metaphors as "it" was being given a name; they were "the end of the monthly" and "change of life" (Tilt). Other American doctors did not consider menopause a proper topic of discussion in medical circles....

However, as the century drew to a close, many physicians expressed the view that certain behavior (such as seeking too much education, attempts at birth control or abortion, seeking undue sexual gratification, insufficient attention to husband or children, or the advocacy of women's suffrage) caused a disease-ridden menopause (Smith-Rosenberg and Rosenberg). There was no doubt that childless women would suffer during menopause. They had thwarted the promise immanent in their bodies' design: they must expect to suffer (Dickson 1989)....

As the twentieth century opened, the mantle of normalization passed from the family doctor to the specialist in diseases of the mind, the psychiatrist. Psychoanalytic "truth" was developed to support and reinforce the power of gynecology over women's lives. Attempts were made to convince women that many problems, including those attending menopause, were primarily intrapsychic, and "talking" could help to relieve those problems.

... Deutsch presented a psychoanalytic interpretation of the psychology of women, illustrated with case studies from her psychiatric practice. The metaphors generated by her research were "natural end as servant of the species," "partial death," and "psychological distress."

The dominant conceptualization of menopause gleaned from the scientific discourses of this time can be expressed as "involutional melancholia." So prevalent was this "disorder occurring in the involutional period and characterized by worry, anxiety, agitation, and severe insomnia" (*Diagnostic and Statistical Manual of Mental Disorders* 36), that it became a psychiatric diagnosis....

Women experiencing a difficult time at menopause were not those seeking education or birth control as earlier described, but those women with "immature personalities" (Petit).... These conceptualizations set the stage for today's "hormone deficiency disease." However, it was the fundamental concept of womanhood as the persona of sexuality with an intrinsic pathology that allowed the conceptualization of menopause as disease to develop (Foucault 1980).

Metaphors of Menopause in the Language of Postmodern Research: The Everyday Discourse

As Foucault (1980) has carefully outlined, "each society has its regime of truth, its 'general politics' of truth: that is, the types of discourses which it accepts and makes function as true" (131). The scientific truth of today is that menopause is a "hormone deficiency disease." In the research I have conducted, evidence of the "truth effects" of the scientific can be heard in the voices of the women interviewed. But evidence of a resistance to this medicalization of menopause also can be heard in the voices. This can be considered an expression of the "woman in the body" (Martin).

Metaphors of menopause, representing both the truth effects and the woman in the body, can be identified from the language of the women interviewed. As women approach fifty and/or begin to notice some menstrual changes, there is a great deal of uncertainty that issues in wondering about and questioning of their experiences and their normalcy.

Some metaphors that the women used to describe this time in life include: "embarrassing and frustrating time," "hot flashes," "feeling blue" and "my change" (Dickson 1989). Others, reflecting a somewhat different perspective, include: "the beginning of a new life," "not a sick kind of thing," "terribly painless time," "end of childbearing years," "having energy," "enjoying life," "taking things into my own hands," and "feeling great" (Dickson 1989).

This postmodern analysis of the language of menopause lays the foundation for further research that would be freeing for women, that would help women gain a mastery of self through the knowledge of their experiences of menopause. The aim of this new research paradigm is to understand the experience of the "woman in the body," rather than seeing menopause through the lens of the biomedical paradigm.

CONCLUSION

... Presenting the results of research in the form of its metaphors allows for a way of shedding new light on an existing phenomenon: menopause. From further studies, such as the one presented here, we can become increasingly conscious of our choices of research processes and the human nature of knowledge. This enables us to make decisions that ensure that our science (a) assumes the same reality as do our convictions, (b) accepts the same definition as our beliefs, (c) allows a similar understanding of the relationship between researchers and their objects of study, and (d) is directed toward ends similar to those of our practice (Moccia).

How we think about metaphors or meanings of a phenomenon determines how we use the words. For example, illness may be expressed as an enemy or as a comfort or as a weakness. The metaphors we hear shape how we perceive, interpret, or define symptom states (Lakoff and Johnson). Similarly, the metaphors of the discourses of menopause research contribute to the experiences of menopause for women. Defining menopause as a disease or as breakdown or as a developmental stage or as a social phenomenon or as rebirth will portend different experiences. It is possible, as Weedon suggests, that bringing to bear a different set of assumptions about science, women, and menopause in the discourses of menopause can transform the meaning of the midlife experiences for women. However, it is acknowledged that the "knowledge" of menopause discussed here represents a moment in history; the discourses and meaning of menopause are already changing.

REFERENCES

Allen, D., P. Benner, and N. L. Diekelmann. 1986. Three paradigms for nursing research: Methodological implications. In *Nursing research methodology: Issues and implementation,* ed. P. L. Chinn, 23–38. Rockville, Md.: Aspen.

Barrett-Connor, E. 1989. Long term estrogen replacement therapy: What we know and what we need to know. (Paper presented at the Eighth Conference of the Society for Menstrual Cycle Research, Salt Lake City, 1 June, 1989.)

Bell, S. E. 1987. Changing ideas: The medicalization of menopause. *Social Science and Medicine* 24:535–42.

Berg, G., and M. Hammar. 1985. Epidemiology of the climacterium. *Acta Obstetricia & Gynecologia of Scandanavica [Supplement]* 132:9–12.

Beyene, Y. 1986. Cultural significance and physiological manifestations of menopause: A biocultural analysis. *Culture, Medicine, and Psychiatry* 10:47–71.

Bleier, R. 1984. *Science and gender: A critique of biology and its theories on women.* New York: Pergamon.

Cohen, L. 1984. *Small expectations: Society's betrayal of older women.* Toronto: McClelland and Stewart.

Cook, T. D. 1983. Quasi-experimentation: Its ontology, epistemology, and methodology. In *Beyond method: Strategies for social research,* ed. G. Morgan, 74–94. Beverly Hills: Sage.

Delaney, J., M. J. Lupton, and E. Toth. 1988. *The curse: A cultural history of menstruation* (revised ed.). Chicago: University of Illinois.

Deutsch, H. 1945. *The psychology of women* (vol. 2). New York: Grune and Stratton.

Diagnostic and statistical manual of mental disorders (2nd ed.). 1968. American Psychiatric Association: Task Force on Nomenclature and Statistics.

Dickson, G. L. 1989. *The knowledge of menopause: An analysis of scientific and everyday discourses.* (Unpublished doctoral dissertation, University of Wisconsin–Madison.)

———. 1990a. A feminist poststructuralist analysis of the knowledge of menopause. *Advances in Nursing Science* 12(3):15–31.

———. 1990b. The metalanguage of menopause research. *IMAGE: Journal of Nursing Scholarship* 22(3):168–73.

Dosey, M. A., and M. F. Dosey. 1980. The climacteric woman. *Patient Counseling* 2(1):14–21.

Ehrenreich, B., and D. English. 1979. *For her own good: 150 years of the experts' advice to women.* New York: Doubleday.

Engel, N. S. 1984. On the vicissitudes of health appraisal. *Advances in Nursing Science* 7(1):12–23.

Fausto-Sterling, A. 1985. *Myths of gender: Biological theories about women and men.* New York: Basic Books.

Fee, E. 1986. Critiques of modern science: The relationship of feminism to other radical epistemologies. In *Feminist approaches to science,* ed. R. Bleier. New York: Pergamon.

Ferguson, K. J., C. Hoegh, and S. Johnson. 1989. Estrogen replacement therapy: A survey of women's knowledge and attitudes. *Archives of Internal Medicine* 149:133–36.

Flint, M. 1975. The menopause: Reward or punishment? *Psychosomatics* 16(4):161–63.

———. 1982. Male and female menopause: A cultural put-on. In *Changing perspectives on menopause,* ed. A. M. Voda, M. Dinnerstein, and S. R. O'Donnell, 363–75. Austin: University of Texas.

Foucault, M. 1977. In *Power/ knowledge: Selected interviews and other writings 1972–1977,* ed./trans. C. Gordon. New York: Pantheon.

———. 1980. *The history of sexuality: Volume 1: An introduction.* New York: Vintage.

Frey, K. A. 1981. Middle-aged women's experience and perceptions of menopause. *Women and Health* 6(1/2):25–36.

Genant, H. K., C. E. Cann, B. Ettinger, and G. S. Gordon. 1982. Quantitative computed tomography of vertebral spongiosa: A sensitive method for detecting early bone loss after oophorectomy. *Annals of Internal Medicine* 97:699–705.

Goldstein, M. Z. 1987. Aspects of gender and ethnic identity in menopause: Two Italian-American women. *Journal of the American Academy of Psychoanalysis* 15(3):383–94.

Harding, S. 1986. *The science question in feminism*. Ithaca: Cornell University.

Henig, R. M. 21 March 1988. Change of view on change of life. *The Milwaukee Journal*, 1D, 3D.

Hotchner, B. 1980. Menopause and sexuality: Gearing up or down? *Topics in Clinical Nursing* 1(4):45–51.

Iatrakis, G., N. Haronis, G. Sakellaropoulos, A. Kourkoubas, and M. Gallso. 1986. Psychosomatic symptoms of postmenopausal women with or without hormonal treatment. *Psychotherapy and Psychosomatics* 46(3):116–21.

Kaufert, P. A. 1982. Anthropology and the menopause: The development of a theoretical framework. *Maturitas* 4:181–93.

———. 1986. Menstrual changes and women in midlife. *Health Care for Women International* 7:63–76.

Kerlinger, F. N. 1986. *Foundations of behavioral research* (3rd ed.). New York: Holt, Rinehart & Winston.

Klaus, H. 1974. The menopause in gynecology: A focus for teaching the comprehensive care of women. *Journal of Medical Education* 49:1186–89. Kuhn, T. S. 1970. *The structure of scientific revolutions* (2nd ed.). Chicago: University of Chicago.

Lakoff, G., and M. Johnson. 1980. *Metaphors we live by*. Chicago: University of Chicago.

Leininger, M. M. (ed.). 1985. *Qualitative research methods in nursing*. New York: Grune & Stratton.

Lennon, M. C. 1982. The psychological consequences of menopause: The importance of timing of a life stage event. *Journal of Health and Social Behavior* 23:353–66.

———. 1987. Is menopause depressing? An investigation of three perspectives. *Sex Roles* 17(1/2):1–16.

Lindsay, R., D. M. Hart, C. Forrest, and C. Baird. 1980. Prevention of spinal osteoporosis in oophorectomised women. *Lancet* 2:1151–53.

Lock, M. 1986. Ambiguities of aging: Japanese experience and perceptions of menopause. *Culture, Medicine, and Psychiatry* 10:23–46.

Lyotard, J. F. 1986. *The postmodern condition: A report on knowledge*. Minneapolis: University of Minnesota.

Macdonell, D. 1986. *Theories of discourse: An introduction*. Oxford, U.K.: Blackwell.

MacPherson, K. I. 1981. Menopause as disease: The social construction of a metaphor. *Advances in Nursing Science* 3(2):95–113.

———. 1985. Osteoporosis and menopause: A feminist analysis of the social construction of a syndrome. *Advances in Nursing Science* 7(4):11–22.

Mann, M. D. 1887. *A system of gynecology, by American authors*. Philadelphia: Lea Brothers.

Martin, E. 1987. *The woman in the body: A cultural analysis of reproduction*. Boston: Beacon.

McCrea, F. B. 1983. The politics of menopause: The "discovery" of a deficiency disease. *Social Problems* 31(1):111–23.

McKinlay, J. B., S. M. McKinlay, and D. J. Brambilla. 1987. Health status and utilization behavior associated with menopause. *American Journal of Epidemiology* 125:110–21.

McKinlay, S. M., and J. B. McKinlay. 1973. Selected studies of the menopause. *Journal of Biosocial Science* 5:533–55.

Moccia, P. 1988. A critique of compromise: Beyond the methods debate. *Advances in Nursing Science* 10(4):1–9.

Morgan, G. 1983. Research strategies: Modes of engagement. In *Beyond method: Strategies for social research*, ed. G. Morgan, 19–42. Beverly Hills: Sage.

Nachtigall, L. E. 1987. Estrogen replacement: Which postmenopausal women benefit? *The Female Patient* 12(8):72ff.

Nicholson, L. J. 1990. Introduction. In *Feminism/Postmodernism*, ed. L. J. Nicholson, 1–16. New York: Routledge.

Petit, M. D. 1955. Management of the menopause. *The Medical Clinics of North America* 39:1725–31.

Polit, D. F., and S. A. LaRocco. 1980. Social and psychological correlates of menopausal symptoms. *Psychosomatic Medicine* 42(3):335–45.

Popkewitz, T. S. 1984. *Paradigm and ideology in educational research: The social functions of the intellectual*. London: Falmer.

Posner, J. 1979. It's all in your head: Feminist and medical models of menopause (strange bedfellows). *Sex Roles* 5:179–90.

Poster, M. 1984. *Foucault, Marxism and history.* Cambridge, U.K.: Polity.

Ravnikar, V. A. 1983. When your patient faces menopause. *Patient Care* 17(11):91–103.

Ricci, J. V. 1945. *One hundred years of gynaecology: 1800 to 1900.* Philadelphia: Blakiston.

Riggs, B. L., and J. Melton. 1986. Involutional osteoporosis. *The New England Journal of Medicine* 314:1676–84.

Riggs, B. L., H. W. Wahner, L. J. Melton, III, L. S. Richelson, H. L. Judd, and K. P. Oxord. 1986. Bone loss in the axial and appendicular skeletons of women: evidence of substantial vertebral bone loss prior to menopause. *Journal of Clinical Investigations* 77:1487–91.

Russett, E. 1989. *Sexual science: The Victorian construction of womanhood.* Cambridge: Harvard University.

Servinghaus, R. L. 1948. *The management of the climacteric: Male or female.* Springfield, Ill.: Charles C. Thomas.

Smith-Rosenberg, C. 1973. Puberty to menopause: The cycle of femininity in nineteenth-century America. *Feminist Studies* 1(3/4):58–73.

———. 1985. *Disorderly conduct: Visions of gender in Victorian America.* New York: Oxford.

Smith-Rosenberg, C., and C. Rosenberg. 1984. The female animal: Medical and biological views of woman and her role in nineteenth-century America. In *Women and health in America,* ed. J. W. Leavitt, 12–27. Madison: University of Wisconsin.

Tilt, E. J. 1882. *The change of life in health and disease* (4th ed.). New York: Bermingham.

Uphold, C. R., and E. J. Susman. 1981. Self-reported climacteric symptoms as a function of the relationships between marital adjustment and childrearing stage. *Nursing Research* 30:84–88.

———. 1985. Child-rearing, marital, recreational and work role integration and climacteric symptoms in midlife women. *Research in Nursing and Health* 8:73–81.

Voda, A. M., and T. George. 1986. Menopause. In *Annual Review of Nursing Research* (vol. 4), ed. H. H. Werley and J. J. Fitzpatrick, 55–75. New York: Springer.

Walfisch, S., H. Antonovsky, and B. Maoz. 1984. Relationship between biological changes and symptoms and health behaviour during the climacteric. *Maturitas* 6:9–17.

Weedon, C. 1987. *Feminist practice and poststructuralist theory.* Oxford, U.K.: Blackwell.

Weideger, P. 1976. *Menstruation and Menopause.* New York: Alfred A. Knopf.

Whatley, M. H. 1986. Integrating sexuality issues into the nursing curriculum. *Journal of Sex Education and Therapy* 12(2):23–26.

Wilbush, J. 1980. Tilt, E. J. and the change of life (1857)—the only work on the subject in the English language. *Maturitas* 2:259–67.

———. 1982. Historical perspectives: Climacteric expression and social context. *Maturitas* 4:195–205.

Wilson, H. S. 1989. *Research in nursing* (2nd ed.). Menlo Park, Calif.: Addison-Wesley.

Wilson, R. A., and T. Wilson. 1963. The fate of nontreated postmenopausal women: A plea for the maintenance of adequate estrogen from puberty to the grave. *Journal of the American Geriatric Society* 11:347–62.

Zita, J. N. 1993. Heresy in the female body: The rhetorics of menopause. In *Menopause: A midlife passage,* ed. J. C. Callahan, 59–78. Bloomington: Indiana University Press.

Karen Messing

Don't Use a Wrench to Peel Potatoes: Biological Science Constructed on Male Model Systems Is a Risk to Women Workers' Health

Recently, researchers at the Centre pour l'étude des interactions biologiques entre la santé et l'environnement (CINBIOSE) applied to a government granting agency for money to study the health problems of women entering nontraditional manual jobs.[1] Our hypothesis was that since these jobs had been designed in relation to the average male body, tools and equipment might be the wrong size and shape for the average woman. Women might get musculo-skeletal problems from trying to perform tasks in awkward positions with badly designed equipment. In collaboration with a sociologist, we would also examine resistance to adapting the jobs so that more women could do them. This question was part of a larger project on musculo-skeletal problems among workers of both sexes.

Some time after submitting the grant, we received a phone call from the project officer. He said he wanted to help us out. The two scientists who had been asked to comment in writing on the quality of the application had reported favorably on all aspects, but he did not think the peer review committee that they reported to would find the subject relevant. He suggested that we change the project resume so the word "women" would be eliminated. We could then deal with the "global" problem of tools and equipment ill-adapted to the diversity of the human body. He mentioned that some men from Asiatic countries were quite small and might also have problems with tools and equipment.

After some soul-searching we changed the resume but not the project description. However, without explanation, funding was refused for the part of the project dealing with women in nontraditional jobs. Some time later I met a member of the peer review committee and asked him why they had cut that part of the project. He explained, "In occupational health, there are central problems and peripheral problems. You were dealing with a peripheral problem." Asked for more examples of each type, he offered "construction workers falling off scaffolding" as central and "stress" as peripheral.

Funny thing: whenever we do educational sessions with women workers, stress is the number one health problem mentioned. . . .

How does it happen that a problem that is considered central by women workers is considered peripheral by those who decide where research money should be concentrated? Why are women's claims for compensation for physical problems caused by stress (heart attacks, for example) refused four times as often as men's?[3] In particular, it seems, the further the workers are from scientists in sex, social class, and race, the more easily the scientists can ignore their needs in deciding on research priorities. But these phenomena are not accidents; they are part of the structure of academic research in occupational health.

Indeed, certain rules and standards of occupational health research support the inhumane treatment of workers, particularly women workers: (1) occupational health research is done in a context that opposes the interests of workers to those of employers and governments, where the workers have many fewer resources; (2) to avoid naming these issues, scientists are encouraged to attribute an abstract scientific value to their studies, which disconnects them from the situation under study; (3) standard practices for the conduct of occupational health research and rules for the determination of scientific quality contain hidden biases against the demonstration of occupational health hazards, particularly those affecting women; the emphasis is on well-controlled studies done in situations that bear little resemblance to real life; (4) judgment of the value of scientific research takes place in the dark anonymously, with no confrontation of judge and judged and no recourse by the scientist whose work is rejected; and (5) myths of excellence, relevance, rigor, and responsibility are used to justify the type of research done and the people allowed to do it.

Some mechanisms exist for breaking loose from this vicious circle, and some workers have succeeded in challenging it. The group of researchers with whom I work at CINBIOSE has developed in a context that facilitates collaboration between women workers and researchers; and this collaboration has led to some new ways of looking at health problems.

WHY THE SCIENCE OF OCCUPATIONAL HEALTH IS NOT GOOD ENOUGH FOR WOMEN WORKERS

Employers' and Employees' Interests in Occupational Health

In North America, research and practice in occupational health have been conditioned by the workers' compensation system. Accidents and illnesses covered by workers' compensation are not subject to other recourse.[4] The compensation system is an insurance-like setup paid into by employers. Employers' payments, like other insurance premiums, are affected by their workers' rates of compensation, as well as by the overall level of compensation paid. Thus, employers have a collective and individual interest in limiting the number of compensable conditions.[5]

Research in occupational health has been influenced by pressure to answer the question, "Was this illness caused by an occupational exposure?" (In other words, is this illness compensable?) Problems that could not result in compensation are not considered to be occupational health problems. Research is concentrated on injuries and illnesses that have a clearly defined cause in a bona fide paid occupation, such as accidents to construction workers and miners. So, for example, the effects of women's unpaid work are not considered to be occupational health problems.[6] Occupational AIDS research has concentrated on health-care workers rather than on the much more heavily exposed sex workers, who are not covered by workers' compensation.

The link to compensation is well illustrated by the situation in Quebec, where the research money available from the occupational health granting agency is explicitly tied to the concept of "priority sectors": those occupational sectors with only 25 per cent of workers, but where compensation has been heaviest in previous years.[7] Research and prevention attempts are thus concentrated in mining, construction, and heavy industry; fewer than 10 percent of workers in the priority sectors are women. This method of determining research priorities ordinarily results in a low scientific interest in women workers.

Women and men have very different jobs,[8] and the study of most traditional men's jobs does not yield information on risks in women's jobs. Since their risks have not been thoroughly studied, women's working conditions have not been integrated into the standards for compensation.[9] It is hard to identify new compensable conditions when funding priorities favor finding low-cost engineering solutions to known problems such as noise and the lifting of heavy weights....

Thus, many health problems of women workers do not fall within the purview of the workers' compensation system, but are relegated to the general health services. At the same time, policies of the Ministry of Health and Social Services (MHSS) fail to identify women's working conditions as a source of health problems.[11] ...

Occupational health research ... is not driven primarily by the necessity to provide information leading to the protection of workers' health, but by a financial incentive: to lower compensation costs for employers and governments. The invisibility of women's occupational health problems permits employers to save money by transferring compensation costs to the public health-care sector.

Criteria for Receiving Research Funds

Occupational health research grants can be obtained directly from employers in industries in which there is concern about human health.... Funds can also be requested from government, private, or university funding agencies, which employ "peer review" (a panel of scientific experts) to determine whose research they will fund. Peer review is also used to judge the quality of research when a scientific paper is presented for publication.

Donna Mergler and I once examined determinants of our own success in getting government grants and found that proposals were more likely to be accepted if the project involved nonhumans or human cells in culture rather than in live humans, if the work was done in a laboratory rather than in the field, if there was a woman on the peer review committee, and if there was no visible worker input at any level of the project.[13] Projects refused (and other proposals accepted by the same granting agency) included: a questionnaire-based study of reproductive problems of health-care workers (a study of their cells was accepted); a study of neurotoxic effects suffered by metal-exposed workers (a comparison of different neurotoxic tests of unexposed people was accepted); a study of ergonomic and social difficulties suffered by women in nontraditional jobs (a study of musculo-skeletal problems of men and women in traditional jobs was accepted). Thus, studies were funded in inverse proportion to the likelihood that their results might support compensation or social change. In particular, all our proposals dealing with problems specific to women were rejected during that time.

Other feminist researchers also have difficulty finding funds for these aspects of their work. Although women now constitute almost half the workforce, research in women's occupational health is strikingly underfunded. In 1989 the Health and Welfare and Labor ministries asked us to prepare a critical review of women's occupational health studies in Canada,[14] and we found that our federal granting agencies did not have much to offer. According to Health and Welfare Canada, it supported sixty-four projects on women's health, of which only three addressed women's occupational health in any way. Only 3.1 per cent of the small amount of money spent in that year on *women's* health was allocated for research on women's occupational health. Many projects supported by Health and Welfare that should have included the health effects of women's jobs did not appear to do so. For example, no occupational determinants were included in studies on premenstrual syndrome, factors associated with outcomes of surgery, risks for development of hypertension during pregnancy, and women and health in the middle years. The situation has not changed dramatically since then....

How does this work? How can supposedly objective committees act with such unanimity to prevent improvement of women's working conditions? Part of the answer to these questions lies in the secrets of the peer review process. Grant applications are sent for review to experts who know the name of the applicant, but the names of these experts are concealed both from the applicants and from other committee members. Their reports are then examined by committees composed of well-established scientists, who make the final decisions on funding. This peer review process takes place almost entirely in the dark. Judgments are irreversible; refusals of grants can never be appealed, even when the grounds for refusal contravene the granting agencies' own published rules for funding.[16] Discussion in committee is confidential; participants are asked to disclose nothing of what is said. In some agencies, committee members vote in secret so that not even the members know the final rating of a project. This leaves the (political) heads of the agencies in a powerful position to make decisions that cannot be reviewed.

The veil lifts occasionally to reveal abusive practices. Recently, a medical researcher described the operation of an "old boys' network" at the Medical Research Council of Canada, suggesting that the network acts to discourage projects from "outsiders."[17] ...

Following are several examples of the practices in funding occupational health research, drawn from comments on grant proposals, submitted papers, and publications. These practices make it very difficult to find funding for studies of interest to women workers.

"Sufficient Evidence to Justify a Study."   Union women often express surprise and dismay after finding out how little we know about many substances to which women are routinely exposed at their jobs. This ignorance of women's exposures can have a self-reinforcing effect. One factor that weighs heavily in the decision to fund a study is, paradoxically, the demonstration that there is sufficient evidence to show that a given exposure-effect link exists. This tendency is particularly pronounced in Canada, where many researchers expect that scientific questions will be generated first in the United States. Refusals of our grant applications and those of our colleagues on the effects of manganese and styrene on chromosomes were justified on the grounds that evidence was insufficient to link these substances with the effects; the same teams were given large amounts to study the neurotoxic effects of these same substances in the same workers, because some evidence already existed to show these effects....

"Relevance to Health."   Another important criterion used to assess proposals for occupational health research is that the research should be relevant to human health. The medically trained committees interpret this to mean that the research must deal with pathologies[18] rather than indicators, signs or symptoms of deterioration in physical or mental states. Occupational health professionals generally come from medical faculties, where they have been trained in the diagnosis of pathologies; no part of their education ensures that they have ever studied exposures in a factory. The length and cost of training these professionals ensure that they usually do not come from working-class families. The pathologies can be studied in either humans or animals, but they must concern diseases with clear diagnoses....

This requirement for pathology has three consequences. First, the pathology must have been diagnosed. Yet, as Lorraine Code points out, ... the diagnosis of pathologies in women has been slowed by bias and stereotyped assumptions.[19] Second, this requirement forces the researcher to consider events that are rare among populations still at work. Ill people often leave the workplace. They can still be studied, but relating their illnesses to their prior working conditions requires a great deal of extrapolation. Third, researchers must study working populations of enormous size in order to find a few cases of illness. Studies become extremely expensive, restricted to the largest workplaces, the very best-recognized scientists, and the best-defined risks. Thus, funds are less available for work on women's occupational health problems, since women tend to work in smaller workplaces and their problems have not interested the best-known scientists.

A still more significant consequence of waiting for pathology to occur is an increase in human suffering. Prevention strategies are most successful before pathology occurs.... Waiting for the disease to happen is a delaying tactic that gets in the way of improving working conditions that could have been related to physiological or psychological effects.

Is This Health Problem Real?   The question of the "reality" of health problems is an especially important issue in occupational health, because employers' decisions about whether to compensate work-related diseases or to invest money in improved working conditions are often based on a cost-benefit analysis. For example, a ventilation system was installed in one twenty-seven-year-old plant only after workers became sensitized to the results of exposure to circulating radioactive dust.[20] This was long after the company was made aware that the dust was radioactive. With women workers, employers can delay recognition of a problem by invoking sexist denials of women's problems....

A good example of a problem treated incorrectly because of sexist bias is heat exposure. Men are typically exposed to heat at dramatic levels in foundries; this type of exposure can produce serious disorders or even death. Legal limits for heat exposure are based on studies of dynamic muscular, heat-generating work typical of these kinds of industries. However, women rarely work in this kind of factory, but often work in badly ventilated kitchens or laundries. When laundry workers complained about the difficulty of ironing sheets in thirty-degree temperatures, the employer replied that existing standards permitted thirty-degree exposures and there was therefore no problem. In fact, such low-level heat exposure does not produce specific heat-related illness. However, when it is coupled with postural and gestural constraints involved in lifting wet sheets or moving cooking pans (rapidly moving upper limbs with little displacement of the lower body), heat puts stress on the heart, resulting in nonspecific symptoms of discomfort and distress....

Compensation can be refused to women on the basis of a "scientific" judgement that the worker is not "really" ill. I still remember with horror the story told by a woman who worked for twenty years on an assembly line in a cookie factory. She was proud of her job and had never been late or absent from work. However, when the repetitive motions she made while wrapping small cakes finally caused shoulder pain that made her unable to work, the company contested her compensation case with scientific testimony that she was not ill....

Objectivity: "Some of These Girls Have Become Rather Anxious."[24]   The type of reasoning that results in restrictive scientific definitions of occupational effects on health can be demonstrated in relation to one of our research areas that has never been specifically funded and for which several grant requests have been refused: the study of workplace effects on menstrual function. Well over half of European and North American women of reproductive age now do paid work, and 30–90 per cent of menstruating women report lower abdominal and lower back pain associated with menstrual periods.[25] It is therefore surprising that the scientific literature on menstruation has rarely concerned itself with the effects of workplace risk factors on menstrual cycle symptoms, and that western occupational health literature has almost never included menstrual symptoms among outcome variables.

One reason could be that sexist researchers have been skeptical about the existence of occupational effects on the menstrual cycle....

"Rigor": The Rules

In the following discussion we present some rules for the standard conduct of occupational health research, drawn from textbooks and comments on grant requests or submissions to learned journals. Although the discussion is technical, we feel it is important to demonstrate that even cold clear rules for statistical significance conceal class- or sex-biased assumptions that increase the suffering of workers....

"Appropriate Study Design."   Epidemiology textbooks suggest two types of study, both of which divide populations into categories.[29] The case-control study divides people into well and not well, looking at the proportions of exposed and not exposed among them. The cohort study divides workers into exposed and not exposed, looking at the proportions of well and not well among them. The relevant other variables are "adjusted for." (Are the workers and controls the same age? Do they smoke and drink to the same extent?) If the differences are statistically significant, a relationship is established.

Most peer-review committees will insist that cohort studies include "reference" populations, groups that differ from workers *only* by not being exposed to the agent or condition thought to be associated with a health effect. However, this is an unrealistic requirement. For example, we presented a study in which 720 poultry-processing workers reported their work schedules and their menstrual cycles in detail.[30] We found that those who had variable schedules (about half) had more irregular cycles than those who went to work and left at the same time every day. Workers' menstrual cycles were also affected by the cold temperatures and fast work-speed in this industry. Reviewers criticized the study because we did not compare poultry-processing workers to workers in some other industry.

... In fact, women factory workers are always exposed to some toxic factors. We think that such comments are evidence that the reviewers (supposedly chosen for their proven expertise in the field) have little notion of what most factory jobs are like. It is hard for us to imagine a real control group that would satisfy these referees.

Keeping the Sample Uniform.   Requirements can be such as to ensure that study populations represent only a very partial view of reality. Researchers insist that populations examined be as "uniform" as possible, and that uniformity be ensured by eliminating any unusual parts of the population. It is interesting to see which criteria are thought to make populations nonuniform. In cancer research, uniformity might be sought by requiring study subjects to share an urban or rural environment, some nutritional habits, or medical history. But women are more often eliminated to make samples uniform. Shelia Zahm has recently published a bibliography of studies of occupational cancer among women. Of 1,233 cancer studies published in 1971–1990 in the eight major occupational health journals, only 14 per cent presented analyses of data on white women and only 10 per cent on nonwhite women.[31]

...

[An] example was a study, paid for with $2 million in public funds, relating cancers to a huge number of occupational exposures. When we asked the researcher why his study excluded women, he replied, "It's a cost-benefit analysis; women don't get many occupational cancers."

He did not react when we suggested that his argument was circular, nor when we pointed out that for women taxpayers, the cost-benefit of a study excluding them was infinitely high....

In fact, there *are* some well-identified occupational cancers among women.... But information is still sadly lacking in this area, because of the "scientific" elimination of women from studies of occupational cancer. Thus, scientists reinforce the notion that women's jobs are safe, that women's concerns about environmental influences on breast cancer (for example) are unfounded, and that it is justifiable to exclude women's jobs from prevention efforts. Is this because scientists feel far removed in sex and/or social class from women factory workers and hairdressers?

"Adjustment for Relevant Variables." "Adjusting" for a variable while analyzing data means using a mathematical procedure to eliminate its effect. It is reasonable, for example, to adjust for smoking when examining the relationship of dust exposure to lung damage, because smoking is an independent determinant of lung damage and might confuse the issue if those exposed to dust smoked more or less than those not exposed. We may need to add a correction factor to the lung function of nonsmokers before testing the relationship between dust exposure and lung damage.[35] This procedure, called "adjusting for smoking," allows us to determine the effect of dust on the lungs while taking into account the deleterious effects of smoking.

(1) Adjusting for Sex: However, such adjusting has been applied widely and abusively to sex differences. Studies that examine the health of workers often find that women workers report more symptoms of poor health or psychological distress than do their male counterparts. The approach to these differences is to "adjust" for sex, by adding a correction factor to the symptoms of male workers....

Adjusting would be appropriate only if sex were an independent determinant of poor health reports, for example, if women were weaker or complained more than men. If we think that "sex" is in itself a determinant of health in the same way as tobacco consumption, we will adjust for sex in relating working condition to health effects. If we think that sex is a surrogate for living or working conditions, we will be forced to carry out more complex analyses.[37]

...

There may be differences between men's and women's bodies that cause them to react differently to the same workplace.[40] For example, women may regulate temperature differently from men. But it is more likely that the disparity is due to the different work activities ascribed to men and women in the home and at work.... In short, adjusting for sex may mean adjusting for important working conditions. Thus, the standard techniques can obscure the types of suffering women experience at their jobs and help maintain the illusion that women are physically, mentally, and emotionally "the weaker sex."[42] Such analyses reduce the amount of money allocated to prevent occupational disease in women.

(2) Adjusting for Socio-Economic Status (SES): Epidemiological studies often refer to subjects' socio-economic status or social class, a loose concept that can mean different things, depending on how it is defined operationally. SES can be determined by reference to individuals' income, occupation, or educational level.

However, these determinations are often made according to the husband's occupation or education. In the past women's jobs have been ignored when determining family SES, with women assigned the same status as their husband or father. This method hides women's contribution to family income, although the additional income may improve the health of the family....

Additional problems result from the fact that a job title may not be associated with the same income or education for women as for men. More education may be required of women, and their job content may be different from men's.

Despite the vagueness and difficulties associated with determining SES, income is definitely associated with health status and with the presence/absence of some risk factors in the physical environment. Pregnancy outcome is much worse among the poorest Canadian women than among the richest.[44] The poor do not eat as well as the rich, they smoke more, and they are more likely to be exposed to certain environmental pollutants.

In studying workplace effects, it is hard to know how to take all of this into account. People of different social classes also have very different work environments. This may be true of people in the same workplace, and even of those with the same job title. Some epidemiologists adjust for social class when they study the effects of work on health. For example, large and often-cited studies on pregnancy and work or fertility and work[45] have used this technique. However, since job status is an important determinant of social class, adjusting for SES can obscure the real effects of a work environment.[46] In fact, some health effects previously attributed to poverty may in fact be due to poor working conditions. In all these ways, adjusting for social class acts to obscure relationships between exposures and effects, resulting in underestimates of occupational disease, especially for women workers.

Accurate Evaluation of Exposure.   Allocating workers dichotomously to ill and well comparison groups can mask biologically important phenomena that could help identify hazardous situations before pathology occurs, but similar false dichotomies can also occur when classifying workers as exposed or unexposed. Such classification (even into several exposure categories) is prone to error and thus to concealment of important occupational hazards.

Exposure to toxic substances or stressful conditions can be monitored in several ways. Taking measurements in the workplace is recognized as the best method, although it does not always relate well to health effects. Workers even a few meters apart can be exposed quite differently. A supervisor may stand back from a tub of solvent while a worker holds her face directly over it. Studies that sample at one time or one site per department may in fact produce very inaccurate results.

Since women and men with the same job title are often assigned very different tasks, they may have different exposures. For example, we recently studied municipal workers' jobs by pairing women and men hired for the same job as near as possible to the same date. At the time of the interview (about six years after hiring), thirty-four of the fifty-three pairs of men and women were assigned to the same jobs. But even among these thirty-four "true" pairs, only half gave similar job descriptions.

Over half (27/52) of the women interviewed reported that they did not do the same tasks as their male colleagues.... [We conclude from these interviews and from examining the literature that there is widespread imprecision in describing women's working conditions. This inaccuracy blurs relationships between exposures and effects and causes the underestimation of effects of working conditions.][49]

These imprecisions are caused in part by a class- and sex-biased reluctance to believe worker reports. In many cases, workers have a fairly good idea of their exposure levels, but their judgements are not considered to be objective and are discounted by researchers. To relate working conditions to illness, researchers refer to "experts." For example, in a study of respiratory symptoms among 13,568 workers, experts were asked to class certain jobs as exposed or not exposed to dust by using tables relating exposures to job title. The tables had been derived seven years previously in another country, but the researchers offered this justification: "Although [an expert exposure estimate] cannot be considered an ideal reference, it is not biased by misclassifications of exposure according to personal factors as it is based only on job titles and industry sectors."[50] This study went on to correlate reported symptoms of dust exposure (difficulty breathing, asthma) with the ratings of experts.... Not surprisingly, the workers' reports were much better correlated with symptoms than were the experts' reports. In fact, for women workers, the correlation with experts' ratings was quite low....

Contempt for nonexperts' reports of exposure has a scientific name: *recall bias,* a supposed tendency of ill people to overreport exposures. It is frequently invoked (as it was in the above case) to contest using workers' reports, but its existence has never been satisfactorily demonstrated.[51] This skepticism with regard to the estimates of interested parties might be comprehensible in scientific terms if it were applied to both workers and employers....

"*Statistical Significance.*" Before a drug, cosmetic, or food product can be marketed in North America, it must undergo extensive testing on animals.... Contrary to the situation with regard to drugs and cosmetics, no law requires employers to be sure that a new work-site condition is safe before exposing workers to it. For example, tens of thousands of women worked with video display terminals (VDTs) before the first study of VDT effects on pregnancy. Even now, no one is yet absolutely sure that VDTs do not pose a danger for pregnant women. But pregnant women have not stopped working with VDTs while waiting for the evidence to come in. In this and many other cases, a decision has been made to place the burden of proof on the worker rather than on the employer....

This antiworker bias has been heartily endorsed by scientists in their requirements for statistical tests. Standard scientific practice is to accept that there is a risk if there is less than one chance in twenty that the observed association was due to happenstance. In other words, in order for scientists to accept the fact that Agent X causes problems for pregnancy (or any other physiological state), a study must establish the toxic effects with "95 per cent certainty." This means that if the researcher would have eighteen chances in twenty of being right in concluding that there is a risk, the study is considered to be "negative," that is, no risk has been demonstrated. This is true even if the group being studied is so small that there is virtually no chance of demonstrating an effect with 95 per cent certainty.[52]

Furthermore, for scientists to be really sure of their conclusions, more than one study must show the same relationship. Given the small numbers of workers in most women's workplaces and the large numbers of potential hazards, it is no wonder that very few dangers for pregnancy or fertility have been established.[53] ...

"*Lack of Bias.*" Probably the most frequent question we hear from other scientists is about our relationship with unions.[54] Our colleagues express concern that we might be forced to falsify our findings in order to support union demands, or that our results may be misrepresented.... The fact that our studies are often initiated by workers is thought to lead to bias.

Our colleagues seem to think that when workers are involved in efforts to improve their working conditions, they will fake symptoms to gain their point. Our work has been criticized on these grounds, even when elaborate study designs are used to take this possibility into account and even when the patterns of physiological change are so specific to the toxic effect that the worker would have to be a specialist in order to produce them.

Many studies are published that have been initiated or inspired by employers, and the major granting agencies have put forward programs for university-industry collaborative research. One is forced to conclude that bias is only perceived when it acts in opposition to the prejudices of "mainstream" scientists. When bias is shared by most scientists, it is invisible and unremarkable.

...

The Supporting Myths: Responsibility and Excellence

The myths of rigor and objectivity justify scientists who conceal life-threatening risks to exposed workers, especially to women and minority workers. But two other myths also act to maintain this system in place: "responsibility" and "excellence."

"Responsibility" is a name often given to concealing risks.... Several of us at CINBIOSE have been criticized and threatened with legal action for giving information to workers about their own cells. A grant request was refused on the grounds that examining sperm counts of metal-exposed workers would be "irresponsible," since it would give them information they "didn't need" (because a low sperm count does not necessarily prevent conception and does not affect the well-being of workers who are not trying to conceive) and would needlessly upset them. Such "responsibility" keeps workers from being able to organize to prevent biological damage.

Lately there has been a lot of pressure from university administrators to hire "excellent" researchers for academic positions. Excellence of candidates is judged by proven grant-getting ability and the ability to publish in peer-reviewed journals with high-impact factors.[56] Thus, the ability to accept the biases of the dominant culture in occupational health is a bona fide occupational qualification for a career in research. In addition, academics in occupational health have already been subjected to a selection process for membership in a privileged class, quite distant from that of the workers they will be studying.... In North America, government affirmative action policies provide the only serious force for including women and ethnic minorities as members of the occupational health establishment; no ways have yet been developed to facilitate the access of working-class people to university positions. But even these minor pressures towards demographic diversity in scientific institutions have recently been opposed by a discourse on "excellence" that suggests "quality" should be the only criterion for hiring.

However, scientists may be perceived as nonexcellent for reasons related to their sex, class, or color.[58] Working-class people or people of color may express themselves in language somewhat different from that of middle-class professionals, language that may be misperceived as inaccurate or sloppy. Women students who combine childrearing with scientific training, or those who need to earn money while studying, may be misperceived as being not serious about science.... Thus, "excellence" can be a name given to exclusionary practices that keep women, working-class people, and minorities out of university departments and thus maintain social distance between researchers and the workers they study....

Forces for Change

We [at CINBIOSE] think that our success is due to the existence of several different structures that have been put in place in Quebec after struggles by working people and progressive scientists: (1) agreements between our university and the three major Quebec labor unions; and (2) provincial granting agencies or programs that include representation from the groups being studied.

Agreements between the University and Community Groups. The Université du Québec à Montreal was founded in 1969 with a mandate to serve the Quebec community, including "those sectors of the community not usually served by universities." It has signed agreements with the three major Quebec unions, the Confédération des syndicats nationaux (CSN), the Fédération des travailleuses et travailleurs du Québec (FTQ), and the Centrale de l'enseignement du Québec (CEQ), providing resources for responding to union requests (such as release time for professors who participate in educational activities, university seed money for research).[59] ...

During the 1970s, professors at the Université du Québec à Montreal joined the CSN. We negotiated clauses in our collective agreement to recognize work done in the context of the university-union agreements. Because our work in occupational health is carried on as part of our regular workload (for forty-five hours of teaching in unions we can be released from forty-five hours of university teaching), many professors have been available to work with unions. The unions gain access to university services and grants. Union-initiated research, which is often received with hostility by the scientific community, *must* be recognized by our employer, at the risk of grievance procedures in the context of our collective agreement. Scientists gain access to interesting and provocative research questions and useful information on working conditions and their effects.[61]

Several features of the university-union agreement have been important in making it productive: explicit recognition of the power imbalance between career researchers and community groups, with structures in place to guarantee that the needs of both are recognized throughout the entire project and guarantees of scientific credibility through peer review. Although peer review committees need to be sensitized to the specific difficulties of community-based research, they provide an important guarantee of quality for the community group and help to maintain the scientific credibility of the researchers. Title to the research results is held by the researcher and by the initiating organization. Seed money is available for feasibility studies, which are often necessary given the radically new questions posed by community groups.

Input from the Community in Granting Agencies. Two Quebec granting agencies include representatives from labor or community groups in the committees that give out funding. The Quebec Institute for Research in Occupational Health and Safety includes representatives from labor and management on its scientific council; the two sides explicitly and openly negotiate to fund research they consider important. This process paradoxically appears to allow for *less* bias in funding, because the practical consequences of the projects are put on the table from the outset....

During the early 1980s, one of the labor representatives was in charge of women's affairs for her union and we were able to get funding for some feminist studies. However, since her departure no such studies have been funded. We (and the union women's committees) have turned to the Quebec Council for Social Research, which incorporates community representatives in its decision-making processes....

Through these institutions we have been able to build relationships with women workers. Over the years, we have been able to count on support, information, and guidance from union members, from health and safety committees, and from the very active women's committees of the three major trade unions in Quebec. With them, we have been able to come to a better understanding of the needs of women in the labor force and provide information that has been helpful to them. Their solidarity has been a source of strength to us over many years, and their insights have been invaluable....

PRACTICAL IMPLICATIONS OF DOING WOMEN-BASED RESEARCH

Since 1978 CINBIOSE scientists have been doing research in collaboration with women workers. Due to the constraints on us and on them, we cannot say that our research agenda is entirely driven by women's questions; rather, it represents a compromise between the needs of women and other workers and the requirements of academia and unions. Still, if we define feminist research as research that responds to questions asked by women and proposes to improve the status of women in society, we have been engaged in feminist research for fifteen years.[63] Through these experiences we have been forced to think and act differently from the ways we had been taught during our scientific training.

We present several examples of this evolution, still in progress: (1) we have learned to think differently from other biologists about male-female biological differences in relation to fitness for specific jobs; (2) we have learned to redefine work activity in studies of occupational health and ergonomics; (3) and we are rethinking questions of expertise and knowledge.

We are not sure whether we have developed specifically feminist methodologies. Feminist studies share the necessity of challenging disciplinary and methodological barriers with other community-oriented research. Community members want answers to their questions, which are not confined to single disciplines or schools of thought. We have therefore had to take seriously the painful task of integrating inputs from social scientists, ergonomists, and biologists. We have been forced to explore combinations of qualitative and quantitative research methods, and interactions between the two.

Some writers consider that feminist methodologies require researcher subjectivity to be explicitly put to use. We in the natural sciences are not yet in a political position from which we could question the official stance of objectivity in our published papers.[64] We are already marginal in our approach to occupational health, because we are women, we work with unions, and we are not doctors.... Most of our studies have therefore employed existing methods. However, many of the questions we have asked have ensured that the methods had to be applied in a new context or in a different situation. We are therefore not proposing new feminist methodologies for biological research, but just demonstrating the new insights we receive when our research is guided by a feminist agenda.

Male/Female Biological Differences from the Point of View of Women Workers

One area in which our collaboration with women's committees has stimulated us to new ways of thinking has been in the area of research on the relative physical strength of women and men. Much current research around women and work has been motivated by questions of equality/inequality and fitness. Can women lift heavy loads?[65] Should pregnant women be exposed to chemicals? However, women workers phrase things differently. How can I get to rest when I'm tired? Whom can I get to help me when a job is too heavy? What is perceived as an equality question by scientists is experienced as a health and safety issue by workers. These two ways of thinking affect research on occupational injuries and illnesses as well as on examinations of the sexual division of labor.

Does the Sexual Division of Labor Protect Women's Health? In many manual occupations there is a rigid sexual division of labor. Women and men are assigned to very different jobs, whose requirements are often quite dissimilar.... One of the explanations often given is that women are biologically different from men and therefore cannot do the same jobs. Jobs held by men are more difficult, and women are not able to do them. Many women workers share this point of view....

We have examined some data relevant to the relative safety of women's jobs. The classic way to compare health risks of men's and women's jobs is by looking at the likelihood of the workers sustaining occupational injuries and illnesses by sex.[68] The interpretation is that women's jobs are safer, due to the fact that women are unfit to be assigned to heavy work.[69] However, one of the reasons why women's traditional work appears to be a safe refuge for them is that its workload and risks have not been characterized. Only recently have ergonomists begun developing ways to represent the extraordinary demands made on women in factories and services....

We have studied a cleaning service assigned to suburban trains in France and employing nineteen men and seventeen women.[71] There was a rigid sexual division of labor, with the task of toilet cleaning assigned exclusively to women. Interviews and observations revealed a number of physical constraints associated with the work, and particularly with toilet cleaning, which involved trajectories of over twenty kilometers a day and work in uncomfortable postures. Some 25 percent of cleaning time was spent in a crouched position. Women employees suffered from many musculo-skeletal problems.... By contrast, men's jobs involved occasional to very occasional lifting of heavy weights, and some work accidents had occurred. Older men, however, were assigned to a job (chrome polishing) that required little energy expenditure or force. Thus, men and women did specific jobs, but only the risks associated with the men's jobs were recognized.

...

We are now selecting dimensions on which to analyze "light" and "heavy" cleaning systematically. Our major problem is that none of the grids currently available in ergonomics can be applied, since the task components that make women's jobs difficult have been unrecognized. For example, we are looking for "objective" correlatives of meticulousness, which hospital cleaners and municipal cleaners alike mentioned as an important characteristic of women's work in cleaning. We will observe the amplitude of movements and the number of times the same surface is cleaned. We will record rubbing and scrubbing incidents as indicators of precision requirements. We hope that these methods can be applied to a variety of women's traditional jobs, in order to represent effectively the difficulties of these jobs. At the same time, it has been necessary to discuss these findings with women workers, because we are suggesting that they redefine their notions of hard work and safe work.

Are Women Wrong When They Say Men's Jobs Are Riskier?
If the sexual division of labor does not prevent women from doing hard jobs, we must ask what purpose it serves. One of the purposes may be to justify health risks by reference to sexual stereotyping. Since work injuries and illnesses occur when the worker's capacity is exceeded by the job requirements, we must consider in this light the fact that men have many more work injuries and illnesses than women. At face value (discounting for the moment the fact that women's occupational health problems have been underreported) the data suggest that men are more apt than women to be in jobs that are ill fitted to their capacities. In other words, risk of injury is an occupational health problem for men, but a reason for exclusion of women.

Our experiences in union training sessions suggest that, although many women accept pain and suffering as chronic components of their jobs,[72] men are in fact more likely to accept acute risk. We observed this in an educational session with textile workers. Sex-typed jobs in their factory, with a 90 per cent male workforce, were eliminated following the enactment of human rights legislation. Changes in the collective agreement abolished seniority by sex and made all jobs accessible to all workers. A single seniority list replaced the separate male and female lists, and all workers were asked to follow the same career path. These changes coincided with heavy cuts in employment due to automation. Since many of the women's jobs on an assembly line were cut, they found themselves "bumped" to entry-level jobs. One of those jobs involved driving a motorized cart with ten 300-pound rolls of fabric. The rolls had to be manipulated onto the cart, and the back end of the cart had to be directed manually, with a lever placed in an awkward position. Many women objected to doing this job because they were afraid they might hurt their backs, and they were laid off, one by one, until 90 per cent of the layoff list was female. The women demanded restoration of the segregated seniority lists. The union women's committee and the company pointed out in vain that the man who had done this job successfully for the previous two years was five feet three inches tall and weighed 130 pounds. The women retorted that they would not accept the risk of back problems.

. . .

Physical strength may in fact be invoked when a health and safety problem should be addressed for all workers. Strength is only mentioned when there is an underlying message that women are not "fit" for some task. But it is erroneous to pose the question of strength just in terms of women's capacities. We do not know whether there would be excess health costs if the "average" woman persisted in doing the manual tasks done by men; women in nontraditional jobs are a small, highly selected group. But we also do not know whether men would be "strong enough" to do the high-speed repetitive tasks done by women, followed by evenings and weekends occupied by domestic tasks. The concept of strength has been limited to women's attempts to enter nontraditional fields and has not included men's intolerance of the physical requirements of women's work.[73] . . . Endurance may be a requirement for women who combine a long paid work day with long hours of child care and domestic work, but this has not been included in the image of strength that emerges from the ergonomics literature.

. . .

Using Sexual Stereotyping to Justify Exploitation Precludes Adequate Methods for Health Protection.
These reactions of workers have led us to understand that sexual stereotypes can be used to justify extreme physical exploitation. The sexual division of manual jobs may result from the fact that some jobs are at the limits of human capacity. The dexterity required to wrap 7,800 cookie packages per day kept men from applying for "women's jobs" in the cookie factory, while the women refused to lift the 40-kilogram bags of sugar up to the top of the mixing machine. . . .

These excessive job requirements may be motivated by economic interest. Employers may save money by keeping working conditions close to the human limit....

In fact, it may be that some jobs are so close to the limit of human capacity that they exceed the capacities of almost all members of one sex. In our study of women in nontraditional municipal jobs, only the largest (male) workers were able to do gardening without suffering pain or excessive fatigue.... In biological terms, men and women are distributed along overlapping normal curves of height, weight, ability to lift weights, endurance, patience, and dexterity.... The degree of overlap varies with the characteristic: there is more overlap in the strength required to push weights than to lift them, for example. However, the degree of overlap can be changed by changing the job characteristics. Use of appropriate equipment can transform lifting motions into pushing, and using different tools can permit smaller workers to take advantage of their greater flexibility....

Thus, there is no job that can be done by all men and no women, or by all women and no men (with some trivial exceptions such as sperm donor or surrogate mother). However, some jobs have extreme requirements, such that they are situated at or near the nonoverlapping portions of the curves of male and female abilities. These jobs nevertheless involve health risks for both sexes....

We have learned from workers that biological differences between women and men should not be studied in isolation. Health is protected when the job is appropriate for workers' capacity, which is affected by their physical abilities and personal and social situations, as well as the tools and equipment available in the workplace.... It can be seen from this representation that attributing male-female differences in work performance to chromosomes is a vast oversimplification.

Thus, we have been led by interactions with workers from a static view of the fitness of women's bodies for their jobs to a dynamic view of job-biology interaction. We therefore are suggesting to the workers as well as to occupational health specialists that questions they are asking about fitness for work be recast as questions about the ability of the work situation to accommodate human diversity and different techniques....

Questioning the Home/Work Dichotomy

As occupational health researchers, we have tended in the past to accept current definitions of "occupations" as including only paid work. One of our current projects is leading us to question this definition. The women's committee of the Fédération des travailleurs et des travailleuses du Québec asked CINBIOSE to do a study of how men and women with young children balance family responsibilities. In an exploratory study, Louise Vandelac and Andrée-Lise Méthot interviewed twenty-three women and four men about techniques used to balance professional and family responsibilities.[80] During the interviews we realized that current work organization segments human existence into two noninterpenetrating spheres. Workers are expected to leave their desires and needs at the door of the workplace. In occupational health jurisprudence, a domestic determinant of a health problem is an accepted reason for denial of compensation.[81] The workplace, however, is allowed to impinge on all areas of the workers' lives by requiring shift work, overtime, and schedule irregularities and by inducing fatigue and health symptoms that follow the worker home. Since in theory workers come to the office without their families, the workplace is organized as if workers had no life outside.[82] Only 15 per cent of a very large sample of French slaughterhouse workers know at the beginning of work the time when they will finish.[83]

The organizational components of tasks may exclude workers with family responsibilities, particularly women. Thus, women may be eliminated from some jobs due to the impossibility of reconciling them with family responsibilities, or women may choose to restrict their family lives to keep their jobs.... Preliminary results from our twenty-three interviews suggested that, at the birth of a child, company policies and pay differentials make it desirable for women to reduce their paid hours or take unpaid leave while men work extra hours to make up the difference in pay.[85] In another CINBIOSE study, municipal workers (90 per cent of them men) do not know where they will be working from one week to the next. Women entering these jobs were significantly less likely than men to be living with children, possibly due to the difficulty of reconciling women's family responsibilities with extremely irregular work hours.[86]

...

Our contacts with workers have led us to suggest that employers include family role requirements in their occupational health programs. It is already recognized that workers have physiological lives that go beyond the immediate requirements of the workplace. For example, employers usually provide lunchrooms, water fountains, and bathrooms. A logical extension of this realization is that workers have families, so they need appropriate shifts, access to telephones, and provision for family illness. We are now trying to induce occupational health specialists to include interactions with family responsibilities in their conceptions of workplace norms and standards. For example, exposure standards for many working conditions suppose an eight-hour working day followed by sixteen hours of rest, a condition not available for many workers or for most women workers. We have also proposed in the scientific literature on ergonomics that family responsibilities be included in a dynamic conception of worker-job interaction.[87]

Using Knowledge of Workers and Professors

We are also exploring issues relating to expertise. Questions of knowledge versus experience are central to the development of feminist research.[88] Respect for women's experiences and perceptions has been proposed as a central element of feminist research methodologies. Incorporating worker knowledge in the data-gathering process poses a specific problem in occupational health, where an immediate money value is attached to credibility. If the worker is believed, she will be paid for her work accident or pregnancy leave (for dangerous work). If not, the employer and government will profit financially. The financial stakes may explain why we have been threatened with lawsuits and prosecution for illegal medical practice for merely reporting to workers what they themselves have told us in questionnaires.

However, our expertise is also critical in assisting workers to gain recognition for their health risks. Any de-emphasizing of our qualifications has proved risky in situations opposing us to employer-paid experts. Both because we are women and because we use non-traditional language about workers, we may be treated with less respect by both workers and employers....

Much of our work has been done with the hospital workers' unions, where the problem of credibility is compounded by authoritative statements from employer representatives who are doctors....

It is sometimes tempting for us to try to oppose the doctors' assertions with our own, in negotiations or during tribunals. After all, we do have some claims to expertise, and it is fun to show how much smarter we are. However, we have learned repeatedly that in occupational health hearings power is knowledge, not the reverse. Although our "expert" testimony has helped gain some rights for women workers, time after time we have seen our work defeated not by being proven false, but by groundless assertions from other "experts" with closer links to employers, or by simple statements from employers that allowing the worker's claim would lead to others and result in enormous costs.[89] These experiences have led us to the conclusion that a transfer of power from us to the women workers is a necessary step in improving working conditions. The transfer of power will be attempted through characterization and valorization of the workload of three groups of women: bank tellers, primary school teachers, and office clerks....

The aim of the project is to create a worker-university partnership that will pool information about the workload in a context that will allow workers to systematize and validate their own experience of their workload. Because the project is being coordinated by the union women's committees, results can be used to focus suggestions for change in the workplace. For example, in the public service sector, women tell us that they no longer take their mid-morning and mid-afternoon breaks. "We don't have enough replacement people, we can't leave a helpless patient alone, saying 'Sorry, it's break time.'" Taking breaks is an important health determinant....

During our project, workers will keep records of the number of breaks they take and what they do on their breaks. We anticipate that this procedure will demonstrate that they are paying with their bodies and minds for the cuts in public sector employment. Needless to say, many scientists will not consider the results of this study to represent an objective estimate of workload. Our project is, rather, intended to give the workers tools that will enable them to recognize and promote recognition of this workload, so they will feel entitled to create conditions for better health. This approach is analogous to those that have been used to support higher salaries for women's work by documenting women's hidden competence.[90] ...

CONCLUSION

Recently the Medical Research Council of Canada invited several researchers to participate in an all-day discussion of a "Women's Health Agenda." It was interesting to hear the dialogue between feminist scientists who recommended "listening to women's voices" and other biomedical experts pleading for "data-driven research priorities" and "measurable outcomes." The latter sounded very reasonable. At a time of pressure on public funds, it is hard to justify working on problems with no measurable effects. Women particularly have a hard time saying outright that money should be invested in an area because we say so. At the same time it seemed absurd to many of us to demand that research be oriented by available data, when in fact few reliable data are available on women's health.

At the end of the day, feeling wounded and uncertain after many compromises and some raised voices, we were not sure that the Council would change its priorities. But the dialogue had made us dream of the day scientists will be given money for sufficient women-oriented data collection to create a new gender-inclusive science of occupational health, including adequate measurement techniques and rules for people-based validation. We do not know whether this process will lead to new methods or new applications of old methods, because it is only just beginning.

NOTES

1. I am grateful to the Social Sciences and Humanities Research Council of Canada, the Conseil québécois de recherche sociale, and the Equality Fund of Labour Canada for research support. I thank Lucie Dumais and Serge Daneault for helpful comments.... Parts of this paper were originally published in K. Messing and D. Mergler, "The Rat Couldn't Speak, but We Can: Inhumanity in Occupational Health Research," in R. Hubbard and L. Birke, eds., *Re-inventing Biology*, Race, Gender, and Science Series (Indianapolis: Indiana University Press, forthcoming). [Karen Messing is Professor of Biological Sciences at the Université du Québec in Montreal.]...

3. Katherine Lippel, *Le stress au travail* (Cowansville, Que.: Les éditions Yvon Blais, 1993), p. 228.

4. This is one reason why employers in the United States have been anxious to restrict women's access to nontraditional jobs thought to cause reproductive damage. A foetus cannot be covered by workers' compensation, and a malformed child could potentially sue an employer for millions of dollars.

5. A historical and political treatment of workers' compensation can be found in Katherine Lippel, *Le droit des accidentes du travail à une indemnité: Analyse historique et critique* (Montreal: Themis, 1986).

6. In fact, women's domestic work overload is often used as a reason for refusing compensation. Recently, the employer presented evidence in a musculo-skeletal injury case purporting to show that the woman had in fact injured herself by carrying heavy loads in her kitchen.

7. Commission de la santé et de la sécurité du travail, *Rapport d'activité 1992* (Quebec: CSST, 1993).

8. See, for example, Pat Armstrong and Hugh Armstrong, *The Double Ghetto* (Toronto: McClelland and Stewart, 1993).

9. Carole Brabant, "Heat Exposure Standards and Women's Work: Equitable or Debatable?" *Women and Health* 18 (1992), pp. 119–30; Karen Messing, Lucie Dumais, and Patrizia Romito, "Prostitutes and Chimney Sweeps Both Have Problems: Toward Full Integration of the Two Sexes in the Study of Occupational Health," *Social Science and Medicine* 36 (1992), pp. 47–55.

. . .

11. Ministère de santé et des services sociaux, *Politique de la santé et du bien-être* (Quebec: Ministère de santé et des services sociaux, 1992).

. . .

13. Karen Messing and Donna Mergler, *Determinants of Success in Obtaining Grants for Action-Oriented Research* in *Occupational Health* (Las Vegas, Nevada: Proceedings of the American Public Health Association, 1986).

14. Messing, *Occupational Health and Safety Concerns*; Karen Messing, *Doing Something about It: Priorities in Women's Occupational Health* (Ottawa: Health Canada, Proceedings of the Round Table on Gender and Occupational Health, 1993), pp. 155–61.

. . .

16. We were once refused a grant on the grounds that our work was too applied, insufficiently related to basic science objectives. We replied by quoting sections of the grant agency's own appeal for projects, which clearly and emphatically stated that applied work should be funded. We were told to submit our grant proposal again the following year. Our new proposal was rejected on the same grounds. We then submitted the same proposal without the applied part: the request was enthusiastically accepted and funded (and was among the top five proposals).

17. Gilles Ste-Marie, "La recherche scientifique au Canada: Un trafic déloyal," *Le devoir,* May 23, 1992.

18. The distinction is made here between diseases diagnosed by a physician (pathologies), symptoms perceptible only to the worker herself, and pre-pathological alterations in the body, which can be revealed by researchers (signs or indicators).

19. Lorraine Code, "How Do We Know? Questions of Method in Feminist Practice," in S. Burt and L. Code, *Changing Methods* (Toronto: Broadview Press, 1995), pp. 13–44.

20. Karen Messing, "Union-Initiated Research in Genetic Effects of Workplace Agents," *Alternatives: Perspectives on Technology, Environment and Society* 15(1) (1988), pp. 14–18.

. . .

24. R.G. Cameron, "Effect of Flying on the Menstrual Function of Air Hostesses," *Aerospace Medicine* (September 1969), pp. 1020–23.

25. N.F. Woods, A. Most, and G.K. Dery, "Prevalence of Premenstrual Symptoms," *American Journal of Public Health* 72 (1982), pp. 1257–64; G. Sundell, I. Milsom, and Anderson, "Factors Influencing the Prevalence of Dysmenorrhea in Young Women," *British Journal of Obstetrics and Gynaecology* 97 (1990), pp. 588–94; and S. Pullon, J. Reinken, and M. Sparrow, "Prevalence of Dysmenorrhea in Wellington Women," *New Zealand Medical Journal* 10 (February 1988), pp. 52–54.

. . .

29. The following section draws heavily for its examples of orthodoxy on Richard R. Monson, *Occupational Epidemiology* (Boca Raton, Fl.: CRC Press, 1980).

30. Messing et al., "Menstrual Cycle Characteristics," pp. 302–9.

31. Shelia Hoar Zahm, *Women's Health: Occupation and Cancer, Selected Bibliography* (Washington, D.C.: National Cancer Institute, 1993); Shelia Hoar Zahm, Linda M. Pottern, Denise Riedel Lewis, Mary H. Ward, and Deborah W. White, "Inclusion of Women and Minorities in Occupational Cancer Epidemiological Research," *J. Occup. Med.* 36(8) (1994): 842–47.

. . .

35. By analogy, if smokers were twice as likely to get cancer, the number of cancers among nonsmokers could be multiplied by two before analysis.

36. Brabant, Mergler, and Messing, "Va te faire soigner," pp. 181–204; Mats Hagberg, Hal Morgenstern, and Michael Kelsh, "Impact of Occupations and Job Tasks on the Prevalence of Carpal Tunnel Syndrome," *Scandinavian Journal of Work Environment and Health* 18 (1992), pp. 337–45, Table 2; and Diana S. Stetson, James W. Albers, Barbara A. Silverstein, and Robert A. Wolfe, "Effects of Age, Sex, and Anthropometric Factors on Nerve Conduction Measures," *Muscle and Nerve* 15 (1992), pp. 1095–104.

...

37. Similar errors are often made when people of different races are studied. See, for example, Nancy Krieger, "Social Class and the Black/White Crossover in the Age-specific Incidence of Breast Cancer," *American Journal of Epidemiology* 131 (1990), pp. 804–14; and Nancy Krieger and Diane L. Rowley, "Re: 'Race, Family Income, and Low Birth Weight,'" *American Journal of Epidemiology* 135 (1992), p. 501.

38. The methods and many results are presented in Saurel-Cubizolles et al., "Enquete dans les abattoirs."

39. These are from unpublished data collected by Marie-Josephe Saurel-Cubizolles and Monique Kaminski of INSERM, Unite 149, Paris, which we are analyzing in collaboration with them. We are grateful for technical help from France Tissot and Marie-Aude Le Berre.

40. Messing, *Occupational Health and Safety Concerns;* and Julie Courville, "Les obstacles ergonomiques à l'integration des femmes dans les postes traditionnellement masculins," M.Sc. thesis, Département des sciences biologiques, Université du Québec à Montréal, 1990.

...

42. The appropriate procedure is to analyze the data separately for both sexes, only considering them together if the same relationships appear to be operating in both sexes. See Margrit Eichler, "Nonsexist Research: A Metatheoretical Approach," *Indian Journal of Social Work* 53(3) (1992), pp. 329–41.

...

44. Russell Wilkins, "Health Expectancy by Local Area in Montreal: A Summary of Findings," *Canadian Journal of Public Health* 77 (1986), pp. 216–20; D. Blanc, G.D. Smith, and Mel Bartley, "Social Class Differences in Years of Potential Life Lost: Size, Trends and Principal Causes," *British Medical Journal* 301, pp. 429–32; and Russell Wilkins, Greg J. Sherman, and P.A.F. Best, "Findings of a New Study Relating Unfavorable Pregnancy Outcomes and Infant Mortality to Income in Canadian Urban Regions in 1986," *Health Reports* 3 (1991), pp. 7–31 (Statistics Canada Catalogue 82-003). This study classes SES according to residence.

45. Alison D. Macdonald, J. Corbett McDonald, Ben Armstrong, Nicola Cherry, C. Delorme, A. Nolin, and D. Robert, "Occupation and Pregnancy Outcome," *British Journal of Industrial Medicine* 44 (1987), pp. 521–26; and P. Rachootin and J. Olsen, "The Risk of Infertility and Delayed Conception Associated with Exposures in the Danish Workplace," *Journal of Occupational Medicine* 25 (1983), pp. 394–402.

46. Chantal Brisson, D. Loomis, and N. Pearce, "Is Social Class Standardisation Appropriate in Occupational Studies?" *Journal of Epidemiology and Community Health* 41 (1987), pp. 290–94; and Jack Siemiatycki, S. Wacholder, R. Dewar, et al., "Degree of Confounding Bias Related to Smoking, Ethnic Group and Socioeconomic Status in Estimates of the Associations between Occupation and Cancer," *Journal of Occupational Medicine* 30 (1988), pp. 617–25.

...

49. N.J. Birkett, "Effect of Nondifferential Misclassification on Estimates of Odds Ratios with Multiple Levels of Exposure," *American Journal of Epidemiology* 136 (1992), pp. 356–62.

50. Mohammed Hsairi, Francine Kauffmann, Michel Chavance, and Patrick Brochard, "Personal Factors Related to the Perception of Occupational Exposure: An Application of a Job Exposure Matrix," *International Epidemiology Association Journal* 21 (1992), pp. 972–80.

51. Michael Joffe, "Male- and Female-mediated Reproductive Effects on Occupation: The Use of Questionnaire Methods," *Journal of Occupational Medicine* 31 (1989), pp. 974–79; Michael Joffe, "Validity of Exposure Data Derived from Interviews with Workers," *Proceedings of the 23rd International Congress on Occupational Health,* Montreal, 1990, p. 61; and Susan MacKenzie and Abby Lippman, "An Investigation of Report Bias in a Case-Control Study of Pregnancy Outcome," *American Journal of Epidemiology* 129 (1989), pp. 65–75.

52. H. L. Needleman, "What Can the Study of Lead Teach Us about Other Toxicants?" *Environmental Health Perspectives* 86 (1990), pp. 183–89; and Karen Messing, "Environnement et santé: La santé au travail et le choix des scientifiques," in *L'avenir d'un monde fini: Jalons pour une éthique du développement durable,* Cahiers de recherche éthique, no. 15 (Montreal: Editions Fides, 1991), pp. 107–10.

53. Not only pregnant women are affected. Any powerless group (among which workers and women are well represented) may have the burden of proof placed on it without explicit justification.

54. The second-most frequent refers to our feminism. A critique of one of our articles on feminist perspectives in occupational health began, "This emotional article ..." We think the emotion was the reviewer's!

...

56. The guesswork has now been taken out of the task of evaluating candidates' curriculum vitaes by the use of impact factors for the journals in which a candidate has published; the impact factor is calculated as the average number of times an article in the given journal is cited in articles published during the current year.

...

58. Karen Messing, "Sois mâle et tais-toi: L'excellence et les chercheures universitaires," *Women's/Education/des femmes* 9 (Autumn 1991), pp. 49–51.

59. The Confédération des syndicats nationaux has 200,000 members, about half of them women; the Fédération des travailleuses et travailleurs du Québec has 350,000 members, about 30 per cent of them women; the Centrale de l'enseignement du Québec represents all of Quebec's primary and secondary school teachers, as well as some junior college and university lecturers and professors, and some support staff, with a large majority of women members. See also Comité conjoint UQAM-CSN-FTQ, *Le protocole d'entente UQAM-CSN-FTQ: Sur la formation syndicale* (1977), Services à la collectivité, Université du Québec à Montréal, CP 8888, Succ. A, Montreal, Quebec H3C 3P8; Comité conjoint UQAM-CSN-FTQ, *Le protocole UQAM-CSN-FTQ: 1976–1986, Bilan et perspectives* (1988), Services à la collectivité, Université du Québec à Montréal; and Karen Messing, "Putting Our Two Heads Together: A Mainly Women's Research Group Looks at Women's Occupational Health," in J. Wine and J. Ristock, eds., *Feminist Activism in Canada: Bridging Academe and the Community* (Toronto: James Lorimer, 1991), reprinted in *National Women's Studies Association Journal* 3 (1991), pp. 355–67.

...

61. Karen Messing and Donna Mergler, "Unions and Women's Occupational Health in Quebec," in L. Briskin and P. McDermott, eds., *Women Challenging Unions* (Toronto: University of Toronto Press, 1993).

...

63. Shulamit Reinharz, *Feminist Methods in Social Research* (New York: Oxford University Press, 1992).

64. Patrizia Romito describes with wry humor the fate of one of her medical research papers, which did not appear sufficiently detached for the U.S. journal that she submitted it to: P. Romito, *Lavoro e salute in gravidanza* (Milan: Franco Angell, 1990), pp. 13–23.

65. Evidence on this point has been reviewed by Courville, "Les obstacles ergonomiques à l'intégration des femmes"; and summarized in Messing, *Occupational Health and Safety Concerns*.

...

68. We have described this phenomenon in K. Messing, J. Courville, M. Boucher, L. Dumais, and A.M. Seifert, "Use of Interview Data to Complement Occupational Accident Reports When Comparing Health and Safety Risks of Blue-collar Jobs by Gender," *Safety Science* 18 (1995). Note that "work accidents" include injuries and illnesses attributable to paid work.

69. G. Laurin, *Féminisation de la main d'oeuvre: Impact sur la santé et la sécurité travail* (Montreal: Commission de la santé et de la sécurité du Québec, 1992), p. 52; C.A. Bell, N.A. Stout, T.R. Bender, C.S. Conroy, W.E. Crouse, and J.R. Myers, "Fatal Occupational Injuries in the United States, 1980 through 1985," *JAMA* 263 (1990), pp. 3047–50; J.E. Cone, D. Makofsky, and R.J. Harrison, "Fatal Injuries at Work in California," *Journal of Occupational Medicine* 33 (1991), pp. 813–817; A. Hough, "Comparison of Losses Due to Accidents Reported by Males and Females," *Journal of Occupational Health and Safety Australia and New Zealand* 5 (1989), pp. 237–42; Laurin, *Féminisation de la main d'oeuvre,* J.C. Robinson, "Trends in Racial Equality and Inequality and Exposure to Work-related Hazards," *AAOHN Journal* 37 (1989), pp. 56–63; and Norman Root and Judy R. Daley, "Are Women Safer Workers?" *Monthly Labor Review* (September 1980), pp. 3–10.

...

71. K. Messing, C. Haentjens, and G. Doniol-Shaw, "L'invisible nécessaire: L'activité de nettoyage des toilettes sur les trains de voyageurs en gare," *Le travail humain* 55 (1992), pp. 353–70; and K. Messing, G. Doniol-Shaw, and C. Haentjens, "Sugar and Spice: Health Effects of the Sexual Division of Labour among Train Cleaners," *International Journal of Health Services* 23 (1993), pp. 133–46.

72. Julie Courville and Nicole Vezina found, in a study of poultry-slaughterhouse workers, that 71 per cent of the women doing a repetitive cutting job had experienced neck and shoulder pain during the previous week and one in five regularly experienced pain during work.

73. Perhaps because job applications have been lacking, no attention has been paid to the capacity of men to do women's traditional work. This situation appears to be changing with the rise in

unemployment among young men. Women's committees complain that men are moving into assembly-line jobs usually held by women.

· · ·

80.   L. Vandelac and A-L. Méthot, *Concilier l'inconciliable* (Montreal: Fédération des travailleuses du Québec, 1993).

81.   We were involved in the case of a woman with shoulder problems that were attributed not to her repetitive task but to the fact that her cupboard shelves at home were too high. Industrial deafness cases invoke the worker's Ski-Doo or presence at a discotheque as reasons to deny compensation.

82.   Workers are not compensated for loss of quality of life due to symptoms, only for illnesses and injuries. The unequal separation of domestic responsibilities within families may have been a response to the extreme demands of the workplace. This point has been recently reviewed in P. Armstrong and H. Armstrong, *Theorizing Women's Work* (Toronto: Garamond Press, 1991), ch. 5.

83.   Marie-Aude Le Berre, "Etude des conditions et des arrêts de travail dans des abattoirs de volaille et des conserveries," report of a project done with CINBIOSE and INSERM, Unité 149 and presented to Département de Statistique, IUT Vannes (1993).

· · ·

85.   Vandelac and Méthot, *Concilier l'inconciliable.*

86.   Karen Messing, Lucie Dumais, Julie Courville, Ana Maria Seifert, Nicole Vézina, "Comment ajuster le "col bleu" à 'Madame Tout (l'Monde': Les obstacles d'ordre physique à l'intégration des femmes dans des postes non-traditionnels," in M. des Rivières, M. de Koninck, and K. Messing, eds., *Dépasser les obstacles et les résistances,* Conseil du statut de la femme du Québec (1994).

87.   See Messing, Dumais, and Romito, "Prostitutes and Chimney Sweeps Both Have Problems," pp. 47–55; and Karen Messing, Andrée-Lise Méthot, and Louise Vandelac, 1994, "Comment inclure les activités de conciliation des responsabilités familiales et professionnelles dans l'analyse du travail?" Proceedings of the 62nd annual meeting of the Association francophone pour le savoir, p. 458.

88.   Lorraine Code, *What Can She Know? Feminist Theory and the Construction of Knowledge* (Ithaca, N.Y.: Cornell University Press, 1991), ch. 6.

89.   For example, our article on the heavy workload of sewing machine operators was used to justify paid early leave *("retrait préventif")* for pregnant operators. However, employers soon challenged this practice, asserting that discomfort was not danger and that there was no risk to a foetus from the mother's discomfort. The issue of the heavy workload was drowned in semantics and the worker lost her case, setting a dangerous precedent.

90.   Jane Gaskell, "What Counts as Skill? Reflections on Pay Equity," in Judy Fudge and Patricia McDermott, eds., *Just Wages: A Feminist Assessment of Pay Equity* (Toronto: University of Toronto Press, 1991); see also Catherine Teiger and Colette Bernier, "Ergonomic Analysis of Work Activity of Data Entry Clerks in the Computerized Service Sector Can Reveal Unrecognized Skills," *Woman and Health* 18(3) (1992), pp. 67–78.

W. A. ROGERS

Evidence-Based Medicine and Justice: A Framework for Looking at the Impact of EBM upon Vulnerable or Disadvantaged Groups

This article examines the implicit promises of fairness in evidence based medicine (EBM), namely to avoid discrimination through objective processes, and to distribute effective treatments fairly. The relationship between EBM and vulnerable groups (such as those disadvantaged by virtue of poverty, ethnicity, age, gender, mental health problems or similar) is examined.... This analysis suggests that EBM turns our attention away from social and cultural factors that influence health and focuses on a narrow biomedical and individualistic model of health. Those with the greatest burden of ill health are left disenfranchised, as there is little research that is relevant to them, there is poor access to treatments, and attention is diverted away from activities that might have a much greater impact on their health.

... We know that the burdens of ill health are unevenly distributed both within and across populations, and that the benefits of health care are not always available to all those who need them. Evidence based medicine (EBM) has been introduced into this already complex situation, with some implicit promise of greater fairness than previously existed. This implicit promise operates in at least two ways. First, the processes of EBM are committed to objectivity through the use of strictly standardized methods, thereby eliminating opportunities for subjective decisions and possible discrimination. Secondly, the findings of EBM can be used to ensure fair distribution of effective interventions across the population, at the individual level through the use of evidence based practice, and at the population level through the use of evidence informed health policy and purchasing decisions.

... This paper examines these promises from the perspective of disadvantaged groups, as it is these who suffer the greatest burden of ill health. "Disadvantaged" is a very general descriptor; here I take the term to include groups subject to social exclusion or deprivation for reasons such as low socioeconomic status, ethnicity, age, gender, mental ill health, or similar. If EBM improves the health care of those with the greatest needs, then we may take seriously the idea that EBM can contribute to health care justice.

One of the major claims of [EBM] is that it provides objective evidence about the effectiveness of interventions. This is achieved through the use of research methods that aim to minimize the risk of bias, such as randomized controlled trials (RCTs). Results from multiple RCTs are pooled, using systematic reviews and meta-analysis to give an overall result that is considered to be the definitive best available evidence about a specific intervention. Evidence synthesized in this way can be used to inform treatment decisions for individual patients, or policy decisions about the provision of interventions at a population level. In theory this should lead to fair and equal decisions about treatments, so that individuals with the same illnesses receive the same effective interventions. Basing treatment decisions solely upon effectiveness may provide the opportunity to eliminate more subjective and possibly discriminatory reasons for giving or withholding treatments, leading to greater overall equity. Before examining the application of EBM, however, it is worth looking in more detail at the way that evidence is generated.

CREATING THE EVIDENCE FOR EBM

The evidence for EBM is created from scientific research. To date the majority of this research relates to testing the effectiveness of treatment interventions on research populations in clinical controlled trials. The first question we should ask is whether and to what extent disadvantaged groups participate in the production of research evidence. The production of research includes commissioning, research design, and participation in clinical trials.

Research Commissioning and Design

Historically, research commissioning and design have been the domain of scientists together with funders of research, either private (such as pharmaceutical companies) or public (such as government funded bodies). Almost by definition, the disadvantaged are not well represented among these groups. Information in this area is scarce. However, one report of a UK survey investigating consumer involvement in designing, conducting, and interpreting RCTs found that one third of specialized trial centers had involved consumers in some part of the process.[1] Consumers were defined as "patients and potential patients, carers, organizations representing consumers' interest, members of the public who are targets of health promotion programs, and groups asking for research because they believe they have been exposed to potentially harmful circumstances, products, or services" (Hanley B, et al., p 520). The commonest form of consumer involvement was drafting or reviewing information for trial participants, followed by promoting recruitment, and membership of the steering committee. This work by consumers was reported in generally positive terms by survey respondents (who were researchers), who felt that consumer contributions helped to ensure that trials addressed questions relevant to consumers. The survey asked for information about the background of consumers who had been involved, but this information was not reported in the published paper. Without this information it is difficult to reach any conclusions about the presence of people from disadvantaged groups, but even without this, the type of consumer involvement reported indicates that their role is largely limited to helping the research run smoothly once the really important decisions have been finalized. There seems little opportunity in this system for substantial input—for example, in determining research topics, or interventions to be tested, or outcomes to be measured, from any consumers, let alone from people whose voices are more generally unheard.[2] A U.S. review of participation of minorities in cancer research reported various barriers such as study duration, cost, time, follow up visits, and side effects, as well as cultural characteristics, and attitudes, beliefs, and knowledge about research.[3] It is reasonable to think that these barriers also operate as much if not more so to exclude disadvantaged groups from participation in research commissioning or design.

Participation in Research

Discussions about the kinds of populations who are generally included as trial participants have been current for some time. The gender imbalance is well known and well reported,[4,5] yet despite this, there continue to be important discrepancies in the number of women participating in—for example—cardiovascular research compared with men.[6-8] Gender is easy to define and record as a variable in trial data. Other potential markers for disadvantage are less so, but there is enough recorded information to suggest that people from ethnic minorities and from low socioeconomic groups are generally underrepresented. Much of the information about the research participation rates of ethnic minorities comes from the US, where study after study reports either underrepresentation or lack of data about ethnicity. Participation rates for minority populations and the medically underserved in adult cancer treatment and prevention trials are lower than those of white non-Hispanics. The most represented group in these trials [is] white, middle class, highly educated men. Breast cancer rates in women vary with race and ethnicity; in the US white non-Hispanic women have the highest rates, closely followed by Hawaiian, African American, Japanese, and Alaska Native.[9] A review of trials of selective estrogen receptor modulators, drugs that may be useful both in the prevention and treatment of breast cancer, found, however, limited ethnic variability amongst the 50,000 women who had participated in the trials, compared with the ethnicity and racial makeup of the population of women who need treatment for breast cancer.[10]

These findings are similar to those of Heiat et al., who compared the characteristics of patients with heart failure in RCTs with those of patients with heart failure in the community, from 1985 to 1999.[11] They identified 59 RCTs and found that the participants in the trials were markedly different from patients in the community. In particular, trial patients with heart failure were younger, more often male, more likely to have a subnormal systolic ejection fraction, and were most commonly white. This represents only a relatively small segment of the heart failure population, with significant underrepresentation of minorities, women, and the elderly. Perhaps most concerning, the authors did not find any marked change in the characteristics of patients in trials over time: RCTs of the 1990s continued to focus on young, white, male patients....

One study looked at sociodemographic markers in recruitment to trials run by the National Cancer Institute over a 12 month period. Sateren et al. found that patients enrolled into clinical trials were significantly less likely to be uninsured and more likely to have Medicare health insurance than the patients with cancer in the community, and that geographical areas with higher socioeconomic levels had higher levels of clinical trial recruitment.[13]

...

The absence of data about ethnicity is also striking. Swanson and Bailar assessed the heterogeneity of subgroups in cancer treatment and prevention trials published in 11 journals between 1990 and 2000. They found that age and gender were reported in over 90% of the 261 published trials, but that less than 30% reported race or ethnicity.[15] This lack of reporting precludes the possibility of any subgroup analysis to identify significant differences in racial or ethnic subgroups. Such subgroup analyses present their own challenges....

What are the implications of the absence of disadvantaged groups in trials, or the lack of identifiable data? First, there is the general observation that people in trials often fare better than people who receive treatment outside a trial. Lack of participation in trials effectively removes this benefit from disadvantaged groups. More importantly however, the lack of participation means there is a paucity of research evidence about which interventions are effective in disadvantaged groups. The generalizability of the findings is limited to people who are sufficiently similar, in relevant respects, to the trial participants. This begs the question as to which respects are relevant; physical, cultural, and structural issues may all be relevant in different ways.

There are two main ways that physical differences may be important in working out whether trial results are applicable to different populations. The first is to do with the presence or absence of comorbidities. Most RCTs exclude people with more than one disease, because the trial aims to find out specific information about the effect of a single intervention on a single disease state. Randomized controlled trials derive proof of effectiveness through strictly controlling as many variables as possible, so that any differences between the intervention and control groups may be attributed to the intervention rather than some other factor. The presence of multiple diseases and their various treatments would weaken this process. Hence the exclusion of people with comorbid conditions. Yet comorbidity is an ever present fact of life in groups with socioeconomic deprivation, which means that many EBM derived guides are inapplicable to their care.[17]

Secondly, there is reason to believe there are some racial or ethnic and gender variations in responses to drug treatments.[18] These variations, due to differences in the metabolism of some drugs, result in variable circulating concentrations of active drug, so that the same doses of particular drugs given to people of different races can have variable effects. The extent and nature of these potentially significant differences have not been fully investigated, but there are several classes of drugs known to have such effects, including cardiovascular, psychotropic, and central nervous system drugs.[19] The consequences of these differences are also not fully understood, but known examples include the increased sensitivity of Asian Americans to beta blockers (used to control high blood pressure), and the decreased effectiveness of ACE inhibitors in African Americans....

It should be relatively easy to create the evidence about correct doses of various drugs where these are relevant for different ethnic groups and for women. More difficult is the task of unravelling cultural and structural issues to do with accepting health care, but this is a crucial part of generating good evidence. We need to know not only that an intervention works in ideal trial circumstances with a well defined population, but also that it works in the context of routine care, with heterogeneous populations. A drug may be very effective at controlling pain, but if it is culturally unacceptable to admit suffering from pain, the drug will not work for that person because they will not be able to articulate the need for it. Giuliano et al. have explored a number of cultural barriers that impact upon screening participation in minority groups and these factors may well affect the expected effectiveness of other health care interventions. Distrust of white dominated institutions is a key factor—for example, in discouraging Native American participation—as is a fatalistic approach to ill health. Fatalism is mentioned as a significant factor for several minority groups, but it has been suggested that fatalism may be less an intrinsic cultural belief than a protective attitude that allows people who have little power to change their material circumstances, to maintain some self-respect.[21]

Some of these problems could be overcome by performing new research which targeted disadvantaged groups, in order to generate evidence about the efficacy of interventions in the trial situation, and also about effectiveness when interventions are delivered as part of normal care in the community. This is unlikely to occur, however, as research that repeats testing of an existing intervention is far less attractive, both to funders and to researchers, than research involving new interventions. Such trials are likely to be small rather than the megatrials currently in vogue, and this raises its own problems. Small trials are methodologically challenging: the smaller a trial, the larger the treatment effect necessary for the results to be significant, so that it is easy to miss small effects that may be clinically, but not statistically, significant.[22] Trials that show no statistically significant benefit are less likely to be published, and so less likely to make their way into systematic reviews and thus into the accepted evidence base. Other reasons why small studies that target disadvantaged populations are unlikely to be performed concern the funding of research and the comparative nature of many studies. Pharmaceutical companies, who are major funders of research worldwide, are interested in products that will find a market, irrespective of the causes and distribution of ill health within populations. There is no incentive for these companies to fund small studies with disadvantaged groups because, even if the research identifies effective drug treatments, the market will be small and therefore unlikely to be profitable in the long run. On the other hand, pharmaceutical companies are interested in developing newer and more effective versions of existing successful drugs, which means comparative trials are an important part of their research and development programs. Comparing new treatments with existing ones leads to clustering of research around a narrow range of interventions in research accessible populations, and again this provides no incentive to perform research with new populations.

In summary, disadvantaged groups rarely have a voice in commissioning and designing research, and have limited participation in trials of new interventions. This results in a lack of research evidence about effective interventions for this group. As the presence of evidence of effectiveness is increasingly a requirement for the provision of health care, this is a serious matter. Health care funders, both government and private, are accountable for their spending; funding interventions that are of proven effectiveness are seen as part of this. Apart from the intuitive attractiveness of funding interventions that work, no health care provider wants to be accused of wasting resources on interventions that do not work. For disadvantaged groups, this can be a vicious circle; to receive the newest and best treatments requires evidence, but exclusion from research prevents the generation of evidence and hence access to treatments. The barriers to performing research with disadvantaged groups are considerable, but unless they are overcome, the disadvantaged will remain disenfranchised from the goods of EBM. The power of EBM to mandate treatment does not function if there is no evidence.

APPLICATIONS OF EBM

Clinical Care

For the reasons outlined above, there can be a lack of evidence about effectiveness for interventions in disadvantaged groups. Where there is applicable evidence, however, we might think this could be used to ensure fair distribution of evidence based interventions for all those who need them. The presence of evidence should ensure access for all, especially in situations where the delivery of care has been variable. In some cases, this has occurred; evidence based guidelines have been used to improve treatment rates in disadvantaged groups. One study found—for example—that before the introduction of evidence based guidelines, African Americans had a 60% greater likelihood of receiving inadequate haemodialysis compared with whites. In the period after the guidelines were introduced, there were dramatic improvements for African American patients, with a 92% increase in the proportion receiving adequate haemodialysis.[23] The use of evidence based guidelines helped to ensure equal treatment for all those needing dialysis, irrespective of race.

This is encouraging; however, other areas of health care are not doing so well. Improved treatment of cardiovascular disease has been one of the flagships of EBM, especially the use of thrombolytics ("clot busting" drugs) in the treatment of acute myocardial infarctions. Despite widespread acceptance of the efficacy of thrombolytic drugs, it is clear that not all those who would benefit do receive these drugs. A review of 26,575 Medicare beneficiaries in the US found that, despite meeting all of the eligibility criteria, and after adjusting for differences in clinical and demographic characteristics and clinical presentation, African Americans with heart attacks were significantly less likely than whites to receive treatment.[24] The situation is not so different in Europe; a review of 4035 patients with acute myocardial infarctions identified a group of eligible patients who did not receive thrombolytic treatment. Statistical analysis of this untreated group found that women and the elderly were less likely to receive thrombolytic treatment compared with younger and male patients.[25] ...

These studies show us that evidence about efficacy has not succeeded in changing patterns of treatment. In particular, disadvantaged groups are less likely than others to receive at least some efficacious treatments. These studies do not explain why this happens; we are left speculating about various reasons. Underrepresentation in research has been suggested as a possible reason. Clinicians might be aware of a lack of research evidence for some groups, and mistake the absence of evidence of efficacy as evidence of no efficacy—that is, they may confuse lack of proof about effectiveness with proof of ineffectiveness. Or perhaps the best evidence in the world is not enough to overcome deeply entrenched patterns of discrimination. Either way, the idea that EBM will lead to fairer treatment is challenged.

The examples discussed here concern variable access to proven treatments in eligible patients. There is less information about withholding treatments because patients do not fit the profiles of the research populations. The presence of other illnesses may have unknown effects on proven therapies, so that clinicians do not know whether evidence based therapies for one condition will work in patients with multiple illnesses. There does not seem to be a way out of this circle, for as we have already seen, the presence of other illnesses, which is more likely in disadvantaged populations, precludes participation in research and hence the generation of applicable evidence.

EBM and Distribution of Health Care

The techniques of EBM are increasingly used to inform purchasing decisions about health care at regional or national levels, as well as informing decisions about health care for individual patients. In the UK, the National Institute for Clinical Excellence (NICE) is the body charged with assessing evidence about efficacy as part of making national recommendations about the introduction of new interventions. This was described by the then Health Secretary, Frank Dobson, in the following terms: "NICE is crucial to our plans for fair and equal treatment of patients within a truly national health service. Internal markets and postcodes were never an acceptable way to run a health service. NICE guidance will provide a common currency of effectiveness for the NHS, to inform and assist decision making about treatment and care at all levels, national, local, and individual." ...

As Dobson mentioned, part of the rationale for NICE was to end uneven access to various treatments across the UK, known as postcode rationing. This was widely perceived to be unfair, as people living in some areas were able to receive treatments that were unavailable in other areas. Health authorities are now obliged to fund interventions that are approved by NICE, guaranteeing nationwide access to approved interventions....

There are now concerns that the aim of equitable distribution is likely to fail, as recommendations from NICE skew health care priorities and as health authorities make cuts in other areas to pay for interventions mandated by NICE.[29] The NICE approved interventions have to be provided by health authorities, but NICE guidance is not accompanied by dedicated funds, so that individual local authorities have to find the funds to pay for these from existing sources.[30] This means either cutting existing services, or using any new monies to implement NICE guidance. Each health authority makes its own decisions, so that as one set of interventions become universally provided because of NICE, others become unavailable, as they are cut to pay for the approved ones. This returns us to the situation of postcode rationing, as each authority responds to its own priorities and withdraws funding from different services.

The overall effects of this on patterns of expenditure and service provision are unknown, and to some extent unknowable: it is just not possible to know what else would have been funded if the money had not been spent on NICE approved treatments. The presence of evidence gives some interventions a spurious advantage over other interventions that are discounted because of a lack of evidence. Given the predominance of pharmaceutical interventions among those reviewed by NICE, we may be concerned about the long term extent of this pharmaceutical creep; and given the way that disadvantaged groups are underrepresented both in research and as recipients of evidence based care, we should be very concerned about the impact of evidence based purchasing on health care for the disadvantaged. There is the risk that services to disadvantaged groups that lack an evidence base are being sacrificed to pay for new, evidence based interventions that do not apply to the disadvantaged.

EBM AND FAIR HEALTH CARE

To be fair or just, we might think that a health care system should take into account various factors, such as need, benefit, equity (of access, of opportunities, of outcomes), or personal preferences. It is almost impossible to rank these; probably the best we can do is try to take account of all of them to some extent. Evidence based medicine addresses only one of these factors: capacity to benefit. A treatment may be effective at preventing something as important as coronary heart disease, or as trivial as premature greying of the hair. There is no logical relationship between proof of effectiveness and the urgency or importance of the condition for which the intervention is effective. Once the capacity to benefit is proved, however, this diverts attention away from more important questions such as whether this is an important health problem, or whether this should be provided, given the impact on other aspects of health care. Rather than starting with a set of priorities, and then performing the research to find out how best to achieve the agreed ends, the system is inverted by EBM. The research is performed, often for largely commercial reasons. and then the presence of this evidence is taken as some kind of imperative. Of course institutions such as NICE have criteria other than proof of effectiveness that enter their considerations, but hard evidence is very seductive, especially when used by lobby groups to argue their cause. Politically it can be very difficult to refuse people access to treatments that are evidence based, even if there are robust justice related reasons for doing so.

If we take into account the social determinants of health, this primacy accorded to capacity to benefit seems particularly invidious, as it does little to address inequalities in health. Much ill health is the result of disadvantage; although the exact mechanisms are not well understood, we can assume they are more to do with the material circumstances of people's lives than individualistic factors. Yet EBM turns our attention away from social and cultural factors that influence health, and focuses on a narrow biomedical model of health and disease that is primarily individualistic. Instead of looking at ways to prevent ill health and ameliorate disadvantage, we are directed towards a system of health care that is very good at delivering highly sophisticated, and often expensive, individual treatments to those who are able to access them. This leaves those with the greatest burden of ill health disenfranchised, as there is little relevant research, poor access to treatments, and attention is diverted away from activities that might have a much greater impact on health.

WHO has recently published *The World Health Report 2002,* which identifies 10 major preventable risks that account for 40% of annual deaths worldwide. The list includes childhood and maternal underweight, unsafe water, and sanitation and hygiene. As we might expect, the greatest burden of health risks is borne by the poor countries, and by the disadvantaged in all societies. A recurrent theme in the report is the need for evidence based interventions. Possible interventions are listed for each risk; interventions for underweight include micronutrient supplementation and fortification.[31] This evidence based advice almost beggars belief: if people are underweight and undernourished, surely they need food, rather than micronutrient supplementation? We are left with the uneasy suspicion that as there are no RCTs to prove that food is an effective method of reducing malnutrition, such a commonsense measure lies outside the evidence base and is therefore excluded from consideration.

CONCLUSION

So far my criticisms of EBM have been of its current processes and applications, but we still need to ask whether EBM is intrinsically inimical to the interests of disadvantaged groups, or whether it is just that its potential is not being realized. This is a difficult question.

Of course there is a place for evidence in health care: we need to know what kinds of interventions improve health outcomes, and which ones do not. And there is no necessary reason why appropriate and applicable evidence (broadly interpreted) cannot be gathered about the effectiveness of interventions for disadvantaged groups. This research will most likely be difficult, expensive, and have little commercial potential, but these are not morally valid reasons for not performing such research. Once performed, the results of this research should inform health care policies and expenditure, and lead to real improvements for the disadvantaged. Understood like this, EBM is a potentially valuable tool.

The current research climate does not, however, inspire optimism about this possible change in the direction of EBM. Medical research reflects the priorities of the rich, with 90% of research funding investigating the diseases of 10% of the world's population. This is according to the *10/90 Report on Health Research* published in Geneva, in 2002, by the Global Forum for Health Research, and cited by R Horton in his Lancet article the following year.[32] This research agenda is shaped by a range of forces, but commercial forces have become dominant, so that research into interventions that are unpatentable is less and less likely.[33] Evidence-based medicine has become a tool for commercial ends, narrowing the range of possible interventions and seeking ever smaller benefits with ever more expensive drugs.

It is possible that EBM could serve the interests of the disadvantaged, but this will only happen with a commitment to justice in health care at the highest possible levels, funded accordingly. Without such commitment, EBM will continue to foster an individualistic treatment oriented approach to health care, using a system that largely excludes the vulnerable and disadvantaged, and may in fact increase inequalities.

This research was supported by the National Health and Medical Research Council of Australia in the form of a Sidney Sax fellowship (ID 007129).

NOTES

1. Hanley B, Truesdale A, King A, et al. Involving consumers in designing, conducting, and interpreting randomized controlled trials: questionnaire survey. *BMJ* 2001;322:519–23.

2. Rogers WA. Evidence based medicine in practice: limiting or facilitating patient choice? *Health Expect* 2002;5:95–103.

3. Giuliano A, Mokuau N, Hughes C, et al. Participation of minorities in cancer research: the influence of structural, cultural and linguistic factors. *Ann Epidemiol* 2000;10(suppl):22–34S.

4. Dresser R. Wanted, single white male. *Hastings Cent Rep* 1992;22:24–9.

5. Sheri. L. Women and clinical trials. In: Sherr L, St Lawrence J, eds. *Women, health and the mind.* Chichester: John Wiley, 2000:47–58.

6. Ebrahim S, Davey Smith G. Systematic review of randomized controlled trials of multiple risk factor interventions for preventing coronary heart disease. *BMJ* 1997;314:1666–74.

7. Rochon P, Clark J, Binns M, et al. Reporting of gender related information in clinical trials of drug therapy for myocardial infarction. *Can Med Assoc J* 1998;159:321–7.

8. Hooper L, Summerbell C, Higgins J, et al. Dietary fat intake and prevention of cardiovascular disease: a systematic review. *BMJ* 2001;322:757–63.

9. Miller B, Kolonel L, Bernstein L, et al. *Racial/ethnic patterns of cancer in the United States 1988–92.* Bethesda, MD: National Cancer Institute, 1996.

10. Taylor AL. SERMs, ethnicity, and clinical trials: opportunities and challenges. *Ann N Y Acad Sci* 2001;949:292–4.

11. Heiat A, Gross C, Krumholz H. Representation of the elderly, women, and minorities in heart failure clinical trials. *Arch Intern Med* 2002;162:1682–8.

    ...

13. Sateren W, Trimble E, Brawley O, et al. How sociodemographics, presence of oncology specialists, and hospital cancer programs affect accrual to cancer treatment trials. *J Clin Oncol* 2002,20:2109–17.

    ...

15. Swanson GM, Bailor III JC. Selection and description of cancer clinical trials participants— science or happenstance? *Cancer* 2002;95:950–9.

    ...

17. Starfield B. New paradigms for quality in primary care. *Br J Gen Prod* 2001;51:303–9.

18. Johnson J. Influence of race or ethnicity on pharmacokinetics of drugs. *J Pharm Sci* 2002;86:1328–33.

19. Matthews H. Racial, ethnic and gender differences in response to medicines. *Drug Metab Drug Interact* 1995;12:77–91.

    ...

21. Kagawa-Singer M. Improving the validity and generalizability of studies with underserved US populations expanding the research paradigm. *Ann Epidemiol* 2000;10(suppl):92–103S.

22. Sterne J, Egge M, Davey Smith G. Investigating and dealing with publication and other biases in meta-analysis. *BMJ* 2001;323:101–5.

23. Owen W, Suzech L, Frankenfield D. Healthcare system interventions for inequality in quality: corrective action through evidence based medicine. *J Natl Med Assoc* 2002;94(suppl): B3–91S.

24. Weissman N. Relation of race and sex to the use of reperfusion therapy in Medicare beneficiaries with acute myocardial infarction. *N Engl J Med* 2000;324:1094–1100.

25. Anon. Translation of clinical trials into practice: a European population based study of the use of thrombolysis for acute myocardial infarction. *Lancet* 1996;347:1203–7.

    ...

29. Burke K. NICE may foil to stop "postcode prescribing," MPs told. *BMJ* 2002;324:191.

30. Sculpher M, Drummond M, O'Brien B. Effectiveness, efficiency, and NICE. *BMJ* 2001;322:993–4.

31. World Health Organization. *The world health report 2002.* Geneva: WHO, 2002. http://www.who.int/whr/en/ (accessed 6 Dec 2002).

32. Horton R. Medical journals: evidence of bias against the diseases of poverty. *Lancet* 2003;361:712–13.

33. Horrobin D. Are large clinical trials in rapidly lethal diseases usually unethical? *Lancet* 2003;361:695–7.

6
Feminist Studies

Since earlier readings have shown that feminist scholarship occurs in many disciplinary loca-tions, one might question why a separate section on feminist studies is included in the present volume. Such a question echoes earlier queries about the need to establish a distinct discipline of women's or gender or feminist studies. As we have seen, the new discipline was originally founded for both academic and political reasons. By establishing a new and distinct discipline, feminist scholars drew attention to issues of gender and encouraged exchange among researchers from a variety of traditional disciplines; they also legitimated research on gender and provided an academic home for embattled feminist scholars. One reason this book includes a separate section on feminist studies is to present some of the discussions on methodology that have taken place within academic arenas that are distinguished explicitly as feminist; another is to demonstrate that even research sailing under a feminist flag is not immune from methodological criticism.

Since the late 1960s, Western feminist scholars have struggled to define the goals and even the name of the discipline that began as women's studies, which today is often called gender studies, and which in my view is properly called feminist studies. Simultaneously, researchers have grappled with questions of feminist methodology. In this introduction, I trace some developments in scholars' thinking about research strategies in feminist studies. For convenience, I link these developments to particular decades, although this division should not be taken too strictly.

THE 1960s: THE DECADE OF DISCOVERY

A primary goal of the Western women's liberation movement, which erupted in the late 1960s, was to establish that women, as a group, suffered severe and distinctively gendered forms of oppression. Of course, this had been recognized for more than one hundred years by suffrage activists, Marxists, and others, but women's activism declined after World War I, following the achievement of the vote in the United States and in many other industrialized countries. In the late 1950s, signs of dissatisfaction began reappearing in the United States and elsewhere, and in the early 1960s President John F. Kennedy rewarded Democratic Party women for their support of his campaign by establishing a Commission on the Status of Women (although it was disappointment in the superficial nature of this commission that led to the founding of the National Organization for Women [NOW] in 1966). A little later in the decade, U.S. women active in such struggles as the civil rights movement and the demonstrations in opposition to the Indochina war found themselves disappointed in their expectations of equality with male comrades. They were often relegated to typing, running the ditto and mimeo machines, fetch-ing pizza and coffee, and providing sexual services: one slogan of the draft resistance movement was "Chicks say yes to men who say no." Treated as "housekeepers to the revolution," women in "the movement" complained that women's specific concerns were disregarded or ridiculed. The so-called second wave of feminism began to swell.

In such a climate of dismissal and ridicule, the first priority of early second-wave feminists was simply to reveal the pervasiveness and severity of women's oppression. They saw this task as simultaneously political and academic and relied on two related methods to accomplish it.

One method was consciousness-raising, which for a time was taken to be the definitive feminist strategy for producing knowledge. In consciousness-raising groups, women shared experiences from their own lives in a supportive and nonjudgmental context. They focused especially on finding similarities or patterns, which they interpreted not as evidence of individual women's inability to cope but rather as evidence that they were trapped in unjust systems of social arrangements. Through the method of consciousness-raising, second-wave feminists revealed that many practices seen at the time as normal and natural, such as employment discrimination and unequal distribution of responsibility for children and house maintenance, had harmful consequences for women. They also discovered "secrets," such as the fact that sexual assault and harassment were endemic to many workplaces as well as social relationships and that domestic violence and incest were rampant in many families.

The second methodological tool that early second-wave feminists invented was the use of gender as a category for analyzing social life. Gender had originally been a category of grammar, but now its meaning was expanded to include the sets of social ideals, norms, and symbols defining the proper behavior and appearance of individuals whose sex assignment was male or female. In the 1960s, gender was often understood as a simple binary construction, which presented "masculinity" as both diametrically opposed to "femininity" and superior to it. Feminists noted that, because masculinity and femininity were not equal in status, masculinity was attributed to things perceived as dominant or more admirable. For instance, they noted that predatory animals were depicted as masculine and prey animals as feminine. Nature was often regarded as feminine, because it was viewed as a resource for human exploitation.

Using the methodological tools of consciousness-raising and gender analysis, second-wave feminists examined the inequities of everyday life. They made connections, saw patterns, and invented new concepts. Now-familiar terms dating from this time include *sexism, sex role, sexual harassment, linguistic sexism, the second shift, sexual politics, sexual objectification, heterosexism, the male gaze, public patriarchy, marital, acquaintance, and date rape, emotional work, caring work, victim shoes, emotional economy, eating disorder, stalking, hostile environment, displaced homemaker, double standard of aging, comparable worth,* and *feminization of poverty.*

The invention of these terms made visible unrecognized social phenomena and established sex and gender as politically and theoretically important categories. This early phase of feminist research, much of which occurred outside the academy, has been described as initiating a revolution in knowledge.

THE 1970s: THE DECADE OF GRAND THEORY

The first "women's studies" courses appeared on U.S. college campuses in the 1970s; they quickly proliferated and soon were followed by the first programs in women's studies. For the first time, the professional identity of "feminist scholar" became available. Some scholars who assumed this identity wanted to move beyond merely describing gendered abuse and exploitation toward understanding these phenomena in a more systematic way. Many had come of age politically in the New Left and were influenced by the Marxist understanding of social theory, even when they were reacting against it. Marxism has a comprehensive perspective on all of human history (the history of class struggle), a theory of historical change (generated by changes in modes of production), a theory of knowledge (historical materialism), a set of distinctive analytical categories (base, superstructure, class, exploitation), and a method (class analysis). The subordination of women is one small problem within the larger Marxist picture of economic exploitation, and it is presented as a problem that can be solved only with the overthrow of the capitalist system. Sometimes, it is presented as a problem that will be solved inevitably with the overthrow of capitalism, although this hope was revealed as illusory by most of the socialist societies that actually existed after World War II. In the 1970s, some feminist scholars aspired to a social theory that would be as sophisticated and comprehensive as Marxism, but in which women's concerns would be central and women would be starring rather than supporting players.

Marxist theory was designed as a tool of social change. Marx famously said, "Philosophers have only understood the world; the point however is to change it." Many feminists of the 1970s had a similarly activist conception of the role of research; their goal was to develop a theory that would identify the deepest underlying causes of women's subordination, which they often regarded as a worldwide phenomenon. If these deep causes could be identified, activists would not waste their energy on issues that were merely symptomatic.

In the 1970s, several large-scale theories were developed that claimed to offer a comprehensive explanation of women's oppression worldwide. One such cluster of theories located the roots of women's subordination in the seemingly universal practice of assigning routine child rearing to women. By some accounts, this practice not only consumed women's energy in low-status though socially indispensable work; it also generated a deep rage against women, because women caretakers were typically the first to introduce infants to the "irreparable grief" of discovering "that circumstance is incompletely controllable and that there exist centers of subjectivity, of desire and will, opposed to or indifferent to one's own" (Dinnerstein 1977: 60). Other accounts located the deep causes of women's subordination in male violence against women, violence that may have been rooted in divisions of labor assigning men responsibility for hunting and warfare or even in men's biologically determined propensity for violence.

Theories such as these were called *radical feminist*. They were characterized by insistence that women's oppression was universal, that "patriarchy" was marked by cross-cultural similarities, and even that a worldwide women's culture existed in colonized form "beneath the surface" of all national, ethnic, and racial cultures (Burris 1971). Radical feminist theories also emphasized the "primacy" of women's oppression, a claim typically taken to mean one or more of the following: that women were historically the first oppressed group, that gender is basic to self-identity because individuals recognize their gender identities before any other identities, that gender oppression is causally fundamental to other kinds of oppression, and that gender discrimination causes more suffering than other types of oppression.

Radical feminist claims about the primacy of women's oppression obviously had political relevance, including the potential to explain why male dominance was so resilient and why so many people were hostile to feminism. If gender was so deep and so pervasive, challenging gender required people to question their core sense of themselves and of what was normal and natural. Shulamith Firestone brilliantly expressed this point in the opening lines of her landmark book *The Dialectic of Sex:* "Sex class is so deep as to be invisible." Claims that women's oppression was primary also implied the political urgency of addressing male dominance, which, according to radical feminists, should become the main focus of revolutionary activity. Rather than waiting to challenge male dominance until "after the revolution," challenging it immediately *became* the revolution.

Much feminist scholarship of the 1970s engaged in bitter contests over rival explanations of women's subordination. Methodologically, the contributions to this debate were distinctly sketchy because the claims being asserted were so ambitious that they were massively underdetermined by the available data. Often, theorists argued from data they found especially significant and filled the epistemic gaps with polemic. Nevertheless, the inconclusive debates raged for years, fueled by many feminists' perception that, in choosing a theory about the cause of women's subordination, they were simultaneously ranking their own social identities and political loyalties. The debates seemed to require answering questions such as whether women of color or working-class women had more in common with white middle-class women than with men of their own class and race or ethnicity, and even determining which women were most oppressed. Many women of color and working-class women felt they were being asked to make agonizing and impossible choices.

The debates of the 1970s were theoretically inconclusive and politically divisive; nevertheless, they were not entirely a waste of time. Feminists' "bold conjectures" drew scholarly as well as popular attention to gendered inequalities, and they inspired feminist science fiction in which authors such as Ursula K. Le Guin, Marge Piercy, and Sally Gearheart explored imaginary worlds with radically different systems of gender arrangements. Perhaps most significantly, the debate stimulated new reflection on the nature of feminist research and the proper methodology for engaging in it. As a result of these reflections, most feminist scholars soon abandoned grand theoretical projects.

THE 1980s: THE DECADE OF DECONSTRUCTION

Despite the seeming variety among 1970s feminist theories, critics in the 1980s saw them as sharing several problematic methodological assumptions. The best known of these was "essentialism." In the context of feminist scholarship, essentialism begins with large-scale generalizations or even universal claims about some phenomenon such as women, men, gender, work, or sexuality. All generalizations are liable to overlook exceptions, of course, and so to be inaccurate or incomplete. For instance, to say that women are trapped in the home ignores women who work outside the home (as many women of color argued they had done for centuries); to say that women are sexually objectified disregards women whose sexuality is socially unacknowledged, such as disabled or old women; to represent women as mothers neglects women without children. However, empirical inaccuracy was not the main problem the 1980s critics raised with essentialism. They recognized that essentialist generalizations might acknowledge exceptional cases but still be problematic precisely because they treated those cases as *exceptions,* thereby refocusing attention on cases that they took to be normative, central, or paradigm.

The critics argued that essentialist generalizations implied claims about the real nature or "essence" of women, men, gender, work, sexuality, and so on. For example, essentialist generalizations might well acknowledge that some women have no children and that some sexual activity is not heterosexual but still suggest that real women are mothers and that normal sex is heterosexual intercourse. Essentialism often lurks in phrases such as "women and blacks" or "women and lesbians," which imply that one group of women is non-normative or not truly women. Thus, the claims made by essentialist generalizations are not simply empirical; they also include overt or covert normative assumptions, which are typically the norms of dominant social groups. Often, essentialist claims represent already disadvantaged groups as deviant and so contribute to their further marginalization.

Many critics pointed out that the supposedly universal woman who was the main protagonist in much 1970s Western feminist theory was often privileged along a number of dimensions; for instance, she was often imagined as white, middle-class, heterosexual, able-bodied, and so on. When the situation of such a privileged woman is taken as the model for understanding the situation of all women, those who are less privileged either become invisible or are "othered," that is, treated as exceptions to the norm. Political strategies recommended on the basis of these models are then likely to disregard the interests of women seen as "other." For instance, no-fault divorce may be liberating for professional women but may condemn to poverty women with few employment credentials. Outlawing prostitution or even surrogate mothering may "protect" some women from exploitation but deprive others of a possible livelihood.

In addition to having exclusionary implications, essentialism, critics charged, was friendly to biological determinism and unfriendly to social constructionism. They argued that it obscured important differences and inequalities among women and masked social privileges. In the 1980s, *essentialist* became a pejorative term used to challenge the grand theoretical projects of the previous decade. It was associated with racism, classism, ethnocentrism, and heterosexism (Fuss 1989; Spelman 1988).

Feminist anti-essentialism emerged primarily from vigorous critiques mounted by lesbians and feminists of color in the late 1970s and early 1980s, but it was also influenced by broader changes in the intellectual atmosphere of Western academies. One of these was the rise of postcolonial studies, especially after the publication of Edward Said's landmark *Orientalism* in 1978. Postcolonial critics charged that Western feminist theory tended to use inappropriately Western categories of analysis such as class, race, and patriarchy to describe the situations of women in non-Western countries. In Western eyes, the situations of such women were as misrepresented as their relationship to Western feminists, which was described presumptuously as "sisterhood" (Carby 1984; Mohanty 1991; Spivak 1988).

In addition to being influenced by postcolonialism, feminist anti-essentialism was influenced by the newly fashionable postmodernism. Postmodernism is a cluster of complex intellectual and cultural phenomena that will be explored in more depth in a later section of this volume. For now, it is sufficient to note that postmodernists view all systems of knowledge as infused with power, simultaneously reflecting and reinforcing specific power relations.

Feminist postmodernists argued that large-scale feminist theories, like other grand theories, were "totalizing" and covertly authoritarian. Theories utilizing broad general concepts such as sexuality and motherhood were charged with ignoring the multitude of alternative ways in which different women interpret or give meaning to their experiences of mothering or sexuality. Postmodern feminists asserted that theories prescribing "orthodox" or "politically correct" meanings of experience implied that women who described their experience differently were unfortunate victims of masculine brainwashing or "false consciousness." Moreover, like the falsely universalizing Enlightenment humanism on which they were said to be modeled, feminist theories were charged with masking the social interests of the theorists themselves. The impulse to theory was equated with the impulse to control and dominate, and "grand theory" was portrayed as imperialist, self-aggrandizing, and terroristic. In the Enlightenment tradition, knowledge had been seen as a *means* to power, but now it was represented as a *product* of power.

The powerful anti-essentialist critiques discouraged large-scale projects of feminist theorizing for a long time. Some feminist researchers avoided broad generalizations by emphasizing "difference," especially differences of class and race, and many began to work on a much smaller scale. For instance, some analyzed specific "discourses" or pursued "micro-analyses" of the exercise of power in specific instances. The period of Kuhnian "revolutionary science" was over, replaced by a period of "normal science."

This "normal science" was increasingly produced by "normal academics." Most second-wave feminist scholars had also been activists, but as younger scholars began to enter the academy without this background, a gap between scholars and activists appeared. As academic theory became more sophisticated and arcane, some feminist activists began to see it as inaccessible, elitist, and opportunist.

THE 1990s: RETHINKING FEMINIST RESEARCH

Not all feminist scholars were content with more modest conceptions of feminist research. Some worried that taking anti-essentialist and postmodern criticisms too literally could shackle feminist scholarship. For instance, Jane Roland Martin observed that all generalizations mask differences but that generalization is still indispensable to thought (1994). She noted the danger of feminists reifying the fashionable categories of difference—namely, race, class, and gender—while ignoring other differences such as ability, age, and religion. She also worried that an overemphasis on difference might obscure commonalities among women.

The feminist research that reemerged in the 1990s was chastened by anti-essentialist criticism, and its methodological assumptions became more sophisticated. First, feminist researchers no longer assumed that human males and females, men and women, were natural, presocial entities. This assumption had been questioned in the 1970s by a few visionary theorists such as Andrea Dworkin and Mary Daly, but many others had viewed gender as a social edifice constructed on a biological foundation that was fixed and universal. By the 1990s, however, work on intersex by Anne Fausto-Sterling and others had revealed that the supposedly exhaustive biological division between the two sexes is itself shaped by gendered norms and assumptions. Men and women are even further away from being "natural kinds" than most earlier feminists had supposed; we are socially constructed all the way down. Similarly, work by Judith Butler and other queer theorists on the instability of gender categories revealed that we are not constructed according to simple gender binaries; instead, we are constructed according to models that are almost infinitely diverse and that we are constantly remaking.

Second, most feminist research in the 1990s had become alert to the perils of hasty generalization and sensitive to diversity. However, feminists no longer interpreted these simply as implying a methodological requirement to study multiple groups; instead, they recognized that group memberships overlapped and that individuals' memberships in some groups affected their experiences in others. Black women, for instance, are not oppressed as black *and* as women *and* as disabled and whatever else; instead, black women suffer a kind of oppression that is *qualitatively distinct* from the oppression suffered by white women or by black men. When Michelle Wallace was distressed because she could not comb her hair like Goldilocks, she was oppressed not just as a (generic) girl or as a (generic) black, but rather specifically as a black girl. By the 1990s, most feminist scholars rejected what Deborah King called *additive* analyses, which assumed that all gender oppression or all race oppression was the same and that their effects could simply be added together. Instead, they recognized that, as King observed, different kinds of oppression interact with each other and *multiply* each other's effects. Class, race, ethnic, gender, and other identities were seen not as separate from each other but rather as intermingled.

The recognition that no class or group is homogeneous, that no generic woman or worker or African American or gay or Third World person exists, has far-reaching consequences for feminist politics. For instance, when race (like class and sexual and other identities) is recognized as an integral component of gender identity, not just something additional, like frosting on cake, it becomes easier to see that all women, not only women of color, have racial/ethnic identities. So-called gender issues are not sharply separable from other injustices, and issues of race (as well as issues of class, sexuality, ability, religion, and so on) must be recognized as central or integral rather than optional for feminism.

A third methodological advance characterizing much feminist research in the 1990s stemmed from recognizing explicitly that no research is undertaken from a neutral or timeless vantage point. Instead, research projects are undertaken for specific reasons by people who are historically and socially situated. In the 1990s, feminist scholars recognized increasingly that their research reflected their own subjectivities; that what they chose to research, what they heard and saw, how they read and interpreted, was conditioned by their specific subject position and the interests related to that, as well as by the categories available to them. Feminist research became increasingly reflexive as scholars more regularly interrogated their own subject positions and the relationship of these to their research projects and practices.

THE 2000s: FEMINIST RESEARCH GOES GLOBAL

At the turn of the twenty-first century, feminist researchers are seeking appropriate methodological strategies for studying gendered issues in a global context. As the world has become ever more integrated on the levels of economics, culture, and governance, it has become increasingly evident that many issues of traditional feminist concern have significant global dimensions. For instance, war and militarism, environmental degradation, climate change, disease, human trafficking, rights violations, and poverty are all gendered issues that can be addressed effectively only by action on a global level. In response to this recognition, feminist politics has become increasingly transnational and so has feminist research. It is premature for this introduction to offer an overview of the methodological approaches that characterize a decade still in progress, but it may be useful to conclude by sketching some of the methodological challenges that feminist researchers currently face.

As we have seen already, an interest in global questions is not new to feminism; early second-wave feminists were extremely interested in what they called cross-cultural comparisons. However, this early work was often methodologically problematic. Sometimes it engaged in facile generalizations about "patriarchy" that ignored deep differences in women's situations across the world. Sometimes it drew equally facile contrasts between women in the so-called First and Third Worlds, portraying First World women as urban, educated, and autonomous and Third World women as rural, ignorant, and dependent. In both cases, the approaches were essentialist, ignoring the enormous diversity among women (and men) both across and within "Worlds." In addition, the contrasting portrayals of First and Third World women typically presented the former as having a privileged perspective on the oppression of the latter, who were shown as uniquely victimized and lacking in agency, almost dehumanized. These portrayals rationalized Western feminists' adoption of a "missionary position," encouraging them to take up the "white women's burden" of enlightening and rescuing women elsewhere in the world.

Today, feminist scholars need methodological tools that will enable us to avoid cultural essentialism and explore in ways that are respectful of how people organize and create meaning in their lives (Narayan 1997). Cultural essentialism offers totalizing and often exoticizing characterizations of whole cultures, presented as internally homogeneous and externally sealed. These characterizations are typically designed to promote political agendas. In contrast with cultural essentialism, contemporary feminist research must begin from the recognition that people across the world share much of our past, present, and future. Unfortunately, our shared history includes processes of colonization, enslavement, and exploitation that created the wealth and "development" of many Western industrialized countries while impoverishing and under-developing countries elsewhere. This history set the stage for our present increasingly inegalitarian global economy, in which already plundered countries are often further disadvantaged by unfair rules imposed by Western-dominated financial, trade, and treaty organizations. In this context, Western culture often appears hegemonic, yet it is confronted everywhere by cultures of resistance. In an era of increasing integration, the local and the global are inseparable, though they are not reducible to each other, and feminist researchers must find ways of exploring each in the context of the other.

In these contexts, feminist researchers must find ways of thinking about women and men across the world that avoid either smothering or othering them. We must recognize that "they" are not radically unlike "us," yet neither are we all sisters and brothers under the skin. We share one world, yet we are situated very differently within it. We are all agents acting within structures of constraint, yet the constraints we face are very different.

Our diverse global positioning has deep implications for the construction of feminist knowledge. People who are variously situated have differential access to a variety of perspectives on the world, even though these perspectives are not closed in principle to others. We speak many languages, even though these are not in principle untranslatable. We have varying degrees of epistemic authority that various audiences respect, and although we all share a responsibility for gender justice, we have different resources for moving toward it. In these circumstances, it seems clear that feminist research must become not only increasingly transnational but also increasingly collaborative. Scholars and activists in a variety of disciplinary and geographical locations must learn how to engage with and build on each other's research, recognizing their shared responsibility for producing knowledge useful in moving toward global gender justice. The second part of this book offers some ideas for addressing these challenges.

REFERENCES

Burris, Barbara. 1973. "The Fourth World Manifesto," in *Radical Feminism*, ed. Anne Koedt, Ellen Levine, and Anita Rapone. New York: Quadrangle/New York Times Books.

Butler, Judith. 1990. *Gender Trouble: Feminism and the Subversion of Identity*. New York: Routledge.

Carby, Hazel. 1997. "White Women Listen," in *Materialist Feminisms*, ed. Rosemary Hennessy and Chrys Ingraham. New York: Routledge.

Dinnerstein, Dorothy. 1977. *The Mermaid and the Minotaur: Sexual Arrangements and Human Malaise*. New York: Harper Colophon.

Fausto-Sterling, Anne. 1999. *Sexing the Body: Gender Politics and the Construction of Sexuality*. New York: Basic Books.

Fuss, Diana. 1989. *Essentially Speaking: Feminism, Nature, and Difference*. New York: Routledge.

King, Deborah. 1988. "Multiple Jeopardy: The Context of a Black Feminist Ideology." *Signs: Journal of Women in Culture and Society* 14, no. 1 (Autumn): 42–72.

Martin, Jane Roland. 1994. "Methodological Essentialism, False Difference, and Other Dangerous Traps." *Signs* 19, no. 3.

Mohanty, Chandra Talpade. 1991. "Under Western Eyes: Feminist Scholarship and Colonial Discourse," in *Third World Women and the Politics of Feminism*, ed. Chandra Talpade Mohanty, Ann Russo, and Lourdes Torres. Bloomington: Indiana University Press, pp. 51–80.

Narayan, Uma. 1997. *Dislocating Cultures: Identities, Traditions, and Third World Feminism*. New York: Routledge.

Said, Edward. 1978. *Orientalism*. New York: Vintage.

Spelman, Elizabeth V. 1989. *Inessential Woman: Problems of Exclusion in Feminist Thought*. Boston: Beacon Press.

Spivak, Gayatri Chakravorty. 1988. "Can the Subaltern Speak?" in *Marxism and the Interpretation of Culture*, ed. Cary Nelson and Lawrence Grossberg. Urbana: University of Illinois Press, pp. 271–313.

Maxine Baca Zinn, Lynn Weber Cannon, Elizabeth Higginbotham, and Bonnie Thornton Dill

The Costs of Exclusionary Practices in Women's Studies

As women who came to maturity during the social upheavals of the late sixties and early seventies, we entered academia to continue—in a different arena—the struggles that our foreparents had begun centuries earlier.... In the tradition of W.E.B. DuBois, Oliver Cox, Joyce Ladner, and other pioneers, we sought to use the tools of history and social science and the media of literature and the arts to improve our people's future and more accurately portray their past.

We each had developed critical perspectives on society and sought theoretical explanations for the continued poverty and oppression of our people. We had different but related foci for our research: on Chicanos and the impact of outside resources on family structure and ethnicity; on working-class consciousness and class conflict; on Black women achieving a college education; and on the relationship of work and family for Black women private household workers. In the process of conducting it, we became acutely aware of the limitations of traditional social science with regard to working-class women and women of color.[1] More profoundly, however, we realized that the experiences of these groups of women were virtually excluded from consideration as vital building blocks in feminist theory.

In the past, many working-class women and women of color have been critical of women's studies for the lack of attention given "their" women.[2] This "Viewpoint" draws from those arguments and adds our own perspectives. Our effort is not only to voice discontent but also to elaborate on some of the implications of the exclusionary nature of women's studies....

THE INSTITUTIONALIZATION OF PRIVILEGE

Many recent studies have documented organizational barriers to women's full and equal participation in society. Institutions are organized to facilitate white middle-class men's smooth entry into and mobility in positions of power. These men establish criteria for the entry of others into similar positions, defining success, the reward system, the distribution of resources, and institutional goals and priorities in a way that perpetuates their power. In higher education, as in other areas, women—even white middle-class women—have been excluded from many of these activities. They continue to struggle to move out of token positions of authority and into the true centers of power....

The obstacles white middle-class women face are compounded many times over for women of color and working-class women. For these two groups, completing college and graduate education itself poses financial, emotional, and intellectual challenges.[3] As students, they are more likely than middle-class white women to attend public institutions—community colleges and state universities—or, in the case of Blacks, traditionally Black institutions. As faculty, they are more likely to be employed in public institutions and in those that do not grant doctorates.... Among these less prestigious schools, few have the financial and other resources necessary to facilitate and encourage research and scholarship. In fact, these settings are characterized by high teaching loads, heavy demand for institutional service, and limited dollars for travel, computer facilities, research libraries, secretarial support, or research assistance.

Most of the scholarly research and writing that take place in the United States are conducted at a relatively small number of institutions. To a large extent, research and other scholarly production in women's studies have also been closely tied to the resources and prestige of these academic centers. Indeed, women's studies, partly because of its marginal position in the academy, has sought to validate the field through association with prestigious institutions of higher education. In these schools, there are very few women of color, and while we cannot know how many of the women faculty at these institutions are from working-class backgrounds, it is safe to assume that their numbers also are relatively small.[5]

The result is that women of color and women from working-class backgrounds have few opportunities to become part of the networks that produce or monitor knowledge in women's studies. In addition, those who have the advantage of being researchers and gatekeepers are primarily located at privileged institutions, where they get little exposure to working-class and ethnically diverse students. As a result, they tend to develop and teach concepts divorced from the realities of women of color and working-class women's lives.

For example, a concept such as the "positive effect of the multiple negative" could not have survived the scrutiny of professional Black women or Black women students. The theory suggests that the negative status of being Black combines with the negative status of being female to give professional Black women an advantage in the labor market.[6] Although this may have appeared to be the case for the researcher isolated from significant numbers of Black women as colleagues or students, Blacks' life experiences would have suggested many alternate interpretations. Such cases clearly illustrate that the current organization of the academy perpetuates the production and distribution of knowledge that is both Anglo and middle-class centered.

To explore further the institutional structures that limit the contributions of women of color and women from working-class backgrounds to the field of women's studies, we engaged in a simple exercise. We looked at the published information about the official gatekeepers of two leading interdisciplinary journals in the field of women's studies: *Signs* and *Feminist Studies*. These groups of editors, associate editors, and consultants make important decisions about which individual pieces of scholarship will be contained in the journals' pages and what special issues will be undertaken, officially sanctioning and defining important concerns and critical scholarship in the field. We asked, "Where are women of color located within these publications generated out of the women's movement and its accompanying scholarship?"

Despite white, middle-class feminists' frequent expressions of interest and concern over the plight of minority and working-class women, those holding the gatekeeping positions at these journals are as white as are those at any mainstream social science or humanities publication. The most important groups within the hierarchies of the two journals—that is, the groups most involved in policy decisions—are the eleven editors of *Feminist Studies* and the editor and eight associate editors of *Signs*. Among those twenty women, in 1983–1984, there was not a single Black woman, there were no Hispanic women, no Native American women, and no Chinese American women. The only woman of color was a Japanese American woman, an associate editor of *Signs*. The new group of associate editors for *Signs*, when it moves to Duke University, will include three Black women, one of whom is a faculty member at a traditionally Black institution. *Feminist Studies* reports that [its] current (1985) group of editors and consultants includes two women of color as editors (out of twelve), one woman of color as an associate editor (out of fifteen), and fifteen women of color as consultants (out of a total of sixty-four).

As reported in Table 6.1, token representation also occurs at positions below those of the editors themselves. The primary function of those in these groups is to review articles and on occasion to give advice to the editors. *Feminist Studies* has fifty-nine whites and five women of color serving as associate editors and consultants, whereas *Signs* has thirty-eight whites and three women of color in those categories. Regardless of position, the total number of editors and consultants for both journals combined shows that there are 119 whites, six Blacks, one Hispanic, and two Asian Americans.

It is much easier to designate the ways that women of color have been excluded than it is to show the ways that white working-class women have been kept out of the mainstream. Furthermore, it is more difficult to delineate the ways that classism excludes both whites and women of color who are from the working class. The information that *Signs* gives about the institutional affiliations of its editors and consultants, however, can be used to illustrate other biases in the gatekeeping positions. None of the fifty women in these positions represents a traditionally Black institution; only about six represent schools whose student bodies are primarily constituted of working-class students (i.e., the first in their families to attend college); and only three are from the South—where the highest concentrations of minorities continue to live.

The major implication of these figures is that women of color are rarely sitting around the table when problems are defined and strategies suggested. They are not in positions to engage in the theoretical discourse behind specific decisions on what will be published. Thus, even when white feminists attempt to include women of color, there are often difficulties because women of color reject the dominant paradigms and approach problems from divergent perspectives. Typically, women of color then find their work rejected on the grounds that it does not conform to the established ways of thinking. This clash of paradigms resounds through the following example.

In 1981, the planners of a conference on communities of women asked Elizabeth Higginbotham to submit an abstract for a paper.[7] The expectation communicated in the letter of invitation was that her research would demonstrate the applicability to Black women of a concept of women's communities set forth by white feminists. Instead of attempting to alter her

Table 6.1   Representation of Minorities on Signs and Feminist Studies Editorial Boards, 1983–84

	Editor(s)		Associate Editor(s)		Consultants		Total	
	Minority	White	Minority	White	Minority	White	Minority	White
Feminist Studies	0	11	2	13	3	46	5	70
Signs	1	8	–	–	3	38	4	46
Both journals	1	19	2	13	6	84	9	116

Note. *Signs*'s associate editors were included under the heading of "Editors" because their functions match more closely those performed by editors of *Feminist Studies*. The data were obtained from the lists published in recent issues of these journals.

work to fit such a model, Higginbotham wrote to the organizers and challenged their narrow definition of communities of women.

Higginbotham noted that, unlike their white sisters who are often excluded from male-dominated spheres or retreat from them, the majority of Black women are ordinarily full participants in mixed-sex spheres and make unique contributions both to the definitions of problems and to solutions. Typically, Black women's vision of their situation leads them not to seek solace from Black males but to create spheres where men, women, and children are relatively protected from racist cultural and physical assaults. Historically, white people, male and female, have rarely validated the humanness of Black people; therefore, it was and is critical for Black people and other people of color to nurture each other. This is a primary fact about the communities of racially oppressed peoples. Thus, as white feminists defined the focus of the conference, only the research of a few Black scholars seemed appropriate—and that research did not necessarily capture the most typical and common experiences of Black women.

THE LIMITATIONS OF POPULAR FEMINIST THEORY

Practices that exclude women of color and working-class women from the mainstream of women's studies have important consequences for feminist theory. Ultimately, they prevent a full understanding of gender and society. The failure to explore fully the interplay of race, class, and gender has cost the field the ability to provide a broad and truly complex analysis of women's lives and of social organization....

Until the past few years, women of color have been virtually hidden in feminist scholarship, made invisible by the erroneous notion of universal womanhood. In an effort to emphasize the shared experiences of sexism, scholars passed over the differences in women's situations.[8] Knowledge assumed to be "universal" was actually based for the most part on the experiences of women who were white and primarily middle class.... As a result, there now exists in women's studies an increased awareness of the variability of womanhood. Women's studies journals and classroom texts are more likely at present to contain material about minority women. Still, such work is often tacked on, its significance for feminist knowledge still unrecognized and unregarded.

A close look at feminist social science reveals three common approaches to race and class. The first treats race and class as secondary features in social organization with primacy given to universal female subordination. Such thinking establishes what is taken to be a common feminist ground and labels any divergence from it, in Phyllis Palmer's phrase, a "diversionary special interest."[9] To make gender relations primary is to assume that they create a set of universal experiences more important than those of other inequalities.

A second approach acknowledges that inequalities of race, class, and gender generate different experiences and that women have a race-specific and a class-specific relation to the sex-gender system. However, it then sets race and class inequalities aside on the grounds that, while they are important, we lack information that would allow us to incorporate them in the analysis. As Bonnie Thornton Dill puts it, inequalities other than sex and gender are recognized, but they are not explicated.[10] ...

The third approach, often found in conjunction with the first two, focuses on descriptive aspects of the ways of life, values, customs, and problems of women in subordinate race and class categories. Here differences are detailed with little attempt to explain their source or their broader meaning. Such discussions of women are "confined to a pretheoretical presentation of concrete problems."[12]

Each of these conceptualizations is inadequate for the development of feminist theory. They create an illusion of comprehensiveness and thereby stifle the development of scholarship about women of color. Moreover, when race and class are set aside, even the analysis of white middle-class women's lives is incomplete. A woman's "place" in society, her opportunities and her experiences, must be understood in relation to the societal placement of men as well as of other classes and races of people.

An approach to the study of women in culture and society should begin at the level of social organization. From this vantage point one can appreciate the complex web of hierarchical social arrangements that generate different experiences for women....

The integration of race and class into the study of gender creates different questions and new conceptualizations of many problems. For instance, in the last few years, there has been a great deal of attention to the entrance of women into professional and managerial occupations. In fact, the levels of female professional and managerial employment are often the standard used to evaluate women's success. In such conceptualizations, Black women are frequently held up as exemplars because they are more concentrated in professional employment than Black males. White women, in contrast, are less concentrated than white males in such positions and are viewed as less "successful" than their Black sisters.[14]

Black professional women understand such seemingly favorable comparisons differently. The analysis behind them lacks a sense of Black history and of racial stratification and thus ignores a number of underlying factors: the racial barriers that limit educational attainment for Black men; a history of limited employment options for Black women who have only a high school education; and the high concentration of Black professional and managerial women in the public sector and in traditionally female occupations.... In short, an analysis of gender and occupation that also incorporates race would have raised a variety of other issues and avoided the narrow focus on Black women's "success."

CLASSISM, RACISM, AND PRIVILEGED GROUPS OF WOMEN

We recognize that there are significant reasons behind the fact that a synthesis of class, race and gender perspectives into a holistic and inclusive feminist theory and practice has not yet taken place. Some derive from both the short- and long-term costs of struggling to overcome institutionally supported and historically reproduced hierarchies of inequality. Others have to do with the benefits that accrue to those in a group with relative power.

White middle-class women profit in several ways from the exclusion of upwardly mobile women and women of color from the ranks of academic equals in their universities, from the pages of women's studies journals, from positions of power in our professional associations, and from a central place in feminist theories. Foremost among these advantages is the elimination of direct competition for the few "women's jobs" in universities; for the limited number of tenure-track and tenured jobs; for the small number of places for women among the higher professorial ranks; for the meager number of pages devoted to research and writing on women in the mainstream professional journals; and for the precious, limited space in women's studies journals. White women, struggling for acceptance by male peers, a secure job, and a living wage in the academy—especially since many are forced to work part-time or on a series of one-year appointments—may not "feel" that they are in a privileged position. Indeed, in many ways and in many cases there is little privilege. However, their relative disadvantage in comparison with white men should not obscure the advantages of race and class that remain.

Despite the benefits to some that derive from exclusionary practices, there are also costs to feminist theory and to women's lives—even to the lives of privileged groups of women. Scholarship that overlooks the diversity of women's experiences cannot reveal the magnitude, complexity, or interdependence of systems of oppression. Such work underestimates the obstacles to be confronted and helps little in developing practical strategies to overcome the sexist barriers that even privileged women inevitably confront.

As women in academia, we are obliged to compete for rewards individually in a system where we are not among the power brokers. Individual competition in a hierarchical scheme based on "merit" may work well to explain the experiences and structure of the lives of middle- or upper-class white men. As a theoretical perspective or guiding principle, it does not explain the life experiences of groups—including that of white middle-class women—who lack power. In this situation, the merit, motivation, and work of an individual who suffers discrimination are not relevant, since discrimination, like all other forms of oppression, operates against a whole group. Thus, as a group, women find themselves up against barriers to success.

Relatively privileged groups of women are nonetheless shielded from awareness of the institutional barriers that their working-class and minority sisters come to recognize early. Many middle-class white women "buy into" the system and assume that it will work for them. Linda Nielsen's comments on her tenure battle show her recognition that she had made just this error: "During those beginning years I was not seriously worried about my future, since I had been exceptionally successful at publishing and teaching, and I believed that this guaranteed my professional security. It did not." She was denied reappointment even though she met objective university criteria.

...

Nielsen also describes herself as experiencing the need for white male approval so common among white women.... After a brief look at some research and at autobiographical accounts, she draws some conclusions about the special difficulties that women have to overcome as a minority group. The characteristics are "overreliance on male approval, passivity or nonassertiveness, ambivalence and anxiety over contradictory female roles, inclination toward self-blame and guilt, affiliative needs which interfere with achievement, motivation, and discrimination from other females."[18]

Unfortunately, although Nielsen's courageous account is a useful analysis of a white middle-class woman's experience, there is not a single reference in her bibliography to a work by a woman of color. Familiarity with research on minority groups immediately reveals that the reactions Nielsen lists contain responses that do not apply *uniquely* to women. Some, such as discrimination from members of one's own group, are common among other minorities, and others—such as overreliance on male approval, ambivalence and anxiety over contradictory female roles, and passivity or nonassertiveness—do not apply to many women of color. For example, numerous Black working-class women have not employed passivity as a survival mechanism—indeed, their aggressive actions in comparison with those of white middle-class women are often viewed antagonistically by whites as "unfeminine."

Thus, Nielsen's conclusions, while somewhat instructive to white middle-class women, actually shed little light on the circumstances and experiences of upwardly mobile women and women of color.... [F]rom this narrow perspective she can only partially glimpse even her own plight, and her observations do little to recognize hers as part of a wider struggle shared with women who are different from her.

SOME GOALS AND STRATEGIES FOR CHANGE

We seek to build a more diverse women's studies and an integrative feminist theory. Achievement of these goals requires many structural changes in the practices and policies of academic communities....

First, we need to establish and maintain heterogeneous college faculties. Frequently, feminists are ready to fight for women colleagues but do not extend such support to minorities and people from working-class backgrounds. We must learn about each other and appreciate our differences in order to form the types of alliances that will transform the composition of faculties at our institutions.... Above all, we must withstand the temptation to secure our individual futures by accommodating to the "principles" of the institution.

Second, we should actively encourage dialogue among academic centers, especially in local areas, by forming close links with faculty in different types of institutions. Faculty in elite schools particularly must reach out beyond their campuses to faculty and students in less prestigious centers of higher education.... Faculty are not distributed among colleges solely by talent and ability; racism, classism, and sexism all function to shape academic careers. Consequently, we have to reject the elitism so prevalent in academe, visit other campuses and learning centers, make friends with new colleagues, and share resources.... The number of women and minorities hired in second-tier, four-year colleges and community colleges makes it imperative that we do everything possible to pull down the structural barriers that block their careers.

Third, efforts should continue to open up the gatekeeping positions in women's studies to include a broad representation of women. Editorial boards need to reject the tokenism that has characterized them so far, and they must strive to solicit and publish feminist scholarship from all corners. Committees and organizations that plan conferences need diverse membership—members who will seriously address issues of age, race, class, and sexual preference in the definition and formation of programs and in the means used to recruit participants....

In everything we attempt, we must strive to welcome diversity rather than gather around us what is comforting and familiar. Without serious structural efforts to combat the racism and classism so prevalent in our society, women's studies will continue to replicate its biases and thus contribute to the persistence of inequality. We must commit ourselves to learning about each other so that we may accomplish our goals without paternalism, maternalism, or guilt. This requires a willingness to explore histories, novels, biographies, and other readings that will help us grasp the realities of class, race, and other dimensions of inequality.[20] At the same time, we must take the personal and professional risks involved in building alliances, listening to and respecting people who have firsthand knowledge of how to cope with oppression, and overcoming the institutionalized barriers that divide us. Within this context, our efforts to develop common goals have the potential to produce a truly diverse community of people who study women and who understand their scholarship as part of the broader quest to arrest all forms of social inequality.

NOTES

The authors wish to thank Barrie Thorne and an anonymous reviewer for their encouragement and helpful suggestions on this piece.

1. Maxine Baca Zinn, "Review Essay: Mexican American Women in the Social Sciences," *Signs: Journal of Women in Culture and Society* 8, no. 2 (Winter 1982): 259–72; "Social Research on Chicanos: Its Development and Directions," *Social Science Journal* 19, no. 2 (April 1982): 1–7; "Sociological Theory in Emergent Chicano Perspectives," *Pacific Sociological Review* 24, no. 2 (April 1981): 255–69; "Field Research in Minority Communities: Ethical, Methodological, and Political Observations by an Insider," *Social Problems* 27, no. 2 (December 1979): 209–19; Lynn Weber Cannon, "Trends in Class Identification among Black Americans from 1952 to 1978," *Social Science Quarterly* 65 (March 1984): 112–26; Reeve Vanneman and Lynn Weber Cannon, "The American Perception of Class" (Memphis State University, Center for Research on Women, 1985, typescript); Elizabeth Higginbotham, "Race and Class Barriers to Black Women's College Attendance," *Journal of Ethnic Studies* (in press); "Issues in Contemporary Sociological Work on Black Women," *Humanity and Society* 4, no. 3 (November 1980): 226–42; "Educated Black Women: An Exploration into Life Chance and Choices" (Ph.D. diss., Brandeis University, 1980); Bonnie Thornton Dill, "We Must Redefine Feminism," *Sojourner, the Women's Forum* (September 1984): 10–11; "Race, Class, and Gender: Prospects for an All-inclusive Sisterhood," *Feminist Studies* 9 (Spring 1983): 131–50; and "On the Hem of Life: Race, Class, and the Prospects for Sisterhood," in *Class, Race, and Sex,* ed. Amy Swerdlow and Hanna Lessingler (Boston: G. K. Hall, 1983), pp. 173–88.

2. See, e.g., Audre Lorde, *Sister Outsider* (Trumansburg, N.Y.: Crossing Press, 1984); Angela Y. Davis, *Women, Race and Class* (New York: Random House, 1981).

3. Higginbotham, "Educated Black Women."

...

5. For a discussion of the experiences of scholars from working-class backgrounds in the academy, see Jake Ryan and Charles Sackrey, *Strangers in Paradise* (Boston: South End Press, 1984); and Carol Sternhell, "The Women Who Won't Disappear," *Ms.* (October 1984): 94–98.

6. Cynthia Epstein, "The Positive Effects of the Multiple Negative: Explaining the Success of Black Professional Women," *American Journal of Sociology* 78, no. 4 (January 1973): 912–33. Although

this article serves as a useful example of failure in the applicability of a theory to reality, we single it out as one among many that could demonstrate the same phenomenon. See below for further discussion of this point in a related context.

7. This conference was held in February 1982. The proceedings can be found in *Signs* 10, no. 4 (Summer 1985).

8. Margaret A. Simons, "Racism and Feminism," *Feminist Studies* 4, no. 2 (1979): 384–401, esp. 388.

9. Phyllis Marynick Palmer, "White Women/Black Women: The Dualism of Female Identity and Experience in the United States," *Feminist Studies* 9 (Spring 1983): 151–70, esp. 152.

10. Dill (n. 1 above), "On the Hem of Life," p. 179.

...

12. Simons, p. 388.

...

14. Marion Kilson, "Black Women in the Professions," *Monthly Labor Review* 100 (May 1977): 38–41. Relevant also is Epstein (n. 6 above).

...

18. Linda L. Nielsen, "Sexism and Self-Healing in the University," *Harvard Educational Review* 49, no. 4 (November 1979): 474. Again this account is singled out as only one among many possible examples, useful because it is so forthright.

...

20. It is important that reading and learning about the diversity of women's experiences are integrated into our lives. You cannot take one week and learn this field, nor does it come from reading one novel. To assist people in this endeavor, the Center for Research on Women at Memphis State University has developed an extensive bibliography on women of color. It has also developed a research clearinghouse on women of color and Southern women. The clearinghouse is a computer-based resource containing up-to-date information on researchers working in these fields and their latest projects, as well as bibliographic references to relevant social science works published in the last ten years on these groups of women. For more information, write to: Research Clearinghouse, Center for Research on Women, Memphis State University, Memphis, Tenn. 38152.

BETTE S. TALLEN

How Inclusive Is Feminist Political Theory? Questions for Lesbians

... Most "feminist theory" today is exclusionary of many groups. As a Jewish lesbian I feel this omission keenly. I begin this paper, then, with a call that it is time to recognize that what we are doing in lesbian theory may be, in fact, far more inclusive than is most feminist theory today.

I also begin this work remembering what happened to me when I entered graduate school in political theory in 1971. I was taking a seminar on modern political theory and one night I was going on and on about my favorite theorist at the time, Jean-Jacques Rousseau and his ideas on man and his environment. My teacher, who was also my dissertation advisor (she became my advisor because she was the only woman on the faculty and I was one of only four female graduate students in my year), finally couldn't take it anymore and asked me, "Tell me, what is the fate of poor woman?" My mouth dropped open—I had never heard such a question. I stammered on and on how man was really a generic term and that clearly Rousseau had meant to include women in his discussion. She asked me if I had ever read Rousseau's *Emile*. I said I hadn't, so she sent me home with her copy that evening. I went home and eagerly opened the book and started to read. Well, *Emile* was all about the education of the ideal citizen, Emile, who of course was male. No problem, I thought, I'm used to identifying with males.... Then I got to Book V of *Emile*, Rousseau's chapter on marriage. Here I met for the first time Sophie, who is there to help complete Emile's education. Imagine how I felt when I read, "In the mating of the sexes each contributes in equal measure to the common end but not in the same way. From this diversity comes the first difference which has to be noted in their personal relations. It is the part of the one to be active and strong, and of the other to be passive and weak. Accept this principle and it follows in the second place that woman is intended to please man."[1]

... I then was forced to reexamine radically all that I thought I knew about any political theorist. Was I to be included in any of their visions and analyses, was I to be liberated along with all the others? ... I began to think of John Locke, the seventeenth century English liberal theorist whose ideas on natural rights and democracy were so critical in the founding of America. I realized that he never really explicitly confronts whether women are truly to be included fully in his theory on natural rights. His silence and the silence of the other political theorists I read spoke volumes.

My second starting place for this work occurred in 1982 when Billie Potts published *Witches Heal: Lesbian Herbal Self-Sufficiency,* the best all-around women's herbal I've seen.[2] ... She subtitled it a lesbian herbal not only because of her extensive work and commitment to lesbian health, but because she meant it to be a complete herbal for a woman's entire body. I have used this book as a text in several courses on women and health. Students loved the book but were, in the main, shocked and uncomfortable with the title. One student went on for pages in her journal yelling about the title and why she, a nonlesbian, should be forced to read this, and then went on to say that the section on arthritis saved her knee. Further, anytime I went into a women's bookstore that stocked the book it was inevitably on the lesbian shelf. Not once did I see a copy on the health shelf, although it clearly belonged on both. That was my first major indication that nonlesbians absolutely refused not only to identify with lesbians, but that many even refuse to utter the word. Recently this perception was reinforced when I was a judge for the Chicago Women in Publishing annual awards. One of the awards that I and another judge recommended was for the Iowa based periodical, *Common Lives, Lesbian Lives*. She and I were amazed at the lengths the other judges, all nonlesbians and all very high-powered women in the world of publishing, went to avoid uttering the L word (and here L stands for lesbian not liberal). It became kind of a game as we tried to get them to say the word and they continued to refuse. As feminists we reject the generic man and refuse to identify with exclusionary language. What does it mean when nonlesbian feminists refuse to identify with the term lesbian?

Do nonlesbians include or exclude us when they use the term woman or the word feminist? We all understand that terms like lady doctor or lady lawyer imply that doctors and lawyers are male. Why is it hard to see that the way nonlesbians use the word feminist may be just as exclusionary? Women of color, such as Alice Walker, have pointed out that white feminists, who never put white in front of feminist, continue to do so for Black women. As a result, many women of color will not identify with the term feminist because they believe that white women are trying to exclude them. Some argue for the term womanist as more inclusive than feminist and in terms of usage they are clearly correct. I think of the times I have heard nonlesbians use terms like lesbian families, lesbian mothers, or the supreme redundancy, lesbian women. When I have pointed out to them that lesbian women as a term implies the existence of the ultimate oxymoron, lesbian men, they look at me as if I was no longer in the realm of the rational. Finally it has dawned on me that perhaps they do not use terms like family, mother, or even woman as inclusive ideas: they do mean to exclude lesbians. A dramatic example of this occurs in an interview with Linda Gordon, a prominent socialist feminist historian, who says, "The word *family* does have an ideological meaning that cannot be defined away simply by the decision of leftists to make it mean something else. The family does *not* mean two lesbians and a child."[3] Let me not be accused of quoting Gordon out of context. She makes it very clear that she does not embrace the profamily politics of some feminist and left theorists. Still her omission of a lesbian defined family from the concept of family is significant. Does it mean that her work on violence within families cannot include a discussion of lesbian battering? ... I believe that woman should be an inclusive term. The very basis of feminist theory and existence is that it applies to all women.... How could woman be an inclusive term if they have to add lesbian to it?

THEORY AND INCLUSIVENESS

Since graduate school I use as my litmus test to evaluate any political theory the issue of inclusiveness and accessibility. Specifically I examine to whom the theory is addressed and how inclusive is the analysis? I have always thought that the best feminist theory attempts to look at the situation of all women. When I began to realize that much of feminist theory, especially kinds of feminist theory that calls itself radical, were not inclusive, I had to radically rethink what is the basis of feminist theory. Is feminist theory only the property of white, middle-class nonlesbians? Is it an enterprise I can work with or must I abandon it?

When I consider how inclusive or exclusionary the practice of feminist theory is I need to think about what I know about political theory and the emergence of feminist theory. Is the process of feminist theory doomed from the start because its roots, especially in liberal theory, are too entrenched in a patriarchal, heterosexualist context? Or can feminist theory speak to the lives and situations of all women? My immediate answer is that I believe that feminist theory can be inclusive, but only if all of us insist that it be and only if we confront and understand the implications of some of the roots of feminist theory. These roots, in English liberal theory, spell out some of the limitations of feminist theory....

Most political theory that calls itself feminist emerged as a reaction to liberal theory. Liberal theory opened up citizenship in the state and full participation in social institutions, in theory, to all men, regardless of class background. Once citizenship in the state was opened up to all men (excluding men who were slaves in the U.S.), women also began to agitate for inclusion. I, among others, have written at length on how the connection between liberal theory and feminist theory has both fueled and limited the emergence of feminism as a political movement.[4] Briefly stated here, according to liberal theory, the exclusion of women from the political state was done not on the basis of divine law, but on practical grounds or grounds of expediency (at least in the eyes of the male theorists). Women were guaranteed some rights (such as life), but were seen as not capable of exercising other rights (such as the right to vote). Women fought back on primarily two grounds: one, that justice demanded their inclusion (that their exclusion from the world of natural rights was arbitrary; an excellent illustration of this argument is seen in the Seneca Falls declaration), and two, that women, if given equal rights, could act as the great reformers of civilization.... I am sure that to no one's surprise lesbians were invisible in this debate. It further should be noted that early liberal feminist theory focused primarily on woman's relationship to the state, a focus that presumed automatically that the state was a given, that the state was and is vitally necessary for the preservation of human peace. Liberal feminist theorists argued that the church and the family need to be preserved, albeit reformed.... Today, some feminist theorists do challenge the hegemony of the state, church, and family of the nineteenth century tradition, but how many nonlesbians challenge the heterosexualism of liberal theory? Socialist feminists, in particular, although often leading the fight against the assumptions of the liberal state, have not seriously questioned compulsory heterosexuality and its institutions. Their failure to do so is striking.

When one looks at modern feminist theory, one is struck by two things. Liberal feminists, such as Betty Friedan, still see the state as natural and vital for human interests. Socialist feminists, such as Linda Gordon or those I discuss below, focus exclusively on women's relations to men, to children, to the family, and to male-defined institutions such as the economy.... The institutions they focus on not only are male-defined and male-dominated; these are also institutions that exclude lesbians and lesbian meaning. It is clear that one of the few things that unites liberal feminists and socialist feminists is their intention to maintain relations with men. Sheila Rowbotham, a prominent socialist feminist, takes this point even further when she says,

> I felt that the concept of patriarchy was one that I really couldn't handle as a historian.... It seemed to me that the idea of patriarchy inevitably inclines toward separatist feminism ... what I was really trying to say was that a feminist theory about the relationships between women and men needs to think in terms of mutual needs and relations, positive reasons for relating as well as conflict. You need the two together ... you need to see why it is not a relation of total conflict, not a Hobbesian situation, otherwise it would deny the experiences of those who have either sexual, work or political relationships with men. I think this is an unreal aspect of separatism.... The term "patriarchy" implies that the forms of male domination are unchanging.[5]

Here women and men become the yin/yang of feminist analysis, the two opposites that unite to form the whole.[6] So much for the dialectic (and this from a socialist feminist), a form of interaction that holds for the dynamic interaction of negation. In Rowbotham's view the dialectic becomes all synthesis and no conflict.

Several other points of interest can be derived from Rowbotham's statement. The first is her view that feminism is meant to facilitate women's relations with men. She equates all women's relations with men, even if they are limited to work relations, and then says that separatism denies all of these women's experiences. Clearly all those relations are not the same. Rowbotham's ignorance of separatism is startling, if not surprising. By denying the existence of women who choose, in whatever ways they can, to define themselves independently of the male context, she reaffirms a yin/yang view of male/female relations. Lesbian meaning and existence have no place in her analysis. What further interests me is Rowbotham's insight that the use of the term patriarchy inevitably inclines toward separatism. She seems to say that once you accept that men seek to dominate, control, and define the lives of women because they are male and because historically men have exercised that right then the only way to free oneself is to separate from men. Her own refusal to separate further underscores the nature of the nonlesbian feminist's dilemma. Rowbotham's last assertion, that the concept of patriarchy implies that forms of male domination are unchanging, is truly absurd. Would she say that the term capitalist implies an unchanging form of economic domination and exploitation and therefore is not a useful term? Perhaps the answer lies in her desertion of the Marxist dialectic for a yin-yang view of male-female relations. This yin/yang view of masculinity/femininity holds that these are universal unchanging principles. Marx's concept of the dialectic is not about the unity of opposites but rather about the nature of the conflict of opposed forces. As a socialist, Rowbotham's embracing of immutable opposites is significant. Why is the sex/gender system immutable in a way capitalism is not? The answer appears to lie in the reality of women who refuse to separate from men and to deny the existence of those women who do.

A survey of major women's studies texts and major nonlesbian theoretical works reveals the same tendency to ignore lesbians altogether or treat them as a special case. Linda Gordon, in the same interview cited above, states that the high point for her at one of the Berkshire Women's History Conferences was a paper on the history of the Buffalo lesbian community. She says we need to do more of this kind of scholarship, but then goes on to say, "since Carroll Smith-Rosenberg's wonderful article, much that has been written about women's culture, particularly in the more popular feminist press, is abstract, rhetorical, polemical or without critical analysis."[7] Earlier, Gordon draws a distinction between lesbian history and women's history when she states, "there is real energy now in lesbian and gay history, as there was in women's history ten years ago and that brings both strength and weakness."[8] Does women's history not include lesbian history? On the one hand, Gordon collapses lesbian history into women's culture and says that since one article on lesbians (written by a nonlesbian), nothing very good has been written. Has she not read Mary Daly, Marilyn Frye, Sarah Hoagland, among many others? . . . Why does Linda Gordon only seem to link lesbian history with the history of gay men; is our history more similar to their history than to the experience of all women?

Perhaps Monique Wittig was right all those years ago when she wrote that lesbians are not women: that to be a woman means that one's existence and context are defined by one's relationship to men. Perhaps all lesbians should abandon the struggle to make feminist theory and the construct of woman inclusive of us. I am not yet ready to give up that struggle, but as each day passes I understand more why many lesbians no longer consider themselves feminists or women. Most nonlesbians who consider themselves feminist are not willing to be seen outside those relations with men, e.g., "I speak to you today as a wife and mother as well as a _____." Their absolute refusal to identify with the word lesbian shows their complicity in male domination.

Nonlesbian feminists, to the degree that they refuse to separate from men and masculine values and identify with lesbian existence, participate in the maintenance of patriarchal values. If the major focus of the feminist revolution is to facilitate women's better relationships with men ("dancing with chains" was my High School principal's description), then one really needs to question the revolutionary nature of feminism.

Feminist theory and process are exclusionary of others in addition to lesbians. As a Jew, I have long been disturbed by what I see as the exclusion of Jewish values and life from feminist politics and process. Evie Beck, in her introduction to *Nice Jewish Girls,* summed up many of my feelings on feminist process. I have long experienced feminist process as subtly anti-Semitic. The focus on not interrupting, not being emotional or loud, are not only feminist priorities, but embody the values of WASP middle and upper class life. Jewish conversational style and cultural values are distinct. In my home to interrupt someone was an indication of interest, not of dismissal. Feminist process also is based on the concept of the "good girl," the one who speaks when spoken to, who is not rowdy and obnoxious, who doesn't talk too fast, who is, well, nice. Within WASP culture Jews are not nice. Within patriarchal culture how many lesbians are nice?

FEMINIST THEORY AND INCLUSIVENESS

As a Jew and a lesbian, I have long rejected the premises of liberal feminism; primarily its belief that adjustments can be made within the current context and that "revolution" can occur without upsetting the applecart. Too many systems of oppression, such as racism, classism, ablism, etc., will still exist unless we confront the entire range of privileges available within the patriarchal construct. Liberal feminism today is based on many of the same premises as the seventeenth century liberalism of John Locke (that people are endowed with natural rights, that the state is necessary for the preservation of human peace). The illusion that one can, by putting pressure on the state, achieve meaningful equality for all women, is a frightening one for me. First, the liberal state was set up to ensure the protection of unequal distribution of property. To imagine that the state, which was set up to protect the interests of wealthy and powerful white men, will protect women, let alone a Jewish lesbian, is absurd. Second, as a Jew, I am all too well aware of what reliance on the state can bring. As Hannah Arendt so convincingly argues in her work, *Anti-Semitism,* one of the primary reasons Jews stayed in Germany, even after Hitler came to power and before the massive deportations to the camps began, is that over the centuries Jews had looked to the secular state to protect them from Christian religious authorities and from the mobs inspired by the Church. To hear liberal feminists embrace the state as the guarantee of my freedom and life is not only foolish but chilling. . . .

If one then turns to socialist feminism to find an inclusive feminist theory, the disappointment is far more bitter. One would expect socialist feminists who do attack the premises of liberal theory and do certainly question systems of economic oppression, to attack other systems of oppression, such as race and heterosexualism, that impact on the lives of women. Their failure to do so underscores the limitations of their own theoretical underpinnings....

This can especially be seen in one of the first, and still most comprehensive anthologies of socialist feminist writings, Zillah Eisenstein's volume, *Capitalist Patriarchy and the Case for Socialist Feminism*. In this long work of over twenty articles there are only two more than superficial references to lesbians. The first is an article by Linda Gordon on reproductive freedom, in which she argues that lesbians and gays will benefit also from reproductive self-determination. Gordon writes,

> In this respect again the lesbian liberation movement has made possibly the most important contribution to a future sexual liberation. It is not that feminism produced more lesbians. There have always been many lesbians, despite high levels of repression; and most lesbians experience their sexual preference as innate and involuntary. What the women's liberation movement did create was a homosexual liberation movement that politically challenged male supremacy in one of its more deeply institutionalized aspects—the tyranny of heterosexuality. The political power of lesbianism is a power that can be shared by all women who choose to recognize and use it: the power of an alternative, a possibility that makes male sexual tyranny escapable, rejectable—possibly even doomed.[9]

Lest I be accused of trashing Linda Gordon, whose work on the whole I admire, it must be noted to her credit that she is the only nonlesbian in the group of women included in the anthology who seriously considers lesbianism as a political issue. Her analysis, though, still links lesbians with gay men, as part of a distinct "homosexual" liberation movement. She states, with no footnote, that most lesbians experience their sexual preference as innate and involuntary. Although the Kinsey research does indicate that is true for most gay men, I have yet to see any serious research that says this is true for most lesbians. My lesbianism was a personal and political choice, a choice to reject heterosexual privilege. So what is positive about Gordon's analysis gets lost as she treats lesbians as a group apart from women, as a group whose closer political ties are with gay men.

The other article in Eisenstein's book that deals with lesbianism is the "Combahee River Collective Statement." Their statement is strongly opposed to any separate lesbian analysis and action, "we are feminists and lesbians, we feel solidarity with progressive black men and do not advocate the fractionalization that white women who are separatists demand."[10] This is the extent of their statement on lesbianism.

The other articles in the anthology systematically ignore lesbianism as they focus on the more "important" subjects of women's work in the family, mothering, and women's role in the work force. Lesbians are clearly not part of the analysis.

... It is perhaps the ultimate irony that socialist feminists appear to be the worst offenders when it comes to the issue of dealing with lesbians and lesbianism. At least liberal feminists deal substantively with the issue of civil rights for gay people and do support lesbian custody fights, etc.

But some nonlesbians are seeing the double bind they are facing. As Erica Jong writes,

> Unless men give up their denial that the society they have created is deeply diseased, most women have no choice but to be either semislaves colluding in their own oppression, or militant separatists à la Dworkin. How to get past male denial when most men have so much to gain by denying the existence of female pain?
>
> Privileged groups seldom give up their privilege without bloody revolution, and it is unthinkable that women will take up arms against their own sons, brothers, husbands. However violent our dreams, we are tied by ties of love and loyalty. Men have always known this and abused it.[11]

Jong is correct when she identifies that unless men give up privileges women face two choices—to collude in their own oppression to get men to be more human and behave themselves, or to separate from men. What a dilemma!

I am not writing this paper to take all lesbian-feminist and lesbian theorists off the hook. Historically, much of our own writing and language has been equally exclusionary. Our theory has seemed at times to assume that all lesbians are white, Christian, middle class, not disabled, but it must be noted that most lesbian theorists and writers have taken seriously the issues of exclusionary theory, privilege, and accessibility. One only has to follow lesbian or predominantly lesbian publications for a short time to realize how diverse are our perspectives and backgrounds. We struggle to take each other's cultures and systems of oppression seriously and attempt to understand the privileges from our own backgrounds and situations. I often think of Alix Dobkin's line when she sings, "We ain't got it easy but we got it."[12] This is far from saying that our work is finished or even mostly successful, for the struggle for inclusiveness in lesbian theory continues. I do think it is accurate to say that lesbians have been at the forefront of every fight in the feminist movement to make it more accessible and inclusive. Further lesbian theory has been far more responsive to charges of omission than has either liberal or socialist theory. The fact that we do so while many of our nonlesbian sisters systematically exclude us from their writing is of great significance.

TOWARD A LESBIAN THEORY

Usually when lesbians write theory they mean to be inclusive of any woman who is willing to identify with a lesbian context. Perhaps it is time that nonlesbians cease to see lesbian as an exclusionary term that does not include them. Lesbian may well be far more inclusive than either feminist or woman, as nonlesbians use those terms.

What would a theory that is explicitly lesbian, and both inclusive and revolutionary, look like? Clearly it cannot start from the assumptions that seem to underlie both liberal and socialist feminist theory. It is not a theory that takes as a given an accommodationist politic with men and male-dominated institutions and it cannot take as its end product the "reconciliation" of men and women. A lesbian theory cannot deny that men do oppress other men, that racism, anti-Semitism, classism, among others, are real for men as well as for women. But it must be a theory that challenges the yin/yang assumption that the end product of theory is the unity of opposites. Such a yin/yang view posits the necessity of both categories, and that either category needs the other in order to achieve meaningful existence. A separate lesbian meaning and existence are invalidated and rendered invisible.

In my opinion, a theory that is explicitly lesbian and revolutionary is a profoundly separatist theory. Such a theory must separate from women's traditional roles in the family and it must challenge the use of "motherhood" as a dominant political metaphor. We need to remember that some feminists of both the nineteenth and twentieth centuries use that metaphor as their primary argument to extend equal rights to women. If we want to define ourselves independently of that context we must seek to create new meaning. Only then can we start with woman as a central focus: woman as a separate and autonomous being, separate from a male-defined reality. We must examine our relations with each other, by analyzing not only the nature of lesbian oppression, but also the issues of bonding, responsibility, ethics, and how other systems of oppression work in our lives.

The necessity for lesbians doing this work can be seen if we examine what happened at the 1988 Sisterfire Music Festival (when two lesbian separatists asked two Black men to leave their crafts area because it was womyn-only space, an altercation ensued and at least one of the womyn was hit by one of the men). When some lesbians defended the actions of these two Black men because of the reality of racism in the U.S.A., they ended up justifying woman-hating. Lesbians (and feminists) must stop excusing men's violent and oppressive behavior because of some men's lack of privilege. We must continue to deal with differences between us, but we can no longer allow our understanding of the oppressions that some men face as an excuse or rationale for their actions.

Events like the Sisterfire incident only teach me how much more theory and understanding we need to do. We also need to continue to confront nonlesbian feminists on their failure to create an inclusive theory. Nonlesbians must begin to identify with the L word. I am not saying they must become lesbians, but that they understand that a lesbian context and meaning can apply to their own lives, the part of their lives they define separate from men. Their continued failure to identify with a lesbian meaning represents the true divisiveness in feminism.

If being a feminist means "working it out" with men, count me out. As long as the practice of feminist theory continues to be exclusionary we must both struggle with nonlesbian feminists and create our own more inclusive lesbian theory. If being a lesbian and being involved with lesbian theory mean working together with other women-identified women to build a community, a movement, and ultimately a safe planet, count me in. The more nonlesbian feminists continue to deny their complicity with male supremacy because of their fear of being labelled a "man-hating" lesbian, the more we all lose.

Let us continue to create our lesbian theory and give voice and meaning to lesbian existence. In so doing let us end the divisiveness and the exclusionary aspects of feminism. Let the nonlesbians among us do more of their own homework and examine their own woman-hating and lesbophobia. Ultimately it is the nonlesbians' fear of us that is the true divisiveness of the feminist revolution.

NOTES

An earlier version of this paper was presented at the 1988 NWSA conference in Minneapolis as one of the papers on the Lesbian Theory panel. A revised version appeared in *Sinister Wisdom* 37 (March 1989).

1. Jean-Jacques Rousseau, *The Emile of Jean-Jacques Rousseau.* Translated by William Boyd. New York: Teachers College, Columbia University, 1962, p. 131.

2. Billie Potts, *Witches Heal: Lesbian Herbal Self-Sufficiency.* Ann Arbor, MI: Du Reve, 1988.

3. "Interview with Linda Gordon." In *Visions of History,* edited by Abelove, Blackmar, Dimock, Schneer. New York: Pantheon, 1983, p. 84.

4. For further discussion of this, see Bette Tallen, *Liberal Equality and Feminism: The Implications of the Thought of John Stuart Mill.* Ann Arbor, MI: University Microfilms, 1980. Also see Juliet Mitchell, "Women and Equality." In *The Rights and Wrongs of Women,* edited by Juliet Mitchell and Ann Oakley. New York: Penguin Books, 1976, pp. 379–399. Also see Zillah Eisenstein, *The Radical Future of Liberal Feminism.* New York and London: Longmans, 1981.

5. "Interview with Sheila Rowbotham." In Abelove et al., *Visions of History,* p. 60.

6. When I use yin/yang here, I am talking about how Rowbotham and many other feminists use male/female as immutable realities meant to be harmonious. This is connected to the New Age version of yin/yang which I believe takes the concept out of context and represents another New Age rip-off of native people's spirituality. While one might think that socialist feminism and New Age spirituality have little in common their influence here is significant.

7. "Interview with Linda Gordon," p. 92.

8. Ibid., p. 88.

9. Linda Gordon, "The Struggle for Reproductive Freedom: Three Stages of Feminism." In *Capitalist Patriarchy and the Case for Socialist Feminism,* edited by Zillah Eisenstein. New York and London: Monthly Review Press, p. 123.

10. "The Combahee River Collective: A Black Feminist Statement." Ibid., p. 365.

11. Erica Jong, "Changing My Mind about Andrea Dworkin." *Ms.* 16, no. 12, p. 64.

12. Alix Dobkin, "Talking Lesbian." From *Lavender Jane Loves Women.* Preston Hollow, NY: Women's Wax Works, 1975.

Uma Narayan
Dislocating Cultures: Identities, Traditions, and Third World Feminism

Dowry-murder is a topic that has surfaced more than a few times during the years I have lived in the United States. The topic's manner of surfacing in social contexts has sometimes left me nonplussed....

When the topic of dowry-murder comes up in academic settings ... I am ... often torn between my desire, both as an academic and as a feminist, to answer questions and respond to work on the topic in "informative" ways, and my apprehension that there are a number of problematic assumptions and understandings about the phenomenon in the minds of those I am engaging with on the issue.... I have in the last few years come across two unrelated papers on dowry-murder that began, "Women are being burned to death every day in India." ...

[T]he central objective of this essay is to call attention to two sorts of problems that often beset the general project of "learning about Other cultures." ... The first cluster of problems has to do with the "effects" that national contexts have on the "construction" of feminist issues and the ways in which understandings of issues are then affected by their "border-crossings" across national boundaries.... The second problem I am concerned with has to do with the ways in which "culture" is invoked in explanations of forms of violence against Third World women, while it is not similarly invoked in explanations of forms of violence that affect mainstream Western women....

Let me begin with an example that helps illuminate both ... problems of "border-crossing" and problems of "cultural explanation." I have referred in a previous essay to the prevalent confusion in Western national contexts between dowry-murders and *sati*.[3] This confusion was evident in a dialogue I came across on the Internet, which began with an American man stating that "suttee is the practice of 'bride-burning' or wives being burned in cooking oil fires ... for having insufficient dowry." This contribution was followed by a man of Indian background attempting to explain the differences between *sati* and dowry-murder, describing *sati* as a traditional, but now rare, practice of voluntary self-immolation on the husband's funeral pyre by widows, and dowry-murders as a recent phenomenon of "burning a bride for insufficient dowry."

While I had problems with many details of this explanation, such as its unproblematic construction of *sati* as "voluntary" and its description of dowry-murders as results of *insufficient* dowry, my biggest worry was that both *sati* and dowry-murders were to a large degree unexplained even after this "explanation."... This conversation helped me see how conversations describing and distinguishing between institutions and practices that are "culturally unfamiliar" might result, often unintentionally, in an understanding of forms of violence against women "specific" to Third World contexts as instances of "death by culture."

This conversation also brought home to me the ways in which understandings of issues are shaped by "border-crossings." The conversation illuminated the ways in which recent Indian feminist engagement with the issue of *sati* seems to have "filtered through" to many members of the American public. It suggested that what often gets edited out when such information engages in "world-traveling" are "facts" well known to many in the Indian context—such as that *sati* is a virtually extinct practice.... The "information" that does "filter through" into the American context often seems to result merely in a vague awareness that "women are being burned to death every day in India," amalgamating *sati* to dowry-murders in a construction of "Indian culture" as one beset with a "cultural habit" of burning its women! ...

I believe it is important for all feminists to think about the general structures that mediate such "border-crossings" and to critically address the specific problems that arise when particular issues cross particular "borders." ...

FEMINIST MOVEMENTS, NATIONAL CONTEXTS, AND THE "MAKING" OF FEMINIST ISSUES

The juxtaposition of domestic violence in Western contexts and dowry-murders in India will likely seem odd to some readers.... It is precisely the fact that the significance of this juxtaposition will not be self-evident to many that prompts me to start with this "joining together" of two phenomena that are taken by many Westerners to be "unconnected." ... What follows is an attempt to make sense of *why* the connection between dowry-murders and domestic violence is not "visible" to many Americans, as well as an attempt to "make" the connection.

Most Americans that I have talked to about dowry-murder know that many U.S. women are killed by their partners as a result of domestic violence. Given that many members of the U.S. public know that domestic violence has fatal forms, why is it that they make no connection between the "foreign" phenomenon of dowry-murder and the "familiar" phenomenon of domestic violence? What are the difficulties that stand in the way of this connection being made? ... In all of the American "domestic violence" readings I initially went through as I began writing this piece, I found no data about the number of women who are annually *killed* as a result of domestic violence....

Although fatalities are often mentioned along with injuries, most discussions do not centrally focus on the most "extreme cases" where the woman dies as a result of domestic violence. There is a striking contrast between the lack of focus on fatal cases that enters into the construction of the category "domestic violence" in the United States context and the focus on deadly cases of domestic violence in the Indian context that has given visibility to the category "dowry-murder." ... I believe that this "asymmetry in focus" contributes to the lack of perceived connection between dowry-murders and domestic violence in the minds of many Americans.

... I think these differences in focus are connected to the different ways in which issues of violence against women emerged within, and were taken up by, feminist movements in India and in the United States. In many areas of U.S. feminist effort around domestic violence, such as challenging police nonresponsiveness to domestic violence complaints, ... there was little reason to single out cases of domestic violence that resulted in death. Rather, the focus was on generating legal and institutional responses that addressed *a wide spectrum* of domestic violence cases, ranging from the fairly minor to the potentially lethal. As a result of U.S. feminist efforts around issues of domestic violence, public attention was certainly drawn to the various ways in which women were often brutally and repeatedly injured in domestic violence attacks, terrorized and stalked, and often additionally endangered if they tried to leave violent relationships. But the bulk of the U.S. feminist responses to domestic violence, quite understandably, seem to have focused on victims who were still alive, who needed either shelters, counseling and assistance or various forms of legal redress.

... The fact that domestic violence situations *can* end in death seems to be used as an indic[ator] of its potential seriousness and danger, rather than as an emblem.... Feminist efforts in the U.S. seem to have moved in the direction of *widening* the scope of what is understood to constitute "domestic violence," pointing out that verbal, emotional, and psychological abuse often constitute components of domestic violence.

If we are to understand the "asymmetry" between feminist engagement with domestic violence in the U.S. and Indian contexts, we also need to understand why the Indian feminist movement focused on domestic violence in the extreme form of "dowry-murder" and did not focus on general issues of domestic violence to the same degree as in the United States.... In an article on the Indian women's movement, Mary Fainsod Katzenstein points out that a report on Indian women, commissioned by the government of India in 1974 in anticipation of the

International Women's Year declared by the United Nations in 1975, played a "catalytic role in the emergence of the contemporary women's movement in India."[9] ...

Although the report sparked an interest in organizing around gender issues, issues of sexual violence were given little attention at the start, as the movement initially focused largely on economic and demographic issues. Members of committees that wrote the 1974 report have, in retrospect, acknowledged their inattention to issues of violence against women....

However, by the late 1970s issues of violence against women began to move to the forefront of the feminist agenda. Katzenstein remarks that "it was the focus on violence against women, beginning in the late 1970s, that propelled the movement forward and endowed it with much of its strength."[12] The two most "visible" issues initially addressed by women's groups were the issue of dowry-murder and that of rape, especially police rape of poor women held in custody.[13] Many women's groups that addressed the issue of dowry-murders did not address the issue in isolation from the general issue of domestic violence, which was also addressed quite apart from dowry-related contexts....

Although the issue of dowry-murder was hardly the only issue pertaining to violence against women that was addressed by the Indian women's movement, it has probably had the most widespread impact on public attention in India and received the most sustained media coverage, resulting in dowry-murders being reported in a more ongoing way than many other issues affecting Indian women. I believe that there are a number of reasons for the public attention that dowry-murders have received. While issues such as that of police rape of women in custody primarily affected poorer women, dowry-murders were predominantly a middle-class phenomenon. And although the political energies of the women's movement were crucial in calling a number of issues of violence against women to public attention and to underlining their prevalence, I suspect that issues such as police rape, or domestic violence as a general problem, were not "surprising" to many Indians, while dowry-murders were.

Let me attempt to clarify what I mean by talking about my own experience around these issues. Like many Indians, I was aware of the existence of domestic violence, and of dowry-related harassment of women, long before these became public issues that women's groups organized around. And even before it elicited organized protest, I suspect that there was a fair degree of general awareness that poor and lower-caste women were vulnerable to rape and sexual exploitation....

In my own case, which I think was not uncharacteristic, one of the two "issues" that I was completely unaware of until they were named, articulated, and publicized by women's groups was the issue of dowry-*murder*.[16] ... Before women's groups named this issue, demonstrated against it, and drew media attention to it, I believe few Indians were aware that there was a growing pattern of women being burnt to death for dowry-related reasons in "respectable middle-class Indian families." I believe that public unfamiliarity with this issue combined with its heinousness and its predominantly middle-class occurrence to make dowry-murder one of the most publicly visible issues of those addressed by women's groups in India.

There also seem to be contextual reasons as to why some other aspects of domestic violence received less organizational attention and effort from women's groups in India than they did in the United States. A significant proportion of feminist efforts around domestic violence in the United States seems to have focused on publicizing the need for shelters for battered women and in setting up and organizing such shelters.... [T]here are considerably *fewer* efforts in [India in] this direction than has been the case in the United States. Understanding the reasons for this difference is, I think, interesting in its capacity to illuminate the degree to which specific feminist policies and solutions are dependent on the background social, economic, and institutional features of the national landscapes within which feminist groups operate.

Why did organizing battered women's shelters not have a central place in Indian feminist agendas? The answer is not, as some Western feminists seem to have assumed, that the Indian women's movement is "less developed." Madhu Kishwar alludes to ... a very different kind of account for this difference, pointing to a number of factors that help make battered women's shelters a feasible strategy for affording assistance to battered women in countries like the United States, factors that play out differently in India....

Enabling some battered women to secure welfare for themselves or their children, assisting others in securing paid employment, state-funded medical care, and legal aid around custody issues, are all ways in which U.S. battered women's shelters can offer more than temporary refuge. The provision of such services enables at least some women to leave relationships they would not otherwise be in a position to leave. The virtual absence in India of state-provided welfare, education, and medical care, the unavailability of state-provided legal services to deal with custody, and far greater levels of unemployment, render it very difficult for feminists to help generate structures that would enable Indian women to leave the family contexts where they are victims of violence.... In addition, as Kishwar suggests, there is much greater stigma in India around issues such as divorce, separation from one's husband, and "women living on their own," factors that might well deter even women who could economically support themselves....

In the Indian context, organizing around issues such as shelters for battered women, which require a variety of state and institutional structures that are not readily available, is not highly feasible.[20] In contrast, dowry-murder was an issue around which Indian women's groups *could* effectively organize in a number of ways. Women's groups in India had the resources to publicize cases of dowry-murders and hold public demonstrations and protests, often in the neighborhood where "suspicious burnings" had occurred. Such public efforts to call the phenomenon of dowry-murder to national attention had the important function of alerting Indian families to the potentially lethal situations in which marriage placed some of their daughters. Such efforts also provoked a considerable amount of public "consciousness raising" on the institution of dowry.... Women's groups in India also engaged in pushing for a variety of legal changes that would enable more efficient prosecution of the family members responsible for these murders, and generated debates on possible changes in property and inheritance laws that might ameliorate the problem of dowry-murders.

The preceding account helps explain why general issues of domestic violence have played a bigger role in Western national contexts than in India, and why dowry-murders were the aspect of domestic violence most widely addressed in the Indian context.... [S]uch explanations ... call attention to economic, social, and institutional features that make certain policies and strategies feasible in some contexts but not in others, features that might be "taken for granted" and remain less visible prior to attempts to account for such differences. They help to make feminists in various national contexts more "contextually self-conscious" about the features of their national landscapes that might shape their engagements with issues of violence against women, and help clarify why "similar problems" might sometimes not permit "similar answers."

The preceding analysis ... challenges the unreflective and naively optimistic view that sees this project primarily in terms of "information retrieval"—as a simple matter of acquiring information and learning "the facts" that illuminate these "problems of women in Other cultures," and then perhaps going on to understand our "commonalities and differences." It suggests that we need to understand the ways in which feminist agendas are shaped by the different conditions that obtain within different national contexts.

In contrast to "dowry-murder," *fatal* forms of domestic violence in the United States are a problem lacking a term that "specifically picks them out" from the general category of "domestic violence." I believe that this "absence" operates to impede Americans from making the connections that would facilitate their seeing dowry-murder as a form of domestic violence.

THE EFFECTS OF "ABSENCES" ON PROJECTS OF CROSS-CULTURAL UNDERSTANDING

... I think it is quite difficult to "notice" that a term like "domestic violence murders" is "absent" in the U.S. context, and to perceive how this "lack" contributes to the phenomenon lacking specificity of a sort it might have had if a term had "picked it out" and made the underlying issue the focused subject of public and political concern.... I believe that the effects of this "absence" go beyond its functioning as an impediment to many Americans making connections between dowry-murders and domestic violence. I would like, in this section, to go on to explore some of the less obvious ways in which this absence works to complicate "cross-cultural understanding" of "similarities and differences" between forms of violence that affect women in Third World nations and violence against women in Western national contexts.

One of the things I hoped to do when I began this essay was to work on making a stronger connection between Indian dowry-deaths and domestic violence in the United States by comparing the number of women annually killed in dowry-murders in India to the numbers of U.S. women annually killed by their partners.... What I completely failed to realize was the degree to which the absence of a term that conferred "specificity" on the phenomenon of "domestic violence murders" in the United States would affect my very attempt to make this comparison. Let me clarify what I mean.

Setting out on this task, I found it easy to locate recent data on the annual numbers of dowry-murders in India. I discovered the numbers quickly after I started looking, and came across them fairly often.... The recent numbers suggest that roughly 5,000 Indian women are killed each year over dowry. On the other hand, in noticeable contrast to information on domestic violence in the United States, I discovered very little national data on other aspects of domestic violence in India. This is not surprising given the lack of infrastructures such as shelters that facilitate in the gathering of such data in the U.S. As a result, I did not find national data on the general incidence of domestic violence, on the numbers of women seriously injured in such incidents, or on how many Indian women are believed to be killed annually for *non-dowry-related* reasons. The conclusion I arrived at was that the construction of "dowry-murder" as a specific public issue had had institutional effects, such as the generation of "official national data" on the phenomenon. On the other hand, the contextual features that work in India to make general issues of "domestic violence" much harder to address institutionally also impede the ability to generate "official data" on the broader facets of domestic violence. One result is that it is easy to find Indian figures for "dowry-murders" but not for the presumably wider category "domestic violence murders."

Moving on to the "other side" of my attempted comparison, finding the statistics for "domestic violence murders" in the U.S. was not easy, as I have previously mentioned.... There was readily available data on the overall annual number of domestic violence cases, on the numbers of battered women seeking assistance from shelters, on the numbers of women seriously injured as a result of domestic violence, and on the numbers of women and children who were homeless as a result of domestic violence, but it was difficult to locate the U.S. figure for "domestic violence murders." I came to the conclusion that the same lack of organizational focus on "domestic violence murders" that leaves it a "phenomenon with no specific name" in the U.S. also works to make it a phenomenon that is not focused on widely in fact sheets and other public information on domestic violence.

In my search, I first arrived at a "ballpark figure" for U.S. "domestic violence murders" indirectly rather than finding the figure stated outright. I worked it out through looking at the FBI's Crime Index, which reports the overall number of U.S. homicides for 1994, and states that 79 percent of murder victims were men. I worked out that the 21 percent of murder victims who were women came to roughly 5,000 women. The FBI statistics also said that 28 percent of female murder victims were "slain by husbands or boyfriends," although they did not go on to specify the number.[21] I worked out from the figures that roughly 1,400 U.S. women annually were victims of "domestic violence murder." When I did begin to find direct information on "domestic violence deaths" in other sources, the numbers I found varied quite widely.

I decided to work with the FBI figure, a figure eventually confirmed by a couple of other sources, that suggested that roughly 1,400 U.S. women annually were victims of "domestic violence murder."[23] However, I began to realize that there were all sorts of problems in attempting what I wished to do next—which was to argue for the "comparative numerical seriousness" of U.S. "domestic violence murders" and Indian dowry-murders. The most obvious problem was that the Indian figures available were for the *narrower* category of "dowry-murder" and not for "domestic violence murders in India," while the U.S. figures I had worked out were for the *inclusive* category of "domestic violence murders." However, on closer examination, it also turned out that the scope of the U.S. figure for "domestic violence murders" might be, in another respect, *narrower* than the scope of the Indian figures for "dowry-murders."

The Indian statistics on dowry-murders, including those put out by the government of India, reflect the number of deaths *suspected* to be dowry-murders, rather than those that have been "proven" to be dowry-murders through the criminal justice process. . . . Some of the incidents that are counted as "dowry-murders" might in fact be the "accidents" or "suicides" or "illnesses" they are inevitably claimed to be, though there is no real way of telling how many. There are also likely to be a number of dowry-murders that do not evoke "suspicion" and fail to be counted in the statistics on dowry-murders, though again it is impossible to know how many.

On the other hand, the U.S. FBI statistics on "domestic violence murders," I believe, reflect only those cases where the partner is *convicted* of the crime.[25] I found out, in addition, that roughly 40 percent of all U.S. homicide cases remained legally "unsolved," though I did not find any data that specified the percentage of murders involving female victims that remained unsolved. One problem, then, with trying to argue that U.S. "domestic violence murders" are comparatively as "numerically serious" as dowry-murders in India is that the Indian figures seem to reflect "suspicions" rather than "legal *convictions*," while the U.S. figures seem to reflect the opposite. While the activism around dowry-murders in India has undoubtedly contributed to the collection of official national data on "suspected dowry-murders," it might well be that the lack of focus on "domestic violence murders" in the United States has resulted in there being no widely available official data on *suspected* domestic violence murders, even though domestic violence activism might well account for FBI statistics now specifying how many female homicides resulted in the *convictions* of the women's partners.

I am arguing that the complicated factors that have shaped different national agendas on issues of domestic violence seem to exert a considerable amount of influence on the kinds of "official data" that are generated on various aspects of the phenomenon. . . .

Such differences of data as well as "absences of data" are, by their nature, difficult to see and to make sense of. However, the ability to see them and make sense of them seems to me to be crucial to attempts to better understand "similarities and differences" between problems women confront in different national contexts.

BORDER-CROSSINGS, LACKS OF CONTEXT, AND THE CONSTRUCTION OF "DEATH BY CULTURE"

. . . I believe that Western feminists interested in the "problems of women in Other cultures" need to think about: (1) the kinds of Third World women's issues that cross Western borders more frequently than others; and (2) the effects of the "editing" and "reframing" such issues undergo when they do cross borders. I will try to address these issues by focusing on dowry-murder.

In thinking about issues of "violence against Third World women" that "cross borders" into Western national contexts, it strikes me that phenomena that seem "Different," "Alien," and "Other" cross these borders with considerably more frequency than problems that seem "similar" to those that affect mainstream Western women. . . . These issues then become "common topics" for academics and feminists, and also cross over to a larger public audience that becomes "familiar" with these issues. It is difficult not to conclude that there is a premium on "Third World difference" that results in greater interest being accorded those issues that seem strikingly "different" from those affecting mainstream Western women. The issues that "cross borders" then become the "Third World gender issues" that are taught about and studied "across the border," reinforcing their "iconic" and "representative" status as issues.

My analysis in the first section of this essay suggested that the issue of dowry-murder has "crossed Western borders" in part because this issue occupied an early and visible place on the agendas of Indian women's groups and remains an ongoing Indian feminist issue today.... I believe [this] can only be a very *partial explanation,* since many other issues that have received sustained attention from Indian women's groups have not acquired the same sort of "familiarity" to many Westerners. Thus, I believe that features of dowry-murder that mark it as "Other" also partly account for its "border-crossing." These features of "Otherness" simultaneously operate to cause the phenomenon to receive "notice" and to distort understandings of the phenomenon.

One factor ... is the history of Western fascination with "the Indian tradition" of *sati* or widow-immolation. This historic association of *sati* and "Indian culture" and "Indian women" results today in a metonymic blurring of *sati* with dowry-murder, generating a confused composite of "burnt Indian women" variously going up in flames as a result of "their Culture." "Women being burnt" thus becomes constituted as a "paradigmatic," "iconic," and "familiar" form of "violence suffered by Indian women." The terms *"sati"* and "dowry-murder" come to have a vaguely familiar ring, even though their exact referents are often not well understood. What is "understood," however, is their ... status as "things that happen elsewhere," which in turn suggests that they are unlike "things that happen here."

This effect is only compounded by the fact that there is little "coverage" or information in the United States about the general issue of domestic violence as it affects women in India, and by the fact that reports about dowry-deaths are seldom framed in terms of the general issue of domestic violence.[26] Given that dowry-related domestic *harassment is* far more widespread in India than *dowry-murder,* and that non-dowry-related forms of domestic violence are likely the most widespread of all, this focus on dowry-murders as a paradigmatic case of "violence suffered by Indian women" is one that centers on the most "extreme" and "spectacular" forms of domestic violence suffered by Indian women. Domestic violence against Indian women thus becomes most widely known in Western contexts in its most *extreme incarnation,* underlining its "Otherness."

The "alien" features of "burning" and "dowry" help to further code the phenomenon as "Indian" and "Other" and intersect to expunge any trace of the phenomenon's connection to the more "familiar" domestic category of "domestic violence." Consider the possible effects on Western understandings of dowry-murder of the "lurid exoticism" of fire and of women being burnt to death. Given the lack of contextual information, Indian women's murder-by-fire seems mysterious, possibly ritualistic, and one of those factors that is assumed to have something to do with "Indian culture." While the use of fire as the preferred instrument of dowry-murder does have much to do with details of the Indian context, these details are less "cultural" and "exotic," and more mundane and material, than they are often assumed to be.

Pointing out that fire is chiefly chosen for "the forensic advantage" it has over other methods of killing a wife, Veena Talwar Oldenburg ... underlines the fact that the use of fire as a murder weapon is far more a matter of expedience than it is a matter of exoticism. Burning a woman to death in the Indian context is no more "exotic" than shooting her to death is in the U.S. context. Conversely, death by shooting in a middle-class domestic context would be rather "exotic" in India, where firearms are not freely available and widely owned, and where widespread ownership of firearms and the prevalence of gun-related violence are often perceived of as "typically American."[27]

I believe that the "exoticizing" features I have mentioned above have contributed to dowry-murder's popularity as a border-crossing issue and have contributed to popular misunderstandings of the issue. In addition, I also believe that such misunderstandings are facilitated by the fact that certain kinds of "contextual information" are often left behind when issues cross national borders....

When the issue of dowry-murders "crosses national borders" and becomes "known" in Western national contexts as an "issue affecting Indian women," it becomes known "out of context." … In traveling across national borders unaccompanied by such contextual information, "dowry-murder" loses its links to the category of "domestic violence" and becomes transmuted into some sort of bizarre … form of violence against women that surely must be "caused by Indian culture." The category "Indian culture" then becomes the diffuse culprit responsible for "women being burned to death every day in India," producing the effect that I call "death by culture."

…

There is often no vantage point from which many members of the American public can "see" some of these factors that contribute to information distortion. To understand, for instance, the different ways in which feminist agendas have shaped the issue of domestic violence in the U.S. and Indian contexts would require historical and political knowledge about India and the Indian women's movement, which is often precisely the kind of knowledge that does not readily travel across borders. The fact that Western reports on "Third World issues" often refer to these issues being matters of public concern and political engagement within Third World nations often only serves to enhance these issues' status as "authentic Third World issues." …While the factual weight of the information testifies to the "reality of the problem," the references to "culture" commonplace in these reports serves to "render intelligible" everything that might otherwise remain "puzzling" to the audience. Thus, while many Western readers might not know exactly what dowry is, or the factors that lead to dowry-murders, or the exact nature of the relationship of either dowry or dowry-murder to "Indian culture," the presence of references to "Indian culture" can provide a swift and convenient "explanation" for what they do not understand. The references to "culture" in these reports can then combine with more "free-floating" ideas of "Third World backwardness" and the tendency to think of Third World contexts as realms of "Very Other Cultures" to make "foreign phenomena" seem comfortingly intelligible while preserving their "foreignness." …

I am suggesting that the "distortions" that occur when "Third World issues" cross over into Western national contexts are not reducible to "ethnocentrism" or "racism." While forms of ethnocentric and stereotypic thinking about "the Third World" do play a part in the perpetuation of such "distortions," there are also other different factors at work. One has to attend to the "multiple mediations" that occur between: (1) the ways in which "related" issues have been shaped in Western national contexts; (2) the "life" these issues have in Third World national contexts, where their coverage and reception occur in a space where members of the national public have a variety of contextual information that puts such issues "in perspective"; and (3) the decontextualization and recontextualization that accompany these issues on their travels across national borders.

… Multicultural education cannot be seen as a simple task of replacing "ignorance about Other cultures" with "knowledge," since problems of the sort I am talking about are precisely not problems of "ignorance" *per se,* but problems related to understanding the "effects" of contexts on issues, and of decontextualized, refracted, and reframed "knowledge." These features of "context" as well as of decontextualization and refraction are, by their very nature, difficult to see and to call attention to, as are their "effects."

Such difficulties complicate the project of "understanding Other cultures." I would like to insist that they cannot be "solved" by simply "deploying" Third World subjects familiar with the articulation of these issues in specific Third World contexts to "point out" the distortions and problems that occur as a result of these border-crossing "mediations." While Third World subjects who are familiar with the representations of an issue in both a Third World and a Western national context might well have a sense of some of the distortions and misrepresentations that occur as a result of "border-crossing," it is hardly *easy* for them to develop a fine-grained sense of the ways in which various "mediations" on particular issues collaborate and cohere to create the widely shared misunderstandings that shape the understanding of the issue in a Western national context.

…

DOWRY-MURDERS AND THE LIMITS AND LIMITATIONS
OF "CULTURAL" EXPLANATIONS

...

What I am calling "cultural explanations" of dowry-murders all too frequently invoke "Hindu religious views on women." I shall begin with an example that helps vividly underline what is problematic about such religious "cultural explanations" of dowry-murder. The example I shall use is a chapter from Elisabeth Bumiller's book, *May You Be the Mother of a Hundred Sons: A Journey Among the Women of India.* I choose this example not because this text is uniquely problematic, but because this is a book whose covers carry glowing review blurbs from *Newsweek, The New York Times Book Review,* and the *Philadelphia Inquirer,* all indicating that the book was a "national bestseller." ... In short, I pick it only because it seems to have had a more significant public presence and influence than most "academic" writing, and not because there are no "scholarly" examples of these same problems.

The third chapter in Bumiller's book is (alas all too predictably) entitled "Flames: A Bride Burning and a Sati." Opening with the line, "When Hindus look at fire, they see many things beyond flames," Bumiller's first paragraph goes on to describe the use of fire in several Hindu ceremonies and rites of passage.[28] The second paragraph opens with the line, "Fire is also a special presence in the lives of Hindu women" and launches into a narration of the mythological story of Sita throwing herself into a fire to prove her chastity to her husband Rama, in the Hindu epic the *Ramayana,* a story that is continued and concluded in the third paragraph.[29]

The fourth paragraph goes on to say: "Sita's ordeal has left an indelible mark on the relationship of women to fire, which remains a major feature of their spiritual lives, a cause of their death and a symbol, in the end, of one of the most shocking forms of oppression. What follows is the story of two Indian women, Surinder Kaur and Roop Kanwar, both of them victims of fire and Hindu tradition."[30]

Let me briefly point to several problems with this "framing" of Bumiller's chapter. The mythological story of Sita, which has occupied two paragraphs, is a story about Sita *proving her chastity through an ordeal by fire,* and its deployment in this chapter is completely gratuitous, given that the Sita story is an instance of neither *sati* nor dowry-murder. Further, given that one of the two Indian women mentioned in the quote above, Roop Kanwar, was a victim of *sati,* and that the other, Surinder Kaur, is a survivor of an attempted dowry-murder, they are hardly victims of "one" form of oppression, as Bumiller claims. Bumiller's failure to make a clear distinction between *sati* and dowry-murder operates as yet one more example of the tedious "metonymic blurring" of completely unrelated phenomena having to do with "burning Indian women." ...

Bumiller also characterizes both women as "victims of Hindu tradition," a characterization that creates different kinds of problems with respect to *sati* and to dowry-murder. *Sati,* the immolation of a widow on her husband's funeral pyre, used to be a "traditional practice" in *some* Indian communities, and was the "exceptional" rather than the "routine" fate of widows even in these communities. Its endorsement by "Hinduism" has been a matter of debate for centuries, and incidents of *sati* have occurred only very rarely in the last half-century.... Dowry-murder is, in contrast, neither Hindu nor a tradition, even in the "qualified" sense in which *sati* might be so characterized. Even in cases where it is Hindu women who are murdered for dowry, Hinduism neither endorses nor condones such murders, allusions to Sita notwithstanding. Dowry-murder can hardly amount to the victimization of Indian women by "Hindu tradition" when there is no such tradition of burning women to death for dowry. In addition, the institution of dowry is not a Hindu institution in at least two important ways. Dowry is not a pan-Hindu practice, given that there are Hindu communities, such as the matrilineal Nair community of Kerala, where dowry was traditionally unknown. It is also a practice that exists within some non-Hindu Indian communities, as Surinder Kaur's case reveals.

Surinder Kaur, who is first invoked by Bumiller as a woman who survived an alleged attempted burning by her husband and sister-in-law, is a Sikh, and not a Hindu. While Bumiller mentions that Surinder Kaur is a Sikh, in the very next paragraph and several times later in the chapter, she seems not to notice its implications.... Few Western readers are likely to unravel themselves from the trail of confusion whereby, in two pages, references to Hindu ceremonies, Sita, and *sati* collaborate to construct dowry-murder as "Indian women's victimization by Hindu tradition" to register the oddity of a Sikh woman being victimized by Hindu tradition, or to register the fact that dowry-murder is neither Hindu nor a tradition!

... The tendency to explain contemporary Indian women's problems by reference to religious views is by no means a tendency exclusive to Western writers, but crops up quite frequently in writings by contemporary Indians. In a context where she is talking about both dowry and dowry-murders, Sushila Mehta asserts, "If the scriptures propound that a woman is a man's property, it is axiomatic that a woman has less value than a man. To compensate she must, therefore, bring something of value along with herself for her husband and his people taking the trouble of marrying her!"[32]

Mehta's discussion exemplifies a common tendency to muddle together discussions of dowry (a traditional practice in some Indian communities) with discussions of dowry-murders (neither a traditional practice nor a historical phenomenon of long standing). Such muddling frequently results in a failure to register that what the scriptures propound may have little explanatory power with respect to the more contemporary of the two phenomena, dowry-murders, even where they have some connection to the traditional practice of dowry.... I wish to argue that Mehta's discussion is only a very mild example of a "problematic genre" of work on India and Indian culture, written by Indians. Such work frequently equates Indian culture to Hindu culture, Hindu culture to Hindu religious views, and Hindu religious views to views propounded in various Hindu scriptures, without any registering of how extremely problematic every step in this equation is.

I believe that the historical genealogy of these several equations lies in the pictures of "Indian culture" generated by both British colonial and Indian nationalist writings of the nineteenth century. Failures to be self-conscious about the existence of such problematic "genres of writing" often result in less-than-lucid explanations of contemporary Third World problems and institutions by Third World subjects themselves. In addition, failing to be aware of the existence of such problematic modes of writing about "Third World cultures" by "native subjects" is an additional handicap to the project of mainstream Westerners "understanding Other cultures" given that such writing then tends to be uncritically quoted, referenced, and "assimilated" by some Western scholars.

Given that dowry-murders are a *contemporary* phenomenon, it seems fairly obvious that explanations for the phenomenon must be sought in the ways in which the "traditional institution of dowry" has changed in recent times. Invoking the "Indian tradition of dowry" does not by itself provide a plausible explanation for dowry-murder, since the "tradition of dowry" has been around a great deal longer than have dowry-murders. I believe that a plausible explanation for dowry-murders must refer to the significant changes that the institution of dowry has undergone in recent decades, changes that have rendered it murderous.

... Mehta's view of dowry as "compensation" for women's scripturally assigned inferiority cannot account for changes in contemporary dowry, since the scriptural views are not of recent vintage, while the changes in dowry are.

I find the explanation of dowry as a form of premortem inheritance that gives daughters a share of family property to be the most plausible explanation of dowry, both traditional and contemporary, even as I think it is only a *partial* account. This explanation regards dowry as an institution that gave daughters a share of the paternal estate at the time of their marriage in the form of "movable property" consisting of gold jewelry and household items, while it simultaneously foreclosed them from inheriting "immovable property" such as land....

I think the view of traditional dowry as premortem inheritance is only a *partial* explanation, since it accounts for what was given to the woman, but does not account for that part of dowry that consisted of gifts to members of the groom's family....

I would like to briefly mention a number of changes that the institution of dowry has undergone as it has come to exist within an increasingly market-dominated modern economy and become increasingly "commercialized." Where dowry used to be something whose components and worth were largely left to the discretion of the woman's parents and their own sense of their social status, these components are increasingly matters of *explicit bargaining* by the parents of bridegrooms.[39] Traditional dowry consisted of three broad sorts of components—clothes and household items for the use of the daughter, household items for the *common use* of the household into which the daughter married, and assets mostly in the form of gold jewelry that belonged exclusively to the daughter. Contemporary "demands" for the latter two components of dowry have escalated due to the emergence of "dowry-bargaining." … Demands for large amounts of expensive jewelry and, increasingly, large sums of outright cash, are part of the new "commercial face" of dowry.[40] If cash is given, it seldom remains in the daughter's control. The jewelry component of dowry, … traditionally … something the daughter retained control of, to be sold only in dire emergencies, now functions virtually as another form of cash, often taken away from the woman with little say-so. … In short, as dowry has become "commercialized," both traditional norms pertaining to women retaining control over their dowry assets, and norms that prescribed that these assets be alienated only in financial emergencies, seem to have significantly eroded.

In addition, where dowry traditionally used to be more or less a "one-shot deal," it seems to be changing into something more like "dowry on the installment plan." Demands for goods and cash nowadays seem to continue for several years after the marriage has taken place, the wife's harassment providing her with an "incentive" to pressure her parents to meet continuing dowry demands by her husband and in-laws. … If a woman's parents are unwilling or unable to meet these ongoing demands, the woman's "utility" is reduced, making it expeditious to murder her. I am arguing that dowry-murders are, in large measure, the killing of women for outright economic gain. …

The sort of explanation for dowry-murders I have sketched refers to the "traditional institution" of dowry, but recognizes that the changing modern context of this institution must help account for its contemporary murderous effects. While it makes reference to several features of the Indian context, it is not a "cultural explanation" of the sort that alludes to Hinduism, Sita, *sati,* or the Laws of Manu, none of which strike me as adding illumination to the sort of explanation I have offered. I can therefore only note with irritation the tendency of many discussions of dowry-murders, both by Westerners and Indians, to be sprinkled with such "religio-cultural explanations" *even when they go on to also provide the sorts of social and economic explanations* I have sketched. There seems to be a fairly widespread tendency in discussions of "Third World issues" to engage in what I increasingly think of as a "schizophrenic analysis," where religious and mythological "explanations" must be woven in willy-nilly, even if they do no real "explanatory work."

… What I find fascinating and puzzling is the persistence of "exoticizing" and "ritualistic" and "religious" elements in accounts where the author knows and acknowledges the quotidian expediencies involved in the use of fire for dowry-murder. Attempts at "cultural explanation" that "weave together" the mundane reasons for the use of fire as a murder weapon with the "spiritual significance of fire to Hindus" end up as "explanations" that need more explanation than the issues they are trying to address. I suspect that Bumiller's ability to remain unaware of the significant tensions between the opening frame of the chapter and her subsequent explanation for the use of fire in the commission of dowry-murders is connected to the widespread tendency to see Third World women as suffering "death by culture" or "victimization by culture."

In the "explanations" that generate "death by culture," religious views or "traditional values" often become virtually synonymous with "culture." While the institution of dowry can certainly be meaningfully connected to "Indian culture" it is not, I think, given a satisfactory "explanation" by references to "religion." …

I do think there are interesting questions (which I am not in the least equipped to answer) about why the institution of dowry has existed in some Indian communities and not in others, and as to why it has persisted in Indian communities when it has disappeared from those Western contexts where it historically existed. While I believe answers to these questions would make reference to many material, social, and cultural aspects of the Indian context, "religious views" alone would hardly suffice as explanation. In addition, while explanations for Indian women's vulnerability to dowry-murder might meaningfully refer to some aspects of "culture," such as underlying marriage and family arrangements that contribute to women's powerlessness, neither dowry-murders nor women's vulnerability to dowry-murder seem explainable as simply the outcome of adherence to a specific set of "religious" views.

. . .

DIFFERENCES OF "CULTURE" AND DIFFERENCES IN "CULTURE AS EXPLANATION"

I would like to end by considering an interesting asymmetry that exists between explanations of violence against women in "mainstream Western culture" and such "death by culture" explanations of violence against women specific to "Third World cultural contexts." The best way I can think of to point to this asymmetry is the following kind of "thought experiment," which is also a kind of wicked fantasy whose "fantastical" elements are actually more interesting than its wickedness. Imagine yourself meeting a young Indian woman journalist who, after reading Bumiller's book, has decided to retaliate by working on a book entitled, *May You Be the Loser of a Hundred Pounds: A Journey Among the Women of the United States.* The young journalist plans to travel throughout the United States talking to an assortment of American women, trying to learn about "American women and American culture." The chapters she hopes to include in her book include vignettes on American women suffering from eating disorders; American women in weight-loss programs; American women who have undergone liposuctions, breast implants, and other types of cosmetic surgery; American women victims of domestic violence; American women in politics; and American women media stars.[45]

Ask yourself, "What are the structures of knowledge production and information circulation that make this book as difficult to imagine as it is impossible to find?" What are the factors that make it unlikely for a young Indian woman to conceive of such a project?[46] What is the likelihood of such a project being taken seriously enough to warrant the various forms of interest that are necessary to enable such a book to be written and published (in the United States *or* in India)? How likely is this book to be considered a serious source of information on "American culture" by the general public, or to appear on the reading list of any course on American culture? . . .

Pursuing my point about "cultural explanation," I shall continue with my fantasy, and go on to imagine how some of the contours of this Indian journalist's book on "women in American culture" would differ from Bumiller's Indian counterpart. I shall concentrate on her attempts to write the chapter linking domestic violence to American culture. Our intrepid Indian journalist would find it difficult, if not impossible, to account for many "American cultural phenomena" by references to Christian doctrines, myths, and practices. While "Christian values" have probably coexisted with domestic violence, fatal and nonfatal, in the United States much longer than "Hinduism" has coexisted with dowry-murder, one doubts that our journalist would be inclined, either on her own or as a result of her conversations with most Americans, to explain contemporary domestic violence in terms of Christian views about women's sinful nature, Eve's role in the Fall, the sanctity of marriage and the family, or the like.

Permit me to imagine the interesting difficulties that would confront our imaginary journalist as she attempted to write this chapter on "domestic violence and American culture." It just doesn't seem plausible, she has realized, to attempt an explanatory link between the two terms "domestic violence" and "American culture" through references to Christianity.... Much of the U.S. literature on domestic violence turns out not very helpful for her particular project, since most of the accounts they give explain the phenomenon in terms of a "non-nation-specific, secularized, general patriarchy" that seems no more distinctively "American" than it is "Christian."

She will find criticisms, most notably by U.S. feminists of color, that the underlying picture of "patriarchy" at work in many U.S. accounts of domestic violence is often overly generalized. She may find the article where Kimberle Crenshaw argues that strands in U.S. domestic violence discourse have "transformed the message that battering is not *exclusively* a problem of poor or minority communities into a claim that it *equally* affects all classes and races,"[48] and that such views impede attention to the specific needs of battered women of color. She will find that Crenshaw argues that women of color suffer disproportionately higher unemployment, lack of job skills, and discriminatory employment and housing practices, that make it harder for them to leave abusive relationships.[50] She will learn that factors such as being non-English speaking and having an immigration status that is dependent on marriage to the abuser further work to disempower a number of battered women of color in the United States.[51] ... She will recognize, however, that such references to features of the American context seem quite different from the sorts of "religious" references to "Indian culture" Bumiller's chapter introduction uses to explain *sati* and dowry-murders.

Among the things she will learn in her readings and conversations are that American men batter their partners for "reasons" that range from sexual jealousy, alcoholism, stress, and pure unmitigated rage, to the desire to control the woman or to "prevent her leaving." She will learn that economic dependency, worries about the custody and welfare of children, low self-esteem due to abuse, and the threats and violence that have followed upon previous attempts at leaving are often given as reasons for American women staying in abusive relationships. With the possible exception of "low self-esteem,"[52] these sorts of reasons will seem similar to those that work to keep Indian women in abusive marriages, though they are often eclipsed in explanations that rely on elements such as Hindu mythology or the status of women in the Laws of Manu. She will notice that in U.S. accounts of domestic violence the sorts of reasons mentioned above appear to provide explanation enough, and that there is no felt need to explain why domestic violence in America is "American." None of this, she realizes, is helping her write a chapter that easily links U.S. domestic violence to "American culture."

. . .

She might, however, acquire some interesting "cross-cultural insights" as a result of her frustrations. She might come to see that while Indian women repeatedly suffer "death by culture" in a range of scholarly and popular works, even as the elements of "culture" proffered do little to explain their deaths, American women seem relatively immune to such analyses of "death or injury by culture."...

Given these difficulties, it is perhaps for the best that this is an imaginary chapter in an improbable book. I would like to end with the suggestion that books that cannot be written and chapters that are oddly difficult to write might have more to teach us about particular cultures and their relationships to "Other cultures" than many books and chapters that face few difficulties in being either imagined or written.

NOTES

...   3. "Restoring History and Politics to 'Third World Traditions': Contrasting the Colonialist Stance and Contemporary Contestations of *Sati*" in Uma Narayan, Dislocating Cultures: ??? (pub info.) Also see Radhika Parameswaran, "Coverage of 'Bride-Burning' in the *Dallas Observer:* A Cultural Analysis of the 'Other,'" *Frontiers* 16, nos. 2–3 (1996)....

    9. Mary Fainsod Katzenstein, "Organizing against Violence: Strategies of the Indian Women's Movement," *Pacific Affairs* 62, no. 1 (Spring 1989): 61....

    12. Ibid., 54.

    13. Katzenstein points out that the Delhi-based group Saheli "concerned itself particularly with issues of dowry and domestic violence" and that the Bombay-based Forum against Oppression of Women took up issues of police rape and dowry-murders. See ibid., pp. 56–57....

16. The other was the issue of the "deficit of women" in the Indian population. Although cause for concern, there are several features that make this issue difficult to organize around. Unlike dowry-murders, this was not a phenomenon whose "causes" were readily clear. It was also less clear how groups might "organize" around this issue....

20. It is interesting to note that feminist groups in many diasporic South Asian communities in Western national contexts have organized shelters for battered women in their communities. For instance, there are shelters organized and operated by South Asian women in New Jersey and in Chicago.

21. Statistics were for 1994 and found in a "Crime Index" based on reports to the Federal Bureau of Investigation's (FBI's) Uniform Crime Reporting Program. The data appear in the FBI's annual publication *Crime in the United States*. The data I obtained were on the Internet, dated November 19, 1995, and reported some "highlights of the 1994 edition" of the FBI publication....

23. The number of women killed by *intimates* (defined as spouses, ex-spouses, or boyfriends) rose from 1,396 in 1977 to 1,510 in 1992, according to "violence between Intimates," Bureau of Justice statistics, U.S. department of Justice, November 1994. These figures seemed close enough to the 1,400 figure I am using, at least for my purposes....

25. I was not at all sure what the FBI's 28 percent statistic did reflect. I wondered whether it reflected criminal convictions, or cases where there had been sufficient evidence for criminal prosecution, or cases where the partner was simply suspected of the murder. My hunch that the FBI statistics reflected criminal convictions was reinforced by the fact that another source cited figures similar to the FBI's and said "28 percent of women murdered were known to be murdered by their partners." I am grateful to my sociologist colleague Marque Miringoff confirming that the FBI statistics reflected criminal convictions.

26. While the Indian journal *Manushi* does cover general issues of domestic violence in India, I do not think it makes much difference at the level of popular U.S. public understanding.

27. Veena Talwar Oldenburg, "Dowry-Murders in India: A Preliminary Examination of the Historical Evidence," in *Women's Lives and Public Policy: The International Experience*, Meredeth Turshen and Briavel Holcomb, eds. (Westport, Conn.: Greenwood Press, 1993), p. 146.

28. Elizabeth Bumiller, *May You Be the Mother of a Hundred Sons: A Journey among the Women of India* (New York: Fawcett Columbine, 1990), p. 44.

29. Ibid., p. 45.

30. Ibid....

32. Sushila Mehta, *Revolution and the Status of Women in India* (New Delhi: Metropolitan Book Co., 1982), p. 208....

39. Contemporary dowry also seems to be becoming a "postnuptial" rather than a "prenuptial" exchange. A recent study of 150 women victimized and harassed over dowry found that in *60 percent* of the cases, dowry was only demanded after the marriage had taken place, a point at which the bride's parents are vulnerable to pressures to "save the marriage ant any cost" and where the husband's family can exert the threat of "desertion." In roughly two-thirds of the cases where dowry was in fact demanded before marriage, it was demanded very shortly before the marriage was solemnized, at a time when arrangements for the marriage had been finalized, and when the woman's family feared social stigma in calling off the wedding. See Ranjana Kumari, *Brides Are Not for Burning*, pp. 44–45.

40. Consumer goods and cash seem to be the two most common components of dowry demands. In about 15 percent of the cases studied by Kumari, there were also demands that the daughter be given a share of her parents' estate, forms of property that women were not traditionally expected to inherit and for which dowry was regarded as a "substitute." Kumari notes that these families are willing to "flout this tradition when it comes to their wives and daughters-in-law" while insisting on tradition when it comes to their own daughters' and sisters' claims to family property! See Kumari, *Brides Are Not for Burning*, p. 48....

48. Kimberle Crenshaw, "Intersectionality and Identity Politics: Learning from Violence against Women of Color," in *Reconstructing Political Theory: Feminist Perspectives*, Mary L. Shanley and Uma Narayan, eds., (Polity Press, year?)....

50. Ibid.

51. See both Crenshaw and Nancy Hirschman's "The Theory and Practice of Freedom: The Case of Battered Women," in *Reconstructing Political Theory*.

52. Initially, discourses about "self-esteem" and "low self-esteem" stuck me as quite American and less likely to be deployed in the Indian context. But considering how rapidly ideas from Western contexts are "exported" to Third World countries, I now do not feel sure about this....

Part II

FEMINISTS RETHINKING METHODOLOGY

7

Feminist Naturalism: Do Women Have Distinctive Ways of Knowing?

OBSTACLES FACED BY WOMEN DOING RESEARCH

Western feminists of the late nineteenth and early twentieth centuries challenged the idea that intellectual inquiry should be conducted exclusively by men. They argued that women who were given appropriate education and training were just as capable as men of producing valuable research, and they pressed for women's admission into institutions of higher education, the primary research institutions of the time. Legal barriers to women's entry into higher education slowly eroded throughout the twentieth century, and by the early 1970s most had fallen, though informal barriers remained strong. However, Title VII of the U.S. Civil Rights Act, passed in 1964, provided a legal basis for "ordering such affirmative action as may be appropriate" to counter employment discrimination. Affirmative action was given no precise legal definition, but was used to refer to an open-ended range of practices designed to make occupational opportunities available to members of previously excluded groups, including women.

In the 1970s, feminists not only drew on new legal strategies to open up research opportunities to women but also added a new strand of argument. Previous generations of feminists had argued primarily in terms of equity, seeing research careers as a chance for women to participate in more prestigious types of employment and in creative and intellectual adventures. By the early 1970s, however, feminists were beginning to develop powerful critiques of accepted bodies of knowledge. They observed that systems of knowledge in the social and natural sciences as well as many great works of art and literature had been created in the service of social control, and they argued that established arts and sciences had often misrepresented women as well as male members of marginalized and stigmatized groups in ways that justified continuing their subordination. In addition, some feminists noted that researchers had often used strategies for producing knowledge that treated their subjects, including women, members of subordinated groups, animals, and nonhuman nature, instrumentally and even abusively.

These emerging critiques led some feminists to reflect that the opportunity to become active scholars, artists, and researchers not only might benefit women by providing new and more fulfilling career openings but also might benefit the fields that they entered. Feminists speculated that women scholars and artists were likely to be less male biased than male scholars and artists and therefore better able to produce more accurate knowledge and works of art that would be more truly universal. Once again, feminists advocated adding women and stirring, but this time, rather than adding new information about women into existing bodies of knowledge, the idea was to add real women as producers of knowledge. However, just as it had become apparent earlier that new perspectives on women were not easily added to existing arts, literatures, and sciences, it now became apparent that women researchers did not always fit smoothly into existing research teams and traditions of scholarship.

Women who sought opportunities to contribute to the sciences, humanities, or arts encountered several difficulties. One was sexual harassment, at this time endemic in research institutions in North America and Western Europe. Another was that the women were typically situated as junior newcomers. Often they were the symbolic daughters of powerful male scholars who had chosen to mentor them; as such, they occupied positions of insecure privilege from which it was extremely difficult to challenge views on which their mentors had built their careers. If aspiring women artists or researchers were not regarded as privileged daughters, they were often seen as tokens of affirmative action, intruders, or undeserving upstarts. Such prejudices were especially strong against women of color and older women.

In addition to discovering that their positions were undermined by these factors, aspiring women scholars in the West found their credibility was also weakened by a pervasive cultural disrespect for women's authority as creators of knowledge. Reliable knowledge, especially scientific knowledge, was imagined as impersonal, universal, and value-neutral. And those who constructed such knowledge were imagined similarly as disinterested, dispassionate, and detached from commitments to particular social groups. In direct contrast with these cultural images of knowledge and its creators, women in general as well as lower-class men and men of color were stereotyped as emotional, subjective, personal, irrational, and dependent. Artifacts, techniques, and bodies of knowledge produced primarily by women were treated disrespectfully; rather than being recognized as art, technology, or science, they were likely to be categorized as folk arts, crafts, or folk wisdom.

EARLY FEMINIST NATURALISM

Not all of the women who entered research institutions in the 1970s viewed themselves as politically supportive of feminism, let alone as feminist scholars, but enough were interested in pursuing questions about gender subordination and bias that lively traditions of feminist research emerged in many existing disciplines. The discipline of women's studies was also founded, with programmatic institutional bases that were at least semi-autonomous in many colleges and universities. As described in the introduction to this volume, feminist scholars viewed their research in a variety of ways. Some saw their mission as that of *expanding* traditional knowledge by adding new information or perspectives on women; others prioritized the need to *reform* traditional knowledge by challenging various male biases; many saw these tasks as complementary. A few feminist scholars even envisioned *transforming* traditional disciplines by prioritizing women's concerns. Regardless of how they viewed their contribution, all insisted on the need to recognize women's authority as creators of knowledge.

Western feminists had always asserted that women were perfectly capable of creating art and science, given the opportunity, but usually the feminist claim had been that women could perform as well as men in fields in which standards and methods were left unquestioned. In the 1980s, however, some Western feminists began to question established standards and methods. They drew on new scholarship that suggested women's abilities to produce knowledge were not only different from men's but in some ways even superior.

The idea that women's minds work differently from men's is a staple of antifeminist thinking. Feminists have long noted that the sensitivity and perceptiveness that many women reveal are frequently labeled "intuition" and discredited as nonrational. In the 1980s, however, emerging feminist scholarship in several disciplines sought to revalue what came to be called women's ways of thinking. Carol Gilligan's articulation of an "ethics of care" was influential both in philosophy and with the general educated public.[1] Meanwhile other feminist psychologists were developing similar theories. One prominent example of this genre was *Women's Ways of Knowing: The Development of Self, Voice, and Mind*, published in 1986, an excerpt from which is reprinted here. The authors of this book, Mary Field Belenky, Blythe McVicker Clinchy, Nancy Rule Goldberger, and Jill Mattuck Tarule, claim that developmental psychology, typified by the work of William Perry (1970), recognizes only a voice that speaks in terms of "separate knowing" as a voice of reason, and they contend that mainstream psychology does not acknowledge the kind of reason represented by "connected knowing." Connected knowing, in their view, is distinguished from separate knowing in that it seeks objectivity not through appeal to impersonal rules but rather by trying to understand how others think *in their own terms*, that is, looking at the circumstances that led a person to hold a certain belief. This is a hermeneutical or phenomenological approach to knowledge more characteristic of the social than of the physical sciences, and is supposed to be preferred by women, though men also may use it. It is also, as Sandra Harding has observed, an approach to knowing that is devalued as less rigorous, less objective, less rational—in short, as feminized.

The idea that research methodology should be derived from studying existing practices of acquiring knowledge is known by philosophers as naturalism—in one of the many meanings of that protean term. The idea that feminist methodology should be derived from studying the work of past feminist scholars is a feminist version of naturalism, though at first it did not represent itself in this way. Its emergence in the 1980s converged with other recent developments in Western philosophy of science.

NATURALIZING METHODOLOGY

For much of the twentieth century, Western philosophy of science was dominated by logical positivism, a philosophical view that held science as the only trustworthy knowledge, distinguished by its exclusive reliance on sensory observation and experiment. The positivist understanding of scientific reasoning was fundamentally challenged in 1962 by the publication of Thomas Kuhn's groundbreaking book, *The Structure of Scientific Revolutions*. Kuhn drew on the history of science to argue that standard philosophical models of scientific reasoning misrepresented the strategies for acquiring knowledge that had actually been used in the physical sciences. He argued that the history of science does not reveal a gradual and steady accumulation of knowledge; instead it reveals periodic revolutionary overthrows of previous theoretical frameworks, illustrated in the shifts from Aristotelian to Newtonian physics and from Newtonian to relativistic physics. When the burden of puzzling cases within one theoretical framework of "paradigm" becomes unbearable, according to Kuhn, a new paradigm emerges, and this provides not just a new set of truths but a whole new way of looking at the subject matter. Kuhn contended that in fact "revolutionary" progress in science had resulted from considerations much more complex than accounting for observational data. For example, the replacement of the Ptolemaic geocentric model by the Copernican heliocentric theory, often taken as emblematic of modern science, was partly motivated by the social pressure for calendar reform. Kuhn rejected the positivist belief in "crucial experiments," writing that "early Copernicans who criticized Aristotle's proofs of the earth's stability ... did not dream that the transition to a relativistic system could have observational consequences." He argued similarly that Newton's conception of absolute space and time followed not so much from empirical observation or from the rigorous requirements of his theory but rather from a prior (theological) framework of belief allied to a deeply conservative sense of cosmopolitical order.

One implication of Kuhn's work is that those who wish to understand scientific methodology would do well to study scientists' actual practices of investigation rather than issuing prescriptions on the basis of models derived mainly from a priori reflection. The challenge to a prioristic approach to scientific methodology was made more explicit with the 1969 publication of Harvard philosopher W. V. O. Quine's landmark essay "Epistemology Naturalized," which disputed the view that the task of epistemology is to set the rules for all inquiry. Modern Western philosophers, such as Descartes, Locke, Hume, and Kant, typically assumed that epistemology came logically prior to the acquisition of knowledge; in other words, that the task of philosophers was to develop rules of inquiry that seekers of knowledge would then apply.

It was in this sense that philosophy was said to be the queen or, in Richard Rorty's phrase, the overseer, of the sciences. By contrast, naturalized epistemology denied the existence of a pure realm of reason to be studied by reason alone, and insisted instead that methodology should begin by studying practices of inquiry, looking empirically at what working researchers actually do and what methods are successful in producing knowledge. In this view, epistemology and the philosophy of science are continuous with empirical studies of scientific practice.

Quine believed that naturalized epistemology should become the student rather than the overseer of the sciences, learning from the work of cognitive scientists, for instance. It should abandon its regulative or normative pretensions and become an entirely empirical discipline. Other philosophers seek to retain an element of normativity in naturalized epistemology and methodology by advocating the selection of the best available practices and methods. Feminists pursuing naturalized approaches to methodology also typically seek to retain normativity.

SOME PROBLEMS OF GENDER NATURALISM

The idea of naturalizing feminist methodology by deriving our methods from women's traditional strategies for gathering or constructing knowledge is very attractive at first sight. Surely models of good literature, art, morality, and science should not be constructed entirely from reflection on what men have done. Despite its attractions, however, the project faces a number of difficulties.

One problem is that it is very difficult to determine how claims that women acquire knowledge differently from men might be empirically substantiated. Such claims not only tend to generalize about enormous populations that are extremely heterogeneous; they also rely on interpretations of what women and men say and do that are highly contestable. It is not at all clear how claims that women have a certain conception of the self-other relation, for instance, might be substantiated conclusively, and it is not surprising that studies of men's and women's thinking have produced divergent findings. For example, several investigations into the empirical validity of care theorists' claims have failed to confirm a link between gender and caring; when subjects are matched for education and occupation, women often achieve almost identical scores with men on justice-oriented tests of moral development, leaving women who work in the home as the main female representatives of the care perspectives. Moreover, many men as well as women have been found to employ care thinking, especially lower-class men and men of color. These findings suggest that the "ways of knowing" attributed to women may reflect divisions of labor and forms of socialization that are associated not only with femininity but also with class and race. Joan Tronto, for example, links the moral perspective of care with the work of cleaning up after bodily functions, tasks that in Western history have been relegated primarily to women but also to working-class people and especially, in most of the West, to people of color (Tronto 1993).

At the beginning of the twenty-first century, Western feminists are finally developing an increasing awareness that generalizations about men or women must be treated with extreme caution. The life situations of both women and men in most societies vary widely according to factors such as class, race, ethnicity, sexuality, and age, and these factors always influence norms and experiences of gender. Patricia Hill Collins exemplifies this awareness in her article "Black Feminist Epistemology." Collins contends that African American women have a distinct approach to epistemology and methodology, which overlaps with but is not identical to the modes of inquiry that some white feminists attribute to women generally.

Naturalized approaches to feminist methodology also face the challenge of the naturalistic fallacy. This is the supposed fallacy of assuming that doing something makes it right. Even if certain types of thinking or "ways of knowing" could be established as associated with biological females or the culturally feminine, feminists might well question whether these types of thinking were adequate for feminist research. Instead, it is possible that the ways of thinking attributed to women merely reflect a subjugated consciousness; for instance, feminist critics of the ethics of care have charged that it is a "slave morality," insufficiently suspicious of the characteristically feminine moral failing of self-sacrifice. In general, because naturalized approaches to methodology build on existing practices, they might well be thought conservative, likely to discourage change and innovation, and likely to maintain the status quo. Simply for this reason, they may be thought inappropriate for feminist critical inquiry.

ADDRESSING THE NATURALISTIC FALLACY

All projects of naturalizing methodology face the challenge of the naturalistic fallacy. Proponents of such projects usually respond that they do not advocate uncritically accepting all established methods of acquiring knowledge; instead, they aim to select only those methods shown to be most successful in generating trustworthy knowledge. This response, however, simply pushes the problem one stage further back: if we take good methods to be those that are most successful in producing trustworthy knowledge, how do we know which knowledge is trustworthy? Frequently, we regard knowledge that is best justified by accepted methods as the most trustworthy, but if accepted methods are brought into question, we lack an independent criterion for assessing them. Instead, we face a circle in which processes of knowledge construction are justified by their products, and the products in turn are justified by the processes used in constructing them.

The idea of reflective equilibrium is helpful in dealing with this conundrum. The term was coined by philosopher Nelson Goodman in his 1955 book *Fact, Fiction, and Forecast*. Goodman was concerned with the foundations of the rules of inference, asking how the rules of deduction were justified. He noted that particular deductions are justified by reference to the rules of inference, but that these in turn are justified by being shown to produce valid inferences. Goodman wrote, "Justification of general rules thus derives from judgments rejecting or accepting particular deductive inferences. This looks flagrantly circular.... But this circle is a virtuous one. The point is that rules and particular inferences alike are justified by being brought into agreement with each other" (1955:66). Another philosopher, John Rawls, later utilized the notion of reflective equilibrium in establishing his theory of justice, explaining moral justification as a feedback process of continuous readjustment between proposed general principles and considered intuitive judgments (Rawls 1970).

Reflections on research methodology cannot begin from any Archimedean point outside the real world of ongoing research, conducted by situated researchers using specific methods. All research, including research into methodology, must operate within a circle of what researchers take to be their best methods and conclusions, continuously reevaluating each in light of the other. We must repair our boat even as we float in it. Circularity cannot be avoided, but not all circles are vicious, and whether a circle of reasoning is vicious or virtuous may be a matter of degree. In general, a circle may be regarded as vicious if elements within it that ought to be contested are held immune to revision, thereby begging significant questions. A circle becomes increasingly virtuous as it becomes increasingly inclusive. Pursuing "wider" equilibria, which take account not only of particular judgments and general principles but also of background theories and discordant particular cases, enlarges the circle of justification and is therefore likely to beg fewer questions and be more virtuous (Daniels 1979).

FROM GENDER NATURALISM TO FEMINIST NATURALISM

Like others seeking to naturalize epistemology and methodology, gender naturalists reject methodological models that are built exclusively on philosophical reflection, which they criticize as empirically misleading and practically inadequate. However, gender naturalists additionally assert that even if such models were accurately to portray the practices used to establish dominant systems of knowledge, they would still ignore or misrepresent women's knowledge and the methods used to establish it. Moreover, they argue, the fact that "male" models are normative or standard serves to delegitimate or devalue women's cognitive practices. They conclude that feminists should use women's practices of inquiry as guides to developing feminist methodologies.

Gender naturalism faces several problems, as we have seen already. One is the danger of essentialism, which equates women's or feminine thinking with what is normative for some subgroup in a particular society. A second problem is that of conservatism, which equates the feminist with the feminine. Both of these problems may be addressed by rethinking the task of feminist methodology, so that it is seen not as the study of women's ways of thinking but instead as the study of feminist practices of inquiry. A naturalized feminist methodology examines the best available practices of feminist research with a view to identifying the implicit or explicit methodological norms that contributed to their success. Even though its title refers to women rather than to feminists, Nancy Tuana's article, "Revaluing Science: Starting from the Practices of Women," moves toward this position as Tuana describes what it means to do science from the politics of feminism.

The project of deriving feminist methods from feminist research practices may appear question begging, or viciously circular, but simple consistency requires that feminist methodology take existing feminist research as its starting point. Vicious circularity can be avoided by careful scrutiny of what is accepted as good feminist research, since not everything advertised as feminist is trustworthy—or even necessarily feminist. Those taking a naturalized approach to feminist methodology must be willing to revise all our assumptions, except for feminism's defining assumption that the subordination of women is morally wrong. We should not hold dogmatically to some specific feminist claim or method as *the* correct feminist position or method. We pursue wide reflective equilibrium by looking for disagreements with the narrow equilibrium, especially dissent by women who have been marginalized and silenced.

Naturalistic approaches to feminist methodology are inspired not only by a desire to acknowledge the importance of feminist work by building on feminist research practices, but also by the conviction that consciously feminist inquiry has frequently produced trustworthy knowledge that resists justifying the subordination of all those defined by oppressive constructions of the feminine.

NOTE

1. Scholars had argued for centuries that women's moral thinking was different from men's and on these grounds had diagnosed women as morally underdeveloped. Developmental psychologist Gilligan (1982) also found that women's moral thinking was different from men's but, rather than interpreting it as immature, she argued that women's thinking offered an alternative way of approaching morality that revealed hitherto neglected but important features of morally difficult situations. She challenged the standard model of moral reasoning, which consisted in deducing particular "applications" from general moral principles. She asserted that women's moral thinking, by contrast, began with concrete, particular cases and that it also prioritized different values, such as connection rather than autonomy. Gilligan's work set off vigorous debate in philosophy about whether the ethics of care was biologically female or culturally feminine and, if it was either, whether this made it feminist.

REFERENCES

Belenky, Mary Field, Blythe McVicker Clinchy, Nancy Rule Goldberger, and Jill Mattuck Tarule. 1986. *Women's Ways of Knowing: The Development of Self, Voice, and Mind.* New York: Basic Books.

Daniels, Norman. 1979. "Wide Reflective Equilibrium and Theory Acceptance in Ethics." *Journal of Philosophy* 76(5): 256–282.

Gilligan, Carol. 1982. *In a Different Voice: Psychological Theory and Women's Development.* Cambridge, MA: Harvard University Press.

Goodman, Nelson. 1955. *Fact, Fiction, and Forecast.* Cambridge, MA: Harvard University Press.

Kuhn, Thomas. 1961. *The Structure of Scientific Revolutions.* Chicago: University of Chicago Press.

Perry, William. 1970. *Forms of Intellectual and Ethical Development in the College Years.* New York: Holt, Rinehart, and Winston.

Quine, Willard Van Orman. 1969. "Epistemology Naturalized," in Willard Van Orman Quine, *Ontological Relativity and Other Essays.* New York: Columbia University Press.

Rawls, John. 1971. *A Theory of Justice.* Cambridge, MA: Harvard University Press.

Tronto, Joan C. 1993. *Moral Boundaries: A Political Argument for an Ethic of Care.* New York: Routledge.

Mary Field Belenky, Blythe McVicker Clinchy, Nancy Rule Goldberger, and Jill Mattuck Tarule

Procedural Knowledge: Separate and Connected Knowing

I never take anything someone says for granted. I just tend to see the contrary, I like playing devil's advocate, arguing the opposite of what somebody's saying, thinking of exceptions to what the person has said, or thinking of a different train of logic.

—A college sophomore

When I have an idea about something, and it differs from the way another person is thinking about it, I'll usually try to look at it from that person's point of view, see how they could say that, why they think that they're right, why it makes sense.

—A college sophomore

The procedures [these college sophomores] use for making meaning, although similar and equally reasonable, are not identical. Their stories illustrate the evolution of two distinctive forms of procedural knowledge. The theme of understanding is more prominent in Patti's story than in Naomi's, and the theme of knowledge is more prominent in Naomi's story than in Patti's, although both themes are present in both stories.

By *understanding* we mean something akin to ... implying personal acquaintance with an object (usually but not always a person). Understanding involves intimacy and equality between self and object, while *knowledge* ... implies separation from the object and mastery over it. Understanding, in Patti's view and the view of other women at this position, entails acceptance. It precludes evaluation, because evaluation puts the object at a distance, places the self above it, and quantifies a response to the object that should remain qualitative....

In Perry's (1970) account of intellectual development, the student discovers critical reasoning as "how They [the upper case 'T' symbolizing authority—here, the professors] want us to think," how students must think in order to win the academic game. The student uses this new mode of thinking to construct arguments powerful enough to meet the standards of an impersonal authority. This is Naomi's story, and most of the women in this chapter tell a similar story. Viewed from a distance, at least, these women might almost be men.

Patti's story is different. Her new mode of thinking emerges not out of a need to conform to the demands of external authorities but out of a need to understand the opinions of other people, opinions that seemed at first obscure, alien, even threatening to her.... In an attempt to achieve a kind of harmony with another person in spite of difference and distance, women like Patti try to enter the other person's frame to discover the premises for the other's point of view.... The focus is not on how They want you to think, as in Perry's account, but on how they (the lower case "t" symbolizing more equal status) think; and the purpose is not justification but connection.

Naomi, like Perry's prototypical male undergraduate at this position, asks herself, "What standards are being used to evaluate my analysis of this poem? What techniques can I use to analyze it?" As with the small boys Piaget (1965) observed playing marbles on the sidewalks of Geneva fifty years ago, the orientation is toward impersonal rules. Borrowing a term from Gilligan (1982), we call this epistemological orientation *separate knowing*. Women at the same position who think more as Patti does ask instead, "What is this poet trying to say to me?" The orientation, as with the little girls Piaget observed playing hopscotch, is toward relationship. We call this epistemological orientation *connected knowing*.

Gilligan (1982) and her colleague Nona Lyons (1983) use the terms *separate* and *connected* to describe two different conceptions or experiences of the self, as essentially autonomous (separate from others) or as essentially in relationship (connected to others). The separate self experiences relationships in terms of "reciprocity," considering others as it wishes to be considered. The connected self experiences relationships as "response to others in their terms" (Lyons 1983, p. 134).

People who experience the self as predominantly separate tend to espouse a morality based on impersonal procedures for establishing justice, while people who experience the self as predominantly connected tend to espouse a morality based on care (Lyons 1983). Similarly, we posit two contrasting epistemological orientations: a separate epistemology, based upon impersonal procedures for establishing truth, and a connected epistemology, in which truth emerges through care.... Although our use of the terms *separate* and *connected* is similar enough to Gilligan's to warrant our adopting them, when we speak of separate and connected knowing we refer not to any sort of relationship between the self and another person, but to relationships between knowers and the objects (or subjects) of knowing (which may or may not be persons).

The relationship between a person and an idea seems doomed to be one-sided since an idea cannot reciprocate the care lavished upon it by a thinker. But, as Noddings says, "When we understand, we feel that this object-other has responded to us" (p. 169). We hear it speak to us....

The voice of separate knowing is easy to hear. Developmentalists like Piaget, Kohlberg, and Perry have tuned our ears to it.... The voice of connected knowing was harder to hear, because our ears were not tuned to it and because we never before listened with such care to relatively unschooled women, like Patti, who speak it most eloquently. We heard the voice, once identified, as at least a minor theme and sometimes the major one in the lives of even the most gifted and privileged women we interviewed, especially at the less traditional colleges....

Separate and connected knowing are not gender-specific. The two modes may be gender-related: It is possible that more women than men tip toward connected knowing and more men than women toward separate knowing....

The women we interviewed were not limited to a single voice. Most of them spoke sometimes in one voice, sometimes in the other....

SEPARATE KNOWING

Most of the women who leaned heavily toward separate knowing were attending or had recently graduated from a traditional, elite, liberal arts college. The majority attended a women's college. . . .

Teachers at traditional, rigorous, liberal arts colleges are bona fide experts with Ph.D.'s in respected disciplines who believe that it is their responsibility to teach their students methods of critical thinking, especially the methods peculiar to their disciplines, and to provide students with regular feedback on the degree to which their work meets the high standards of the institution. In such a setting students may be expected to discover separate *knowing* as "the way They want you to think" and to learn how to do it.

Some of the separate knowers, in having chosen and having been chosen to attend such institutions, already showed a penchant for separate knowing. In one sense, these were highly conventional women. They met the standards of academic achievement and conformed to the expectations set by their parents and their teachers. But they also violated conventional feminine stereotypes. Many reported that as children they were tomboys. . . . These women conformed to a pattern observed in a study by Norman Livson and Harvey Peskin (1981): Girls who behaved like tomboys in early adolescence exhibited high intellectual competence in late adolescence. . . . Separate knowers refuse to play the conventional female role, choosing instead to play a game that has belonged traditionally to boys—the game of impersonal reason.

Doubting

At the heart of separate knowing is critical thinking, or, as Peter Elbow (1973) puts it, "the doubting game." . . .

Separate knowers are tough-minded. They are like doormen at exclusive clubs. They don't want to let anything in unless they are pretty sure it is good. They would rather exclude someone who belongs to the club than admit someone who does not. As Elbow says, the doubting game involves "putting something on trial to see whether it is wanting or not" (p. 173). Presented with a proposition, separate knowers immediately look for something wrong—a loophole, a factual error, a logical contradiction, the omission of contrary evidence.

Separate knowing is in a sense the opposite of subjectivism. While subjectivists assume that everyone is right, separate knowers assume that everyone—including themselves—may be wrong. If something feels right to subjectivists, they assume it to *be* right. Separate knowers, on the other hand, are especially suspicious of ideas that feel right; they feel a special obligation to examine such ideas critically, whether the ideas originate in their own heads or come from someone else. . . .

Listening to Reason

"I'll not listen to reason," says a woman servant in Elizabeth Gaskell's novel *Cranford*. "Reason always means what someone else has to say" (1894, p. 242). The women in this chapter, like all the women we interviewed, were wary of other people's words and reasons, because people had battered them with words and reasons. Separate knowers remain suspicious; but as they develop techniques for analyzing and evaluating arguments, they become less vulnerable to attack. Because other people's reasons threaten them less, they are more able to listen to them. They can detect specious reasoning and find rational grounds for disagreement; but, like hidden subjectivists, they find it difficult to give voice to their disagreement, unless they can couch it in the method. . . .

In general, few of the women we interviewed, even among the ablest separate knowers, found argument—reasoned critical discourse—a congenial form of conversation among friends. . . . Women find it hard to see doubting as a "game"; they tend to take it personally.

Teachers and fathers and boyfriends assure them that arguments are not between *persons* but between *positions,* but the women continue to fear that someone may get hurt.

A woman may avoid debates with peers, but her professors force her to construct arguments. Sometimes they invite her to argue with them. Faith, in her sophomore year, said, "Last night, the professor gave us his interpretation of Henry James's *Turning [sic] of the Screw,* and after it he said, 'All right. This is my interpretation. You should be ripping it apart. You're sitting there. Come on, start ripping at it.'" The interviewer asked, "Did you?" and Faith replied, "Well, I did a little, but basically I agreed with what he was saying." Faith had not yet learned how to play the doubting game. It does not matter whether you agree with an interpretation or not; you must still try to find something wrong with it. In fact, as Elbow (1973) says, the more believable the interpretation is, the harder you must try to doubt it.

Separate knowing is essentially an adversarial form. If played among peers, the game is fair; but in the "games" the women described, as in Faith's case, the woman was nearly always pitted against an authority, usually a professor and usually male. These were unequal contests. The teacher wields very real power over the student, although masked with genial camaraderie; and it is dangerous for the relatively powerless to rip into the interpretations of the powerful....

Teachers, being professionals, are much more skilled than students at playing the game....

When we asked Faith to tell us about an important learning experience in her life, she recalled a time when she successfully challenged her seventh-grade physics teacher's assertion that Mount Everest was the highest mountain on earth. This seemingly trivial incident stuck in her mind, she thought, because it taught her that "you don't have to accept people's words." But seven years later Faith continued to wrestle with issues concerning acceptance of teachers' words.... Just beginning to trust her own reasoning, she was easily intimidated by displays of brilliance. "Whenever I'm around anyone I perceive as being very, very intelligent, I'm always afraid of saying something stupid. And so I tend to be silent."

This loss of voice is common, especially when separate knowing is the only voice allowed and especially when that voice is just beginning to emerge. Faith had trouble doubting her teacher's polished interpretations, but she had no trouble doubting her own....

Faith believed that the only way people could say something important was by weighing its importance in advance. But how could she help but think before she spoke? She knew her thinking was inadequate; teachers told her so in person and in the margins of her papers....

Faith had adopted for herself the standards teachers used in evaluating her thoughts....

Although the process of learning can be painful, many students become adept in playing the academic game of separate knowing. Daphne is one of them.... "You take a point of view, and then you address the points of view that might most successfully challenge your point of view. You try to disqualify those." Using this procedure, she consistently received A's on her papers and occasionally reached "common ground" with her teachers, at least to the degree that she could engage in friendly arguments with them. This is not the common ground of genuine colleagues.... The teachers still wield the power: They write the rules of the game and rate the players' performances. But teachers and students can now speak a common language, and they can at least play at being colleagues.

Separate knowers use these new skills to defend themselves against the authorities in their lives.... In their academic lives students sometimes come to feel like pawns in the doubting game. They are the "something" put on trial to see whether or not "it" is wanting.

In accepting authorities' standards, separate knowers make themselves vulnerable to their criticism. The authorities have a right to find fault with the reasoning of separate knowers; and since there is nothing personal in their criticism, the separate knowers must accept it with equanimity. On the other hand, separate knowers move toward a collegial relationship with the authorities. Armed with new powers of reason, separate knowers can criticize the reasoning of authorities. Laws, not men, govern the world of separate knowers, at least in theory. Authority is nonarbitrary; it rests on reason rather than power or status.... Experts are only as good as their arguments. According to Perry (1970), the paradox is that, although attempting merely to conform to authorities' standards, the student is developing the capacity for independent thought....

At this point in development the woman exercises her capacity for independent thought only at the behest of authority. Separate knowers speak a public language. They exhibit their knowledge in a series of public performances, and they address their messages not to themselves or to intimate friends but to an audience of relative strangers. Often, the primary purpose of their words is not to express personally meaningful ideas but to manipulate the listener's reactions, and they see the listener not as an ally in conversation but as a potentially hostile judge....

We asked another student, Simone, what she thought the purpose of class discussion was. We meant what purpose it served for *her*, but she answered from the teacher's perspective: "It helps to see if the students are doing the reading. There's not much else to grade on." According to Simone, the purpose of discussion was to provide data that authority could use for evaluation....

"Good papers" to Simone were papers teachers liked. Simone, herself, did not like them much: "I can write a good paper, and someday I may learn to write one that I like, that is not just bullshit, but I still feel that it's somewhat pointless. I do it, and I get my grade, but it hasn't proved anything to me."

Simone reminds us of the two Ivy League women students in Joan Bolker's (1979) composition class, who got good grades on their papers but sensed in them "a lack of personality" and felt a "sense of nonownership and of disappointment at not being able to make [themselves] heard." According to Bolker, although these young women "have both learned how to write papers, they have not yet learned to write—that is, to be able to communicate by expressing their own ideas, feelings, and voices on paper" (p. 906). Simone and her separate knowing sisters have developed a public voice that aims to please the teacher and pays no attention to the speaker....

Self-Extrication

One of the meanings of *objectivity* is that people do not project the contents of their own heads into the external object. Both separate and connected knowers are wary of projection, but they avoid it by different means. Separate knowers avoid it by suppressing the self, taking as impersonal a stance as possible toward the object....

Feelings and personal beliefs are rigorously excluded. These procedures have been most highly elaborated and explicitly codified in the sciences, but they exist in some form and with some degree of specificity in all disciplines. Faith, interviewed in her first and second years, articulated especially clearly the view that in order to really analyze an event you had to divorce yourself from your emotions about it....

To be objective, here, means to speak dispassionately, to exclude your own concerns and to adopt a perspective that your adversaries may respect, as in their own self-interest. It also means to exclude *all* feelings, including those of the adversary, examining the issue from a strictly pragmatic, strategic point of view....

Disinterested reason is, of course, one of the highest of human achievements, and separate knowers appreciate it. They deplore the egocentricity of their earlier judgments. They believe that they can see more and see more clearly than they could when blinded by their own passions and opinions. But some of the young women we interviewed carry disinterest too far; it degenerates into absence of interest, anomie, and monotony....

"The problem," Simone says, "is that I don't feel terribly strongly about one point of view, but that point of view seems to make more sense. It's easier to write the paper, supporting that point of view than the other one, because there's more to support it. And it's not one of my deep-founded beliefs, but it writes the paper." Simone did not write the paper; it wrote the paper. Reasons wrote the paper, and words and reasons seemed unrelated to personal truth.

Forced to choose between a personal belief she could not reasonably articulate and a position she did not believe but could defend, she felt she had to choose the reasonable, the "acceptable lie" (Rich 1979, p. 239).

Simone's A-minus arguments seemed to her unrelated not only to personal truth but to objective truth. It seemed to her that you could write a good argument in support of a bad interpretation. Simone could tell a well-reasoned argument from a poorly reasoned one, but she remained suspicious of reason. "It's just rhetoric," she said. "It's just a game. It doesn't prove anything." The person who won the argument was the person with the greater rhetorical skill, not the person closer to the truth.

Some of the women we interviewed were proud of their rhetorical skill, but for many it was an empty exercise that did not, as Simone said, "prove anything." Ceremonial combat, to women, often seems just silly....

These young women had little sense that their words and reasons could have powerful effects. Their arguments did not convince them; why should they influence anyone else? We asked one undergraduate what she would do if she were opposed to nuclear power and her boss ordered her to write a report favoring it. She saw no problem in writing the report. "Just saying I'm in favor of it would never change my idea," nor, she implied, would it change anyone else's.

But when they leave school and enter the real world, many of these women find themselves in situations in which it is necessary to fight; and they are grateful, then, to find themselves equipped with words that they can wield effectively as weapons of attack. One alumna said, "I think I can set up an argument very well, so that I've got a much better chance of winning it. I'll start one out from a position of offense, rather than all the time trying to get back on my feet."

. . .

In her sophomore year, Faith took a philosophy course on feminism, which helped her to formulate her own feminist convictions and to articulate her own anger about the position of women. In addition, she felt the course taught her to argue "without getting too emotional": "On the first part of the midterm exam we were given this article that, for me at least, inspired nothing but blind rage. I was so infuriated reading it. And then I had to sit down and write a critique of it. And it teaches you to have the anger there, but also the reasoning. And not lose the reasoning. So people can't tell you, 'You're just being overemotional—typically female.'"

Faith's last sentence suggested that she still tailored her messages to withstand the doubts of powerful authorities; but this passage has a very different flavor from the ones taken from her earlier interview. Although she was careful not to get "too emotional," she did not extricate herself entirely from the argument. She argued in favor of her own convictions; and she allowed herself to "have the anger there." It was rare, in our experience, for undergraduates at this institution to do this. More often, like Naomi, they kept their feelings out of the classroom. But Naomi, like most of her fellow students, was strongly tipped toward separate knowing; while in Faith the two modes were more evenly balanced. And in connected knowing, the self is allowed to participate.

CONNECTED KNOWING

Connected knowing builds on the subjectivists' conviction that the most trustworthy knowledge comes from personal experience rather than the pronouncements of authorities. Among extreme subjectivists this conviction can lead to the view that they can know only their own truths, access to another person's knowledge being impossible.

Connected knowers develop procedures for gaining access to other people's knowledge. At the heart of these procedures is the capacity for empathy. Since knowledge comes from experience, the only way they can hope to understand another person's ideas is to try to share the experience that has led the person to form the idea. A college senior, discussing *The Divine Comedy* with us, said, "You shouldn't read a book just as something printed and distant from you, but as a real experience of someone who went through some sort of situation. I tend to try and read the mind of the author behind it, and ask, 'Why did he write that? What was happening to him when he wrote that?'"

Connected knowers know that they can only approximate other people's experiences and so can gain only limited access to their knowledge. But insofar as possible, they must act as connected rather than separate selves, seeing the other not in their own terms but in the other's terms. Elbow (1973) calls this procedure the "believing game," and he says it is very hard to play. Although it may be difficult for men, many women find it easier to believe than to doubt....

And, while women frequently do experience doubting as a game, believing feels real to them, perhaps because it is founded upon genuine care and because it promises to reveal the kind of truth they value—truth that is personal, particular, and grounded in firsthand experience. This comes through most clearly in their accounts of conversations.

Conversing: In the Connected Mode

A first-year student recalled a "wonderful conversation" with a student from Ethiopia who explained why her people had accepted communism and described the effects of the new regime: "It was great to get another view on it from someone who's right there in the situation and who can see it differently from the American view that communism is bad, although I still feel it is."

We have in our records innumerable reports of conversations like this, especially among students in their first year of college. These conversations differed in both form and substance from the competitive bull sessions mentioned earlier. These young women did not engage in metaphysical debate. They did not argue about abstractions or attack or defend positions. No one tried to prove anything or to convert anyone....

The differences between the women's conversation and the male bull session were strikingly reminiscent of the differences Janet Lever (1976) noted between the play of fifth-grade girls and boys: intimate rather than impersonal, relatively informal and unstructured rather than bound by more or less explicit formal rules. Women have been practicing this kind of conversation since childhood.

An alumna recalled spending much of her first year "just sitting around and talking." ... She began to engage in less facile and more energetic forms of listening, interviewing her new acquaintances. And she discovered that "if you listen to people, you can understand why they feel the way they do. There are reasons. They're not just being irrational."

The reasons mentioned here have to do not with propositional logic but with experience. "Why do you think that?" they ask, meaning not "What were the steps in your reasoning?" but "What circumstances led you to that perception?" This is not like an oral examination in which the respondent must prove that she knows what she is supposed to know.... It is more like a clinical interview. By inviting the respondent to tell her story, without interruption, the questioner allows the respondent to control and develop her own response.

These conversations occur with special frequency whenever women encounter people who hold and practice beliefs that seem exotic, intriguing, bizarre, alien, even frightening. Naomi, for example, was initially shattered when, late in her first year at college, a woman who had become a close friend revealed that she had discovered she was a lesbian. The friend talked, and Naomi listened until she understood.

If one can discover the experiential logic behind these ideas, the ideas become less strange and the owners of the ideas cease to be strangers. The world becomes warmer and more orderly. Sometimes, but not always, a woman adopts another person's ideas as her own. Through empathy she expands her experiential base; she acquires vicarious (secondhand, firsthand) experience and so expands her knowledge....

Connected knowers begin with an interest in the facts of other people's lives, but they gradually shift the focus to other people's ways of thinking. As in all procedural knowing, it is the form rather than the content of knowing that is central. Separate knowers learn through explicit formal instruction how to adopt a different lens—how, for example, to think like a sociologist. Connected knowers learn through empathy. Both learn to get out from behind their own eyes and use a different lens, in one case the lens of a discipline, in the other the lens of another person....

Sharing Small Truths

Conversations among intimates do not always concern such weighty matters as communism and higher education. More often they consist of what the literary critic Patricia Spacks calls "small shared truth[s]" (1982, p. 24). Usually, women share these truths with other women, occasionally with friends and lovers of the opposite sex. Sometimes they talk directly about their own feelings, and sometimes they talk about other people. We call the latter gossip.

Spacks contrasts *gossip* with *discourse:* "People discourse *to* one another; they gossip *with....* One discourses from a height, gossips around the kitchen table" (p. 24). Gossip concerns the personal, the particular, and frequently the petty; but it does not follow that it is a trivial activity. "Gossip, like poetry and fiction, penetrates to the truth of things" (p. 25). The explicit information gossipers share concerns the behavior of other people; but, implicitly, gossipers tell each other about themselves by showing how they interpret the information they share. In gossip, as Spacks says, "responses to news matter more than news itself." As the gossiper observes her friend's responses she learns about the friend's ways of making meaning. And the gossipers collaborate in practicing this "special mode of knowing" (p. 28), which moves back and forth between large and small, particular and general.

Refusing to Judge

Spacks (1982) says that gossip proceeds from trust and builds trust. This is true of all conversations conducted in the connected mode: These conversations grow out of connection, and they cement connections. Connected knowers begin with an attitude of trust; they assume the other person has something good to say. This trustfulness builds on the subjectivist notion that because all opinions come from experience and you cannot call anyone's experience wrong, you cannot call the opinion wrong....

Women seem to take naturally to a nonjudgmental stance. In teaching undergraduates we have found it necessary to ask many of the males to refrain from making judgments until they understood the topic. On the other hand, we have often had to prod the females into critical examination: Even when they disagreed vehemently with an opinion, they hesitated to judge it wrong until they had tried hard to understand the reasoning behind it.

These women start, like the women Gilligan (1982) describes, from a premise of connection.... Ideally—although not always in practice—they take the stance that nothing human is alien to them.... Within their own frameworks, these women said that they could make moral judgments, but they did not wish to impose these judgments on others. When someone said something they disagreed with or disapproved of, their instinct was not to argue but to "look at it from that person's point of view, see how they could say that, why they think that they're right, why it makes sense."

It is easy to condemn women's refusal to make judgments as evidence of passivity or absence of agency, and indeed, in a sense, it is.... But, as the philosopher Carol McMillan (1982) reminds us, "Agency need not involve control over events" (p. 131). McMillan quotes the philosopher Georg von Wright: "Action has a 'passive' counterpart which is usually called forbearance. Forbearance can be distinguished from mere passivity, not acting, by being intentional passivity.... The immediate outer aspect of forbearance is, normally, a state of muscular rest or, exceptionally, muscular activity which one 'lets go on' although one could restrain the movements" (pp. 131–32). McMillan cites as an illustration of the coexistence of forbearance and control the relaxation of the woman who refuses medication in order to participate as an active agent in the birth of her child.

Connected knowing requires forbearance. "Patience," says the writer Simone de Beauvoir, is one of those "'feminine' qualities which have their origin in our oppression but should be preserved after our liberation" (1976, p. 153)....

Collaborating in Connected-Knowing Groups

It is helpful for both separate and connected knowers to meet in groups of two or more people. Separate knowers bring to their group propositions that they have developed as fully as possible and that they hope to sell in the free marketplace of ideas. Members must know the rules, but they need not know each other. In connected-knowing groups people utter half-baked half-truths and ask others to nurture them. Since no one would entrust one's fragile infant to a stranger, members of the group must learn to know and trust each other. In such an atmosphere members do engage in criticism, but the criticism is "connected." A sophomore we call Bess helped us understand connected criticism by describing her studio art course. She told us that everyone was scared and no one wanted to "cut up" anyone's work. As the class went along, although people became more and more supportive, they also grew more and more critical: "But if you've gone along since the beginning with the same people it never comes across as this awful criticism. It's very supportive." ...

People could criticize each other's work in this class and accept each other's criticisms because members of the group shared a similar experience.... Authority in connected knowing rests not on power or status or certification but on commonality of experience....

Separate knowers try to subtract the personality of the perceiver from the perception, because they see personality as slanting the perception or adding "noise" that must be filtered out. Connected knowers see personality as adding to the perception, and so the personality of each member of the group enriches the group's understanding. Each individual must stretch her own vision in order to share another's vision. Through mutual stretching and sharing the group achieves a vision richer than any individual could achieve alone.

...

In most educational institutions there is no chance to form such family groups. Each course starts with a new cast of characters, runs for thirteen weeks or so, and then disperses. Often, members of the class do not even know each other's names, much less their styles of thinking.

Many women first experience collaborative connected knowing in their families. Bess, like Patti, believed that family crisis transformed her into a thinker. Her parents' separation, just after she entered high school, caused "a sudden awakening." Before that, she had been "just sort of floating along, feeling things. All of a sudden I became more aware of my personal situation, my family feelings, what was going on, what I had to think about." She and her three sisters stayed with their mother. "We started to verbalize problems. We felt very much that it was just the four of us. We bought our first car together. My father had always bought the car before. My mother had to say, 'You've got to help me. We've got to buy a car.' And I realized, yeah, I really have to know how to do these things. I have to help."

Bess's family has become a collaborative enterprise. Each member regularly asks for and receives support from each other member. "We've gone through enough problems together that we're always supporting each other." Bess's family sounds very much like her sculpture class. Indeed, her experience within the family may have enabled her to appreciate the class....

Using Personal Knowledge

When we asked the women we interviewed "Why be objective?" they often answered that unless you were objective you could not help a friend. Suppose, for example, your friend is considering an abortion. You may find that horrifying, but you have to look at it in her terms, as one student said, "in terms of her situation and what *she* wants. Help her figure out what *she* wants, rather than tell her what you want for her." Women who act on knowledge received from authority know what a friend should do without consulting her; if they believe that abortion is wrong, they tell the friend to keep the child. Women who trust subjective knowledge, on the other hand, advise their friends to do whatever feels right to them. Connected knowers make it their responsibility to understand how their friends feel and to help them think the problem through. When we asked procedural knowers to tell us about moral dilemmas in their lives, they often told us about friends who were contemplating actions that they believed were not in the friends' best interests. Their own task, as they saw it, was to help their distraught friends think through their decisions.

Although connected knowing may begin as a procedure for understanding people, it does not end there. The mode of knowing is personal, but the object of knowing need not be. It may be a painting, for example (or even, as we shall see, an ear of corn [Keller 1983]). Connected knowers try to understand texts by imagining themselves into the author's mind....

Many women take naturally to connected knowing, finding it easier to follow authors than to attack them, easier to get close to them than to stand apart; but they do not always find it easy to enter perspectives very different from their own. This requires real skill and effort. It is important to distinguish between the effortless intuition of subjectivism (in which one identifies with positions that feel right) and the deliberate, imaginative extension of one's understanding into positions that initially feel wrong or remote. Connected knowing involves feeling, because it is rooted in relationship; but it also involves thought. Like Noddings's "care," it entails "generous thinking" (1984, p. 186) and "receptive rationality" (p. 1).

Connected knowing is just as *procedural* as separate knowing, although its procedures have not yet been as elaborately codified. Faith, in her first year at college, saw what her history professor wanted her to do, but she could not see how to do it: "He's trying to get us to divorce ourselves from modern ways of thinking and look at it as it was, say, in 1700, when the event occurred. Which is fine. But I have difficulty doing that, because I can't place myself back in the proper time period. I come from a middle-class family, and back then you would either have been peasantry or aristocracy. And I can't imagine being either. Now that we've gotten into the late 1800s I'm doing a little better, I think."

... Her problem in the history course was not so much to extricate herself from the situation as to connect with it. Elbow would say that Faith must "insert" herself into the seventeenth-century mind: "It takes practice over time to learn not to 'project' in the bad sense—not to see only your own preconceptions or preoccupations; and to learn to 'project' more in the good sense—to see more of what's really there by getting more of the self into every bit of it" (1973, p. 171).

Elbow's notion is close to the *Oxford Universal Dictionary*'s definition of *empathy:* "the power of projecting one's own personality into, and so fully understanding, the objective of contemplation." This phallic imagery may capture the masculine experience of empathy, but it strikes many women—Nel Noddings, for example—as a peculiar description of "feeling with." Empathy, for Noddings, "does not involve projection but reception." "I do not project," she says. "I receive the other into myself, and I see and feel with the other" (1984, p. 30).

In describing connected knowing the women we interviewed used images not of invading another mind but of opening up to receive another's experience into their own minds. One undergraduate said, "When I'm reading a book, I can open my mind to the point where I see what the author was all about, see the *isness* of what he was trying to say." ...

Judging from the stories Faith and her classmates told, the kind of self-analysis required for complex connected knowing has been largely excluded from the traditional liberal arts curriculum and relegated to "counseling." In institutions that are more progressive, or less rigorous (depending upon one's point of view), students may be encouraged to develop their own curricula, exploring their own self-interests, and to use their own personal experience as a source of knowledge. Under these circumstances, women find it easier (although still not easy) to identify and articulate their needs and desires and preoccupations....

BEYOND PROCEDURAL KNOWLEDGE

Some of the women we interviewed seemed content, for the moment at least, with procedural knowledge as a mode of approaching the world. Others had begun to chafe against the constraints of the position.

Procedural knowledge is "objective" in the sense of being oriented away from the self—the knower—and toward the object the knower seeks to analyze or understand. In Piagetian language, procedural knowledge is tilted toward "accommodation" to the shape of the object rather than "assimilation" of the object to the shape of the knower's mind. This is true of both the connected and the separate forms; connected knowers seek to understand other people's ideas in the other people's terms rather than in their own terms.

Although this selfless aspect of procedural knowledge is its glory, some women began to experience it as alienation. This was especially and perhaps exclusively true of our most separate knowers. They no longer felt any personal involvement in the pursuit of knowledge.... Connected knowers, on the other hand, were attached to the objects they sought to understand; they *cared* about them. This being so, it seems likely that connected knowers can make the transition beyond purely procedural knowledge more smoothly than those who are tipped toward separate knowing. But this speculation is based on very little data, because we have in our sample very few highly reflective women who relied more heavily on connected than separate procedures.

In any case, the following section mainly describes the travails of transition the more separate knowers experience. These women hear themselves speaking in different voices in different situations. They hear themselves echoing the words of powerful others. And, like so many women, they feel like frauds (Clance and Imes 1978; McIntosh 1985). They yearn for a voice that is more integrated, individual, and original—a voice of their own.

Searching for a Single Voice

In the institutions of higher learning most of these women attended, the subjective voice was largely ignored; feelings and intuitions were banished to the realm of the personal and private. It was the public, rational, analytical voice that received the institutions' tutelage, respect, and rewards. Most of these women profited from the tutelage, respect, and rewards, and most were grateful to their colleges for nurturing their analytical powers. In acquiring the skills of separate knowing, women at this position did, indeed, transcend the stereotypes of women as creatures ruled by instinct and emotion, incapable of reason; but they also adopted a stereotyped view of reason as detached from feeling and remote from everyday experience.

Naomi is a case in point. Although she took pride in her analytical skills, she exercised them only on academic tasks, only when required to submit material for judgment. She told us that she would be "stretching it" to try to apply her analytical skills to her personal life.... Naomi felt that it was appropriate to be objective and unbiased in academic life, but in personal life it "would be like being a robot, having no feelings."

Just as Naomi found no room for dispassionate reason in personal life, she found no place for passion in academic life....

But ... there were signs that Naomi's two worlds—the public world of reason and the private world of feeling and unjustifiable insight—were beginning to intersect. For the first time, she spoke of bringing analysis to bear upon her personal life. "I want some time to think about myself," she said, and she resigned all her extracurricular posts in order to provide time for introspection the following year.

During her senior year Naomi did devote time to introspection; she grew more and more "emotionally distraught" until she was "unable to function." With the help of a counselor she began to *think* about personal issues, to "take a very close-up look" at her problematic relationship with her mother—something she had never mentioned in her three previous interviews. She told us that her mother needed to believe that she and Naomi were identical. "She wants a merger of the two selves. If she cries, I have to cry. There just isn't any separateness. She's really confused about how to deal with emotions." She accused Naomi of changing, "as if," Naomi said, "change is bad."

Several other women who were searching for something beyond procedural knowledge told of being utterly submerged in relationships, sometimes, as in Naomi's case, in relationships with their mothers....

These women had treated their mothers and even their friends and lovers, as well as their teachers, as authorities whom they were obliged to please. They had never experienced active partnership in a truly equal relationship. Finally, they have begun to imagine such relationships with friends and lovers and even with mothers and teachers.

Again, Naomi's story illustrates the point. As she began to function again, she found that for the first time she was really enjoying her academic work, "maybe because I'm running ahead of the game, and I don't have to prove anything any more." (She was elected to Phi Beta Kappa during her junior year.) Although still "motivated to do well by traditional standards," she felt she was "putting more personal effort into it." ...

In the past Naomi portrayed her academic life as "sort of a battle" between two unequal and impersonal forces, "me and the professors." Now, she could imagine a student-teacher relationship of reciprocal care, built around a common concern for work. She could begin to envision an integration of thinking and feeling in a voice that spoke both in private and in public.

Leaving the System

Women who rely on procedural knowledge are systematic thinkers in more than one sense of the term. Their thinking is encapsulated within systems. They can criticize a system, but only in the system's terms, only according to the system's standards. Women at this position may be liberals or conservatives, but they cannot be radicals. If, for example, they are feminists, they want equal opportunities for women within the capitalistic structure; they do not question the premises of the structure. When these women speak of "beating the system," they do not mean violating its expectations but rather exceeding them....

But some of the women we interviewed were taking steps toward breaking out of the systems that had governed their lives. Naomi dropped a busy agenda in order to allow herself time to think about herself. As graduation approached Naomi found herself shedding old commitments and avoiding new ones.... To her "total surprise" she had no idea what she would do after college. Earlier, not knowing was frightening. Now, she welcomed it, "because I've always felt so directed. Right now I have little direction. I feel like I'm at a point where I want to become awfully selfish. I kind of look forward to living alone and not answering to anyone and not being judged by anyone."

Women like Naomi found it especially difficult to take the initiative in disengaging themselves from systems that they had struggled to maintain in the past. Emily, daughter of a distinguished family and graduate of a distinguished coeducational college, never spoke to anyone in the family about the continual sexual assaults she suffered during childhood from her father. Her mother tried repeatedly to commit suicide. Emily perceived her mother as manipulative and her father as irresponsible; nevertheless, she worked hard to keep the system going....

The week before our interview, Emily's mother made another suicide attempt, and Emily decided she had had enough. She marched into her mother's hospital room and, for the first time, told her off.

...

Emily, like Naomi and others beginning to break out of the systems in which they were embedded, described herself as "selfish," She felt, as many did, that she had swung from one extreme to another, from utterly selfless to utterly selfish, "very callous." The swing did not feel entirely good, but it did feel necessary.

"Selfishness" is required because the sense of identity is weak.... Procedural knowers feel like chameleons; they cannot help but take on the color of any structure they inhabit. In order to assume their own true colors, they must detach themselves from the relationships and institutions to which they have been subordinated.... As women move out of procedural knowing, they begin to put more faith in unjustifiable intuitions than they once did. But they do not abandon reason. They are aware that reason is necessary; but they know, too, that it is insufficient, that to ignore the role of feeling in making judgments is to be guilty of something like "romantic rationalism" (Noddings 1984, p. 3). What is needed is not reversion to sheer feeling but some sort of integration of feeling and thinking. The task is clear, although the solution is not.

Patricia Hill Collins
Black Feminist Epistemology

...

As critical social theory, U.S. Black feminist thought reflects the interests and standpoint of its creators.... Because elite White men control Western structures of knowledge validation, their interests pervade the themes, paradigms, and epistemologies of traditional scholarship. As a result, U.S. Black women's experiences as well as those of women of African descent transnationally have been routinely distorted within or excluded from what counts as knowledge.

U.S. Black feminist thought as specialized thought reflects the distinctive themes of African-American women's experiences. Black feminist thought's core themes of work, family, sexual politics, motherhood, and political activism rely on paradigms that emphasize the importance of intersecting oppressions in shaping the U.S. matrix of domination. But expressing these themes and paradigms has not been easy because Black women have had to struggle against White male interpretations of the world.

In this context, Black feminist thought can best be viewed as subjugated knowledge. Traditionally, the suppression of Black women's ideas within White-male-controlled social institutions led African-American women to use music, literature, daily conversations, and everyday behavior as important locations for constructing a Black feminist consciousness. More recently, higher education and the news media have emerged as increasingly important sites for Black feminist intellectual activity. Within these new social locations, Black feminist thought has often become highly visible, yet curiously, despite this visibility, it has become differently subjugated (Collins 1998a, 32–43).

...

Epistemology constitutes an overarching theory of knowledge (Harding 1987). It investigates the standards used to assess knowledge or *why* we believe what we believe to be true. Far from being the apolitical study of truth, epistemology points to the ways in which power relations shape who is believed and why....

In producing the specialized knowledge of U.S. Black feminist thought, Black women intellectuals often encounter two distinct epistemologies: one representing elite White male interests and the other expressing Black feminist concerns. Whereas many variations of these epistemologies exist, it is possible to distill some of their distinguishing features that transcend differences among the paradigms within them. Epistemological choices about whom to trust, what to believe, and why something is true are not benign academic issues. Instead, these concerns tap the fundamental question of which versions of truth will prevail.

EUROCENTRIC KNOWLEDGE VALIDATION
PROCESSES AND U.S. POWER RELATIONS

In the United States, the social institutions that legitimate knowledge as well as the Western or Eurocentric epistemologies that they uphold constitute two interrelated parts of the dominant knowledge validation processes. In general, scholars, publishers, and other experts represent specific interests and credentialing processes, and their knowledge claims must satisfy the political and epistemological criteria of the contexts in which they reside (Kuhn 1962; Mulkay 1979). Because this enterprise is controlled by elite White men, knowledge validation processes reflect this group's interests. Although designed to represent and protect the interests of powerful White men, neither schools, government, the media and other social institutions that house these processes nor the actual epistemologies that they promote need be managed by White men themselves. White women, African-American men and women, and other people of color may be enlisted to enforce these connections between power relations and what counts as truth. Moreover, not all White men accept these power relations that privilege Eurocentrism. Some have revolted and subverted social institutions and the ideas they promote.

Two political criteria influence knowledge validation processes. First, knowledge claims are evaluated by a group of experts whose members bring with them a host of sedimented experiences that reflect their group location in intersecting oppressions. No scholar can avoid cultural ideas and his or her placement in intersecting oppressions of race, gender, class, sexuality, and nation. In the United States, this means that a scholar making a knowledge claim typically must convince a scholarly community controlled by elite White avowedly heterosexual men holding U.S. citizenship that a given claim is justified. Second, each community of experts must maintain its credibility as defined by the larger population in which it is situated and from which it draws its basic, taken-for-granted knowledge. This means that scholarly communities that challenge basic beliefs held in U.S. culture at large will be deemed less credible than those that support popular ideas. For example, if scholarly communities stray too far from widely held beliefs about Black womanhood, they run the risk of being discredited.

When elite White men or any other overly homogeneous group dominates knowledge validation processes, both of these political criteria can work to suppress Black feminist thought. Given that the general U.S. culture shaping the taken-for-granted knowledge of the community of experts is permeated by widespread notions of Black female inferiority, new knowledge claims that seem to violate this fundamental assumption are likely to be viewed as anomalies (Kuhn 1962). Moreover, specialized thought challenging notions of Black female inferiority is unlikely to be generated from within White-male-controlled academic settings because both the kinds of questions asked and the answers to them would necessarily reflect a basic lack of familiarity with Black women's realities. Even those who think they are familiar can reproduce stereotypes. Believing that they are already knowledgeable, many scholars staunchly defend controlling images of U.S. Black women as mammies, matriarchs, and jezebels, and allow these commonsense beliefs to permeate their scholarship.

The experiences of African-American women scholars illustrate how individuals who wish to rearticulate a Black women's standpoint through Black feminist thought can be suppressed by prevailing knowledge validation processes.... Black women have long produced knowledge claims that contested those advanced by elite White men. But because Black women have been denied positions of authority, they often relied on alternative knowledge validation processes to generate competing knowledge claims....

Black women with academic credentials who seek to exert the authority that our status grants us to propose new knowledge claims about African-American women face pressures to use our authority to help legitimate a system that devalues and excludes the majority of Black women. When an outsider group ... recognizes that the insider group ... requires special privileges from the larger society, those in power must find ways of keeping the outsiders out and at the same time having them acknowledge the legitimacy of this procedure.... One way of excluding the majority of Black women from the knowledge validation process is to permit a few Black women to acquire positions of authority in institutions that legitimate knowledge, and to encourage us to work within the taken-for-granted assumptions of Black female inferiority shared by the scholarly community and the culture at large....

African-American women academicians who persist in trying to rearticulate a Black women's standpoint also face potential rejection of our knowledge claims on epistemological grounds. Just as the material realities of powerful and dominated groups produce separate standpoints, these groups may also deploy distinctive epistemologies or theories of knowledge. Black women scholars may know that something is true—at least, by standards widely accepted among African-American women—but be unwilling or unable to legitimate our claims using prevailing scholarly norms. For any discourse, new knowledge claims must be consistent with an existing body of knowledge that the group controlling the interpretive context accepts as true....

Though I describe Western or Eurocentric epistemologies as a single cluster, many interpretive frameworks or paradigms are subsumed under this category. Moreover, my focus on positivism should be interpreted neither to mean that all dimensions of positivism are inherently problematic for Black women nor that nonpositivist frameworks are better.

Positivist approaches aim to create scientific descriptions of reality by producing objective generalizations.... [G]enuine science is thought to be unattainable unless all human characteristics except rationality are eliminated from the research process. By following strict methodological rules, scientists aim to distance themselves from the values, vested interests, and emotions generated by their class, race, sex, or unique situation. By decontextualizing themselves, they allegedly become detached observers and manipulators of nature (Jaggar 1983; Harding 1986).

Several requirements typify positivist methodological approaches. First, research methods generally require a distancing of the researcher from her or his "object" of study by defining the researcher as a "subject" with full human subjectivity and by objectifying the "object" of study (Keller 1985; Asante 1987). A second requirement is the absence of emotions from the research process (Jaggar 1983). Third, ethics and values are deemed inappropriate in the research process, either as the reason for scientific inquiry or as part of the research process itself (Richards 1980). Finally, adversarial debates, whether written or oral, become the preferred method of ascertaining truth: The arguments that can withstand the greatest assault and survive intact become the strongest truths (Moulton 1983).

Such criteria ask African-American women to objectify ourselves, devalue our emotional life, displace our motivations for furthering knowledge about Black women, and confront in an adversarial relationship those with more social, economic, and professional power. On the one hand, it seems unlikely that Black women would rely exclusively on positivist paradigms in rearticulating a Black women's standpoint....

On the other hand, many Black women have had access to another epistemology that encompasses standards for assessing truth that are widely accepted among African-American women. An experiential, material base underlies a Black feminist epistemology, namely, collective experiences and accompanying worldviews that U.S. Black women sustained based on our particular history.... The historical conditions of Black women's work, both in Black civil society and in paid employment, fostered a series of experiences that when shared and passed on become the collective wisdom of a Black women's standpoint. Moreover, a set of principles for assessing knowledge claims may be available to those having these shared experiences. These principles pass into a more general Black women's wisdom and, further, into what I call here a Black feminist epistemology.

This alternative epistemology uses different standards that are consistent with Black women's criteria for substantiated knowledge and with our criteria for methodological adequacy. Certainly this alternative Black feminist epistemology has been devalued by dominant knowledge validation processes and may not be claimed by many African-American women....

LIVED EXPERIENCE AS A CRITERION OF MEANING

"My aunt used to say, 'A heap see, but a few know,'" remembers Carolyn Chase, a 31-year-old inner-city Black woman (Gwaltney 1980, 83). This saying depicts two types of knowing—knowledge and wisdom—and taps the first dimension of Black feminist epistemology. Living life as Black women requires wisdom because knowledge about the dynamics of intersecting oppressions has been essential to U.S. Black women's survival. African-American women give such wisdom high credence in assessing knowledge.

Allusions to these two types of knowing pervade the words of a range of African-American women.... In describing differences separating African-American and White women, Nancy White invokes a similar rule: "When you come right down to it, white women just *think* they are free. Black women *know* they ain't free" (Gwaltney 1980, 147)....

This distinction between knowledge and wisdom, and the use of experience as the cutting edge dividing them, has been key to Black women's survival. In the context of intersecting oppressions, the distinction is essential. Knowledge without wisdom is adequate for the powerful, but wisdom is essential to the survival of the subordinate.

For most African-American women those individuals who have lived through the experiences about which they claim to be experts are more believable and credible than those who have merely read or thought about such experiences. Thus lived experience as a criterion for credibility frequently is invoked by U.S. Black women when making knowledge claims. For instance, Hannah Nelson describes the importance that personal experience has for her: "Our speech is most directly personal, and every black person assumes that every other black person has a right to a personal opinion. In speaking of grave matters, your personal experience is considered very good evidence. With us, distant statistics are certainly not as important as the actual experience of a sober person" (Gwaltney 1980, 7)....

Experience as a criterion of meaning with practical images as its symbolic vehicles is a fundamental epistemological tenet in African-American thought systems (Mitchell and Lewter 1986). "Look at my arm!" Sojourner Truth proclaimed: "I have ploughed, and planted, and gathered into barns, and no man could head me! And ain't I a woman?" (Loewenberg and Bogin 1976, 235). By invoking examples from her own life to symbolize new meanings, Truth deconstructed the prevailing notions of woman. Stories, narratives, and Bible principles are selected for their applicability to the lived experiences of African-Americans and become symbolic representations of a whole wealth of experience.... The narrative method requires that the story be told, not torn apart in analysis, and trusted as core belief, not "admired as science" (Mitchell and Lewter 1986, 8).

. . .

Some feminist scholars claim that women as a group are more likely than men to use lived experiences in assessing knowledge claims. For example, a substantial number of the 135 women in a study of women's cognitive development were "connected knowers" and were drawn to the sort of knowledge that emerges from firsthand observation (Belenky et al. 1986). Such women felt that because knowledge comes from experience, the best way of understanding another person's ideas was to develop empathy and share the experiences that led the person to form those ideas. In explaining these patterns, some feminist theorists suggest that women are socialized in complex relational nexuses where contextual rules versus abstract principles govern behavior (Chodorow 1978; Gilligan 1982). This socialization process is thought to stimulate characteristic ways of knowing (Hartsock 1983a; Belenky et al. 1986). These theorists suggest that women are more likely to experience two modes of knowing: one located in the body and the space it occupies and the other passing beyond it. Through multiple forms of mothering, women mediate these two modes and use the lived experiences of their daily lives to assess more abstract knowledge claims (D. Smith 1987). These forms of knowledge allow for subjectivity between the knower and the known, rest in the women themselves (not in higher authorities), and are experienced directly in the world (not through abstractions).

African-American women's lives remain structured at the convergence of several factors: Black community organizations reflecting principles of African-influenced belief systems; activist mothering traditions that stimulate politicized understandings of Black women's motherwork; and a social class system that relegates Black women as workers to the bottom of the social hierarchy. . . .

In traditional African-American communities Black women find considerable institutional support for valuing lived experience. Black women's centrality in families, churches, and other community organizations allows us to share with younger, less experienced sisters our concrete knowledge of what it takes to be self-defined Black women. "Sisterhood is not new to Black women," asserts Bonnie Thornton Dill, but "while Black women have fostered and encouraged sisterhood, we have not used it as the anvil to forge our political identities" (1983, 134). Though not expressed in explicitly political terms, this relationship of sisterhood among Black women can be seen as a model for a series of relationships African-American women have with one another (Gilkes 1985; Giddings 1988).

Given that Black churches and families are often woman-centered, African-influenced institutions, African-American women traditionally have found considerable institutional support for this dimension of Black feminist epistemology. While White women may value lived experience, it is questionable whether comparable support comes from White families—particularly middle-class families where privatization is so highly valued—and other social institutions controlled by Whites that advance similar values. Similarly, while Black men participate in the institutions of Black civil society, they cannot take part in Black women's sisterhood. In terms of Black women's relationships with one another, African-American women may find it easier than others to recognize connectedness as a primary way of knowing, simply because we have more opportunities to do so and must rely upon it more heavily than others.

THE USE OF DIALOGUE IN ASSESSING KNOWLEDGE CLAIMS

"Dialogue implies talk between two subjects, not the speech of subject and object. It is a humanizing speech, one that challenges and resists domination," asserts bell hooks (1989, 131). For Black women new knowledge claims are rarely worked out in isolation from other individuals and are usually developed through dialogues with other members of a community. A primary epistemological assumption underlying the use of dialogue in assessing knowledge claims is that connectedness rather than separation is an essential component of the knowledge validation process (Belenky et al. 1986, 18).

This belief in connectedness and the use of dialogue as one of its criteria for methodological adequacy has African roots. Whereas women typically remain subordinated to men within traditional African societies, these same societies have at the same time embraced holistic worldviews that seek harmony. "One must understand that to become human, to realize the promise of becoming human, is the only important task of the person," posits Molefi Asante (1987, 185). People become more human and empowered primarily in the context of a community, and only when they "become seekers of the type of connections, interactions, and meetings that lead to harmony" (p. 185). The power of the word generally, and dialogues specifically, allows this to happen.

. . .

The widespread use of the call-and-response discourse mode among African-Americans illustrates the importance placed on dialogue. Composed of spontaneous verbal and nonverbal interaction between speaker and listener in which all of the speaker's statements, or "calls," are punctuated by expressions, or "responses," from the listener, this Black discourse mode pervades African-American culture. The fundamental requirement of this interactive network is active participation of all individuals (Smitherman 1977, 108). For ideas to be tested and validated, everyone in the group must participate. To refuse to join in, especially if one really disagrees with what has been said, is seen as "cheating" (Kochman 1981, 28).

...

Black women's centrality in families, churches, and other community organizations provides African-American women with a high degree of support for invoking dialogue as a dimension of Black feminist epistemology. However, when African-American women use dialogues in assessing knowledge claims, we might be invoking ways of knowing that are also more likely to be used by women. Feminist scholars contend that men and women are socialized to seek different types of autonomy—the former based on separation, the latter seeking connectedness—and that this variation in types of autonomy parallels the characteristic differences between how men and women understand ideas and experiences (Chodorow 1978; Keller 1985; Belenky et al. 1986)....

THE ETHICS OF CARING

"Ole white preachers used to talk wid dey tongues widdout sayin' nothin', but Jesus told us slaves to talk wid our hearts" (Webber 1978, 127). These words of an ex-slave suggest that ideas cannot be divorced from the individuals who create and share them. This theme of talking with the heart taps the ethic of caring, another dimension of an alternative epistemology used by African-American women. Just as the ex-slave used the wisdom in his heart to reject the ideas of the preachers who talked "wid dey tongues widdout sayin' nothin'," the ethic of caring suggests that personal expressiveness, emotions, and empathy are central to the knowledge validation process.

One of three interrelated components of the ethic of caring is the emphasis placed on individual uniqueness. Rooted in a tradition of African humanism, each individual is thought to be a unique expression of a common spirit, power, or energy inherent in all life....

A second component of the ethic of caring concerns the appropriateness of emotions in dialogues. Emotion indicates that a speaker believes in the validity of an argument. Consider Ntozake Shange's description of one of the goals of her work: "Our [Western] society allows people to be absolutely neurotic and totally out of touch with their feelings and everyone else's feelings, and yet be very respectable. This, to me, is a travesty.... I'm trying to change the idea of seeing emotions and intellect as distinct faculties" (Tate 1983, 156)....

A third component of the ethic of caring involves developing the capacity for empathy.... Black women writers often explore the growth of empathy as part of an ethic of caring....

These components of the ethic of caring—the value placed on individual expressiveness, the appropriateness of emotions, and the capacity for empathy—reappear in varying combinations throughout Black civil society. One of the best examples of the interactive nature of the importance of dialogue and the ethic of caring in assessing knowledge claims occurs in the use of the call-and-response discourse mode in many Black church services. In such services both the minister and the congregation routinely use voice rhythm and vocal inflection to convey meaning. The sound of what is being said is just as important as the words themselves in what is, in a sense, a dialogue of reason and emotion. As a result it is nearly impossible to filter out the strictly linguistic-cognitive abstract meaning from the sociocultural psychoemotive meaning (Smitherman 1977, 135, 137). While the ideas presented by a speaker must have validity (i.e., agree with the general body of knowledge shared by the Black congregation), the group also appraises the way knowledge claims are presented.

The emphasis placed on expressiveness and emotion in African-American communities bears marked resemblance to feminist perspectives on the importance of personality in connected knowing. Belenky et al. (1986) point out that two contrasting orientations characterize knowing: one of separation based on impersonal procedures for establishing truth, and the other of connection in which truth emerges through care. While these ways of knowing are not gender specific, disproportionate numbers of women rely on connected knowing. Separate knowers try to subtract the personality of an individual from his or her ideas because they see personality as biasing those ideas. In contrast, connected knowers see personality as adding to an individual's ideas and feel that the personality of each group member enriches a group's understanding. The significance of individual uniqueness, personal expressiveness, and empathy in African-American communities thus resembles the importance that some feminist analyses place on women's "inner voice" (Belenky et al. 1986).

The convergence of African-influenced and feminist principles in the ethic of caring seems particularly acute. White women may have access to women's experiences that encourage emotion and expressiveness, but few White-controlled U.S. social institutions except the family validate this way of knowing. In contrast, Black women have long had the support of the Black church, an institution with deep roots in the African past and a philosophy that accepts and encourages expressiveness and an ethic of caring. Black men share in this Black cultural tradition. But they must resolve the contradictions that confront them in redefining Black masculinity in the face of abstract, unemotional notions of masculinity imposed on them (Hoch 1979). Thus, the differences distinguishing U.S. Black women from other groups, even those close to them, lie less in Black women's race or gender identity than in access to social institutions that support an ethic of caring in their lives.

THE ETHIC OF PERSONAL ACCOUNTABILITY

An ethic of personal accountability also characterizes Black feminist epistemology. Not only must individuals develop their knowledge claims through dialogue and present them in a style proving their concern for their ideas, but people are expected to be accountable for their knowledge claims....

Assessments of an individual's knowledge claims simultaneously evaluate an individual's character, values, and ethics. Within this logic, many African-Americans reject prevailing beliefs that probing into an individual's personal viewpoint is outside the boundaries of discussion. Rather, all views expressed and actions taken are thought to derive from a central set of core beliefs that cannot be other than personal (Kochman 1981, 23). "Does Aretha really *believe* that Black women should get 'respect,' or is she just mouthing the words?" is a valid question in Black feminist epistemology. Knowledge claims made by individuals respected for their moral and ethical connections to their ideas will carry more weight than those offered by less respected figures.

. . .

Traditional Black church services also illustrate the interactive nature of all four dimensions of this alternative epistemology. The services represent more than dialogues between the rationality used in examining biblical texts and stories and the emotion inherent in the use of reason for this purpose. The reason such dialogues exist is to examine lived experiences for the presence of an ethic of caring. Neither emotion nor ethics is subordinated to reason. Instead, emotion, ethics, and reason are used as interconnected, essential components in assessing knowledge claims. In this alternative epistemology, values lie at the heart of the knowledge validation process such that inquiry always has an ethical aim. Moreover, when these four dimensions become politicized and attached to a social justice project, they can form a framework for Black feminist thought and practice.

BLACK WOMEN AS AGENTS OF KNOWLEDGE

Social movements of the 1950s, 1960s, and 1970s stimulated a greatly changed intellectual and political climate in the United States. Compared to the past, many more U.S. Black women became legitimated agents of knowledge. No longer passive objects of knowledge manipulated within prevailing knowledge validation processes, African-American women aimed to speak for ourselves.

African-American women in the academy and other positions of authority who aim to advance Black feminist thought now encounter the often conflicting epistemological standards of three key groups. First, Black feminist thought must be validated by ordinary African-American women who, in the words of Hannah Nelson, grow to womanhood "in a world where the saner you are, the madder you are made to appear" (Gwaltney 1980, 7). To be credible in the eyes of this group, Black feminist intellectuals must be personal advocates for their material, be accountable for the consequences of their work, have lived or experienced their material in some fashion, and be willing to engage in dialogues about their findings with ordinary, everyday people.

Historically, living life as an African-American woman facilitated this endeavor because knowledge validation processes controlled in part or in full by Black women occurred in particular organizational settings. When Black women were in charge of our own self-definitions, these four dimensions of Black feminist epistemology—lived experience as a criterion of meaning, the use of dialogue, the ethic of personal accountability, and the ethic of caring—came to the forefront. When the core themes and interpretive frameworks of Black women's knowledge were informed by Black feminist epistemology, a rich tradition of Black feminist thought ensued.

Traditionally women engaged in this overarching intellectual and political project were blues singers, poets, autobiographers, storytellers, and orators. They became Black feminist intellectuals both by doing intellectual work and by being validated as such by everyday Black women. Black women in academia could not openly join their ranks without incurring a serious penalty. In racially segregated environments that routinely excluded the majority of African-American women, only a select few were able to defy prevailing norms and explicitly embrace Black feminist epistemology....

The community of Black women scholars constitutes a second constituency whose epistemological standards must be met. As the number of Black women academics grows, this heterogeneous collectivity shares a similar social location in higher education, yet finds a new challenge in building group solidarities across differences. African-American women scholars place varying amounts of importance on furthering Black feminist scholarship. However, despite this newfound diversity, since more African-American women earn advanced degrees, the range of Black feminist scholarship has expanded. Historically, African-American women may have brought sensibilities gained from Black feminist epistemology to their scholarship. But gaining legitimacy often came with the cost of rejecting such an epistemology. Studying Black women's lives at all placed many careers at risk. More recently, increasing numbers of African-American women scholars have chosen to study Black women's experiences, and to do so by relying on elements of Black feminist epistemology in framing their work....

A third group whose epistemological standards must be met consists of dominant groups who still control schools, graduate programs, tenure processes, publication outlets, and other mechanisms that legitimate knowledge. African-American women academics who aim to advance Black feminist thought typically must use dominant Eurocentric epistemologies for this group. The difficulties these Black women now face lie less in demonstrating that they could master White male epistemologies than in resisting the hegemonic nature of these patterns of thought in order to see, value, and use existing alternative Black feminist ways of knowing. For Black women who are agents of knowledge within academia, the marginality that accompanies outsider-within status can be the source of both frustration and creativity. In an attempt to minimize the differences between the cultural context of African-American communities and the expectations of mainstream social institutions, some women dichotomize their behavior and become two different people. Over time, the strain of doing this can be enormous. Others reject Black women's accumulated wisdom and work against their own best interests by enforcing the dominant group's specialized thought. Still others manage to inhabit both contexts but do so critically, using perspectives gained from their outsider-within social locations as a source of insights and ideas. But while such women can make substantial contributions as agents of knowledge, they rarely do so without substantial personal cost. "Eventually it comes to you," observes Lorraine Hansberry, "the thing that makes you exceptional, if you are at all, is inevitably that which must also make you lonely" (1969, 148).

Just as migrating between Black and White families raised special issues for Black women domestic workers, moving among different and competing interpretive communities raises similar epistemological concerns for Black feminist thinkers. The dilemma facing Black women scholars, in particular, engaged in creating Black feminist thought illustrates difficulties that can accompany grappling with multiple interpretive communities. A knowledge claim that meets the criteria of adequacy for one group and thus is judged to be acceptable may not be translatable into the terms of a different group. . . . Although both worldviews share a common vocabulary, the ideas themselves defy direct translation.

Once Black women scholars face the notion that on certain dimensions of a Black women's standpoint, it may be fruitless to try to translate into other frameworks truths validated by Black feminist epistemology, then other choices emerge. Rather than trying to uncover universal knowledge claims that can withstand the translation from one epistemology to another (initially, at least), Black women intellectuals might find efforts to rearticulate a Black women's standpoint especially fruitful. Rearticulating a Black women's standpoint refashions the particular and reveals the more universal human dimensions of Black women's everyday lives. "I date all my work," notes Nikki Giovanni, "because I think poetry, or any writing, is but a reflection of the moment. The universal comes from the particular" (1988, 57). Lorraine Hansberry expresses a similar idea: "I believe that one of the most sound ideas in dramatic writing is that in order to create the universal, you must pay very great attention to the specific. Universality, I think, emerges from the truthful identity of what is" (1969, 128).

TOWARD TRUTH

The existence of Black feminist thought suggests another path to the universal truths that might accompany the "truthful identity of what is." In this volume I place Black women's subjectivity in the center of analysis and examine the interdependence of the everyday, taken-for-granted knowledge shared by African-American women as a group, the more specialized knowledge produced by Black women intellectuals, and the social conditions shaping both types of thought. This approach allows me to describe the creative tension linking how social conditions influenced a Black women's standpoint and how the power of the ideas themselves gave many African-American women the strength to shape those same social conditions. I approach Black feminist thought as situated in a context of domination and not as a system of ideas divorced from political and economic reality. Moreover, I present Black feminist thought as subjugated knowledge in that African-American women have long struggled to find alternative locations and epistemologies for validating our own self-definitions. In brief, I examined the situated, subjugated standpoint of African-American women in order to understand Black feminist thought as a partial perspective on domination.

Because U.S. Black women have access to the experiences that accrue to being both Black and female, an alternative epistemology used to rearticulate a Black women's standpoint should reflect the convergence of both sets of experiences. Race and gender may be analytically distinct, but in Black women's everyday lives, they work together. The search for the distinguishing features of an alternative epistemology used by African-American women reveals that some ideas that Africanist scholars identify as characteristically "Black" often bear remarkable resemblance to similar ideas claimed by feminist scholars as characteristically "female." This similarity suggests that the actual contours of intersecting oppressions can vary dramatically and yet generate some uniformity in the epistemologies used by subordinate groups. Just as U.S.

Black women and African women encountered diverse patterns of intersecting oppressions yet generated similar agendas concerning what mattered in their feminisms, a similar process may be at work regarding the epistemologies of oppressed groups. Thus the significance of a Black feminist epistemology may lie in its ability to enrich our understanding of how subordinate groups create knowledge that fosters both their empowerment and social justice.

This approach to Black feminist thought allows African-American women to explore the epistemological implications of transversal politics. Eventually this approach may get us to a point at which, claims Elsa Barkley Brown, "all people can learn to center in another experience, validate it, and judge it by its own standards without need of comparison or need to adopt that framework as their own" (1989, 922). In such politics, "one has no need to 'decenter' anyone in order to center someone else; one has only to constantly, appropriately, 'pivot the center'" (p. 922).

Rather than emphasizing how a Black women's standpoint and its accompanying episte-mology differ from those of White women, Black men, and other collectivities, Black women's experiences serve as one specific social location for examining points of connection among multiple epistemologies. Viewing Black feminist epistemology in this way challenges additive analyses of oppression claiming that Black women have a more accurate view of oppression than do other groups. Such approaches suggest that oppression can be quantified and com-pared and that adding layers of oppression produces a potentially clearer standpoint (Spelman 1988). One implication of some uses of standpoint theory is that the more subordinated the group, the purer the vision available to them. This is an outcome of the origins of standpoint approaches in Marxist social theory, itself reflecting the binary thinking of its Western origins. Ironically, by quantifying and ranking human oppressions, standpoint theorists invoke criteria for methodological adequacy that resemble those of positivism. Although it is tempting to claim that Black women are more oppressed than everyone else and therefore have the best standpoint from which to understand the mechanisms, processes, and effects of oppression, this is not the case.

Instead, those ideas that are validated as true by African-American women, African-Ameri-can men, Latina lesbians, Asian-American women, Puerto Rican men, and other groups with distinctive standpoints, with each group using the epistemological approaches growing from its unique standpoint, become the most "objective" truths. Each group speaks from its own stand-point and shares its own partial, situated knowledge. But because each group perceives its own truth as partial, its knowledge is unfinished. Each group becomes better able to consider other groups' standpoints without relinquishing the uniqueness of its own standpoint or suppressing other groups' partial perspectives. "What is always needed in the appreciation of art, or life," maintains Alice Walker, "is the larger perspective. Connections made, or at least attempted, where none existed before, the straining to encompass in one's glance at the varied world the common thread, the unifying theme through immense diversity" (1983, 5). Partiality, and not universality, is the condition of being heard; individuals and groups forwarding knowledge claims without owning their position are deemed less credible than those who do.

… Alternative epistemologies challenge all certified knowledge and open up the question of whether what has been taken to be true can stand the test of alternative ways of validating truth. The existence of a self-defined Black women's standpoint using Black feminist epistemology calls into question the content of what currently passes as truth and simultaneously challenges the process of arriving at that truth.

Nancy Tuana

Revaluing Science:
Starting from the Practices of Women

Work in the social studies of science in the last twenty years has undermined the belief common to positivist models of science that value-neutrality is both a hallmark and goal of scientific knowledge. The ideal of a value-free science was linked to the tenet that neither the individual beliefs or desires of a scientist nor the social values of a scientific community are relevant to the production of knowledge, and models of scientific method were constructed with the goal of factoring out such contaminating influences.... Questions in the philosophy of science have shifted from the "pure" epistemological question "How do we know?" to questions that reflect the locations of science within society and the relationships between power and knowledge: "Why do we know what we know?" "Why don't we know what we don't know?" "Who benefits or is disadvantaged from knowing what we know?" "Who benefits or is disadvantaged from what we don't know?" "Why is science practiced in the way that it is and who is advantaged or disadvantaged by this approach?" "How might the practice of science be different?"

... One of the central insights of feminist science studies has been the increased awareness of the ways in which social locations, locations that include political and ethical dimensions, are gendered. Through this attention to gender we have contributed to the transformation of the traditional question "How do we know?" in numerous ways, including investigating whether traditional models of rationality and of the scientific method have been gender biased, ... documenting the ways in which scientific theories have reinforced sexist and/or racist biases, ... and analyzing the impact of the exclusion, as well as the inclusion, of women in science.

... Many feminist theorists, particularly those who embrace a feminist standpoint epistemology, have argued that the distinctive experiences of women in a gender-stratified society provide an important resource, a resource typically overlooked by nonfeminist theorists, that, in the words of Sandra Harding, enables "feminism to produce empirically more accurate descriptions and theoretically richer explanations than does conventional research" (Harding, 1991, p. 119). One of my goals in this essay is to illustrate the ways in which the experiences of women, particularly women scientists, provide a resource for feminist critiques of the ideal of value-neutrality in science.

Women's differences, both their differences from men and their differences from one another, can highlight overlooked or minimized aspects of the knowledge process in science. I will here limit my analysis to three of these, each of which is relevant to transformations of the traditional epistemological question "How do we know?" and the rejection of the ideal of value-neutrality in science:

1. replacing the traditional model of the knower as a detached, disinterested individual with the dynamic model of engaged, committed individuals in communities;
2. recognition of the epistemic value of affective processes;
3. examination of the role of embodiment in the knowledge process.

INDIVIDUALS IN COMMUNITIES

...

Although Descartes was hardly an empiricist, it is the Cartesian subject that is designed to hold the subject position in S-knows-that-p models of knowledge. This is a model of knowledge that aims ideally at removing all individual traces of the knowing subject. Both perception and cognition are assumed to be invariant from knower to knower, at least in the ideal case. All other factors such as personal beliefs, desires, and bodily configurations are deemed irrelevant at best, contaminating at worst....

This model of the knowing subject is in tension with the feminist acknowledgement of the fact that as humans we are always in relations of interdependence and that these relationships are crucial not simply for personal satisfaction, but also for moral, political, and scientific deliberation. In the words of Seyla Benhabib, "the self only becomes an I in a community of other selves who are also I's. Every act of self-reference expresses simultaneously the uniqueness and difference of the self as well as the commonality among selves" (Benhabib, 1987, p. 94).

A careful study of the actual practice of science also discloses a different model of the knowing subject, one that necessitates a rejection of the model of the isolated knower and replaces it with a dynamic model of individuals in communities. An examination of the complexity of the communities relevant to the production of knowledge in science also reveals that the production of good science does not require disinterested, dispassionate scientists. As Sandra Harding has convincingly argued, objectivity does not require neutrality.[2] ... The ideal of a pure science, a science uninfluenced by values, and the scientist as a neutral recorder of facts are myths, ones that can be rejected without abandoning objectivity.

Changing the Subject of Evolution

The development of "woman, the gatherer" ... is an excellent illustration of not only the inescapable fact of value within the construction of scientific theories, but also the potential epistemic significance of the various communities, including political communities, in which the knower participates.[3]

...

To understand the androcentrism of traditional "man, the hunter" accounts of evolution, we need only attend to the respective roles of women and men. "Man, the hunter" theories of human evolution attribute the evolution of *Homo sapiens* to those activities and behaviors engaged in and exhibited by male ancestors. Males, the explanation goes, having the important and dangerous task of hunting big animals to provide the central food source, invented not only tools but also a social organization. Hunting behavior is posited as the rudimentary beginnings of social and political organization....

Such accounts do not omit women, but place them firmly "at home." While men are out hunting, women are taking care of hearth and children, dependent upon the men for sustenance and protection. Note the assumptions embedded in this account. Only male activities are depicted as skilled or socially oriented. Women's actions are represented as biologically oriented and based on "nature." This definition of woman's functions as natural curtails any analysis of them, such as their relation to the physical and social environments or the role they might play in determining other social arrangements....

The alternative origin stories told by feminist primatologists transform women from a passive, sexual resource for males to active agents and creators....

Feminist attention to perceptions of women's roles and the linkage of woman and nature provided the basis for a rethinking of evolution for a number of scientists. The anthropologist Sally Linton Slocum, for example, in her 1970 essay "Woman the Gatherer: Male Bias in Anthropology" identified ways in which females were being obscured within evolutionary theories by the association of their actions with nature and began to question the assumption that women's actions were unimportant because they were derived from instinct and thus not relevant to the evolutionary process.... This shift of attention was the result not of any biological difference between women and men scientists, but because women scientists were more likely to be affected by and participate in the feminist community—a community that had been actively exposing the history and the impact of the androcentric bias of associating women with nature and men with culture, as well as working to revalue the socially defined work of women, including childcare and housework.[4] ...

But it would be inaccurate to see the accounts of these scientists as influenced only by their participation in communities that were redefining woman's nature. These women were also influenced by their membership in scientific communities and the then current theories of evolution. The point is that accounts by women primatologists, particularly feminist primatologists, while marked both by their gender and their politics as they attempt to carve a role for women out of the standard narrative of evolution, nevertheless evolve out of and are influenced by the accepted narratives and standards of evidence of their scientific communities.

Nor should alternative evolutionary accounts such as "woman, the gatherer" be seen simply as feminist "correctives," that is, as an ideological image imposed onto the data. I will argue that this alternative model of evolution arose in response to changes within the scientific community, provided more accurate accounts of the evidence, and was therefore the result of better science. But this is not incompatible with saying that the model emerged from the practice of feminist scientists who, because of the impact of their communities, attended differently to the data. To say that the practice of science is marked by gender and by politics is not the same as claiming that it arises out of wishful thinking or ideological concerns. A scientific theory can provide consistent methods for obtaining reliable knowledge, yet be influenced by certain values or interests. Objectivity and neutrality are not the same thing.

Although it is an error to ignore the influence of the feminist community on Adrienne Zihlman's development of the "woman, the gatherer" account, it was hardly the only or the most important community of which she was a part. Being a student of Washburn, she was influenced by his belief in a human/chimpanzee/gorilla divergence of only 5 million years, rather than the previously accepted 20 million years....

Zihlman's accounts were thus strongly influenced by contemporaneous scientific accounts. Based on chimpanzee studies of diet and tool use, Zihlman denied the evolutionary importance of hunting as inscribed in "man, the hunter" accounts. For similar reasons she rejected a sharp division of labor between females and males, arguing that both sexes shared food gathering activities, and denounced the image of females as basically confined to a "home-base." ...

"Woman, the gatherer" accounts of human evolution were not reversals of "man, the hunter" accounts in which women are seen as agents of evolution and men's activities are relegated to the realm of nature. Rather, "woman, the gatherer" theories recast accounts of human evolution such that both female and male roles are seen as important and did so primarily by denying radical differences between them.... In other words, these activities are constructed as social and skilled rather than individual and unskilled. Hominid evolution arising from the increased importance of gathering is depicted as a central factor in the development of greater social skills, including communication, as well as the development of tools. Zihlman thus depicts gathering as creating the conditions for the evolution of the importance of hunting, a conclusion more consistent with the archaeological evidence for hunting tools.

What this example illustrates is the importance of beliefs acquired from one's participation in various communities for the development of knowledge. Zihlman's creation of an alternative to the androcentric "man, the hunter" theory was made possible by the knowledge she gained from the communities of which she was a member, in this case both scientific and nonscientific.... Being a feminist scientist can affect one's practice of science. In the words of Lynn Hankinson Nelson, "it makes a difference to one's observations, appraisals of theories, and one's own theorizing.... In short, it makes a difference if one is working from a feminist perspective" (Nelson, 1990, p. 224). But Zihlman's participation within particular scientific communities was also a crucial factor in the development of her research. The point is that a scientist is simultaneously a member of a number of different epistemic communities and subcommunities.... Fully understanding the development of knowledge then requires an appreciation of the interactive effects of all relevant communities and an understanding of the underlying presuppositions, metaphysical as well as aesthetic and moral values, of each community's system of beliefs.

ENGAGED KNOWERS

Acknowledging that social values enter into the practice of science problematizes the traditional model of the knower as detached, disinterested, and autonomous. Both the individualism as well as the goal of neutrality posited by traditional accounts of knowledge must be questioned. Many feminist theorists of science contend that women's relative absence from the practice of science is not due simply to institutional barriers, ... but is also an aspect of a model of the scientist that privileges traits that have historically been associated with masculinity (autonomous, detached, disinterested) and suppress those traditionally associated with femininity (dependent, connected, engaged).[6] ...

Feminist studies of science thus reveal the myopia of traditional individualist accounts of the knowing subject. On the traditional S-knows-that-p model of knowledge, we need have no knowledge of S. Knowers, while envisioned as distinct individuals, are not seen as *distinctive*. ... This model of knowledge is linked to the belief in a universal faculty of reason common to all potential knowers.... S-knows-that-p models thus embrace the vision of the generic "man"—a sameness that removes the threat of allegedly biased or partial perspectives.

Feminist investigations of science are resulting in what Helen Longino labels the strategy of "changing the subject" of knowledge. We are finding that S-knows-that-p models of knowledge are inadequate to the actual practice of science. The conception of the subject of knowledge as "generic" and hence not itself a subject of study does not fit the epistemic importance of differences between subjects. Such a model, for example, does not account for the epistemic role of the complex relationships between agents of knowledge as evidenced in examples like that of "woman, the gatherer" theories of human evolution. Equally problematic, this model overlooks the epistemic significance of subjective aspects of the relationship between scientists and the subject of inquiry, such as the scientist's commitments, desires, and interests. It also ignores the fact and nature of a scientist's embodiment....

A Feeling for the Organism

Evelyn Fox Keller offers a portrait of the geneticist Barbara McClintock that provides a very different image of the scientist than that of the disinterested, detached observer. McClintock describes herself as having developed a close relationship with the objects of her investigation. "I start with the seedling [of maize], I don't want to leave it. I don't feel I really know the story if I don't watch the plant all the way along. So I know every plant in the field. I know them intimately, and I find it a great pleasure to know them" (Keller, 1983, p. 198). McClintock viewed the complexity of nature as being beyond full human comprehension.... In holding to this belief—a metaphysical value—McClintock deviated from the positivist assumption—yet another metaphysical value—that there were underlying regularities of nature, the laws of nature, that were discrete and individually knowable by humans. This difference in basic values contributed to McClintock's commitment of developing a close relationship with the material she was studying.... "I feel that much of the work [in science] is done because one wants to impose an answer on it. They have the answer ready, and they [know what they] want the material to tell them. [Anything else it tells them] they don't really recognize as there, or they think it's a mistake and throw it out.... *If you'd only just let the material tell you*" (Keller, 1983, p. 179).

...

McClintock's emphasis on nature's complexity led to her belief that scientists must at all costs "take the time and look" (Keller, 1983, p. 206)....

McClintock's values, particularly her belief in nature's complexity and the corresponding method of taking the time to look, resulted in her being particularly sensitive to difference. Rather than minimizing anomalies, McClintock believed they were to be listened to carefully, for by finding out why they do not fit the model, one is challenged to develop a more complex model which will account for them. This value led her to criticize the emphasis on quantitative analysis in science arguing that the focus on making everything numerical often resulted in overlooking what was different ... (Keller, 1983, p. 97)....

McClintock's description of the process of observation reads very differently from the accounts of the detached, disinterested observer.... In addition to her admonition to take time to listen ... McClintock's approach was a blend of reason and passion.... According to Keller what is significant about McClintock's method and constitutes the wellspring of her powers as a scientist is the intimacy of the relationship that she develops with the object she is studying, a relationship that requires empathy and cultivated attentiveness.

Knowing Other People

Feminist studies of science, particularly the detailed studies of the practices of women scientists, have served as an important resource for feminist epistemologists. Influenced by examples like that of McClintock, many feminists are developing epistemologies that include the tenet that subjectivity is an important and indispensable component of the process of gaining knowledge.[7] ... Lorraine Code has offered such an alternative, the model of "knowing other people." While S-knows-that-p models of knowledge are based on what Code calls ordinary knowledge of medium-sized objects in the immediate environment—the red book, the open door—Code's model is based on the centrality of our relationships with others.... Code presents this model as an *addition* to the S-knows-that-p epistemologies that perhaps work for simple objects in simple settings. She argues that the latter model is not sufficient for more complex instances in which knowledge requires constant learning, is open to interpretation at various levels, admits of degree, and is not primarily propositional. For such cases, a standard of knowledge modeled after our knowledge of other people would be more accurate.

Code ... argues for a remapping of the epistemic terrain. A model that posits knowing other people as a paradigmatic kind of knowing challenges the desirability or even possibility of the disinterested and dislocated view from nowhere. Code's model of knowing other people is a dynamic, interactive model. It is a vision of a process of coming to know, "knowing other people in relationships requires constant learning: how to be with them, respond to them, and act toward them" (Code, 1993, p. 33). It is a model of knowledge that admits of degree, that is not fixed or complete, that is not primarily propositional, and is acquired interactively.

... Code's alternative model, unlike S-knows-that-p models, embraces McClintock's metaphysical belief that nature, like other people, is far too complex to allow for complete and universal knowledge. For McClintock, our knowledge of nature will always be partial, always changing, always in process—just as is our knowledge of people. This is not a critique or belittlement of our knowledge capacities, but rather a recognition and appreciation of the extraordinary complexity and continual evolution both of nature and of people. Such recognition leads to a model of knowledge that embraces the importance of empathy and imagination as a resource for "letting the material tell you." It is a model that, while acknowledging the importance of categories and theories, does not privilege them over and above the importance of listening attentively and responsibly to the stories told to us—accounting for the differences rather than imposing a model upon the world.

Code's point and one that is shared by many feminist epistemologists is that the traditional image of the dispassionate scientist removed from her or his object of study has blinded us to the complexity of the possible relationships between subjects and objects. Code argues that McClintock gained her knowledge *because* of her engaged relationship with the object of her study. That is, McClintock's fascination with the maize is epistemically significant....

Code posits nothing like an essential femininity that entails that all and only women will embrace an engaged style of knowledge production. She argues rather that McClintock's femaleness is one aspect of the complex conjunction of subjective factors at play in her practice of science.... Code's intention is to reclaim subjective components of the knowledge process, components often defined as "feminine" and suppressed from traditional accounts. The aim is not to create a "feminine" science, but "to make a space in scientific research for suppressed practices and values that, coincidentally or otherwise, are commonly associated with 'the feminine'" (Code, 1991, p. 152).

EMBODIED KNOWERS

The feminist rejection of the supposedly "generic" knower thus requires that attention be paid to the characteristics and situation of the knower as an important part of the knowledge process.... [T]he various communities of which one is a part, including one's political beliefs, can be epistemically significant to the knowledge process. As we see with McClintock, a knower's emotive capacities and her or his openness to their relevance to the knowing process can also be epistemically significant. This is the content of Code's claim that a person's gender can be epistemically significant. In contemporary Western culture, one who is female is more likely than one who is male to be socialized in such a way as to make her more proficient in and accepting of the usefulness of emotions such as empathy and imagination. Just as a feminist is more likely to question the categorization of female activities as "natural" and male activities as "cultural," a woman in contemporary Western culture is more likely to be accepting of and skilled in the employment of emotions in the knowledge process.

But an additional aspect of the knowing subject that is epistemically significant is the fact of and nature of their embodiment. The model of the generic knower has traditionally rejected the relevance of our bodily differences. Attention to the body calls attention to the specificities and partiality of human knowledge, as well as reminding us of the importance of acknowledging the body, and its variations, in the knowledge process. Once we admit the body into our theories of knowledge, we must also recognize its variations; we must, for example, examine the ways in which bodies are "sexed."[8]

Vision

Traditional models of knowledge privilege vision over the other senses. The association of knowledge and vision provides a model of knowledge as disembodied. Vision, perceived as the most detached of the senses, is employed in such a way as to conceal the action of the body. The world appears to my gaze without any apparent movement or action on my part. The action of the body disappears into the background and with it as a model of knowledge, the philosopher places the world at a distance from the observer, thereby dematerializing knowledge. The perceived scene, as well as the perceiver, is to be physically unaffected by the gaze.

... The construction of an image of reason based on metaphors of vision has led to the notion of a "mind's eye" and a conception of knowledge in which the world is separated from the observer who sees it and thereby gains knowledge of it, without in any way contaminating it or being affected by it.

But these disembodied images of vision are possible only by "forgetting" the fact of our embodiment. What we are capable of seeing and what we attend to are part of our location within the world. Let me begin by using a very different case study than those I've so far employed. Let us think about frogs and dogs.[10]

There are many ways to remember the significance of the situatedness of vision and thereby inhibit the tendency to use visual metaphors to construct allegedly generic images of reason. One of these is to reflect upon the significance of the specificities of human vision. A frog's visual cortex is different from ours. Neural response is linked to small objects in rapid, erratic motion. Objects at rest elicit little neural response and large objects evoke a qualitatively different response than small ones. Although this makes sense for frogs, let us imagine, along with Katherine Hayles, that a frog is presented with Newton's law of motion:

> The first law, you recall, says that an object at rest remains so unless acted upon by a force. Encoded into the formulation is the assumption that the object stays the same: the new element is the force. This presupposition, so obvious from a human point of view, would be almost unthinkable from a frog's perspective, since for the frog moving objects are processed in an entirely different way than stationary ones. Newton's first law further states, as a corollary, that an object moving in a straight line continues to move so unless compelled to change by forces acting upon it. The proposition would certainly not follow as a corollary for the frog, for variation of motion rather than continuation counts in his perceptual scheme. Moreover, it ignores the *size* of the object, which from a frog's point of view is crucial to how information about movement is processed. (Hayles, 1993, p. 28)

The point is that bodily differences in perceptual organs and neural patterns organize perception in highly specific, in this case species specific, ways. Far from being the neutral receptor or static mirroring of the visual metaphors informing traditional accounts of knowledge, observation is a dynamic process of organization in which our bodily being plays a central role.

...

When we consider the human specificities of vision, those mandated by our bodies as well as by the social contexts which shape our experiences of it, we are reminded that the privileging of an image of vision which views it as passive, detached, and disinterested is itself a partial and biased perspective. As any loving parent who looks into the eyes of her or his six month old child or any lover who gazes into the eyes of the person she or he loves knows, vision can also be a way in which we actively connect and interact with other people. It can be a way in which we express feelings and negotiate our relationships. Such vision is active, engaged, and recipro-cal. An emphasis on vision as passive, detached, and disinterested is a situated vision, one that arises out of particular social situations and values. We are reminded again that vision, as well as objectivity, is not about neutrality, but is embedded in particular and specific embodiments.

A recognition of the epistemic importance of our embodiment requires a conception of knowledge as embodied, in which the emphasis on vision as the primary source of knowledge is replaced by an appreciation of the multiplicity of senses involved in the process of knowledge and an understanding of the ways in which faculties such as empathy, intuition, and reason enter into and interact in this process. I think that Code's model of knowing other people can be fleshed out in actual practice by looking at the science and practice of primary care health providers—nurses, physicians, midwives, etc.—as an alternative to the paradigm of the autono-mous, detached, disinterested scientist.[11] Health providers provide a model of an inquirer who is both engaged and objective, whose knowledge is embodied, and whose methods illustrate Code's model of knowing other people. It is important to note that I do not claim that this new image of scientific rationality is gynecentric. In fact I would argue that it is neither andro-centric nor gynecentric, but tries instead to more accurately portray the nature of rationality in all its complexity.

Knowledge with and of the Body

Carefully trained in the latest theories and techniques, the primary health care provider will be successful in her or his diagnoses and treatments only to the extent that she or he can come to fully understand the person she or he is attending. The process of coming to such an understand-ing is complex. The health provider often begins by looking carefully, even when the source of the malady is not obvious. She or he watches how patients hold themselves, examining their complexion, their eyes, looking for tell-tale signs.

But vision is only one source of information for health providers and often not the most important. Touch enters into the process of diagnosis as well as treatment. The training of health care providers involves an elaborate education of their hands.... As important as touch is for diagnosis, the health care provider also understands that it serves an important role in both comforting and reassuring the individual, for the process of diagnosis works best when the provider is able to establish a relationship with the patient.[12]

The health care provider also learns from listening. But this listening works best when it can go beyond the stethoscope or monitor and includes dialogue between the provider and the patient. Through trust and empathy, the health care provider develops a relationship with the patient that allows for communication, for she or he views the patient's own experiences as an important source of knowledge.... Since successful treatment often involves transformation of life-style choices, health care providers are most successful when they develop relationships with patients that enable patients to become subjects of knowledge—both of the manifestations of their illness as well as how their life-style affects their health.[13] In all these ways the health care provider works with a blend of intellect, imagination, and emotion. The subjective components in this case, far from being a barrier to knowledge and understanding, enhance the process.[14]

My suggestion is that the example of the engaged, embodied scientist we find illustrated so well in the primary care health provider offers a more adequate model of scientific inquiry than the image of the detached, disinterested, autonomous scientist.... I ... believe that the legacy of positivism has obscured the variety of ways scientific practice is in fact a blend of subjective and objective factors, and has resulted in a bias in the way in which science is both conceived of and how it is taught to practitioners. McClintock's loving attention to maize is hardly unique among scientists, nor is it limited to women scientists....

Granted, feminists are not the only epistemologists questioning the positivist model of scientific rationality. Michael Polanyi, to cite just one of the many theorists, offered an analysis of the tacit dimension in science that is in many ways compatible with feminist approaches to knowledge. "It is not by looking at things," he explained, "but by dwelling in them, that we understand" (Polanyi, 1966, p. 18). Given this Polanyi concludes that "the ideal of eliminating all personal elements of knowledge, would, in effect, aim at the destruction of all knowledge" (Polanyi, 1966, p. 20). But the feminist concern with gender dynamics and the historical inter-connections between power and knowledge has made us particularly attentive to developing alternative models that do not suppress women's cognitive authority....

CONCLUSION

... I and many other feminists came to positions like these because of our participation in feminist communities. This obviously was not the only epistemically significant community; we are also philosophers, historians, sociologists, and scientists. Nor does it mean that *only* feminists will hold such views. There are many theorists of science who do not participate in feminist communities who argue for versions of the above tenets. But a difference of feminist analyses is the persistent attention to gender as a variable of analysis. This is how our feminism is epistemologically significant.

... Scientific research, as well as all cognitive endeavors, begins with metaphysical and methodological commitments. It arises out of and is conditioned by our participation in various epistemic communities. Each of us, in being part of a community and a number of subcommunities, participates in an evolving conceptual scheme that makes intersubjective experience possible, influences our interests and desires, and also sets the standards of what constitutes evidence.

The acceptance of the essentially relational nature of knowledge and the inseparability of subjective and objective components of knowledge does not result in relativism, though it does require an abandonment of the traditional "view from nowhere" conception of objectivity. This alternative notion of objectivity has been the research program of many feminist philosophers of science including a number of those whose work appears in this anthology (see Harding, Longino, Nelson). Although I will refer you to their work for the details of feminist accounts of objectivity, let me call attention to yet another way the development of feminist epistemologies are compatible with the model offered. Although there are significant differences between feminist epistemologies, one common tenet is the emphasis on diversity within the scientific community to ensure objectivity. To cite just one of many possible examples, consider Helen Longino's claim that

> ... because background assumptions can be and most frequently are invisible to the members of the scientific community for which they are background and because unreflective acceptance of such assumptions can come to define what it is to be a member of such a community (thus making criticism impossible), effective criticism of background assumptions requires the presence and expression of alternative points of view. This sort of account allows us to see how social values and interests can become enshrined in otherwise acceptable research programs (i.e., research programs that strive for empirical adequacy and engage in criticism). As long as representatives of alternative points of view are not included in the community, shared values will not be identified as shaping observation or reasoning. (Longino, 1993, pp. 111–12)

Once again we see the impact of the politics of feminism upon the development of feminist epistemology, for a central emphasis of feminism has been the importance of inclusion of previously excluded groups and viewpoints. Earlier feminist accounts focused on the impact of including women and attention to gender upon society, scholarly methods, politics, and so on. The last decade has intensified this commitment as feminists have become aware of the differences between women and have acknowledged the ways in which attention to such factors as class, race, and sexuality, as well as gender, reveals previously hidden assumptions and opens up new research programs.

Feminist philosophers of science have thus actively developed research programs consistent with the values and commitments we express in the rest of our lives. In this sense we are creating "feminist sciences," the doing of science from the politics of feminism. We also acknowledge the need for science to be open to diverse groups of individuals and to have these groups engage in what Longino calls "an interactive dialogic community" (Longino, 1993, p. 113). This is not a simple pluralism, but one in which critical interchange between communities is highly valued. This, of course, does not mean that "anything goes." Although scientific standards are not seen as unchanging or unresponsive to such critical interaction, they do provide standards for acceptability. The "woman, the gatherer" model in human evolution studies arises out of a feminist political agenda yet meets the standards set by the field in which it is proposed. And this is important. Only if these alternative models receive a hearing within the scientific community will they ever secure serious attention.

A value implicit in this vision of science is that the best form of science will be that which is the product of the most inclusive scientific community. This suggests that the problem of developing a new science is the problem of creating a new social and political reality.

NOTES

...

2. Harding, 1992. See also Proctor, 1991.

3. Accounts of "woman, the gatherer" theories can be found in Haraway, 1989; Longino, 1990; and Nelson, 1990. My analysis here is thoroughly influenced by Haraway's *Primate Visions*.

4. For a more detailed argument in support of this position see Haraway, 1989.

...

6. See Keller, 1984 and 1992.

7. See Code, 1991 and 1993; Jaggar, 1989; Keller, 1984; Longino, 1990; Nelson, 1990; and Rose, 1983 and 1994.

8. Although I do not have the time to develop this point, I feel it is too important not to mention and to urge readers to explore the work done on this topic in the writings of feminists such as Rosi Braidotti, Elizabeth Grosz, and Luce Irigaray.

...

10. My account here is influenced by Haraway, 1988 and Hayles, 1993, dogs and frogs respectively.

11. Just as there are positivist social scientists, so are there positivist primary health care providers. My argument here is that when health care is done well the provider is engaged, embodied, interested, and objective. In other words, objectivity does not require the suspension of subjectivity.

12. Discussions of doctor-patient relationships in family practice journals often involve the suggestion that the physician touch the patient, even if doing so is not needed for diagnosis. The reason given is that such touch reassures and comforts the patient, thus allowing a relationship of trust to develop between them.

13. There have been numerous feminist critiques of modern medicine that discuss the ways in which medical institutions reinforce sexism. Vrinda Dalmiya and Linda Alcoff (1993), for example, have argued that modern obstetrics has emphasized propositional knowledge to the exclusion of the practical knowledge of midwifery. I would argue that these accounts, although certainly pointing out problematic areas in contemporary medicine, are not reflective of primary care medicine (as distinct from surgery and other specialty areas). The training, experience, and institutions of primary care physicians are antithetical to a strict division between knowing how and knowing that, and involve an explicit acknowledgement of the importance of the physician/patient relationship both for diagnosis and for treatment. I do not claim that all primary care doctors in fact successfully embody this model, but I do think it is one that the majority of primary care physicians strive for. (But perhaps it is only fair to reveal that my partner is a primary care physician.)

14. In developing my model of the primary health care provider as a paradigm of scientific practice, I focused on the provider/patient relationship. But given my discussion of the agent of knowledge as individuals in communities, it should be understood that my discussion is only partial. To complete it would require adding the relationships between providers and their research/practitioner communities, and any other epistemically relevant communities.

...

REFERENCES

Benhabib, Seyla. 1987. "The Generalized and the Concrete Other: The Kohlberg-Gilligan Controversy and Feminist Theory," in Seyla Benhabib and Drucilla Cornell (eds.), *Feminism as Critique: On the Politics of Gender.* University of Minnesota Press, Minneapolis.

Code, Lorraine. 1991. *What Can She Know? Feminist Theory and the Construction of Knowledge.* Cornell University Press, Ithaca.

Code, Lorraine. 1993. "Taking Subjectivity into Account," in Linda Alcoff and Elizabeth Potter (eds.), *Feminist Epistemologies.* Routledge, New York, pp. 15–48.

Dalmiya, Vrinda and Linda Alcoff. 1993. "Are 'Old Wives' Tales' Justified?," in Linda Alcoff and Elizabeth Potter (eds.), *Feminist Epistemologies.* Routledge, New York, pp. 217–44.

Haraway, Donna. 1989. *Primate Visions: Gender, Race and Nature in the World of Modern Science.* Routledge, New York.

Haraway, Donna. 1991. "Situated Knowledges: The Science Question in Feminism and the Privilege of Partial Perspective," in *Simians, Cyborgs, and Women: The Reinvention of Nature.* Routledge, New York.

Harding, Sandra. 1991. *Whose Science? Whose Knowledge?* Cornell University Press, Ithaca.

Harding, Sandra. 1992. "After the Neutrality Ideal: Science, Politics, and 'Strong Objectivity,'" *Social Research,* 59, 567–87.

Harding, Sandra. 1993. *The "Racial" Economy of Science: Toward a Democratic Future.* Indiana University Press, Bloomington.

Hayles, N. Katherine. 1993. "Constrained Constructivism: Locating Scientific Inquiry in the Theater of Representation," in George Levine (ed.), *Realism and Representation*. University of Wisconsin Press, Madison.

Jaggar, Alison. 1989. "Love and Knowledge: Emotion in Feminist Epistemology," in Susan Bordo and Alison Jaggar (eds.), *Gender/Body/Knowledge*. Rutgers University Press, New Brunswick.

Jonas, Hans. 1966. *The Phenomenon of Life*. University of Chicago Press, Chicago.

Keefer, Chester. 1994. "Skillful Listening," *Cortland Forum,* June, 74.

Keller, Evelyn Fox. 1983. A *Feeling for the Organism*. W. H. Freeman and Company, New York.

Keller, Evelyn Fox. 1984. *Reflections on Gender and Science*. Yale University Press, New Haven.

Keller, Evelyn Fox. 1992. *Secrets of Life, Secrets of Death: Essays on Language, Gender and Science*. Routledge, New York.

Keller, Evelyn Fox and Christine R. Grontkowski. 1983. "The Mind's Eye," in Sandra Harding and Merrill B. Hintikka (eds.), *Discovering Reality*. D. Reidel, Dordrecht, pp. 207–24.

Leder, Drew. 1990. *The Absent Body*. University of Chicago Press, Chicago.

Lloyd, Genevieve. 1984. *The Man of Reason: "Male" and "Female" in Western Philosophy*. University of Minnesota Press, Minneapolis.

Lloyd, Genevieve. 1993. "Maleness, Metaphor, and the 'Crisis' of Reason," in Louise M. Anthony and Charlotte Witt (eds.), *A Mind of One's Own: Feminist Essays on Reason and Objectivity*. Westview Press, Boulder.

Longino, Helen. 1990. *Science as Social Knowledge*. Princeton University Press, Princeton.

Longino, Helen. 1993. "Subjects, Power, and Knowledge: Description and Prescription in Feminist Philosophies of Science," in Linda Alcoff and Elizabeth Potter (eds.), *Feminist Epistemologies*. Routledge, New York, pp. 101–120.

Merleau-Ponty, Maurice. 1962. *Phenomenology of Perception,* trans. Colin Smith. Routledge and Kegan Paul, London.

Nelson, Lynn Hankinson. 1990. *Who Knows: From Quine to a Feminist Empiricism*. Temple University Press, Philadelphia.

Polanyi, Michael. 1966. *The Tacit Dimension*. Doubleday and Co., Garden City, NY.

Proctor, Robert N. 1991. *Value-Free Science? Purity and Power in Modern Knowledge*. Harvard University Press, Cambridge.

Ratty, Richard. 1979. *Philosophy and the Mirror of Nature*. Princeton University Press, Princeton.

Rose, Hilary. 1983. "Hand, Brain and Heart: A Feminist Epistemology for the Natural Sciences," *Signs,* 9, 73–90.

Rose, Hilary. 1994. *Love, Power, and Knowledge: Towards a Feminist Transformation of the Sciences*. Indiana University Press, Bloomington.

Slocum, Sally Linton. 1971. "Woman the Gatherer: Male Bias in Anthropology," in Sue-Ellen Jacobs (ed.), *Women in Perspective: A Guide for Cross Cultural Studies*. University of Illinois Press, Urbana.

Washburn, Sherwood L. and C. S. Lancaster. 1976. "Evolution of Hunting," in R. B. Lee and I. DeVore (eds.), *Kalahari Hunter-Gatherers*. Harvard University Press, Cambridge.

8
Feminist Empiricism: Experience and Interpretation

Empiricism is the epistemological theory that holds that all knowledge is based on experience, specifically the experience of our senses. Although the belief that sensory experiences are the only trustworthy sources of information defines empiricism, many empiricists have made several additional assumptions. They include the following:

1. Sensory experiences constitute the building blocks or foundation of knowledge, a view known as *foundationalism*.
2. Knowers are typically solitary individuals, a view known as epistemological *individualism*.
3. Finally, knowers are essentially similar in the sense that, if their sensory apparatus is in good working order, they will have similar experiences in the same situations. If the last assumption is correct, experience and observation do not depend in any significant way on the subjectivity of the knower and normal knowledge seekers are *interchangeable*.

When empiricism is construed in this way, it generates certain methodological prescriptions. They include the requirements that knowledge be based on observations that are as "simple" and indisputable as possible and that the observations be replicable by multiple researchers in order to ensure that they are not influenced by individual idiosyncrasies.

Logical positivism was an extreme version of empiricism. It emerged in Vienna in the 1920s and early 1930s and came to dominate English-speaking philosophy shortly before and after World War II. Logical positivism held that the only true knowledge was scientific, and it took the paradigm of science to be physics, which it regarded as constructed entirely on the basis of sensory perceptions and strict logical inferences from these. According to logical positivism, assertions that could not be validated by reference to sensory experience were meaningless; thus positivism disqualified as meaningful all metaphysical, religious, aesthetic, and ethical assertions. Positivism was discredited in the last half of the twentieth century, and today the term is often used in a pejorative sense, rather like essentialism. Nevertheless, just as traces of essentialism survive unacknowledged, scientific and popular culture still contains many vestiges of positivism.

SOME CHALLENGES TO CLASSICAL EMPIRICISM

Many challenges to positivism focused on problems in the notions of perception and experience. As long ago as the eighteenth century, the philosopher Kant noted that experience of the physical world is always mediated by some conceptual framework and so always includes an element of interpretation. In 1953, W. V. O. Quine published his landmark article "Two Dogmas of Empiricism," in which he argued that the distinction between analytic and synthetic statements was negotiated rather than fixed. In the 1960s, some philosophers of science argued that observations were theory laden and that what counted as a veridical observation or "brute fact" was determined by the particular theoretical framework of which it was a part.

The idea that knowledge has "foundations" is now widely questioned, especially in the humanities. Today, experiences and perceptions are less likely to be regarded as discrete, indisputable building blocks for constructing knowledge, and the so-called evidence of the senses is regarded more frequently as revisable; hence, theories and observations are more likely to be seen as negotiated and balanced in processes of reflective equilibrium. As noted earlier, positivist accounts are no longer accepted as accurate descriptions even of method in the physical sciences.

Recent European philosophers have emphasized that empirical facts and experiences are not simply observed but also created through language. In addition, they have asserted that these constructions are infused with social values and affected by social power. For example, Foucault's *History of Sexuality* famously traced the invention of the so-called discourses of sexuality, with their creation, pathologization, and criminalization of new sexual types, such as the homosexual, and the complementary creation of new professional types, such as the sexologist. Foucault argued that what gets authorized and legitimated as knowledge reflects social power and social interests.

BASING THEORY ON EXPERIENCE: "SPONTANEOUS" FEMINIST EMPIRICISM IN THE 1960s AND 1970s

Just as Western philosophers were losing confidence in traditional formulations of empiricism, with its postulation of "raw experience" and "brute facts," feminist scholars in the 1960s and 1970s expressed new interest in women's experience. Many feminists undertook to revise existing bodies of knowledge by introducing new information about women's experience, which was said to have been neglected or even falsified by male theorists, and they had a fairly specific conception of what it meant to include women's experience in their theory. They emphasized listening to women's first-person narratives, and they were interested not only in experiences of victimization but also in women's agency, creativity, and resistance to oppression. The two were not unrelated; people who recount their own experience typically talk about what they did and how they felt about it—highlighting their own agency even in situations of extreme victimization and duress. So often the focus on women's experience revealed not only unhappiness hidden beneath the bland surface of masculine accounts but also hitherto unrecognized resistance to oppression.

The idea of using women's experience as a test of established knowledge was immediately fruitful. Women's narratives revealed that violence against women was systematic, not just a problem for individuals; that housework was real work, hard, skilled, and socially productive; that so-called sexual teasing and flirting were often harassing and threatening; that supposedly light work was often very strenuous; and that many women did not experience orgasm in heterosexual intercourse. The new focus on women's experience transformed many academic disciplines; for instance, a focus on women as historical agents stimulated the emergence of the subfields of social and family history and suggested alternative ways of identifying historical periods; a focus on women as producers of culture challenged "man, the hunter" accounts of cultural evolution in anthropology; and a focus on women as economic producers stimulated some economists to pay more attention to subsistence labor and the informal economy as well as to ways in which women's work subsidized male wages. Attention to women's literature and art raised questions about the standards of canon construction in those fields, and attention to women's health care issues led to new standards of medical research and the revaluation of the importance of nursing care relative to more drastic interventions intended to cure. Attention to women's accounts of their moral experience raised similar challenges to traditional philosophical accounts of moral psychology and the domain of politics.

The proposal to use experience as the basis or touchstone of theory rings pleasantly in modern ears. Trust in experience and observation is central to modernity's self-conception. It invokes the values of the Protestant Reformation and the Scientific Revolution, of intellectual independence and anti-authoritarianism, of reliance on the so-called scientific method and the importance of experimentation. The proposal to trust women's experiences and perceptions rings even more pleasantly for feminists because it expresses several deeply held feminist convictions. These include the beliefs that women's experiences matter, that women are the authorities on those experiences, and that attention to women's experiences and perceptions is conducive to producing knowledge superior to traditional accounts because it is more complete and comprehensive and less biased and partial.

For these reasons, the aspiration to ground feminist theory in women's experience is not easily dismissed. However, when 1970s feminists spontaneously adopted an initially naive empiricism, they were likely unaware that many tenets of classical empiricism were already under pressure. These challenges were soon extended to early versions of feminist empiricism.

SOME CHALLENGES FOR SPONTANEOUS FEMINIST EMPIRICISM

One obvious problem for the project of grounding feminist research in women's experience is that the data supposedly provided by this experience are not indisputable. Even first-person accounts of experience, even when the informant is telling the truth to the best of her ability, are not necessarily reliable. Individuals' experience is affected by subjective factors such as their mood, values, and expectations; it is also shaped by the language available. For instance, after "consciousness-raising," when they had a new vocabulary available, women often changed their accounts of their experience from those they had given earlier.

These complexities in the idea of experience challenged several familiar assumptions of traditional empiricist epistemology. For instance:

1. They challenged the idea that experience comes in discrete and indisputable chunks.
2. Moreover, if experiences are constructed through language, then the empiricist assumption that people acquire knowledge as solitary individuals is untenable, since language, by definition, is a social product.
3. In addition, second-wave feminists' emphasis on "women's" specific experience presupposed that individuals' perceptions were affected by their social positions; for instance, whether they saw flirting as harassment was likely to be influenced by their gender. This presupposition conflicted with the further empiricist assumption that experience and observation did not depend in any significant way on the subjectivity of the knower, since "normal" knowledge seekers are similar or interchangeable.

Bringing into question several assumptions of classical empiricism does not refute the basic empiricist conviction that knowledge must be based on experience, but it does complicate the task of feminists seeking to develop empiricist methodologies. For instance, when we speak of "women's experience," how do we select which women's experience to investigate? Women's heterogeneity makes it extremely implausible that any subgroup represents all women, but are some groups' experiences more "typical" or even more important than others? How can we justify the inevitable exclusion of some women's questions and experiences? Why indeed should feminist research be limited to women's experiences; why not also investigate men's experiences through a feminist lens? How can we justify the ways we identify persons as men and women—and why does it matter?

A further set of complications arises from the fact that experience is not simply reported by its subjects. These reports also have to be heard, read, understood, and interpreted. How can feminist researchers learn to listen, hear, read, and represent the experience of other women and even of men without distorting or misrepresenting it? Which criteria can researchers use to determine whether they have succeeded? If experience is socially constructed, is there any sense in which each of us is an authority on her own experience? If power is inherent in the construction of experience, how can feminist researchers struggle against dominant categories of interpretation or decide whose account is authoritative?

EMPIRICISM AND FEMINIST METHODOLOGY

The existence of these and other difficulties does not mean that feminists must necessarily abandon empiricist approaches to methodology; the notion of gendered experience remains central to feminism. However, if experience is taken to be more complex than simple sensory perception, it becomes evident that feminists need to develop better accounts of the relationships between experience and knowledge. Feminist philosophers such as Helen Longino and Lynn Hankinson Nelson are now replacing the spontaneous empiricism of early second-wave feminism with more sophisticated and flexible versions (Longino 1990, 2002; Nelson 1990). Contemporary feminist empiricists do not assume that it is possible to identify discrete experiences that constitute the building blocks of knowledge. They recognize that experience is always constructed and contested in circumstances of inequality, and that existing language is not always adequate to contain it.

The complexities of basing research on gendered experience not only raise epistemic questions of identifying reliable data, developing trustworthy guides to interpreting that data, and drawing inferences from it, but also raise ethical and political questions. For instance, when reports of experience conflict or when researchers interpret experience differently from informants, the question of which account to take as authoritative has political and ethical as well as epistemic dimensions. Does proffering an alternative account mean disrespecting our research subjects? How can researchers recognize and give accounts of their own roles in the construction of other people's experience? What are the ethical responsibilities of feminists toward their informants? How can they avoid disappointment, broken trust, betrayal, exploitation, and invasion of privacy? Which research projects should have priority?

Many of these questions are explored in the following readings from Joan Scott, Renee White, and Lorraine Code. They address issues of epistemic authority between researchers and the subjects of their research, and they explore the question of what it means for feminist researchers to be responsive and responsible to their research subjects, their findings, and their feminist principles.

REFERENCES

Harding, Sandra. 1993. "Rethinking Standpoint Epistemology: What Is 'Strong Objectivity'?" in *Feminist Epistemologies*, ed. Linda Alcoff and Elizabeth Potter. New York: Routledge. [Au: page numbers?]

Longino, Helen E. 1990. *Science as Social Knowledge: Values and Objectivity in Scientific Inquiry*. Princeton, NJ: Princeton University Press.

———. 2002. *The Fate of Knowledge*. Princeton, NJ: Princeton University Press.

Nelson, Lynn Hankinson. 1990. *Who Knows: From Quine to a Feminist Empiricism*. Philadelphia: Temple University Press.

JOAN W. SCOTT
"Experience"

BECOMING VISIBLE

There is a section in Samuel Delany's magnificent autobiographical meditation, *The Motion of Light in Water*,[1] that dramatically raises the problem of writing the history of difference, the history, that is, of the designation of "other," of the attribution of characteristics that distinguish categories of people from some presumed (and usually unstated) norm.[2] Delany (a gay man, a black man, a writer of science fiction) recounts his reaction to his first visit to the St. Marks bathhouse in 1963. He describes standing on the threshold of a "gym-sized room" dimly lit by blue bulbs. The room was full of people, some standing, the rest "an undulating mass of naked male bodies, spread wall to wall." "My first response," he writes, "was a kind of heart-thudding astonishment, very close to fear. . . . I have written of a space at certain libidinal saturation before. That was not what frightened me. It was rather that the saturation was not only kinesthetic but visible" (173).

Watching the scene establishes for Delany a "fact that flew in the face" of the prevailing representation of homosexuals in the 1950s as isolated perverts, subjects gone awry. The "apprehension of massed bodies" gave him (as it does, he argues, anyone, "male, female, working or middle class") a "sense of political power": "[W]hat this experience said was that there was a population—not of individual homosexuals . . . not of hundreds, not of thousands, but rather of millions of gay men, and that history had actively and already, created for us whole galleries of institutions, good and bad, to accommodate our sex" (174).

. . . He emphasizes not the discovery of an identity, but a sense of participation in a movement. . . . Numbers—massed bodies—constitute a movement and this, even if subterranean, belies enforced silences about the range and diversity of human sexual practices. Making the movement visible breaks the silence about it, challenges prevailing notions, and opens new possibilities for everyone. . . .

The point of Delany's description, indeed of his entire book, is to document the existence of those institutions in all their variety and multiplicity, to write about and thus to render historical what has hitherto been hidden from history.

A metaphor of visibility as literal transparency is crucial to his project. The blue lights illuminate a scene he has participated in before (in darkened trucks parked along the docks under the West Side Highway, in men's rooms in subway stations), but understood only in a fragmented way. "No one ever got to see its whole" (174). . . . Seeing enables him to comprehend the relationship between his personal activities and politics. "[T]he first direct sense of political power comes from the apprehension of massed bodies." . . . Knowledge is gained through vision; vision is a direct, unmediated apprehension of a world of transparent objects. In this conceptualization of it, the visible is privileged; writing is then put at its service.[3] Seeing is the origin of knowing. Writing is reproduction, transmission—the communication of knowledge gained through (visual, visceral) experience.

This kind of communication has long been the mission of historians documenting the lives of those omitted or overlooked in accounts of the past. It has produced a wealth of new evidence previously ignored about these others and has drawn attention to dimensions of human life and activity usually deemed unworthy of mention in conventional histories. It has also occasioned a crisis for orthodox history, by multiplying not only stories, but subjects, and by insisting that histories are written from fundamentally different—indeed irreconcilable—perspectives or standpoints, no one of which is complete or completely "true." Like Delany's memoir, these histories have provided evidence for a world of alternative values and practices whose existence gives the lie to hegemonic constructions of social worlds, whether these constructions vaunt the political superiority of white men, the coherence and unity of selves, the naturalness of heterosexual monogamy, or the inevitability of scientific progress and economic development. The challenge to normative history has been described, in terms of conventional historical understandings of evidence, as an enlargement of the picture, a corrective to oversights resulting from inaccurate or incomplete vision, and it has rested its claim to legitimacy on the authority of experience, the direct experience of others, as well as of the historian who learns to see and illuminate the lives of those others in his or her texts.

Documenting the experience of others in this way has been at once a highly successful and limiting strategy for historians of difference. It has been successful because it remains so comfortably within the disciplinary framework of history, working according to rules which permit calling old narratives into question when new evidence is discovered. The status of evidence is, of course, ambiguous for historians. On the one hand, they acknowledge that "evidence only counts as evidence and is only recognized as such in relation to a potential narrative, so that the narrative can be said to determine the evidence as much as the evidence determines the narrative."[4] On the other hand, their rhetorical treatment of evidence, and their use of it to falsify prevailing interpretations, depends on a referential notion of evidence which denies that it is anything but a reflection of the real.[5]

When the evidence offered is the evidence of "experience," the claim for referentiality is further buttressed.... It is precisely this kind of appeal to experience as uncontestable evidence and as ... a foundation upon which analysis is based that weakens the critical thrust of histories of difference. By remaining within the epistemological frame of orthodox history, these studies lose the possibility of examining those assumptions and practices that excluded considerations of difference in the first place. They take as self-evident the identities of those whose experience is being documented and thus naturalize their difference. They locate resistance outside its discursive construction, and reify agency as an inherent attribute of individuals, thus decontextualizing it. When experience is taken as the origin of knowledge, the vision of the individual subject (the person who had the experience or the historian who recounts it) becomes the bedrock of evidence upon which explanation is built. Questions about the constructed nature of experience, about how subjects are constituted as different in the first place, about how one's vision is structured—about language (or discourse) and history—are left aside. The evidence of experience then becomes evidence for the fact of difference, rather than a way of exploring how difference is established, how it operates, how and in what ways it constitutes subjects who see and act in the world.[6]

To put it another way, the evidence of experience, whether conceived through a metaphor of visibility or in any other way that takes meaning as transparent, reproduces rather than contests given ideological systems.... But the project of making experience visible precludes critical examination of the workings of the ideological system itself, its categories of representation (homosexual/heterosexual, man/woman, black/white as fixed immutable identities), its premises about what these categories mean and how they operate, its notions of subjects, origin, and cause.

The project of making experience visible precludes analysis of the workings of this system and of its historicity; instead it reproduces its terms.... Making visible the experience of a different group exposes the existence of repressive mechanisms, but not their inner workings or logics; we know that difference exists, but we don't understand it as constituted relationally. For that we need to attend to the historical processes that, through discourse, position subjects and produce their experiences. It is not individuals who have experience, but subjects who are constituted through experience. Experience in this definition then becomes not the origin of our explanation, not the authoritative (because seen or felt) evidence that grounds what is known, but rather that which we seek to explain, that about which knowledge is produced. To think about experience in this way is to historicize it as well as to historicize the identities it produces. This kind of historicizing ... implies critical scrutiny of all explanatory categories usually taken for granted, including the category of "experience."

THE AUTHORITY OF EXPERIENCE

History has been largely a foundationalist discourse. By this I mean that its explanations seem to be unthinkable if they do not take for granted some primary premises, categories, or presumptions. These foundations ... are unquestioned and unquestionable; they are considered permanent and transcendent. As such they create a common ground for historians and their objects of study in the past and so authorize and legitimize analysis; indeed analysis seems not to be able to proceed without them.[7] ...

"Experience" is one of the foundations that have been reintroduced into historical writing in the wake of the critique of empiricism; unlike "brute fact" or "simple reality," its connotations are more varied and elusive. It has recently emerged as a critical term in debates among historians about the limits of interpretation and especially about the uses and limits of poststructuralist theory for history.

The evocation of "experience" by historians committed to the interpretation of language, meaning, and culture appears to solve a problem of explanation for professed antiempiricists even as it reinstates a foundational ground. For this reason it is interesting to examine the uses of "experience" by historians. Such an examination allows us to ask whether history can exist without foundations and what it might look like if it did.

In *Keywords* Raymond Williams sketches the alternative senses in which the term "experience" has been employed in the Anglo-American tradition.[9] These he summarizes as "(i) knowledge gathered from past events, whether by conscious observation or by consideration and reflection; and (ii) a particular kind of consciousness, which can in some contexts be distinguished from reason or knowledge" (126). Until the early eighteenth century, he says, experience and experiment were closely connected terms, designating how knowledge was arrived at through testing and observation (here the visual metaphor is important). In the eighteenth century, experience still contained within it this notion of consideration or reflection on observed events, of lessons gained from the past, but it also referred to a particular kind of consciousness. This consciousness, in the twentieth century, has come to mean a "full, active awareness" including feeling as well as thought. The notion of experience as subjective witness, writes Williams, "is offered not only as truth, but as the most authentic kind of truth," as "the ground for all (subsequent) reasoning and analysis" (128). According to Williams, experience has acquired another connotation in the twentieth century different from these notions of subjective testimony as immediate, true, and authentic. In this usage it refers to influences external to individuals—social conditions, institutions, forms of belief or perception—"real" things outside them that they react to, and does not include their thought or consideration.[10]

In the various usages described by Williams, "experience," whether conceived as internal or external, subjective or objective, establishes the prior existence of individuals. When it is defined as internal, it is an expression of an individual's being or consciousness; when external, it is the material upon which consciousness then acts. Talking about experience in these ways leads us to take the existence of individuals for granted (experience is something people have) rather than to ask how conceptions of selves (of subjects and their identities) are produced.[11] It operates within an ideological construction that not only makes individuals the starting point of knowledge, but that also naturalizes categories such as man, woman, black, white, heterosexual, or homosexual by treating them as given characteristics of individuals.

Teresa de Lauretis's redefinition of experience exposes the workings of this ideology: "Experience [she writes] is the process by which, for all social beings, subjectivity is constructed.

Through that process one places oneself or is placed in social reality and so perceives and comprehends as subjective (referring to, originating in oneself) those relations—material, economic, and interpersonal—which are in fact social, and, in a larger perspective, historical."[12]

The process that de Lauretis describes operates crucially through differentiation; its effect is to constitute subjects as fixed and autonomous, and who are considered reliable sources of a knowledge that comes from access to the real by means of their experience.[13] When talking about historians and other students of the human sciences, it is important to note that this subject is both the object of inquiry—the person one studies in the present or the past—and the investigator him- or herself—the historian who produces knowledge of the past based on "experience" in the archives or the anthropologist who produces knowledge of other cultures based on "experience" as a participant observer.

The concepts of experience described by Williams preclude inquiry into processes of subject construction; and they avoid examining the relationships between discourse, cognition, and reality, the relevance of the position or situatedness of subjects to the knowledge they produce, and the effects of difference on knowledge.... His knowledge, reflecting as it does something apart from him, is legitimated and presented as universal, accessible to all. There is no power or politics in these notions of knowledge and experience.

An example of the way "experience" establishes the authority of the historian can be found in R. G. Collingwood's *The Idea of History.* ... For Collingwood, the ability of the historian to "reenact past experience" is tied to his autonomy, "where by autonomy I mean the condition of being one's own authority, making statements or taking action on one's own initiative and not because those statements or actions are authorized or prescribed by anyone else."[15] The question of where the historian is situated—who he is, how he is defined in relation to others, what the political effects of his history may be—never enters the discussion. Indeed, being free of these matters seems to be tied to Collingwood's definition of autonomy....

For Collingwood it is axiomatic that experience is a reliable source of knowledge because it rests on direct contact between the historian's perception and reality (even if the passage of time makes it necessary for the historian to imaginatively reenact events of the past). Thinking on his own means owning his own thoughts and this proprietary relationship guarantees an individual's independence, his ability to read the past correctly, the authority of the knowledge he produces. The claim is not only for the historian's autonomy, but also for his originality. Here "experience" grounds the identity of the researcher as an historian.

Another, very different use of "experience" can be found in E. P. Thompson's *Making of the English Working Class,* the book that revolutionized social and labor history.... For him experience meant "social being"—the lived realities of social life, especially the affective domains of family and religion and the symbolic dimensions of expression. This definition separated the affective and the symbolic from the economic and the rational. "People do not only experience their own experience as ideas, within thought and its procedures," he maintained. "[T]hey also experience their own experience as *feeling*" (171). This statement grants importance to the psychological dimension of experience, and it allows Thompson to account for agency. Feeling, Thompson insists, is "handled" culturally as "norms, familial and kinship obligations, ... values or ... within art and religious beliefs." At the same time it somehow precedes these forms of expression and so provides an escape from a strong structural determination....

And yet in his use of it, experience, because it is ultimately shaped by relations of production, is a unifying phenomenon, overriding other kinds of diversity. Since these relations of production are common to workers of different ethnicities, religions, regions, and trades, they necessarily provide a common denominator and they emerge as a more salient determinant of "experience" than anything else. In Thompson's use of the term, experience is the start of a process that culminates in the realization and articulation of social consciousness, in this case a common identity of class. It serves an integrating function, joining the individual and the structural and bringing together diverse people into that coherent (totalizing) whole which is a distinctive sense of class (170–71).[17]

The unifying aspect of experience excludes whole realms of human activity by simply not counting them as experience at least with any consequences for social organization or politics. When class becomes an overriding identity, other subject positions are subsumed by it, those of gender for example (or, in other instances of this kind of history, race, ethnicity, and sexuality). The positions of men and women and their different relationships to politics are taken as reflections of material and social arrangements rather than as products of class politics itself.

In Thompson's account class is finally an identity rooted in structural relations that preexist politics. What this obscures is the contradictory and contested process by which class itself was conceptualized and by which diverse kinds of subject positions were assigned, felt, contested, or embraced. As a result, Thompson's brilliant history of the English working class, which set out to historicize the category of class, ends up essentializing it.... Working-class "experience" is now the ontological foundation of working-class identity, politics, and history.[18]

This use of experience has the same foundational status if we substitute women or African American or lesbian or homosexual for working-class in the previous sentence. Among feminist historians, for example, "experience" has helped to legitimize a critique of the false claims to objectivity of traditional historical accounts. Part of the project of some feminist history has been to unmask all claims to objectivity as an ideological cover for masculine bias by pointing out the shortcomings, incompleteness, and exclusiveness of "mainstream" history. This has been achieved by providing documentation about women in the past which calls into question existing interpretations made without consideration of gender. But how authorize the new knowledge if the possibility of all historical objectivity has been questioned? By appealing to experience, which in this usage connotes both reality and its subjective apprehension—the experience of women in the past and of women historians who can recognize something of themselves in their foremothers.

Judith Newton, a literary historian, writing about the neglect of feminism by contemporary critical theorists, argues that women, too, arrived at the critique of objectivity usually associated with deconstruction or the New Historicism. This feminist critique "seemed to come straight out of reflection on our own, that is, [on] women's experience, out of the contradictions we felt between the different ways we were represented even to ourselves, out of the inequities we had long experienced in our situations."[19] Newton's appeal to experience seems to bypass the issue of objectivity (by not raising the question of whether feminist work can be objective), but it rests firmly on a foundational ground (experience). In her work the relationship between thought and experience is represented as transparent (the visual metaphor combines with the visceral) and so directly accessible, as it is in historian Christine Stansell's insistence that "social practices" in all their "immediacy and entirety" constitute a domain of "sensuous experience" (a prediscursive reality directly felt, seen, and known) that cannot be subsumed by "language."[20] The effect of these kinds of statements, which attribute an indisputable authenticity to women's experience, is to establish incontrovertibly women's identity as people with agency. It is also to universalize the identity of women and so to ground claims for the legitimacy of women's history in the shared experience of historians of women and those women whose stories they tell. In addition, it literally equates the personal with the political, for the lived experience of women is seen as leading directly to resistance to oppression, to feminism.[21] Indeed, the possibility of politics is said to rest on, to follow from, a preexisting women's experience.

"Because of its drive towards a political massing together of women," writes Denise Riley, "feminism can never wholeheartedly dismantle 'women's experience,' however much this category conflates the attributed, the imposed, and the lived, and then sanctifies the resulting melange."[22] The kind of argument for a women's history (and for a feminist politics) that Riley criticizes closes down inquiry into the ways in which female subjectivity is produced, the ways in which agency is made possible, the ways in which race and sexuality intersect with gender, the ways in which politics organize and interpret experience—the ways in which identity is a contested terrain, the site of multiple and conflicting claims. In Riley's words again, "it masks the likelihood that ... [experiences] have accrued to women not by virtue of their womanhood alone, but as traces of domination, whether natural or political" (99). I would add as well that it masks the necessarily discursive character of these experiences.

But it is precisely the discursive character of experience that is at issue for some historians, because attributing experience to discourse seems somehow to deny its status as an unquestionable ground of explanation. This seems to be the case for John Toews, writing a long review article in the *American Historical Review* in 1987, called "Intellectual History after the Linguistic Turn: The Autonomy of Meaning and the Irreducibility of Experience."[23] The term "linguistic turn" is a comprehensive one used by Toews to refer to approaches to the study of meaning which draw on a number of disciplines, but especially on theories of language ... (881). The question for Toews is how far linguistic analysis has gone and should go especially in view of the poststructuralist challenge to foundationalism.

By definition, he argues, history is concerned with explanation; it is not a radical hermeneutics, but an attempt to account for the origin, persistence, and disappearance of certain meanings at "particular times and in specific sociocultural situations" (882). For him explanation requires a separation of experience and meaning; experience is that reality which demands meaningful response. "Experience" in Toews's usage is taken to be so self-evident that he never defines the term....

Experience, for Toews, is a foundational concept. While recognizing that meanings differ and that the historian's task is to analyze the different meanings produced in societies and over time, Toews protects "experience" from this kind of relativism. In so doing he establishes the possibility for objective knowledge and so for communication among historians, however diverse their positions and views. This has an effect (among others) of removing historians from critical scrutiny as active producers of knowledge.

... Toews's "experience" thus provides an object for historians that can be known apart from their own role as meaning makers and it then guarantees not only the objectivity of their knowledge, but their ability to persuade others of its importance. Whatever diversity and conflict may exist among them, Toews's community of historians is rendered homogeneous by its shared object (experience). But as Ellen Rooney has so effectively pointed out, this kind of homogeneity can exist only because of the exclusion of the possibility that "historically irreducible interests divide and define ... communities."[24] Inclusiveness is achieved by denying that exclusion is inevitable, that difference is established through exclusion, and that the fundamental differences that accompany inequalities of power and position cannot be overcome by persuasion. In Toews's article no disagreement about the meaning of the term "experience" can be entertained, since experience itself lies somehow outside its signification. For that reason, perhaps, Toews never defined it.

Even among those historians who do not share all of Toews's ideas about the objectivity or continuous quality of history, writing the defense of "experience" works in much the same way: it establishes a realm of reality outside of discourse and it authorizes the historian who has access to it. The evidence of experience works as a foundation providing both a starting point and a conclusive kind of explanation, beyond which few questions need to or can be asked. And yet it is precisely the questions precluded—questions about discourse, difference, and subjectivity, as well as about what counts as experience and who gets to make that determination—that would enable us to historicize experience, to reflect critically on the history we write about it, rather than to premise our history upon it.

HISTORICIZING "EXPERIENCE"

How can we historicize "experience"? How can we write about identity without essentializing it? Answers to the second question ought to point toward answers to the first, since identity is tied to notions of experience, and since both identity and experience are categories usually taken for granted in ways that I am suggesting they ought not to be. It ought to be possible for historians to, in Gayatri Spivak's terms, "make visible the assignment of subject-positions," not in the sense of capturing the reality of the objects seen, but of trying to understand the operations of the complex and changing discursive processes by which identities are ascribed, resisted, or embraced and which processes themselves are unremarked, indeed achieve their effect because they aren't noticed.[25] To do this a change of object seems to be required, one which takes the emergence of concepts and identities as historical events in need of explanation.... This mean[s] assuming that the appearance of a new identity is not inevitable or determined, not something that was always there simply waiting to be expressed, not something that will always exist in the form it was given in a particular political movement or at a particular historical moment....

Treating the emergence of a new identity as a discursive event is not to introduce a new form of linguistic determinism, nor to deprive subjects of agency. It is to refuse a separation between "experience" and language and to insist instead on the productive quality of discourse. Subjects are constituted discursively, but there are conflicts among discursive systems, contradictions within any one of them, multiple meanings possible for the concepts they deploy.[28] And subjects have agency. They are not unified, autonomous individuals exercising free will, but rather subjects whose agency is created through situations and statuses conferred on them. Being a subject means being "subject to definite conditions of existence, conditions of endowment of agents and conditions of exercise."[29] These conditions enable choices, although they are not unlimited. Subjects are constituted discursively, experience is a linguistic event (it doesn't happen outside established meanings), but neither is it confined to a fixed order of meaning. Since discourse is by definition shared, experience is collective as well as individual. Experience is a subject's history. Language is the site of history's enactment. Historical explanation cannot, therefore, separate the two.

The question then becomes how to analyze language, and here historians often ... confront the limits of a discipline that has typically constructed itself in opposition to literature. (These limits have to do with a referential conception of language, the belief in a direct relationship between words and things.) The kind of reading I have in mind would not assume a direct correspondence between words and things, nor confine itself to single meanings, nor aim for the resolution of contradiction. It would not render process as linear, nor rest explanation on simple correlations or single variables. Rather it would grant to "the literary" an integral, even irreducible, status of its own. To grant such status is not to make "the literary" foundational, but to open new possibilities for analyzing discursive productions of social and political reality as complex, contradictory processes.

The reading I offered of Delany at the beginning of this essay is an example of the kind of reading I want to avoid. I would like now to present another reading—one suggested to me by literary critic Karen Swann—as a way of indicating what might be involved in historicizing the notion of experience.

For Delany, witnessing the scene at the bathhouse ... was an event. It marked what in one kind of reading we would call a coming to consciousness of himself, a recognition of his authentic identity, one he had always shared, would always share with others like himself. Another kind of reading, closer to Delany's preoccupation with memory and the self in this autobiography, sees this event not as the discovery of truth (conceived as the reflection of a prediscursive reality), but as the substitution of one interpretation for another. Delany presents this substitution as a conversion experience, a clarifying moment, after which he sees (that is, understands) differently. But there is all the difference between subjective perceptual clarity and transparent vision.... Moreover (and this is Swann's point), "the properties of the medium through which the visible appears—here, the dim blue light, whose distorting, refracting qualities produce a wavering of the visible," make any claim to unmediated transparency impossible.[31] Instead, the wavering light permits a vision beyond the visible, a vision that contains the fantastic projections ("millions of gay men" for whom "history had, actively and already, created ... whole galleries of institutions") that are the basis for political identification.[32] "In this version of the story," Swann notes, "political consciousness and power originate, not in a presumedly unmediated experience of presumedly real gay identities, but out of an apprehension of the moving, differencing properties of the representational medium—the motion of light in water."[33]

The question of representation is central to Delany's memoir. It is a question of social categories, personal understanding, and language, all of which are connected, none of which are or can be a direct reflection of the others.... The answer is that the social and the personal are imbricated in one another and that both are historically variable. The meanings of the categories of identity change and with them possibilities for thinking the self.... [T]he available social categories aren't sufficient for Delany's story. It is difficult, if not impossible to use a single narrative to account for his experience. Instead he makes entries in a notebook, at the front about material things, at the back about sexual desire. These are "parallel narratives, in parallel columns."[35] Although one seems to be about society, the public, the political, and the other about the individual, the private, the psychological, in fact both narratives are inescapably historical; they are discursive productions of knowledge of the self, not reflections either of external or internal truth.... The two columns are constitutive of one another, yet the relationship between them is difficult to specify. Do the social and economic determine the subjective? Is the private entirely separate from or completely integral to the public? Delany voices the desire to resolve the problem: "Certainly one must be the lie that is illuminated by the other's truth."[37] And then he denies that resolution is possible since answers to these questions do not exist apart from the discourses that produce them....

It is finally by tracking "the appropriation of language ... in both directions, over the gap," and by situating and contextualizing that language that one historicizes the terms by which experience is represented, and so historicizes "experience" itself.

CONCLUSION

Reading for "the literary" does not seem at all inappropriate for those whose discipline is devoted to the study of change. It is not the only kind of reading I am advocating, although more documents than those written by literary figures are susceptible to such readings. Rather, it is a way of changing the focus and the philosophy of our history, from one bent on naturalizing "experience" through a belief in the unmediated relationship between words and things, to one that takes all categories of analysis as contextual, contested, and contingent. How have categories of representation and analysis—such as class, race, gender, relations of production, biology, identity, subjectivity, agency, experience, even culture—achieved their foundational status? What have been the effects of their articulations? What does it mean for historians to study the past in terms of these categories; for individuals to think of themselves in these terms? What is the relationship between the salience of such categories in our own time and their existence in the past? Questions such as these open consideration of what Dominick LaCapra has referred to as the "transferential" relationship between the historian and the past, that is, of the relationship between the power of the historian's analytic frame and the events that are the object of his or her study. And they historicize both sides of that relationship by denying the fixity and transcendence of anything that appears to operate as a foundation, turning attention instead to the history of foundationalist concepts themselves. The history of these concepts (understood to be contested and contradictory) then becomes the evidence by which "experience" can be grasped and by which the historian's relationship to the past she writes about can be articulated. This is what Foucault meant by genealogy:

If interpretation were the slow exposure of the meaning hidden in an origin, then only metaphysics could interpret the development of humanity. But if interpretation is the violent or surreptitious appropriation of a system of rules, which in itself has no essential meaning, in order to impose a direction, to bend it to a new will, to force its participation in a different game, and to subject it to secondary rules, then the development of humanity is a series of interpretations. The role of genealogy is to record its history: the history of morals, ideals, and metaphysical concepts, the history of the concept of liberty or of the ascetic life; as they stand for the emergence of different interpretations, they must be made to appear as events on the stage of historical process.[39]

Experience is not a word we can do without, although it is tempting, given its usage to essentialize identity and reify the subject, to abandon it altogether. But experience is so much a part of everyday language, so imbricated in our narratives that it seems futile to argue for its expulsion. It serves as a way of talking about what happened, of establishing difference and similarity, of claiming knowledge that is "unassailable."[40] Given the ubiquity of the term, it seems to me more useful to work with it, to analyze its operations and to redefine its meaning. This entails focusing on processes of identity production, insisting on the discursive nature of "experience" and on the politics of its construction.... The study of experience, therefore, must call into question its originary status in historical explanation. This will happen when historians take as their project *not* the reproduction and transmission of knowledge said to be arrived at through experience, but the analysis of the production of that knowledge itself. Such an analysis would constitute a genuinely nonfoundational history, one which retains its explanatory power and its interest in change but does not stand on or reproduce naturalized categories.[41] It also cannot guarantee the historian's neutrality, for the choice of which categories to historicize is inevitably "political," necessarily tied to the historian's recognition of his/her stake in the production of knowledge. Experience is, in this approach, not the origin of our explanation, but that which we want to explain. This kind of approach does not undercut politics by denying the existence of subjects; it instead interrogates the processes of their creation, and, in so doing, refigures history and the role of the historian, and opens new ways for thinking about change.[42]

NOTES

A longer version of this paper appeared in *Critical Inquiry,* 17 (Summer 1991) pp. 773–97. I am grateful for their critical advice to Judith Butler, Christina Crosby, Nicholas Dirks, Christopher Fynsk, Clifford Geertz, Donna Haraway, Susan Harding, Gyan Prakash, Donald Scott, William Sewell, Jr., Karen Swann, and Elizabeth Weed.

1. Samuel R. Delany, *The Motion of Light in Water: Sex and Science Fiction Writing in the East Village, 1957–1965* (New York: New American Library, 1988). Page numbers of citations from this book are indicated in the text.

2. Martha Minow, "Foreword: Justice Engendered," *Harvard Law Review,* 101 (November 1987), pp. 10–95.

3. On the distinction between seeing and writing in formulations of identity see Homi K. Bhabha, "Interrogating Identity," in *Identity: The Real Me,* ICA Documents (London) 6 (1987), pp. 5–11.

4. Lionel Gossman, "Towards a Rational Historiography," in *Transactions of the American Philosophical Society,* 79, 3 (1989), p. 26.

5. On the "documentary" or "objectivist" model used by historians, see Dominick LaCapra, "Rhetoric and History," in Dominick LaCapra, *History and Criticism* (Ithaca: Cornell University Press, 1985), pp. 15–44.

6. On vision as not passive reflection, see Donna Haraway, "Situated Knowledges," typescript p. 9, and Donna Haraway, "The Promises of Monsters: Reproductive Politics for Inappropriate/d Others," unpublished paper, Summer 1990, p. 9. See also Minnie Bruce Pratt, "Identity: Skin Blood Heart," in *Yours in Struggle: Three Feminist Perspectives on Anti-Semitism and Racism* (Brooklyn, N.Y.: Long Haul Press, 1984) and the analysis of Pratt's autobiographical essay by Biddy Martin and Chandra Talpade Mohanty, "Feminist Politics: What's Home Got to Do with It?," in Teresa de Lauretis, *Feminist Studies/Critical Studies* (Madison: University of Wisconsin Press, 1986), pp. 191–212.

7. I am grateful to Judith Butler for discussions on this point.

. . .

9. Raymond Williams, *Keywords* (New York: Oxford University Press, 1983), pp. 126–29. My discussion in this paragraph paraphrases much of Williams's definition. Page numbers of citations are indicated in parentheses in the text.

10. On the ways knowledge is conceived "as an assemblage of accurate representations," see Richard Rorty, *Philosophy and the Mirror of Nature* (Princeton: Princeton University Press, 1979), especially p. 163.

11. Homi Bhabha puts it this way: "To see a missing person, or to look at Invisibleness, is to emphasize the subject's transitive demand for a direct object of self-reflection; a point of presence which would maintain its privileged enunciatory position qua subject," in "Interrogating Identity," p. 5.

12. Teresa de Lauretis, *Alice Doesn't* (Bloomingtom: Indiana University Press, 1984), chapter 6, "Semiotics and Experience," p. 159.

13. Gayatri Spivak describes this as positing a metalepsis, that is, substituting an effect for a cause. See Gayatri Chakravorty Spivak, *In Other Worlds: Essays in Cultural Politics* (New York: Routledge, 1987), p. 204.

. . .

15. R. G. Collingwood, *The Idea of History* (New York: Oxford University Press, 1956), pp. 274–75. Page numbers of citations are indicated in parentheses in the text.

. . .

17. On the integrative functions of "experience," see Judith Butler, *Gender Trouble: Feminism and the Subversion of Identity* (New York: Routledge, Chapman and Hall, 1990), pp. 22–25.

18. For a different reading of Thompson on experience see William Sewell, Jr., "How Classes Are Made: Critical Reflections on E. P. Thompson's Theory of Working-Class Formation," in Harvey J. Kaye and Keith McClelland, eds., *E. P. Thompson: Critical Perspectives* (Philadelphia: Temple University Press, 1990); see also, Sylvia Schafer, "Writing about 'Experience': Workers and Historians Tormented by Industrialization," unpublished paper, May 1987.

19. Judith Newton, "History as Usual? Feminism and the 'New Historicism,'" *Cultural Critique,* 9 (1988), p. 93.

20. Christine Stansell, "Response," *International Labor and Working Class History,* 31 (Spring 1987), p. 28. Often this kind of invocation of experience leads back to the biological or physical "experience" of the body. See, for example, the arguments about rape and violence offered by Mary Hawkesworth, "Knowers, Knowing, Known: Feminist Theory and Claims of Truth," *Signs,* 14, 3 (Spring 1989), pp. 533–57.

21. For critiques of this position, see Chandra Talpade Mohanty, "Feminist Encounters: Locating the Politics of Experience," *copyright,* 1 (Fall 1987), p. 32; and Katie King, "The Situation of Lesbianism as Feminism's Magical Sign: Contests for Meaning and the U.S. Women's Movement, 1968–1972," *Communication,* 9 (1986), pp. 65–91. Catharine MacKinnon's work is probably the best example of the uses of "experience" Mohanty, King, and I are criticizing; see her *Feminism Unmodified: Discourses on Life and Law* (Cambridge, Mass.: Harvard University Press, 1987).

22. Denise Riley, *"Am I That Name?" Feminism and the Category of Women in History* (Minneapolis: University of Minnesota Press, 1988), p. 100.

23. John Toews, *American Historical Review,* 92, 4 (October 1987), pp. 879–907.

24. Ellen Rooney. *Seductive Reasoning: Pluralism as the Problematic of Contemporary Theory* (Ithaca, N.Y.: Cornell University Press, 1989), pp. 5–6.

25. Gayatri Spivak, "A Literary Representation of the Subaltern: A Woman's Text from the Third World," in *Other Worlds,* p. 241.

. . .

28. For discussions of how change operates within and across discourses, see James Bono, "Science, Discourse, and Literature: The Role/Rule of Metaphor in Science," in Stuart Peterfreund, ed., *Literature and Science: Theory and Practice* (Boston: Northeastern University Press, 1990), pp. 59–89. See also, Mary Poovey, *Uneven Developments: The Ideological Work of Gender in Mid-Victorian England* (Chicago: University of Chicago Press, 1988), pp. 1–23.

29. Parveen Adams and Jeff Minson. "The Subject of Feminism," *m/f,* 2 (1978), p. 52. On the constitution of the subject, see Michel Foucault, *The Archaeology of Knowledge* (New York: Harper and Row, 1972), pp. 95–96; Felicity A. Nussbaum, *The Autobiographical Subject: Gender and Ideology in Eighteenth-Century England* (Baltimore: Johns Hopkins University Press, 1989); and Peter de Bolla, *The Discourse of the Sublime: Readings in History, Aesthetics, and the Subject* (Oxford and New York: Basil Blackwell, 1989).

. . .

31. Karen Swarm, Comment, p. 4.

32. Samuel R. Delany, *The Motion of Light,* p. 174.

33. Karen Swann, Comment, p. 4.

. . .

35. Samuel R. Delany, *The Motion of Light,* p. 29.

. . .

37.   Ibid.

...

39.   Michel Foucault, "Nietzsche, Genealogy, History," in D. F. Bonchard, ed., *Language, Counter-Memory, Practice* (Ithaca, NY: Cornell University Press, 1977), pp. 151–52.

40.   Ruth Roach Pierson, "Experience, Difference and Dominance in the Writings of Women's History," unpublished paper, 1989, p. 32.

41.   Conversations with Christopher Fynsk helped clarify these points for me.

42.   For an important attempt to describe a poststructuralist history, see Peter de Bolla, "Disfiguring History," *Diacritics,* 16 (Winter 1986), pp. 49–58.

Renée T. White
Talking about Sex and HIV: Conceptualizing a New Sociology of Experience

... Capturing the essence of life, in all its complexities, is a challenge that can be answered by ethnographic research and oral narratives. Learning how to ask questions and listen to those in our communities and neighborhoods is a method of study that is still new to many in the social sciences. Understanding the way people live their lives can result in a greater understanding of how the social world functions.

Field research enables the search for more personal, "everyday" meanings and explanations of the social problems with which we often find ourselves identifying. For example,

> Some ethnographers have constructed their accounts almost exclusively through the first-person narratives of their informants. The strategy can be a powerful one. In the hands of a skillful author, the resulting text can appear as a vivid and privileged reconstruction of the speaker's experience. A variety of narrative accounts can provide a shifting point of view: a kaleidoscope of contrasting or complementary perspectives is provided through a variety of voices. (Atkinson, 1992, p. 24)

Field research, ethnography, and other qualitative methods are effective in the development of research questions that can be addressed with large-scale surveys....

Determining how to use oral narratives within an ethnographic project can result in a new set of methodological, ethical, and ideological questions. As a sociologist, my training prepared me for a quantitative and meta-theoretical world. What was I to make of the one I was to encounter through fieldwork? This chapter is informed by the years spent collecting data in New Haven, Connecticut, for a project on AIDS, race, and teenage females' sexuality....

This chapter focuses on the theoretical and philosophical issues that emerged as a result of using an exploratory research process. This also requires reviewing the process of data collection. Such a process includes developing strategies for entry and access to key individuals in the field, sampling from the available adolescents in the community, generating methods for data collection and recording, and interpreting/analyzing findings....

"IS THERE EVEN A SLIGHT POSSIBILITY THAT YOU'LL FIND OUT SOMETHING NEW?": THE UNIQUE VALUE OF NARRATIVE STUDIES

Social scientists are often received with skepticism outside disciplinary circles. This is a result, at least in part, of the way research is conducted and the results are interpreted. In the case of research on black women's sexuality and AIDS, both the generation of hypotheses and data collection have been rife with problems and controversy (Winter & Brekenmaker, 1991). Sexual behavior and related outcomes are so often interpreted within racial-ethnic parameters that it is assumed that race determines or explains what is found.

Traditional ways of confronting and addressing sociological questions appeared to fall short of providing truly revelatory accounts of why so many men and women of color in certain urban areas were living with and dying from AIDS. . . . Claiming that racial differences in rates of infection are explained by race and class in statistical modeling cannot answer a difficult question: Why?

The body of research on AIDS and sexual behavior usually falls into three categories: (a) tracking the incidence of infection and the rates of sexual activity; (b) measuring AIDS/STD knowledge; and (c) identifying cultural differences in sexual behavior and attitudes (Chavkin, 1990; Herz & Reis, 1987; Winter & Brekenmaker, 1991). These three areas of research rely on surveys, epidemiological data, and interviews. They do not include the long-term investigation of participants' lives. Consequently, none of these approaches can capture the range of societal factors associated with black women's risk of HIV infection.

Confronting a complicated yet imperative question such as the association between AIDS and race necessitates shifting the analytic lens from the phenomenon or behavior being studied to the "subject" or "actor." . . . [T]raditional social science methods identify the *what*, but not the *how* or *why*.

Using a method inspired by ethnography and drawing on sociological theory, I was able to illustrate how people develop their sexual identities within specific social contexts. In this particular project, using field methods was essential because the issue of interest was the interaction of socioeconomic and sociocultural factors in the *lives* of young women. Such an intricate issue could not be comprehensively studied with a survey or questionnaire.

"BUT WHERE'S YOUR HYPOTHESIS? WHAT ARE YOU GOING TO PROVE?": POSING QUESTIONS WITH FIELDWORK

Ethnography is open-ended and exploratory. You do not need any preconceived notions about what you will find. . . .

The methodological focus of the research centers on developing concepts through observation and in-depth interviews. As such, the results are time- and context-specific. This specificity is extremely valuable when one is interested in clearly understanding the social space or context in which attitudes are formed and acted on by individuals. Concern for generalizing findings, though relevant, does not diminish the usefulness of this approach.

Although I had a clearly defined interest, as well as some broadly outlined expectations (in terms of the in-depth nature of the information I sought), the method I used had to introduce me to the social practices among teenagers, which eventually could be used to develop hypotheses, if necessary. . . . Rather than state that race and class explain the association between race and HIV infection among adolescents, I wanted to ask a question.

The goal was to investigate why young women of color were (and still are) overrepresented among those at greatest risk for HIV infection. My main assumption was that a variety of social and material elements influenced this decision-making process. Thus, the goal was to determine whether and how these elements affected decision making. Although surveys and interviews can generate data concerning correlations and associations among variables, these methods do not always provide insights into why people behave as they do.

Many ethnographic, life history, and narrative studies use grounded theory because this inductive approach highlights potential associations and recurring patterns in the recorded life histories. By using grounded theory, a study begins with a general topic, which is addressed by the empirical data (field notes), and then ends in developing hypotheses and concepts (Burawoy,

1991; Kaplan, 1964). Extracting general principles from particular observations provides the foundation for theorizing the existence of social phenomena. It does not start with rigidly defined associations among elements, factors, or variables.... Instead, this type of investigation assumes that discovering and uncovering the interesting and unexpected is an end in itself.

By combining ethnography and oral narrative with other methods, I gained a more complete view of what young black women encountered on a day-to-day basis and how their sexuality and sexual behavior fit into this overall picture. Sex and sexuality are among the most private facets of our lives.... Gathering such sensitive information requires trust between the young women and me, which can only occur once we have developed relationships and they feel comfortable enough with me to be honest about their experiences.

Conducting extensive, open-ended interviews (narratives) incorporated ethnographic strategies because I had to spend as much time with the young women in their real-life contexts as they would allow....

Because the girls' parents were not included in the study, my exposure to their home lives was somewhat limited. In many cases, I was able to see their homes and meet some of their friends. These moments were informative precisely because I remained a silent observer of the young women's daily experiences and interactions. The study had ethnographic elements because, having lived in New Haven for many years before initiating the project, I had a reasonable understanding of the city and was able to observe interactions among adolescents in public spaces over a long period of time. The insights emerging from these observations were to contribute to my sensitivity to the needs and concerns of young women in the project.

This approach enabled me to spend long periods of time with these girls in both structured (controlled) and unstructured settings. By becoming acquainted with the girls, I learned about their sexual behavior and decision-making processes, as well as the impact of their sexual identities, poverty, and perceptions of family and motherhood on these processes. Using such a flexible and adaptable method for primary data collection provided a comprehensive picture of the experience and meaning of adolescence in the 1990s....

"THE THING IS, HOW DID YOU GET MY NAME, ANYWAY?": CONFRONTING THE SAMPLING QUESTION

By requiring frequent and extensive contact with young women, the sample size had to be limited. At the same time, it had to be large enough to highlight possible trends in behavior and attitudes; the findings could definitively either challenge or confirm existing research. In addition, the sample had to be demographically representative of other young women in the city; in this way, the findings could arguably represent, or at least reflect, the experiences of other adolescent females.

An additional selection requirement was that I approach white and other nonblack female adolescents. Although black women were the focus of the project, contact with other young women would help illuminate what issues were common to all racial-ethnic groups and which ones might be influenced by racial-ethnic or cultural differences. Ultimately, I wanted to oversample the number of black teenagers—having a group that was 70% to 80% black. The target number of participants was a minimum of 20 and a maximum of 40 young women. My goal was to contact organizations and programs that attracted various kinds of teenagers from different racial-ethnic groups, neighborhoods, educational levels, socioeconomic backgrounds, and households.

My selection process was largely nonrandom, in that I approached any young woman who expressed interest in this project. At the same time, however, I remained cognizant of the importance of generating a group of discussants who reflected various social, economic, educational, and ethnic backgrounds. By using a snowball selection process, a few participants introduced me to additional friends who were included in the sample; in turn, these girls introduced me to their friends and acquaintances.

To minimize sampling bias in my nonrandom selection process, I approached four organizations for participants.... In deciding which programs to approach, I required that (a) they include participants who, in addition to being residents of New Haven, were representative of the background characteristics in which I was interested; (b) the administrators and outreach staff express enthusiasm for the topics I wanted to study; (c) an educational or outreach component be part of the program; (d) the group meet at least once a week; and (e) discussions include sexual behavior and/or dating.

The groups I selected differed in composition, organizational structure or administrative style, operating philosophy, and prerequisites for participation. One was an academic enrichment program. Another was a pilot project, initiated in a local high school, that addressed cultural differences. The last two were affiliated with local health clinics.... Participation in the study depended on whether the young women were comfortable and was therefore completely voluntary. I offered no financial incentive for participating.

It should be clear that this is not a random or anonymous sampling process. Although variance is sought, it is also important to find participants who will ultimately tell their stories. Even if there is less heterogeneity among the participants, the potential wisdom and insight to be gained from their stories still remains. What has to change is the way this information is used. We cannot expect to conduct narratives in a social vacuum; participants, if they are from the same community or neighborhood, may know each other and will probably talk about some parts of the interview process. This sharing would be highly problematic if one were using other methods; such contact would skew how people respond. In narrative research, however, interactions among participants might stimulate thoughts and memories they wish to share with you.

"I'D LIKE TO INTRODUCE YOU ALL TO ...": MAKING CONTACTS WITH ORGANIZATIONS IN THE COMMUNITY

Many organizations in New Haven focus on youth issues.... To make an informed decision, I had to collect information on as many groups as I could find and then contact program directors.

Initial efforts to speak with concerned individuals prepared me for later contacts with organizations. First, I had to confront the political terrain in which the social issues of adolescents were located. Each individual or organization involved with teenagers envisioned him- or herself or themselves as having the definitive view of what teenagers in New Haven require for healthy social and sexual development. As a result, there appeared to be ideological, political, and policy boundaries that they would not cross when addressing social issues. It was necessary that I understand what and where these divisions were early in the research and interview process so as to minimize the risk of alienating the people I contacted.

Second, I had to learn how to communicate effectively with youth professionals and the teenagers. Contacting the professionals involved learning the language that social workers, health care providers, educators, and other youth advocates use on a regular basis. Most of this language was removed from the discourse found in social science theory. Recognizing this language enabled me to eventually prove myself aware of general adolescent issues, as well as those issues more specific to black teenage females in New Haven....

Inclusion in the project depended on the willingness of case managers, outreach workers, and administrators to introduce me to the young women and to encourage ongoing interaction among us. Before this was feasible, I had to establish a strong relationship with as many of the professionals as possible.... In the early stages of the project, I always emphasized that my primary role was as a researcher who was also interested in and committed to contributing to the organization in whatever ways they deemed most appropriate. I presented myself as willing to learn from and report on their experiences, as well as those of their peers and clients.

This acknowledgment points to the continuing ethical debate about how forthright a researcher should be about her intentions. The ethical demands are different in any type of study in which researcher and participant have any sort of contact. In field research, this is particularly true because self-disclosure and one's very presence within a setting can have long-term effects on participants and nonparticipants alike.

"ARE YOU SERIOUS ABOUT ALL THIS? WHAT ARE YOU REALLY DOING WITH ALL THIS STUFF?": TRANSFORMING AND CHALLENGING MY ROLE AS RESEARCHER

Most of my early professional contacts expressed frustration and mistrust because they believed they worked in agencies and organizations that had been overstudied, especially by nonminority social scientists. These studies, though sometimes brief and generally noninvasive, were nonetheless viewed as intrusive and uninformative. Some of the observations made by these professionals clarify the tension between the academic and local advocates' communities: "I have developed a reputation as unapproachable with people doing research because I make it difficult for them to just swoop down and study my kids and then swoop back to their ivory tower without leaving us something in return." . . .

Racial-ethnic conflict mingles not only with issues of informational and experiential territory but also with cynicism about the proper role that researchers should and do play in the community. "Gatekeepers, sponsors, and the like (indeed, most of the people who act as hosts to the research) will operate in terms of expectations about the ethnographer's identity and intentions" (Hammersly & Atkinson, 1995, p. 77). I suspect that, as a black woman, I encountered more skepticism from these early contacts precisely because of this "town-gown" tension.

My presence had to be ambiguous because I was a black woman like them, yet one who seemed to enjoy certain privileges. Many saw my status as a reflection of an elite lifestyle—one shaped by my membership in an exclusive Ivy League social club that was perceived as anti-black, anti–working class, and ultimately anti–New Haven. As such, how else could I have been regarded? If people saw me as actively participating in a social reality that fundamentally rejected them, by extension this meant that my own racial-ethnic-gender identity had to be compromised. There also was the issue of my research status. Any involved, intimate kind of project presumes some sensitivity and commitment to the participants. If my presence is, at best, questionable, then my integrity as a researcher will also be questioned.

. . . A basic tenet of social science research is to be clear about one's status in the group under study. As a black woman, I was part of the racial group of interest in the study, but as a representative of a major university, I represented the mainstream (nonblack society).

Even though my contacts expressed support for the project, they also needed reassurance that I retained a strong enough ethnic identity and sense of community that I would not ask questions or interpret findings without any cultural sensitivity. . . . After passing what were clearly meant as tests, being black clearly became an asset in further contacts with the advocates, most of whom were black women or Latina. They considered me both an outsider and an insider. Having links with the university was no longer considered a drawback or a problem, but a potential resource.

When first meeting with the young women, I faced their curiosity and resistance. I was usually introduced during the first meeting by whoever facilitated that day's discussion. I was always introduced as what I was—someone interested in researching their attitudes, beliefs, and experiences by documenting their memories and daily experiences. As expected, they were very cynical concerning what I could offer them. Most were uncomfortable with the idea of talking about personal issues with a stranger. Some said that I could not be interested in them, that my interests had to lie in sensationalizing teens' sexual behavior. . . .

At first, I remained an observer, noting which young women were particularly vocal or were treated as peer group leaders. My silence was important because I had presented myself as someone who wanted to learn from them, who did not have all the answers. The extent of my participation was determined by the professionals. . . .

Once my presence was less intrusive during group meetings, I began to initiate conversations with different girls concerning popular culture issues of interest to most adolescents—music, clothing, and sports. I initially approached only those who had made efforts to talk with me or who allowed me within their personal space (this was usually expressed by saving me a seat, letting me play with their children, or smiling at me). During these discussions, I reiterated that I was interested in learning about their experiences and opinions of popular views of adolescence (by *popular*, I mean media representations, as well as academic ones). Among the factors I expressed a wish to explore were dating, sex, and male-female relationships. Anyone who appeared interested was invited to participate in group discussions on any topic of interest to them. This participation constituted the initial focus group discussions. I purposely left topics undefined because I wanted the participants to believe that they had some control over this process and that I had no negative, predetermined motives.

… Using these structured settings as the sites of my first encounters with them, however, actually made it more difficult for them to see me as someone they could spend time with on other days. Because the downtown shopping mall was one popular social spot for many teenagers, I had to spend hours there, sometimes alone, sometimes speaking with one or two young women I might see who knew me. I had to create circumstances and environments outside the boundaries of the programs in order to see them in other social settings.

Not all the participants appreciated seeing me during their off-time. … On the one hand, it is often difficult to separate the researcher and "average person" roles for all those participating in the project. Can there be moments of social contact when data collection is either warranted or expected? On the other hand, living in this kind of social space enables the researcher to even engage in "passive" modes of data collection through simple participation in the rhythm and flow of the community.

"YES, I HAVE HEARD ABOUT WHAT HAPPENED": DEVELOPING A RAPPORT

The transition in the reception of one's presence is simultaneously slow and enlightening. Because collecting these narratives required first developing trusting relationships, I had to let the young women dictate the paths this process might take. Reading the cues that indicate their willingness to delve into personal issues is usually difficult and requires having a working knowledge of the teenagers' personality styles. Once I had permission from them to include them in the study, I entered this new phase in our relationships: juggling for control and testing each other's truthfulness/trustworthiness.

… As the personal narrative process was to emerge out of group discussions, much of the testing I faced occurred within groups. In one case, a group of Latina teenagers were talking about their day. They used "Spanglish," a hybrid of Spanish and English. None of these teenagers was willing to speak with me in the beginning. They would slip between Spanglish and Spanish when speaking to each other; they had assumed I knew no Spanish and thus could be excluded from their discussions.

… I "showed my hand" one day by laughing at a joke one of them told in Spanish. Even though this reaction was not completely self-conscious, it did facilitate the relationship I was to develop with one young woman. I had indicated that I knew Spanish, that I was not going to chastise them for things previously said, and that I had a sense of humor.

In another case, young men devised dramatic stories to test my sensibilities. They wanted to prove their sexual experience through telling shocking stories. …

Working within groups where people know each other involves both benefits and drawbacks. On occasion, participants would serve as screeners or fact-checkers: If one person misrepresented information, another might interject and challenge her. Having grown up together also meant that some young women already felt comfortable with each other. As a result, they would either protect each other from seemingly invasive questions or maintain a sense of camaraderie, thus creating a safe discussion environment. These dynamics placed a great deal of control with the participants. They could choose to either actively include or exclude me from their inner sanctum.

After a few weeks, some teenagers started to meet with me individually. Initiating this stage required being sensitive to the ways each young woman expressed herself and how private she had seemed in previous group discussions. Willingness to delve into personal life issues is as varied as can be imagined. Some people will volunteer personal experiences; others need encouragement.... This process is time-consuming because it involves individualized attention. Each participant is her own person and has her own boundaries. Discovering what these are may take trial-and-error. This approach is often discomforting for those with formal training in data collection who are used to more stable and predictable timetables and reliable research formats.

Determining how and when to guide individual interviews involves an element of openness. Both preliminary literature review and early interviews should shape what general topics are to be addressed, but it is also important to allow flexibility within discussions.... Seemingly unrelated discussions may eventually touch on the heart of the research question (this may become immediately apparent, or only after reflection). The strength of narrative is that the participant's life is the resource, and she is your intermediary.

For example, one young woman was describing a move her family had made to a different street. This was the seventh move in about 2 years. In reality, this conversation ended up highlighting the kinds of social isolation that teenagers might experience and the dangers of having an adult exploit this fact. In Cathy's case, the result was sexual assault....

After an extended discussion of how much we both disliked moving, Cathy shared this account: "I was crying 'cause I just wanted to stay in one place, and he came over and told me it was okay and that it would get better and he came from behind and hugged me and touched my breasts.... He's disgusting, and I won't let him near those girls so he'll have to make do with me." Allowing the narrator to guide some of the discussion can be unexpectedly fruitful and thus requires some intuition, or reading within and between the lines of discourse.

There is no way to predict when and how enough intimacy will have developed for a participant to relate her own memories as truthfully as she can. This will be a mutually determined moment, one emerging from possibly many months of interactions. Because narrative research involves sharing the most personal elements in a person's life, any number of strategies may be needed....

"OK, WHAT TO DO WITH ALL THIS INFORMATION?": RECORDING AND PRESENTING NARRATIVES

... Shifting from a record of what people said to a set of conclusions requires a few stages. Obviously, the first stage involves the actual collecting and recording of data. In the second stage, field notes have to be reviewed and analyzed (what I call the presentation stage). Finally, all these reflections have to be formally reported. During this representation stage, one has to decide what findings are relevant and why. To some extent, judgments and evaluations must be made. Each of these stages is especially complex because most one-on-one interactions are open-ended (unstructured) interviews, and not unguided monologue. The issues that guide the questions also shape how responses are recorded during the interviews.

The question of recording and taking notes is a complex one. Because life histories are the focus, it is imperative that they be recorded as completely and accurately as possible. Ideally, this imperative points to tape recording during interviews. Not all people are willing and interested participants.... This is where the issue of trust is relevant, for if the narrator believes that you are going to protect her privacy, she is more likely to agree to some form of record keeping.

... Tape recording may or may not be feasible, but field notes are necessities. They can fill in the gaps in interview notes, add commentary to previous observations, and encourage self-reflection. Being self-conscious of one's presence within a community or group is an important part of collecting data. Writing down and reviewing what happened during the course of that day will facilitate what bell hooks (1990, 1994) recommends: self-interrogation. Reviewing notes is part of the analytical process as much as creating them.

The level of detail in field notes largely depends on how much time one has to engage in their construction and reconstruction. Eventually, they will be a combination of in-the-moment perceptions, after-the-fact elaborations, and down-the-line interpretations. Obviously, this process can be problematic if interpretation obscures presentation. Going from recording to presentation to representation involves the interpretation of narratives. Collecting field notes occurs in the first stage of investigation—recording information—and will be instrumental in the second stage, in which you analyze what you have noted. When you are deeply involved with a person or group and the social role of researcher appears fuzzy, it is easy for interpretations to replace the narratives themselves. The mediator of the author's story, as the expert in social sciences, becomes the true storyteller in this sense—and thus the narrator's experience becomes lost. One possible solution, which was effective in this project, is to check for accuracy by sharing small segments of field notes with the narrator.

CONCLUSION: REFLECTING ON THE UNEXPECTED IN ORAL NARRATIVE STUDIES

There is much more to this story than can be shared here. Working with young women in the construction and presentation of their life histories affected me on many levels. Embarking on this project required studying and learning about a method of research previously unknown to me. Although I had read narratives and analyses of them, I had not known how to engage in narrative and ethnographic research in a systematic way. As a result, parts of the process were more experimental than I had anticipated.

Working in the community where I lived was ultimately a self-revelatory process. In addition to gathering descriptive information that illuminated more than I had hoped, the method also forced me to question my role as objective researcher....

Any social contact with another person has to affect the two of you. In narrative research, one engages in very personal, in-depth, and often sensitive territory. The simple exercise of reflection has to affect a participant. In other situations, women may find themselves confiding things they have never confronted before. This disclosure leaves the researcher with a moral dilemma, particularly when the confidence concerns something in the present. What do you do if someone tells you something that is placing her at risk? In such a case, the "objective" researcher confronts the "subjective" confidant. You may not be a close friend, but you have certainly been entrusted with intimate details of a woman's life. As a friend, you want to intervene, which is tantamount to tampering with the research setting—but only in the most literal sense. There is no one solution. How we respond has to be situation-specific.

As these issues illustrate, for black women concerned with the lives of other black women (or for any individual investigating the experiences of someone with whom an alliance is shared), self-interrogation and self-consciousness are ongoing processes. The data collection, recording, and analysis stages will involve reflection, analysis, reinvention, and discovery. In my case, I found that my perceptions of myself as a black woman changed.... By using oral narratives, we have the opportunity to both contribute to the depictions of black women in our disciplines and expand our social, political, professional, and personal selves.

REFERENCES

Anderson, E. (1990). *Streetwise: Race, class, and change in an urban community.* Chicago: University of Chicago Press.

Atkinson, P. (1992). *Understanding ethnographic texts.* Newbury Park, CA: Sage.

Burawoy, M. (Ed.). (1991). *Ethnography unbound: Power and resistance in the modern metropolis.* Berkeley: University of California Press.

Chavkin, W. (1990, Spring). Women, AIDS, and reproductive rights: Preventing AIDS, targeting women. *Health/PAC Bulletin,* pp. 19–23.

Collins, P. H. (1990). *Black feminist thought: Knowledge, consciousness, and the politics of empowerment.* Winchester, MA: Unwin Hyman.

Dash, L. (1989). *When children want children.* New York: William Morrow.

Geertz, C. (1980). *Negara.* Princeton, NJ: Princeton University.

Hammersly, M., & Atkinson, P. (1995). *Ethnography: Principles in practice.* New York: Routledge.

Herz, E. J., & Reis, J. (1987). Family life education for young inner-city teens: Identifying needs. *Journal of Youth and Adolescence, 4,* 361–376.

Holden, C. (1979). Ethics in social science research. *Science, 206,* 537–538, 540.

hooks, b. (1990). *Yearning: Race, gender, and cultural politics.* Boston: South End.

———. (1994). *Outlaw culture.* New York: Routledge.

Kaplan, A. (1964). *The conduct of inquiry.* San Francisco: Chandler.

Ladner, J. A. (1973). *Tomorrow's tomorrow.* Garden City, NY: Doubleday.

Walker, A. (1983). *In search of our mothers' gardens.* Orlando, FL: Harcourt Brace.

Whitten, N. E., & Szwed, J. F. (1970). *Afro-American anthropology.* New York: Free Press.

Winter, L., & Brekenmaker, L. C. (1991). Tailoring family planning services to the special needs of adolescents. *Family Planning Perspectives, 1,* 24–30.

Yow, V. R. (1994). *Recording oral history: A practical guide for social scientists.* Thousand Oaks, CA: Sage.

LORRAINE CODE

Incredulity, Experientialism, and the Politics of Knowledge

PRODUCING "THE TRUTH"

Writing in the first volume of *The History of Sexuality* about the nineteenth-century confessional as a mechanism of power, Michel Foucault observes that the "work of producing the truth" in a confession was "obliged to pass through [a] relationship" with a listener who was at the same time an interpreter, "if it was to be scientifically validated." He continues: "The truth did not reside solely in the subject who, by confessing, would reveal it wholly formed. It was constituted in two stages: present but incomplete, blind to itself, in the one who spoke, it could only reach completion in the one who assimilated and recorded it.... The one who listened was not simply the forgiving master, the judge who condemned or acquitted; he was the master of truth."[1]

In this essay I examine some places where comparable spoken truths do not "reach completion," not because the utterances are false, but because of power-infused practices of "mastery": of condemnation or acquittal. I take Foucault's remarks about the confessional as emblematic for analyses of the *incredulity* that works, unevenly across the social order, to invalidate some processes of would-be truth production, and to disqualify certain speakers, individually or collectively, from full membership in companies of truth-tellers. I speak of "testimony" where Foucault speaks of "confession," and I treat the social-political mechanisms that acknowledge or dismiss testimonial evidence as analogous to those he finds in the confessional.

... [Foucault] ... writes of truth being *produced*—not just told. Yet his language will sit uneasily with epistemologists trained in a tradition for which knowledge is "justified true belief." Foucault is, in effect, marking a rupture—signalling a reversal—in this taken-for-granted order of things. He is maintaining that justification, validation do not occur simply through the verification procedures to which "individual" knowers committed to methodological rigor will submit their beliefs. He is as interested ... in the situations where [truth's] failure to reach completion causes the speaker/testifier to doubt the veracity, the validity even of her/his "own" experiences. The confessional or testimonial moment becomes the place at which truth is formed in the telling, where adverse or hostile circumstances can block its production. The "master of truth" literally allows—or refuses to allow—the truth to establish itself.

In my investigation here, I attempt to explicate the epistemological issues—and hence to understand the effects of the alleged "knowledge" that operate within everyday and institutional testimonial processes, to inform consequent moral-political actions and attitudes. My inquiry is prompted by the impotence of mainstream theories of knowledge to address situations where testimony amounts not simply to requesting or offering a piece of information, but where a speaker/testifier puts him/her self, her/his reputation on the line. There are numerous examples. Women often testify as clearly and straightforwardly as they can about a sexual assault or an abusive relationship, only to face systematic incredulity that undermines not just the "truth" of the experiences, but their sense of self, of credibility, of trustworthiness.[2] A black male student tells of being stopped by the police and asked to account for himself when he is walking at night in the city, only to find himself immobilized when his "account" is discredited in the incredulity of their reception.... My contention will be that mere quirks of individual psychology are not the issue in instances like this. Rather, I will suggest that the rhetorical spaces that a society legitimates generate presumptions of credibility and trust that attach differentially according to how speakers and interpreters are positioned within them. Philosophical assumptions about the veracity of first-person privileged access and automatic uptake bypass these everyday occurrences, which are shaping forces in the ongoing construction of subjectivity and agency, especially in places of unequal power and authority.... The term [incredulity] expands, in this analysis, to cover places where testifiers find that they are not being listened to, indeed not even noticed, and where these occurrences are located within hierarchical structures that position one person or group of people in such a way that they can obliterate or destabilize the credibility of the other(s).

In this [reading] I examine some rhetorical-testimonial-experiential disadvantages that women and other marginalized speakers face in the legitimized and legitimating discursive spaces of late-twentieth-century capitalist societies, where their testimony is as often dismissed, discounted, and disbelieved as it is taken seriously into account or validated. I draw on two texts where testimony, in an elaborated sense, is crucial to the production of knowledge, judgment, and informed action: Toni Morrison's *Race-ing Justice, En-gendering Power,* a collection of essays about the confrontation between Anita Hill and Clarence Thomas in the 1991 U.S. Senate Hearings on the confirmation of Thomas as Supreme Court Justice; and Shoshana Felman and Dori Laub's *Testimony,* a study of testimony in general and of Holocaust testimonials in particular.[3] In my reading of the Morrison collection, ... for purposes of this analysis (self-referentially to the argument of this essay) I assume Hill's commitment to testifying as accurately as she could. I cite the Felman and Laub text to reinforce, and to offer a different version of, this sense of the inhibiting effects of incredulity in a fragile testimonial process.

These two books document some of the disempowering effects of incredulity for people who present themselves as *bona fide* testifiers, co-conversants and interlocutors, yet fail to gain acknowledgment from the masters of truth.[4] Kimberle Crenshaw, for example, attests to Anita Hill's "inability to be heard outside the rhetorical structures within which cultural power has been organized"; and refers to the "lack of available and widely comprehended narratives to communicate the reality of her experience as a black woman to the world." She observes: "The particularities of black female subordination are suppressed as the terms of racial and gender discrimination law require that we mold our experience into that of either white women or black men in order to be legally recognized."[5] Laub remarks that "The absence of an empathic listener, or more radically, the absence of an addressable other, an other who can hear the anguish of one's memories and thus affirm and recognize their realness, annihilates the story."[6] These books record, piece by piece, and in painstaking detail, how "truths" of the most compelling kind can simply fail to compel assent when the available rhetorical spaces are either closed against them, or so constrained in the possibilities they offer that what is "really" being said is slotted automatically into categories, ready-made places, where the fit is at best crude, at worst distorting and damaging....

Interesting for a project of developing an *epistemological* analysis of testimony and the incredulity it often occasions is that there is a sense in which these complex testimonial moments are not really about knowledge at all. Hence the issue seems not to be an epistemological one, but to have more to do with social interaction: with power and the distribution of cognitive authority. So mapping the rhetorical spaces that legitimate or discredit testimony—that foster or forestall incredulity—seems rather to be a way of mapping social-political power structures. Yet it also is an issue about knowledge at the most basic level, where what is at stake is the nature and status of empirical evidence. This is a place within the social expectations of a liberal-democratic society where the claims of a straightforward empiricist realism press most urgently, yet where, as Donna Haraway puts it, "politics and ethics ground struggles for the contests over what may count as rational knowledge."[8] ...

Epistemologically, Foucault's remark suggests that, in these complex testimonial and confessional practices, the epistemologist's taken-for-granted line of reasoning from "true belief" to knowledge does not always map the most obvious direction. Sometimes knowledge comes first, and needs belief to establish—to "complete"—it. Consider some familiar locutions: "I always knew that there were people like that, but I never believed it." "I knew that there was sexism/racism at work in that incident, but I didn't believe it." Standard epistemologies, appealing to amateur psychiatry, might discount such utterances as mere instances of denial; but there is more at stake. In some contexts such initial knowings, based in empirical evidence, reach (or fail to reach) completion only in the dynamics of communicative interaction, where the contributions of listeners/interpreters enable a testifier/confessor to believe the "truth" that she/he might previously have known as detached information, not as a truth that demands assent; or might have known but not realized that she/he did.... The testimonial process—for the occupants of both the testifying and the listening position(s)—assimilates the propositional-informational substance of the exchange, and inscribes (records) it into the ongoing doxastic stories of these lives. Yet the incredulity of the listeners can block its passage altogether.

At this point it is worth adding one more twist to this story. For incredulity is multidimensional: it is not all bad, and indeed it has a positive, emancipatory, strategic aspect. Feminist consciousness-raising and interpretive-genealogical projects have demonstrated the power of an ongoing, strategic skepticism[10] that is integral to transformative political discussion, and to advice-giving and -taking in situations of unequal power and authority. They have appealed to the effectiveness of incredulity as a parodic mode of "refusal" ... that can function as a peculiarly effective political tool. So the solution to the problems I am addressing cannot be to recommend a naive "experientialism," according to which experience is always to be regarded as a pure unmediated given, and first-person experiential reports are treated as inviolate, sacrosanct, closed to interpretation, challenge, and debate.[11] ... I am suggesting that some version of a principle of charity, belief, and trust has to govern discursive encounters marked by a power/privilege differential, if confrontational impasse and might overriding right are to be avoided. But that principle may manifest itself as propitiously in interpretive debate as in simply taking a testifier at her word. And it will not always be clear from the outset whether interpretation or straightforward credulity is required.

The questions generated by discriminatory incredulity, then, are located at the intersection of mainstream epistemology's analyses of testimony as a source of knowledge, philosophical prohibitions on *ad hominem* argumentation, and taken-for-granted assumptions about the "nature" of knowers and of cognitive agency. They are neither strictly epistemological nor strictly moral-political questions: indeed, they point to the artificiality of drawing boundaries between these areas of inquiry.[12] The problem I am addressing is that of how feminists and others, who know they are not operating on a level playing field, can negotiate the legitimate demands that they (we) take one another's experiences seriously, and yet can resist the temptation to substitute a new tyranny of "experientialism" immune to discussion for the old and persistent tyrannies of incredulity, denigration, and distrust....

EPISTEMOLOGY AND TESTIMONY

Anglo-American epistemologists commonly name perception, memory, and testimony as the sources of human knowledge. Of this trio, they tend to represent perception as the most secure and reliable source; memory as more fallible, less stable; and testimony as the least reliable, most uncertain of the three. This ranking derives from presuppositions central to positivist-empiricist theories of knowledge ... where stylized, propositional, observational knowledge claims based in first-personal, perceptual events count as paradigmatic for knowledge in general. It is reinforced by a concomitant conception of the epistemic agent, whose presumed self-sufficiency and open receptivity are thought to ensure that his immediate perceptions, in "normal" or ideal observation conditions, will yield the best possible knowledge. Memory enables him to sort and match perceptions; both for classical empiricists—most notably Hume and Russell—and for their recent successors, such as Goldman and Foley, its reliability appears to vary only with the vividness of the sensory experiences in which it originates. Testimony, even in the restricted form of "knowledge by description" tends, by contrast, to be an altogether dicey affair: its esteem ranks more with hearsay, gossip, mere opinion than with perceptions reported at one remove, even when it amounts to communally confirmed and corroborated reports of perceived events. In short, knowledge of matters unavailable to direct observation does not fare well in the dominant classical and post-positivist empiricist traditions.

This distrust of testimony is curious because only a minute proportion both of communal and of "individual" knowledge indeed derives from firsthand experiences. It is still more puzzling when inquiry moves from the rarefied places where epistemologists work, and the sanitized examples on which they base their conclusions, into the places where testimony, in a much richer than merely information-reporting sense, becomes the principal stuff of which knowledge is made and on which policies, practices, and actions depend. Courts of law, media reportage, classrooms, consulting rooms, confessionals, professional and intimate conversations are just some of the more obvious places where the knowledge constitutive of attitudes and actions derives principally from testimony.

In all of these places, and in others like them, testimony would seem to be the epistemic mode in which "the knower" cannot easily be represented as an isolated, self-sufficient creature, even on a traditional "one man, one knowledge claim" conception of knowledge. Whereas perception- and memory-stating knowledge claims commonly pose as purely monologic, as though no interlocutor were necessary to their completion, a testimonial report looks to its listener(s) for evidence of comprehension, acknowledgment. For testimony is, inherently, a form of address in which epistemic interaction, intersubjectivity are explicitly invoked. Hence it would appear to be a place where epistemic individualism could no longer hold, and where ethical-political questions would quite naturally enter the discourse of epistemology. Yet epistemologists have sought to assimilate testimony to the monologic model rather than allowing it to pose difficulties for the assumptions on which such a model is based. They have tended to concentrate on circumstances where a testimonial utterance becomes another perception—this time an auditory one—in a personal set of knowledge-producing observations.[14] The speaker may be lying or mistaken, and hence the testimonial process may fail to transmit knowledge;[15] but in this failure it does not differ significantly from perceptual error or faulty memory. Such approaches do not merely fail to notice the constitutive role of an interpreter/listener in fostering or thwarting validation of a testimonial knowledge claim; they actually work to subsume that role under an observational model. Hence they preserve the self-centered character of most standard epistemologies, reinforcing the assumption that giving or hearing testimony invokes no more significant moral-political issues than do acts of perceiving tables and chairs. In these analyses, hearing, like seeing, is believing.

Plainly, such analyses of testimony operate just as closely with an interchangeability-substitutability picture of the interpreter/listener, to whom any testimonial utterance is at least implicitly addressed, as purely observational analyses work with assumptions about the neutral observer. Nor are they simply to be condemned for so doing, for people in everyday situations often, and appropriately, assume some degree of neutral and ubiquitous availability of testimonial knowledge. On occasions when a straightforward exchange of information is involved, the appeal of such a model is clear. I should be able to ask any number of a diverse group of judiciously selected acquaintances, peers, and even strangers, interchangeably, who won the election, or where the film is playing, and to receive the same (testimonial) information anyone else would. I may have to search a little for someone who knows, but the assumption that governs such exchanges is that anyone who does know will tell me as accurately as she/he can, and that her or his willingness to offer information will be a matter-of-course aspect of social cognitive interaction.... When analyses of testimony are based in such exchanges—on which large parts of most people's everyday lives depend—it is easy to see why philosophers would consider them merely to be somewhat complex, and less-than-ideally secure, variants on a standard perceptual model.... Their apparent reducibility reinforces the impression that no special analysis is needed.

Reducing testimony to disengaged moments of information exchange flattens the inter-subjective dimension of such moments, so that it becomes little more than a formal necessity in an information-conveying process. And when these simple exchanges are represented as para-digmatic for testimonial—and confessional—events in circumstances and locations of greater complexity, the apolitical presumption they sustain works to deflect questions about differences of power and epistemic privilege among testifiers and listeners. Yet such differences, in fact, contest any assumption to the effect that interlocutors, in general, are simply interchangeable. On the contrary, testimonial exchanges are often tangled negotiations where it matters who the participants are, and where issues of differential credulity and credibility cannot be ignored. Such exchanges require assessment not just of the warrant of the knowledge claims that circulate within them, but of the credibility of the "master of truth," and of the power-saturated processes that enable or obstruct its production.

Now some critics will object that few epistemologists, nowadays, operate with so stark a model as I have sketched; hence that few would endorse so bare and experientially inadequate an account of testimony. I want, however, to introduce another twist into the discussion.... A "hearing is believing" presumption has trickled down from positivist-empiricist thinking to inform everyday folk wisdom, in lateearly twenty-first-century affluent societies, about what it means to know, and about what "we" should be able to expect from testimonial—especially "eyewitness"—reports. It prompts outrage when testimony is not taken at face value. And the assumption captures an element of liberal-democratic common sense which, I believe, is worthy of preservation. Yet the uneasy place that testimony occupies within these same epistemologies generates a curious tension which the protagonists in the Hill/Thomas hearings were able to turn to strategic ends. The hearings were presented to the North American public as inquiries conducted according to positivist-empiricist principles which ensured that everyone would say what she or he had to say, and that all the statements would be weighed fairly, equivalently, and openly. This presentational format produced the possibility of exploiting the resources of a power structure that obscured its own power behind a mask of monologic epistemic neutrality. Hence the very idea that who was believed and who met merely with incredulity had anything to do with who—specifically—they were could be represented as preposterous. Yet it was precisely the denial that such processes were at work that created a space in which they could proceed in all apparent innocence. And this mask of disinterested neutrality remained available even after the conclusion of the formal hearings. To cite just one example, Jane Mayer and Jill Abramson detail the ease with which investigative journalist David Brock donned that same mask in preparing his book, *The Real Anita Hill: The Untold Story.* They show how the packaging of the book as an "unbiased, revisionist look at the explosive hearings, which the author claims to have approached as an agnostic, willing to go wherever the facts led him"[16] creates a presumption of credibility for a work of research that is at best sloppy, at worst demonstrably duplicitous in its failures to report some pieces of evidence and its tendency to falsify others. Now Mayer's and Abramson's report has equally to be evaluated: my point is not that theirs automatically supersedes his. It is, rather, that such situations of weighing conflicting information, divergent testimonials that issue from contestable motivations and investments, are far more common in people's epistemic lives than uttering or receiving monologic knowledge claims. But Anglo-American epistemology alone does not have the resources to explicate the inhibiting and productive effects of such tensions. It informs and captures the "commonsense" for which "seeing is believing," even while it works to mask the structural implications of systematic incredulity.

Epistemological ambivalence about the reliability of testimony notwithstanding, liberal-democratic societies that take some version of post-positivist empiricism implicitly for granted foster the belief that if people just "tell it as it is," "speak the truth," "stick to the facts," then they will be heard and believed.... Moreover, the tacit rhetoric that shapes such societies promotes the assumption that would-be knowers are equally distributed across the epistemic terrain; and that everyone has equal and equivalent access to the discursive spaces where knowledge is claimed, corroborated, and contested. These assumptions count in favor of the perceptual model of testimony....

Yet feminists and other critics of empiricist-Enlightenment projects have demonstrated that "hearing is believing" expectations do not hold uniformly across the epistemic terrain. Indeed, where they hold at all—and such places are far fewer than adherents to this tradition optimistically assume—they tend to attach differentially according to the credibility of the testifier(s) and their solidarity with or differences from their interlocutors, rather than according to the simple strength of "the evidence." And credibility is by no means conferred only on the basis of a good epistemic record. Epistemologically, these issues are as much about subjectivity as they are about knowledge, and questions about who is speaking figure centrally in their analysis. Patricia Williams tells of her futile attempts to file a complaint about a racist incident. She observes: "I could not but wonder ... what it would take to make my experience verifiable. The testimony of an independent white bystander?" And she comments on "how the blind application of principles of neutrality ... acted either to make me look crazy or to make the reader participate in old habits of cultural bias."[17]

Such issues are not easily addressed within the discourse of mainstream epistemology, with its established presumption against granting credence to *ad hominem (ad feminam?)* argumentation, yet where the "who knows?" question evidently invites an *ad hominem* response.[18] When philosophy presents itself as a disinterested and universal/impartial pursuit of truth—indeed of the underlying and overarching truth of all truths—or as a quasi-scientific inquiry, the assumption is that the philosopher-as-thinker is a neutral vehicle through whom the truth passes untainted.... Yet a reevaluation of the traditional fallacy of the *ad hominem* argument is integral to any inquiry into the politics of knowledge.[19] And the need for that reevaluation renders too crude any clear distinction between simple observational knowledge claims and "invested" ones—those where the speaker has something of her/himself at stake. To show how this distinction becomes blurred in a revisioning of *ad hominem* arguments, I need to make an excursus through feminist and postmodern critiques of subjectivity as these pertain to questions of epistemic agency and accountability.

Prohibitions against appeals to *ad hominem* evidence derive their persuasiveness from a tacit endorsement of the interchangeability model of epistemic agency that I have referred to. These prohibitions assume that the truth merely passes, willy-nilly, through the cognitive (= observational) processes of the knowing subject. Would-be knowledge would be tainted, and hence weakened in its claim to truth, if in its passage it were to acquire the stamp of the knower's idiosyncrasies and/or invested interests. And indeed, one of the principal tasks of mainstream epistemology has been to devise ways of separating "pure" knowledge claims from sullied, tainted ones.... In this context, the *ad hominem* fallacy is a fallacy of asserting that the knower and his or her personal investments determine the truth or falsity of his or her claims to know; and in practice, any suggestion that a knower's specificities bear upon the status of her or his knowledge has come to amount to a commission of this fallacy and thus to count as a reason for discrediting the alleged knowledge....

I am proposing that a reevaluation of *ad hominem* evidence is central to the projects of developing the emancipatory epistemologies that many feminists and other post-Enlightenment critics (I among them) are engaged in: epistemologies, that is to say, that focus, among other things, upon the "whose knowledge?" question. And in consequence I am assuming that most knowledge claims—including observational ones—are indeed to some extent invested claims, and in ways that cannot always be determined before the fact.... Such critical investigations depend for their structure and content, at least in part, on the conception of subjectivity operative within them.

Despite their persuasiveness, postmodern critiques of the uniform and coherent conceptions of subjectivity, which they attribute to humanism or to the Enlightenment tradition, bypass a vital feature of the very possibility of human survival to chronological maturity. I am referring to the fact that it is not possible to lead a minimally coherent human life unless one's environment, both material and human, sustains a core of realist-empiricist assumptions. Developmentally, children learn to negotiate the world through processes of establishing reasonably fixed, constant expectations about the behaviors and "natures" of the people and things around them. Could they not do so, their survival would be in constant jeopardy; could they do so only erratically, their sanity would be similarly in jeopardy. Most of what people come to know, from the language into which they are born and educated, to the manners, customs, and cultural expectations they ingest, are items and ways of being that they learn from other people.... In societies where people are surrounded by predictable events, objects, and other people, these processes generate a fundamental, commonsense presumption in favor of a quotidian empiricism/realism whose implications are as ontologically as they are epistemologically, and morally/politically, significant. Hence "most people" (leaving the extension of that phrase vague) are—and have to be—empiricists/realists in their everyday lives; and contestations of uniform subjectivity take place around a core of relative stability.[20]

Ontologically, for all the evanescence of subjectivity, I could not be the person I am without a relational, cultural-historical-racial history, a fairly constant set of relationships or lack thereof, a fairly well-defined place—or lack of place—in a network of overlapping expectations: without a sense, however blurred, revisable, or evolving about who I am and what the world is that I am part of. Epistemologically, the very possibility of experiencing the world as "this person," knowing my surroundings, and interacting with other "this (those) person(s)" is produced by and produces expectations that things and other people are really there or not there, independent of my wishes and fantasies. It presupposes that I can know how things are reliably enough to move about them, and to negotiate/be with other people. These epistemological expectations are likewise constitutive of subjectivity; they frame its fluidity and its fixity.[21] And they are equally constitutive of the possibilities of moral-political actions, just as such actions in turn, are ontologically formative and epistemologically crucial. Because of the extent to which everyday knowledge is a product of testimony, of teaching, the cognitive core of a viable subjectivity has to be built around expectations that other people will testify "truly," and that I can act, even to the point of entrusting my life, on the basis of information I gain from them.... Both reaffirmations of the reasonableness of placing one's trust in such circumstances, and refusals to do so, commonly—and correctly—are based in *ad hominem* assertions.... It is now a commonplace in feminist and other critiques of post-Enlightenment epistemology and moral-political theory that when a stark, often atomistic, conception of subjectivity shapes theories of knowledge and action, sociality is erased for theoretical purposes, treated as incidental or intrusive; as something to be overcome in processes of maturation from the inevitable dependency of infancy and childhood....

I have proposed, by contrast, that persons are essentially second persons, and have offered a dialogic, fundamentally relational reading of subjectivity that starts from acknowledging the enabling—indeed, the *sine qua non*—features of intersubjectivity in the production of human selves, even as it acknowledges their constraining aspects.[23]... I am claiming that human beings are social creatures all the way down; and sociality is embedded in and shaped by all of the myriad story lines into which each of us is thrust at birth. Subjectivity is produced and continually reproduced out of a multiplicity of crisscrossing, sometimes mutually supportive and sometimes conflictual, discursive, dialogic relations which are lived not on a geographic analogue of a *tabula rasa,* but in specific rhetorical locations—spatial, historical, racial, cultural, gendered—themselves embedded in and part of the ongoing stasis and flux of narrative ways of making sense. Hence every life is always already partially scripted, partially contained within preexisting narrative lines.... So the incredulity issue becomes an issue about stories, scripts, and improvisations: about how some story lines pull people back from being able "freely and honestly" to speak the truth, tell it as it is, about even the simplest of everyday things. And about the inertia that some story lines foster in their resistance to improvisation, even as they assure "us" of a place in the world, a sense of where and how and who to be, without which we might be utterly at sea. Thus Wahneema Lubiano comments that "in [the Hill-Thomas] debate 'Anita Hill' and 'Emma Mae Martin' were not actually existing individuals as much as they were narrative stand-ins for certain properties of the mythic black-lady and welfare-queen categories. The names of the two actually existing women became increasing [sic] unimportant as the 'names' for their 'types' took over the discourse."[25]

And Shoshana Felman writes (referring to Camus): "The Plague (the Holocaust) is disbelieved because it does not enter, and cannot be framed by, any existing frame of reference (be it of knowledge or belief)."[26] Incredulity may not threaten all the way down, but when there is a presumption in its favor—and some story lines generate just such a presumption—then even the simplest of utterances may be heard "askance," skeptically. And the apparent distinction between observational and "invested" knowledge claims is noticeably blurred.

LIFE STORIES, TESTIMONIAL OPTIONS

The idea that lives are embedded in and lived along received, culturally sanctioned story lines is not a new one. Indeed, a "narrative" model of subjectivity and selfhood has enjoyed considerable favor in Anglo-American philosophy, especially since the 1981 publication of Alasdair MacIntyre's *After Virtue.* MacIntyre argues that cultures are shaped around certain stock characters who become models of emulation and aspiration, exemplars of ways of living.... For him, characters are more and other than mere social roles. They embody current moral, political, social thinking, and are the principal actors in the social scripts that articulate the ways of life available in any society—both those that should be achieved, and those that should be avoided.

Advanced in the interests of advocating a return to traditional moral values in an era where Nietzschean chaos threatens, it is no wonder that MacIntyre's argument—despite the appeal of its central insight—should have a decidedly conservative flavor. Not only are the exemplars he holds up for emulation without exception male, they are also "respectable public figures" whose values are those of the white, propertied, educated classes of the heyday of colonial imperialism. Yet he does not doubt that they represent the best of human possibilities. Hence Sabina Lovibond asks, ironically, "whether the female half of the population can reasonably be asked to piece itself together out of the semiotic fallout from [MacIntyre's] sources." She continues:

> our *effective* mythology, the one which actually determines the customary ethics of the (post)modern world, invites us to interpret ourselves and our neighbours in terms of a rather more topical range of "imputed characters": good mothers, bad mothers, ruthless career women, gorgeous (dumb) blondes, ordinary housewives, *women who are no better than they should be,* loony lesbian feminists covered with badges ... anyone who ever reads a newspaper or watches TV can continue the list.[28]

In the Anita Hill/Clarence Thomas encounter and—albeit differently—in the testimonial analyses of Holocaust literature, the protagonists exploited and/or were exploited by "effective mythologies" peopled by "imputed characters" into whose scripts their testimony was molded, or against which it was contrasted, as though to ensure that they would be unable to produce the "truth" about what happened.... This media-saturated age offers a plethora of such ready-mades into which to fit "new" experiences, evidence—to tame their newness, their potentially unsettling effects, their "danger." "Mammy, welfare cheat, Jezebel, period. These were the roles available to Anita Hill."[30]

As I have argued elsewhere, stereotypes are the bearers of attributes and characteristics that have congealed into instruments for summing up and managing the unmanageables that startling or challenging testimony might present.[31] In the Hill-Thomas hearings, stereotypes circulate out of control, blocking access to the evidence Hill speaks. And the situation is more complex than a mere listing of available roles and stereotypes can convey. For stereotyping cannot be contested or erased by simple personal refusals to comply. On the contrary, there is a peculiar elasticity to stereotypical roles and options, which produces the result that their occupant is damned either way. Nellie McKay notes that "because Anita Hill is black and a woman, but fits none of the stereotypes of black women to which most white people are accustomed (the mammy, the slut, the virago, etc.) these men could find no reference point for her, and therefore she had no believability for them."[32] She has no believability because she does not fit the scripts, even as she has no believability when she does.... One further note needs to be added to this scenario: Wahneema Lubiano's observation about the curious process by which narratives and the stock characters within them become naturalized so that they can be read as depicting how women, men, blacks really, naturally are. "Such narratives are so naturalized, so pushed by the momentum of their ubiquity, that they seem to be reality."[34] In brief, Hill's plausibility in the role of a woman complaining about sexual harassment was "dependent upon the degree to which she could be fit within the dominant images of sexual victimization."[35]

What is at issue here is not simply prejudice, of which a "good liberal" could be cautioned to disencumber himself. Rather it is a question of coherent prejudgments that are sanctioned and maintained by dominant social narratives.... Claudia Lacour argues that, in declaring himself a victim of racism, Thomas erased Hill's charges, disempowered her testimony. She remarks: "If the threat of the use of the word 'racism' kept even the mention of Professor Hill out of the proceedings to begin with, the actual use of the word made her eventual testimony insignificant ... 'racism,' the literally meaningless speech act aimed at a black woman, freed white (and many black) Americans from thinking about racism."[37] And according to Manning Marable, "Senator Strom Thurmond of South Carolina declared Hill's allegations to be 'totally without merit,' even *before* listening to her testimony!"[38]

The Holocaust testimonials produce an analogous aporia in the place of the acknowledgment on which knowledge depends. And those who maintain silence are as fully implicated as those who actively refuse to hear. Thus Felman, writing of the narrator in Camus's *The Fall:* "Silence ... is not a simple absence of an act of speech, but a positive avoidance—and erasure—of one's hearing, the positive *assertion* of a deafness, in the refusal not merely to know but to *acknowledge* ... what is being heard or witnessed."[39]

What is of especial pertinence for thinking, then, about incredulity is how these already-running narratives with their takeaway metaphors and images provide and constrain possibilities of self-interpretation and self-presentation, and—more crucially—how they shape and constrain listening.... Listeners, too, listen through available narratives, stories, character possibilities, stereotypes. Sometimes such narratives perform the preliminary work that ensures that they are open, prepared and able to hear (on the model of good therapy). But in the tangled situations where incredulity prevails, they work rather to ensure that the listeners do not hear. And they work across the whole range from simple information-giving to the places where the "truth" is indeed generated, produced in the telling. A black man is asked at an accident scene: "Were you wearing a seat belt?" When his affirmative response is heard askance, the incredulity is not about the information conveyed, but about him, about the story into which he is slotted.... Here a simple informational exchange is no longer just that, in the structures of credulity and incredulity that inform the social order. And here, too, the appeal of an empiricist analysis of testimony is strongest: the interests of justice seem to demand such a model.

Yet the situation does not call just for individual self-improvement either on the part of the teller or the listener. It is a matter of working out, collectively, how to produce and circulate new scripts, how to devise improvisational possibilities that can unsettle and disrupt story lines that are apparently seamless, unable to admit of unexpected or novel twists in the plot. And that working out, both in the Hill-Thomas hearing and the Holocaust testimonials (albeit quite differently in each) has to occur in largely uncharted territory, where the rules for how to listen, how to hear, how to act are not properly in place. For at these moments whole clusters of taken-for-granted social assumptions are under strain. These situations recall Cheshire Calhoun's thought-provoking analysis of what she calls "abnormal moral contexts": places where, she believes, most feminist moral critique—and, I would add, most socially transformative critique—occurs. Calhoun observes that "average moral citizens [seem to be] ... responsible for applying accepted moral canons (e.g. against exploiting others) to cases not covered, or incorrectly covered, in the social stock of moral knowledge.... [T]heir ignorance is not simply due to an uncooperative world. Their participation in oppressive social practices helps sustain the social acceptance of those practices."[41]

In this [reading] I have been discussing situations in which the testifiers are speaking at the limits of available moral knowledge; at a moral frontier where assumptions of shared, communal rules and expectations break down and have to be reshaped. The participants cannot simply be exonerated with the excuse that they could not have known differently: naming the reasons cannot be permitted to "backfire into sanctioning."[42] Calhoun's is a persuasive argument for requiring moral transformation, for ongoing political activism committed to disrupting sedimented oppressive practices, not so much individually as socially, communally; and not as single, monologic refusals, but as ongoing, critical, dialogic negotiations.

In his book *Inconvenient Fictions*, Bernard Harrison draws a useful distinction between what he calls "knowledge as amenity," and "*dangerous* knowledge," the latter defined as knowledge that "has the potentiality to set the established structures of my self in motion towards change."[43] Noting that dominant paradigms of knowledge in western societies restrict knowledge to impersonal facts—knowledge as amenity—Harrison names literature in general, and especially narrative fiction, as a source of dangerous knowledge. He suggests that "the peculiar value of literature in a culture such as ours, the thing which really does make it essential to a civilized society, is its power to act as a standing rebuke and irritant to the dominant paradigm of knowledge."[44] The distinction between the two "kinds" of knowledge is not, I think, so neat as Harrison suggests. Some knowledge that seems to be purely factual can unsettle in much the same way as dangerous knowledge; and some situations erect analogous blocks against acknowledging it. And other "stories" can be equivalently dangerous, disruptive.[45] These points do not detract from Harrison's distinction, but they suggest refinements that could enhance its heuristic potential. By contrast with MacIntyre, who looks to narrative for examples of safety—in confirmed and confirming narrative possibilities—Harrison lauds its unsettling powers; its capacities to break with traditions, standards, entrenched opinions and presuppositions. His proposals cast another light on incredulity, too, suggesting that some forms of incredulity work as defenses—perhaps subconscious defenses, and in any case not always properties of individual psychologies—but collective (at least for some part of the collectivity) defenses against unsettling truths, dangerous truths, that threaten the stability of story lines, categories, explanatory possibilities that are firmly in place and constitutive of the self-construction of the culture or of relevant sections thereof.

Framed within these general lines of inquiry, then, Morrison's collection and the Felman-Laub book emerge as (Foucauldian) genealogical investigations of some of the local effects of power within knowledge-producing practices and social structures. They show how certain truths and certain would-be truth-tellers simply cannot get past the gatekeepers to the rhetorical spaces where what "really" happened could be told.

Whereas MacIntyre holds exemplars out in front of his readers like mirrors, goals, a *telos* toward which, well-intentioned, "we" strive, Foucault digs beneath the surface of everyday and extraordinary discourse, showing how the everyday seeks to tame the extraordinary, to find a place for it that subsumes and assimilates its very extraordinariness, making it possible to "record" it within preexisting categories. Hence, moving to the psychological level, the sheer amazement and frustration of saying just what happened and finding one's statement moved sideways, slotted in elsewhere, no longer conveying what it is meant to say.

As I have picked up these story lines here I have simplified them, perhaps unjustly. Barbara Houston, for example, remarks that the question "What is the truth of Anita Hill's experience?" is more complex than I allow, and that the responses the hearings have generated do not divide neatly into those would-be truths that go through, and those that do not.[46] Questions persist about where to place belief—and culpability—in the multilayered issues of truth and falsity that are at play, where the discourse of testimonial evidence is stretched beyond what any available epistemic analysis can accommodate. Her observations are well taken: this essay, as I see it, is only a beginning of a long, complex inquiry.

CONCLUSION

... Reading across the residual empiricism that produces expectations that should issue in a confirmation that I can mean what I say and be heard accordingly, I have tried to show—phenomenologically—how things do not in fact work so easily. But at the end of this initial tracing of the genealogies, what do we have? Perhaps only a better map of one or two localities; a sense of some interconnections; a realization of how much work needs to be done. Perhaps also a sense of the impotence of mere personal outrage; and of the need always to look beneath the surface before taken-for-granted categories are scripted into the putative knowledge that informs and generates action. Dislodging the entrenched and nearly ossified story lines that produce ongoing incredulity is not a matter just of saying it isn't so, but of finding more and ever more communally crafted stories, more and ever more ways of fueling a strategic skepticism....

Ontologically, at the level of subjectivity and selfhood, these are questions about what it is to be believ*able*. They differ from simpler questions about being believed, which are merely episodic, evoking a model of an autonomous knower face to face with possibilities and options which it is prudent to choose or not to choose. Being believable is about how one is, how one puts together one's sense of self within the improvisation possibilities that the multiple stories in which one is a participant can allow....

Donna Haraway aptly observes that "struggles over what will count as rational accounts of the world are struggles over *how* to see."[50] Still more complex, I am suggesting, are struggles over how to hear and be heard; questions about how people can devise strategies for survival when they occupy marginalized and disempowered positions where they are muted by incredulity to the point that silence becomes their only viable option.

NOTES

1. Michel Foucault, *The History of Sexuality,* Volume I: *An Introduction.* Translated by Robert Hurley. New York: Vintage, 1980, pp. 66–67. Joseph Rouse discusses some epistemological implications of this passage in his *Knowledge and Power: Toward a Political Philosophy of Science.* Ithaca: Cornell University Press, 1987, pp. 218–220.

2. Manning Marable cites a 1991 study according to which only "one out of eight women who had been sexually harassed actually reported the incident. Like [Anita] Hill, they knew that without hard evidence their assertions were unlikely to be believed." Manning Marable, "Clarence Thomas and the Crisis of Black Political Culture." In Toni Morrison, ed., *Race-ing Justice, En-gendering Power: Essays on Anita Hill, Clarence Thomas, and the Construction of Social Reality.* New York: Pantheon Books, 1992, p. 66.

3. See Toni Morrison, *Race-ing Justice, En-gendering Power,* and Shoshana Felman and Dori Laub, *Testimony: Crises of Witnessing in Literature, Psychoanalysis, and History.* New York: Routledge, 1992.

4. I address issues of acknowledgement also in chapter 5, "Women and Experts," of my *What Can She Know?* where my discussion centers on Wittgenstein's observation that "knowledge is in the end based on acknowledgement." (See Ludwig Wittgenstein, *On Certainty*. Edited by G.E.M. Anscombe and G.H. von Wright. Translated by Denis Paul and G.E.M. Anscombe. New York: Harper Torchbooks, 1971. #378.)

5. Kimberle Crenshaw, "Whose Story Is It Anyway? Feminist and Antiracist Appropriations of Anita Hill." In Toni Morrison, ed., *Race-ing Justice, En-gendering Power,* pp. 403–404.

6. *Testimony,* p. 68. Italics in original.

...

8. Donna Haraway, "Situated Knowledges: The Science Question in Feminism and the Privilege of Partial Perspective." In Donna Haraway, *Simians, Cyborgs, and Women: The Reinvention of Nature.* New York: Routledge, 1991, p. 193.

...

10. By "strategic skepticism" I mean, for example, the "healthy skepticism" that parents teach their children about media advertising, and that marks cautiously informed attitudes to political promises which I refer to in chapter two.

11. For a pertinent critique of experientialism, see Judith Grant, "I Feel Therefore I Am: A Critique of Female Experience as the Basis for a Feminist Epistemology." *Women and Politics* 7, No. 3, 1987, pp. 99–114. Donna Haraway observes: "We are not immediately present to ourselves." "Situated Knowledges," p. 192.

12. I discuss the artificiality of such boundaries in my *Epistemic Responsibility.*

...

14. See especially Elizabeth Fricker, "The Epistemology of Testimony," *Aristotelian Society Supplementary Volume,* 1987. Fricker acknowledges an indebtedness in her analysis to C.A.J. Coady, "Testimony and Observation," *American Philosophical Quarterly,* 1973; and to John McDowell, for his "Meaning, Communication, and Knowledge," in Z. Van Straaten, ed., *Philosophical Subjects.* Oxford: Clarendon Press, 1980, and his "Antirealism and the epistemology of understanding," in H. Parret and J. Bouveresse, eds., *Meaning and Understanding.* Berlin: Gruyter, 1981.

15. Cf. Fricker, p. 68.

16. Jill Mayer and Jill Abramson, "The Surreal Anita Hill." *The New Yorker,* May 24, 1993, p. 90. The book in question is David Brock, *The Real Anita Hill: The Untold Story.* New York: Macmillan, Free Press, 1992.

17. Patricia Williams, *The Alchemy of Race and Rights,* pp. 47, 48.

18. But see Alan Brinton, "A Rhetorical View of the *Ad Hominem." Australasian Journal of Philosophy* 63, No. 1, March 1985, pp. 50–63. Brinton concludes: "There are in general, but also relative to particular contexts, certain presuppositions of discourse and of argumentation. Especially important ... are some having to do with the credentials, commitments, and intentions of those who participate, and especially of those who take the lead. The *ad hominem* typically raises doubts about whether these ethotic presuppositions have been fulfilled," p. 62.

19. In this suggestion I part company with Foucault's oft-cited endorsement of Samuel Beckett's comment: "What matter who's speaking, someone said, what matter who's speaking." Foucault observes: "In an indifference such as this we must recognize one of the fundamental ethical principles of contemporary writing." Michel Foucault, "What Is an Author?" In Donald F. Bouchard, ed., *Language, Counter-Memory, Practice: Selected Essays and Interviews by Michel Foucault.* Translated by Donald Bouchard and Sherry Simon. Ithaca: Cornell University Press, 1977, pp. 115–16. Yet Foucault takes a somewhat different tack in "The Functions of Literature," translated by Alan Sheridan. In Lawrence D. Kritzman, ed., *Michel Foucault: Politics, Philosophy, Culture: Interviews and Other Writings 1977–1984.* New York: Routledge, 1988, where he remarks that before 1970 the writer was a revolutionary, p. 310.

20. There is, I think, no tension between these claims and the mitigated relativism that I espouse in the last chapter of my *What Can She Know?* in chapter two of this book, "Taking Subjectivity into Account," and in chapter nine, "Must a Feminist Be a Relativist after All?" In all of these places I argue that relativism is, in fact, compatible with realism.

21. I envisage some effects of the breakdown of such expectations in chapter four of this book, "Persons, and Others."

...

23. See *What Can She Know?* especially chapter three.

...

25.   Wahneema Lubiano, "Black Ladies, Welfare Queens, and State Minstrels: Ideological War by Narrative Means." In Toni Morrison, ed., *Race-ing Justice, En-gendering Power,* p. 344.

...

28.   Sabina Lovibond, "Feminism and Postmodernism." *New Left Review* 178 (November–December 1989), 5–28, p. 23. Italics in original.

...

30.   Nell Irvin Painter, "Hill, Thomas, and the Use of Racial Stereotype." In Toni Morrison, ed., *Race-ing Justice, En-gendering Power,* p. 210.

31.   See *What Can She Know?* especially pp. 188–203 and 228–231.

32.   Nellie Y. McKay, "Remembering Anita Hill and Clarence Thomas: What Really Happened When One Black Woman Spoke Out." In Toni Morrison, ed., *Race-ing Justice, En-gendering Power,* p. 285.

...

34.   Lubiano, p. 329,

35.   Crenshaw, p. 407.

...

37.   Claudia Brodsky Latour, "Doing Things with Words: 'Racism' as Speech Act and the Undoing of Justice." In Toni Morrison, ed., *Race-ing Justice, En-gendering Power,* pp. 136, 140.

38.   Ibid., p. 68. Italics in original.

39.   *Testimony,* p. 183. Italics in original.

...

41.   Cheshire Calhoun, "Responsibility and Reproach." In Cass R. Sunstein, ed., *Feminism and Political Theory.* Chicago: University of Chicago Press, 1990, p. 248. Barbara Houston reminded me of the pertinence of Calhoun's discussion to these issues.

42.   Ibid., p. 255.

43.   Bernard Harrison, *Inconvenient Fictions: Literature and the Limits of Theory.* New Haven: Yale University Press, 1991, p. 3.

44.   Ibid., p. 4. Consider also Claudia Lacour's reference to "Socrates' scandalous exclusion of poets from his 'just' republic ... for a poet has the verbal power to play any part, to throw the 'justly' functioning machine of the republic into chaos by making us believe a function is being fulfilled—a part played rather than play-acted—when it is not." In Lacour, "Doing Things with Words," p. 153.

45.   With thoughts such as these in mind I argue for the value of a "storied epistemology" in chapter eight of this book, "Voice and Voicelessness: A Modest Proposal."

46.   Barbara Houston, "Commentary on 'Incredulity,'" paper presented at the Canadian Society for Women in Philosophy conference, Calgary, Canada, September 1993. I am grateful to Barbara Houston for her careful and insightful comments.

...

50.   "Situated Knowledges," p. 194. Italics in original.

9
Feminist Standpoint Theory: Social Location and Epistemic Privilege

Feminist standpoint epistemology goes beyond feminist empiricism in its account of knowledge creation. It seeks to give due weight not only to experience but also to the epistemic roles played by both social location and political commitment. It aims to develop an alternative to neopositivist objectivism, on the one hand, and to relativism, on the other. Feminist standpoint theory is sometimes traced back to Dorothy Smith's classic 1974 article, "Women's Perspective as a Radical Critique of Sociology," reprinted in this volume. However, the first explicit formulation was provided by political theorist Nancy Hartsock (1983). The theory has received its fullest development in the work of Sandra Harding (1991, 2004).

MARXIST STANDPOINT EPISTEMOLOGY

Hartsock borrowed the basic idea of standpoint epistemology from the 1930s Hungarian Marxist theoretician Georg Lukacs. Like other Marxists, Lukacs believed that people acquire knowledge not through a relatively passive process of observation but instead by engaging actively in the world in order to satisfy their distinctively human needs. For Marxists, knowledge is not the purely intellectual product of a detached spectator but instead is produced collectively through practical human involvement in changing the world; this involvement also changes humans themselves. Because knowledge is a social construction and its expansion a social project, it is never the achievement of a single isolated individual. It is true that individuals often contribute to the growth of knowledge, but their contributions are made possible and have meaning only as parts of larger socially constructed systems of knowledge.

Marxists believe that acquiring knowledge requires that people engage in the world both physically and intellectually. People must organize their experience by conceptual frameworks, which are influenced by the human physical apparatus and also by the needs and interests generated originally by our bodies. Since knowledge is one aspect of human productive activity, which is always purposive, the basic categories of knowledge are shaped by human purposes and values. Thus, even empirical and scientific knowledge is never entirely value-free. The conceptual frameworks by which we make sense of ourselves and our world are shaped and limited by the interests and values of the society that we inhabit. For instance, the Inuit people are said to make many more fine distinctions among types of snow than do people whose lives do not depend so closely on snow conditions.

Marxists are not alone in believing that knowledge is socially constructed through practical labor and shaped by human interests; pragmatists also hold a view something like this. However, Marxism is distinguished by its claim that economic class has epistemic relevance. Specifically, Marxism identifies the working class as occupying a social location that is in some respects epistemically privileged.

THE EPISTEMIC PRIVILEGE OF THE WORKING CLASS

Marxists view all knowledge as growing out of specific ways of life and in particular as emerging from specific modes of production, a view said to characterize materialist as opposed to idealist approaches to epistemology. In Marx's famous words, it is not consciousness that determines existence but existence that determines consciousness.

According to Marxist social analysis, all except the earliest societies are divided by class. The interests of the members of various classes are systematically opposed to each other, and many of their values conflict. In class-divided societies, prevailing systems of knowledge never reflect the interests and values of the society as a whole but instead reflect the interests and values of the dominant class. This is partly because, according to Marx in *The German Ideology,* "The class which has the means of material production at its disposal has control at the same time over the means of mental production, so that thereby, generally speaking, the ideas of those who lack the means of mental production are subject to it." For instance, the ruling class controls education and the media. In addition to these direct dominations over thought, the forms of daily life characteristic of particular societies generate historically specific forms of consciousness; people's life experiences make dominant systems of ideas seem more plausible or even inescapable. For instance, peasants who experience little personal mobility or power and limited technological change tend to think fatalistically of social circumstances as immutable; by contrast, many people under capitalism experience social circumstances as changing constantly and unpredictably and human nature as self-aggrandizing and competitive.

Although Marxists believe that class societies are governed by ruling systems of ideas, they think that such societies also contain ideas that are subversive of those systems. Foucault later came to call these ideas "subjugated knowledges," and noted that they may be developed by groups such as slaves or prisoners. In relatively stable times these ideas are suppressed by methods such as denying education and literacy to slaves and other likely dissenters; by funding and legitimating ideas that justify the status quo; by ridiculing dissenting ideas as superstitious, crazy, or subversive; by directly censoring dissenting ideas; and by persecuting dissenters. However, in periods of social upheaval, dissenting ideas are likely to surface, and they typically provide a stark contrast to dominant systems of knowledge. From the point of view of the capitalist, for instance, society looks very different from the way it appears to the working class. Members of the capitalist class typically portray life under capitalism as a world of freedom, human rights, and material abundance, and they view technology as a tool of progress. By contrast, capitalism often appears to members of the working class as a system of coercion, violence, and material scarcity, and technology often appears as a means of domination or enslavement.

Marxist standpoint epistemology is distinguished by its claim that the view of the world from the standpoint of the working class is not just different from that of the capitalist standpoint; it is also superior to it. For Marxists, the working class is the universal class, whose interests are those of humanity as a whole; unlike the capitalist class, therefore, the working class does not have an interest in presenting mystifying and distorted models of human nature and social reality, and so its ideas are likely to be less partial and more trustworthy. Marxists sometimes express this as a claim that the view of the world developed from the standpoint of the working class is scientific rather than ideological.

Marxist standpoint epistemology contrasts with classical empiricism in several ways. It denies that facts are sharply distinct from values and that science is value-neutral; it also denies the epistemic irrelevance of social location and the associated view that knowers are interchangeable. Like empiricism, however, Marxist standpoint epistemology rejects relativism and remains strongly committed to distinguishing between appearance and reality. The more positivist interpretations of Marxist standpoint theory seem also to preserve a commitment to the view that trustworthy knowledge must in some way correspond to or "mirror" reality; however, we will see shortly that feminist versions of standpoint theory tend to develop less objectivist, more pragmatist, conceptions of truth and objectivity.

THE STANDPOINT OF WOMEN

In the 1980s, some Western feminists drew on the Marxist idea of an epistemic standpoint to develop their own concept of the standpoint of women. They used this concept to explain how some systems of belief may be justified, relative to other systems, even though knowledge is always constructed in specific historical circumstances by particular social groups and embodies those groups' specific values and interests. Feminist standpoint theorists recognize that multiple ways of conceptualizing social reality, rationality, and justification exist, but they deny that this multiplicity necessarily entails cultural (or subjective) relativism.

To understand feminist standpoint theory, it is crucial to recognize that a standpoint is not an empirical perspective. It is not a bundle of beliefs actually held by any individual or group of individuals. Feminist standpoint theorists believe that the perceptions of most people in male-dominated societies, including most women, are distorted both by dominant systems of knowledge and by the structure of everyday life. For instance, they recognize that many women are not feminists, that many women think it is men's responsibility to "provide" for them and men's right to expect sexual services in return, that many women oppose the "choice" of abortion and often regard harassment as flattery, and that many women blame themselves when they are raped or subjected to domestic violence. Thus standpoint theorists do not equate the standpoint of women with the existing beliefs and attitudes of empirical women. No survey of women's actual thinking can reveal the standpoint of women, in the theoretical sense, although such a survey would be likely to identify commonalities that the standpoint would illuminate.

A standpoint is unlike a perspective in that it is a theoretical system of beliefs that incorporates some of the views held by members of a particular group but rejects other views. The system is said to express the group's standpoint not because it reflects every detail of what members of the group actually believe but because it presents issues of concern to them in ways that allow their objective interests to be revealed. Feminist standpoint theorists contend that the standpoint of women is epistemically superior to that of men because women have less interest than men in concealing inequality and injustice. The standpoint of women is more impartial than male-dominated systems of ideas because it comes closer to representing the interests of the society as a whole; it is more inclusive or comprehensive because it recognizes and demystifies dominant systems of knowledge.

Feminist standpoint theorists assert that the standpoint of women is discovered through collective political struggle on behalf of women. Women's distinctive social experiences generate insights incompatible with men's perceptions of reality, and these insights provide clues as to how reality might be interpreted from the standpoint of women. Political struggle provides an opportunity to test these insights and develop them into a systematic representation of reality that does not promote the interests of men above the interests of women. In the end, the epistemological superiority of women's standpoint can be demonstrated conclusively only through a distinctively feminist reconstruction of reality in which women's interests are promoted equally with those of men, a reconstruction that must be practical as well as theoretical.

FEMINIST CHALLENGES TO EARLY STANDPOINT THEORY

Like other epistemological theories, standpoint theory has been controversial among feminists. Because of the growing influence of postmodernism and anti-essentialism, the brief popularity that standpoint theory enjoyed in the early 1980s declined by the end of the decade.

Some critics objected to the implausibility of what they took to be standpoint theory's assertion that members of subordinated and marginalized groups automatically know more simply by virtue of their social/political location. However, the single most serious problem many feminists found with standpoint theory was that it seemed to postulate a distinct and unified category of "women," identified by biology or by a common experience of subordination. Standpoint theory was criticized for failing to recognize women's vast heterogeneity and the problematic character of the category "woman"; it was said to be essentialist in ignoring differences and especially inequalities among women. Its critics rejected what they took to be standpoint theory's "totalizing" aspirations to provide a single unified and comprehensive account of social reality. In their view, standpoint epistemology resembled other essentialist theories by providing yet another rationalization for privileged white women to speak on behalf of all women, and yet another rationalization for elitism and authoritarianism.

If standpoint theorists responded to these charges by postulating multiple standpoints of women, they faced the challenge of providing criteria for distinguishing among them. How could the supposed standpoint of women avoid fragmenting into innumerable individual perspectives? Even if nonarbitrary criteria for distinguishing among groups were provided, how could standpoint theorists determine which social location was the most privileged epistemically? Did recourse to standpoint theory require raising again the unanswerable and bitterly divisive question of which group of women was most oppressed? Standpoint theory seemed to be able to avoid authoritarianism or dogmatism only at the cost of falling into group relativism or even individual subjectivism.

THE PROMISE OF STANDPOINT THEORY

At the turn of the twenty-first century, some feminists developed responses to the criticisms of standpoint theory that had been made in the 1980s (Wylie 2004). They asserted that many of these criticisms rested on misreadings and misunderstandings, and were sometimes traceable to the critics' limited acquaintance with Marxist theory. They pointed out that Marxist epistemology is not concerned with individual beliefs and their relation to idiosyncratic life experiences but rather with the collective construction of knowledge and the ways in which this process is shaped and limited by social structures such as gender, class, and race. Standpoint theory does not claim that individual members of subordinated groups have automatic knowledge of the structure of social reality; it simply claims that occupying a certain social location may facilitate or block the achievement of certain insights. For instance, Patricia Hill Collins describes how black women domestics, whose social location compels them to negotiate the world of the privileged, are likely to know things that their employers, because of their social location and social interests, are invested in systematically ignoring and denying.

Recent standpoint theorists disavow any commitment to a reified or unified category of women. They recognize that individuals belong to multiple and overlapping social groups, and they assert that the insights made available by an individual's membership in a particular group are not necessarily incompatible with each other but instead may be convergent and complementary; for this reason, using standpoint theory does not require asking which group is the most oppressed. Some standpoint theorists have acknowledged the importance of insights from members of groups that are not identifiable exclusively by gender, such as ethnic and racial minorities or people with disabilities; indeed men may make distinctive contributions to the construction of feminist knowledge.

Concerns about competition among various standpoints may be reduced by recognizing that particular social locations confer epistemic advantage only with respect to particular epistemic projects. Uma Narayan notes that the oppressed "have epistemic privilege when it comes to immediate knowledge of everyday life under oppression" (1988:36), but that this epistemic advantage is neither automatic nor all-encompassing. Alison Wylie observes that although *maquiladora* workers are likely to know how work disciplines are manipulated to extract maximum profit and are likely to be familiar with specific injustices, they may well not understand the movements of international capital that bring a factory to Mexico from West Virginia and then move it to Indonesia. So standpoint theory does not assert that the oppressed are infallible authorities even on their own oppression, and certainly it does not assert that they are authorities on everything.

SOME METHODOLOGICAL IMPLICATIONS OF STANDPOINT THEORY

Standpoint theory offers an approach to assessing the epistemic reliability of knowledge claims by taking into account the circumstances in which these claims were produced. Specifically, standpoint theory offers an approach to assessing the credibility of particular knowers in particular subject areas. Typically, it asserts the epistemic authority of individuals who have been discredited as knowers, especially those who are economically dispossessed, politically oppressed, and socially marginalized, and whose status as knowers is therefore likely to be doubted as unreliable, uneducated, and uninformed. Standpoint theory emphasizes that marginal social locations in fact offer certain epistemic advantages; it explains that by virtue of having to know how the world looks from more than one perspective, an insider-outsider has available a set of comparisons that make visible the assumptions underpinning dominant worldviews. Thus, standpoint theory asserts that it is precisely the occupation of marginal social locations that facilitates recognition of certain insights, yet concedes that these insights are limited and that insider-outsiders' claims to knowledge are fallible.

Standpoint theory also asserts that political commitments have epistemic relevance and so offers an explanation of how feminists, among others, have been able to make contributions to many fields. Feminists' political commitments have enabled them to recognize evidence that others have thought unimportant, to discern patterns that others have ignored, to question assumptions that have gone unnoticed and unchallenged, and sometimes to reframe the research agendas of their disciplines in the light of different questions. Their solidarity with those suffering from gender oppression enables them to dissociate critically from the accepted rationalizations of gender inequality.

Several methodological prescriptions are generated from standpoint theory's account of when reliance on particular knowledge claims is warranted by the conditions of those claims' production. First, standpoint theory gives us direction in selecting research projects, advising us to begin with questions that are problematic for those on society's underside, people who are impoverished or otherwise marginalized. Second, it recommends questioning the categories of ruling elites and managing bureaucracies. Third, it advises us to award varying degrees of credibility to different knowers, depending on their social location and political engagement relative to particular subjects. Finally, it requires that researchers approach their research reflexively, looking critically at their own social locations, interests, and commitments and critically assessing their own reliability as knowers.

REFERENCES

Harding, Sandra. 1991. *Whose Science? Whose Knowledge? Thinking from Women's Lives.* Ithaca, NY: Cornell University Press.
———. 2004. *The Feminist Standpoint Theory Reader: Intellectual and Political Controversies.* New York and London: Routledge.
Hartsock, Nancy C. M. 1983. *Money, Sex, and Power: Toward a Feminist Historical Materialism.* New York: Longman.
Narayan, Uma. 1989. "The Project of Feminist Epistemology: Perspectives from a Nonwestern Feminist," in *Gender/Body/Knowledge: Feminist Reconstructions of Being and Knowing,* ed. Uma Narayan with Susan R. Bordo. New Brunswick, NJ: Rutgers University Press, 1989, pp. 256–269.
Wylie, Alison. 2004. "Why Standpoint Matters," in *Whose Science? Whose Knowledge? Thinking from Women's Lives,* ed. Sandra Harding. Ithaca, NY: Cornell University Press, pp. 339–351.

PATRICIA HILL COLLINS
Learning from the Outsider Within: The Sociological Significance of Black Feminist Thought

Afro-American women have long been privy to some of the most intimate secrets of white society. Countless numbers of Black women have ridden buses to their white "families," where they not only cooked, cleaned, and executed other domestic duties, but where they also nurtured their "other" children, shrewdly offered guidance to their employers, and frequently became honorary members of their white "families." These women have seen white elites, both actual and aspiring, from perspectives largely obscured from their Black spouses and from these groups themselves.[1]

On one level, this "insider" relationship has been satisfying to all involved. The memoirs of affluent whites often mention their love for their Black "mothers," while accounts of Black domestic workers stress the sense of self-affirmation they experienced at seeing white power demystified—of knowing that it was not the intellect, talent, or humanity of their employers that supported their superior status, but largely just the advantages of racism.[2] But on another level, these same Black women knew they could never belong to their white "families." In spite of their involvement, they remained "outsiders."[3]

This "outsider within" status has provided a special standpoint on self, family, and society for Afro-American women.[4] A careful review of the emerging Black feminist literature reveals that many Black intellectuals, especially those in touch with their marginality in academic settings, tap this standpoint in producing distinctive analyses of race, class, and gender.... Black feminist historian E. Frances White (1984) suggests that Black women's ideas have been honed at the juncture between movements for racial and sexual equality and contends that Afro-American women have been pushed by "their marginalization in both arenas" to create Black feminism. Finally, Black feminist critic bell hooks captures the unique standpoint that the outsider within status can generate. In describing her small-town Kentucky childhood, she notes, "living as we did—on the edge—we developed a particular way of seeing reality. We looked both from the outside in and from the inside out ... we understood both" (1984:vii).

In spite of the obstacles that can confront outsiders within, such individuals can benefit from this status. Simmel's (1921) essay on the sociological significance of what he called the "stranger" offers a helpful starting point for understanding the largely unexplored area of Black female outsider within status and the usefulness of the standpoint it might produce. Some of the potential benefits of outsider within status include (1) Simmel's definition of "objectivity" as "a peculiar composition of nearness and remoteness, concern and indifference"; (2) the tendency for people to confide in a "stranger" in ways they never would with each other; and (3) the ability of the "stranger" to see patterns that may be more difficult for those immersed in the situation to see. Mannheim (1936) labels the "strangers" in academia "marginal intellectuals."...

Sociologists might benefit greatly from serious consideration of the emerging cross-disciplinary literature that I label Black feminist thought, precisely because, for many Afro-American female intellectuals, "marginality" has been an excitement to creativity.... Bringing this group—as well as others who share an outsider within status vis-à-vis sociology—into the center of analysis may reveal aspects of reality obscured by more orthodox approaches....

THREE KEY THEMES IN BLACK FEMINIST THOUGHT

Black feminist thought consists of ideas produced by Black women that clarify a standpoint of and for Black women. Several assumptions underlie this working definition. First, the definition suggests that it is impossible to separate the structure and thematic content of thought from the historical and material conditions shaping the lives of its producers (Berger and Luckmann, 1966; Mannheim, 1936). Therefore, while Black feminist thought may be recorded by others, it is produced by Black women. Second, the definition assumes that Black women possess a unique standpoint on, or perspective of, their experiences and that there will be certain commonalities of perception shared by Black women as a group. Third, while living life as Black women may produce certain commonalities of outlook, the diversity of class, region, age, and sexual orientation shaping individual Black women's lives has resulted in different expressions of these common themes.... Finally, the definition assumes that, while a Black woman's standpoint exists, its contours may not be clear to Black women themselves. Therefore, one role for Black female intellectuals is to produce facts and theories about the Black female experience that will clarify a Black woman's standpoint for Black women.

...

No one Black feminist platform exists from which one can measure the "correctness" of a particular thinker; nor should there be one. Rather, as I defined it above, there is a long and rich tradition of Black feminist thought.... The three themes I have chosen [in Black feminist thought] are not exhaustive but, in my assessment, they do represent the thrust of much of the existing dialogue.

The Meaning of Self-Definition and Self-Valuation

An affirmation of the importance of Black women's self-definition and self-valuation is the first key theme that pervades historical and contemporary statements of Black feminist thought. Self-definition involves challenging the political knowledge-validation process that has resulted in externally defined, stereotypical images of Afro-American womanhood. In contrast, self-valuation stresses the content of Black women's self-definitions—namely, replacing externally derived images with authentic Black female images.

Both Mae King's (1973) and Cheryl Gilkes's (1981) analyses of the importance of stereotypes offer useful insights for grasping the importance of Black women's self-definition. King suggests that stereotypes represent externally defined, controlling images of Afro-American womanhood that have been central to the dehumanization of Black women and the exploitation of Black women's labor. Gilkes points out that Black women's assertiveness in resisting the multifaceted oppression they experience has been a consistent threat to the status quo. As punishment, Black women have been assaulted with a variety of externally defined negative images designed to control assertive Black female behavior.

The value of King's and Gilkes's analyses lies in their emphasis on the function of stereotypes in controlling dominated groups. Both point out that replacing negative stereotypes with ostensibly positive ones can be equally problematic if the function of stereotypes as controlling images remains unrecognized. John Gwaltney's (1980) interview with Nancy White, a 73-year-old Black woman, suggests that ordinary Black women may also be aware of the power of these controlling images in their everyday experiences. In the following passage, Ms. White assesses the difference between the controlling images applied to Afro-American and white women as being those of degree, and not of kind: "My mother used to say that the black woman is the white man's mule and the white woman is his dog. Now, she said that to say this: we do the heavy work and get beat whether we do it well or not. But the white woman is closer to the master and he pats them on the head and lets them sleep in the house, but he ain't goin' treat neither one like he was dealing with a person" (1980:148). This passage suggests that while both groups are stereotyped, albeit in different ways, the function of the images is to dehumanize and control both groups. Seen in this light, it makes little sense, in the long run, for Black women to exchange one set of controlling images for another even if, in the short run, positive stereotypes bring better treatment.

The insistence on Black female self-definition reframes the entire dialogue from one of determining the technical accuracy of an image to one stressing the power dynamics underlying the very process of definition itself.... When Black women define themselves, they clearly reject the taken-for-granted assumption that those in positions granting them the authority to describe and analyze reality are entitled to do so. Regardless of the actual content of Black women's self-definitions, the act of insisting on Black female self-definition validates Black women's power as human subjects.

... While Black female self-definition speaks to the power dynamics involved in the act of defining images of self and community, the theme of Black female self-valuation addresses the actual content of these self-definitions. Many of the attributes extant in Black female stereotypes are actually distorted renderings of those aspects of Black female behavior seen as most threatening to white patriarchy (Gilkes, 1981; White, 1985). For example, aggressive Afro-American women are threatening because they challenge white patriarchal definitions of femininity. To ridicule assertive women by labeling them Sapphires reflects an effort to put all women in their place....

When Black females choose to value those aspects of Afro-American womanhood that are stereotyped, ridiculed, and maligned in academic scholarship and the popular media, they are actually questioning some of the basic ideas used to control dominated groups in general.... By defining and valuing assertiveness and other "unfeminine" qualities as necessary and functional attributes for Afro-American womanhood, Black women's self-valuation challenges the content of externally defined controlling images.

Black women's insistence on self-definition, self-valuation, and the necessity for a Black female-centered analysis is significant for two reasons. First, defining and valuing one's consciousness of one's own self-defined standpoint in the face of images that foster a self-definition as the objectified "other" is an important way of resisting the dehumanization essential to systems of domination....

One of the best examples of this process is described by Judith Rollins (1985). As part of her fieldwork on Black domestics, Rollins worked as a domestic for six months. She describes several incidents where her employers treated her as if she were not really present.... Rollins notes, "It was this aspect of servitude I found to be one of the strongest affronts to my dignity as a human being.... These gestures of ignoring my presence were not, I think, intended as insults; they were expressions of the employers' ability to annihilate the humanness and even, at times, the very existence of me, a servant and a black woman" (1985:209).

Racist and sexist ideologies both share the common feature of treating dominated groups—the "others"—as objects lacking full human subjectivity.... But if Black women refuse to accept their assigned status as the quintessential "other," then the entire rationale for such domination is challenged.

A second reason that Black female self-definition and self-valuation are significant concerns their value in allowing Afro-American women to reject internalized, psychological oppression (Baldwin, 1980). The potential damage of internalized control to Afro-American women's self-esteem can be great even to the prepared. Enduring the frequent assaults of controlling images requires considerable inner strength. Nancy White ... notes, "Now, you know that no woman is a dog or a mule, but if folks keep making you feel that way, if you don't have a mind of your own, you can start letting them tell you what you are" (Gwaltney 1980:152). Seen in this light, self-definition and self-valuation are not luxuries—they are necessary for Black female survival.

The Interlocking Nature of Oppression

Attention to the interlocking nature of race, gender, and class oppression is a second recurring theme in the works of Black feminists (Beale, 1970; Davis, 1981; Dill, 1983; hooks, 1981; Lewis,

1977; Murray, 1970; Steady, 1981).[9] While different sociohistorical periods may have increased the saliency of one or another type of oppression, the thesis of the linked nature of oppression has long pervaded Black feminist thought.... Black women's absence from organized feminist movements has mistakenly been attributed to a lack of feminist consciousness. In actuality, Black feminists have possessed an ideological commitment to addressing interlocking oppression yet have been excluded from arenas that would have allowed them to do so (Davis, 1981).

As Barbara Smith points out, "the concept of the simultaneity of oppression is still the crux of a Black feminist understanding of political reality and ... is one of the most significant ideological contributions of Black feminist thought" (1983:xxxii). This should come as no surprise since Black women should be among the first to realize that minimizing one form of oppression, while essential, may still leave them oppressed in other equally dehumanizing ways.... [U]nlike white women, they have no illusions that their whiteness will negate female subordination, and unlike Black men, they cannot use a questionable appeal to manhood to neutralize the stigma of being Black.

The Black feminist attention to the interlocking nature of oppression is significant for two reasons. First, this viewpoint shifts the entire focus of investigation from one aimed at explicating elements of race or gender or class oppression to one whose goal is to determine what the links are among these systems. The first approach typically prioritizes one form of oppression as being primary, then handles remaining types of oppression as variables within what is seen as the most important system.... In contrast, the more holistic approach implied in Black feminist thought treats the interaction among multiple systems as the object of study. Rather than adding to existing theories by inserting previously excluded variables, Black feminists aim to develop new theoretical interpretations of the interaction itself.

Black male scholars, white female scholars, and more recently Black feminists like bell hooks, may have identified one critical link among interlocking systems of oppression. These groups have pointed out that certain basic ideas crosscut multiple systems of domination. One such idea is either/or dualistic thinking, claimed by hooks to be "the central ideological component of all systems of domination in Western society" (1984:29).

... Either/or dualistic thinking, or what I will refer to as the construct of dichotomous oppositional difference, may be a philosophical lynchpin in systems of race, class, and gender opposition. One fundamental characteristic of this construct is the categorization of people, things, and ideas in terms of their difference from one another. For example, the terms in dichotomies such as black/white, male/female, reason/emotion, fact/opinion, and subject/object gain their meaning only in *relation* to their difference from their oppositional counterparts. Another fundamental characteristic of this construct is that difference is not complementary in that the halves of the dichotomy do not enhance each other. Rather, the dichotomous halves are different and inherently opposed to one another. A third and more important characteristic is that these oppositional relationships are intrinsically unstable. Since such dualities rarely represent different but equal relationships, the inherently unstable relationship is resolved by subordinating one half of each pair to the other. Thus, whites rule Blacks, males dominate females, reason is touted as superior to emotion in ascertaining truth, facts supercede opinion in evaluating knowledge, and subjects rule objects. Dichotomous oppositional differences invariably imply relationships of superiority and inferiority, hierarchical relationships that mesh with political economies of domination and subordination.

The oppression experienced by most Black women is shaped by their subordinate status in an array of either/or dualities. Afro-American women have been assigned the inferior half of several dualities, and this placement has been central to their continued domination. For example, the allegedly emotional, passionate nature of Afro-American women has long been used as a rationale for their sexual exploitation....

Either/or dualistic thinking is so pervasive that it suppresses other alternatives. As Dill points out, "the choice between identifying as black or female is a product of the patriarchal strategy of divide and conquer and the continued importance of class, patriarchal, and racial divisions, perpetuates such choices both within our consciousness and within the concrete realities of our daily lives" (1983:136). In spite of this difficulty, Black women experience oppression in a personal, holistic fashion and emerging Black feminist perspectives appear to be embracing an equally holistic analysis of oppression.

Second, Black feminist attention to the interlocking nature of oppression is significant in that this view implicitly involves an alternative humanist vision of societal organization.... Black feminists who see the simultaneity of oppression affecting Black women appear to be more sensitive to how these same oppressive systems affect Afro-American men, people of color, women, and the dominant group itself. Thus, while Black feminist activists may work on behalf of Black women, they rarely project separatist solutions to Black female oppression.

The Importance of Afro-American Women's Culture

A third key theme characterizing Black feminist thought involves efforts to redefine and explain the importance of Black women's culture. In doing so, Black feminists have not only uncovered previously unexplored areas of the Black female experience, but they have also identified concrete areas of social relations where Afro-American women create and pass on self-definitions and self-valuations essential to coping with the simultaneity of oppression they experience.

In contrast to views of culture stressing the unique, ahistorical values of a particular group, Black feminist approaches have placed greater emphasis on the role of historically specific political economies in explaining the endurance of certain cultural themes. The following definition of culture typifies the approach taken by many Black feminists. According to Mullings, culture is composed of "the symbols and values that create the ideological frame of reference through which people attempt to deal with the circumstances in which they find themselves. Culture ... is not composed of static, discrete traits moved from one locale to another. It is constantly changing and transformed, as new forms are created out of old ones. Thus culture ... does not arise out of nothing: it is created and modified by material conditions" (1986a:13).

Seen in this light, Black women's culture may help provide the ideological frame of reference—namely, the symbols and values of self-definition and self-valuation—that assist Black women in seeing the circumstances shaping race, class, and gender oppression. Moreover, Mullings' definition of culture suggests that the values which accompany self-definition and self-valuation will have concrete, material expression: they will be present in social institutions like church and family, in creative expression of art, music, and dance, and, if unsuppressed, in patterns of economic and political activity. Finally, this approach to culture stresses its historically concrete nature. While common themes may link Black women's lives, these themes will be experienced differently by Black women of different classes, ages, regions, and sexual preferences as well as by Black women in different historical settings. Thus there is no monolithic Black women's culture—rather, there are socially constructed Black women's cultures that collectively form Black women's culture.

The interest in redefining Black women's culture has directed attention to several unexplored areas of the Black female experience. One such area concerns the interpersonal relationships that Black women share with each other. It appears that the notion of sisterhood—generally understood to mean a supportive feeling of loyalty and attachment to other women stemming from a shared feeling of oppression—has been an important part of Black women's culture (Dill, 1983:132).... For example, Debra Gray White (1985) documents the ways Black slave women assisted each other in childbirth, cared for each other's children, worked together in sex-segregated work units when pregnant or nursing children, and depended on one another when married to males living on distant farms. White paints a convincing portrait of Black female slave communities where sisterhood was necessary and assumed....

The attention to Black women's culture has stimulated interest in a second type of interpersonal relationship: that shared by Black women with their biological children, the children in their extended families, and with the Black community's children. In reassessing Afro-American motherhood, Black feminist researchers have emphasized the connections between (1) choices available to Black mothers resulting from their placement in historically specific political economies, (2) Black mothers' perceptions of their children's choices as compared to what mothers thought those choices should be, and (3) actual strategies employed by Black mothers both in raising their children and in dealing with institutions that affected their children's lives. For example, Janice Hale (1980) suggests that effective Black mothers are sophisticated mediators between the competing offerings of an oppressive dominant culture and a nurturing Black value structure....

Another dimension of Black women's culture that has generated considerable interest among Black feminists is the role of creative expression in shaping and sustaining Black women's self-definitions and self-valuations.... Alice Walker's (1974) classic essay, "In Search of Our Mothers' Gardens," explains the necessity of Black women's creativity, even if in very limited spheres, in resisting objectification and asserting Black women's subjectivity as fully human beings. Illustrating Walker's thesis, Willie Mae Ford Smith, a prominent gospel singer featured in the 1984 documentary, "Say Amen Somebody," describes what singing means to her. She notes, "it's just a feeling within. You can't help yourself ... I feel like I can fly away. I forget I'm in the world sometimes. I just want to take off." For Mother Smith, her creativity is a sphere of freedom, one that helps her cope with and transcend daily life.

This third key theme in Black feminist thought—the focus on Black women's culture—is significant for three reasons. First, the data from Black women's culture suggest that the relationship between oppressed people's consciousness of oppression and the actions they take in dealing with oppressive structures may be far more complex than that suggested by existing social theory. Conventional social science continues to assume a fit between consciousness and activity; hence, accurate measures of human behavior are thought to produce accurate portraits of human consciousness of self and social structure (Westkott, 1979). In contrast, Black women's experiences suggest that Black women may overtly conform to the societal roles laid out for them, yet covertly oppose these roles in numerous spheres, an opposition shaped by the consciousness of being on the bottom. Black women's activities in families, churches, community institutions, and creative expression may represent more than an effort to mitigate pressures stemming from oppression. Rather, the Black female ideological frame of reference that Black women acquire through sisterhood, motherhood, and creative expression may serve the added purpose of shaping a Black female consciousness about the workings of oppression.... That these activities have been obscured from traditional social scientists should come as no surprise. Oppressed peoples may maintain hidden consciousness and may not reveal their true selves for reasons of self-protection.[15]

A second reason that the focus on Black women's culture is significant is that it points to the problematic nature of existing conceptualizations of the term "activism." While Black women's reality cannot be understood without attention to the interlocking structures of oppression that limit Black women's lives, Afro-American women's experiences suggest that possibilities for activism exist even within such multiple structures of domination. Such activism can take several forms. For Black women under extremely harsh conditions, the private decision to reject external definitions of Afro-American womanhood may itself be a form of activism. If Black women find themselves in settings where total conformity is expected, and where traditional forms of activism such as voting, participating in collective movements, and officeholding are impossible, then the individual women who in their consciousness choose to be self-defined and self-evaluating are, in fact, activists. They are retaining a grip over their definition as subjects, as full humans, and rejecting definitions of themselves as the objectified "other." ... In this sense, consciousness can be viewed as one potential sphere of freedom, one that may exist simultaneously with unfree, allegedly conforming behavior (Westkott, 1979). Moreover, if Black women simultaneously use all resources available to them—their roles as mothers, their participation in churches, their support of one another in Black female networks, their creative expression—to be self-defined and self-valuating and to encourage others to reject objectification, then Black women's everyday behavior itself is a form of activism. People who view themselves as fully human, as subjects, become activists, no matter how limited the sphere of their activism may be. By returning subjectivity to Black women, Black feminists return activism as well.

A third reason that the focus on Black women's culture is significant is that an analytical model exploring the relationship between oppression, consciousness and activism is implicit in the way Black feminists have studied Black women's culture....

Several features pervade emerging Black feminist approaches. First, researchers stress the interdependent relationship between the interlocking oppression that has shaped Black women's choices and Black women's actions in the context of those choices. Black feminist researchers rarely describe Black women's behavior without attention to the opportunity structures shaping their subjects' lives (Higginbotham, 1985; Ladner, 1971; Myers, 1980). Second, the question of whether oppressive structures and limited choices stimulate Black women's behavior characterized by apathy and alienation, or behavior demonstrating subjectivity and activism, is seen as ultimately dependent on Black women's perceptions of their choices.... Finally, this relationship between oppression, consciousness, and action can be seen as a dialectical one. In this model, oppressive structures create patterns of choices which are perceived in varying ways by Black women. Depending on their consciousness of themselves and their relationships to these choices, Black women may or may not develop Black female spheres of influence where they develop and validate what will be appropriate Black female sanctioned responses to oppression. Black women's activism in constructing Black female spheres of influence may, in turn, affect their perceptions of the political and economic choices offered to them by oppressive structures, influence actions actually taken, and ultimately alter the nature of oppression they experience.

THE SOCIOLOGICAL SIGNIFICANCE OF BLACK FEMINIST THOUGHT

... The sociological significance of Black feminist thought lies in two areas. First, the content of Black women's ideas has been influenced by and contributes to ongoing dialogues in a variety of sociological specialties. While this area merits attention, it is not my primary concern in this section. Instead, I investigate a second area of sociological significance: the process by which these specific ideas were produced by this specific group of individuals. In other words, I examine the influence of Black women's outsider within status in academia on the actual thought produced....

Two Elements of Sociological Paradigms

Kuhn defines a paradigm as the "entire constellation of beliefs, values, techniques, and so on shared by the members of a given community" (1962:175). As such, a paradigm consists of two fundamental elements: the thought itself and its producers and practitioners.[16] In this sense, the discipline of sociology is itself a paradigm—it consists of a system of knowledge shared by sociologists—and simultaneously consists of a plurality of paradigms (e.g., functionalism, Marxist sociology, feminist sociology, existential sociology), each produced by its own practitioners.

Two dimensions of thought itself are of special interest to this discussion. First, systems of knowledge are never complete. Rather, they represent guidelines for "thinking as usual." Kuhn (1962) refers to these guidelines as "maps," while Schutz (1944) describes them as "recipes." ... Second, while thought itself contains diverse elements, I will focus mainly on the important fact/theory relationship. As Kuhn (1962) suggests, facts or observations become meaningful in the context of theories or interpretations of those observations. Conversely, theories "fit the facts" by transforming previously accessible observations into facts....

Several dimensions of the second element of sociological paradigms—the community formed by a paradigm's practitioners—are of special interest to this discussion. First, group insiders have similar worldviews, acquired through similar educational and professional training, that separate them from everyone else. Insider worldviews may be especially alike if group members have similar social class, gender, and racial backgrounds....

A second dimension of the community of practitioners involves the process of becoming an insider. How does one know when an individual is really an insider and not an outsider in disguise? ... One becomes an insider by translating a theory or worldview into one's own language until, one day, the individual converts to thinking and acting according to that worldview.

A final dimension of the community of practitioners concerns the process of remaining an insider. A sociologist typically does this by furthering the discipline in ways described as appropriate by sociology generally, and by areas of specialization particularly. Normal foci for scientific sociological investigation include: (1) determining significant facts; (2) matching facts with existing theoretical interpretations to "test" the paradigm's ability to predict facts; and (3) resolving ambiguities in the paradigm itself by articulating and clarifying theory (Kuhn, 1962).

Black Women and the Outsider Within Status

Black women may encounter much less of a fit between their personal and cultural experiences and both elements of sociological paradigms than that facing other sociologists. On the one hand, Black women who undergo sociology's lengthy socialization process, who immerse themselves in the cultural pattern of sociology's group life, certainly wish to acquire the insider skills of thinking in and acting according to a sociological worldview. But on the other hand, Black women's experienced realities, both prior to contact and after initiation, may provide them with "special perspectives and insights available to that category of outsiders who have been systematically frustrated by the social system" (Merton, 1972:29). In brief, their outsider allegiances may militate against their choosing full insider status, and they may be more apt to remain outsiders within.[17]

In essence, to become sociological insiders, Black women must assimilate a standpoint that is quite different from their own. White males have long been the dominant group in sociology, and the sociological worldview understandably reflects the concerns of this group of practitioners.... It should come as no surprise that Black women's efforts in dealing with the effects of interlocking systems of oppression might produce a standpoint quite distinct from, and in many ways opposed to, that of white male insiders.

Seen from this perspective, Black women's socialization into sociology represents a more intense case of the normal challenges facing sociology graduate students and junior professionals in the discipline. Black women become, to use Simmel's (1921) and Schutz's terminology, penultimate "strangers." ... Like everyone else, Black women may see sociological "thinking as usual" as partially organized, partially clear, and contradictory, and may question these existing recipes. However, for them, this questioning process may be more acute, for the material that they encounter—white male insider–influenced observations and interpretations about human society—places white male subjectivity at the center of analysis and assigns Afro-American womanhood a position on the margins.

In spite of a lengthy socialization process, it may also be more difficult for Afro-American women to experience conversion and begin totally to think in and act according to a sociological worldview. Indeed, since past generations of white male insiderism have shaped a sociological worldview reflecting this group's concerns, it may be self-destructive for Black women to embrace that worldview. For example, Black women would have to accept certain fundamental and self-devaluing assumptions: (1) white males are more worthy of study because they are more fully human than everyone else; and (2) dichotomous oppositional thinking is natural and normal. More importantly, Black women would have to act in accordance with their place in a white male worldview. This involves accepting one's own subordination or regretting the accident of not being born white and male....

Remaining in sociology by doing normal scientific investigation may also be less complicated for traditional sociologists than for Afro-American women. Unlike Black women, learners
from backgrounds where the insider information and experiences of sociology are more familiar
may be less likely to see the taken-for-granted assumptions of sociology and may be more prone
to apply their creativity to "normal science." ... [T]hose Black women with a strong foundation
in Black women's culture (e.g., those that recognize the value of self-definition and self-valuation,
and that have a concrete understanding of sisterhood and motherhood) may be more apt to take
a critical posture toward the entire sociological enterprise. In brief, where traditional sociologists
may see sociology as "normal" and define their role as furthering knowledge about a normal
world with taken-for-granted assumptions, outsiders within are likely to see anomalies.

... Two types of anomalies are characteristically noted by Black female scholars. First,
Black female sociologists typically report the omission of facts or observations about Afro-
American women in the sociological paradigms they encounter.... Where white males may
take it as perfectly normal to generalize findings from studies of white males to other groups,
black women are more likely to see such a practice as problematic, as an anomaly. Similarly,
when white feminists produce generalizations about "women," Black feminists routinely ask
"which women do you mean?" ...

A second type of anomaly typically noted by Black female scholars concerns distortions of
facts and observations about Black women. Afro-American women in academia are frequently
struck by the difference between their own experiences and sociological descriptions of the
same phenomena. For example, while Black women have and are themselves mothers, they
encounter distorted versions of themselves and their mothers under the mantle of the Black
matriarchy thesis.... The response to these perceived distortions has been one of redefining
distorted images—for example, debunking the Sapphire and Mammy myths.

Since facts or observations become meaningful in the context of a theory, this emphasis
on producing accurate descriptions of Black women's lives has also refocused attention on
major omissions and distortions in sociological theories themselves. By drawing on the strengths
of sociology's plurality of subdisciplines, yet taking a critical posture toward them, the work
of Black feminist scholars taps some fundamental questions facing all sociologists. One such
question concerns the fundamental elements of society that should be studied. Black feminist
researchers' response has been to move Black women's voices to the center of the analysis, to
study people, and by doing so to reaffirm human subjectivity and intentionality. They point
to the dangers of omission and distortion that can occur if sociological concepts are studied
at the expense of human subjectivity. For example, there is a distinct difference between conducting a statistical analysis of Black women's work, where Afro-American women are studied
as a reconstituted amalgam of researcher-defined variables (e.g., race, sex, years of education,
and father's occupation), and examining Black women's self-definitions and self-valuations
of themselves as workers in oppressive jobs. While both approaches can further sociological
knowledge about the concept of work, the former runs the risk of objectifying Black women,
of reproducing constructs of dichotomous oppositional difference, and of producing distorted
findings about the nature of work itself.

A second question facing sociologists concerns the adequacy of current interpretations
of key sociological concepts. For example, few sociologists would question that work and
family are two fundamental concepts for sociology. However, bringing Black feminist thought
into the center of conceptual analysis raises issues of how comprehensive current sociological
interpretations of these two concepts really are.... For example, labor theories that relegate
Afro-American women's work experiences to the fringe of analysis miss the critical theme
of the interlocking nature of Black women as female workers (e.g., Black women's unpaid
domestic labor) and Black women as racially oppressed workers (e.g., Black women's unpaid
slave labor and exploited wage labor). Examining the extreme case offered by Afro-American
women's unpaid and paid work experiences raises questions about the adequacy of generalizations about work itself....

Similarly, sociological generalizations about families that do not account for Black women's experience will fail to show how the public/private split shaping household composition varies across social and class groupings, how racial/ethnic family members are differentially integrated into wage labor, and how families alter their household structure in response to changing political economies (e.g., adding more people and becoming extended, fragmenting and becoming female-headed, and migrating to locate better opportunities). Black women's family experiences represent a clear case of the workings of race, gender, and class oppression in shaping family life....

While Black women who stand outside academia may be familiar with omissions and distortions of the Black female experience, as outsiders to sociology, they lack legitimated professional authority to challenge the sociological anomalies. Similarly, traditional sociological insiders, whether white males or their nonwhite and/or female disciples, are certainly in no position to notice the specific anomalies apparent to Afro-American women, because these same sociological insiders produced them. In contrast, those Black women who remain rooted in their own experiences as Black women—and who master sociological paradigms yet retain a critical posture toward them—are in a better position to bring a special perspective not only to the study of Black women, but to some of the fundamental issues facing sociology itself.

TOWARD SYNTHESIS: OUTSIDERS WITHIN SOCIOLOGY

Black women are not the only outsiders within sociology. As an extreme case of outsiders moving into a community that historically excluded them, Black women's experiences highlight the tension experienced by any group of less powerful outsiders encountering the paradigmatic thought of a more powerful insider community. In this sense, a variety of individuals can learn from Black women's experiences as outsiders within: Black men, working-class individuals, white women, other people of color, religious and sexual minorities, and all individuals who, while from social strata that provided them with the benefits of white male insiderism, have never felt comfortable with its taken-for-granted assumptions.

... Outsiders within occupy a special place—they become different people, and their difference sensitizes them to patterns that may be more difficult for established sociological insiders to see....

The approach suggested by the experiences of outsiders within is one where intellectuals learn to trust their own personal and cultural biographies as significant sources of knowledge. In contrast to approaches that require submerging these dimensions of self in the process of becoming an allegedly unbiased, objective social scientist, outsiders within bring these ways of knowing back into the research process. At its best, outsider within status seems to offer its occupants a powerful balance between the strengths of their sociological training and the offerings of their personal and cultural experiences. Neither is subordinated to the other. Rather, experienced reality is used as a valid source of knowledge for critiquing sociological facts and theories while sociological thought offers new ways of seeing that experienced reality.

What many black feminists appear to be doing is embracing the creative potential of their outsider within status and using it wisely. In doing so, they move themselves and their disciplines closer to the humanist vision implicit in their work—namely, the freedom both to be different and to be part of the solidarity of humanity.

NOTES

1. See Rollins (1985) for a discussion of Black domestic work.
2. For example, in *Of Women Born: Motherhood as Experience and Institution*, Adrienne Rich has fond memories of her Black "mother," a young, unstereotypically slim Black woman she loved.

3. For example, in spite of Rich's warm memories of her Black "mother," she had all but forgotten her until beginning research for her book. Similarly, the Black domestic workers in both Dill's (1980) and Rollins' (1985) studies discussed the limitations that their subordinate roles placed on them.

4. For a discussion of the notion of a special standpoint or point of view of oppressed groups, see Hartsock (1983). See Merton's (1972) analysis of the potential contributions of insider and outsider perspectives to sociology. For a related discussion of outsider within status, see his section "Insiders as 'Outsiders'" (1972:29–30).

…

9. Emerging Black feminist research is demonstrating a growing awareness of the importance of including the simultaneity of oppression in studies of Black women; studies such as those by Dill (1980), Rollins (1985), Higginbotham (1983), and Mullings (1986b) indicate a new sensitivity to the interactive nature of race, gender, and class. By studying Black women, such studies capture the interaction of race and gender.

…

15. Audre Lorde (1984:114) describes this conscious hiding of one's self as follows: "in order to survive, those of us for whom oppression is as American as apple pie have always had to be watchers, to become familiar with the language and manners of the oppressor, even sometimes adopting them for some illusion of protection."

16. In this sense, sociology is a special case of the more generalized process discussed by Mannheim (1936). Also, see Berman (1981) for a discussion of Western thought as a paradigm, Mulkay (1979) for a sociology of knowledge analysis of the natural sciences, and Berger and Luckmann (1966) for a generalized discussion of how everyday knowledge is socially constructed.

17. Jackson (1974) reports that 21 of the 145 Black sociologists receiving doctoral degrees between 1945 and 1972 were women. Kulis et al. (1986) report that Blacks comprised 5.7 percent of all sociology faculties in 1984. These data suggest that historically, Black females have not been sociological insiders, and currently, Black women as a group comprise a small portion of sociologists in the United States.

REFERENCES

Andrews, William L. (ed.) 1986. *Sisters of the Spirit.* Bloomington: Indiana University Press.

Asante, Molefi Kete. 1980. "International/intercultural relations." Pp. 43–58 in Molefi Kete Asante and Abdulai S. Vandi (eds.), *Contemporary Black Thought.* Beverly Hills, CA: Sage.

Baldwin, Joseph A. 1980. "The psychology of oppression." Pp. 95–110 in Molefi Kete Asante and Abdulai S. Vandi (eds.), *Contemporary Black Thought.* Beverly Hills, CA: Sage.

Beale, Frances. 1970. "Double jeopardy: to be Black and female." Pp. 90–110 in Toni Cade (ed.), *The Black Woman.* New York: Signet.

Berger, Peter L., and Thomas Luckmann. 1966. *The Social Construction of Reality.* New York: Doubleday.

Berman, Morris. 1981. *The Reenchantment of the World.* New York: Bantam.

Brittan, Arthur, and Mary Maynard. 1984. *Sexism, Racism and Oppression.* New York: Basil Blackwell.

Chodorow, Nancy. 1978. *The Reproduction of Mothering.* Berkeley, CA: University of California Press.

Christian, Barbara. 1985. *Black Feminist Criticism: Perspectives on Black Women Writers.* New York: Pergamon.

Davis, Angela. 1981. *Women, Race and Class.* New York: Random House.

Dill, Bonnie Thornton. 1980. "'The means to put my children through': child-rearing goals and strategies among Black female domestic servants." Pp. 107–23 in LaFrances Rodgers-Rose (ed.), *The Black Woman.* Beverly Hills, CA: Sage.

———. 1983. "Race, class, and gender: prospects for an all-inclusive sisterhood." *Feminist Studies* 9:131–50.

Giddings, Paula. 1984. *When and Where I Enter . . . the Impact of Black Women on Race and Sex in America.* New York: William Morrow.

Gilkes, Cheryl Townsend. 1980. "'Holding back the ocean with a broom': Black women and community work." Pp. 217–31 in LaFrances Rodgers-Rose (ed.), *The Black Woman*. Beverly Hills, CA: Sage.

———. 1981. "From slavery to social welfare: racism and the control of Black women." Pp. 288–300 in Amy Smerdlow and Helen Lessinger (eds.), *Class, Race, and Sex: The Dynamics of Control*. Boston: G. K. Hall.

———. 1985. "'Together and in harness': Women's traditions in the sanctified church." *Signs* 10:678–99.

Gwaltney, John Langston. 1980. *Drylongso, a self-portrait of Black America*. New York: Vintage.

Hale, Janice. 1980. "The Black woman and child rearing." Pp. 79–88 in LaFrances Rodgers-Rose (ed.), *The Black Woman*. Beverly Hills, CA: Sage.

Hartsock, Nancy M. 1983. "The feminist standpoint: developing the ground for a specifically feminist historical materialism." Pp. 283–310 in Sandra Harding and Merrill Hintikka (eds.), *Discovering Reality*. Boston: D. Reidel.

Higginbotham, Elizabeth. 1982. "Two representative issues in contemporary sociological work on Black women." Pp. 93–98 in Gloria T. Hull, Patricia Bell Scott, and Barbara Smith (eds.), *But Some of Us Are Brave*. Old Westbury, NY: Feminist Press.

———. 1983. "Laid bare by the system: work and survival for Black and Hispanic women." Pp. 200–15 in Amy Smerdlow and Helen Lessinger (eds.), *Class, Race, and Sex: The Dynamics of Control*. Boston: G. K. Hall.

———. 1985. "Race and class barriers to Black women's college attendance." *Journal of Ethnic Studies* 13:89–107.

hooks, bell. 1981. *Ain't I a Woman: Black Women and Feminism*. Boston: South End Press.

———. 1984. *From Margin to Center*. Boston: South End Press.

Jackson, Jacquelyn. 1974. "Black female sociologists." Pp. 267–98 in James E. Blackwell and Morris Janowitz (eds.), *Black Sociologists*. Chicago: University of Chicago Press.

Keller, Evelyn Fox. 1983. "Gender and science." Pp. 187–206 in Sandra Harding and Merrill Hintikka (eds.), *Discovering Reality*. Boston: D. Reidel.

King, Mae. 1973. "The politics of sexual stereotypes." *Black Scholar* 4:12–23.

Kuhn, Thomas S. 1970. *The Structure of Scientific Revolutions*. 2d Edition. [1962] Chicago: University of Chicago Press.

Kulis, Stephen, Karen A. Miller, Morris Axelrod, and Leonard Gordon. 1986. "Minority representation of U.S. departments." *ASA Footnotes* 14:3.

Ladner, Joyce. 1971. *Tomorrow's Tomorrow: The Black Woman*. Garden City, NY: Anchor.

Lee, Alfred McClung. 1973. *Toward Humanist Sociology*. Englewood Cliffs, NJ: Prentice-Hall.

Lewis, Diane. 1977. "A response to inequality: Black women, racism and sexism." *Signs* 3:339–61.

Loewenberg, Bert James, and Ruth Bogin (eds.). 1976. *Black Women in Nineteenth-Century Life*. University Park, PA: Pennsylvania State University.

Lords, Audre. 1984. *Sister Outsider*. Trumansburg, NY: The Crossing Press.

Mannheim, Karl. 1954. *Ideology and Utopia: An Introduction to the Sociology of Knowledge*. [1936] New York: Harcourt, Brace & Co.

Merton, Robert K. 1972. "Insiders and outsiders: a chapter in the sociology of knowledge." *American Journal of Sociology* 78:9–47.

Mulkay, Michael. 1979. *Science and the Sociology of Knowledge*. Boston: George Allen & Unwin.

Mullings, Leith. 1986a. "Anthropological perspectives on the Afro-American family." *American Journal of Social Psychiatry* 6:11–16.

———. 1986b. "Uneven development: class, race and gender in the United States before 1900." Pp. 41–57 in Eleanor Leacock and Helen Safa (eds.), *Women's Work, Development and the Division of Labor by Gender*. South Hadley, MA: Bergin & Garvey.

Murray, Pauli. 1970. "The liberation of Black women." Pp. 87–102 in Mary Lou Thompson (ed.), *Voices of the New Feminism*. Boston: Beacon Press.

Myers, Lena Wright. 1980. *Black Women: Do They Cope Better?* Englewood Cliffs, NJ: Prentice-Hall.

Paris, Peter J. 1985. *The Social Teaching of the Black Churches*. Philadelphia: Fortress Press.

Park, Robert E. 1950. *Race and Culture*. Glencoe, IL: Free Press.

Rich, Adrienne. 1976. *Of Woman Born: Motherhood as Experience and Institution*. New York: Norton.

Richards, Dona. 1980. "European mythology: the ideology of 'progress.'" Pp. 59–79 in Molefi Kete Asante and Abdulai S. Vandi (eds.), *Contemporary Black Thought.* Beverly Hills, CA: Sage.

Rollins, Judith. 1985. *Between Women: Domestics and Their Employers.* Philadelphia: Temple University Press.

Rosaldo, Michelle Z. 1983. "Moral/analytic dilemmas posed by the intersection of feminism and social science." Pp. 76–96 in Norma Hann, Robert N. Bellah, Paul Rabinow, and William Sullivan (eds.), *Social Science as Moral Inquiry.* New York: Columbia University Press.

Schutz, Alfred. 1944. "The stranger: an essay in social psychology." *American Journal of Sociology* 49:499–507.

Scott, Patricia Bell. 1982. "Debunking sapphire: toward a non-racist and non-sexist social science." Pp. 85–92 in Gloria T. Hull, Patricia Bell Scott, and Barbara Smith (eds.), *But Some of Us Are Brave.* Old Westbury, NY: Feminist Press.

Simmel, Georg. 1921. "The sociological significance of the 'stranger.'" Pp. 322–27 in Robert E. Park and Ernest W. Burgess (eds.), *Introduction to the Science of Sociology.* Chicago: University of Chicago Press.

Smith, Barbara (ed.). 1983. *Home Girls: A Black Feminist Anthology.* New York: Kitchen Table, Women of Color Press.

Steady, Filomina Chioma. 1981. "The Black woman cross-culturally: an overview." Pp. 7–42 in Filomina Chioma Steady (ed.), *The Black Woman Cross-culturally.* Cambridge, MA: Schenkman.

Tate, Claudia. 1983. *Black Women Writers at Work.* New York: Continuum.

Walker, Alice (ed.). 1974. "In search of our mothers' gardens." Pp. 231–43 in *In Search of Our Mothers' Gardens.* New York: Harcourt Brace Jovanovich.

Walker, Alice. 1979. *I Love Myself When I Am Laughing . . . A Zora Neal Hurston Reader.* Westbury, NY: Feminist Press.

Westkott, Marcia. 1979. "Feminist criticism of the social sciences." *Harvard Educational Review* 49:422–30.

White, Deborah Gray. 1985. *Ain't I a Woman? Female Slaves in the Plantation South.* New York: W.W. Norton.

White, E. Frances. 1984. "Listening to the voices of Black feminism." *Radical America* 18:7–25.

Maria Mies

The Need for a New Vision:
The Subsistence Perspective

The Earth Summit in Rio de Janeiro (UNCED, June 1992) again made clear that solutions to the present worldwide ecological, economic and social problems cannot be expected from the ruling elites of the North or the South. As Vandana Shiva points out, . . . a new vision—a new life for present and future generations, and for our fellow creatures on earth—in which praxis and theory are respected and preserved can be found only in the survival struggles of grassroots movements. The men and women who actively participate in such movements radically reject the industrialized countries' prevailing model of capitalist-patriarchal development. They do not want to be developed according to this blueprint, but rather want to preserve their subsistence base intact, under their own control.

This quest for a new vision, however, is to be found not only among people in the South, who cannot ever expect to reap the fruits of "development"; the search for an ecologically sound, nonexploitative, just, nonpatriarchal, self-sustaining society can also be found among some groups in the North. Here, too, this search for a new perspective involves not only middle-class people, disenchanted and despairing about the end result of the modernization process, but even by some at the bottom of the social pyramid.

We have called this new vision the *subsistence perspective,* or the *survival perspective.*

This concept was first developed to analyze the hidden, unpaid or poorly paid work of housewives, subsistence peasants and small producers in the so-called informal sector, particularly in the South, as the underpinning and foundation of capitalist patriarchy's model of unlimited growth of goods and money. Subsistence work as life-producing and life-preserving work in all these production relations was and is a necessary precondition for survival; and the bulk of this work is done by women.[1]

With increasing ecological destruction in recent decades, however, it becomes obvious that this subsistence—or life production—was and is not only a kind of hidden underground of the capitalist market economy, it can also show the way out of the many impasses of this destructive system called industrial society, market economy or capitalist patriarchy.

This has become particularly clear since the alternative to capitalist industrialism, which the socialist version of catching-up development had provided, collapsed in Eastern Europe and what was the USSR.... In their efforts to emulate the capitalist model of industrial society these systems caused greater environmental destruction than have their capitalist counterparts; their relationship to nature was based on the same exploitative principles as in the West. Furthermore, as Kurz points out, they were based on the same economic model of alienated, generalized commodity production first developed by capitalism,[2] which, as we have shown elsewhere,[3] is based on the colonization of women, nature and other peoples....

Kurz does not identify the inherent need for colonies in the capitalist or socialist versions of commodity-producing systems; rather he sees the reason for the breakdown of erstwhile "Actually Existing Socialism" (AES) in the dilemma of generalized commodity production as such. Before trying to delineate the contours of a subsistence perspective as an alternative to generalized commodity production it may be useful to look again at the contradictions of this strange economic system which is now propagated as the only possible way of satisfying human needs.

THE SCHIZOPHRENIA OF COMMODITY-PRODUCING SOCIETIES

The logic of commodity-producing systems consists in the principle of surplus value production and the impetus for permanent growth. This logic is/was the same in both capitalist and AES states, differing only in so far as in capitalist societies the surplus is accumulated privately and in the AES countries it was accumulated by the state. In both systems people are in principle *subjects,* both as producers and as consumers.... In both systems there is a fundamental contradiction between production and consumption, because the sphere of production of commodities is principally separated from that of consumption by the sphere of circulation or the market.

But also the individuals, the economic subjects, are dichotomized into producers and consumers with contradictory interests....

For the producer his own products are desensualized, have become abstract "work amalgams [gallerts] ... because they are nothing but potential money."[5] It makes no difference to them whether they produce Sachertortes or neutron bombs, writes Kurz. But as consumer, the same person has a quite opposite interest in the sensuous, concrete use-value of the things bought "as individuals who eat, drink, need a house, wear clothes, people have to be sensuous."[6]

It is this contradiction between production and consumption, between exchange and use-values, which is ultimately responsible for the destruction of nature in industrial, commodity-producing society. The exclusive concern of people as producers is maximizing the money output of their production and they will therefore continue to produce poisonous substances, nuclear power, weapons, more and more cars. But as consumers they want clean air, unpolluted food, and a safe place for their waste, far away from their home.

As long as production and consumption are structured in this contradictory way, inherent in generalized commodity production, no solution of the various economic, ecological and political/ethical/spiritual crises can be expected.

Some people think that the solution lies in substituting environmentally noxious substances, technologies and commodities with nature-friendly, life-preserving ones. They propose harnessing commodity production and market forces to the service of sustainable development, replacing the production and marketing of destructive goods by "eco-marketing." They want to mobilize funds from the corporate sector, even from those firms known for ruthless environmental pollution, to sponsor the activities of environmental organizations.... But the fundamentally contradictory relationships inherent in commodity production and consumption are not criticized. Nor is there a critique of the basic principles of capitalist production: individual self-interest, generalized competition and the system's need for permanent growth. On the contrary, eco-marketing and eco-sponsoring are seen as a new area of investment, a new opportunity to extend commodity production and marketing....

A way out of this destructive and irrational system of commodity production cannot be found in catching-up development and technological fixes, even if technological alternatives could be quickly found to end and to repair some of the environmental damage caused by industrialism....

Nevertheless, this utopia of the modern industrial society is not fundamentally criticized even in those countries where it has already collapsed and a deindustrialization process has begun. This is the case in, for example, Peru, Argentina, Mexico, Brazil and many other countries of the South which tried to catch up with the North through credit-based industrialization. These countries are now caught in the debt trap, victims of the structural adjustment policy of the World Bank and the IMF.

But this deindustrialization process has also begun in Eastern Europe, in the erstwhile Soviet Union and in Cuba whose economy and modernization policy was totally dependent on imports from and exports to the Soviet Union. Since the collapse of the USSR these imports, particularly of oil and machinery, stopped. Cuba now faces the dilemma either of becoming a neocolony of the USA or of trying to survive economically and politically as an independent entity by reviving subsistence technologies and production.

To make up for the lack of oil, Fidel Castro imported 100,000 bicycles from China and replaced the tractors in agriculture by 100,000 oxen as draught animals.... The survival of Cuba as an independent society will depend on whether the people can see this compulsory return to subsistence production as a chance rather than a defeat. But this would entail the people's acceptance of a different concept of socialism or of a "good society," based on regional self-sufficiency, ecological sustainability and social equality.

...

Such survival strategies are also the only way out of the deindustrialization crisis in Africa. But unlike the postsocialist societies in Eastern Europe most sub-Saharan African societies cannot assume that deindustrialization and enforced demodernization is only a temporary affair and that the "world community"—20 per cent of the world's rich nations—will come to their rescue....

At a conference at the University of Dar es Salaam in December 1989, representatives of the academic community, churches, trade unions, women's organizations, NGOs, students and government officials across the African continent discussed alternative development strategies, particularly after the new East-West detente which leads to an "involuntary delinking" of Africa from the aid and trade flows of the world market. At the end of the conference the participants adopted the Dar es Salaam Declaration: Alternative Development Strategies for Africa.[8]

...

People-centered development, popular democracy and social justice on the basis of effective African integration at subregional and regional levels as well as South-South Cooperation. This reorientation of African development should focus on planned disengagement from international capitalism, regional food self-sufficiency, satisfaction of basic needs for all, development from below through the termination of antirural bias as well as concentration on relevant small and medium scale enterprises.[9]

Conference participants were able, it seems, to transform the "involuntary delinking from the capitalist world market" into a voluntary new social, economic and political/cultural strategy in which self-reliance, self-provisioning, food self-sufficiency, regionality, the need for reruralization, participatory democracy, interregional cooperation are the key concepts.

...

As mentioned earlier, the new vision of a nonexploitative, noncolonial, nonpatriarchal society which respects, not destroys nature, did not emanate from research institutes, UN organizations or governments, but from grassroots movements, in both the South and the North, who fought and fight for survival. And in these movements it is women who more than men understand that a subsistence perspective is the only guarantee of the survival of all, even of the poorest, and not integration into and continuation of the industrial growth system.

Many recent studies on the impact of ecological deterioration on women, particularly the poorest women in the South, have highlighted not only the fact that women and children are the main victims of this war against nature but also that women are the most active, most creative, and most concerned and committed in movements for conservation and protection of nature and for healing the damage done to her.[10] While women's role as "saviors of the environment" may be welcomed by many, including those who want to combine sustainability of ecosystems with permanent economic growth, few voices emphasize that these grassroots women's movements also implicitly and explicitly criticize the prevailing capitalist, profit- and growth-oriented, patriarchal development paradigm and that they advocate a new alternative; a subsistence alternative.

This perspective was most clearly spelt out by the women of the Chipko Movement, who in Vandana Shiva's interview with some of its leaders in Garwhal ... clearly said that they expect nothing from "development" or from the money economy. They want only to preserve their autonomous control over their subsistence base, their common property resources: the land, water, forests, hills. From history and their own experience they know that their survival (their bread) as well as their freedom and dignity—all essentials for survival—can be maintained only as long as they have control over these resources. Their concept of freedom and the good life differs from that offered by the global supermarket of the capitalist patriarchal industrial system....

The conflict between a subsistence and survival, and a market and money perspective is frequently a source of conflict between men and women, even in some of the Chipko struggles. Whereas the women participated in hugging the trees and wanted to preserve their subsistence base, their men wanted modernization and waged work.... But the women claimed their right to leadership because of their responsibility for daily survival. They said: "As the men do not collect fuel or fodder they are not concerned about the maintenance of the forests. They are more interested to earn money, even if they have to cut trees for that. But the forests are the women's wealth."[11]

Elsewhere in the world too, women are more concerned about a survival subsistence perspective than are men, most of whom continue to believe that more growth, technology, science and "progress" will simultaneously solve the ecological and economic crises; they place money and power above life. At a conference on women and ecology in Sweden in February 1992 a Samo woman, reporting on tribal people's efforts to create global networks and groups, said that at such global gatherings the men were mainly interested in competing for political power in the organization, whereas the women's concern centered on preserving their cultural and survival base, independent of governmental or NGO development programs. Vandana Shiva also observed this women/men opposition at the conference: "What it Means to be Green in South Africa" (September 1992), organized by the ANC. While the male leaders and speakers seemed to expect South Africa's economic and ecological problems to be solved through full integration into the growth-oriented world economy, the women, who had so far borne the burden of modernization and development, were much more skeptical. One 60-year-old woman said that, "The [government's] betterment scheme has been the best strategy to push us into the depth of poverty. It accelerated the migratory system."

The men were forced to migrate to the cities in search of jobs, whereas the women, together with the old and the children, had to try to survive in the rural areas. Meanwhile, the white government destroyed all assets and possessions by which the women tried to maintain their subsistence: "We were dispossessed of our goats, donkeys and other animals. They were taken away by force and we got only 20 cents as compensation per head."

This woman had experienced the contradictory impact of "betterment" or development as the government understood it. She knew that some must always pay the price for this development and that usually its victims are the women. Therefore she was not enthusiastic about further integration of the new nonracist, democratic South Africa into the world market. Rather she demanded land and the security of independent subsistence. (*Source:* Vandana Shiva.)

One reason why women are becoming increasingly critical of modern development and integration into the world market is the recognition that this has led to more and more violence against women, particularly in areas where it was successful. . . . In the industrialized North too, many women's projects and initiatives implicitly or explicitly seek to develop an alternative to the destructive patriarchal and capitalist system. These groups sprang up in the course of the women's, peace, and ecology movements, which found campaigns and protests not enough but wanted to put their beliefs into practice. . . .

To subsume all these practical and theoretical efforts to find an alternative to the existing destructive system under the rubric "subsistence perspective" would be incorrect; many differences exist, in detail and perhaps also in perspective. But there is a commonality in these initiatives: the need for a qualitative, not simply a quantitative change in what we are accustomed to call the economy. Men, increasingly, also begin to understand that an ecologically sound, just, women-and-children friendly, peaceful society cannot be built up by a continuation of the growth oriented industrial society.

Rather than developing an abstract model, . . . I shall present two accounts of how people have tried to put this subsistence perspective into practice. One, in the South, is the case of a people's movement towards water preservation and subsistence in India. The other is an account of a commune in Germany which tries to solve the ecological problem of waste disposal within the framework of a subsistence perspective. These are particular cases, but they encapsulate the main elements of a society which is no longer based on industrialism and generalized commodity production for profit, permanent growth and consumerism.

People's Dams: The Baliraja Dam, India

Projects for the construction of megadams in many Southern countries is one strategy designed to harness nature's resources in the service of modern industrial development. These projects have been opposed almost everywhere by strong, people's movements, particularly of peasants, tribals and others whose ancestral lands and livelihood bases will be flooded or submerged by these dams. Ecologically concerned people also oppose the construction of these dams because, in most cases, primeval forests, ancient temples, ecologically and culturally unique areas will be destroyed forever by these "temples of modernity" as Nehru called the big dams. One of the better-known resistance movements is that against the Narmada Valley Project (NVP) in India, a megaproject financed by the World Bank. . . .

Apart from such movements there have for several years been initiatives seeking an alternative solution to the water and energy problems of drought-prone areas in India, solutions which would restore both the ecological and social balance without sacrificing the future for short-term present gains.

The People's Dams movement in Khanapur in Sangli district in Maharashtra is an outcome of this search for alternative water management, stemming from an alternative concept of development; this movement started during the prolonged textile workers' strike in Bombay. Many who returned to their villages in search of support for the strike, found that for several years the people of Khanapur had been suffering from severe drought, crop failures and water shortage. Before the strike these workers had tried to help their villages by sending money home to build or repair temples. But, as Bharat Patankar points out, they showed scant solidarity with the poor peasants, the class from which they originated. The simultaneous strike and drought situation changed this....

An organization of the workers and poor, landless peasants—the Mukti Sangarsh—was formed which successfully agitated for proper wages and against corruption on the EGS schemes.... The Mukti Sangarsh and the people, in the belief that droughts should be eradicated, then began to study the reasons for their recurrence.... What had happened? Since the 1980s private contractors had excavated sand from the dried-up riverbeds and sold it to construction firms in the cities. Consequently, water percolation was further reduced and the wells dried up.

Moreover, since the mid-1970s this area had been transformed from more or less subsistence-oriented agriculture to Green Revolution capitalist farming. Old subsistence crops like *bajra* and *jowar* (millets) were replaced by commercial crops like sugarcane, which not only need chemical fertilizers and pesticides, but also vast quantities of water. In this process the old farming methods disappeared. The peasants became dependent on seed, fertilizer and chemical companies, on banks and market fluctuations. Due to the compulsions to produce for the market, small peasants became increasingly indebted and many had to migrate to the city in search of work. The big farmers survived and used up most of the water. This agroindustrial development was supported by the Maharashtra government because it had a stable vote base in the area.

The Mukti Sangarsh and the People's Science Organization of Maharashtra organized science fairs and discussions in the villages during which people studied water management from an historical perspective. The old cropping methods, the geological conditions and the vegetation of the area were also examined and viable schemes for an alternative agriculture were proposed.

. . .

After a conference on drought organized in 1985 peasants of two villages produced a plan to build a people's dam, the Baliraja Dam. They also demonstrated at Kolhapur University, demanding that scientists and students should help the drought-affected peasants. As a result a Drought Eradication Committee was formed, and professors and students helped with surveys.

Controlling Their Own Resources

To finance construction of the dam the people decided that they themselves would sell a small quantity of sand from the Yerala riverbed; according to law, the sand in the rivers belongs to the government. They also wanted to stop all commercial sand excavation by outside contractors....

They demanded no help from the government, except its permission to build the dam and stop commercial excavation of their sand.

They received the government sanction in 1988 and in 1990 the dam was completed. The Baliraja Dam is an example of how people can use their own resources and at the same time conserve the ecological balance. They take from nature but they also give back to nature.

A New Water Distribution System

In discussing their water problems the people had identified that one reason for recurring droughts was the unequal water distribution system that prevailed so far: those who possessed most land also got most water to irrigate their commercial crops. Water collected in the Baliraja Dam, however was, from the beginning, to be distributed equitably, based on the following principles:

- Water as a resource belongs to everybody and must be distributed on a per capita basis, not on a landholding basis.
- Every person, including landless people and women, to receive the same share.
- Landless people can either lease land on a sharecropping basis and use their water share or lease it out or sell it.
- Each water share costs Rs 10, or is equivalent to one day's *shramdan* (free labor) on the dam site.

...

Thus, the people not only wanted to regain control over their own resources and restore the ecological balance in their area, they also began to change the unequal social relationships between the classes and genders. For the first time women received a share in a resource which actually belongs to everyone and to nature.

A New Cropping System—and an Alternative Agriculture

The Mukti Sangarsh Movement also wanted to change the socially and ecologically disastrous capitalist farming system. A new cropping system was proposed in which the various resources—land, water, different species—should be used to facilitate an ecologically, socially and economically sustainable system. The crops, the land and the water should be divided in an alternative way: a family of five would possess an average of three acres of land (which is the average in Maharashtra).

...

In the course of the movement for people's dams, people not only reevaluated their old subsistence knowledge and skills, but also began to question the role of science and technology in the "development" of apparently backward areas, and when the people are treated as passive and ignorant. In this movement the people participated fully in developing an alternative technology, and scientists and engineers who supported the movement were able to use the people's knowledge creatively as well as combine it with modern science....

The Baliraja Dam in Khanapur is evidence of the fruitfulness of such a subsistence-oriented, integrated, synergic approach in which the key elements are:

- social organization of the people;
- recovery of their subsistence knowledge and skills;
- active participation in the development process;
- a serious attempt to change structures of social inequality and exploitation, including sexual inequality and exploitation;
- a critique of mainstream science and technology and the development of locally based, ecologically sustainable alternatives;
- an effort to end further privatization of the commons, and instead, a move to re-create community control over common resources like water, sand, and so on.

These component parts of an integrative strategy are all centered around the main goal of this approach: to regain self-reliance and subsistence security, that is, to become ecologically, socially and economically more independent from external market forces.

FROM GARBAGE TO SUBSISTENCE

Phase 1: From Students' Movement to Squatter Movement

The Sozialistische Selbsthilfe Köln (SSK) is one of the oldest self-help initiatives in Cologne (Germany); its beginning dates back to the Students Movement in the early 1970s. Inspired by Herbert Marcuse's argument that the "revolution," the alternative to capitalist, industrial society, could no longer be expected from the working class in industrialized, affluent societies, but rather from drop-outs, marginalized groups and the colonized in the Third World, a group of students in Cologne initiated a scheme whose objective was to give shelter to youngsters who had run away from authoritarian homes, remand homes or even prisons. They claimed that they could offer a better education and better prospects for life to these young people than could the establishment institutions.... Initially, the project was supported by the Social Welfare Department of the Municipality of Cologne, who not only gave a house to the SSK but also agreed to pay the same amount for a boy or a girl, which they would have paid to a remand home. Eventually however, it became evident that this project was too expensive for the municipality....

About 30 people decided to continue the SSK and to depend only on their own work and the help of friends and sympathizers. They henceforth changed the name to: Sozialistische Selbsthilfe Koln (Socialist Self-Help, Cologne, SSK) and laid down a series of strict rules for all who wished to become members. The most important of these were:

- No money is accepted from the state, not even social welfare money. Self-reliance is the main principle.
- Everybody, men and women, must work for the livelihood of all. Every morning this work is distributed by the whole commune.
- All income is pooled and distributed equally.
- No violence (beating, harassing etc.) is allowed within the SSK.
- No drugs and alcohol are allowed.
- Everybody must participate in political work and actions.
- The SSK has no leadership. All problems are discussed in plenary sessions and decisions are taken according to the consensus principle.

The SSK commune saw these rules and principles not only as necessary for their own survival but also as the beginning of a truly socialist society in which both the capitalist and the centralist and bureaucratic socialist models of society, then prevailing in Eastern Europe, were to be transcended. They saw their own commune as a model of such a society.

For their livelihood the SSK did various odd jobs, such as: transporting coal; collecting and reselling old furniture, clothes or household equipment; repair jobs; cleaning houses; gardening, and so on. They virtually lived off the garbage of our rich society.

The SSK's political activities centered around the problems created by the modernization strategy of the commercial community and the city planners, which penalized mainly the poor, the elderly, and foreign workers....

In these and many other political struggles the SSK's strength lay in its potential for quick, direct, nonbureaucratic action, innovative publicity by means of wall-newspapers, a direct link between action and reflection, and their commitment to live by their own strength and be open to all the downtrodden, the social "garbage" of our industrial society....

Phase 2: From Chernobyl to the Ecology Question and the Discovery of Subsistence

About 1986, after the meltdown at Chernobyl, the SSK commune became aware of the ecology problem. They began to question their model of socialism and asked themselves what was its use in an environment poisoned and polluted by radioactivity and other toxic wastes of industrial society. They held many discussions on how to change the SSK in order to contribute to a more ecologically sound society. But they failed to arrive at a consensus, and the organization faced a grave crisis, while several members left the commune.

Around this time my friend Claudia v. Werlhof and I organized a conference at the Evangelische Akademie, Bad Boll—Die Subsistenzperspektive, ein Weg ins Freie (The Subsistence

Perspective—a Path into the Open). The conference's objective was to bring together activists and theoreticians from the women's movement, the alternative and ecology movements and the Third World in order to clarify our ideas about a possible common strategy or perspective: the Subsistence Perspective. Three members of the SSK were also invited because I felt that they had practiced this perspective for years. This conference later proved to have indeed opened a "path into the open" for the SSK, because not only did the three activists discover the global interconnections between their own work and ideals and such diverse movements as a peasants' movement in Venezuela, the people's struggles against modernization and industrialization in Ladakh, the Chipko movement in India, but they also discovered the richness encapsulated in the concept subsistence. They realized that it encompassed what they had been aspiring to during all those years. In an SSK brochure called "Land in Sight" Lothar Gothe (one of SSK's founders) and Maggie Lucke defined the concept as follows: "The word [subsistence] is derived from the Latin word *subsistere,* which has several meanings: 'to stand still, to make a halt, to persist, to resist, to stay back, to remain backward.' Today the word means: 'to be able to live on (by) the basic (minimum) necessities of life' or: 'to exist and sustain oneself by one's own strength.'"

Today we include all these meanings and connotations when we talk of the Subsistence Perspective as the way out, the emergency exit out of our blockaded, overgrown, industrial society.

To live according to the guiding star of subsistence means no longer to live off the exploitation of the environment or of foreign peoples. For human life it means a new balance between talking and giving, between each one of us and other people, our people and other peoples, our species and the other species in nature.[21]

Phase 3: From Garbage to Compost

The Subsistence Conference at Bad Boll not only meant the discovery of a new guiding concept but also the beginning of a new process in which their old utopia could be re-created within a new ecological framework....

Phase 4: From Compost to Subsistence Agriculture

From the beginning the SSK had stressed the interconnections between the various problems with which they dealt: joblessness; the ecology problem; the inanity of most work; a sense of futility; loneliness; health problems; lack of dignity and recognition; overconsumption and addictions; and so on. Therefore also in their practical, political work similar also synergetic solutions should be sought.

...

Work in the Duster Grundchen, the logical continuation of the strategy of consumption critique, the use of organic garbage for compost-making, began to reveal the interconnected character of the holistic social and ecological approach we called "subsistence perspective."

It not only sparked off a new sense of enthusiasm, enjoyment, meaningfulness, political and personal purpose in SSK members and others, particularly some younger people, but also a new wave of reflection, theorizing and political creativity. In a paper produced in this process of action and reflection sent to the chairman of the local authority (Regierungspräsident), Lothar Gothe pointed out that neither the government nor any official party had succeeded in solving so many interrelated problems in one single project, namely: combining ecological with social problem-solving; healing the earth as well as people and communities by creating meaningful work; giving a new sense of purpose to socially marginalized women and men; developing a new, appropriate technology out of discarded, obsolete objects; recultivating wasteland; reestablishing a new community sense among people who are concerned and feel responsible for the future of life on this planet; and finally, creating new hope not only for those directly involved in the project but for many who have lost a sense of orientation.

It is this project's *synergic* character which was not planned but which developed out of necessity and which guarantees its survival. Had it been developed as a monocultural one-issue project, planned by experts, it could not have survived....

CONCLUSION

In summarizing the main features of the subsistence perspective which has informed and inspired the initiatives described above, as well as many ecological and feminist grassroots movements referred to in this book, we can see that these struggles for survival are a practical critique not only of an aggressive, exploitative, ecologically destructive technology, but of commodity-producing.... These women's and men's concept of what constitutes a "good life," of "freedom" is different, as is their concept of economics, politics and culture. Their utopia may not yet be spelt out explicitly, but its components are already being tested in everyday practice; it is a potentially *concrete utopia*. What are the main characteristics of this subsistence perspective?

1. The aim of *economic activity* is not to produce an ever-growing mountain of commodities and money (wages or profit) for an anonymous market but the creation and re-creation of *life*, that means, the satisfaction of fundamental human needs mainly by the production of use-values not by the purchase of commodities. Self-provisioning, self-sufficiency, particularly in food and other basic needs; regionality; and decentralization from a state bureaucracy are the main economic principles. The local and regional resources are used but not exploited; the market plays a subordinate role.

2. These economic activities are based on new *relationships:* (a) to *nature:* Nature is respected in her richness and diversity, both for her own sake and as a precondition for the survival of all creatures on this planet. Hence, nature is not exploited for the sake of profit; instead, wherever possible, the damage done to nature by capitalism is being healed. Human interaction with nature is based on respect, cooperation and reciprocity. Man's domination over nature—the principle that has guided Northern society since the Renaissance—is replaced by the recognition that humans are part of nature, that nature has her own subjectivity; and (b) *among people:* As man's domination over nature is related to man's domination over women and other human beings[23] a different, nonexploitative relationship to nature cannot be established without a change in human relationships, particularly between *women and men*. This means not only a change in the various *divisions of labor* (sexual division; manual/mental and urban/rural labor, and so on) but mainly the substitution of money or commodity relationships by such principles as reciprocity, mutuality, solidarity, reliability, sharing and caring, respect for the individual and responsibility for the "whole." The need for *subsistence security* is satisfied not by trust in one's bank account or a social welfare state, but by trust in the reliability of one's community. A subsistence perspective can be realized only within such a network of reliable, stable human relations; it cannot be based on the atomized, self-centered individuality of the market economy.

3. A subsistence perspective is based on and promotes participatory or grassroots democracy—not only in so far as political decisions per se are concerned, but also with regard to all economic, social and technological decisions. Divisions between politics and economics, or public and private spheres are largely abolished. The personal is the political. Not only the parliament but also everyday life and lifestyle are battlefields of politics. Political responsibility and action are no longer expected solely from elected representatives but assumed by all in a communal and practical way.

4. A subsistence perspective necessarily requires a multidimensional or synergic problem-solving approach. It is based on the recognition that not only the different dominance systems and problems are interconnected, but also that they cannot be solved in isolation or by a mere technological fix. Thus social problems (patriarchal relations, inequality, alienation, poverty) must be solved together with ecological problems. This interconnectedness of all life on earth, of problems and solutions is one of the main insights of ecofeminism.[24]

5. A subsistence perspective demands a new paradigm of science, technology and knowledge. Instead of the prevailing instrumentalist, reductionist science and technology—based on dualistic dichotomies which have constituted and maintain man's domination over nature, women and other people—ecologically sound, feminist, subsistence science and technology will be developed in participatory action with the people. Such a grassroots, women- and people-based knowledge and science will lead to a reevaluation of older survival wisdom and traditions and also utilize modern knowledge in such a way that people maintain control over their technology and survival base. Social relations are not external to technology but rather incorporated in the artefacts as such. Such science and technology will therefore not reinforce unequal social relationships but will be such as to make possible greater social justice.

6. A subsistence perspective leads to a reintegration of culture and work, of work as both burden and pleasure. It does not promise bread without sweat nor imply a life of toil and tears. On the contrary, the main aim is happiness and a fulfilled life. Culture is wider than specialized activity exclusive to a professional elite—it imbues everyday life.

This also necessitates a reintegration of spirit and matter, a rejection of both mechanical materialism and of airy spirituality. This perspective cannot be realized within a dualistic worldview.

7. A subsistence perspective resists all efforts to further privatize and/or commercialize the commons: water, air, waste, soil, resources. Instead it fosters common responsibility for these gifts of nature and demands their preservation and regeneration.

8. Most of the characteristics in the foregoing would also be appropriate to the conception of an ecofeminist society. In particular, the practical and theoretical insistence on the interconnectedness of all life, on a concept of politics that puts everyday practice and experiential ethics, the consistency of means and ends, in the forefront. And yet, the two examples previously documented are not feminist projects in the narrow sense in which this term is often understood, namely, all-women initiatives in which men have no role to play. In fact, the initiators of these projects were men.... As ecofeminists emphasize overcoming established dualisms and false dichotomies, as they want to put the interdependence of all life at the center of a new ethic and politics,[25] it would be quite inconsistent to exclude men from this network of responsibility for the creation and continuation of life. Ecofeminism does not mean, as some argue, that women will clean up the ecological mess which capitalist-patriarchal men have caused; women will not eternally be the *Trümmerfrauen* (the women who clear up the ruins after the patriarchal wars). Therefore, a subsistence perspective necessarily means men begin to share, *in practice,* the responsibility for the creation and preservation of life on this planet. Therefore, men must start a movement to redefine their identity. They must give up their involvement in destructive commodity production for the sake of accumulation and begin to share women's work for the preservation of life. In practical terms this means they have to share unpaid subsistence work: in the household, with children, with the old and sick, in ecological work to heal the earth, in new forms of subsistence production.

In this respect it is essential that the old sexist division of labor criticized by the feminists in the 1970s—that is, men become the theoreticians of the subsistence perspective while women do the practical work—is abolished. This division between mental and manual labor is contrary to the principles of a subsistence perspective....

9. Moreover, if the dichotomy between life-producing and -preserving and commodity-producing activities is abolished, if men acquire caring and nurturing qualities which have so far been considered women's domain, and if, in an economy based on self-reliance, mutuality, self-provisioning, not women alone but men too are involved in subsistence production they will have neither time nor the inclination to pursue their destructive war games. A subsistence perspective will be the most significant contribution to the demilitarization of men and society....

Finally, it must be pointed out that we are not the first to spell out a subsistence perspective as a vision for a better society. Wherever women and men have envisaged a society in which all—women and men, old and young, all races and cultures—could share the "good life," where social justice, equality, human dignity, beauty and joy in life were not just utopian dreams never to be realized (except for a small elite or postponed to an afterlife), there has been close to what we call a subsistence perspective.... This was already clear to Mahatma Gandhi 60 years ago, who, when asked by a British journalist whether he would like India to have the same standard of living as Britain, replied: "To have its standard of living a tiny country like Britain had to exploit half the globe. How many globes will India need to exploit to have the same standard of living?"[27] From an ecological and feminist perspective, moreover, even if there were more globes to be exploited, it is not even desirable that this development paradigm and standard of living was generalized, because it has failed to fulfill its promises of happiness, freedom, dignity and peace, even for those who have profited from it.

NOTES

1. Mies, Maria, et al, *Women: The Last Colony,* Zed Books, London, 1988; Mies, M. (1991) *Patriarchy and Accumulation on a World Scale: Women in the International Division of Labor,* Zed Books, London, 1991.

2. Kurz, R. *Der Kollaps der Modernisierung, vom Zusammenbruch des Kasernensozialismus zur Krise der Weltökonomie.* Eichborn Verlag, Frankfurt, 1991.

3. Mies, et al, *Women.*

...

5. Kurz, R. *Der Kollaps der Modernisierung,* p. 101.

6. Ibid., p. 102.

...

8. Dar es Salaam Declaration: Alternative Development Strategies for Africa. Institute for African Alternatives (IFAA), London, 1989.

9. Ibid.

10. Dankelman, I. and J. Davidson, *Women and Environment in the Third World. Alliance for the Future.* Earthscan Publications, London, 1988. Women's Feature Service (ed.) *The Power to Change: Women in the Third World Redefine their Environment.* Kali for Women, New Delhi, 1992; Zed Books, London, 1993.

11. Joshi, Gopal (1988) Alltag im Himalya, in: Tüting, Ludmilla (ed.), *Menschen, Bäume, Erosionen, Kahlschlag im Himalya; Wege aus der Zerstörung.* Der Grune Zweig, Lohrbach, pp. 38–41.

...

21. Gothe, Lothar and Meggie Lucke, *Land in Sight,* Cologne, 1990.

...

23. Bookchin, Murray, *Toward an Ecological Society.* Black Rose Books, Montreal, Buffalo, 1986. Mies, 1991, op. cit. Ackelsberg, Martha and Irene Diamond, "Is Ecofeminism a New Phase of Anarchism?" Paper presented at Eighth Berkshire Conference on the History of Women, Douglass College, New Brunswick, New Jersey, 8–10 June, 1990.

24. Ackelsberg and Diamond, op. cit.

25. Diamond, Irene and Gloria Feman-Orenstein, *Reweaving the World: The Emergence of Ecofeminism,* Sierra Club Books, San Francisco, 1990.

...

27. Quoted by Kamla Bhasin, op. cit., p. 11.

SANDRA HARDING
Borderlands Epistemologies

TWO PROBLEMATIC EPISTEMOLOGICAL STRATEGIES

The new kinds of science and technology studies that emerged after World War II were created out of the systematic gaps in modern science's self-understanding.[1] ... Of course no humans are ever able to understand fully "what we are doing," since we lack the historical long view, the awareness of larger economic, political, and social patterns, and an understanding of the causes of our collective fears, interests, preferences, and desires that subsequent histories, sociologies, political economies, and psychologies reveal.

... [I]n the early 1960s historian Thomas Kuhn had called for more of the kind of social history of modern science that could "display the historical integrity of ... science in its own time." These histories were to explain scientific and technological change in ways that the prevailing intellectual histories could not.... Of course these social histories would not turn out to be merely an additive project that left untouched conventional understandings of how the sciences have worked, for Kuhn's account revealed a different pattern to the growth of knowledge than the intellectual histories had detected....

The older, "internalist" histories and philosophies of science that many of us learned were not just accidentally silent about such matters. Rather, they had denied the relevance and legitimacy of such accounts to understanding how science "really works." Such social accounts might explain how societies provided many of the resources scientific research requires, how they sometimes influenced the selection of which scientific projects were to be pursued, and how they applied the information science produced. And they could explain how politics sometimes managed to lead science down wrong paths, as with Lysenkoism and Nazi so-called science. But they could not explain science's successes, the internalist histories and epistemologies claimed, since these were the product not of such social factors, but of nature's order and the powerful features of scientific inquiry that lay entirely *inside* scientific processes. A distinctive scientific method of research, high standards of objectivity and of what can count as good reasoning, a critical attitude toward traditional belief, the distinctive metaphysics of nature that distinguished primary and secondary qualities, the use of mathematics to express nature's order, the particular way modern scientific communities have been organized—these and other features *internal* to science were especially suited to discovering nature's order.... The post–World War II science and technology studies pointed out, however, that this internalist dogma, as some referred to it, left mysterious the answers to kinds of historical questions that are considered necessary to understand each and every other product of human activity.[3]

The internalist epistemology obscured why modern science emerged when and where it did, how it changed over time, and how its culture and practices coevolved with those of other social institutions, such as the economy and state. Of course it was this epistemology of modern science—its method, standards of objectivity and rationality, the necessity of such features for social progress—that had long been used to justify the unique authority of the modern West in global political relations. Consequently, the discovery of these systematic and suspicious gaps were one source of rising global skepticism about the desirability and legitimacy of the authority of the West more generally. Widespread recognition of such failures has produced what is referred to as the epistemological crisis of the modern West.

...

Two strategies for resolving the "crisis" that have been favored in post-Kuhnian science studies appear problematic from the perspective of postcolonial and feminist science and technology studies.[4] One project has been to try to patch up this conventional epistemology by responding to some criticisms of it and dismissing others without abandoning its fundamental internalist principle.... These revisionists think that the prevailing epistemology of modern science should be retained in a modified form....

Another project, characteristic of many northern sociologists and ethnographers of sciences, is to agree with much more of the criticism of internalist epistemology—indeed, these theorists have themselves produced a great deal of it. But they presume that the only reasonable solution is to abandon epistemological projects completely and forswear the arrogance of presuming the political and intellectual appropriateness of the "policing of thought" that they think this requires.[5] They conceptualize all epistemological projects as necessarily internalist.[6] The only alternatives to such epistemologies are to be descriptive histories, sociologies, and ethnographies of science that disavow the normative stance taken by epistemologies. They try to substitute "sciences" of natural sciences, namely social sciences and more accurate historical accounts of natural sciences, for epistemologies of science. . . .

While revised internalist epistemologies or the "abandonment" of epistemology have sometimes been the favored strategies in postcolonial and feminist science studies, a third approach has clearly emerged in both, which makes use of the resources of "borderlands" locations and states of mind. This is the approach of standpoint epistemologies. . . .

WHAT IS A STANDPOINT? CULTURAL AND POLITICAL EPISTEMOLOGICAL RESOURCES

. . . The concept of a standpoint arose from women's political struggles to see their concerns represented in public policy and in the natural and social science disciplines that have shaped such policy. These epistemologies propose that there are important resources for the production of knowledge to be found in starting off research projects from issues arising in women's lives rather than only from the dominant androcentric conceptual frameworks of the disciplines and the larger social order. Two kinds of "difference" provide independent arguments for abandoning the internalist epistemology of the modern West. One appeals to *politically* assigned locations in social hierarchies, such as those created by class, racism, imperialism, or sexism. The other appeals to *culturally* created locations, such as Chinese versus Puerto Rican, or Confucian versus Catholic. Though analytically distinguishable, in daily life the pervasiveness of political relations within and between cultures insures that different cultural resources almost never have equal political status.[9]

Intellectual and Social Histories of Standpoint Epistemologies

The intellectual history of feminist standpoint theory conventionally is traced to Hegel's reflections on what can be known about the master/slave relationship from the standpoint of the slave's life in contrast to the far more distorted understanding of it available from the perspective of the master's life. From the perspective of the master's activities, everything the slave does appears to be the consequence either of the master's will or of the slave's lazy and brutish nature. The slave does not appear fully human. However, from the standpoint of the slave's activities, one can see her smiling at the master when she in fact wishes to kill, playing lazy as the only form of resistance she can get away with, and scheming with the slave community to escape. The slave can be seen as fully human. Marx, Engels, and Lukacs subsequently developed this insight into the "standpoint of the proletariat," from which were produced theories of how class society operates.[10] In the 1970s, several feminist thinkers independently began reflecting on how the Marxian analysis could be transformed to explain how structural and symbolic gender relations had consequences for the production of knowledge. . . .

A *social* history of standpoint theory would focus on the kinds of criticisms of prevailing institutions, their cultures, and practices that appear when formerly silenced peoples begin to gain public voice. On the one hand, these voices argue for applying the existing methods, rules, and procedures more fairly in order to eliminate what they think of as the biases in the prevailing views. However, they also frequently argue that the existing conceptual frameworks, methods, rules, and procedures for inquiry are themselves constituted only from the perspective of ruling-group interests. The standpoint of some particular marginalized group can point the way to less partial and distorted conceptual frameworks, methods, rules, and procedures of inquiry. What the standpoint of any particular group consists in must be determined by empirical observation and theoretical reflection. A standpoint is an objective position in social relations as articulated through one or another theory or discourse. . . .

The Conceptual Practices of Power[14]

Standpoint theory is not much concerned with the biases of individuals or of subgroups within the dominant culture (one laboratory or research group versus another), which are the conventional focus of internalist epistemological thinking. Rather, its concern is with the assumptions generated by "ways of life" and apparent in discursive frameworks, conceptual schemes, and epistemes, within which entire dominant groups tend to think about nature and social relations, and to use such frameworks to structure social relations for the rest of us, too.... A standpoint is not the same as a viewpoint or perspective, for it requires both science and political struggle, as Nancy Hartsock puts the point, to see beneath the surfaces of social life to the "realities" that structure it.[15]

We can pick out several major themes in standpoint approaches. First, the starting point of standpoint theory, and its claim that is most often misread, is that in societies stratified by race, ethnicity, class, gender, sexuality, or some other such politics shaping the very structure and meanings of social relations, the *activities* or lives ("labor" in the Marxian account) of those at the top both organize and set limits on what persons who perform such activities can understand about themselves and the world around them.... In contrast, the activities of those who are exploited by such social hierarchies can provide starting points for thought—for everyone's research and scholarship—from which otherwise obscured relations that people have with each other and with the natural world can become visible.

... [D]ifferent cultures are led to ask different questions about nature and social relations because of their distinctive locations in the natural world (in deserts, on waterways, in the Arctic, or on the equator), their distinctive cultural interests even in "the same" environment, their culturally local discursive legacies (the metaphors, models, narratives, and the like through which they have defined themselves as a culture and come to see the world around them), and their distinctive ways of organizing the work of producing knowledge. Chinese and Puerto Rican patterns of knowledge and ignorance will differ because of such cultural differences. However, power differences within or between cultures will also create different opportunities for systematic knowledge and systematic ignorance. The experience and lives of marginalized peoples, as they understand them, provide distinctive *problems to be explained* or research agendas that are not visible or not compelling to the dominant groups. Marginalized experiences and lives have been devalued or ignored as a source of important questions about nature and social relations, especially objectivity-maximizing ones.... It is valuable new questions that thinking from the perspective of such lives can generate.

However, the answers to such questions are never completely to be found in those experiences or lives. For the answers, one must examine critically the dominant conceptual frameworks that reflect disproportionately the interests of dominant groups. It is dominant groups who, in making what appear to them to be perfectly reasonable policies, shape marginal lives in ways not always visible within those lives. For example, women, too, have tended to see their household labor as not really work.... Thus, standpoint theories argue that it is certainly the case that each group's social situation enables and sets limits on what it can know. However, the critically unexamined dominant ones tend to be more limiting than others in this respect. What makes these social locations more limiting is their inability to generate—indeed, their interests in avoiding, devaluing, silencing—the most critical questions about the dominant conceptual frameworks. Marginalized groups have interests in asking such questions, and dominant groups have interests in not hearing them.

Of course this does not mean that all women will be able to ask the most critical questions of androcentric frameworks.... Nor does it mean that no men can ever ask them; there are plenty of examples of men doing so in the history of feminist political activism, research, and scholarship.... Standpoint theory is only pointing to how people tend to perceive their own best interests in predictable ways, though they can always find reason to pursue other interests that make exceptions to such predictions.

... Women's lives (our many different lives and different experiences) can provide the starting point for asking new, critical questions about not only those lives, but also about men's lives and the social institutions designed primarily by men to serve "humanity." Most importantly, [Dorothy] Smith argues, a sociology that is to be *for* women, rather than for the dominant social institutions and their beneficiaries must ask new questions about the causal relations between women's lives, on the one hand, and men's lives and public institutions, on the other hand.

For example, [Smith] points out that if we start thinking from women's lives, we (anyone) can see that women are assigned the work that men do not want to do for themselves, especially the care of everyone's bodies—the bodies of men, of babies and children, of old people, of the sick, and of their own bodies. And they are assigned responsibility for the local places where those bodies exist as they clean and maintain their own and others' houses and workplaces.... And men in marginalized groups often perform certain kinds of such work in restaurants, hospitals, and janitorial jobs. This kind of work, she shows, frees men in the ruling groups to immerse themselves in the world of abstract concepts. The more successful women are at this concrete work, the more invisible it becomes to men as distinctively social labor. Caring for bodies and for the places in which bodies exist disappears into nature....

She points out that if we start from women's lives, we can generate questions about why primarily women are assigned such activities and what the consequences are for the economy, the state, the family, the educational system, and other social institutions of assigning body and emotional work to one group and head work to another.[18] Such questions lead to less partial and distorted understandings of women's worlds, men's worlds, and the causal relations between them than do questions originating only in that part of human activity that men in the dominant groups reserve for themselves—the abstract mental work of management and administration.[19]

Similar accounts of the tendency of the eurocentric, colonial, or imperial mentality to conceptualize "natives" as part of nature, of their labor as not really social labor, not really part of human history, their land as empty or wasteland, are common.[20] ...

Thus, standpoint epistemology sets the relationship between knowledge and politics at the center of its account in the sense that it tries to explain the effects that different kinds of political arrangements have on the production of knowledge. Of course, the older empiricist theories of knowledge were also concerned with the effects politics have on the production of knowledge, but prefeminist empiricism conceptualizes politics as entirely a threat to the purity of scientific knowledge.[21] Empiricism tries to purify science of all such bad politics by adherence to what it takes to be rigorous methods for the testing of hypotheses.... Thought that begins from the lives of the marginalized has no chance to get its critical questions voiced or heard within such an empiricist conception of the way to produce knowledge, nor can the positive value of such "political" questions be detected within empiricist frameworks....

Thus, the standpoint claims that all knowledge attempts are socially situated, and that some of these objective social locations are better than others as starting points for knowledge projects, challenge some of the most fundamental assumptions of the scientific worldview and the western thought that take science as their model of how to produce knowledge. It sets out guidelines for a "logic of discovery" intended to maximize the objectivity of the results of research, and thereby to produce knowledge that can be for marginalized people and for those who would know what they can know....

How Can the Lives of the "Weak" Provide Resources for the Growth of Knowledge in the Natural Sciences?

Most conventional histories, sociologies, and philosophies of science assumed that science's social relations are constituted fundamentally by public, official, visible, and dramatic role players and situations—scientists and their critics who were recognized as such in their own day, for example.... Of course, it is those who are public, official, visible, and dramatic role players ... who would make such limited and distorting assumptions about the constitution of a culture such as scientific culture.... So it was by starting off analyses from the unofficial, supportive, less dramatic, private, and invisible spheres of social life "outside science," ones that support and sustain public, official, visible, and dramatic *scientific* role players and organizations, that it has been possible to produce more accurate and comprehensive accounts of the historical integrity of sciences with their cultures. Feminist and postcolonial critiques of the conceptual frameworks of each discipline contributing to the social studies of science—history, economics, political philosophy, anthropology, sociology, psychology—draw our attention to unacknowledged aspects of the culture and practices of both modern sciences and the scientific and technological traditions of other cultures....

One can learn much by starting off thought from the lives of those who perform the daily routines necessary for everyone's bodily and social survival. Insofar as different groups are assigned different daily activities, they will tend to know different things about natural and social worlds.

Another way this "power of the weak" has been discussed is in terms of the advantages of the stranger or outsider. The stranger brings to research just the combination of nearness and remoteness, concern and indifference, that are central to maximizing objectivity.[24] Women, racial/ethnic minorities, the victims of imperialism and colonialism, and the poor are in some respects functionally "strangers" to the dominant cultures and practices that structure their lives—including such scientific and technological cultures and practices. Their needs and desires are not the ones that have found expression in the design and functioning of the dominant institutions.... And yet these groups are not completely outside the dominant institutions—they are no longer off in Africa or barefoot and pregnant in the kitchen. They are instead on the margins, the periphery; they are "outsiders within" or on the "borderlands," in two influential standpoint phrases.[25]

... Anyone who starts out thinking about science funding, or environmental destruction, or medical research from the perspective of the lives of those who bear a disproportionate share of the costs of these activities can learn to "follow the interests" of the latter to arrive at less partial and distorted accounts of science and technology institutions and practices.

...

The older Marxian accounts argued that certain social formations only became easily visible at certain historical moments.... Feminist theorists have described the emergence into visibility only after World War II of what has been called the "gender system"—a system that is not entirely an effect of biology, of class relations, or of some other social arrangements.[26] Of course class and gender relations are far older than the 1840s and 1950s, respectively; but their relative independence from other social formations only becomes visible at these points.... Thus, epistemic advantage with respect to any particular social formation of sciences and technologies can wax and wane at different historical moments. The ability to identify and think from those sites—to identify the contradictions within the dominant ways of organizing social life—is to enhance one's chances for more accurate and comprehensive accounts of nature and social relations.

Finally, a whole range of interpretive strategies in literary, cultural, and historical studies draws our attention to alternative readings not only of conventional texts—of spoken or written words—but also of cultural formations.... Starting from marginalized lives makes it easier to see the discursive formations that construct and continuously relegitimate dominant conceptual frameworks in the sciences and the larger societies that evolve together.

WHAT STANDPOINT EPISTEMOLOGIES ARE NOT

For those who still hold that maximizing objectivity requires maximizing neutrality ... standpoint epistemologies will appear relativist. From such a perspective they appear as a kind of special pleading or unreasonably claimed privileged positionality. On such a reading, empiricism is politics-free, and standpoint theory is asserting epistemological/scientific privilege for one group at the expense of the equally valuable and/or equally distorted perceptions of other groups. All groups are "biased," they are willing to admit, so standpoint approaches are simply claiming privilege for one kind of such bias....

This interpretation of difference as mere diversity is a serious misunderstanding of social relations, as well as of political standpoint claims about the effects of power on knowledge claims. It reduces power relations to mere cultural differences. Standpoint theory leads us to turn such a way of posing the issue into a topic for historical analysis: "what forms of social relations make this conceptual framework—the view from nowhere versus special pleading—so useful, and for what purposes?" Let us look at some of these common misunderstandings of standpoint theory.

Not Only about Marginal Lives

First, standpoint theory is not only about how to get a more accurate understanding of marginal lives.... Instead, research is to *start off* from such locations in order to explain the relationship between those lives and the rest of social relations, including human interactions with nature.... The point is to produce systematic causal accounts of how the natural and social orders are organized such that the everyday lives of women and men, Europeans and those they encounter, end up in the forms that they do.

"Grounded," but Unconventionally So

The phrases "peasant experiences" and "women's experiences" can be read in an empiricist way such that these experiences are assumed to be constituted prior to the social. Major strains of standpoint theory challenge this kind of reading.[29] For a researcher to start from marginalized lives is not necessarily to take one's research problems in the terms in which marginalized people perceive or articulate their problems—and this is as true for researchers who come from these groups as it is for those who do not. The dominant discourses, their institutions, practices, favored conceptual frameworks, and languages, restrict what everyone is permitted to see and shape everyone's consciousness. Fortunately, they are not perfect at these projects, for subjugated discourses always also exist; power always also produces in its subjects visions, dreams, plans for its end. Women, like men, have had to learn to think of their domestic work not just as a "labor of love," but as a contribution to the local and national economy. Many citizens of so-called developing countries have had to reassess just who is benefitting from the "progress" that the transfer to their cultures of modern sciences and technologies is supposed to be bringing.... It is obvious that "peasant experience" or "women's experience" does not automatically generate counterhegemonic analyses, since the former often exists but only occasionally does the latter emerge. Standpoint theorists are not making the absurd claim that the new postcolonial and feminist analyses simply flow naturally from these groups' experiences.

Postcolonial and feminist analyses are not culturally neutral elaborations of people's social experiences, or what members of marginalized groups say about their lives; they are theoretical reflections on them. Marginalized experiences, and what marginalized peoples say, are crucial guides to the new questions that can be asked about nature, sciences, and social relations. Such questions arise out of the gap between marginalized interests and consciousness, on the one hand, and the way the dominant conceptual schemes organize social relations, including those of scientific and technological change. Moreover, the answers to such research questions cannot be found simply by examining more carefully marginalized lives, since marginalized interests and experiences are shaped by national and international policies and practices that are formulated and enacted far away from marginalized people's daily lives.... Standpoint theory is not calling for phenomenologies or merely rational interpretations of marginalized worlds. Nor is it arguing that only members of marginalized groups can generate knowledge that is useful to such groups—that is *for* them. Standpoint epistemology is not an "identity politics" project for knowledge production—unless "identity" is taken as one's commitment to who one wants to be rather than only to where one has come from.

Men, too, can learn to start their thought from women's lives, and northern peoples from southern lives, as many have done. Misunderstandings come about because objectivism insists that the only alternative to its "view from nowhere" is special interest biases and ethnoknowledges that can be understood only within a relativist epistemology....

Much of the debate over just what "grounds" standpoint accounts is a consequence of the different ways feminist (and postcolonial) analyses have theorized what was problematic about internalist epistemologies. Where the internalist epistemologies insisted on the scientific priority, the greater objectivity, of outsiders' descriptions over "the natives," the new social movements have insisted that such descriptions greatly lacked objectivity, and that marginalized groups should get to express their concerns in their own terms. Their "experiences" were at least as good as the experiences of their "masters" in providing objective descriptions and explanations of the social relations between them. There was no innocent, disembodied view from nowhere possible with respect to gender, class, or race relations in which everyone was implicated, whether or not they chose to recognize such loss of innocence. The site from which more objective analyses were to emerge was not individuals' consciousness, but collective histories. One's position in such histories was crucial.... The suggestion here is that it is more important to understand how the pattern of these claims was created by what they were opposed to and how they were devalued in the mainstream epistemologies than to try to settle on one or another as the really only defensible one.

No Essential Marginalized Lives

Next, standpoint theory is not arguing that there is some kind of essential, universally adequate model of the marginalized life from which research should start off.... "Racially marginalized," "poor," and "women" are not homogenous categories; they include groups whose activities are differently shaped by their class, race, gender, ethnicity, historical period, and cultural milieu. Any presumption of uniform experiences and activities would distort the accounts that ensued. Though the conventional way of thinking about power relations tends to enshrine an oppositional, two-party relationship between a homogenized "us" and a homogenized "them," power functions in far more complex ways.

Consciousness Not Determined by Social Location

According to standpoint theorists, we each have a specific location, albeit often a complex one, in such a social matrix; but that location does not determine one's consciousness. The availability of competing discourses enables some men, for example, to think and act in feminist ways. Yet they still obviously remain men, who are thereby in determinate relations to women and men in every class and race. They can work to eliminate male supremacy, but no matter what they do, they will still be treated with the privilege (or suspicion!) accorded to men by students, sales people, coworkers, family members, and others.... The point of standpoint theory is to help move people toward liberatory standpoints, whether one is in a marginalized or dominant social location. It is an achievement, not a "natural property," of women to develop a feminist standpoint, or a standpoint of women, no less than it is for a man to do so.

An Epistemology, a Philosophy of Science, a Sociology of Knowledge, and a Method for Doing Research

Several disciplines have competed to disown (and in one case not only to claim, but to monopolize) standpoint theory....

Reflection on such rejections of standpoint theory can be illuminating, for they reveal how severely this theory diverges from the standard disciplinary models that conceptualize representations of knowledge seeking. It is more useful, I suggest, to see it as all of these projects: a philosophy of knowledge, a philosophy of science, a sociology of knowledge, a moral/political advocacy of the expansion of democratic rights to participate in making the social decisions that will affect one's life, and a proposed research method for the natural and social sciences. Each such project must always make assumptions about the others.... Our beliefs face the tribunal of experience as a network, and none are immune from possible revision when a misfit between belief and observation arises, as philosopher W. V. O. Quine put the point. Postcolonial, feminist, and post-Kuhnian social studies of science and technology have been raising challenges to conventional conceptual frameworks that have led to reexamination of empiricist assumptions about the organization of scientific communities, ideals of the knower, the known, and how knowledge should be produced, rational reconstructions of the growth of scientific knowledge, and scientific method in the sense of "how to do good research." Standpoint theory's claims have effects on and must draw resources from all of these fields.

Not Damagingly Relativist

... In everyday talk, "standpoint" is used interchangeably with "view," "perspective," and other such locational terms that are relativist not only in that they are socially located, but also in that all have equal authority; none is inherently more advantaged or privileged than any other. However, in the originating analyses on which standpoint theorists reflected, starting off thought from the master's life was not just as good as starting off from the slave's life to understand the master/slave relationship. Nor was the view from bourgeois lives supposed to be just as good as the view from workers' lives to explain how capitalist economic relations worked. In these cases, the exploited social position offered the possibility of a critical perspective on the dominant institutional and conceptual systems. Thanks to African American history and labor history we have come to understand systems of slavery and of class societies in ways that were not visible from the lives of those benefiting from such systems.

Claims can be sociologically or historically "relativist" in the sense of locating a distinctive pattern of thought in its historical and social context: different cultures (classes, genders, historical epochs) tend to favor different patterns of thought. But that still leaves us with the possibility of adopting a position of cognitive or epistemological relativism, or not; it does not force us to a relativist position.... [Standpoint epistemology] argues that such different local knowledge systems each have their own distinctive resources for and limitations on understanding ourselves and the natural and social worlds around us. The practical challenge raised by post–World War II science and technology studies is to understand which are the resources and which the limitations for any given knowledge system, and which systems are best for which knowledge production projects.

CONCLUSION

... Standpoint approaches can show us how to detect values and interests that constitute scientific projects, ones that do not vary between legitimated observers, and the difference between those values and interests that enlarge and those that limit our descriptions, explanations, and understandings of nature and social relations. Standpoint approaches provide a map, a method, for maximizing a "strong objectivity" in the natural and social sciences. They provide more objective ways of explaining the limitations of standard accounts of nature and social relations, and the surprising strengths of the post-Kuhnian, postcolonial, and feminist studies of science and technology that have emerged since World War II.

However, they may not always be the best way to articulate why a particular knowledge seeking strategy is preferable.... My point here is that the preference for one epistemology over another can reasonably be as strategic as the preference for one scientific theory over another: it provides the kind of map we need to get us where we want to go. Of course we then must justify why it is *there* that we want to go. Borderlands have emerged as expanding and crowded territories of contemporary social life. Standpoint epistemologies articulate how important forms of knowledge can be produced from such "territories." ...

NOTES

1. Langdon Winner made this point in his "The Gloves Come Off: Shattered Alliances in Science and Technology Studies," *Social Text* 46–47 (1996), 81–92.

...

3. See, for example, W. V. O. Quine, "Two Dogmas of Empiricism," in his *From a Logical Point of View* (Cambridge, MA: Harvard University Press, 1953). See chapter 15 of Peter Novick, *That Noble Dream: The "Objectivism Question" and the American Historical Profession* (Cambridge: Cambridge University Press, 1988) for a good overview of the historical changes and intellectual ferment of the post–World War II period that produced and surrounded the emerging "epistemological crisis of the modern West," including major streams of the science and technology studies examined here. Richard Bernstein's *Beyond Objectivism and Relativism* (Philadelphia: University of Pennsylvania Press, 1983) and Richard Rorty's *Philosophy and the Mirror of Nature* (Princeton, NJ: Princeton University Press, 1979) were two immensely influential books by philosophers that diagnosed how "the crisis" was emerging across broad swaths of European and North American natural and social sciences and their philosophies.

4. As noted in earlier chapters, these three streams of science and technology studies are by no means entirely separate; they have interacted and their arguments often coincide. Some writers and writings, such as the latest stages of the gender and sustainable development debates and Donna Haraway's work, for example, clearly have been shaped by all three tendencies. Nevertheless, most of the post–World War II science and technology writings have not drawn on this full range of analyses; they are still constrained by pre-Kuhnian, Eurocentric, and/or androcentric understandings of modern science.

5. The idea is Michel Foucault's. See, for example, his *Power/Knowledge: Selected Interviews and Other Writings, 1972–1977,* trans. Cohn Gordon, Leo Marshall, John Mepham, and Kate Soper (New York: Random House, 1980).

6. As I have argued in a somewhat different context, in this respect they are as conservative as the internalists, who agree that there is no reasonable epistemological alternative to their own program. See my chapter 7, "Feminist Epistemology after the Enlightenment," in *Whose Science? Whose Knowledge?* (Ithaca, NY: Cornell University Press, 1991).

...

9. The resources of such culturally specific standpoints were explored especially in chapter 4. Early feminist standpoint theories were explicitly concerned with the effects on knowledge of the politics of men's and women's culturally distinctive activities. How have the systematic patterns of knowledge and ignorance in the modern West reflected the exclusion of women from the conceptualization of sociological or philosophical problems, for example, and the relative absence of men from the childcare, household labor, and emotional labor which had been assigned primarily to women? See, e.g., Nancy Hartsock, "The Feminist Standpoint: Developing the Ground for a Specifically Feminist Historical Materialism," in *Discovering Reality: Feminist Perspectives on Epistemology, Metaphysics, Methodology, and Philosophy of Science,* ed. Sandra Harding and Merrill Hintikka (Dordrecht: Reidel/Kluwer, 1983); Alison Jaggar, *Feminist Politics and Human Nature* (Totowa, N.J.: Rowman and Allanheld, 1983), chapter 11; Hilary Rose, "Hand, Brain, and Heart: A Feminist Epistemology for the Natural Sciences," *Signs* 9:1 (1983); Dorothy Smith, *The Everyday World as Problematic: A Sociology for Women* (Boston: Northeastern University Press, 1987); and *The Conceptual Practices of Power: A Feminist Sociology of Knowledge* (Boston: Northeastern University Press, 1990). Smith's essays collected in these volumes had been appearing since the mid-1970s. See also my discussions of standpoint theories in *The Science Question in Feminism* (Ithaca, NY: Cornell University Press, 1986), and in *Whose Science? Whose Knowledge?*

10. Of course, there were many problems with the way the proletarian standpoint was conceptualized. After Lukacs's work on it, feminist theorists were the next to try to use the resource of a specifically Marxian understanding of the relationship between "doing" and knowing to develop an epistemology. Of course Foucault had meanwhile been exploring power/knowledge relations in ways that lead readers to the disavowal of any epistemological projects at all. See his *Power/Knowledge.* Fredric Jameson has argued that the feminist standpoint theorists are the only contemporary thinkers currently working explicitly with the Marxian epistemological legacy. See George Lukacs, *History and Class Consciousness* (Cambridge: Massachusetts Institute of Technology Press, 1971); Jameson, "History and Class Consciousness as an 'Unfinished Project,'" *Rethinking Marxism* 1 (1988): 49–72; F. Engels, "Socialism: Utopian and Scientific," in *The Marx and Engels Reader,* ed. R. Tucker (New York: Norton, 1972).

...

14. The heading is borrowed from Smith's book, *Conceptual Practices.*

15. Hartsock, "The Feminist Standpoint."

...

18. Of course body work and emotional work also require head work—contrary to the long history of sexist, racist, and class biased views. See, e.g., Sara Ruddick, *Maternal Thinking* (Boston: Beacon, 1989). And the kind of head work required in administrative and managerial work—what Smith means by "ruling"—also involves distinctive body and emotional work, though it is not acknowledged as such. Think of how much of early childhood education of middle-class children is really about internalizing a certain kind of (gender specific) regulation of bodies and emotions.

19. See the very similar accounts, independently produced, in Hartsock's "Feminist Standpoint" and Rose's "Hand, Brain, and Heart." Feminist standpoint theory was an idea whose time had arrived in Canada, the United States, and the United Kingdom.

20. See, for example, Amin, *Eurocentrism;* J. M. Blaut, *The Colonizers' Model of the World* (New York: Guilford Press, 1993); and Vandana Shiva, *Staying Alive: Women, Ecology, and Development* (London: Zed, 1989).

21. I specify "prefeminist empiricism" here since some of the feminist philosophical empiricists, such as Helen Longino, who have always understood the importance of progressive politics for "eliminating bias" from purportedly value-free claims, have recently begun to permit somewhat more expanded contributions for such politics, while nevertheless drawing a firm line between their projects and the standpoint centering of relations between politics and knowledge that directs us all to "start off thought from marginal lives" in order to gain more accurate and comprehensive accounts. See her *Science as Social Knowledge* (Princeton, NJ: Princeton University Press, 1990).

...

24. Patricia Hill Collins has discussed this in *Black Feminist Thought.*

25. "Outsider within" is Patricia Hill Collins's phrase; see her *Black Feminist Thought.* As indicated above, *Borderlands* is Gloria Anzaldúa's term.

26. See my "Why Has the Sex/Gender System Emerged into Visibility Only Now?" in *Discovering Reality: Feminist Perspectives on Epistemology, Metaphysics, Methodology, and Philosophy of Science,* ed. Sandra Harding and Merrill Hintikka (Dordrecht: Reidel, 1983).

...

29. Feminist standpoint ambiguities and ambivalences about the role to be assigned to women's experiences have been the topic of innumerable discussions. See, for example, Rosemary Hennessy, *Feminist Materialism and the Politics of Discourse* (New York: Routledge, 1993); and many discussions in sociology journals of Smith's work in particular. However, one strain throughout standpoint theory's history within feminism, more strongly emphasized in some writings than in others, has been that women's experiences are themselves generated from within discourses—prevailing, or subjugated, or newly constructed through feminisms. Neither women's experiences nor their subjectivities are constituted prior to "the social." Accessible discussions of this topic more generally can be found in Chris Weedon, *Feminist Practice and Poststructuralist Theory* (Cambridge, MA: Blackwell, 1987).

...

10
Feminist Postmodernism: Knowledges as Partial, Contingent, and Politically Informed

Postmodernism did not originate as an academic epistemological theory produced by scholars in philosophy. Instead, it emerged as a broad stylistic or aesthetic movement, beginning in architecture and then migrating to other arts. Later, theoretical writings in the humanities and eventually the social sciences sought to explicate and justify that style. Postmodernism's conceptions of knowledge and reality are most easily explained by contrasting them with the conceptions associated with modernity.

SOME ONTOLOGICAL AND EPISTEMOLOGICAL THEMES OF MODERNITY

Modern ways of thinking appeared in the West in the seventeenth century. They sprang from the intellectual, social, and cultural transformations of the Renaissance, the Reformation, and the Scientific and Industrial Revolutions. Modern thought is characterized by confidence in the ability of secular reason to understand the world, confidence that contrasts with the medieval acceptance of mystery and reliance on faith. Within Western modernity, reason was construed in various ways: for rationalists, it is a priori deduction from first principles; for empiricists, it is induction from data given directly to experience. Despite these variations, Western epistemology increasingly came to conceptualize reason in instrumental terms, regarding it as a tool for assessing various means to achieving ends that were valued subjectively but not open themselves to rational evaluation. This view of reason obviously assumed a sharp distinction between facts and values and suggested that reason must be value-neutral. In this view, the knowledge produced by reason must also be value-neutral, in sharp contrast with medieval ideas that knowledge and science provided insight into laws that were natural in the sense of being divinely ordained.

According to the modern worldview, reality exists objectively, that is, independently of human thoughts or beliefs about it, and the goal of knowledge is to discover the true nature of objective reality. Genuine knowledge must be absolutely certain or at the very least highly probable, and this certainty can be achieved only by basing knowledge claims on indubitable premises, an approach to epistemology known as foundationalism. Certain knowledge is best achieved through the methods of science, which is distinguished by its use of the experimental method and especially by its insistence on replicable observations and experiments, a requirement designed to eliminate possible bias on the part of individual observers. Modern thought aspires to produce a view of reality as it appears from nowhere in particular and so from everywhere in general. Truth is thought to be universal and particular perspectives are seen as biased.

342

The requirement that observations be replicable presupposes that knowers or observers are very similar in their capacities to acquire knowledge and therefore interchangeable. Within the modern epistemological tradition, knowers' social locations and specific perspectives are at best irrelevant to their ability to know and at worst subversive of it. Knowing selves are unified subjects of consciousness, fully transparent to themselves.

SOME MORAL AND POLITICAL THEMES OF MODERNITY

With the advent of modernity, Western modes of thinking became increasingly secular and humanistic, emphasizing achievement in this world rather than the next. They tended to represent both knowledge and social life in teleological terms, as progressively evolving or developing, rather than conceiving human life and thought in terms of repeating cycles or even a process of degeneration. Progress could be made through the modern virtues of work, productivity, and efficiency.

Modernity also produced the secular ideal of a universal humanity. According to this ideal, human individuals are equal not only in moral worth but also in their capacity to reason and acquire knowledge. Ironically, this ideal developed at a time when the history of modern Europeans and their North American descendants was marked by conquest, colonization, slavery, exploitation, and even genocide; nevertheless, the ideal of a universal humanity has inspired countless struggles for impartial justice, equality, and democracy, including feminist ones.

SOME CHARACTERISTICS OF POSTMODERN THINKING

As noted above, the term *postmodern* was first used in architecture and the arts to refer to an aesthetic style that departed radically from high modernism. This style rejected modernism's assumptions of universally valid standards and values, its understanding of art as a separate and privileged realm, its search for logic and order, and its distinction between high and low culture. "Postmodernism" was later used to connote aspects of late twentieth-century culture that seemed to match this style. Such aspects included loss of a sense of connection among past, present, and future; rejection of universal values; and, more generally, loss of meaning, breakdown of traditional cultural values and expectations, and rejection of fixed categories and of attempts to impose analytic frameworks or moral judgments.

Postmodern thinking thus challenges the central assumptions of modernism. It abandons belief in the transcendent or universal, including transcendent reason, universal humanity, transhistorical progress, and objective science. It also rejects any idea that social reality is orderly or teleological and that progress is inevitable. It denies "grand narratives" of history such as those presented by religion and Marxism, and instead portrays reality as uncontrolled and directionless, lacking unity, order, or direction. The philosopher Foucault emphasizes the constant struggle of humans "caught in webs of contingency."

Postmodernism resists postulating any underlying, mind-independent reality or any natural kinds whose "essence" could be discovered by science. Rejecting essences and natural kinds, postmodernism contends that things exist only insofar as humans "construct" them through language and discourse. Language and discourse are historically contingent and changeable; there is no reason to believe that they reflect a single underlying reality. For postmodernism, therefore, truth is always relative to specific discourses, of whose rules it is a product. Objectivity is simply conformity to agreements contingently made by those who control discourse, and reason is simply a set of conventions that license certain inferences but do not express any universal laws of thought. For postmodernists, meaning is always "deferred," and no account of reality is ever complete; claims to present the full story are "totalizing" pretensions.

Postmodernism Is Fascinated with Style, Language, Symbolism, Theater, and Play

Discourses are not only multiple and contingent; they are also not politically innocent. On the contrary, postmodernism regards discourses as "regimes of power," which promote specific social interests; thus, postmodernism denies that systems of knowledge could ever be neutral among competing social interests. Foucault famously inverts the traditional relation between knowledge and power, presenting knowledge as produced by power rather than power as produced by knowledge.

Even though postmodernists do not aspire to universal ideals, they are often critics who advocate social change; however, they deny Marxist models of how social change occurs. They reject not only economic determinism but also Marxism's priority of transforming society's "economic base"; instead, postmodernists stress the importance of changing elements that Marxism regards as "superstructural," such as language and culture. "Hegemonic" discourses reflect the interests of those who control the society, and it is crucial that they be challenged by hitherto "subjugated" knowledges, which express the perceptions of those who are socially powerless and marginalized.

FEMINISM AND POSTMODERNISM

Western feminism was inspired by the distinctively modern ideal of a universal humanity. However, just as the Marxist concept of class simultaneously invoked and undermined this ideal, so too did the feminist concept of gender.

We have seen already that Western feminists of the late 1960s and early 1970s began to use the previously grammatical category of gender to analyze social phenomena. Some asserted that gender divisions were evident in all areas of life in all societies, dividing humanity into two basic classes on the basis of male or female sex as assigned at birth. They noted that the gender categories of masculine and feminine were used to characterize not only human individuals but also many aspects of the human and nonhuman worlds; for instance, they observed that some work is considered masculine and other work feminine and that some styles of dress, deportment, and speech are masculine and other styles feminine. Feminists also noted that, because masculinity and femininity are not equal in status, masculinity is typically attributed to things perceived as dominant or more admirable and femininity is attributed to whatever is perceived as inferior or subordinate.

For many feminists of the 1970s, the language of gender expressed a revolutionary discovery. They thought that it revealed that the deep underlying structure of social reality was one of male dominance. Different feminists responded differently to this "revelation." Some argued that women were as capable as men of realizing values culturally coded as masculine; some embraced the hitherto devalued feminine values; others challenged the rationale for these dichotomies. However, none doubted that the categories of masculinity and femininity captured deep divisions in social life and thought. Polemical contrasts between women's and men's situations were commonplace, and feminists frequently spoke in very general terms about "women's" and sometimes "men's" lives, interests, and experiences, sometimes seeming to postulate a universal manhood and womanhood.

Postmodernism challenges feminism's tendencies to universalize and naturalize. It emphasizes that such categories as man, woman, masculinity, and femininity do not refer to natural kinds of things that exist prior to discourse or independently of being named. Instead those categories have meaning only in the context of historically contingent and culturally specific discourses or ways of speaking, which construct the social realities that they purport to describe. This is true also of other identity categories, such as those pertaining to race, ethnicity, nationality, and sexuality. Because postmodernists regard social identities and forms of subjectivity as constructed through discourse, rather than prior to it, they deny the possibility of any inherent, authentic, or universal experience of being black, indigenous, or lesbian. Instead, they view the experiences of those categorized as black, indigenous, or lesbian as shaped and limited by the available discourses of race, ethnicity, and sexuality. Similarly, postmodernists deny any universal women's or men's experience; instead, they view the experience of those who happen to be categorized as women or men as depending on the gendered discourses available at the time. These discourses are always intertwined with other discourses, such as those of race, class, and religion.

Since discourses are constantly evolving and changing, the identities they define are in constant flux. Postmodernism emphasizes that social identities are not only multiple and overlapping but also disunified, fragmented, discontinuous, and contradictory. Changes in the discourses that construct identities do not typically result from new discoveries about the nature of social groups but rather from new ways of thinking about their social and power relations. In the United States, for instance, the category "black" came to displace the category "Negro" as a result of struggles against racism; similarly, the category "woman of color" emerged from feminist alliances against gendered racism. Because social groups such as classes are defined through processes of social interaction, such groups have no inherent character or set of interests; their destiny is not governed by any discoverable laws of history or social science, and they have no trajectory that can be predicted with any confidence. Unlike Martin Luther King, Jr., postmodernists have no confidence that the arc of history bends toward justice. They therefore tend to reject vanguardist political strategies and prefer "identity" politics even as they recognize that because identities are shifting and unstable, so are alliances based on them.

SOME METHODOLOGICAL IMPLICATIONS OF POSTMODERNISM

Postmodernism challenges the conceptions of knowledge and method advocated by some feminists. As Donna Haraway's article makes clear, feminists influenced by postmodernism cannot conceive the goals of their research as the discovery of essences or underlying realities, nor can they aim to reveal any simple truths about women's experience. Postmodern feminist researchers cannot pretend to offer one true story, but instead must recognize that many stories may be told, each incorporating a partial truth. They cannot hope to aggregate these partial truths into some comprehensive or impartial theory because more stories will always emerge. Instead, researchers can aspire only to tell a story acknowledged to be partial and perspectival, one story among others.

Although postmodern feminism is especially interested in subjugated knowledges, it cannot aim to present the epistemic standpoint of any particular social group. Within postmodernism, the very idea of social location is problematic, since individuals occupy multiple locations within structures that are not rigid but always shifting; mothers are also daughters and the meaning of "mother" and "daughter" is not static. Social life is too complex and ambiguous to be presented in broad brushstrokes as a large, overarching narrative; instead, postmodern feminist research tends to focus on the details of small slices of reality, including inconsistencies and anomalies.

For postmodernism, unmarked standpoints that are presented as "objective" typically mask the partial perceptions and specific interests of historically and socially situated subjects. Postmodern feminists therefore recognize that their research reflects their own subjectivity; what they hear and see, how they read and interpret, is conditioned by the interests linked with their specific subject positions and by the categories available to them. Therefore, rather than presenting their research in the passive voice and themselves as disembodied and dislocated observers, they aim to reveal their relationship to their research processes. Postmodernist researchers may reflect explicitly on how they came to choose their research topic, select their techniques for gathering evidence and their criteria for interpreting this evidence, along with any stake they may have in arriving at particular conclusions.

One aspect of the relationship between knowledge and power emphasized by postmodernism is that doing research is a way of assuming authority over a particular field of study. Often, researchers come from or aspire to the more privileged social classes, and they frequently "study down." Especially in the social sciences, they offer interpretations of the lives of those who are less privileged and in this way exercise significant power over them. Anne Opie offers some suggestions for empowering research subjects in the social sciences and mitigating the potential for appropriating their voices. Her article illustrates the concern of postmodernist feminist researchers not only for the epistemic implications of their situatedness but also for the ethical and political responsibilities that arise from it.

Donna Haraway
Situated Knowledges:
The Science Question in Feminism and the Privilege of Partial Perspective

. . .

It has seemed to me that feminists have both selectively and flexibly used and been trapped by two poles of a tempting dichotomy on the question of objectivity. Certainly I speak for myself here, and I offer the speculation that there is a collective discourse on these matters. Recent social studies of science and technology, for example, have made available a very strong social constructionist argument for *all* forms of knowledge claims, most certainly and especially scientific ones.[1] According to these tempting views, no insider's perspective is privileged, because all drawings of inside-outside boundaries in knowledge are theorized as power moves, not moves toward truth. So, from the strong social constructionist perspective, why should we be cowed by scientists' descriptions of their activity and accomplishments; they and their patrons have stakes in throwing sand in our eyes. . . . Social constructionists make clear that official ideologies about objectivity and scientific method are particularly bad guides to how scientific knowledge is actually *made*. Just as for the rest of us, what scientists believe or say they do and what they really do have a very loose fit.

. . .

From this point of view, science—the real game in town—is rhetoric, a series of efforts to persuade relevant social actors that one's manufactured knowledge is a route to a desired form of very objective power. Such persuasions must take account of the structure of facts and artefacts, as well as of language-mediated actors in the knowledge game. Here, artefacts and facts are parts of the powerful art of rhetoric. Practice is persuasion, and the focus is very much on practice. All knowledge is a condensed node in an agonistic power field. . . . History is a story Western culture buffs tell each other; science is a contestable text and a power field; the content is the form. Period.

. . . We would like to think our appeals to real worlds are more than a desperate lurch away from cynicism and an act of faith like any other cult's, no matter how much space we generously give to all the rich and always historically specific mediations through which we and everybody else must know the world. But the further I get in describing the radical social constructionist program and a particular version of postmodernism, coupled with the acid tools of critical discourse in the human sciences, the more nervous I get. . . .

Some of us tried to stay sane in these disassembled and dissembling times by holding out for a feminist version of objectivity. Here, motivated by many of the same political desires, is the other seductive end of the objectivity problem. Humanistic Marxism was polluted at the source by its structuring theory about the domination of nature in the self-construction of man and by its closely related impotence in relation to historicizing anything women did that didn't qualify for a wage. But Marxism was still a promising resource as a kind of epistemological feminist mental hygiene that sought our own doctrines of objective vision. Marxist starting points offered a way to get to our own versions of standpoint theories, insistent embodiment, a rich tradition of critiquing hegemony without disempowering positivisms and relativisms and a way to get to nuanced theories of mediation. . . .

Another approach, "feminist empiricism," also converges with feminist uses of Marxian resources to get a theory of science which continues to insist on legitimate meanings of objectivity and which remains leery of a radical constructivism conjugated with semiology and narratology.[4] Feminists have to insist on a better account of the world; it is not enough to show radical historical contingency and modes of construction for everything. Here, we, as feminists, find ourselves perversely conjoined with the discourse of many practicing scientists, who, when all is said and done, mostly believe they are describing and discovering things *by means of* all their constructing and arguing. Evelyn Fox Keller has been particularly insistent on this fundamental matter, and Sandra Harding calls the goal of these approaches a "successor science." Feminists have stakes in a successor science project that offers a more adequate, richer, better account of a world, in order to live in it well and in critical, reflexive relation to our own as well as others' practices of domination and the unequal parts of privilege and oppression that make up all positions. In traditional philosophical categories, the issue is ethics and politics perhaps more than epistemology.

So, I think my problem, and "our" problem, is how to have *simultaneously* an account of radical historical contingency for all knowledge claims and knowing subjects, a critical practice for recognizing our own "semiotic technologies" for making meanings, *and* a no-nonsense commitment to faithful accounts of a "real" world, one that can be partially shared and that is friendly to earth-wide projects of finite freedom, adequate material abundance, modest meaning in suffering, and limited happiness.

. . .

Natural, social, and human sciences have always been implicated in hopes like these. Science has been about a search for translation, convertibility, mobility of meanings, and universality . . . There is, finally, only one equation. That is the deadly fantasy that feminists and others have identified in some versions of objectivity, those in the service of hierarchical and positivist orderings of what can count as knowledge. That is one of the reasons the debates about objectivity matter, metaphorically and otherwise. Immortality and omnipotence are not our goals. But we could use some enforceable, reliable accounts of things not reducible to power moves and agonistic, high-status games of rhetoric or to scientistic, positivist arrogance. . . . In our efforts to climb the greased pole leading to a usable doctrine of objectivity, I and most other feminists in the objectivity debates have alternatively, or even simultaneously, held on to both ends of the dichotomy, a dichotomy which Harding describes in terms of successor science projects versus postmodernist accounts of difference and which I have sketched in this essay as radical constructivism versus feminist critical empiricism. It is, of course, hard to climb when you are holding on to both ends of a pole, simultaneously or alternatively. It is, therefore, time to switch metaphors.

THE PERSISTENCE OF VISION

I would like to proceed by placing metaphorical reliance on a much maligned sensory system in feminist discourse: vision. Vision can be good for avoiding binary oppositions. I would like to insist on the embodied nature of all vision and so reclaim the sensory system that has been used to signify a leap out of the marked body and into a conquering gaze from nowhere. This is the gaze that mythically inscribes all the marked bodies, that makes the unmarked category claim the power to see and not be seen, to represent while escaping representation. This gaze signifies the unmarked positions of Man and White, one of the many nasty tones of the world "objectivity" to feminist ears in scientific and technological, late-industrial, militarized, racist, and male-dominant societies, that is, here, in the belly of the monster, in the United States in the late 1980s. I would like a doctrine of embodied objectivity that accommodates paradoxical and critical feminist science projects: Feminist objectivity means quite simply *situated knowledges.*

The eyes have been used to signify a perverse capacity—honed to perfection in the history of science tied to militarism, capitalism, colonialism, and male supremacy—to distance the knowing subject from everybody and everything in the interests of unfettered power. The instruments of visualization in multinationalist, postmodernist culture have compounded these meanings of disembodiment. The visualizing technologies are without apparent limit. The eye of any ordinary primate like us can be endlessly enhanced by sonography systems, magnetic reasonance imagining, artificial intelligence–linked graphic manipulation systems, scanning electron microscopes, computed tomography scanners, color-enhancement techniques, satellite surveillance systems.... Vision in this technological feast becomes unregulated gluttony; all seems not just mythically about the god trick of seeing everything from nowhere, but to have put the myth into ordinary practice.

...

I would like to suggest how our insisting metaphorically on the particularity and embodiment of all vision (although not necessarily organic embodiment and including technological mediation), and not giving in to the tempting myths of vision as a route to disembodiment and second-birthing allows us to construct a usable, but not an innocent, doctrine of objectivity. I want a feminist writing of the body that metaphorically emphasizes vision again, because we need to reclaim that sense to find our way through all the visualizing tricks and powers of modern sciences and technologies that have transformed the objectivity debates. We need to learn in our bodies, endowed with primate color and stereoscopic vision, how to attach the objective to our theoretical and political scanners in order to name where we are and are not, in dimensions of mental and physical space we hardly know how to name. So, not so perversely, objectivity turns out to be about particular and specific embodiment and definitely not about the false vision promising transcendence of all limits and responsibility. The moral is simple: only partial perspective promises objective vision.... Feminist objectivity is about limited location and situated knowledge, not about transcendence and splitting of subject and object. It allows us to become answerable for what we learn how to see.

... The "eyes" made available in modern technological sciences shatter any idea of passive vision; these prosthetic devices show us that all eyes, including our own organic ones, are active perceptual systems, building on translations and specific *ways* of seeing, that is, ways of life. There is no unmediated photograph or passive camera obscura in scientific accounts of bodies and machines; there are only highly specific visual possibilities, each with a wonderfully detailed, active, partial way of organizing worlds. All these pictures of the world should not be allegories of infinite mobility and interchangeability but of elaborate specificity and difference and the loving care people might take to learn how to see faithfully from another's point of view, even when the other is our own machine....

Many currents in feminism attempt to theorize grounds for trusting especially the vantage points of the subjugated; there is good reason to believe vision is better from below the brilliant space platforms of the powerful.[5] Building on that suspicion, this essay is an argument for situated and embodied knowledges and an argument against various forms of unlocatable, and so irresponsible, knowledge claims.... There is a premium on establishing the capacity to see from the peripheries and the depths. But here there also lies a serious danger of romanticizing and/or appropriating the vision of the less powerful while claiming to see from their positions. To see from below is neither easily learned nor unproblematic, even if "we" "naturally" inhabit the great underground terrain of subjugated knowledges. The positionings of the subjugated are not exempt from critical reexamination, decoding, deconstruction, and interpretation; that is, from both semiological and hermeneutic modes of critical inquiry. The standpoints of the subjugated are not "innocent" positions. On the contrary, they are preferred because in principle they are least likely to allow denial of the critical and interpretive core of all knowledge. They are knowledgeable of modes of denial through repression, forgetting, and disappearing acts—ways of being nowhere while claiming to see comprehensively.... "Subjugated" standpoints are preferred because they seem to promise more adequate, sustained, objective, transforming accounts of the world. But *how* to see from below is a problem requiring at least as much skill with bodies and language, with the mediations of vision, as the "highest" technoscientific visualizations.

Such preferred positioning is as hostile to various forms of relativism as to the most explicitly totalizing versions of claims to scientific authority. But the alternative to relativism is not total-ization and single vision, which is always finally the unmarked category whose power depends on systematic narrowing and obscuring. The alternative to relativism is partial, locatable, criti-cal knowledges sustaining the possibility of webs of connections called solidarity in politics and shared conversations in epistemology. Relativism is a way of being nowhere while claiming to be everywhere equally. The "equality" of positioning is a denial of responsibility and critical inquiry. Relativism is the perfect mirror twin of totalization in the ideologies of objectivity; both deny the stakes in location, embodiment, and partial perspective; both make it impossible to see well....

A commitment to mobile positioning and to passionate detachment is dependent on the impossibility of entertaining innocent "identity" politics and epistemologies as strategies for seeing from the standpoints of the subjugated in order to see well. One cannot "be" either a cell or molecule—or a woman, colonized person, laborer, and so on—if one intends to see and see from these positions critically. "Being" is much more problematic and contingent. Also, one cannot relocate in any possible vantage point without being accountable for that movement. Vision is *always* a question of the power to see—and perhaps of the violence implicit in our visualizing practices.... These points also apply to testimony from the position of "oneself." We are not immediately present to ourselves.... Self-identity is a bad visual system. Fusion is a bad strategy of positioning....

The split and contradictory self is the one who can interrogate positionings and be accountable, the one who can construct and join rational conversations and fantastic imaginings that change history. Splitting, not being, is the privileged image for feminist epistemologies of scientific knowledge. "Splitting" in this context should be about heterogeneous multiplicities that are simultaneously salient and incapable of being squashed into isomorphic slots or cumulative lists. This geometry pertains within and among subjects. Subjectivity is multidimensional; so, therefore, is vision. The knowing self is partial in all its guises, never finished, whole, simply there and original; it is always constructed and stitched together imperfectly, and *therefore* able to join with another, to see together without claiming to be another. Here is the promise of objectivity: a scientific knower seeks the subject position, not of identity, but of objectivity, that is, partial connection. There is no way to "be" simultaneously in all, or wholly in any, of the privileged (i.e. subjugated) positions structured by gender, race, nation, and class. And that is a short list of criti-cal positions. The search for such a "full" and total position is the search for the fetishized perfect subject of oppositional history, sometimes appearing in feminist theory as the essentialized Third World Woman.[6] Subjugation is not grounds for an ontology; it might be a visual clue. Vision requires instruments of vision; an optics is a politics of positioning. Instruments of vision medi-ate standpoints; there is no immediate vision from the standpoint of the subjugated. Identity, including self-identity, does not produce a science; critical positioning does, that is, objectivity. Only those occupying the positions of the dominators are self-identical, unmarked, disembodied, unmediated, transcendent, born again. It is unfortunately possible for the subjugated to lust for and even scramble into that subject position—and then disappear from view. Knowledge from the point of view of the unmarked is truly fantastic, distorted, and irrational. The only position from which objectivity could not possibly be practiced and honored is the standpoint of the master, the Man, the One God, whose Eye produces, appropriates, and orders all difference....

I am arguing for politics and epistemologies of location, positioning, and situating, where partiality and not universality is the condition of being heard to make rational knowledge claims.... I am arguing for the view from a body, always a complex, contradictory, structuring, and structured body, versus the view from above, from nowhere, from simplicity....

Feminism loves another science: the sciences and politics of interpretation, translation, stuttering, and the partly understood. Feminism is about the sciences of the multiple subject with (at least) double vision. Feminism is about a critical vision consequent upon a critical positioning in unhomogeneous gendered social space. Translation is always interpretive, critical, and partial. Here is a ground for conversation, rationality, and objectivity—which is power-sensitive, not pluralist, "conversation." ... There is no single feminist standpoint because our maps require too many dimensions for that metaphor to ground our visions. But the feminist standpoint theorists' goal of an epistemology and politics of engaged, accountable positioning remains eminently potent. The goal is better accounts of the world, that is, "science."

... Rational knowledge is a process of ongoing critical interpretation among "fields" of interpreters and decoders. Rational knowledge is power-sensitive conversation.[7] Decoding and transcoding plus translation and criticism; all are necessary. So science becomes the paradigmatic model, not of closure, but of that which is contestable and contested.... Situated knowledges are about communities, not about isolated individuals. The only way to find a larger vision is to be somewhere in particular. The science question in feminism is about objectivity as positioned rationality. Its images are not the products of escape and transcendence of limits (the view from above) but the joining of partial views and halting voices into a collective subject position that promises a vision of the means of ongoing finite embodiment, of living within limits and contradictions—of views from somewhere.

OBJECTS AS ACTORS: THE APPARATUS OF BODILY PRODUCTION

... Situated knowledges require that the object of knowledge be pictured as an actor and agent, not as a screen or a ground or a resource, never finally as slave to the master that closes off the dialectic in his unique agency and his authorship of "objective" knowledge. The point is paradigmatically clear in critical approaches to the social and human sciences, where the agency of people studied itself transforms the entire project of producing social theory. Indeed, coming to terms with the agency of the "objects" studied is the only way to avoid gross error and false knowledge of many kinds in these sciences. But the same point must apply to the other knowledge projects called sciences. A corollary of the insistence that ethics and politics covertly or overtly provide the bases for objectivity in the sciences as a heterogeneous whole, and not just in the social sciences, is granting the status of agent/actor to the "objects" of the world. Actors come in many and wonderful forms. Accounts of a "real" world do not, then, depend on a logic of "discovery" but on a power-charged social relation of "conversation." The world neither speaks itself nor disappears in favor of a master decoder. The codes of the world are not still, waiting only to be read.... [T]he world encountered in knowledge projects is an active entity.... The approach I am recommending is not a version of "realism," which has proved a rather poor way of engaging with the world's active agency.

... Acknowledging the agency of the world in knowledge makes room for some unsettling possibilities.... Feminist objectivity makes room for surprises and ironies at the heart of all knowledge production; we are not in charge of the world. We just live here and try to strike up noninnocent conversations by means of our prosthetic devices, including our visualization technologies....

Another rich feminist practice in science in the last couple of decades illustrates particularly well the "activation" of the previously passive categories of objects of knowledge. This activation permanently problematizes binary distinctions like sex and gender, without eliminating their strategic utility. I refer to the reconstructions in primatology (especially, but not only, in women's practice as primatologists, evolutionary biologists, and behavioral ecologists) of what may count as sex, especially as female sex, in scientific accounts.[8] The *body*, the object of biological discourse, becomes a most engaging being. Claims of biological determinism can never be the same again. When female "sex" has been so thoroughly retheorized and revisualized that it emerges as practically indistinguishable from "mind," something basic has happened to the categories of biology. The biological female peopling current biological behavioral accounts has almost no passive properties left. She is structuring and active in every respect; the "body" is an agent, not a resource. Difference is theorized *biologically* as situational, not intrinsic, at every level from gene to foraging pattern, thereby fundamentally changing the biological politics of the body. The relations between sex and gender need to be categorically reworked within these frames of knowledge. I would like to suggest that this trend in explanatory strategies in biology is an allegory for interventions faithful to projects of feminist objectivity. The point is not that these new pictures of the biological female are simply true or not open to contestation and conversation—quite the opposite. But these pictures foreground knowledge as situated conversation at every level of its articulation....

So I will close with a final category useful to a feminist theory of situated knowledges: the apparatus of bodily production. In her analysis of the production of the poem as an object of literary value, Katie King offers tools that clarify matters in the objectivity debates among feminists. King suggests the term "apparatus of literary production" to refer to the emergence of literature at the intersection of art, business, and technology. The apparatus of literary production is a matrix from which "literature" is born. Focusing on the potent object of value called the "poem," King applies her analytic framework to the relation of women and writing technologies.[9] I would like to adapt her work to understanding the generation—the actual production and reproduction—of bodies and other objects of value in scientific knowledge projects. At first glance, there is a limitation to using King's scheme inherent in the "facticity" of biological discourse that is absent from literary discourse and its knowledge claims. Are biological bodies "produced" or "generated" in the same strong sense as poems? ... I wish to translate the ideological dimensions of "facticity" and "the organic" into a cumbersome entity called a "material-semiotic actor." This unwieldy term is intended to portray the object of knowledge as an active, meaning-generating part of apparatus of bodily production, without *ever* implying the immediate presence of such objects or, what is the same thing, their final or unique determination of what can count as objective knowledge at a particular historical juncture. Like "poems," which are sites of literary production where language too is an actor independent of intentions and authors, bodies as objects of knowledge are material-semiotic generative nodes. Their *boundaries* materialize in social interaction. Boundaries are drawn by mapping practices; "objects" do not preexist as such. Objects are boundary projects. But boundaries shift from within; boundaries are very tricky. What boundaries provisionally contain remains generative, productive of meanings and bodies. Siting (sighting) boundaries is a risky practice.

Objectivity is not about disengagement but about mutual *and* usually unequal structuring, about taking risks in a world where "we" are permanently mortal, that is, not in "final" control. We have, finally, no clear and distinct ideas....

NOTES

1. For example, see Karin Knorr-Cetina and Michael Mulkay (eds.), *Science Observed: Perspectives on the Social Study of Science* (London: Sage, 1983); Wiebe E. Bijker, Thomas P. Hughes, and Trevor Pinch (eds.), *The Social Construction of Technological Systems* (Cambridge: MIT Press, 1987); and esp. Bruno Latour's *Les microbes, guerre et paix, suivi de irréductions* (Paris: Métailié, 1984) and *The Pasteurization of France, Followed by Irreductions: A Politico-Scientific Essay* (Cambridge: Harvard University Press, 1988)....

...

4. Harding, 24–26, 161–62.

5. See Hartsock, "The Feminist Standpoint: Developing the Ground for a Specifically Feminist

Historical Materialism"; and Chela Sandoral, *Yours in Struggle: Women Respond to Racism* (Oakland: Center for Third World Organizing, n.d.); Harding; and Gloria Anzaldúa, *Borderlands/La Frontera* (San Francsico: Spinsters/Aunt Lute, 1987).

6. Chandra Mohanty, "Under Western Eyes," *Boundary,* 2 and 3 (1984): 333–58.

7. Katie King, "Canons without Innocence" (Ph.D. diss., University of California at Santa Cruz, 1987).

8. Donna Haraway, *Primate Visions: Gender, Race, and Nature in the World of Modern Science* (New York: Routledge & Kegan Paul, 1989).

9. Katie King, prospectus for "The Passing Dreams of Choice … Once Before and After: Audre Lorde and the Apparatus of Literary Production" (MS, University of Maryland, College Park, Maryland, 1987).

Nancy Fraser and Linda J. Nicholson

Social Criticism without Philosophy: An Encounter between Feminism and Postmodernism

Feminism and postmodernism have emerged as two of the most important political-cultural currents of the last decade. So far, however, they have kept an uneasy distance from one another....

Initial reticences aside, there are good reasons for exploring the relations between feminism and postmodernism.... Other differences notwithstanding, one could say that during the last decade feminists and postmodernists have worked independently on a common nexus of problems: They have tried to rethink the relation between philosophy and social criticism so as to develop paradigms of criticism without philosophy.

The two tendencies have proceeded from opposite directions.... Postmodernists have focused primarily on the philosophy side of the problem. They have begun by elaborating antifoundational metaphilosophical perspectives and from there have drawn conclusions about the shape and character of social criticism. For feminists, on the other hand, the question of philosophy has always been subordinate to an interest in social criticism. Consequently, they have begun by developing critical political perspectives and from there have drawn conclusions about the status of philosophy. As a result of this difference in emphasis and direction, the two tendencies have ended up with complementary strengths and weaknesses. Postmodernists offer sophisticated and persuasive criticisms of foundationalism and essentialism, but their conceptions of social criticism tend to be anemic. Feminists offer robust conceptions of social criticism, but they tend at times to lapse into foundationalism and essentialism.

Thus, each of the two perspectives suggests some important criticisms of the other. A postmodernist reflection on feminist theory reveals disabling vestiges of essentialism while a feminist reflection on postmodernism reveals androcentrism and political naivete.

It follows that an encounter between feminism and postmodernism will initially be a trading of criticisms. But there is no reason to suppose that this is where matters must end. In fact, ... each is in possession of valuable resources which can help remedy the deficiencies of the other. Thus, the ultimate stake of an encounter between feminism and postmodernism is the prospect of a perspective which integrates their respective strengths while eliminating their respective weaknesses. It is the prospect of a postmodernist feminism.

In what follows, we aim to contribute to the development of such a perspective by staging the initial, critical phase of the encounter. In the first section, we examine the ways in which one exemplary postmodernist, Jean-François Lyotard, has sought to derive new paradigms of social criticism from a critique of the institution of philosophy. We argue that the conception of social criticism so derived is too restricted to permit an adequate critical grasp of gender dominance and subordination.... In the second section, we examine some representative genres of feminist social criticism. We argue that in many cases feminist critics continue tacitly to rely on the sorts of philosophical underpinnings which their own commitments, like those of the postmodernists, ought in principle to rule out. We identify some points at which such underpinnings could be abandoned without any sacrifice of social-critical force. Finally, in a brief conclusion, we consider the prospects for a postmodernist feminism. We discuss some requirements which constrain the development of such a perspective, and we identify some pertinent conceptual resources and critical strategies.

POSTMODERNISM

Postmodernist seek, *inter alia,* to develop conceptions of social criticism which do not rely on traditional philosophical underpinnings.... Writers like Richard Rorty and Jean-François Lyotard begin by arguing that Philosophy with a capital *P* is no longer a viable or credible enterprise. They go on to claim that philosophy and, by extension, theory in general, can no longer function to *ground* politics and social criticism. With the demise of foundationalism comes the demise of the view that casts philosophy in the role of *founding* discourse vis-à-vis social criticism. That "modern" conception must give way to a new "postmodern" one in which criticism floats free of any universalist theoretical ground. No longer anchored philosophically, the very shape or character of social criticism changes; it becomes more pragmatic, *ad hoc,* contextual, and local....

Thus, in the postmodern reflection on the relationship between philosophy and social criticism, the term "philosophy" undergoes an explicit devaluation; it is cut down to size, if not eliminated altogether. Yet, even as this devaluation is argued explicitly, the term "philosophy" retains an implicit structural privilege. It is the changed condition of philosophy which determines the changed character of social criticism and of engaged intellectual practice. In the new postmodern equation, then, philosophy is the independent variable while social criticism and political practice are dependent variables. The view of theory which emerges is not determined by considering the needs of contemporary criticism and engagement. It is determined, rather, by considering the contemporary status of philosophy. This way of proceeding has important consequences, not all of which are positive. Among the results is a certain underestimation and premature foreclosing of possibilities for social criticism and engaged intellectual practice. This limitation of postmodern thought will be apparent when we consider its results in the light of the needs of contemporary feminist theory and practice.

Let us consider as an example the postmodernism of Jean-François Lyotard, since it is genuinely exemplary of the larger tendency.... His book *The Postmodern Condition* has become the *locus classicus* for contemporary debates, and it reflects in an especially acute form the characteristic concerns and tensions of the movement.[2]

For Lyotard, postmodernism designates a general condition of contemporary Western civilization. The postmodern condition is one in which "grand narratives of legitimation" are no longer credible. By grand narratives he means overarching philosophies of history like the Enlightenment story of the gradual but steady progress of reason and freedom, Hegel's dialectic of Spirit coming to know itself, and, most importantly, Marx's drama of the forward march of human productive capacities via class conflict culminating in proletarian revolution. For Lyotard, these metanarratives instantiate a specifically modern approach to the problem of legitimation. Each situates first-order discursive practices of inquiry and politics within a broader totalizing metadiscourse which legitimates them. The metadiscourse narrates a story about the whole of human history which purports to guarantee that the pragmatics of the modern sciences and of modern political processes—the norms and rules which govern these practices, determining what counts as a warranted move within them—are themselves legitimate. The story guarantees that some sciences and some politics have the *right* pragmatics and, so, are the *right* practices.

We should not be misled by Lyotard's focus on narrative philosophies of history. In his conception of legitimating metanarrative, the stress properly belongs on the *meta* and not on the *narrative*. For what most interests him about the Enlightenment, Hegelian, and Marxist stories is what they share with other nonnarrative forms of philosophy. Like ahistorical epistemologies and moral theories, they aim to show that specific first-order discursive practices are well formed and capable of yielding true and just results. *True* and *just* here mean something more than results reached by adhering scrupulously to the constitutive rules of some given scientific and political games. They mean, rather, results which correspond to Truth and Justice as they really are in themselves independently of contingent, historical social practices. Thus, in Lyotard's view, a metanarrative is *meta* in a very strong sense. It purports to be a privileged discourse capable of situating, characterizing, and evaluating all other discourses but not itself to be infected by the historicity and contingency which render first-order discourses potentially distorted and in need of legitimation.

In *The Postmodern Condition*, Lyotard argues that metanarratives, whether philosophies of history or nonnarrative foundational philosophies, are merely modem and dépassé. We can no longer believe, he claims, in the availability of a privileged metadiscourse capable of capturing once and for all the truth of every first-order discourse.... A so-called metadiscourse is in fact simply one more discourse among others. It follows for Lyotard that legitimation, both epistemic and political, can no longer reside in philosophical metanarratives. Where, then, he asks, does legitimation reside in the postmodern era?

... The answer, in brief, is that in the postmodern era legitimation becomes plural, local, and immanent. In this era, there will necessarily be many discourses of legitimation dispersed among the plurality of first-order discursive practices.... Instead of hovering above, legitimation descends to the level of practice and becomes immanent in it.... [P]ractitioners assume responsibility for legitimizing their own practice.

Lyotard intimates that something similar is or should be happening with respect to political legitimation. We cannot have and do not need a single, overarching theory of justice. What is required, rather, is a "justice of multiplicities."[3] What Lyotard means by this is not wholly clear. On one level, he can be read as offering a normative vision in which the good society consists in a decentralized plurality of democratic, self-managing groups and institutions whose members problematize the norms of their practice and take responsibility for modifying them as situations require. But paradoxically, on another level, he can be read as ruling out the sort of larger-scale, normative political theorizing which, from a modern perspective at least, would be required to legitimate such a vision. In any case, his justice of multiplicities conception precludes one familiar, and arguably essential, genre of political theory; identification and critique of microstructures of inequality and injustice which cut across the boundaries separating relatively discrete practices and institutions. There is no place in Lyotard's universe for critique of pervasive axes of stratification, for critique of broad-based relations of dominance and subordination along lines like gender, race, and class.

Lyotard's suspicion of the large extends to historical narrative and social theory as well. Here, his chief target is Marxism.... The problem with Marxism, in his view, is twofold. On the one hand, the Marxian story is too big, since it spans virtually the whole of human history. On the other hand, the Marxian story is too theoretical, since it relies on a *theory* of social practice and social relations which claims to *explain* historical change. At one level, Lyotard simply rejects the specifics of this theory. He claims that the Marxian conception of practice as production occludes the diversity and plurality of human practices; and that the Marxian conception of capitalist society as a totality traversed by one major division and contradiction occludes the diversity and plurality of contemporary societal differences and oppositions. But Lyotard does not conclude that such deficiencies can and should be remedied by a better social theory. Rather, he rejects the project of social theory *tout court*.

Once again, Lyotard's position is ambiguous, since his rejection of social theory depends on a theoretical perspective of sorts of its own. He offers a postmodern conception of sociality and social identity, a conception of what he calls "the social bond." What holds a society together, he claims, is not a common consciousness or institutional substructure. Rather, the social bond is a weave of crisscrossing threads of discursive practices, no single one of which runs continuously throughout the whole. Individuals are the nodes or posts where such practices intersect, and so, they participate in many practices simultaneously. It follows that social identities are complex and heterogeneous. They cannot be mapped onto one another nor onto the social totality. Indeed, strictly speaking, there is no social totality and *a fortiori* no possibility of a totalizing social theory.

Thus, Lyotard insists that the field of the social is heterogeneous and nontotalizable. As a result, he rules out the sort of critical social theory which employs general categories like gender, race, and class. From his perspective, such categories are too reductive of the complexity of social identities to be useful. There is apparently nothing to be gained, in his view, by situating an account of the fluidity and diversity of discursive practices in the context of a critical analysis of large-scale institutions and social structures.

Thus, Lyotard's postmodern conception of criticism without philosophy rules out several recognizable genres of social criticism. From the premise that criticism cannot be grounded by a foundationalist philosophical metanarrative, he infers the illegitimacy of large historical stories, normative theories of justice, and social-theoretical accounts of macrostructures which institutionalize inequality. What, then, *does* postmodern social criticism look like?

Lyotard tries to fashion some new genres of social criticism from the discursive resources that remain. Chief among these is smallish, localized narrative. He seeks to vindicate such narrative against both modern totalizing metanarrative and the scientism that is hostile to all narrative. One genre of postmodern social criticism, then, consists in relatively discrete, local stories about the emergence, transformation, and disappearance of various discursive practices treated in isolation from one another. Such stories might resemble those told by Michel Foucault, although without the attempts to discern larger synchronic patterns and connections that Foucault sometimes made.[4] ...

This genre of social criticism is not the whole postmodern story, however. For it casts critique as strictly local, *ad hoc,* and ameliorative, thus supposing a political diagnosis according to which there are no large-scale, systemic problems which resist local, *ad hoc,* ameliorative initiatives. Yet, Lyotard recognizes that postmodern society does contain at least one unfavorable structural tendency which requires a more coordinated response. This is the tendency to universalize instrumental reason, to subject *all* discursive practices indiscriminately to the single criterion of efficiency, or "performativity." In Lyotard's view, this threatens the autonomy and integrity of science and politics, since these practices are not properly subordinated to performative standards. It would pervert and distort them, thereby destroying the diversity of discursive forms.

Thus, even as he argues explicitly against it, Lyotard posits the need for a genre of social criticism which transcends local mininarrative. Despite his strictures against large, totalizing stories, he narrates a fairly tall tale about a large-scale social trend. Moreover, the logic of this story, and of the genre of criticism to which it belongs, calls for judgments which are not strictly practice-immanent. Lyotard's story presupposes the legitimacy and integrity of the scientific and political practices allegedly threatened by performativity. It supposes that one can distinguish changes or developments which are *internal* to these practices from externally induced distortions. But this drives Lyotard to make normative judgments about the value and character of the threatened practices. These judgments are not strictly immanent in the practices judged. Rather, they are metapractical.

Thus, Lyotard's view of postmodern social criticism is neither entirely self-consistent nor entirely persuasive. He goes too quickly from the premise that Philosophy cannot ground social criticism to the conclusion that criticism itself must be local, *ad hoc,* and nontheoretical. . . .

We began this discussion by noting that postmodernists orient their reflections on the character of postmodern social criticism by the falling star of foundationalist philosophy. They posit that, with philosophy no longer able credibly to ground social criticism, criticism itself must be local, *ad hoc,* and untheoretical. Thus, from the critique of foundationalism, they infer the illegitimacy of several genres of social criticism. For Lyotard, the illegitimate genres include large-scale historical narrative and social-theoretical analyses of pervasive relations of dominance and subordination.[6]

Suppose, however, one were to choose another starting point for reflecting on postfoundational social criticism. Suppose one began, not with the condition of Philosophy, but with the nature of the social object one wished to criticize. Suppose, further, that one defined that object as the subordination of women to and by men. Then, we submit, it would be apparent that many of the genres rejected by postmodernists are necessary for social criticism. For a phenomenon as pervasive and multifaceted as male dominance simply cannot be adequately grasped with the meager critical resources to which they would limit us. On the contrary, effective criticism of this phenomenon requires an array of different methods and genres. It requires at minimum large narratives about changes in social organization and ideology, empirical and social-theoretical analyses of macrostructures and institutions, interactionist analyses of the micropolitics of everyday life, critical-hermeneutical and institutional analyses of cultural production, historically and culturally specific sociologies of gender, and so on. The list could go on.

Clearly, not all of these approaches are local and untheoretical. But all are nonetheless essential to feminist social criticism. Moreover, all can in principle be conceived in ways that do not take us back to foundationalism, even though, as we argue in the next section, many feminists have not wholly succeeded in avoiding that trap.

FEMINISM

Feminists, like postmodernists, have sought to develop new paradigms of social criticism which do not rely on traditional philosophical underpinnings. They have criticized modern foundationalist epistemologies and moral and political theories, exposing the contingent, partial, and historically situated character of what has passed in the mainstream for necessary, universal, and ahistorical truths. They have called into question the dominant philosophical project of seeking objectivity in the guise of a "God's eye view" which transcends any situation or perspective.[7]

However, if postmodernists have been drawn to such views by a concern with the status of philosophy, feminists have been led to them by the demands of political practice. This practical interest has saved feminist theory from many of the mistakes of postmodernism: Women whose theorizing was to serve the struggle against sexism were not about to abandon powerful political tools merely as a result of intramural debates in professional philosophy.

Yet, even as the imperatives of political practice have saved feminist theory from one set of difficulties, they have tended at times to incline it toward another. Practical imperatives have led some feminists to adopt modes of theorizing which resemble the sorts of philosophical metanarrative rightly criticized by postmodernists. To be sure, the feminist theories we have in mind here are not pure metanarratives; they are not ahistorical normative theories about the transcultural nature of rationality or justice. Rather, they are very large social theories ... [that] claim, for example, to identify causes and constitutive features of sexism that operate cross-culturally. Thus, these social theories purport to be empirical rather than philosophical. But, as we hope to show, they are actually quasimetanarratives. They tacitly presuppose some commonly held but unwarranted and essentialist assumptions about the nature of human beings and the conditions for social life. In addition, they assume methods and concepts which are uninflected by temporality or historicity and which therefore function *de facto* as permanent, neutral matrices for inquiry. Such theories, then, share some of the essentialist and ahistorical features of metanarratives: They are insufficiently attentive to historical and cultural diversity, and they falsely universalize features of the theorist's own era, society, culture, class, sexual orientation, and ethnic or racial group.

On the other hand, the practical exigencies inclining feminists to produce quasimetanarratives have by no means held undisputed sway. Rather, they have had to coexist, often uneasily, with counterexigencies which have worked to opposite effect, for example, political pressures to acknowledge differences among women. In general, then, the recent history of feminist social theory reflects a tug of war between forces which have encouraged and forces which have discouraged metanarrative-like modes of theorizing. We can illustrate this dynamic by looking at a few important turning points in this history.

When in the 1960s, women in the New Left began to extend prior talk about women's rights into the more encompassing discussion of women's liberation, they encountered the fear and hostility of their male comrades and the use of Marxist political theory as a support for these reactions. Many men of the New Left argued that gender issues were secondary because they were subsumable under more basic modes of oppression, namely, class and race.

In response to this practical-political problem, radical feminists such as Shulamith Firestone resorted to an ingenious tactical maneuver: Firestone invoked biological differences between women and men to explain sexism. This enabled her to turn the tables on her Marxist comrades by claiming that gender conflict was the most basic form of human conflict and the source of all other forms, including class conflict.[8] Firestone drew on the pervasive tendency within modern culture to locate the roots of gender differences in biology. Her coup was to use biologism to establish the primacy of the struggle against male domination rather than to justify acquiescence to it,

The trick, of course, is problematic from a postmodernist perspective in that appeals to biology to explain social phenomena are essentialist and monocausal. They are essentialist insofar as they project onto all women and men qualities which develop under historically specific social conditions. They are monocausal insofar as they look to one set of characteristics, such as women's physiology or men's hormones, to explain women's oppression in all cultures. These problems are only compounded when appeals to biology are used in conjunction with the dubious claim that women's oppression is the cause of all other forms of oppression.

Moreover, as Marxists and feminist anthropologists began insisting in the early 1970s, appeals to biology do not allow us to understand the enormous diversity of forms which both gender and sexism assume in different cultures.... Gayle Rubin aptly described this dual requirement as the need to formulate theory which could account for the oppression of women in its "endless variety and monotonous similarity."[9] How were feminists to develop a social theory adequate to both demands?

One approach which seemed promising was suggested by Michelle Zimbalist Rosaldo and other contributors in the influential 1974 anthropology collection, *Woman, Culture, and Society.* They argued that common to all known societies was some type of separation between a domestic sphere and a public sphere, the former associated with women and the latter with men. Because in most societies to date, women have spent a good part of their lives bearing and raising children, their lives have been more bound to the domestic sphere. Men, on the other hand, have had both the time and mobility to engage in those out of the home activities which generate political structures. Thus, as Rosaldo argued, while in many societies women possess some or even a great deal of power, women's power is always viewed as illegitimate, disruptive, and without authority.[10]

This approach seemed to allow for both diversity and ubiquity in the manifestations of sexism. A very general identification of women with the domestic and of men with the extradomestic could accommodate a great deal of cultural variation both in social structures and in gender roles. At the same time, it could make comprehensible the apparent ubiquity of the assumption of women's inferiority above and beyond such variation. This hypothesis was also compatible with the idea that the extent of women's oppression differed in different societies....

However, this explanation turned out to be problematic in ways reminiscent of Firestone's account. Although the theory focused on differences between men's and women's spheres of activity rather than on differences between men's and women's biology, it was essentialist and monocausal nonetheless. It posited the existence of a domestic sphere in all societies and thereby assumed that women's activities were basically similar in content and significance across cultures. (An analogous assumption about men's activities lay behind the postulation of a universal public sphere.) ... The theory thus failed to appreciate that, while each individual property may be true of many societies, the conjunction is not true of most.[11]

One source of difficulty in these early feminist social theories was the presumption of an overly grandiose and totalizing conception of theory. Theory was understood as the search for the one key factor which would explain sexism cross-culturally and illuminate all of social life. In this sense, to theorize was by definition to produce a quasimetanarrative.

Since the late 1970s, feminist social theorists have largely ceased speaking of biological determinants or a cross-cultural domestic/public separation. Many, moreover, have given up the assumption of monocausality. Nevertheless, some feminist social theorists have continued implicitly to suppose a quasimetanarrative conception of theory. They have continued to theorize in terms of a putatively unitary, primary, culturally universal type of activity associated with women, generally an activity conceived as domestic and located in the family.

One influential example is the analysis of mothering developed by Nancy Chodorow. Setting herself to explain the internal, psychological dynamics which have led many women willingly to reproduce social divisions associated with female inferiority, Chodorow posited a cross-cultural activity, mothering, as the relevant object of investigation. Her question thus became: How is mothering as a female-associated activity reproduced over time? How does mothering produce a new generation of women with the psychological inclination to mother and a new generation of men not so inclined? The answer she offered was in terms of gender identity: Female mothering produces women whose deep sense of self is relational and men whose deep sense of self is not.[12]

... [T]he theory has clear metanarrative overtones. It posits the existence of a single activity, mothering, which, while differing in specifics in different societies, nevertheless constitutes enough of a natural kind to warrant one label. It stipulates that this basically unitary activity gives rise to two distinct sorts of deep selves, one relatively common across cultures to women, the other relatively common across cultures to men. It claims that the difference thus generated between feminine and masculine gender identity causes a variety of supposedly cross-cultural social phenomena, including the continuation of female mothering, male contempt for women, and problems in heterosexual relationships.

From a postmodern perspective, all of these assumptions are problematic because they are essentialist. But the second one, concerning gender identity, warrants special scrutiny, given its political implications. Consider that Chodorow's use of the notion of gender identity presupposes three major premises. One is the psychoanalytic premise that everyone has a deep sense of self which is constituted in early childhood through one's interactions with one's primary parent and which remains relatively constant thereafter. Another is the premise that this deep self differs significantly for men and for women but is roughly similar among women, on the one hand, and among men, on the other hand, both across cultures and within cultures across lines of class, race, and ethnicity. The third premise is that this deep self colors everything one does; there are no actions, however trivial, which do not bear traces of one's masculine or feminine gender identity.

One can appreciate the political exigencies which made this conjunction of premises attractive. It gave scholarly substance to the idea of the pervasiveness of sexism. If masculinity and femininity constitute our basic and ever present sense of self, then it is not surprising that the manifestations of sexism are systemic. Moreover, many feminists had already sensed that the concept of sex-role socialization, an idea Chodorow explicitly criticized, ignored the depth and intractability of male dominance.... Finally, Chodorow's depth-psychological approach gave a scholarly sanction to the idea of sisterhood. It seemed to legitimate the claim that the ties which bind women are deep and substantively based.

Needless to say, we have no wish to quarrel with the claim of the depth and pervasiveness of sexism nor with the idea of sisterhood. But we do wish to challenge Chodorow's way of legitimating them. The idea of a cross-cultural, deep sense of self, specified differently for women and men, becomes problematic when given any specific content. Chodorow states that women everywhere differ from men in their greater concern with "relational interaction." But what does she mean by this term? Certainly not any and every kind of human interaction, since men have often been more concerned than women with some kinds of interactions, for example, those which have to do with the aggrandizement of power and wealth. Of course, it is true that many women in modern Western societies have been expected to exhibit strong concern with those types of interactions associated with intimacy, friendship, and love, interactions which dominate one meaning of the late twentieth-century concept of relationship. But surely this meaning presupposes a notion of private life specific to modern Western societies of the last two centuries....

Equally troubling are the aporias this theory generates for political practice. While gender identity gives substance to the idea of sisterhood, it does so at the cost of repressing differences among sisters. Although the theory allows for some differences among women of different classes, races, sexual orientations, and ethnic groups, it construes these as subsidiary to more basic similarities. But it is precisely as a consequence of the request to understand such differences as secondary that many women have denied an allegiance to feminism.

...

The difficulty here is that categories like sexuality, mothering, reproduction, and sex-affective production group together phenomena which are not necessarily conjoined in all societies while separating off from one another phenomena which are not necessarily separated. As a matter of fact, it is doubtful whether these categories have any determinate cross-cultural content. Thus, for a theorist to use such categories to construct a universalistic social theory is to risk projecting the socially dominant conjunctions and dispersions of her own society onto others, thereby distorting important features of both. Social theorists would do better first to construct genealogies of the *categories* of sexuality, reproduction, and mothering before assuming their universal significance.

Since around 1980, many feminist scholars have come to abandon the project of grand social theory. They have stopped looking for *the* causes of sexism and have turned to more concrete inquiry with more limited aims. One reason for this shift is the growing legitimacy of feminist scholarship. The institutionalization of women's studies in the United States has meant a dramatic increase in the size of the community of feminist inquirers, a much greater division of scholarly labor, and a large and growing fund of concrete information....

Even in this phase, however, traces of youthful quasimetanarratives remain. Some theorists who have ceased looking for *the* causes of sexism still rely on essentialist categories such as gender identity. This is especially true of those scholars who have sought to develop gynocentric alternatives to mainstream androcentric perspectives but who have not fully abandoned the universalist pretensions of the latter.

Consider, as an example, the work of Carol Gilligan. Unlike most of the theorists we have considered so far, Gilligan has not sought to explain the origins or nature of cross-cultural sexism. Rather, she set herself the more limited task of exposing and redressing androcentric bias in the model of moral development of psychologist Lawrence Kohlberg. Thus, she argued that it is illegitimate to evaluate the moral development of women and girls by reference to a standard drawn exclusively from the experience of men and boys. She proposed to examine women's moral discourse on its own terms in order to uncover its immanent standards of adequacy.[15]

Gilligan's work has been rightly regarded as important and innovative. It challenged mainstream psychology's persistent occlusion of women's lives and experiences and its insistent but false claims to universality.... On the one hand, by providing a counterexample to Kohlberg's model, she cast doubt on the possibility of any single, universalist developmental schema. On the other hand, by constructing a female countermodel, she invited the same charge of false generalization she had herself raised against Kohlberg, although now from other perspectives such as class, sexual orientation, race, and ethnicity....

Thus, vestiges of essentialism have continued to plague feminist scholarship, even despite the decline of grand theorizing. In many cases, including Gilligan's, this represents the continuing subterranean influence of those very mainstream modes of thought and inquiry with which feminists have wished to break.

On the other hand, the practice of feminist politics in the 1980s has generated a new set of pressures which have worked against metanarratives. In recent years, poor and working-class women, women of color, and lesbians have finally won a wider hearing for their objections to feminist theories which fail to illuminate their lives and address their problems. They have exposed the earlier quasimetanarratives, with their assumptions of universal female dependence and confinement to the domestic sphere, as false extrapolations from the experience of the white, middle-class, heterosexual women who dominated the beginnings of the second wave.... Thus, as the class, sexual, racial, and ethnic awareness of the movement has altered, so has the preferred conception of theory. It has become clear that quasimetanarratives hamper rather than promote sisterhood, since they elide differences among women and among the forms of sexism to which different women are differentially subject. Likewise, it is increasingly apparent that such theories hinder alliances with other progressive movements, since they tend to occlude axes of domination other than gender. In sum, there is growing interest among feminists in modes of theorizing which are attentive to differences and to cultural and historical specificity.

In general, then, feminist scholarship of the 1980s evinces some conflicting tendencies.... [F]eminist scholarship has remained insufficiently attentive to the *theoretical* prerequisites of dealing with diversity, despite widespread commitment to accepting it politically.

By criticizing lingering essentialism in contemporary feminist theory, we hope to encourage such theory to become more consistently postmodern. This is not, however, to recommend merely any form of postmodernism.... Rather, as we argue next, a robust postmodern feminist paradigm of social criticism without philosophy is possible.

TOWARD A POSTMODERN FEMINISM

How can we combine a postmodernist incredulity toward metanarratives with the social-critical power of feminism? How can we conceive a version of criticism without philosophy which is robust enough to handle the tough job of analyzing sexism in all its endless variety and monotonous similarity?

A first step is to recognize, *contra* Lyotard, that postmodern critique need forswear neither large historical narratives nor analyses of societal macrostructures. This point is important for feminists, since sexism has a long history and is deeply and pervasively embedded in contemporary societies. Thus, postmodern feminists need not abandon the large theoretical tools needed to address large political problems. There is nothing self-contradictory in the idea of a postmodern theory.

However, if postmodern feminist critique must remain theoretical, not just any kind of theory will do. Rather, theory here would be explicitly historical, attuned to the cultural specificity of different societies and periods and to that of different groups within societies and periods. Thus, the categories of postmodern feminist theory would be inflected by temporality, with historically specific institutional categories like the modern, restricted, male-headed, nuclear family taking precedence over ahistorical, functionalist categories like reproduction and mothering. Where categories of the latter sort were not eschewed altogether, they would be genealogized, that is, framed by a historical narrative and rendered temporally and culturally specific.

Moreover, postmodern feminist theory would be nonuniversalist. When its focus became cross-cultural or transepochal, its mode of attention would be comparativist rather than universalizing, attuned to changes and contrasts instead of to covering laws. Finally, postmodern feminist theory would dispense with the idea of a subject of history. It would replace unitary notions of woman and feminine gender identity with plural and complexly constructed conceptions of social identity, treating gender as one relevant strand among others, attending also to class, race, ethnicity, age, and sexual orientation.

In general, postmodern feminist theory would be pragmatic and fallibilistic. It would tailor its methods and categories to the specific task at hand, using multiple categories when appropriate and forswearing the metaphysical comfort of a single feminist method or feminist epistemology....

The most important advantage of this sort of theory would be its usefulness for contemporary feminist political practice. Such practice is increasingly a matter of alliances rather than one of unity around a universally shared interest or identity. It recognizes that the diversity of women's needs and experiences means that no single solution, on issues like child care, social security, and housing, can be adequate for all. Thus, the underlying premise of this practice is that, while some women share some common interests and face some common enemies, such commonalities are by no means universal; rather, they are interlaced with differences, even with conflicts. This, then, is a practice made up of a patchwork of overlapping alliances, not one circumscribable by an essential definition. One might best speak of it in the plural as the practice of feminisms. In a sense, this practice is in advance of much contemporary feminist theory. It is already implicitly postmodern. It would find its most appropriate and useful theoretical expression in a postmodern feminist form of critical inquiry. Such inquiry would be the theoretical counterpart of a broader, richer, more complex, and multilayered feminist solidarity, the sort of solidarity which is essential for overcoming the oppression of women in its "endless variety and monotonous similarity."

NOTES

...

2. Jean-François Lyotard, *The Postmodern Condition: A Report on Knowledge,* trans. G. Bennington and B. Massumi (Minneapolis: University of Minnesota Press, 1984).

3. Ibid. Cf. Jean-François Lyotard and Jean-Loup Thebaud, *Just Gaming* (Minneapolis: University of Minnesota Press, 1987); also Jean-François Lyotard, "The Differend," *Diacritics,* Fall 1984, trans. Georges Van Den Abbeele, pp. 4–14.

4. See, for example, Michel Foucault, *Discipline and Punish: The Birth of the Prison,* trans. Alan Sheridan (New York: Vintage Books, 1979).

...

6. It should be noted that, for Lyotard, the choice of philosophy as a starting point is itself determined by a metapolitical commitment, namely, to antitotalitarianism. He assumes erroneously, in our view, that totalizing social and political theory necessarily eventuates in totalitarian societies. Thus, the "practical intent" that subtends Lyotard's privileging of philosophy (and which is in turn attenuated by the latter) is anti-Marxism. Whether it should also be characterized as neoliberalism is a question too complicated to be explored here.

7. See, for example, the essays in *Discovering Reality: Feminist Perspectives on Epistemology, Metaphysics, Methodology, and Philosophy of Science,* ed. Sandra Harding and Merrill B. Hintikka (Dordrecht, Holland: D. Reidel, 1983).

8. Shulamith Firestone, *The Dialectic of Sex* (New York: Bantam, 1970).

9. Gayle Rubin, "The Traffic in Women," *Toward an Anthropology of Women,* ed. Rayna R. Reiter (New York: Monthly Review Press, 1975), p. 160.

10. Michelle Zimbalist Rosaldo, "Woman, Culture, and Society: A Theoretical Overview," *Woman, Culture, and Society,* ed. Michelle Zimbalist Rosaldo and Louise Lamphere (Stanford: Stanford University Press, 1974), pp. 17–42.

11. These and related problems were soon apparent to many of the domestic/public theorists themselves. See Rosaldo's self-criticism, "The Use and Abuse of Anthropology: Reflections on Feminism and Cross-cultural Understanding," *Signs: Journal of Women in Culture and Society,* Vol. 5, No. 3, 1980, pp. 389–417....

12.   Nancy Chodorow, *The Reproduction of Mothering: Psychoanalysis and the Sociology of Gender* (Berkeley: University of California Press, 1978).

...

15.   Carol Gilligan, *In a Different Voice: Psychological Theory and Women's Development* (Cambridge, MA: Harvard University Press, 1983).

ANNE OPIE

Qualitative Research, Appropriation of the "Other" and Empowerment

The issues I want to explore in this essay have arisen in the context of my qualitative research into the everyday experiences of twenty-eight family caregivers caring for elderly confused spouses or relatives at home.[1] My interpretation of the interview data, derived from lengthy and unstructured interviews, has drawn extensively on feminist comment and research on caring in order to challenge conventional political and social knowledge about caring. Yet, in constructing an analysis which adequately represents the complexity of the experiences in which the interview texts are grounded, I have also become conscious of limitations in feminist interpretations. Although at one point they are liberatory because they open to inspection what has been previously hidden, they are also restrictive in the sense that they can appropriate the data to the researcher's interests, so that other significant experiential elements which challenge or partially disrupt that interpretation may also be silenced.

The significance of feminist analyses of social policy and caregiving (for example Croft, 1986; Dailey, 1988; Finch and Groves, 1980, 1983; Gibson and Allen, 1989; Pascall, 1986; Williams, 1989) lies in their challenge to the conventional construction of family and gender in social policy and in particular their elaboration of the need for integration of the dual surface of the hitherto privatized domain of the home and the public arena across which these analyses must move. Importantly, the feminist perspective has emphasized the exploitative relationship between the carer and the state and opened for scrutiny contradictions within the notion of "care" by identifying the oppositional character of "taking charge" and "feeling concern" (Graham, 1983), and of affection and physical management and work in contrast to its delineation as intuitive and essentialist.

My position is that the complexities of power relations and ideologies are identified within the feminist researcher/researched relationship because a major feminist objective has been to "undermin[e] existing conventions of representations" (Felski, 1989: 31). Although feminist researchers have questioned many aspects of the construction and management of these relationships within mainstream social science research, there is a need for further, more reflexive analysis to avoid textual appropriation of the researched; and to focus attention on difference as a means of more fully representing the complexities of the social world. Where issues of social policy are concerned, it becomes all the more necessary as Statham *et al.* have stated, that these policies, often "formulated on the macrosocial level" should "translate effectively on the microlevel of individual and group experience" (1988: 4). Avoiding appropriation and highlighting difference are crucial means by which a researcher may empower participants in her research....

THE INTERVIEW TEXT

In many respects, the texts of informal caregivers participating in my research, i.e., spouses and adult children, represent caring as work and as destructive of personal relationships, and confirm feminist readings of the exploitation of family obligation by the health system. Because of the degree of stress under which these caregivers labored it is easy to respond to the material primarily on that basis and highlight the exploitative nature of the role. But interspersed through a number of texts are different moments which speak of love and affection and regard, which mitigate temporarily the tensions of the role, and which disrupt and qualify the subjective experience of exploitation. These moments by no means negate that reading but they indicate points of complication and of contradiction which the analysis must additionally identify and explain.

These moments are, significantly, very largely restricted to the spouses' texts rather than those of the adult children. Quantitatively speaking, even in the spouses' texts, these alternative affectionate moments pale into insignificance in relation to the accounts of the stress and monotony of the everyday. Yet it is these brief and ambiguously positioned moments that allow caregivers to reaffirm the value of their role. One 71-year-old woman, whose voice throughout our two interviews was very flat, tired and slow, said: "Well, as I say, um, my husband is happy at home and I am happy to have him at home ... and I feel that ... once he went away perhaps it wouldn't be the same and I think he's getting to that stage now that perhaps if he went away as long as he was fed and looked after, it wouldn't really matter." She begins with a strong statement of her intentions and her perceptions of her husband's well-being then suddenly moves off in an unexpected direction. After having stated that joint happiness as sufficient reason for her husband to stay at home, her first clause in the second line breaks her line of thought and turns the emotional content on its head. Her *raison d'être* for her role (her husband's happiness) which seemed secure in her opening words is suddenly cast into doubt.

My reading of this quotation is that her satisfaction with her role, with all its very real trials and tribulations, depends on the extent of her husband's cognitive awareness and thus on his ability to discriminate. What becomes difficult for her is the point at which she has to take account of the possibility that it is not just a question of whether he would be unhappy in continuing care, but when he would no longer be able to discriminate between the two environments and (very pertinently) no longer discriminate between her personal care and that given by another. She returned to the subject later:

> *Sometimes* I think to myself, "Well, you know, if you were in hospital, I don't think that it would make much difference. I don't think you'd ... *really care* as long as you ... were being fed ... and looked after," and then I think, "Well, I don't know. Why would you put your arm around me at night, if you didn't know that it wasn't me?" And I always said, "Well, as soon as he forgets who I am," but I don't really think that he has ever ... because—now the other night he tried to wake me up ... I was awake, but I thought, "I won't say too much" ... and then he said, "Dear" ... Then he said it again ... and I thought, "Oh, I had better say something," so I answered. Oh, but before I did, he said ... "It's your husband, Steve, talking," so I thought, "Oh, I had better come to" and ... So I thought, "Well, you know, he can't have forgotten who I am."

Here her doubts have become more substantial (*"sometimes," "really care"*) about whether her husband should be institutionalized. She appears to be making a more definite and despondent movement towards deciding for hospital care. Her words indicate recognition of *her* increasing absence from her husband's world. But this movement towards an acceptance of institutionalization is arrested, initially by her reading of his placing his arm around her as confirming his presence and his validation of her as *known* and then by the poignant event of his speaking, all the more so because his speech has almost entirely gone. A sentence such as "It's your husband, Steve, talking" represents for her a triumph of determination to assert himself and their relationship. It allows her to reaffirm the point of her personal sacrifices, that she is still remembered, that their joint life has meaning—which itself then indicates a complex *interdependent* relationship.

Extracts such as this one derive their significance from the hesitation, contradictoriness and recursiveness of the spoken voice (Barthes, 1973) and because of the light they cast on the painful moving across the surfaces of remembrance/nonremembrance, presence/absence. They also point to the significance of events about which little was said but which were crucial especially to an appreciation of the elderly spouses' experience of caregiving and to their ability and desire to sustain their role. Furthermore, they raise important questions about the weight that sociology has traditionally assigned to data which occurs only momentarily because of its deeply engrained valorizing of quantity.

In relation to developing fuller representations of caring, the tension arising from the duality of positioning (willing/exploited) has to be simultaneously maintained so that women (and men) who derive significant positive affectional and personal meaning from their role are not defined as imbued with "false consciousness" as Croft has noted (1986: 24). The disjunction between the experiential (where caring is not always defined as exploitative) and ideology (where it is) should not only be remarked but incorporated into the analysis. Rather than representing the caring body as uniformly (monolithically) exploited or alternatively uniformly (monolithically) willing, the data from my research suggests that its constituents are unstable and are differently constituted by, for example, generational positioning, age, gender, ideology, prior experience of acting as a caregiver, the past and current relationship with the elderly person, and ability to command resources (Opie, 1990a). All these different dimensions require elaboration. Furthermore, part of the representation of that body requires the exploration of the manner and extent of "tactics" of resistance to the role (de Certeau, 1984: xix) and the elaboration of the degree to which the body is more or less fully inscribed in a particular micropolitics of power focused around only one orientation to caring.

Appropriation is a term which conventionally defines social relations in terms of power relations. More recently, and notably in the work of Edward Said (1978, 1989), the critical importance of textual representation in the work of appropriation has been demonstrated. Although Said has concentrated upon the relations of colonizer and colonized in his analysis, his argument is very informative for research on the elderly because the characteristic features of the colonizer/colonized relationship are clearly replicated in the relationship of health system/informal caregiver and researcher/researched.

APPROPRIATION OF THE "OTHER"

Said (1978) defines "appropriation" as the means by which the experiences of the "colonized" (a term used to link those colonized in the imperialistic sense of the word and those "located in zones of dependency and peripherality" (Said, 1989: 207) are interpreted by a (more) dominant group to sustain a particular representation or view of the "other" as part of an ideological stance. This practice is complex, interlocking, self-fulfilling and constraining.... Adopting a Foucauldian stance, Said argues that language cannot be regarded as a transparent, truthful medium through which the world is simply apprehended as it is but, instead, that it is fully implicated in power relations.

He identifies two ways by which textual authority is constituted. The first he calls "strategic location" which defines the location of the author in relation to the material about which she writes; and the second is a process called "strategic formation" which defines how texts acquire "mass, density, and referential power among themselves and thereafter in the culture at large" (20). Arguing that the author's location is indicated by the narrative voice adopted, by structure, images, themes and motifs, he goes on to critique, within the historical development of the discipline of Orientalism, the notion of scholarship as facilitating the development of new knowledge. He suggests instead that the affiliation of each work to others within the field increases its own referential power and equally disguises its own modes of representation; and within that process of reference and representation, the impact of the novel is reduced by a series of comparisons between the new and the familiar. This is achieved through a filtering of the new through the old so that the new is suppressed in favor of the old; and the potentially destabilizing impact of new knowledge is subverted by a process which permits the established view to retain its dominance.[2] This continual mediation of interpretative attitudes, where each builds upon and sustains the authoritative position of self and others in the same field, leads to a situation where "knowledge no longer requires application to reality; knowledge is what gets passed on, silently, without comment, from one text to another.... [W]hat matters is that [ideas] are *there*, to be repeated, echoed and re-echoed uncritically" (Said, 1978: 116).

... Feminist social research needs to be highly aware of the potential for appropriation which accompanies the researcher's ideological positioning and that initiating a new "strategic form" within a research field implies modifying the "strategic location" of the researcher.... The force of Said's argument is that developing new knowledge in an established field requires modifying the conventional textual practices in that field particularly as those practices constitute a colonizing or appropriative relationship between the researcher and the participants in the research. What this means is that the problem of appropriation and its solution lie within the researcher's way of working with the texts produced by that research; in other words, by the researcher's textual practice.

TEXTUAL PRACTICES

In this section I want to discuss the contribution of deconstructive textual practice to the reduction of appropriation. I suggest that this can be made across several planes through: (1) an identification of the constraints ideology can impose on data; (2) the indirect empowerment of participants by writing texts which represent a range of positionings within the field under investigation; and (3) a discussion of ways in which interpretive control can be shared between researcher and participants.

My discussion of the significance of a deconstructive reading of participants' texts is premised on research practice which is closed to more quantitative modes of working. A deconstructive analysis requires the detailed accessing of the participant's world. It depends on the taping and full transcription of interviews which, although "unstructured," generate their own coherence through their responsiveness to the concerns of the participant. The researcher, in the analysis and writing of her text, is engaged in a fluid process of identifying and questioning ideology (her own, not merely the other's), her location within the literature, the nature of her textual practice and the personal and political implications of methodology for the participants in the study.

What I am suggesting is that a deconstructive reading may mitigate the issues of authority and ideological appropriation which Said has identified, but never entirely overcome them because of the impossibility of avoiding suppression or of writing beyond ideology (Threadgold, 1986). Mitigation is possible because a deconstructive reading does not attempt to be definitive. In order to maximize a nonappropriable stance towards participants the writer of a deconstructive sociological text should be explicit about its limitations and the implications of participants' locations (including the writer's). Furthermore, the writer should consciously attempt to move away from a uniform textual surface, which represents only the researcher's voice, to the creation of a report which is more fissured, that is, one in which different and often competing voices within a society are recognized. Nor is it sufficient to posit one's ideological position. It is necessary, I believe, to continually reexamine the extent to which that ideology contributes to a failure to see beyond it, and to question particular truths which adhere to it and the stereotypes which develop from it.

As (partial) alternatives to Said's representation of conventional academic research as characterized by textual closure and appropriation I have identified four practices assisting in the creation of differently structured texts. These alternative practices, which make available the evidence on which one's interpretations are based and which attempt to move beyond the "subject-become-object" status of the participant in relation to the researcher, are: (i) recognition of the limitations of the researcher's research and knowledge; (ii) the analytic reading of the participants' texts; (iii) some principles in relation to the incorporation of quotations from the participants' texts—what I am calling here the "writing in of voices"; and (iv) issues of empowerment.

LIMITATIONS OF RESEARCH AND KNOWLEDGE

In a discussion of the nature of ethnographic research, Clifford displaces the ethnographer to a position "at the edge of the frame" (1986: 1), a felicitous phrase which undermines the authoritativeness of the research and introduces elements of incompleteness and contingency. Historically, however, Clifford argues that anthropological (and sociological) studies have disguised their inherent limitations, claiming instead an ability to portray what he describes as the "essence" (Clifford, 1983: 124ff) of the society through the use of various devices or textual strategies. One such device was an emphasis on observation which allowed the ethnographer, through a typifying procedure, to record characteristic behaviors and cultural ceremonies; another, the use of "powerful abstractions" which enabled ethnographers to assert their possession of the "heart" of the culture (125). Such practices go together with the conviction that true statements about another culture can be made. They serve to validate the representation of the other culture, which it is the task of the ethnographer's text to produce, yet work to conceal the fact, as Said (1978: 273) notes, that all representations are "implicated, intertwined, embedded, interwoven with a great many other things besides the 'truth' which is itself a representation," being "embedded first in the language and then in the culture, institutions and political ambience of the representer."

Yet to present one's research outcomes as contingent and incomplete goes against very strong Western notions of objectivity and truth and raises questions about the authority of texts and modes of writing in which limitations are overtly acknowledged. Taking up a strategic location "at the edge of the frame" has fundamental implications for the practice of social research.

THE ANALYTIC READING

A deconstructive or postmodernist reading is a distinctive mode of reading and interpretation of textual data. It is constituted by attention to the paradoxical, the contradictory, the marginal, and by the foregrounding (not suppression) of these elements. Its focus on difference and on marginality within a text means that it specifically attends to what may be quantifiably insignificant but whose (remarked) presence may question a more conventional interpretation and expand theoretical understanding. It demands reflexivity from researchers, and a challenge to their ideological positions from the data may be recognized. It accepts that the research report is limited in its representation of actuality, despite its apparent fullness....

WRITING IN VOICES

Following postmodernist theory I have argued for the production of texts which incorporate multiple voices, citing its value for theory and the empowerment of participants (Opie, 1988a [especially Chapters 2 and 3] and b). Such a practice, however, raises at least three issues: (1) the criteria for the selection of quotations; (2) the question whether including extracts from interviews is a sufficient means of weaving other voices into the research report; and (3) the question whether the researcher should be solely responsible for the interpretation.

Selection of Quotations

Because qualitative research often involves the analysis of thousands of lines of transcripts, principles for selection of quotations must be defined. The principles underpinning a deconstructive analysis depend upon thinking of language as nontransparent, as deeply involved in ideology, paradox, contradiction and ephemerality. The researcher must attend not only to the content of the texts of the interviews but also their textual features which may affect the reception and representation of that content because of their contribution to the interpretation.

The principles (which I am not claiming are exhaustive) that I have identified as augmenting the common practice in social research of illustrative quotation are:

The intensity of the speaking voice. I rely heavily on an aural recollection of passages since recalling or rehearing the intensity with which a point is spoken can significantly influence the analysis. During my research on shared parenting or joint custody after separation or divorce (Opie, 1988a) one woman, in talking about how she arrived at the decision to try shared parenting, said in a rather matter of fact voice, "I knew what I wanted." She then launched into a page and a half of an intense and very detailed account of what "*I didn't want,*" repeating this clause persistently. The emphasis and intensity with which she spoke in addition to the content of her speech [illustrate the] extent to which the women in the study had been responsible for the decision. This contributed to a gender analysis of power and to the recognition of the paradox of women acting traditionally in taking responsibility for the children, yet radically in that the mode of custody they chose was potentially destabilizing of traditional gender roles within the family.

The contradictory moment. There will be times when speakers, often apparently without any sign of awareness, contradict themselves in midsentence. On other occasions, the actual moment of contradiction is not so closely positioned. My understanding of the importance of an awareness of contradiction is located in a philosophical reading of self and identity. Acknowledgement of contradiction challenges the notion of rationality, affirms instead a much more unstable, decentered notion of self and calls for the representation of this self within the written text.... A frequent sociological practice is to valorize one side or element of the contradiction, a device like those Clifford has identified, which serves to make the contradiction disappear rather than encourages the discovery of the ground "in between" (Poovey, quoting Derrida, 1988: 53).

Emotional content or tone. The emotional content of the voice contributes significantly to the implications of what is said....

A concentration on the differences in emotion between the speakers assists in a finely grained analysis of carers' experiences. It contributes, too, to a more complex gender analysis (Jacobus, 1986), since intertextual comparisons between elderly carers' texts in tone and emotional content indicate points at which male and female carers cross gender-specific boundaries. Furthermore, it suggests that specific verbal content, such as the repeated denigratory comments about the demented person (as well as the abusive emotional content) may help in identifying situations of potential psychological and physical abuse.

The extent to which the participant uses whole sentences, rather than the more usual recursive speech patterns. Conversational speech is marked by redundancy, repetitiveness and incompleteness and depends extensively on the listener's ability to interpret a range of nonverbal communicative features. Under these circumstances the use of a nonredundant mode of speech is extremely powerful (Barthes, 1973/86). Focusing on the nonredundant speech act may assist in the identification of a particular ideological moment, inform the readers of the manner in which issues of power and control affect the process of data collection and indicate the unstable ground of the researcher/researched relationship (Opie, 1988b).

The identification of examples of these four points in interview texts relies on a close textual reading and the inclusion by the transcriber of some of the characteristics of the spoken word—sudden movements of emphasis, breaks in a sentence and changes of direction, and movement through a range of emotions. One of the implications of such speech behavior is that the reproduction of the voice only in a transcript of the word spoken is inadequate and that a more powerful means of presentation should be found so that the voice actually speaking may be evidenced within the text....

The Control of the Interpretation

Recently, the practice has developed, particularly among anthropologists, of giving a draft of a report to research participants and asking them to comment on its validity. The point of this practice is to realign the balance of power in the research relationship by minimizing appropriation through a deliberate attempt to avoid misrepresentation and stereotype and by the expansion of the researcher's appreciation of the situation as a result of discussing and reworking the text with the participants. However, I am unclear how agreement over the final version is reached when there is more than one participant. If agreement cannot be reached, one course of action is that the contentious material is removed; another, that the interpretation of some of the participants is privileged. However, I believe the situation to be more complicated. Removal of the material does not permit it to be discussed; while subordination of one reading raises several problems.

The problematic areas are located in: (i) the implied claim that there is a final or "deep" truth which research can reveal; (ii) the notion of "consensus" when the processes of how consensus has been achieved and whose account privileged are left unexplored with the result that it is assumed that the participant's group is speaking in a united voice; (iii) the implications for interpretation of the different perspectives of the researcher and the researched; and (iv) the nature and/or physical appearance of the final text.

Because a postmodernist analysis highlights competing voices and raises critical appreciation of the presence of ideologies within a text, accepting an interpretation which implies a single or unified representation of an event is problematic, especially since this implies that all participants are similarly located. A further implication, that participants and researchers occupy an identical relationship to the data, is also problematic since participants may occupy a less analytic and more descriptive position, while researchers may be more aware of alternative interpretations.

Although anthropologists have suggested (Clifford, 1983, 1986) that a coauthorship relationship with respondents should be developed or have achieved this mode of working relationship (Mbilinyi, 1989), such a relationship is difficult to achieve when participants, while constituting a community of interest, do not form a close-knit physical community. For instance, it is impossible to develop a coauthorial relationship with the informal carers whom I have interviewed because of their geographical spread and the difficulty in attending drafting meetings because of the elder's need for supervision.

The physical appearance of texts which reflect difference and seek to avoid textual smoothness has generated little comment. One example, however, is Benterrak, Muecke and Roe's (1984) *Reading the Country* in which three very different visual and physically structured texts coexist, each representing alternative modes of reading, each claiming very different genealogies. The writerly intention, then, is not necessarily to achieve a consensus but to highlight the points of difference and the tensions between competing accounts as well as shared interpretations. Addressing difference would create a much more broken and fissured text and would focus much more attention on the nature of the interpretive processes. It would also have the effect of highlighting the sociological and ideological locations of those involved—not merely differences between the researcher and the participants, but also differences between the participants themselves and the implications of location on interpretation (Rosaldo, 1986). The consequences of such practices would reinforce the significance of textuality as an integral part of research, indicate the instability of (sociological) knowledge, and challenge "strateg[ies] of authority" (Clifford, 1983: 120).

EMPOWERMENT

I want to move now from the means of diminishing textual appropriation to look at more direct means of empowerment through research design and the researcher's assumptions about some of the purposes of research. I have chosen to address more the personal benefit to participants (while also noting how the ramifications spread beyond the individual) because I do not think that this area has been discussed extensively....

Finally, I focus on strategies and research design specifically intended to empower participants and discuss problems within feminist action-oriented research in which unacknowledged appropriative tendencies can be located. I suggest that disempowerment is located within textual appropriation. This appropriation can be partially avoided by the use of qualitative research methods which can lead to an empowerment of participants on a personal and broadly therapeutic plane. Deconstructive textual practice can importantly assist in political empowerment, through the incorporation in published research of participants' multiple and very different voices, so that the way that ideology can smooth over differences is disrupted and questioned; and through the encouragement, as a result of participation in the research, of individual and collective challenging of the system.

The Private Dimension of Research

There are at least three ways in which a participant may be individually empowered through participation in a research project where the style of interviewing is not hindered by rigid interview schedules, and where points of specific interest can be followed in detail. I suggest that this mode of unstructured and responsive interviewing, when used reflexively, can enable especially the socially marginalized (Said's "colonized") to be empowered because it assumes they can contribute significantly to the description and analysis of a social issue; and indeed, nearly every participant in my caregiving study agreed to take part because of their desire to help others through making their experience available and through their critique of the health system. By taking part in the research they lifted the veil of invisibility surrounding carers' everyday lives, and the experience of marginality from their existence (by becoming "center" even if briefly), thus opening what is generally a socially obscured experience to a more public gaze.

Because the interviews were responsive to individual preoccupations, there was an inbuilt therapeutic dimension to the process which I would also characterize as empowering. Some participants were able to reflect on and reevaluate their experience as part of the process of being interviewed. For some, this reevaluation had important personal as well as political consequences.

...

When qualitative research incorporates the voices of marginal and hence previously silenced groups into the text it can become subversive along a number of fronts. For example, the texts of the interviews with the caregivers challenge the ascription of caring as intuitive, affirm the existence of a world which is emotionally extraordinarily complex and contradictory, and indicate that caring is constituted within several affective positions within the field of caring, none of which are peculiar to a particular kin relationship and where the positioning of the individual carer is likely to change over time (Opie, 1990a). My interpretation of these texts, then, confirms much of the feminist critique of caring, but demonstrates aspects of that critique requiring further theorizing.

The Praxis Dimension of Research

The final question I want to pose is: does the researcher's adoption of a praxis orientation (Ortner, 1984; Smith, 1987) avoid appropriation and support the political empowerment of the inevitably objectified "subject," or is it merely a "reductively pragmatic response," where practice is viewed as if it "were a domain of actuality unencumbered by agents, interests, and contentions" (Said, 1989: 211)?

Lather's work (1986, 1988) can be read as an exemplar of an overtly political model of feminist research practice which valorizes research leading to collective social action. Her model of research has some similarities to my concept of a significant research methodology. She embraces firmly a praxis/empowerment/reciprocity paradigm, where she affirms the need to expand the knowledge base through the problemization of what is taken for granted through nondogmatic, grounded research into the mundane lives of the dispossessed. She quotes Heron to the effect that the ability of the dispossessed to "participate in decisions that claim to generate knowledge about them" (1986: 262) avoids their manipulation. She argues that reciprocity, achieved through interactive, sequential interviewing and a negotiation of meaning through sharing of drafts, helps "participants to understand and change their situations" (263). She also refers approvingly to a number of praxis-oriented research projects that resulted in women being able to set up organizations or centers which addressed their previously unmet and unrecognized needs. So far, so good. However, there are three points where I think her approach is open to question.

On a number of occasions Lather makes reference to the concept of "false consciousness" which she defines (1986: 264) as a "denial of how our commonsense ways of looking at the world are permeated with meanings that sustain our disempowerment"; she further suggests that one of the main purposes of research is to assist participants in self-reflection and understanding (her words) or self-criticism (my words). A full appreciation of false consciousness among participants is achieved by running groups for the women whom one is researching with the implication that they can be helped on from their false, to a true, state of consciousness. This is to be achieved by engaging in an "ideology critique," the purpose being to create conditions where a questioning of beliefs, authority and culture hitherto taken for granted becomes possible and where the "researcher joins the participants in a theoretically guided program of action" (268).

One of the difficulties about taking a critical approach to Lather's work is its current political correctness; for example, the research projects which she cites as leading to a praxis outcome include the establishment of Rape Crisis Centers. My argument is not about the outcome, but with the positioning of the various women in the research process. My discomfort with her argument derives from: (i) her failure to recognize her own processes of appropriation; (ii) her failure to treat women as other than a generic whole; and (iii) a lack of reflexivity in her research paradigm. Let me expand on these points. Critical enquiry, as Lather defines it, is that which, in a complex series of interactions, begins as a response to the experiences and desires of the oppressed. The researcher guides the dispossessed in "a process of cultural transformation," itself a mutually educative process where the researcher and the researched both contribute to the expansion of the other's knowledge—a process whereby the respondents are liberated from "ideologically frozen understandings" (Lather, 1986: 268) and become aware that these no longer serve their interests. During the period of the research, the critical researcher submits her work to participants for their evaluation of its accuracy but at the same time must have reference beyond their assessments because of the contamination of "false consciousness" (269) and must then negotiate meanings with the participants *without becoming impositional* (269; Lather's italics).

What concerns me is that there is a considerable tension between her intention to liberate women and her failure to recognize her own ideological location (however positively valued that may currently be) which is itself taken for granted and is therefore seen as true, rather than apprehended as ideological. I think that the assumption of correctness introduces a further tension between all participants. There is a pretense of equality where the researched are understood to have some knowledge not yet possessed/appropriated by the researcher (but the superiority of some of that knowledge is not affirmed by Lather since, ultimately, the researcher is guide). The researcher is consistently privileged, particularly through her location in a more ideologically correct position—in terms of Said's concept of the colonized it could be argued that she has missionary status (with all of its unfortunate and well-meaning connotations)—thus raising doubts about the extent of the mutually transformative process that has been promised, a doubt compounded by the admission at the end that the participants' viewpoint cannot be completely relied on and that further external evidence must be sought, which one presumes will offer a higher degree of reliability.

This notion of research, then, appears to me also to disempower participants (even if differently) as do the research paradigms it seeks to displace. The object is apprehended through a particular predetermined textual attitude, the adherence to which may preclude the possibility of modification through interaction between knowledge and theory. There appears, in this somewhat rigid practice, to be less room, on the researcher's part, for reflexivity and for change; for a recognition that a single ideological position may deny and distort the experience of some women while validating that of others. We cannot engage in research divested of ideology. We can come with an overt consciousness of ideology and an awareness that all ideology can obscure as well as enlighten. Appropriation of the other can therefore be minimized by a constant, sensitive reflection on the way that the texts of the participants are created by ideology and yet at some points challenge it.

CONCLUSION

I have argued throughout this paper that textual appropriation of the other is an inevitable consequence of research. I have demonstrated that a qualitative, deconstructive, theoretical and methodological approach with its emphasis on a close textual reading can counterbalance (although by no means eliminate) this inevitability. I have suggested that this is because it facilitates the researcher's entry into complex, recursive and contradictory worlds, and because of its potential for empowerment of the participants. To return to Said's distinction which I introduced at the beginning of this paper: How do we as social researchers understand our "strategic location" with respect to the participants in our research, and how do we define the "strategic formation" within which we think and research? I have argued that qualitative research using a deconstructive methodology permits a more reflexive, flexible understanding of our location and it obviously introduces a new "strategic formation" for sociological research. In particular, it helps focus fundamental questions in a new way: Who are we writing for? What kinds of authority should we claim for our texts? What kind of texts should we be producing?

NOTES

1. For a more detailed account of the REACH research (Research with Elders and Carers at Home) see Opie (1990b). This research has been funded by the New Zealand University Grants Committee and supported by additional grants from the Internal Research Committee of Victoria University of Wellington.

2. See also Barthes's (1971/86) comments on issues of textual authority.

REFERENCES

Barthes, Roland (1971/1986) "From work to text" in *The Rustle of Language* trans. by Richard Howard, New York: Hill & Wang.

————. (1973/1986) "The war of language" in *The Rustle of Language* trans. by Richard Howard, New York: Hill & Wang.

Benterrak, Kim, Muecke, Stephen and Roe, Paddy (1984) *Reading the Country: Introduction to Nomadology* Fremantle: Fremantle Arts Centre Press.

Briggs, Charles (1986) *Learning How to Ask: A Sociolinguistic Appraisal of the Role of the Interview in Social Science Research* Cambridge: Cambridge University Press.

Certeau de, Michel (1984) *The Practice of Everyday Life* trans. by Stephen Rendall, Berkeley: University of California Press.

Clifford, James (1983) "On ethnographic authority" *Representations* Vol. 1, No. 2: 118–46.

————. (1986) "Introduction: partial truths" in Clifford and Marcus (1986).

Clifford, James and Marcus, George (1986) editors, *Writing Culture: The Poetics and Politics of Ethnography* Berkeley: University of California Press.

Close, Paul (1989) "Policy, domestic labour and gender" *National Conference on Social Policy in Australia: What Future the Welfare State?*

Croft, Suzy (1986) "Women, caring and the recasting of need—a feminist reappraisal" *Critical Social Policy* Vol. 16: 23–39.

Dalley, Gillian (1988) *Ideologies of Caring: Rethinking Community and Collectivism* London: Macmillan Educational Books.

Eco, Umberto and Sebeok, Thomas (1983) *The Sign of the Three: Dupin, Holmes and Pierce* Bloomington: Indiana University Press.

Felski, Rita (1989) *Beyond Feminist Aesthetics: Feminist Literature and Social Change* Cambridge, Mass: Harvard University Press.

Finch, Janet and Groves, Dulcie (1980) "Community care and the family: a case for equal opportunities" *Journal of Social Policy* Vol. 9, No. 4: 487–511.

————. (1983) editors, *A Labour of Love: Women, Work and Caring* London: Routledge & Kegan Paul.

Gibson, Diane and Allen, Judith (1989) "Parasitism and phallocentrism: a critique of social policy provisions for the aged" University of Queensland, Australia.

Ginzburg, Carlo (1983) "Clues: Morelli, Freud, & Sherlock Holmes" in Eco and Sebeok (1983).

Graham, Hilary (1983) "Caring: a labour of love" in Finch and Groves (1983).

Jacobus, Mary (1986) "Reading woman (reading)" in Mary Jacobus, *Reading Woman: Essays in Feminist Criticism* London: Methuen.

Lather, Patti (1986) "Research as praxis" *Harvard Educational Review* Vol. 56, No. 3: 257–77.

———— (1988) "Feminist research perspectives on empowering research methodologies" *Women's Studies International Forum* Vol. 11, No. 6: 569–82.

Mbilinyi, Marjorie (1989) "'I'd have been a man': politics and the labour process in producing personal narratives" in Personal Narratives Group (1989).

Opie, Anne (1988a) *Shared Parenting in New Zealand after Separation and Divorce*, Ph.D. thesis, Wellington: Victoria University of Wellington, New Zealand.

———— (1988b) "Moving beyond local colour: the voices of qualitative research" *Sites*, Vol. 17: 83–99.

———— (1990a) "The instability of the caring body: gender and caregivers of the confused elderly" paper presented at the Sociological Association Conference of Aoteanoa (New Zealand) Christchurch, December.

————. (1990b) "Caring for the confused elderly at home: report on work in progress" *New Zealand Women's Studies Journal* Vol. 6, No. 1/2: 48–64.

Ortner, Sherry (1984) "Theory in anthropology since the sixties" *Comparative Studies in Society and History*, Vol. 26, No. 1: 126–66.

Pascall, Gillian (1986) *Social Policy: A Feminist Analysis* London and New York: Tavistock.

Personal Narratives Group (1989) *Interpretating Women's Lives: Feminist Theory and Personal Narratives* Bloomington: Indiana University Press.

Poovey, Mary (1988) "Feminism and deconstruction" *Feminist Studies* Vol. 14, No. 1: 51–65.

Rosaldo, Renato (1986) "From the door of his tent" in Clifford and Marcus (1986).

Said, Edward (1978) *Orientalism* London: Penguin.

————. (1989) "Representing the colonized: anthropology's interlocutors" *Critical Inquiry* Vol. 15: 205–25.

Smith, Dorothy (1987) *The Everyday World as Problematic: A Feminist Sociology* Boston: N.E. University Press.

Statham, Anne, Miller, Eleanor and Mauksch, Hans (1988) editors, "Women's approach to work: the creation of knowledge" in Statham, Miller, and Mauksch, *The Worth of Women's Work: A Qualitative Synthesis* Albany: State University of New York Press.

Threadgold, Terry (1986) "Semiotics—ideology—language" in Threadgold, Grosz, Kress, and Halliday (1986) *Language, Semiotics, Ideology* Sydney: Pathfinder Press.

Williams, Fiona (1989) *Social Policy: A Critical Introduction. Issues of Race, Gender and Class* Cambridge: Polity Press.

11
Objectivity and Validation

Questions of method have been intertwined with questions of validation at least since the philosopher Rene Descartes initiated the so-called epistemological turn in the seventeenth century. Two of Descartes's most famous works, *Rules for the Direction of the Mind* and *A Discourse on the Method of Rightly Conducting the Reason and Seeking for Truth in the Sciences,* assume that the central task of epistemology is to prescribe methods for establishing objective truth. Thus, the best methods are defined as those most successful in producing objective knowledge—and objective knowledge is defined as that supported by the best available methods.

Objectivity is an honorific concept that confers respect; in this, it is like other concepts such as justice, goodness, democracy, and freedom. Objectivity also resembles ethical and political terms in that its operational meaning is "essentially contested." Just as alternative interpretations of justice, goodness, democracy, and freedom are perennially debated within ethics and political philosophy, so modern epistemologists and philosophers of science have been preoccupied with debates over objectivity. Some Western feminist scholars have abandoned the ideal of objectivity, which some associate with objectification, and some have embraced relativism. However, many feminist scholars wish to develop a viable conception of objectivity or validation because they want to assert that feminist claims offer a corrective and not just an alternative to male-biased knowledge claims. The readings in this section offer enlarged conceptions of objectivity, validation, and method.

THE PARAMETERS OF FEMINIST DEBATES ABOUT OBJECTIVITY

Feminist discussions of objectivity and validation occur on terrain lying between two poles, neopositivism at one pole and various versions of relativism at the other. Frequently though not necessarily, neopositivism is associated with more conservative political views and relativism is associated with political views that are more left-leaning.

As we saw earlier, positivism is generally disavowed but neopositivism still has wide influence. Neopositivists tend to view objectivity as a kind of correspondence between knowledge claims and the mind-independent reality that the claims purportedly describe, and they regard empiricism as the only trustworthy methodology. Neopositivists contend that objectivism and empiricism must be supported as the only alternatives to the epistemic chaos of pluralism, perspectivalism, relativism, and skepticism.

A few feminist scholars are sympathetic to positivism, but many, as we have seen, are developing alternative approaches to epistemology and methodology. Critics who misunderstand or misinterpret these alternative approaches often cast the feminists who adopt them as relativists. For instance, they may misconstrue feminist naturalized epistemology as claiming that women's ways of knowing are biologically or socially determined and so unavailable to men, who have a different biology or socialization. The critics then attribute to feminists the relativist view that what men and women respectively can know is not only radically different but also incommunicable to each other. Similarly, critics may misrepresent standpoint theory as claiming that people's consciousness is entirely determined by their social location and that the consciousness of those in the lowest social classes is always correct;

from this they may infer that feminists are committed to the relativist view that what women (or working-class people or people of color) claim to know is unchallengeable by—indeed, forever unknowable to—men (or persons from the ruling classes or whites). Finally, critics may misconstrue postmodernist claims that reality is "constructed" by discourse as saying that anything goes.

Despite such misrepresentations, feminist theorists have developed their various epistemological approaches precisely because they seek methods of producing knowledge that will be better supported and more objective than the knowledge produced by traditional approaches. Thus feminist naturalized epistemologists defend their interest in women's (and other disrespected groups') practices of inquiry on the grounds that such practices have often produced valuable knowledge even when they have not accorded with dominant research models. Similarly, feminist empiricists argue that investigating the experience of women (and other subordinated groups) has produced important information, even as they recognize that women (and other groups) are diverse and that first-person reports of experience are not beyond question. Again, standpoint theorists argue that focusing inquiry on issues problematic for the most marginalized is likely to suggest fruitful new research agendas that will generate less partial and more comprehensive understandings than those generated from the perspectives of the rulers. Finally, postmodernist feminists argue that recognizing all knowledge as historically situated, contingent, and shaped by social power enables researchers to avoid misleading universalizations. By drawing on all these insights, feminists have sought to develop methodological strategies that will enable researchers to create knowledge that is more objective in being less biased by the interests of dominant social groups.

In addition to seeking knowledge that is more epistemically reliable, feminist researchers typically wish to produce knowledge *for* women in the sense of being addressed to women's concerns, perhaps capable of providing a reliable guide to action. They also wish to avoid utilizing knowledge-generating strategies that are incompatible with feminist ethical values. Neopositivist epistemology sees these three desiderata of knowledge production as entirely separate from each other. In other words, it distinguishes:

1. the epistemic trustworthiness of knowledge claims from
2. their social applicability or usefulness

and distinguishes both of these from

3. the ethics of research

However, some feminist scholars have argued that these three issues are connected, so that better values may produce better research. For instance, addressing problems that some groups of women (or other subordinated groups) find pressing and that incorporate egalitarian or democratic values into the process of inquiry may be likely to promote findings that are more epistemically reliable. One theme of the readings in this section is that the three conditions we have been considering necessary for research to be regarded as feminist, namely, that such research be reliable, emancipatory, and ethically conducted, are not entirely independent of each other.

TWO CONTRASTING APPROACHES TO OBJECTIVITY AND METHODOLOGY: NEOPOSITIVISM AND THE SOCIAL STUDIES OF SCIENCE

Within the positivist tradition, the question of method is interpreted exclusively as a question of how to justify hypotheses presented for investigation. A sharp distinction is made between the "context of discovery" and the "context of justification."

1. The context of discovery refers to the circumstances from which hypotheses are derived; it may include many sources, even dreams or religious revelations. According to positivism, the source from which a hypothesis is generated is independent of the epistemic validity of that hypothesis, which instead depends entirely on the context of justification.

2. The context of justification refers to the set of experiments designed for testing hypotheses. Neopositivist methodology is characterized by its exclusive focus on the context of justification and its disregard for the context of discovery. Its theorists have developed elaborate "logics" or methodological models for justifying hypotheses. They include the hypothetico-deductive method, according to which the implications deduced from hypotheses are tested against experience, and the falsification method, which requires that every effort be made to find counterinstances to theoretical claims. In order to rule out individual biases, all the methodological models require that observations and experiments be replicable by other investigators. When no experiment can be devised that will validate one hypothesis over another, positivists select among hypotheses by appeal to criteria such as consistency with other accepted theories, explanatory fruitfulness, and simplicity.

The positivist tradition assesses objectivity exclusively on the basis of what it calls "internal" grounds, namely, the relations between a hypothesis and the evidence that tends to support or undermine it. According to "internalist" approaches to methodology, knowing the social context within which knowledge claims are produced is irrelevant to assessing the objectivity of these claims, since social circumstances are "external" to reason. Thus, the social context of knowledge production is excluded from methodological reflections. Methodology begins only after hypotheses are formulated; no "logic of discovery" can exist.

In contrast with neopositivism's exclusive focus on considerations it regards as internal to knowledge claims, the intellectual tradition known as social studies of science includes consideration of so-called external factors. It studies how the construction of knowledge has been shaped by its social context, including the interests and values of researchers and their funders. The origins of the social studies of science are quite diverse; they include Marxism, American pragmatism, German critical theory, the historiography and analytic philosophy of science, and postmodernism. All share a commitment to naturalizing epistemology in the broad sense of investigating how knowledge actually is produced, believing that science must be used to study the practice of science itself. Scholars working in the social studies of science tradition reject the kind of armchair philosophizing that produces a priori normative models or "rules for the direction of the understanding" without looking first at how scientists actually work. They see such armchair philosophizing as "idealist" in the invidious sense of ungrounded, unrealistic, and impractical. On the basis of empirical investigation, those who pursue the social studies of science deny that the development of science can be fully understood by reference only to so-called internal factors. They trace how social values and interests have influenced the choice of problems for research, the selection of techniques for gathering evidence, the interpretation of the evidence, and the conclusions drawn from it. Their methodological reflections are not restricted to what positivists call the logic of justification; they seek in addition to develop possible logics of discovery.

IS SUBJECTIVITY THE ENEMY OF OBJECTIVITY?

The more inclusive approach to methodology adopted by scholars pursuing the social studies of science obviously relies on a conception of objectivity different from that of positivism. Rather than seeing objective knowledge as guaranteed by nonperspectival and value-neutral reason, the alternative conception assumes that objectivity is always situated, partial, provisional, and incomplete. It also resists portraying objectivity as entirely opposed to subjectivity.

Within the positivist tradition, subjectivity is the mirror image of objectivity. Subjectivity is everything that objectivity is not: private rather than public, value-laden rather than value-free, emotional rather than rational, partial and biased rather than total or comprehensive. Thus, within the positivist tradition, "subjective knowledge" is close to being a contradiction in terms; if it means anything, it means claims based on private feelings that are incapable in principle of being intersubjectively validated and that, because they resist revision by others, can be no more than matters of personal opinion. Positivism therefore associates subjectivism with relativism and with the abandonment of objectivity.

Western culture has tended to associate reason and objectivity symbolically with men and the masculine; by contrast, it has symbolically associated women and the feminine with subjectivity and so with irrationality, chaos, emotion, and the private. Typically, men have been portrayed as the paradigm knowers and women's epistemic authority has been suspect (Lloyd 1984). Contemporary critics of feminist approaches to epistemology and methodology have drawn on these symbolic associations in portraying feminism as hostile to reason and science, as relativistic, or as a set of "politically correct" orthodoxies that are immune to empirical evidence. They have argued that recognizing the influence of subjective and social factors in shaping the construction of knowledge would at best reduce epistemology, methodology, and the philosophy of science to sociology and at worst promote relativism and irrationalism.

In response to these charges, Elisabeth Lloyd and others have argued that the critics misrepresent the epistemological projects of feminists influenced by the social studies of science (Lloyd 1997). Specifically, the critics mistakenly characterize the social studies of science as committed to what Lloyd calls "the exclusivity thesis," the view that the only considerations relevant to determining objectivity are what the critics call external and that so-called internal considerations are irrelevant. This is a caricature of epistemological approaches drawing on the social studies of science. In fact, feminists sympathetic to this tradition challenge the whole positivist opposition between "internal" and "external," which they regard as a false dilemma. They resist being relocated at the subjective pole of the objective/subjective dichotomy, and instead seek to undermine the old contrasts between so-called internal and external, objectivity and subjectivity. As Sandra Harding has put it, rather than seeing subjective factors only as a source of bias, they are exploring ways to utilize the social situatedness of subjects of knowledge systematically as a resource for maximizing objectivity.

COMBINING "INTERNALISM" AND "EXTERNALISM" IN FEMINIST METHODOLOGY

Many contemporary feminists see so-called internal and external explanations of knowledge as complementary; for example, Elisabeth Lloyd (1997) has argued that, in anthropology, a fuller comprehension of the beliefs of another culture comes from understanding *both* what they mean to believers *and* what role they play in the culture. Thus, most contemporary feminists contend that more inclusive understandings of rationality can be developed by studying considerations that are both internal and external, logical and social. They regard the contexts of both justification and discovery as not sharply separable.

The view that social values shape the construction of knowledge at many levels has methodological implications; for instance, it challenges the traditional distinction between cognitive and noncognitive values in science (Longino 1997). It implies that developing feminist methods requires attending not only to the logical requirements of investigative projects but also to their broader social context. Thus, feminist researchers should certainly devise tests for their hypotheses, but they should also reflect on how hypotheses are generated and what they might mean within a particular social context. Feminists certainly do not advise abandoning tried-and-true methods such as double-blind studies, but many recommend construing methodology more inclusively so that it also takes social context into account. For instance, they advocate that researchers should take everyday life as problematic, develop research agendas that address the concerns of the subjugated and marginalized, find ways of including researchers from diverse backgrounds, and reflect on how their research is affected by their own positionality.

The readings in this chapter of the book all offer suggestions for broadening traditional conceptions of methodology in order to attain greater objectivity. Alison Jaggar discusses how some emotions might be useful in developing more objective understandings of social reality, Helen Longino argues that objectivity requires a kind of intellectual democracy, and Naomi Scheman contends that a context of trust is indispensable for objectivity.

If more inclusive approaches to methodology are warranted, then the three aspects of knowledge production that positivism views as separate are in fact interrelated: the question of the objective content of knowledge claims is independent neither of the question of its usefulness nor of the ethical standards used in the research. Emancipatory purposes and more ethical methods not only are valuable in their own right but are also more likely to produce objective knowledge.

REFERENCES

Lloyd, Elisabeth A. 1997. "Science and Anti-Science: Objectivity and Its Real Enemies," in *Feminism, Science, and the Philosophy of Science,* ed. Lynn Hankinson Nelson and Jack Nelson. Dordrecht, Netherlands: Kluwer Academic Publishers.

Lloyd, Genevieve. 1984. *The Man of Reason: "Male" and "Female" in Western Philosophy.* Minneapolis: University of Minnesota Press.

Longino, Helen E. 1997. "Cognitive and Noncognitive Values in Science: Rethinking the Dichotomy," in *Feminism, Science, and the Philosophy of Science,* ed. Lynn Hankinson Nelson and Jack Nelson. Dordrecht, Netherlands: Kluwer Academic Publishers.

Alison M. Jaggar
Love and Knowledge: Emotion in Feminist Epistemology

This reading argues that, by construing emotion as epistemologically subversive, the Western tradition has tended to obscure the vital role of emotion in the construction of knowledge.

INTRODUCTION: EMOTION IN WESTERN EPISTEMOLOGY

Within the Western philosophical tradition, emotions have usually been considered potentially or actually subversive of knowledge; reason rather than emotion has been regarded as the indispensable faculty for acquiring knowledge.[2]

Typically, the rational has been contrasted with the emotional, with reason associated with the mental, the cultural, the universal, the public and the male, whereas emotion has been associated with the irrational, the physical, the natural, the particular, the private and, of course, the female.

Although Western epistemology has tended to give pride of place to reason rather than emotion, it has not always excluded emotion completely from the realm of reason. In the *Phaedrus,* emotions were not seen as needing to be totally suppressed, but rather as needing direction by reason.... [T]he emotions were thought of as providing indispensable motive power that needed to be channelled appropriately....

The contrast between reason and emotion was sharpened in the seventeenth century by redefining reason as a purely instrumental faculty. For both the Greeks and the medieval philosophers, reason had been linked with value in so far as reason provided access to the objective structure or order of reality, seen as simultaneously natural and morally justified. With the rise of modern science, however, the realms of nature and value were separated: nature was stripped of value and reconceptualized as an inanimate mechanism of no intrinsic worth. Values were relocated in human beings, rooted in their preferences and emotional responses. The separation of supposedly natural fact from human value meant that reason, if it were to provide trustworthy insight into reality, had to be uncontaminated by or abstracted from value. Increasingly, therefore, though never universally, reason was reconceptualized as the ability to make valid inferences from premises established elsewhere, the ability to calculate means but not to determine ends. The validity of logical inferences was thought independent of human attitudes and preferences; this was now the sense in which reason was taken to be objective and universal.[5]

The modern redefinition of rationality required a corresponding reconceptualization of emotion. This was achieved by portraying emotions as nonrational and often irrational urges that regularly swept the body. The common way of referring to the emotions as the "passions" emphasized that emotions happened to or were imposed upon an individual, something she suffered rather than something she did.

The epistemology associated with this new ontology rehabilitated sensory perception that, like emotion, typically had been suspected or even discounted by the Western tradition as a reliable source of knowledge. British empiricism, succeeded in the nineteenth century by positivism, took its epistemological task to be the formulation of rules of inference that would guarantee the derivation of certain knowledge from the "raw data" supposedly given directly to the senses. Empirical testability became accepted as the hallmark of natural science; this, in turn, was viewed as the paradigm of genuine knowledge. Often epistemology was equated with the philosophy of science, and the dominant methodology of positivism prescribed that truly scientific knowledge must be capable of intersubjective verification. Because values and emotions had been defined as variable and idiosyncratic, positivism stipulated that trustworthy knowledge could be established only by methods that neutralized the values and emotions of individual scientists.

Recent approaches to epistemology have challenged some fundamental assumptions of the positivist epistemological model. Contemporary theorists of knowledge have undermined once rigid distinctions between analytic and synthetic statements, between theories and observations and even between facts and values. However, few challenges have been raised thus far to the purported gap between emotion and knowledge. In this paper, I wish to begin bridging this gap through the suggestion that emotions may be helpful and even necessary rather than inimical to the construction of knowledge.

EMOTION

What Are Emotions?

Several problems confront someone trying to answer the deceptively simple philosophical question, "What are emotions?" One set of difficulties results from the variety, complexity, and even inconsistency of the ways in which emotions are viewed, both in daily life and in scientific contexts. A second difficulty is the wide range of phenomena covered by the term "emotion": these extend from apparently instantaneous "knee-jerk" responses of fright to lifelong dedication to an individual or a cause; from highly civilized aesthetic responses to undifferentiated feelings of hunger and thirst;[6] from background moods such as contentment or depression to intense and focused involvement in an immediate situation. It may well be impossible to construct a manageable account of emotion to cover such apparently diverse phenomena.

A further problem concerns the criteria for preferring one account of emotion to another. The more one learns about the ways in which other cultures conceptualize human faculties, the less plausible it becomes that emotions constitute what philosophers call a "natural kind." Not only do some cultures identify emotions unrecognized in the West, but there is reason to believe that the concept of emotion itself is a historical invention. If this is true, then we have even more reason to wonder about the adequacy of ordinary Western ways of talking about emotion. Yet we have no access either to our own emotions or to those of others independent of or unmediated by the discourse of our culture.

In the face of these difficulties, I shall sketch an account of emotion with the following limitations. First, it will operate within the context of Western discussions of emotion: I shall not question, for instance, whether it would be possible or desirable to dispense entirely with anything resembling our concept of emotion. Second, this account is intended to cover only a limited domain, not every phenomenon that may be called an emotion. On the contrary, it excludes as genuine emotions both automatic physical responses and nonintentional sensations, such as hunger pangs. Third, I do not pretend to offer a complete theory of emotion; instead, I focus on a few specific aspects of emotion that I take to have been neglected or misrepresented, especially in positivist and neopositivist accounts. Finally, I would defend my approach not only on the ground that it illuminates aspects of our experience and activity that are obscured by positivist and neopositivist construals, but also on the ground that it is less open than these to ideological abuse. In particular, I believe that recognizing certain neglected aspects of emotion makes possible a better and less ideologically biased account of how knowledge is, and so ought to be, constructed.

Emotions as Intentional

Early positivist approaches to understanding emotions assumed that an adequate account required analytically separating emotion from other human faculties. [P]ositivist accounts of emotion tried to separate emotion conceptually from both reason and sense perception. As part of their sharpening of these distinctions, positivist construals of emotion tended to identify emotions with the physical feelings or involuntary bodily movements that typically accompany them; or to the subduing of physiological function or movement. The continuing influence of such supposedly scientific conceptions of emotion can be seen in the fact that "feeling" is often used colloquially as a synonym for emotion, even though the more central meaning of "feeling" is physiological sensation. On such accounts, emotions were not seen as being *about* anything: instead, they were contrasted with and seen as potential disruptions of other phenomena that *are* about some thing, phenomena such as rational judgments, thoughts, and observations. The positivist approach to understanding emotion has been called the Dumb View (Spelman [1982]).

The Dumb View of emotion is quite untenable. For one thing, the same feeling or physiological response is likely to be interpreted as various emotions, depending on the context of experience. Another problem with the Dumb View is that identifying emotions with feelings would make it impossible to postulate that a person might not be aware of her emotional state, because feelings by definition are a matter of conscious awareness. Finally, emotions differ from feelings, sensations or physiological responses in that they are dispositional rather than episodic. For instance, we may assert truthfully that we are outraged by, proud of or saddened by certain events, even if at that moment we are neither agitated nor tearful.

In recent years, contemporary philosophers have tended to reject the Dumb View of emotion and have substituted more intentional or cognitivist understandings, [which] emphasize that intentional judgments as well as physiological disturbances are integral elements in emotion.[7] They define or identify emotions not by the quality or character of the physiological sensation that may be associated with them, but rather by their intentional aspect, the associated judgment. Thus, it is the content of my associated thought or judgment that determines whether my physical agitation and restlessness are defined as "anxiety about my daughter's lateness" rather than as "anticipation of tonight's performance."

Cognitivist accounts of emotion have been criticized as overly rationalist, inapplicable to allegedly spontaneous, automatic or global emotions, such as general feelings of nervousness, contentedness, *Angst,* ecstasy or terror. Certainly, these accounts entail that infants and animals experience emotions, if at all, in only a primitive, rudimentary form. Far from being unacceptable, however, this entailment is desirable because it suggests that humans develop and mature in emotions as well as in other dimensions, increasing the range, variety and subtlety of their emotional responses in accordance with their life experiences and their reflections on these.

Cognitivist accounts of emotion are not without their own problems. A serious difficulty with many is that they end up replicating an artificial split between emotion and thought because most cognitivist accounts explain emotion as having two "components": an affective or feeling component and a cognition that supposedly interprets or identifies the feelings. Such accounts, therefore, unwittingly perpetuate the positivist distinction between the shared, public, objective world of verifiable calculations, observations, and facts and the individual, private, subjective world of idiosyncratic feelings and sensations. This sharp distinction breaks any conceptual links between our feelings and the "external" world: if feelings are still conceived as blind or raw or undifferentiated, then we can give no sense to the notion of feelings fitting or failing to fit our perceptual judgments, that is, being appropriate or inappropriate. When intentionality is viewed as intellectual cognition and moved to the center of our picture of emotion, the affective elements are pushed to the periphery and become shadowy conceptual danglers whose relevance to emotion is obscure or even negligible.

Moreover, in so far as they prioritize the intellectual over the feeling aspects, they reinforce the traditional Western preference for mind over body.[8] Nevertheless, they do identify a vital feature of emotion overlooked by the Dumb View, namely, its intentionality.

Emotions as Social Constructs

We tend to experience our emotions as involuntary individual responses to situations, responses that are often private in the sense that they are not perceived as directly and immediately by other people as they are by the subject of the experience. The apparently individual and involuntary character of our emotional experience is often taken as evidence that emotions are presocial, instinctive responses, determined by our biological constitution. This inference, however, is quite mistaken. Although it is probably true that the physiological disturbances characterizing emotions (facial grimaces, changes in the metabolic rate, sweating, trembling, tears, and so on) are continuous with the instinctive responses of our prehuman ancestors and also that the ontogeny of emotions to some extent recapitulates their phylogeny, mature human emotions can be seen neither as instinctive nor as biologically determined. Instead, they are socially constructed on several levels.

The most obvious way in which emotions are socially constructed is that children are taught deliberately what their culture defines as appropriate responses to certain situations: to fear strangers, to enjoy spicy food or to like swimming in cold water. On a less conscious level, children also learn what their culture defines as the appropriate ways to express the emotions that it recognizes. Although there may be cross-cultural similarities in the expression of some apparently universal emotions, there are also wide divergences in what are recognized as expressions of grief, respect, contempt or anger. On an even deeper level, cultures construct divergent understandings of what emotions are.

Further aspects of the social construction of emotion are revealed through reflection on emotion's intentional structure. If emotions necessarily involve judgments, then obviously they require concepts, which may be seen as socially constructed ways of organizing and making sense of the world. For this reason, emotions are simultaneously made possible and limited by the conceptual and linguistic resources of a society. This philosophical claim is borne out by empirical observation of the cultural variability of emotion. Although there is considerable overlap in the emotions identified by many cultures (Wierzbicka [1986]), at least some emotions are historically or culturally specific, including perhaps *ennui, Angst,* the Japanese *amai* (in which one clings to another, affiliative love), and the response of "being a wild pig," which occurs among the Gururumba, a horticultural people living in the New Guinea Highlands (Averell [1980], p. 158]). Even apparently universal emotions, such as anger or love, may vary cross-culturally. Romantic love was invented in the Middle Ages in Europe and since that time has been modified considerably. . . . In some cultures, romantic love does not exist at all.[9]

Thus there are complex linguistic and other social preconditions for the experience, that is, for the existence of human emotions. The emotions that we experience reflect prevailing forms of social life. . . . [I]t is inconceivable that any distinctively human emotion could be experienced by a solitary individual in some hypothetical presocial state of nature. There is a sense in which any individual's guilt or anger, joy or triumph, presupposes the existence of a social group capable of feeling guilt, anger, joy, or triumph. This is not to say that group emotions historically precede or are logically prior to the emotions of individuals; it is to say that individual experience is simultaneously social experience.[10]

Emotions as Active Engagements

We often interpret our emotions as experiences that overwhelm us rather than as responses we consciously choose: that emotions are to some extent involuntary is part of the ordinary meaning of the term "emotion." Even in daily life, however, we recognize that emotions are not entirely involuntary and we try to gain control over them in various ways ranging from mechanistic behavior modification techniques designed to sensitize or desensitize our feeling responses to various situations to cognitive techniques designed to help us to think differently about situations.

Some psychological theories interpret emotions as chosen on an even deeper level, interpreting them as actions for which the agent disclaims responsibility. For instance, the psychologist Averell likens the experience of emotion to playing a culturally recognized role we ordinarily perform so smoothly and automatically that we do not realize we are giving a performance. Averell notes, however, that emotions often are useful in attaining their goals only if they are interpreted as passions rather than as actions.

The action/passion dichotomy is too simple for understanding emotion, as it is for other aspects of our lives. Perhaps it is more helpful to think of emotions as habitual responses that we may have more or less difficulty in breaking. We claim or disclaim responsibility for these responses depending on our purposes in a particular context. We could never experience our emotions entirely as deliberate actions, for then they would appear nongenuine and inauthentic, but neither should emotions be seen as nonintentional, primal or physical forces with which our rational selves are forever at war.

Emotions, then, are ways in which we engage actively and even construct the world. They have both "mental" and "physical" aspects, each of which conditions the other; in some respects they are chosen but in others they are involuntary; they presuppose language and a social order. Thus, they can be attributed only to what are sometimes called "whole persons," engaged in the ongoing activity of social life.

Emotion, Evaluation, and Observation

Emotions and values are closely related. The relation is so close, indeed, that some philosophical accounts of what it is to hold or express certain values reduce these phenomena to nothing more than holding or expressing certain emotional attitudes. When the relevant conception of emotion is the Dumb View, then simple emotivism is certainly too crude an account of what it is to hold a value; on this account, the intentionality of value judgments vanishes and value judgments become nothing more than sophisticated grunts and groans. Nevertheless, the grain of important truth in emotivism is its recognition that values presuppose emotions to the extent that emotions provide the experiential basis for values. If we had no emotional responses to the world, it is inconceivable that we should ever come to value one state of affairs more highly than another.

Just as values presuppose emotions, so emotions presuppose values. The object of an emotion (that is, the object of fear, grief, pride, and so on) is a complex state of affairs that is appraised or evaluated by the individual.

Emotions and evaluations, then, are logically or conceptually connected. Certainly it is true (*pace* J. S. Mill) that the evaluation of a situation as desirable or dangerous does not entail that it is universally desired or feared, but it does entail that desire or fear is viewed generally as an appropriate response to the situation. Thus, every emotion presupposes an evaluation of some aspect of the environment while, conversely, every evaluation or appraisal of the situation implies that those who share that evaluation will share, *ceteris paribus,* a predictable emotional response to the situation.

The rejection of the Dumb View and the recognition of intentional elements in emotion already incorporate a realization that observation influences and indeed partially constitutes emotion. Without characteristically human perceptions of and engagements in the world, there would be no characteristically human emotions.

Just as observation directs, shapes, and partially defines emotion, so too emotion directs, shapes, and even partially defines observation. Observation is not simply a passive process of absorbing impressions or recording stimuli; instead, it is an activity of selection and interpretation. What is selected and how it is interpreted are influenced by emotional attitudes. On the level of individual observation, this influence has always been apparent to common sense, which notes that we remark very different features of the world when we are happy, depressed, fearful, or confident. This influence of emotion on perception is now being explored by social scientists. One example is the so-called Honi phenomenon, named after a subject called Honi who, under identical experimental conditions, perceived strangers' heads as changing in size but saw her husband's head as remaining the same.

The most obvious significance of this sort of example is in illustrating how the individual experience of emotion focuses our attention selectively, directing, shaping, and even partially defining our observations, just as our observations direct, shape, and partially define our emotions. In addition, the example has been taken further in an argument for the social construction of what are taken in any situation to be undisputed facts, showing how these rest on intersubjective agreements that consist partly in shared assumptions about "normal" or appropriate emotional responses to situations (McLaughlin [1985]). Thus these examples suggest that certain emotional attitudes are involved on a deep level in all observation, in the intersubjectively verified and so supposedly dispassionate observations of science as well as in the common perceptions of daily life. In the next section, I shall elaborate this claim.

EPISTEMOLOGY

The Myth of Dispassionate Investigation

The derogatory Western attitude toward emotion, like the earlier Western contempt for sensory observation, fails to recognize that emotion, like sensory perception, is necessary to human survival. Emotions prompt us to act appropriately, to approach some people and situations and to avoid others, to caress or cuddle, fight or flee. Moreover, emotions have an intrinsic as well as an instrumental value. Although not all emotions are enjoyable or even justifiable, as we shall see, life without any emotion would be life without any meaning.

Within the context of Western culture, however, people have often been encouraged to control or even suppress their emotions. Consequently, it is not unusual for people to be unaware of their emotional state or to deny it to themselves and others. This lack of awareness, especially combined with a neopositivist understanding of emotion that construes it as just a feeling of which one is aware, lends plausibility to the myth of dispassionate investigation. But lack of awareness of emotions certainly does not mean that emotions are not present subconsciously or unconsciously, or that subterranean emotions do not exert a continuing influence on people's articulated values and observations, thoughts, and actions.

Within the positivist tradition, the influence of emotion is usually seen only as distorting or impeding observation or knowledge. Certainly it is true that contempt, disgust, shame, revulsion or fear may inhibit investigation of certain situations or phenomena. Furiously angry or extremely sad people often seem quite unaware of their surroundings or even of their own conditions; they may fail to hear or may systematically misinterpret what other people say. People in love are notoriously oblivious to many aspects of the situation around them.

In spite of these examples, however, positivist epistemology recognizes that the role of emotion in the construction of knowledge is not invariably deleterious and that emotions may make a valuable contribution to knowledge. But the positivist tradition will allow emotion to play only the role of suggesting hypotheses for investigation. Emotions are allowed this because the so-called logic of discovery sets no limits on the idiosyncratic methods that investigators may use for generating hypotheses.

When hypotheses are to be tested, however, positivist epistemology imposes the much stricter logic of justification. The core of this logic is replicability, a criterion believed capable of eliminating or cancelling out what are conceptualized as emotional as well as evaluative biases on the part of individual investigators. The conclusions of Western science thus are presumed "objective," precisely in the sense that they are uncontaminated by the supposedly "subjective" values and emotions that might bias individual investigators (Nagel [1968, pp. 33–34]).

But if, as has been argued, the positivist distinction between discovery and justification is not viable, then such a distinction is incapable of filtering out values in science. For example, although such a split, when built into the Western scientific method, is generally successful in neutralizing the idiosyncratic or unconventional values of individual investigators, it has been argued that it does not, indeed, cannot, eliminate generally accepted social values. These values are implicit in the identification of the problems that are considered worthy of investigation, in the selection of the hypotheses that are considered worthy of testing and in the solutions to the problems that are considered worthy of acceptance. The science of past centuries provides ample evidence of the influence of prevailing social values, whether seventeenth-century atomistic physics (Merchant [1980]) or nineteenth-century competitive interpretations of natural selection (Young [1985]).

Of course, only hindsight allows us to identify clearly the values that shaped the science of the past and thus to reveal the formative influence on science of pervasive emotional attitudes, attitudes that typically went unremarked at the time because they were shared so generally. Because we are closer to them, however, it is harder for us to see how certain emotions, such as sexual possessiveness or the need to dominate others, are currently accepted as guiding principles in twentieth-century sociobiology or even defined as part of reason within political theory and economics (Quinby [1986]).

Values and emotions enter into the science of the past and the present not only at the level of scientific practice but also at the metascientific level, as answers to various questions: What is science? How should it be practiced? And what is the status of scientific investigation versus nonscientific modes of inquiry? For instance, it is claimed with increasing frequency that the modern Western conception of science, which identifies knowledge with power and views it as a weapon for dominating nature, reflects the imperialism, racism, and misogyny of the societies that created it.

Positivism views values and emotions as alien invaders that must be repelled by a stricter application of the scientific method. If the foregoing claims are correct, however, the scientific method and even its positivist construals themselves incorporate values and emotions. Moreover, such an incorporation seems a necessary feature of all knowledge and conceptions of knowledge. Therefore, rather than repressing emotion in epistemology it is necessary to rethink the relation between knowledge and emotion and construct conceptual models that demonstrate the mutually constitutive rather than oppositional relation between reason and emotion. Far from precluding the possibility of reliable knowledge, emotion as well as value must be shown as necessary to such knowledge. Despite its classical antecedents and as in the ideal of disinterested inquiry, the ideal of dispassionate inquiry is an impossible dream, but a dream none the less or perhaps a myth that has exerted enormous influence on Western epistemology. Like all myths, it is a form of ideology that fulfills certain social and political functions.

The Ideological Function of the Myth

So far, I have spoken very generally of people and their emotions, as though everyone experienced similar emotions and dealt with them in similar ways. It is an axiom of feminist theory, however, that all generalizations about "people" are suspect. The divisions in our society are so deep, particularly the divisions of race, class, and gender, that no one is simply a person but instead is constituted fundamentally by race, class, and gender. Race, class, and gender shape every aspect of our lives, and our emotional constitution is not excluded. Recognizing this helps us to see more clearly the political functions of the myth of the dispassionate investigator.

Feminist theorists have pointed out that the Western tradition has not seen everyone as equally emotional. Instead, reason has been associated with members of dominant political, social, and cultural groups and emotion with members of subordinate groups. Prominent among those subordinate groups in our society are people of color, except for supposedly "inscrutable Orientals" and women.

Although the emotionality of women is a familiar cultural stereotype, its grounding is quite shaky. Women appear to be more emotional than men because they, along with some groups of people of color, are permitted and even required to express emotion more openly. In contemporary Western culture, emotionally inexpressive women are suspect as not being real women, whereas men who express their emotions freely are suspected of being homosexual or in some other way deviant from the masculine ideal. Modern Western men are required to present a facade of coolness, lack of excitement, even boredom, to express emotion only rarely. Thus, women in our society form the main group allowed or even expected to express emotion.

White men's control of their emotional expression may go to the extremes of repressing their emotions, failing to develop emotionally or even losing the capacity to experience many emotions. Not uncommonly, these men are unable to identify what they are feeling, and even they may be surprised, on occasion, by their own apparent lack of emotional response to a situation, such as a death, where emotional reaction is perceived to be appropriate. In therapeutic situations, men may learn that they are just as emotional as women but less adept at identifying their own or others' emotions. In consequence, their emotional development may be relatively rudimentary; this may lead to moral rigidity or insensitivity.

Although there is no reason to suppose that the thoughts and actions of women are any more influenced by emotion than the thoughts and actions of men, the stereotypes of cool men and emotional women continue to flourish because they are confirmed by an uncritical daily experience. In these circumstances, where there is a differential assignment of reason and emotion, it is easy to see the ideological function of the myth of the dispassionate investigator. It functions, obviously, to bolster the epistemic authority of the currently dominant groups, composed largely of white men, and to discredit the observations and claims of the currently subordinate groups including, of course, the observations and claims of many people of color and women. The more forcefully and vehemently the latter groups express their observations and claims, the more emotional they appear and so the more easily they are discredited. The alleged epistemic authority of the dominant groups then justifies their political authority.

The previous section of this paper argued that dispassionate inquiry was a myth. This section has shown that the myth promotes a conception of epistemological justification vindicating the silencing of those, especially women, who are defined culturally as the bearers of emotion and so are perceived as more "subjective," biased and irrational. In our present social context, therefore, the ideal of the dispassionate investigator is a classist, racist, and especially masculinist myth.[18]

Emotional Hegemony and Emotional Subversion

Like everything else that is human, emotions in part are socially constructed; like all social constructs, they are historical products, bearing the marks of the society that constructed them. Within the very language of emotion cultural norms and expectations are embedded. Simply describing ourselves as angry, for instance, presupposes that we view ourselves as having been wronged, victimized by the violation of some social norm. Thus, we absorb the standards and values of our society in the very process of learning the language of emotion, and those standards and values are built into the foundation of our emotional constitution.

Within a hierarchical society, the norms and values that predominate tend to serve the interests of the dominant groups. Within a capitalist, white supremacist, and male-dominant society, the predominant values will tend to be those that serve the interests of rich white men. Consequently, we are all likely to develop an emotional constitution that is quite inappropriate for feminism. Whatever our color, we are likely to feel what Irving Thalberg has called "visceral racism"; whatever our sexual orientation, we are likely to be homophobic; whatever our class, we are likely to be at least somewhat ambitious and competitive; whatever our sex, we are likely to feel contempt for women. Such emotional responses may be rooted in us so deeply that they are relatively impervious to intellectual argument and may recur even when we pay lip service to changed intellectual convictions.[19]

By forming our emotional constitution in particular ways, our society helps to ensure its own perpetuation. The dominant values are implicit in responses taken to be precultural or acultural, our so-called gut responses. Not only do these conservative responses hamper and disrupt our attempts to live in or prefigure alternative social forms but also, and in so far as we take them to be natural responses, they blinker us theoretically. For instance, they lend plausibility to the belief that greed and domination are inevitable human motivations; in sum, they blind us to the possibility of alternative ways of living.

This picture may seem at first to support the positivist claim that the intrusion of emotion only disrupts the process of seeking knowledge and distorts the results of that process. The picture, however, is not complete; it ignores the fact that people do not always experience the conventionally acceptable emotions. They may feel resentment rather than gratitude for welfare payments and hand-me-downs. They may be attracted to forbidden modes of sexual expression. In other words, the hegemony that our society exercises over people's emotional constitution is not total.

People who experience conventionally unacceptable, or what I call "outlaw" emotions often are subordinated individuals who pay a disproportionately high price for maintaining the *status quo*. The social situation of such people makes them unable to experience the conventionally prescribed emotions: for instance, people of color are more likely to experience anger than amusement when a racist joke is recounted, and women subjected to male sexual banter are less likely to be flattered than uncomfortable or even afraid.

When unconventional emotional responses are experienced by isolated individuals, those concerned may be confused, unable to name their experience; they may even doubt their own sanity. Women may come to believe that they are "emotionally disturbed" and that the embarrassment or fear aroused in them by male sexual innuendo is prudery or paranoia. When certain emotions are shared or validated by others, however, the basis exists for forming a subculture defined by perceptions, norms, and values that systematically oppose the prevailing perceptions, norms, and values. By constituting the basis for such a subculture, outlaw emotions may be politically because epistemologically subversive.

Outlaw emotions are distinguished by their incompatibility with the dominant perceptions and values, and some, though certainly not all, of these outlaw emotions are potentially or actually feminist emotions. Emotions become feminist when they incorporate feminist perceptions and values, just as emotions are sexist or racist when they incorporate sexist or racist perceptions and values. For example, anger becomes feminist anger when it involves the perception that the persistent importuning endured by one woman is a single instance of a widespread pattern of sexual harassment.[20] ...

Outlaw emotions stand in a dialectical relation to critical social theory: at least some are necessary for developing a critical perspective on the world, but they also presuppose at least the beginnings of such a perspective. Feminists need to be aware of how we can draw on some of our outlaw emotions in constructing feminist theory, and also of how the increasing sophistication of feminist theory can contribute to the reeducation, refinement, and eventual reconstruction of our emotional constitution.

Outlaw Emotions and Feminist Theory

The most obvious way in which feminist and other outlaw emotions can help in developing alternatives to prevailing conceptions of reality is by motivating new investigations. This is possible because, as we saw earlier, emotions may be long-term as well as momentary. Feminist emotions provide a political motivation for investigation and so help to determine the selection of problems as well as the method by which they are investigated.

As well as motivating critical research, outlaw emotions may enable us to perceive the world differently from its portrayal in conventional descriptions. They may provide the first indications that something is wrong with the way alleged facts have been constructed, with accepted understandings of how things are. Conventionally unexpected or inappropriate emotions may precede our conscious recognition that accepted descriptions and justifications often conceal as much as reveal the prevailing state of affairs. Only when we reflect on our initially puzzling irritability, revulsion, anger or fear may we bring to consciousness our "gut-level" awareness that we are in a situation of coercion, cruelty, injustice or danger. Thus, conventionally inexplicable emotions, particularly though not exclusively those experienced by women, may lead us to make subversive observations that challenge dominant conceptions of the *status quo*. ...

But why should we trust the emotional responses of women and other subordinated groups? How can we determine which outlaw emotions are to be endorsed or encouraged and which rejected? In what sense can we say that some emotional responses are more appropriate than others? What reason is there for supposing that certain alternative perceptions of the world, perceptions informed by outlaw emotions, are to be preferred to perceptions informed by conventional emotions? Here I can indicate only the general direction of an answer, whose full elaboration must await another occasion.[21]

I suggest that emotions are appropriate if they are characteristic of a society in which all humans (and perhaps some nonhuman life too) thrive, or if they are conducive to establishing such a society. For instance, it is appropriate to feel joy when we are developing or exercising our creative powers, and it is appropriate to feel anger and perhaps disgust in those situations where humans are denied their full creativity or freedom....

This suggestion, obviously, is extremely vague and may even verge on the tautologous. How can we apply it in situations where there is disagreement over what is or is not disgusting or exhilarating or unjust? Here I appeal to a claim for which I have argued elsewhere: the perspective on reality that is available from the standpoint of the subordinated, which in part at least is the standpoint of women, is a perspective that offers a less partial and distorted and therefore more reliable view (Jaggar [1983, ch. 11]). Subordinated people have a kind of epistemological privilege in so far as they have easier access to this standpoint and therefore a better chance of ascertaining the possible beginnings of a society in which all could thrive. For this reason, I would claim that the emotional responses of subordinated people in general, and often of women in particular, are more likely to be appropriate than the emotional responses of the dominant class. That is, they are more likely to incorporate reliable appraisals of situations.

Even in contemporary science, where the ideology of dispassionate inquiry is almost overwhelming, it is possible to discover a few examples that seem to support the claim that certain emotions are more appropriate than others in both a moral and epistemological sense. For instance, Hilary Rose claims that women's practice of caring, even though warped by its containment in the alienated context of a coercive sexual division of labor, has nevertheless generated more accurate and less oppressive understandings of women's bodily functions, such as menstruation (Rose [1983]). Examples like these prompt Hilary Rose to assert that a feminist science of nature needs to draw on heart as well as hand and brain.

Some Implications of Recognizing the Epistemic Potential of Emotion

Accepting that appropriate emotions are indispensable to reliable knowledge does not mean, of course, that uncritical feeling may be substituted for supposedly dispassionate investigation. Nor does it mean that the emotional responses of women and other members of the underclass are to be trusted without question. Although our emotions are epistemologically indispensable, they are not epistemologically indisputable. Like all our faculties, they may be misleading, and their data, like all data, are always subject to reinterpretation and revision. Because emotions are not presocial, physiological responses to unequivocal situations, they are open to challenge on various grounds. They may be dishonest or self-deceptive, they may incorporate inaccurate or partial perceptions, or they may be constituted by oppressive values. Accepting the indispensability of appropriate emotions to knowledge means no more (and no less) than that discordant emotions should be attended to seriously and respectfully rather than condemned, ignored, discounted or suppressed.

Just as appropriate emotions may contribute to the development of knowledge, so the growth of knowledge may contribute to the development of appropriate emotions. For instance, the powerful insights of feminist theory often stimulate new emotional responses to past and present situations. Inevitably, our emotions are affected by the knowledge that the women on our faculty are paid systematically less than the men. We are likely to feel different emotions toward older women or people of color as we reevaluate our standards of sexual attractiveness or acknowledge that black is beautiful. The new emotions evoked by feminist insights are likely in turn to stimulate further feminist observations and insights, and these may generate new directions in both theory and political practice. There is a continuous feedback loop between our emotional constitution and our theorizing such that each continually modifies the other and is in principle inseparable from it.

The ease and speed with which we can reeducate our emotions is unfortunately not great. Emotions are only partially within our control as individuals. Although affected by new information, they are habitual responses not quickly unlearned. These unwelcome, because apparently inappropriate, emotions should not be suppressed or denied; instead, they should be acknowledged and subjected to critical scrutiny. The persistence of such recalcitrant emotions probably demonstrates how fundamentally we have been constituted by the dominant world view, but it may also indicate superficiality or other inadequacy in our emerging theory and politics.[22] We can only start from where we are—beings who have been created in a cruelly racist, capitalist and male-dominated society that has shaped our bodies and our minds, our perceptions, our values and our emotions, our language, and our systems of knowledge.

The alternative epistemological models that I suggest would display the continuous interaction between how we understand the world and who we are as people. They would show how our emotional responses to the world change as we conceptualize it differently and how our changing emotional responses then stimulate us to new insights. They would demonstrate the need for theory to be self-reflexive, to focus not only on the outer world but also on ourselves and our relation to that world, to examine critically our social location, our actions, our values, our perceptions, and our emotions....

A corollary of the reflexivity of feminist and other critical theory is that it requires a much broader construal than positivism accepts of the process of theoretical investigation. In particular, it requires acknowledging that a necessary part of theoretical process is critical self-examination. Time spent in analyzing emotions and uncovering their sources should be viewed, therefore, neither as irrelevant to theoretical investigation nor even as a prerequisite for it. Instead, we must recognize that our efforts to reinterpret and refine our emotions are necessary to our theoretical investigation. Critical reflection on emotion is not a self-indulgent substitute for political analysis and political action. It is itself a kind of political theory and political practice, indispensable for an adequate social theory and social transformation.

Finally, the recognition that emotions play a vital part in developing knowledge enlarges our understanding of women's claimed epistemic advantage. We can now see that women's subversive insights owe much to women's outlaw emotions, themselves appropriate responses to the situations of women's subordination. In addition to their propensity to experience outlaw emotions, at least on some level, women are relatively adept at identifying such emotions, in themselves and others, in part because of their social responsibility for caretaking, including emotional nurturance. It is true that women, like all subordinated peoples, especially those who must live in close proximity with their masters, often engage in emotional deception and even self-deception as the price of their survival. Even so, women may be less likely than other subordinated groups to engage in denial or suppression of outlaw emotions. Women's work of emotional nurturance has required them to develop a special acuity in recognizing hidden emotions and in understanding the genesis of those emotions. This emotional acumen can now be recognized as a skill in political analysis and validated as giving women a special advantage both in understanding the mechanisms of domination and in envisioning freer ways to live.

CONCLUSION

The claim that emotion is vital to systematic knowledge is only the most obvious contrast between the conception of theoretical investigation that I have sketched here and the conception provided by positivism. For instance, the alternative approach emphasizes that what we identify as emotion is a conceptual abstraction from a complex process of human activity that also involves acting, sensing, and evaluating. This proposed account of theoretical construction demonstrates the simultaneous necessity for and interdependence of faculties that our culture has abstracted and separated from each other: emotion and reason, evaluation and perception, observation and action. The model of knowing suggested here is appropriately symbolized by the radical feminist metaphor of the upward spiral. Emotions are neither more basic than observation, reason or action in building theory, nor secondary to them. Each of these human faculties reflects an aspect of human knowing inseparable from the other aspects. Thus, to borrow a famous phrase from a Marxian context, the development of each of these faculties is a necessary condition for the development of all.

NOTES

...
2. The Western tradition as a whole has been profoundly rationalist.
...

5. … [T]he variability, rather than the commonality, of human preferences and responses was emphasized; values gradually came to be viewed as individual, particular and even idiosyncratic rather than as universal and objective. The only exception to the variability of human desires was the supposedly universal urge to egoism and the motive to maximize one's own utility, whatever that consisted in. The value of autonomy and liberty, consequently, was seen as perhaps the only value capable of being justified objectively because it was a precondition for satisfying other desires.

6. For instance, Julius Moravcsik has characterized as emotions what I would call "plain" hunger and thirst, appetites that are not desires for any particular food or drink (Moravcsik [1982, pp. 207–24]). I would view so-called instinctive, nonintentional feelings as the biological raw material from which full-fledged human emotions develop.

7. Even adherents of the Dumb View recognize, of course, that emotions are not entirely random or unrelated to an individual's judgments and beliefs. On the Dumb View, however, the judgments or beliefs associated with an emotion are seen as its causes and thus as related to it only externally.

8. Cheshire Calhoun pointed this out to me in private correspondence.

9. Recognition of the many levels on which emotions are socially constructed raises the question whether it makes sense even to speak of the possibility of universal emotions. Although a full answer to this question is methodologically problematic, one might speculate that many of what we Westerners identify as emotions have functional analogues in other cultures.

10. The relationship between the emotional experience of an individual and the emotional experience of the group to which the individual belongs may perhaps be clarified by analogy with the relation between a word and the language of which it is a part. That a word has meaning presupposes that it is part of a linguistic system without which it has no meaning; yet the language itself has no meaning over and above the meaning of the words of which it is composed together with their grammatical ordering. Words and language presuppose and mutually constitute each other. Similarly, both individual and group emotion presuppose and mutually constitute each other. (Averell [1980, p. 157]).

…

14. It is now widely accepted that the suppression and repression of emotion has damaging if not explosive consequences. Psychotherapy, which purports to help individuals recognize and "deal with" their emotions, has become an enormous industry, especially in the USA. Once emotions have been discharged or vented, they are supposed to be experienced less intensely, or even to vanish entirely, and consequently to exert less influence on individuals' thoughts and actions. This approach to psychotherapy clearly retains the traditional Western assumption that emotion is inimical to rational thought and action. Thus, such approaches fail to challenge and indeed provide covert support for the view that "objective" knowers are not only disinterested but also dispassionate.

…

18. Someone might argue that the viciousness of this myth was not a logical necessity. In an egalitarian society, where the concepts of reason and emotion were not gender-bound in the way they still are today, it might be argued that the ideal of the dispassionate investigator could be epistemologically beneficial. Is it possible that, in such socially and conceptually egalitarian circumstances, the myth of the dispassionate investigator could serve as a heuristic device, an ideal never to be realized in practice but nevertheless helping to minimize "subjectivity" and bias? My own view is that counterfactual myths rarely bring the benefits advertised and that this one is no exception. This myth fosters an equally mythical conception of pure truth and objectivity, quite independent of human interests or desires, and in this way it functions to disguise the inseparability of theory and practice, science and politics. Thus, it is part of an antidemocratic worldview that mystifies the political dimension of knowledge and unwarrantedly circumscribes the arena of political debate.

19. Of course, the similarities in our emotional constitutions should not blind us to systematic differences. For instance, girls rather than boys are taught fear and disgust for spiders and snakes, affection for fluffy animals and shame for their naked bodies. It is primarily, though not exclusively, men rather than women whose sexual responses are shaped by exposure to visual and sometimes violent pornography. As we shall see shortly, differences in the emotional constitution of various groups may be epistemologically significant in so far as they both presuppose and facilitate different ways of perceiving the world.

20. A necessary condition for experiencing feminist emotions is that one already be a feminist in some sense, even if one does not consciously wear that label. But many women and some men, even those who would deny that they are feminist, still experience emotions compatible with feminist values. For instance, they may be angered by the perception that someone is being mistreated just because she is a woman, or they may take special pride in the achievement of a woman. If those who experience such emotions are unwilling to recognize them as feminist, their emotions are probably described better as potentially feminist or prefeminist emotions.

21. I owe this suggestion to Marcia Lind.

22. Within a feminist context, Berenice Fisher suggests that we focus particular attention on our emotions of guilt and shame as part of a critical reevaluation of our political ideals and our political practice (Fisher [1984]).

HELEN LONGINO
Values and Objectivity

Objectivity is a characteristic ascribed variously to beliefs, individuals, theories, observations, and methods of inquiry. It is generally thought to involve the willingness to let our beliefs be determined by "the facts" or by some impartial and nonarbitrary criteria rather than by our wishes as to how things ought to be. A specification of the precise nature of such involvement is a function of what it is that is said to be objective. . . .

Some part of the popular reverence for science has its origin in the belief that scientific inquiry, unlike other modes of inquiry, is by its very nature objective. . . . Science is thought to provide us with a view of the world that is objective in two seemingly quite different senses of that term. In one sense objectivity is bound up with questions about the truth and referential character of scientific theories, that is, with issues of scientific realism. In this sense to attribute objectivity to science is to claim that the view provided by science is an accurate description of the facts of the natural world as they are. . . . In the second sense objectivity has to do with modes of inquiry. In this sense to attribute objectivity to science is to claim that the view provided by science is one achieved by reliance upon nonarbitrary and nonsubjective criteria for developing, accepting, and rejecting the hypotheses and theories that make up the view. The reliance upon and use of such criteria as well as the criteria themselves are what is called scientific method. Common wisdom has it that if science is objective in the first sense it is because it is objective in the second.

At least two things can be intended by the ascription of objectivity to scientific method. Often scientists speak of the objectivity of data. By this they seem to mean that the information upon which their theories and hypotheses rest has been obtained in such a way as to justify their reliance upon it. This involves the assumption or assurance that experiments have been properly performed and that quantitative data have not been skewed by any faults in the design of survey instruments or by systematic but uncharacteristic eccentricities in the behavior of the sample studied. . . . What can be reliable is the relation of measurements one to another within a particular dimension or kind of scale—for example, the relation between what we label as the pressure and temperature of a gas. Here what is reliable is a certain covariance in the measurements obtained by the use of certain instruments. . . . While objective, that is, reliable, measurement is indeed one crucial aspect of objective scientific method,[2] it is not the only dimension in which questions about the objectivity of methods can arise. In ascribing (or denying) objectivity to a method we can also be concerned about the extent to which it provides means of assessing hypotheses and theories in an unbiased and unprejudiced manner.

In this [reading] I will explore more deeply the nature of this second mode of scientific objectivity and its connection with the logic of discourse in the natural sciences.... My analysis makes no pretense to totality or completion. It suggests, rather, a framework to be filled in and developed both by epistemologists whose task is to develop criteria and standards of knowledge, truth, and rational belief and by historians and sociologists whose task is to make visible those historical and institutional features of the practice of science that affect its content....

OBJECTIVITY, SUBJECTIVITY, AND INDIVIDUALISM

The positivist analysis of confirmation guaranteed the objectivity of science by tying the acceptance of hypotheses and theories to a public world over whose description there can be no disagreement. Positivists allow for a subjective, nonempirical element in scientific inquiry by distinguishing between a context of discovery and a context of justification.[3] The context of discovery for a given hypothesis is constituted by the circumstances surrounding its initial formulation—its origin in dreams, guesses, and other aspects of the mental and emotional life of the individual scientist. Two things should be noted here. First, these nonempirical elements are understood to be features of an individual's psychology. They are treated as randomizing factors that promote novelty rather than as beliefs or attitudes that are systematically related to the culture, social structure, or socioeconomic interests of the context within which an individual scientist works. Secondly, in the context of justification these generative factors are disregarded, and the hypothesis is considered only in relation to its observable consequences, which determine its acceptability. This distinction enables positivists to acknowledge the play of subjective factors in the initial development of hypotheses and theories while guaranteeing that their acceptance remains untainted, determined not by subjective preferences but by observed reality. The subjective elements that taint its origins are purged from scientific inquiry by the methods characteristic of the context of justification: controlled experiments, rigorous deductions, et cetera. When one is urged to be objective or "scientific," it is this reliance on an established and commonly accepted reality that is being recommended....

As long as one takes the positivist analysis as providing a model to which any inquiry must conform in order to be objective and rational, then to the degree that actual science departs from the model it fails to be objective and rational.... The only disagreement with respect to objectivity seems to be over the question of whether actual, historical science does or does not realize the epistemological ideal of objectivity. Defenders of the old model have argued that science ("good science") does realize the ideal. Readers of Kuhn and Feyerabend take their arguments to show that science is not objective, that objectivity has been fetishized by traditionalists. These authors themselves have somewhat more subtle approaches. While Kuhn has emphasized the role of such subjective factors as personality, education, and group commitments in theory choice, ... he suggests that values such as relative simplicity and relative problem-solving ability can and do function as nonarbitrary criteria in theory acceptance. Such values can be understood as internal to inquiry, especially by those to whom scientific inquiry just is problem solving.[4] Feyerabend, on the other hand, has rejected the relevance to science of canons of rationality or of general criteria of theory acceptance and defends a positive role for subjectivity in science.[5]

... How can the contextualist analysis of evidence, with its consequent denial of any logically guaranteed independence from contextual values, be accommodated within a perspective that demands or presupposes the objectivity of scientific inquiry?

As a first step in answering this question it is important to distinguish between objectivity as a characteristic of scientific method and objectivity as a characteristic of individual scientific practitioners or of their attitudes and practices. The standard accounts of scientific method tend to conflate the two, resulting in highly individualistic accounts of knowledge. Both philosophical accounts assume that method, the process by which knowledge is produced, is the application of rules to data. The positivist or traditional empiricist account of objectivity attributes objectivity to the practitioner to the extent that she or he has followed the method. Scientific method, on this view, is something that *can* be practiced by a single individual: sense organs and the capacity to reason are all that are required for conducting controlled experiments or practicing rigorous deduction. For Kuhn and for the contextualist account sketched above rationality and deference to observational data are not sufficient to guarantee the objectivity of individuals. For Kuhn this is because these intellectual activities are carried out in the context of a paradigm assented to by the scientific community. But, although Kuhn emphasizes the communitarian nature of the sciences, the theory of meaning he developed to account for the puzzling aspects of scientific change that first drew his attention reduces that community to a solipsistic monad incapable of recognizing and communicating with other monads/communities. Kuhn's account is, thus, as individualist as the empiricist one. The contextualist account makes the exercise of reason and the interpretation of data similarly dependent on a context of assumptions. Why is it not subject to the same problems?

OBJECTIVITY, CRITICISM, AND SOCIAL KNOWLEDGE

Two shifts of perspective make it possible to see how scientific method or scientific knowledge is objective even in the contextualist account. One shift is to return to the idea of science as practice. The analysis of evidential relations outlined above was achieved by thinking about science as something that is done, that involves some form of activity on the part of someone, the scientist. Because we think the goal of the scientist's practice is knowledge, it is tempting to follow tradition and seek solutions in abstract or universal rules. Refocussing on science as practice makes possible the second shift, which involves regarding scientific method as something practiced not primarily by individuals but by social groups.

The social nature of scientific practice has long been recognized. In her essay "Perception, Interpretation and the Sciences" Marjorie Grene discusses three aspects of the social character of science.[6] One she sees as the existence of the scientific disciplines as "social enterprises," the individual members of which are dependent on one another for the conditions (ideas, instruments, et cetera) under which they practice. Another related aspect is that initiation into scientific inquiry requires education. One does not simply declare oneself a biologist but learns the traditions, questions, mathematical and observational techniques, "the sense of what to do next," from someone who has herself or himself been through a comparable initiation and then practiced. One "enters into a world" and learns how to live in that world from those who already live there. Finally, as the practitioners of the sciences all together constitute a network of communities embedded in a society, the sciences are also among a society's activities and depend for their survival on that society's valuing what they do.... What I wish particularly to stress is that the objectivity of scientific inquiry is a consequence of this inquiry's being a social, and not an individual, enterprise.

The application of scientific method, that is, of any subset of the collection of means of supporting scientific theory on the basis of experiential data, requires by its nature the participation of two or more individuals. Even ... scientific knowledge is, after all, the product of many individuals working in (acknowledged or unacknowledged) concert. As noted earlier, scientific inquiry is complex in that it consists of different kinds of activities.... The integration and transformation of these activities into a coherent understanding of a given phenomenon are a matter of social negotiations.

One might argue that this is at least in principle the activity of a single individual. But, even if we were to imagine such group efforts as individual efforts, scientific knowledge is not produced by collecting the products of such imagined individuals into one whole. It is instead produced through a process of critical emendation and modification of those individual products by the rest of the scientific community. Experiments get repeated with variations by individuals other than their originators hypotheses and theories are critically examined, restated, and reformulated before becoming an accepted part of the scientific canon....

The social character of scientific knowledge is made especially apparent by the organization of late twentieth-century science, in which the production of knowledge is crucially determined by the gatekeeping of peer review. Peer review determines what research gets funded and what research gets published in the journals, that is, what gets to count as knowledge. The function of peer review is not just to check that the data seem right and the conclusions well-reasoned but to bring to bear another point of view on the phenomena, whose expression might lead the original author(s) to revise the way they think about and present their observations and conclusions. To put this another way, it is to make sure that, among other things, the authors have interpreted the data in a way that is free of their subjective preferences.

... Peer review prior to publication is not the only filter to which results are subjected. The critical treatment *after* publication is crucial to the refining of new ideas and techniques. While institutional bias may also operate in the postpublication reception of an idea, other factors, such as the attempt to repeat an experiment or to reconcile incompatible claims, can eventually compensate for such misplaced deference. Publication in a journal does not make an idea or result a brick in the edifice of knowledge. Its absorption is a much more complex process, involving such things as subsequent citation, use and modification by others, et cetera. Experimental data and hypotheses are transformed through the conflict and integration of a variety of points of view into what is ultimately accepted as scientific knowledge.[9]

What is called scientific knowledge, then, is produced by a community (ultimately the community of all scientific practitioners) and transcends the contributions of any individual or even of any subcommunity within the larger community.[10] ...

The social character of hypothesis acceptance underscores the publicity of science. This publicity has both social and logical dimensions. We are accustomed to thinking of science as a public possession or property in that it is produced for the most part by public resources—either through direct funding of research or through financial support of the education of scientists. The social processes described underscore another aspect of its publicity; it is itself a public resource—a common fund of assertions presumably established to a point beyond question. It thereby constitutes a body of putative truths that can be appealed to in defense or criticism of other claims.

From a logical point of view the publicity of science includes several crucial elements. First, theoretical assertions, hypotheses, and background assumptions are all in principle public in the sense of being generally available to and comprehensible to anyone with the appropriate background, education, and interest. Second, the states of affairs to which theoretical explanations are pegged (in evidential and explanatory relationships) are public in the sense that they are intersubjectively ascertainable.... Both features are consequences of the facts (1) that we have a common language which we use to describe our experience and within which we reason and (2) that the objects of experience which we describe and about which we reason are purported to exist independently of our seeing and thinking about them.[11]

These two aspects of the logical publicity of science make criticism of scientific hypotheses and theories possible in a way that is not possible, for instance, for descriptions of mystical experience or expressions of feeling or emotion. First, a common language for the description of experience means that we can understand each other, which means in turn that we can accept or reject hypotheses, formulate and respond to objections to them. Second, the presupposition of objects existing independently of our perception of them imposes an acceptance of constraints on what can be said or reasonably believed about them. Such acceptance implies the relevance of reports and judgments other than our own to what we say or believe. There is no way, by contrast, to acquire the authority sufficient to criticize the description of a mystical experience or the expression of a particular feeling or emotion save by having the experience or emotion in question, and these are not had in the requisite sense by more than one person. By contrast, the logical publicity of scientific understanding and subject matter makes them and hence the authority to criticize their articulation accessible to all.[12] It should be said that these constitute necessary but not sufficient conditions for the possibility of criticism, a point I shall return to later. It is the possibility of intersubjective criticism, at any rate, that permits objectivity in spite of the context dependence of evidential reasoning. Before developing this idea further let me outline some of the kinds of criticism to be found in scientific discourse.

There are a number of ways to criticize a hypothesis. For the sake of convenience we can divide these into evidential and conceptual criticism to reflect the distinction between criticism proceeding on the basis of experimental and observational concerns and that proceeding on the basis of theoretical and metatheoretical concerns.[13] Evidential criticism ... questions the degree to which a given hypothesis is supported by the evidence adduced for it; questions the accuracy, extent, and conditions of performance of the experiments and observations serving as evidence; and questions their analysis and reporting.[17]

Conceptual criticism, on the other hand, ... has received less attention in a tradition of discourse dominated by empiricist ideals. At least three sorts can be distinguished. The first questions the conceptual soundness of a hypothesis—as Einstein criticized and rejected the discontinuities and uncertainties of the quantum theory.[18] ... A second sort of criticism questions the consistency of a hypothesis with accepted theory—as traditionalists rejected the heliocentric theory because its consequences seemed inconsistent with the Aristotelian physics of motion still current in the fifteenth and sixteenth centuries.[20] ... A third sort questions the relevance of evidence presented in support of a hypothesis: relativity theorists could deny the relevance of the Michelson-Morley interferometer experiment to the Lorentz-Fitzgerald contraction hypothesis by denying the necessity of the ether.[22] ... This last form of criticism, though related to evidential considerations, is grouped with the forms of conceptual criticism because it is concerned not with how accurately the data has been measured and reported but with the assumptions in light of which that data is taken to be evidence for a given hypothesis in the first place. Here it is not the material presented as evidence itself that is challenged but its relevance to a hypothesis.

All three of these types of criticism are central to the development of scientific knowledge and are included among the traditions of scientific discourse into which the novice is initiated. It is the third type of criticism, however, which amounts to questioning the background beliefs or assumptions in light of which states of affairs become evidence, that is crucial for the problem of objectivity. Objectivity in the sense under discussion requires a way to block the influence of subjective preference at the level of background beliefs. While the possibility of criticism does not totally eliminate subjective preference either from an individual's or from a community's practice of science, it does provide a means for checking its influence in the formation of "scientific knowledge." Thus, even though background assumptions may not be supported by the same kinds of data upon which they confer evidential relevance to some hypothesis, other kinds of support can be provided, or at least expected.[25] And in the course of responding to criticism or providing such support one may modify the background assumption in question. Or if the original proponent does not, someone else may do so as a way of entering into the discourse. Criticism is thereby transformative. In response to criticism, empirical support may be forthcoming (subject, of course, to the limitations developed above). At other times the support may be conceptual rather than empirical.... The contextual analysis of evidential relations shows the limits of purely empirical considerations in scientific inquiry....

As long as background beliefs can be articulated and subjected to criticism from the scientific community, they can be defended, modified, or abandoned in response to such criticism. As long as this kind of response is possible, the incorporation of hypotheses into the canon of scientific knowledge can be independent of any individual's subjective preferences. Their incorporation is, instead, a function in part of the assessment of evidential support. And while the evidential relevance to hypotheses of observations and experiments is a function of background assumptions, the adoption of these assumptions is not arbitrary but is (or rather can be) subject to the kinds of controls just discussed. This solution incorporates as elements both the social character of the production of knowledge and the public accessibility of the material with which this knowledge is constructed.

Sociologically and historically, the molding of what counts as scientific knowledge is an activity requiring many participants. Even if one individual's work is regarded as absolutely authoritative over some period—as for instance, Aristotle's and later Newton's were—it is eventually challenged, questioned, and made to take the role of contributor rather than sole author—as Aristotle's and Newton's have been. From a logical point of view, if scientific knowledge were to be understood as the simple sum of finished products of individual activity, then not only would there be no way to block or mitigate the influence of subjective preference but scientific knowledge itself would be a potpourri of merrily inconsistent theories. Only if the products of inquiry are understood to be formed by the kind of critical discussion that is possible among a plurality of individuals about a commonly accessible phenomenon, can we see how they count as knowledge rather than opinion.

Objectivity, then, is a characteristic of a community's practice of science rather than of an individual's, and the practice of science is understood in a much broader sense than most discussions of the logic of scientific method suggest. These discussions see what is central to scientific method as being the complex of activities that constitute hypothesis testing through comparison with experiential data—in principle, if not always in reality, an activity of individuals. What I have argued here is that scientific method involves as an equally central aspect the subjection of hypotheses and the background assumptions in light of which they seem to be supported by data to varieties of conceptual criticism, which is a social rather than an individual activity.[26]

The respect in which science is objective, on this view, is one that it shares with other modes of inquiry, disciplines such as literary or art criticism and philosophy.[27] The feature that has often been appealed to as the source of the objectivity of science, that its hypotheses and theories are accepted or rejected on the basis of observational, experimental data, is a feature that makes scientific inquiry empirical. In the positivist account, for instance, it was the syntactically and deductively secured relation of hypotheses to a stable set of observational data that guaranteed the objectivity of scientific inquiry. But, as I've argued, most evidential relations in the sciences cannot be given this syntactic interpretation. In the contextual analysis of evidential relations, however, that a method is empirical in the above sense does not mean that it is also objective. A method that involved the appeal to observational or experimental data but included no controls on the kinds of background assumptions in light of which their relevance to hypotheses might be determined, or that permitted a weekly change of assumptions so that a hypothesis accepted in one week on the basis of some bit of evidence *e* would be rejected the next on the same basis, would hardly qualify as objective. Because the relation between hypotheses and evidence is mediated by background assumptions that themselves may not be subject to empirical confirmation or disconfirmation, and that may be infused with metaphysical or normative considerations, it would be a mistake to identify the objectivity of scientific methods with their empirical features alone. The process that can expose such assumptions is what makes possible, even if it cannot guarantee, independence from subjective bias, and hence objectivity.... The formal requirement of demonstrable evidential relevance constitutes a standard of rationality and acceptability independent of and external to any particular research program or scientific theory. The satisfaction of this standard by any program or theory, secured, as has been argued, by intersubjective criticism, is what constitutes its objectivity.

Scientific knowledge is, therefore, social knowledge....

OBJECTIVITY BY DEGREES

I have argued both that criticism from alternative points of view is required for objectivity and that the subjection of hypotheses and evidential reasoning to critical scrutiny is what limits the intrusion of individual subjective preference into scientific knowledge. Are these not two opposing forms of social interaction, one dialogic and the other monologic? Why does critical scrutiny not simply suppress those alternative points of view required to prevent premature allegiance to one perspective? How does this account of objectivity not collapse upon itself? The answer involves seeing dialogic and monologic as poles of a continuum. The maintenance of dialogue is itself a social process and can be more or less fully realized. Objectivity, therefore, turns out to be a matter of degree. A method of inquiry is objective to the degree that it permits *transformative* criticism. Its objectivity consists not just in the inclusion of intersubjective criticism but in the degree to which both its procedures and its results are responsive to the kinds of criticism described.... Scientific communities will be objective to the degree that they satisfy four criteria necessary for achieving the transformative dimension of critical discourse: (1) there must be recognized avenues for the criticism of evidence, of methods, and of assumptions and reasoning; (2) there must exist shared standards that critics can invoke; (3) the community as a whole must be responsive to such criticism; (4) intellectual authority must be shared equally among qualified practitioners. Each of these criteria requires at least a brief gloss.

Recognized Avenues for Criticism

The avenues for the presentation of criticism include such standard and public forums as journals, conferences, and so forth. Peer review is often pointed to as the standard avenue for such criticism, and indeed it is effective in preventing highly idiosyncratic values from shaping knowledge. At the same time its confidentiality and privacy make it the vehicle for the entrenchment of established views. This criterion also means that critical activities should receive equal or nearly equal weight to "original research" in career advancement. Effective criticism that advances understanding should be as valuable as original research that opens up new domains for understanding; pedestrian, routine criticism should be valued comparably to pedestrian and routine "original research."

Shared Standards

In order for criticism to be relevant to a position it must appeal to something accepted by those who hold the position criticized. Similarly, alternative theories must be perceived to have some bearing on the concerns of a scientific community in order to obtain a hearing. This cannot occur at the whim of individuals but must be a function of public standards or criteria to which members of the scientific community are or feel themselves bound. These standards can include both substantive principles and epistemic, as well as social, values. Different subcommunities will subscribe to different but overlapping subsets of the standards associated with a given community. Among values the standards can include such elements as empirical adequacy, truth, generation of specifiable interactions with the natural or experienced world, the expansion of existing knowledge frameworks, consistency with accepted theories in other domains, comprehensiveness, reliability as a guide to action, relevance to or satisfaction of particular social needs. Only the first of these constitutes a necessary condition that any research program must meet or aspire to meet, and even this requirement may be temporarily waived and is subject to interpretation.

... The particular weighting and interpretation assigned these standards will vary in different social and historical contexts as a function of cognitive and social needs. Furthermore, they are not necessarily consistent.

Standards do not provide a deterministic theory of theory choice. Nevertheless, it is the existence of standards that makes the individual members of a scientific community responsible to something besides themselves. It is the open-ended and nonconsistent nature of these standards that allows for pluralism in the sciences and for the continued presence, however subdued, of minority voices.

Community Response

This criterion requires that the beliefs of the scientific community as a whole and over time change in response to the critical discussion taking place within it. This responsiveness is measured by such public phenomena as the content of textbooks, the distribution of grants and awards, the flexibility of dominant world views.... What is required is that community members pay attention to the critical discussion taking place and that the assumptions that govern their group activities remain logically sensitive to it.

Equality of Intellectual Authority

This Habermasian criterion is intended to disqualify a community in which a set of assumptions dominates by virtue of the political power of its adherents.[30] ... The bureaucratization of United States science in the twentieth century tends ... to privilege certain points of view.[31] The exclusion, whether overt or more subtle, of women and members of certain racial minorities from scientific education and the scientific professions has also constituted a violation of this criterion.... Other scholars have documented the role of racial assumptions in the sciences.[32] The long-standing devaluation of women's voices and those of members of racial minorities means that such assumptions have been protected from critical scrutiny.

The above are criteria for assessing the objectivity of communities. The objectivity of individuals in this scheme consists in their participation in the collective give-and-take of critical discussion and not in some special relation (of detachment, hardheadedness) they may bear to their observations. Thus understood, objectivity is dependent upon the depth and scope of the transformative interrogation that occurs in any given scientific community. This communitywide process ensures (or can ensure) that the hypotheses ultimately accepted as supported by some set of data do not reflect a single individual's idiosyncratic assumptions about the natural world. To say that a theory or hypothesis was accepted on the basis of objective methods does not entitle us to say it is true but rather that it reflects the critically achieved consensus of the scientific community. In the absence of some form of privileged access to transempirical (unobservable) phenomena it's not clear we should hope for anything better.

... Several conditions can limit the extent of criticism and hence diminish a scientific community's objectivity without resulting in a completely or intentionally closed society (for example, such as characterized Soviet science under Stalin or some areas of Nazi science).

First of all, if scientific inquiry is to have any effect on a society's ability to take advantage of natural processes for the improvement of the quality of its life, criticism of assumptions cannot go on indefinitely. From a logical point of view, of course, criticism of background assumptions, as of any general claim, can go on ad infinitum. The philosophical discussion of inductive reasoning is an example of such unending (though not useless) debate. The utility of scientific knowledge depends on the possibility of finding frameworks of inquiry that remain stable enough to permit systematic interactions with the natural world. When critical discussion becomes repetitive and fixed at a metalevel, or when criticism of one set of assumptions ceases to have or does not eventually develop a connection to an empirical research program, it loses its relevance to the construction of empirical knowledge....

Secondly, these critical activities, however crucial to knowledge building, are deemphasized in a context that rewards novelty and originality, whether of hypotheses or of experimental design. The commoditization of scientific knowledge—a result of the interaction of the requirements of career advancement and of the commercial value of data—diminishes the attention paid to the criticism of the acquisition, sorting, and assembling of data. It is a commonplace that in contemporary science papers reporting negative results do not get published.

In the third place, some assumptions are not perceived as such by any members of the community. When, for instance, background assumptions are shared by all members of a community, they acquire an invisibility that renders them unavailable for criticism. They do not become visible until individuals who do not share the community's assumptions can provide alternative explanations of the phenomena without those assumptions, as, for example, Einstein could provide an alternative explanation of the Michelson-Morley interferometer experiment. Until such alternatives are available, community assumptions are transparent to their adherents. In addition, the substantive principles determining standards of rationality within a research program or tradition are for the most part immune to criticism by means of those standards.

From all this it follows again that the greater the number of different points of view included in a given community, the more likely it is that its scientific practice will be objective.... Because points of view cannot simply be allowed expression but must have an impact on what is ultimately thought to be the case, such diversity is a necessary but not a sufficient condition for objectivity. Finally, these conditions reinforce the point that objectivity is a matter of degree. While the conditions for objectivity are at best imperfectly realized, they are the basis of an ideal by reference to which particular scientific communities can be evaluated. Ascertaining in greater detail the practices and institutional arrangements that facilitate or undermine objectivity in any particular era or current field, and thus the degree to which the ideal of objectivity is realized, requires both historical and sociological investigation....

CONCLUSION

... The contextualist view produces a framework within which it is possible to respect the complexity of science, to do justice to the historical facts and to the current practice of science, and to avoid paradox. In addition, it is possible to articulate a standard of comparison independent of and external to any particular theory or research project. In making intertheoretic comparison possible it offers the basis (an expanded basis) upon which to develop criteria of evaluation. Finally, the social account of objectivity and scientific knowledge to which the contextualist account of evidence leads seems more true to the fact that scientific inquiry is not always as free from subjective preference as we would wish it to be. And even though the resulting picture of objectivity differs from what we are used to, our intuition that scientific inquiry at its best is objective is kept intact by appealing to the spirit of criticism that is its traditional hallmark.[35]

NOTES

...

2. Compare Broad (1981).

3. Hempel (1966), pp. 3–18, and Popper (1962), pp. 41–59.

4. Laudan (1977) does articulate criteria for what counts as progress. These are not' necessarily criteria or standards for truth.

5. Feyerabend (1975).

6. Grene (1985).

...

9. In what I take to be a similar vein, Bruno Latour (1987) claims that in science a statement made by an individual becomes a fact only as a consequence of what others do with the statement. Latour, however, emphasizes the agonistic as opposed to the cooperative dimension of social relations in the sciences.

10. The precise extension of "scientific community" is here left unspecified. If it includes those interested in and affected by scientific inquiry, then it is much broader than the class of those professionally engaged in scientific research. For a discussion of these issues and some consequences of our current restricted understanding of the scientific community see Addelson (1983).

11. One might say that the language game of science presupposes the independent existence of objects of experience. Contemporary arguments about scientific realism can be understood as arguments about (1) the nature of this presupposition and (2) what categories of objects it covers.

12. To avoid possible confusion about the point being made here, I wish to emphasize that I am contrasting the descriptive statements of science with expressions of emotion.... Objectivity as it is being discussed here involves the absence (or control) of subjective *preference* and is not necessarily divorced from our beliefs about our subjective states. Locke (1968) discusses the different ways in which privacy is properly and improperly attributed to subjective states (pp. 5–12).

13. The distinction between the different kinds of concerns relevant to the development and evaluation of theories is discussed for different purposes and with significant differences in detail by Buchdahl in a discussion of criteria choice, by Laudan in a discussion of the problems that give rise to the development of theory, and by Schaffner in a discussion of categories for comparative theory evaluation. A more complete categorization of concerns and types of criticism than that offered here requires a more thorough study of past and present scientific practice. See Gerd Buchdahl (1970); Larry Laudan (1977); and Kenneth Schaffner (1974).

...

17. The latter two kinds of questions are concerned with the objectivity of data, a notion mentioned above.

18. Bernstein (1973), pp. 137–177.

...

20. Kuhn (1957), pp. 100–133, 185–192.

...

22. Jaffe (1960), pp. 95–103.

...

25. Conceptual criticism of this sort is a far cry from the criticism envisaged by Popper. For him metaphysical issues must be decided empirically, if at all. (And if they cannot be so tested, they lack significance.)

26. This is really a distinction between the number of points of view (minds) required. Many individuals (sharing assumptions and points of view) may be involved in testing a hypothesis (and commonly are in contemporary experiments). And though this is much rarer, one individual may be able to criticize her or his own evidential reasoning and background assumptions from other points of view.

27. This is not to deny the importance of distinguishing between different modes of understanding—for instance, between scientific, philosophical, and literary theories—but simply to deny that objectivity can serve as any kind of demarcation criterion.

...

30. Invocation of this criterion confirms the kinship of this account of objectivity with the account of truth that Jürgen Habermas has developed as part of his theory of communicative competence....

31. See Levins and Lewontin (1985), pp. 197–252, for further discussion of this point.

32. See Gould (1981); Lewontin, Rose, and Kamin (1984); Richardson (1984).

...

35. ... Three books ... draw attention in varying degrees to the social character of cognitive processes in science: Peter Galison, *How Experiments End* (Chicago, IL: University of Chicago Press, 1987); David Hull, *Science as a Process* (Chicago, IL: University of Chicago Press, 1988); and Sharon Traweek, *Beamtimes and Lifetimes: The World of High Energy Physicists* (Cambridge, MA: Harvard University Press, 1988).

REFERENCES

Addelson, Kathryn Pyne. 1983. "The Man of Professional Wisdom." In *Discovering Reality: Feminist Perspectives on Epistemology, Metaphysics, Methodology, and Philosophy of Science,* ed. Sandra Harding and Merrill Hintikka, pp. 165–186. Dordrecht, Netherlands: Reidel.

Bernstein, Jeremy. 1973. *Einstein.* Bungay: William Collins and Son.

Broad, William. 1981. "Fraud and the Structure of Science." *Science* 212: 137–141.

Buchdahl, Gerd. 1970. "History of Science and Criteria of Choice." In *Minnesota Studies in the Philosophy of Science,* ed. Roger Steuwer, 5:204–230. Minneapolis: University of Minnesota Press.

Feyerabend, Paul K. 1975. *Against Method.* London: Verso.

Gould, Stephen J. 1981. *The Mismeasure of Man.* New York: W. W. Norton.

Grene, Marjorie. 1985. "Perception, Interpretation, and the Sciences." In *Evolution at a Crossroads,* ed. David Depew and Bruce Weber, pp. 1–20. Cambridge, MA: Massachusetts Institute of Technology Press.

Hempel, Carl Gustav. 1966. *Philosophy of Natural Science.* Englewood Cliffs, NJ: Prentice-Hall.

Jaffe, Bernard. 1960. *Michelson and the Speed of Light.* Garden City, NY: Doubleday.

Kuhn, Thomas. 1957. *The Copernican Revolution.* New York: Random House.

Latour, Bruno. 1987. *Science in Action.* Cambridge, MA: Harvard University Press.

Laudan, Larry. 1977. *Progress and Its Problems.* Berkeley, CA: University of California Press.

Levins, Richard, and Richard Lewontin. 1985. *The Dialectical Biologist.* Cambridge, MA: Harvard University Press.

Lewontin, Richard, Steven Rose, and Leon Kamin. 1984. *Not in Our Genes: Biology, Ideology, and Human Nature.* New York: Pantheon Books.

Locke, Don. 1968. *Myself and Others.* Oxford: Oxford University Press.

Richardson, Robert C. 1984. "Biology and Ideology: The Interpenetration of Science and Values." *Philosophy of Science* 51, no. 2: 396–420.

Rowell, Thelma. 1974. "The Concept of Dominance." *Behavioral Biology* 11: 131–154.

Schaffner, Kenneth. 1974. "Einstein versus Lorentz: Research Programmes and the Logic of Theory Evaluation." *British Journal for the Philosophy of Science* 25: 45–78.

Naomi Scheman

Epistemology Resuscitated: Objectivity as Trustworthiness

INTRODUCTION: WITH FRIENDS LIKE THESE, WHO NEEDS ENEMIES?

... I want to argue that feminist epistemologists and philosophers of science are not the enemies of objectivity they are made out to be by the critics.... What the critics misidentify as a threat is better understood as an attempt to save objectivity by understanding why it matters and why and how it is truly threatened.

Objectivity, along with reason, truth, and rationality, is a normative concept with which we evaluate our own and each other's assertions and beliefs. Central to what we do when we call an argument, conclusion, or decision "objective" is to recommend it to others, and, importantly, to suggest that they *ought* to accept it, that they would be doxastically irresponsible to reject it without giving reasons that made similar claims to universal acceptability. Objective claims, that is, are always disputable, but they are not, without dispute, rejectable.... I'm concerned not with feminist arguments *against* objectivity, but rather with those feminist arguments that explicitly take their aims to be the articulation and defense of alternative conceptions of objectivity, and with the critics who insist that these feminists cannot possibly mean what they say.

In order to break up the logjam of disputes over who the "real enemies" of objectivity are, I am suggesting that we start by asking what it is about objectivity that makes a sustainable claim to being a real friend so valuable, why it is that objectivity and its similarly endangered relatives *matter*.... Rather than defending relativism (or some other alternative to objectivity as an ideal), I want to start with the fact that we (diversely) do often want or need knowledge claims to be acceptable by broader constituencies, or criticizable by those constituencies. I take it to be an open question, not to be answered in advance or in general, ... how broad a consensus we ought to seek or can plausibly expect for particular sorts of knowledge claims.... I will focus on the case that can be made for the objectivity (the universal acceptability) of the paradigm cases—namely, the claims of the sciences. Stated more broadly, the issue is: When, and insofar as, it actually matters that knowledge claims be acceptable to—or criticizable by—a broader constituency, what do we actually have to *do,* and what counts as doing it right? ...

In the disputes over who are the real friends and who the real enemies of objectivity one point of agreement is that other things that we care about depend on it and are imperiled by its actual or perceived enfeeblement or demise.... What are these other things, and why might their well-being depend on the well-being of objectivity? According to Paul Gross and Norman Levitt, "What is threatened [by, *inter alia,* feminist science studies, which, they allege, attack or repudiate objectivity] is the capability of the larger culture, which embraces the mass media as well as the more serious processes of education, to interact fruitfully with the sciences, to draw insight from scientific advances, and, above all, to evaluate science intelligently."[3] The underlying assumptions here are that the sciences produce something of value ("advances"), and ("above all") that "science" ought not to be accepted uncritically but ought to be subject to intelligent evaluation by "the larger culture." While the details of this formulation will turn out to be contentious ... the general formulation and the assumptions behind it would, I think, be acceptable to the feminist epistemologists and philosophers of science who are cited as objectivity's alleged enemies.

... Rather than defining what objectivity is, I want to propose an answer to a different question, one about what objectivity *does* (what it's good for). The proposal is this: A sustainable attribution of objectivity serves to underwrite a significant degree of—objectively refutable—authority, and it does so by rationally grounding trust. When we characterize something (an epistemic practice or product) as objective, we commend it or its results to others than those who engaged in or produced it, including to those whose perspectives and interests might differ.[4] It comes into importance as a virtue to the extent that we are epistemically dependent on others who are in a range of ways—spatially, temporally, culturally, attitudinally, cognitively—distant from us. Given the extraordinary and increasing degree of both interconnectedness and technological complexity of the contemporary world, the need for objectivity cannot be overstated.... If objective judgments are judgments we can rationally trust, we need them more than ever; and the "we"s that need them are, especially, the "we"s least in a position either to identify with or to independently check out the judgments produced by socially recognized authorities. Furthermore, and perhaps even more importantly, we (diversely located "we"s) need to be able to enter into dialogue with authoritative knowledge producers, to become and be recognized as credible even if nonexpert critics—to, in Gross and Levitt's terms, "evaluate science intelligently"—and to have our perspectives recognized as potentially contributing to fuller, more adequate accounts.

... The antifeminist friends of objectivity are, I want to argue, the sorts of friends alleged to render enemies superfluous. Like snake oil salesmen, they purvey a quack remedy for a real problem. And like most quack remedies, this one is worse than useless: worse, because in purporting to be the real thing, it effectively diverts us from pursuing an effective remedy for what actually ails us.[5] By contrast, feminist epistemologists and philosophers of science, along with others engaged in related projects of what can be called "liberatory epistemology," are developing accounts of objectivity that take seriously our need for it: If objectivity is an instrumental good, then it has actually to function so as to produce the good it promises; what we label "objective" has actually to be worthy of our trust and the trust of a diverse range of others.

In the tradition of analytic philosophers' giving acronyms to the theses they argue for, I want to suggest "CPR" as an acronym (sort of) for the projects of liberatory epistemology.... [T]hose letters jointly cover a large number of the central concepts that characterize epistemology resuscitated: critical, contextual,[7] committed, "corresponsible,"[8] and commonable;[9] perspectival, pragmatic,[10] practical, political, participatory, pluralist,[11] and partial;[12] and radical, relational, and responsible[13]—all of which characterize revised notions of reason, rationality, and realism.[14]

... Briefly, my argument will be that liberatory politics such as feminism are intrinsically related to objectivity in their commitment to struggling for social institutions that are worthy of trust on the part of all those whose lives are affected by them: A "bias" in favor of such struggles is a bias in favor of the conditions that would make objectivity a real possibility, rather than a merely theoretical gesture.[15] ...

THE CASE FOR SCIENTIFIC OBJECTIVITY

... For the critics of feminist science studies, science is the paradigm example of objectivity; hence such arguments are taken to be an attack on objectivity itself. There is, in fact, good reason for thinking of objectivity as the defining virtue of modern science—that is, as the guiding aim of scientific method and practice—but it doesn't follow from that connection that we cannot meaningfully ask about how it is that scientific practices achieve that aim to the extent that they do and why and how they might fall short of it, or even about whether the particular conceptions of objectivity embedded in scientific method as usually understood (especially by philosophers of science) might not be fundamentally flawed. By attending to the function of objectivity in rationally grounding the trust we are called on to have in what scientists do, we can get a handle on understanding both why and how scientific practices are objective and why and how they are not.

We can start by noting that objectivity has a history—one intimately and honorably bound up with the democratization of knowledge, the wresting of epistemic authority away from those with entrenched religious, political, or economic power—and a track record—comprising all of the successes of modern science.... There is no reason why those defenders have to argue that anything about the doing of science can entirely rule out any of those influences, nor even that good science could possibly thrive in a seriously unjust society. That there are external conditions that set the stage for the effective working of scientific methods is surely something that can be conceded by those who nonetheless maintain that it is adherence to those methods, whenever and whyever they are adhered to, that constitutes objectivity and gives us good reason to believe what scientists come up with.

Furthermore, the critics can grant that the plural ("scientific *methods*") is crucial: There is no one such method, nor is there even a codifiable range of them. Science is a complex set of social practices governed by a complex set of norms that share little more than the aim precisely of ensuring that the results of scientific investigation will be trustworthy, meaning that those results will be credible not only to the scientists who came up with them but also to others who may not share their particular experiences, biases, perspectives, interests, and the like. The norms of science work—when and to the extent that they *do* work—by factoring out of scientific knowledge claims the biasing effects of, among other things, the sorts of injustices that characterize the world in which science is done. When the rest of us trust what scientists come up with, what we are trusting them to do is to conform to the norms of good scientific practice; and we trust their results to the extent that we believe that they have done so and because we trust that conforming to those norms reliably tends to lead to the truth.

Certainly (the critics can concede), political considerations come into play around questions of research priorities, notably decisions about funding; and there is reason to argue for the greater involvement of a diverse range of scientists and nonscientists in these decisions, and for specific attention to the perspectives of those whose voices have been silenced, ignored, or distorted. But when it comes to the research itself, and to the evaluation of research results, it will be claimed that such diversity is idle. Certainly, it is a loss to science that some potentially productive researchers are undiscovered or unsuccessful for reasons having to do with discrimination and other social inequities, but there is no reason to believe that the loss is of some *distinctive* contribution.... If they bring anything *else* from the specificities of their lives into the doing of science, they are importing the same sort of bias that has led to sexist, racist, or homophobic science....

The central point is this: According to the critics, feminists are claiming that trust in scientific method is misplaced, amounting to trust in those who wield unjust forms of privilege and who use that privilege—buttressed by the cultural capital of scientific expertise—to shield themselves from possibly legitimate forms of criticism. Rather, the critics claim, trust in scientific method is trust in a set of mechanisms and practices that are designed precisely to *rule out* these sort of abuses.... Given the extraordinary difficulty and complexity of contemporary science, we have no choice but to delegate epistemic authority to those who understand what we never will and to trust that what they come up with is what we would come up with if we had the talent, time, and energy to acquire their expertise....

DEPENDENCY AND TRUST

... I want to focus on a central and (so far as I can tell) indisputable but oddly underacknowledged fact about the vast majority of what we know or believe; namely, the extent to which we are irremediably dependent on others. I want to argue that taking this fact seriously gives us good reason to be suspicious of what I will call "internalist" defenses of scientific objectivity, such as those of the critics of feminist science studies.

The fact of epistemic dependency might not be contestable, but its centrality to epistemology is hardly universally acknowledged. Taking trust to be a central epistemological issue tends to mark one as belonging to a particular, still academically marginal, subfield—that of social epistemology.[18] It is, as usual, interesting to note what is and what is not linguistically marked: the contrast (unmarked epistemology proper) is presumably nonsocial, individualist, taking as its subject the generic knower-as-such—what Lorraine Code (1991) has dubbed "S knows that p" epistemology. The issue of epistemic dependency, when it arises in "unmarked" epistemology, is addressed as the specific and separable problem of "testimony"—whether and, if so, when and how and why and to what extent S (the generic knower) should believe some particular claim because someone else says it is so.[19]

What is masked by S's generic nature are not so much S's individual properties but rather the particularities of S's relationships to others as a fully social being, including the relationships that constitute S's gender, race, class, sexual identity, and so on. With respect to generic knowers, if "trust" is used at all, it is only as (roughly) a synonym for "believe," as in "I trust the train will be here any minute." ... But it is one of the central claims of this chapter that thinking about objectivity requires thinking about diversely situated subjects and about the possibilities for and barriers to trust between them. What is needed for that task is a much more full-blown notion of trust, involving an indefinite range of moral, political, and interpersonal factors that we can never fully spell out.... Such dependence, I want to argue, is ineliminable, but it can be more or less rational, and the trust that rests on it more or less justified....

The marginality of epistemic dependence within epistemology reflects the emergence of the field in its distinctively modern form in the seventeenth century, in the attempts to liberate the individual knower from dependence on various, particularly religious, forms of authority. The strongly individualist slant of the field reflects the religious, political, and economic individualism of early modernity; and the fact that on the most fundamental theoretical level individuals were and are taken to be generic reflects modernity's democratic egalitarianism.... The crises of trust out of which modern science arose—the need to find foundations for knowledge that would survive challenges to authority—were resolved by finding firm ground on which such individual generic knowers could stand.... In the first instance, this guarantee is meant to underwrite extreme epistemic autonomy....

In practice, however, what the guarantee has underwritten is our dependence, oddly grounded in the denial of the relationships that make us different from each other. We are meant to trust each other epistemically only to the extent that we are assured that each of us is acting in ways uninflected by any of our actual relationships....

Such extreme epistemic autonomy is of a piece with Descartes's rationalism. Though observation had a place in his scientific method, that place was subsidiary to the workings of reason, which in his view were not in any essential way social.[21] Considerations of trust, specifically of those one took to be peers, were, by contrast, central to the development of experimental science, as Steven Shapin argues in *The Social History of Truth* (1994). As important as it was that experimental results be replicable, it was clearly impractical for every knower actually to replicate every experiment the results of which contributed to something he took himself to know. That, by and large, knowers were men was, in fact, one of the consequences of the need to provide socially salient signs of one's credibility, signs that rested on indications of competence and character that were, most explicitly, focused on class, with consequences for gender....

No one thought, of course, that some experimental result was true *because* it was reported by a gentleman, still less that being so reported was what truth *was*. But we can say that a significant part of the justification for believing such a report was that it was made by a gentleman.... Epistemologically, issues of honorable character and the ways of giving recognizable demonstrations of such character were in practice ineliminable—as are the present-day ways of ensuring the integrity of scientific results: peer review of research and researchers, replication of experimental results, and the like. To argue for a distinctively feminist epistemology, therefore, is not to argue for some dubious claim about sex differences in individual cognitive capacities: Rather, it is to argue, far more plausibly, for the relevance of gender to the ways in which different people regard—and ought to regard—others as more or less worthy of trust.[23] And whatever one wants to say about the nature of truth claims, claims to credibility—what makes our beliefs justified—rest in large part on such socially grounded reasons for trusting.[24]

...

THE INELIMINABILITY OF TRUST

... What we can do is to put in place practices that we have good reason to believe are effective in certifying the trustworthiness—the competence and integrity—of those on whom we are dependent. Despite our having, even in theory, no independent way of checking on the effectiveness of those practices, we do have ways of ... constructing overlapping ropes of trust that make our dependency reasonable, not abject. But, as Hardwig points out (1991), such trust-grounding practices are just that: actual practices, engaged in by actual people, and subject to all the vagaries that affect other forms of social interaction. Hardwig's analysis, however, focuses on the importance of individual character and on the role to be played by the teaching of ethics to researchers. He doesn't address my central concern here, namely, the systematically trust-eroding effects of various forms of social, political, and economic injustice. Who, for a start, are the "we" who put in place the mechanisms meant to ensure the integrity of scientific results?

One way of framing the dispute between feminist objectivity theorists and their critics is with the question of whether we ought to understand objectivity (as exemplified by science) in terms of the norms and methods of scientific practice (an internalist account), or whether we can and should go beneath or beyond those norms and methods and the practices that embody them to find critical ground (an externalist account).[26] ... Going beneath or beyond the precincts of science is seen as leaving the domain of objectivity, allowing into the conversation just the sorts of differences in interest and perspective that are seen as damaging to the trustworthiness of science's knowledge claims. Those of us on the outside of science are urged to trust what goes on within its domains not despite but precisely because of our not participating in its innermost practices....[27]

Much of the appeal of the internalist account has to do with its rootedness in the democratic egalitarianism of modernity (it is not supposed to matter that some of us discover truths for the rest of us to take on trust, because we are all supposed, in all relevant respects, to be interchangeable); and it suffers fatally from the flaws and limits of that egalitarianism. As Shapin's study shows, the actual practices of demonstrating scientific credibility have always been shaped … by more general practices of judging people as worthy of trust, practices that have not been … immune from the practices that structure and maintain various forms of privilege.[28] It is quite likely that those whose economic exploitation grounded the economic "independence" of gentlemen would not have found a gentlemanly readiness to duel a sign of trustworthiness, or, if they did, it is hard not to see that trust as misplaced....

I'm not denying (at this point in the argument) that even socially unjust codes of trustworthiness might actually be reliable as "trackers of truth": That's a different question from whether or not someone in particular has good reason to think that they are. And to the extent that such codes are articulated and enforced by, accessible to, and understood by an unjustly privileged elite, those excluded from those privileges have, in fact, little reason to trust them. It does not help to be told that you are included in the "we" in whose name those norms are set and enforced—that you are, in all important respects, the same as those who actually do the setting and enforcing—when what you know is that the chances are minuscule that someone like you (however you understand that) might actually participate in that "we," and, furthermore, that the structures that keep you from participation are the same ones that provide the participants with the means of recognizing each other's trustworthiness....

The central problem with the internalist account is thus that it fails to seriously confront the problem of justification as it actually arises. Epistemic dependency means that justification requires rationally grounded trust, and trust needs to be convincingly demonstrated—not just abstractly demonstrable. The world of contemporary science is large and impersonal, and the practices that ground and demonstrate trust are embedded in the workings of institutions such as universities, corporate research departments, government agencies, and academic journals. The trustworthiness of scientific methods derives, in practice, from the effective working of those institutional structures; and justified belief in that trustworthiness derives from the justified belief that those institutions do in practice what they are supposed to do in theory: ground knowledge claims that are acceptable to all of us, not just to those of us with certain forms of privilege, who see the world through certain lenses, from certain biased perspectives. If you believe (as presumably those on the political left *do* believe) that the institutions in question are problematically complicit in society's racism, sexism, classism, heterosexism, and so on, then you ought to be suspicious of the ability of those institutions to ground the trustworthiness of scientific knowledge—even if it seems to you clear that such complicity has no discernible effect on the specific trust-ensuring practices themselves....

The situation is analogous to the one facing the criminal justice system, notably when it comes to seeking convictions for Black defendants. The task of the prosecution is to convince a jury that the prosecution's case demonstrates the defendant's guilt beyond a reasonable doubt. Meeting that epistemic standard is in general impossible without the jury's having a great deal of trust in the competence and integrity of those who are presenting the state's case.... When, as arguably in the O. J. Simpson case, the jury is convinced that those institutions are corrupt—that they are, specifically, racist—there does not have to be a story to tell about just how that corruption could have tainted the specific evidence on which the case rests. Rather, all that is necessary for the standard of persuasion beyond a reasonable doubt to be unreachable is that the jury not find the institutions of the state trustworthy.[33]

… The credibility of science suffers, and, importantly, *ought* to suffer—just as the credibility of the prosecution suffers and ought to suffer—when its claims to trustworthiness are grounded in the workings of institutions that are demonstrably unjust—even when those injustices cannot be shown to be responsible for particular lapses in evidence gathering or reasoning. Credibility will suffer especially when the scientists in question, or those to whom they are believed to be close or beholden, are thought to have a stake in what they are reporting, as, for example, in research on racial differences in IQ, on the safety of drugs or food additives, or on the reliability of nuclear reactors. Those who are concerned (as, for example, scientists should be) that the results of science be not just true but justifiably believed to be true by the lay public as well as by other scientists need to be concerned about the systematic complicities with unjust privilege that systematically undermine the trustworthiness of the institutions on which such justified belief depends....

To lay such skepticism about science at the door of the "academic left" is to blame the messenger: Rather than blaming the academic theorists who attempt to understand this mistrust, it makes much more sense to blame the practices in and around science that engender it.... The problem isn't the theories of the academic left: The problem is racism....

The critics' insistence that nonetheless internalist epistemological resources provide the only proper tools for identifying and remedying such trust-destroying activities looks less like the high-minded defense of objectivity than like the defensive warding off of an appropriately democratic demand for accountability.

BEYOND HEURISTICS: IF YOU WANT TRUTH, FIGHT FOR JUSTICE

One might object at this point that, while what I've said might well be true when it comes to the *credibility* of science, it doesn't affect the question of scientific *truth,* provided that science is working as it should, according to its own norms.... The problem (admittedly a large and important one) would be to find ways of convincing the lay public—especially those among them who are understandably alienated from the institutions of the epistemic establishment—that those institutions are worthy of their trust, or at least that they would be if they lived up to their own, internally justified norms. One could further agree that the solution cannot and should not be seen as a matter of image manipulation: Possibly the only effective but certainly the only proper way of producing such confidence would be to work to make the institutions in question—and, generally, the broader society within which they exist—more genuinely just, more truly worthy of everyone's trust. One could concede all this and still argue that the results of scientific research, conducted according to internal norms, are in fact, objectively, true (or, more reasonably, leading toward the truth), and justifiably believed by anyone who is in a position—as the lay public lamentably is not—to see how it is that the practices of trust-grounding work, despite the injustices of the institutions in which they are housed.

But how *do* those practices work, and why should *anyone* trust them? Why, specifically, do *I* trust them?—because the fact is that, to a very great extent, I do.... What I want to suggest is that an externalist focus on epistemic dependency and the epistemological centrality of trust enables both better prescriptive accounts of how justification ought to work and better descriptive accounts of how it actually does work, including when its working is apparently accounted for in internalist terms.

... Sue Campbell argues against the efforts of the False Memory Syndrome Foundation and its supporters to systematically undermine the confidence of those who experience what they take to be recovered memories of childhood sexual abuse. She compares such efforts to Descartes's evocation of the evil demon: In both cases we are urged to see ourselves as systematically defective, as unable to trust our own faculties, or those of others relevantly like us.... Campbell's point is not that false memories are impossible, or that feminist therapists are always trustworthy: Rather, she argues, the interpretive frame provided by the FMSF undercuts the trust without which even accurate memories cannot be retrieved. "We require," she concludes, "an account of objectivity that can endorse the contexts in which knowledge emerges only through relationships of trust, the influence of imagination, and protection from premature criticism. The cost of supporting these contexts may indeed often be uncertainty about whether our beliefs or commitments are fully justified; the cost of withdrawing our support from these contexts will be the silencing of these perspectives." ...

Sarah Hoagland ... raises for feminist philosophers of science extremely challenging questions about the limits of trustworthiness: How ought we think about our commitment—in the name of objectivity—to broadening the critical context within which scientific claims are articulated and evaluated, when some of the women whose voices and perspectives we are bringing into the conversation have good reasons for not wanting their stories told to those whom they do not trust not to misuse them? ... Are we, she asks, dangerously naive, in trusting the powerful to hear the stories of the powerless, and in trusting our own ability to tell those stories in ways that will enfranchise, rather than endanger, those who trusted us with them? ...

She characterizes "the scientific move to 'objectivity' [as] an effort to exclude others from meaning-making, deauthorizing all voices it has not trained/tamed," ... arguing that feminist projects to achieve greater objectivity by bringing into the conversation silenced or marginalized voices ignore the ways in which such voices get distorted by the reframing necessary to make them scientifically intelligible, and the ways in which, so distorted, those voices get used against those from whose mouths they come.

Part of Hoagland's point is that it is a mistake to think that dominant discourses have no use for what the nondominant might have to say: The roles of the "native informant" and the research "subject" (i.e., object) are well recognized. That's part of the problem: The voices of the subordinated are all too easy to slot into predetermined places, as producers of "data" the interpretation of which remains in the hands of the dominant.... Exclusion from meaning-making has never meant that one's life, culture, and body were off limits for "incorporation" by epistemological omnivores, who have always acknowledged that objectivity requires extensive, wide-ranging data collection....

Hoagland's separatism is grounded in her pessimism about the possibilities of trust between the dominant and those they dominate. Specifically *epistemological* separatism follows from her recognition of the epistemic importance of trust. If we accept, as I argue that we should, the conception of objectivity articulated by its feminist friends, then Hoagland poses a deep and serious challenge: We may be barred from pursuing more objective knowledge so long as the conditions of trust are lacking—so long, that is, as some pieces of the perspectival puzzle cannot be added to dominant accounts without betraying those whose perspectives they are.[35] ... In the absence of good grounds for trust, the critical work of striving toward objectivity cannot (and *should* not) go on.

OBJECTIVITY, DEPENDENCY, AND INEQUALITY

Return to the democratic ideals that motivated and provided the theoretical underpinnings for the epistemology of modern science. According to those ideals, all knowers are ideally interchangeable, meaning both that individually arrived-at results should be the same for all reasoners and that we can effectively function as each other's surrogate knowers. Our epistemic dependency, that is, is either eliminable or benign. But that assumption ... is, in the real world, false, and not only because many of us have been expected to be irrationally dependent on those who have been our oppressors. The dependency of scientists on other scientists—of peers on peers within shared institutional settings—while less obviously irrational, needs also to be called into question in the light of what are widely acknowledged to be the problematic ways in which power and privilege shape the workings of the practices meant to ensure trustworthiness. But there is an additional, deeper problem than those involving the trustworthiness of scientists and of scientific practices. All along, those who have been the authorized knowers have been, in subtle and complex ways, dependent on those whom they would not have acknowledged, except, perhaps, in the most purely theoretical of terms, as their peers; and those forms of dependency have gone unacknowledged and unaccounted for in terms of assessing the trustworthiness of knowledge claims.

The norms of epistemic self-sufficiency and, failing that, dependency on trusted peers, were connected to the individualism of early modernity not just through the ideal of theoretical egalitarianism but also through the picture of persons as essentially competent adults—Hobbes's men sprung up like mushrooms, to take that picture's most striking evocation. If the sort of extreme dependency that characterizes infancy and childhood is acknowledged at all, it is to mark it as something that has, intellectually, to be superseded.... Projects of rational reconstruction and the distinction between the realm of discovery and the realm of justification are versions of this project, which has as one of its aims the demonstration that a route to knowledge that in fact crossed over swamps and bogs and very shaky bridges could have been undertaken proceeding solely on firm ground; in other words, that any trusting of those whose trustworthiness cannot be independently verified can be shown to be dispensable.[37] Beyond parents and teachers (those Descartes, for example, charges with having filled his head with unverifiable beliefs before he reached the age of reason), there are those whose unrecognized labor goes into grounding the trustworthiness of scientific endeavors: the workers who make or clean laboratory equipment, for example, or set the type for scientific publications, or, for that matter, the informants who are presumed not to be making up funny stories to tell the various social scientists who pry into their lives.

...

Thus, to acknowledge the complex webs of dependencies—of laypersons on scientists, of scientists on other scientists, and of scientists on nonscientists—that undergird the workings of objectivity is to acknowledge the necessity, throughout those webs, for trust to be both psychologically possible and rationally justifiable. If we cannot trust those on whom we are epistemically dependent, we will not believe when we should; and if we ought not to trust them, we risk believing when we should not. Much of what goes into both the psychological possibility and the rational justifiability of trust lies both below and outside of (as well as, in each of our lives, temporally prior to) the explicit norms of scientific practice; and without such grounding, we are powerless to effectively answer the skeptic, who speaks to us from a place of alienation from that ground—whether that alienation be a philosophical conceit or a material reality....

It is the task of the projects I have collectively referred to as "CPR" to argue for the dependence of objectivity on the conditions of social justice that would justify this faith; for the claim that, in the absence of such conditions, objectivity is inevitably compromised; and for the necessity for those who would be objectivity's true friends to struggle for social justice. Such a view of objectivity differs from an internalist account largely in being far more rigorous and demanding: Sandra Harding's term "strong objectivity" is not just a rhetorical ploy (Harding 1993, 69). The internalist provides an account of rational credibility that rests on the suitability of some people to serve as surrogate knowers for the rest of us, who are ineliminably dependent on their expertise, while denying the relevance of many of the questions we might be inclined to ask if we were to take seriously the issue of their trustworthiness. It is, in short, irrational to expect people to place their trust in the results of practices about which they know little and that emerge from institutions—universities, corporations, government agencies—which they know to be inequitable....

Charges of irrationalism are oddly directed at those who point out—correctly, from their perspective—that they do not have good reason to believe what experts say. And it is simply arrogant to be certain that the effort genuinely to engage with those who have been excluded could be of only heuristic value, that all the worthwhile criticisms and advances are generated from within. Objectivity on an externalist account is not an all or nothing matter, settled by rules laid down in advance; it is, rather, a rolling horizon we move toward as we increasingly democratize our epistemic practices.

Hoagland's separatist epistemology is, therefore, a challenge to CPR theorists, who, I want to suggest, can be seen as arguing for a *diasporic* epistemology, one that is sufficiently hopeful about universalist liberatory politics to sustain, and even to encourage less privileged others to sustain, faith in a not-yet-existent human community.[40] That we (feminist academics) might be fools is the least of our worries, Hoagland warns; if our faith is misplaced, we'll be guilty of betrayal. To be a friend of objectivity and simultaneously a friend to those who do not share one's relatively privileged social location is a moral and political risk. I am inclined to think that it is one worth taking, though I urge those of us who take it to also take Hoagland's warnings to heart. What I am certain of is that no defense of objectivity can be made on ground less politically contentious than this.

Those who hold on to internalist conceptions of scientific objectivity do so in part because they believe that a naturalized account of science as a social practice is a wholly different endeavor from a normative account of it as truth producing. Historical and sociological studies such as Shapin's (1994) do typically eschew what is taken to be the central epistemological question: How *ought* we to pursue knowledge? My contention in this chapter has been that it is precisely as a social practice, naturalistically understood, that science needs to be evaluated—especially if what we care about is its objectivity. The normativity that characterizes epistemology can be found not in ahistorical canons of rationality but in the normativity of politics.[41]

NOTES

Over the past few years, a number of graduate students at the University of Minnesota have been working on issues of trust and testimony. I have learned a lot from them: Nancy Nyquist Potter, Heidi Grasswick, Peg O'Connor, Lisa Bergin, Amanda Vizedom, and Jan Binder. I owe a special debt to students, colleagues, and friends in Gothenburg, Örebro, and Helsinki, where I taught short graduate courses in 1997 and 1998, in which I developed these ideas in dialogue; and to the Feminist Studies Department at the University of Gothenburg for a wonderfully congenial work environment. Thanks to Michael Root and Stephen Kellert for comments on earlier drafts.

. . .

3. Gross and Levitt 1994, 9; quoted in Lloyd 1996, 220; and Gross 1998, 102.

4. My point here is related to Carl Ginet's distinction between interested and disinterested justification. Beliefs, Ginet argues, can reasonably be counted as justified even if their justification is tied to the subject's desire that the belief be true; but *disinterested* justification, which is required for knowledge—that is, belief that anyone at all has reason to accept—cannot so depend. See Ginet 1975, 28–31.

5. For an account of the role of central philosophical theses as in this sense quack remedies, see Scheman, forthcoming.

. . .

7. On the connection of critical and contextual values, see Longino 1990.

8. A term used by Lisa Heldke (1988).

9. See Code 1987.

10. See Heldke 1987 for connections between feminist epistemology and John Dewey's, and see Siegfried 1996 on the connections between feminist philosophy and pragmatism generally.

11. On the need to have pluralism from the beginning, in the structure of a theory—not as a footnote at the end—see Lugones 1991.

12. See Haraway 1988.

13. See Heldke and Kellert 1995.

14. The intended scope of "CPR" is illustrated by what I take to be two exemplary texts: Collins 1990 and Dupre 1993. (I've characterized Dupre's position as "Committed Promiscuous Realism.")

15. Sabina Lovibond comes to a similar conclusion at the end of her *Realism and Imagination in Ethics* (1983).

. . .

18. On the failure of much, even explicitly social, epistemology to appreciate the importance of feminist perspectives, see Rooney 1998.

19. Michael Root, following Hume, has argued that, while testimony is epistemologically important, our reliance on it can and should be understood not in terms of trust but as straightforwardly evidential: We ought to believe, on Root's view, when and to the extent that we have good reason to take our informant to be both sincere and relevantly competent (1998). For an argument against a similar position, see Hardwig 1991.

...

21. Annette Baier argues against a disembodied, asocial reading of Descartes on the nature of the mind, but she notes that "our genuine theoretical need for a standard of excellence, or correctness, in thought, is met, on Descartes's account, not by fellow finite thinkers, but by that divine mind to which we have direct innate nonmediated access" (1985, 77).

...

23. For a discussion of how to understand the projects of feminist epistemology, see Scheman 1995, and the following critical response by Louise Antony (1995).

24. See Root 1998 for an account of the role played by policing norms in science in underwriting the credibility of scientific reports, and reasons for thinking that such norms work far more effectively among scientists than they do between scientists and the lay public. See Fricker 1998 for an illuminating argument, using Shapin 1994 and Craig 1990, for the need to attend to the ways in which political factors are inevitably—albeit through political change, reparably—implicated in our conceptions of knowledge.

...

26. It might seem that, by framing the discussion around the question of the instrumental value of objectivity I am, if not begging the question, at least stacking the deck in favor of the externalists. I do think that such a frame does, if one takes it seriously, support the externalist position, but the frame itself is suggested strongly by the tenor of the critics' attacks on feminist objectivity theories, as well as by their defense of internalism: They emphasize repeatedly that the acceptance of scientific method as the best guarantor of objectivity is something we all benefit from and would suffer from attacks on.

27. See Kellert 1999 for a "situated defense of universalism," an argument specifically from the perspective of Jewish intellectuals for a conception of knowledge that abstracts from the social location of knowers.

28. For a thoughtful discussion of the resulting "epistemic injustice," see Fricker 1998.

...

33. For discussions of the epistemological issues raised by the Simpson case, see Morrison and Lacour 1997.

...

35. It should be clear that it is not just "add women and stir" projects that are threatened: Even the far more critical engagements of more theoretically sophisticated feminist scholars are subject to the same critique. It is dangerously naive, on Hoagland's view, for us to think that we control the terms of the discourse or even to think that the dominant *don't*. She asks: "If feminist scientists are going to study women, I want to know who, and who is the audience? To whose understanding are you attending as you write? In what frame of reference are you trying to make sense? Who are you trying to represent to whom and why?" ...

...

37. Thanks to Jennifer Hornsby for reminding me of this point, that is, of how dependent the most presumptively independent of the early moderns in fact were.

...

40. For a fuller account of what I mean by a "diasporic" epistemology, see Scheman 1997.

41. Here and elsewhere, my indebtedness to Helen Longino will be evident to all who have read her work. To those who haven't: Do.

REFERENCES

Alcoff, Linda, and Elizabeth Potter, eds. 1993. *Feminist epistemologies*. New York: Routledge.

Antony, Louise. 1995. Comment on Naomi Scheman. *Metaphilosophy* 26, 3: 191–98.

Baier, Annette. 1980. Secular faith. *Canadian Journal of Philosophy* 10, 1: 131–48. Reprinted in *Postures of the mind*. See Baier 1985b.

———. 1985a. Cartesian persons. In *Postures of the mind*. See Baier 1985b.

———. 1985b. *Postures of the mind: Essays on mind and morals.* Minneapolis: University of Minnesota Press.

Campbell, Sue. 2001. Memory, suggestibility, and social skepticism. In *Engendering Rationalities,* edited by Nancy Tuana and Sandra Morgan. Albany: SUNY Press.

Code, Lorraine. 1987. *Epistemic responsibility.* Hanover, N.H.: University Press of New England.

———. 1991. *What can she know? Feminist theory and the construction of knowledge.* Ithaca, N.Y.: Cornell University Press.

———. 1995. Incredulity, experientialism, and the politics of knowledge. In *Rhetorical spaces.* See Code 1995b.

———. 1995a. Must a feminist be a relativist after all? In *Rhetorical spaces.* See Code 1995b.

———. 1995b. *Rhetorical spaces: Essays on gendered location.* New York: Routledge.

———. 1995d. Taking subjectivity into account. In *Rhetorical spaces.* See Code 1995b.

Collins, Patricia Hill. 1986. "Learning from the outsider within: The social significance of Black feminist thought. *Social Problems* 33, 8: 14–32. Reprinted in *Beyond methodology: Feminist scholarship as lived research,* ed. Mary Margaret Fonow and Judith A. Cook. Bloomington: Indiana University Press, 1991.

———. 1990. *Black feminist thought: Knowledge, consciousness, and the politics of empowerment.* Boston: Unwin Hyman.

Craig, Edward. 1990. *Knowledge and the state of nature: An essay in conceptual synthesis.* Oxford: Clarendon.

Dupre, John. 1993. *The disorder of things: Metaphysical foundations of the disunity of science.* Cambridge, Mass.: Harvard University Press.

Fine, Arthur. 1998. The viewpoint of no one in particular. *Proceedings and Addresses of the American Philosophical Association* 72, 2: 9–20.

France, David. 1998. Challenging the conventional stance on AIDS. *New York Times* 22 December: F6.

Fricker, Miranda. 1998. Rational authority and social power: Towards a truly social epistemology. *Proceedings of the Aristotelian Society* 98, 2: 159–77.

Ginet, Carl. 1975. *Knowledge, perception, and memory.* Dordrecht, Holland; Boston: D. Reidel.

Gross, Paul R. 1998. Evidence-free forensics and enemies of objectivity. In *A house built on sand.* See Koertge 1998.

Gross, Paul, and Norman Levitt. 1994. *Higher superstition: The academic left and its quarrels with science.* Baltimore: Johns Hopkins University Press.

Haraway, Donna. 1988. Situated knowledges and the privilege of partial perspective. *Feminist Studies* 14, 3: 575–99. Reprinted in *Feminism and science.* See Keller and Longino 1996.

Harding, Sandra. 1986. *The science question in feminism.* Ithaca, N.Y.: Cornell University Press.

———. 1991. *Whose science? Whose knowledge? Thinking from women's lives.* Ithaca, N.Y.: Cornell University Press.

———. 1993. Rethinking standpoint epistemology. In *Feminist epistemologies.* See Alcoff and Potter 1993.

Hardwig, John. 1991. The role of trust in knowledge. *Journal of Philosophy* 88: 693–70.

Heldke, Lisa. 1987. John Dewey and Evelyn Fox Keller: A shared epistemological tradition. *Hypatia* 2: 129–40.

———. 1988. Recipes for theory-making. *Hypatia* 3: 15–30.

Heldke, Lisa, and Stephen H. Kellert. 1995. Objectivity as responsibility. *Metaphilosophy* 26, 4: 360–78.

Hoagland, Sarah Lucia. 2001. Resisting rationality. In *Engendering Rationalities,* edited by Nancy Tuana and Sandra Morgan. Albany: SUNY Press.

Jones, Karen. 1998. Trust in science and in scientists: A response to Kane. In *NOMOS XL: Integrity and conscience,* ed. Ian Shapiro and Robert Adams. New York: New York University Press.

———. 2000. The politics of credibility. In *A mind of one's own,* 2nd edition, ed. Louise Antony and Charlotte Witt. Boulder, CO: Westview.

Keller, Evelyn Fox. 1985. *Reflections on gender and science.* New Haven, Conn.: Yale University Press.

Keller, Evelyn Fox, and Helen Longino. 1996. *Feminism and science.* Oxford: Oxford University Press.

Kellert, Stephen. 1999. Never coming home: Positivism, ecology, and rootless cosmopolitanism. In *The meaning of being human,* ed. Michelle Stoneburner and Billy Catchings. Indianapolis: University of Indianapolis Press.

Kitcher, Philip. 1998. Truth or consequences. *Proceedings and Addresses of the American Philosophical Association* 72, 2: 49–63.

Koertge, Noretta, ed. 1998. *A house built on sand.* New York: Oxford University Press.

Lloyd, Elisabeth A. 1996. Science and antiscience: Objectivity and its real enemies. In *Feminism, science, and the philosophy of science.* See Nelson and Nelson 1996.

Longino, Helen. 1990. *Science as social knowledge: Values and objectivity in scientific inquiry.* Princeton, N.J.: Princeton University Press.

Lovibond, Sabina. 1983. *Realism and imagination in ethics.* Oxford: Blackwell.

Lugones, Maria. 1991. On the logic of pluralist feminism. In *Feminist ethics,* ed. Claudia Card. Lawrence: University Press of Kansas.

Morrison, Toni, and Claudia Brodsky Lacour, eds. 1997. *Birth of a nation'hood: Gaze, script, and spectacle in the O. J. Simpson case.* New York: Pantheon.

Nelson, Lynne Hankinson, and Jack Nelson, eds. 1996. *Feminism, science, and the philosophy of science.* Dordrecht; Boston: Kluwer.

Nozick, Robert. 1998. Invariance and objectivity. *Proceedings and Addresses of the American Philosophical Association* 72, 2: 21–48.

Porter, Bernard. 1999. Review of David Vincent, *The culture of secrecy in Britain 1832–1998. London Review of Books* 21, 14: 13–15.

Rooney, Phyllis. 1998. Putting naturalized epistemology to work. In *Epistemology: The big questions,* ed. Linda Martin Alcoff. Oxford: Blackwell.

Root, Michael. 1998. How to teach a wise man. In *Pragmatism, reason, and norms,* ed. Kenneth R. Westphal. New York: Fordham University Press.

Scheman, Naomi. 1991. Who wants to know? The epistemological value of values. In *(En)gendering knowledge: Feminists in academe,* ed. Joan E. Hartman and Ellen Messer-Davidow. Knoxville: University of Tennessee Press.

———. 1995. Feminist epistemology and Reply to Antony. *Metaphilosophy* 26, 3: 177–90, 199–200.

———. 1997. Forms of life: Mapping the rough ground. In *Cambridge companion to Wittgenstein,* ed. Hans Sluga and David Stern. Cambridge: Cambridge University Press.

———. Forthcoming. Nonnegotiable demands: Metaphysics, politics, and the discourse of needs. In *Future pasts,* ed. Juliet Floyd and Sanford Shieh. Oxford: Oxford University Press.

Seigfried, Charlene Haddock. 1996. *Pragmatism and feminism: Reweaving the social fabric.* Chicago: University of Chicago Press.

Shapin, Steven. 1994. *A social history of truth: Civility and science in seventeenth-century England.* Chicago: University of Chicago Press.

Specter, Michael. 1999. Decoding Iceland. *The New Yorker* 18 January: 50–51.

Tuana, Nancy, ed. 1987. *Feminism and science.* Bloomington: Indiana University Press.

Waldron, Jeremy. 1999. Review of John Rawls, *Collected papers,* ed. Samuel Freeman. *London Review of Books* 21, 14: 3–6.

Wylie, Alison. 2000. Rethinking objectivity: Nozick's neglected third option. *International Studies in the Philosophy of Science* 14, 1: 5–10.

12
Democratizing Research

Many readings in this volume have addressed the complex connections between knowledge, on the one hand, and sociopolitical power, on the other. The readings in this chapter consider whether it is possible to utilize sociopolitical power in ways that promote the feminist research goals not only of epistemic trustworthiness but also of social usefulness, gender equity, and ethical decency.

KNOWLEDGE, POWER, AND THE MARKETPLACE OF IDEAS

In modern Western culture, knowledge is often seen as a means for increasing control not only over one's individual life and over nature but also over other people's lives. Developments in the physical sciences have often resulted from quests to improve transportation and the production of food and other goods, but they have also resulted from quests for more powerful weaponry. Similarly, developments in the social sciences have often resulted from aspirations to control the social world; in earlier readings, Dorothy Smith noted that the discipline of sociology has long been involved with administration and ruling, and Linda Tuhiwai Smith showed how both history and anthropology have often been linked with colonial enterprises. The idea that truth is what works, associated with U.S. pragmatism among other traditions, is often interpreted to mean that truth is whatever we can use to control the world.

Although Western culture regards knowledge as a means to power, it does not regard power, or at least sociopolitical power, as a useful means to knowledge. Instead, it views sociopolitical power as more likely to corrupt the search for knowledge. It portrays reliable knowledge as a product of dispassionate, disinterested inquiry, arguing that only such inquiry can provide insight into the workings of physical or social reality independent of human desires, fears, and values. In this view, knowledge is valuable as a tool for control precisely because it is autonomous and value-neutral.

The view that the influence of sociopolitical power undermines the production of reliable knowledge is very plausible. One familiar cautionary tale is that of Trofim Denisovic Lysenko in the former Soviet Union. Lysenko responded to Stalinist pressure by advocating the Lamarckian view that evolution could occur very rapidly in response to changing environmental conditions; this mistaken view, promoted by political authorities, had disastrous consequences for Soviet and Chinese biology and agriculture. Readings in this volume have provided many other examples of ways in which the influence of gender, class, race, and empire have generated mistaken and biased views in various fields of knowledge. More contemporary examples abound. Until recently, political authorities in South Africa denied that AIDS was caused by a virus; in the United States, a recent article in the *New York Times* (2004) described "Bush science," conclusions supported by government officials that included the claims that women who have abortions are more likely to suffer from mental health problems, that the climate is not really warming, and that the world could not have resulted from evolution unaided by intelligent design.

If the influence of political power typically undermines the reliability of knowledge claims, it seems to follow that such influence should be eradicated, as far as possible, from research. The ideal of free inquiry is often interpreted as requiring that the pursuit of knowledge should be untrammeled by authority and its production freed from power and politics. This conception of free inquiry was famously argued by nineteenth-century philosopher John Stuart Mill in his classic work *On Liberty*. Mill contended that no opinions should be suppressed because even those that turned out to be mistaken made a contribution by inspiring stronger arguments for the truth. A conception of free inquiry that permits and even welcomes voices of dissent is obviously friendly to feminism, and a number of later feminists have followed Mill in arguing that truth is most likely to emerge from free competition in the marketplace of ideas. Research conclusions produced in this way are thought to approach the modern epistemic ideals of purity, value neutrality, and transcendence of social interests.

THE LIMITS OF FREE INQUIRY IN THE MARKETPLACE

Construing free inquiry as competition in the marketplace of ideas assumes that research is best conducted when it is insulated from the influence of politics. But is this assumption justified? Can values and power ever entirely be excluded from the knowledge-seeking enterprise? Even if so, is the marketplace the arena in which this is most likely to occur?

Several epistemological theories claim, as we have seen, that it is impossible in principle to eradicate the influence of external sociopolitical factors on the production of knowledge. Marxism and postmodernism both contend that inquiry is never purely disinterested, but instead is always produced with a purpose; we approach the understanding of nature and society with questions that depend on our interests and values. Moreover, they say, powerful interests always influence which knowledge claims are accepted and how they are interpreted and developed. In these views, knowledge is always shaped by sociopolitical power, whether this is immediately evident.

Even if these epistemological theories are interpreted as offering no more than diagnoses of how past research has been corrupted by power, it remains indisputable that, in many fields, the search for knowledge is no longer a spare-time activity for leisured individuals. Today, research in most fields of knowledge is conducted by professional researchers who depend on institutional funding. The production of scientific knowledge in particular typically relies on massive investments of resources, which often can be provided only by large corporations or by governments. Inevitably, these sources of funding encourage directions in research that are thought likely to be either profitable or to promote the national interest, too often perceived as an interest in militarization. The article in this chapter by Vandana Shiva traces how such interests have influenced research in biology and medicine in ways that have not promoted the well-being of all equally.

If research is never free in principle from social interests and values, or even if, more weakly, it is usually shaped in practice by the influence of powerful funders, must we therefore resign ourselves to the view that truth is what pays off? Some feminists have responded to this challenge by reinterpreting the idea of free inquiry in a way that seeks to draw on sociopolitical power as an epistemic resource. If power cannot be eliminated from research, either in principle or in practice, then perhaps it may be harnessed to promote research that serves wider rather than narrower social interests. An increasing focus of feminist methodology has been to reinterpret the ideal of free inquiry as inquiry in which production is democratized.

DEMOCRATIZING RESEARCH

The idea of democratizing the production of knowledge was raised already in Chapter 11 on objectivity, where Helen Longino argues that objectivity in science is maximized when scientific communities practice a kind of intellectual democracy. Longino takes this intellectual democracy to be defined by the following conditions: the existence of publicly recognized fora for the criticism of evidence, methods, assumptions, and reasoning; uptake of criticism as opposed to simple toler-ance of dissent; shared standards of discourse, which are not static but may themselves be criticized and transformed by reference to other standards, goals, or values held temporarily constant; and equality of intellectual authority. Longino argues that meeting these conditions is likely to increase objectivity by mitigating the influence of subjective preferences on background assumptions and by increasing the chances that shared assumptions will become visible and become open to critical examination. Although Longino is talking primarily about scientific communities, her views seem naturally transferable to communities of experts in the humanities and arts.

Yet, the democracy that Longino advocates is democracy is only at the level of research processes—democracy in the *internal* processes of knowledge production. In this volume, however, we have interpreted feminist methodology more broadly than as simply a concern for methods in the sense of gathering evidence; we have also looked at the larger social context in which projects are selected, practiced, and utilized. Some of the feminist methodological propos-als that we have considered address so-called external as well as internal aspects of knowledge production; for instance, they advocate broadening research agendas to address the concerns of the subjugated and marginalized and including researchers from "other" backgrounds. This chapter considers what it might mean to promote democratization also in the so-called *external* processes of knowledge production.

The readings in this chapter discuss proposals for democratizing methods at several levels. Patricia Maguire's notion of feminist participatory research suggests ways of democra-tizing the selection of research projects, the choice of research processes, and the use made of research findings. Vandana Shiva argues that democratizing biology would require recovering and genuinely assessing indigenous and non-Western knowledge traditions and recognizing the rights of all citizens to determine how we relate to diverse species. Jan Bootinand provides an excellent example of feminist participatory action research that involves research subjects in designing the focus and methods of studies of their lives and in deciding how to use the findings.

These methodological recommendations suggest that democratization may promote research that is not only more epistemically trustworthy but also investigates questions of concern to subordinated groups, including many women. In addition, democratizing research increases the likelihood that it will be conducted in accord with feminist ethical principles.

SOME DIFFICULTIES FOR DEMOCRATIZING RESEARCH

The ideal of democracy is notoriously problematic, and a number of familiar problems reemerge in the project of democratizing research. Some of these problems are especially salient for mem-bers of social minorities or those, such as feminists, who hold views outside the mainstream.

One familiar problem is that of intervention by know-nothings. Democratic research cannot mean equal participation by people who are unqualified, whose interventions may well impede the advancement of knowledge. Helen Longino seems correct in her assertion that not everyone has equal authority on every matter—but the difficulty comes in determining who has authority on which matters. Individuals from historically subordinated groups, including women, have often faced difficulties in acquiring officially recognized credentials; feminist and other criticism has often been discredited by claims that the critics are unqualified. The readings in this chapter and many in previous chapters describe how people with a stake in various research projects nevertheless have been excluded from commenting on those projects on the grounds that they are stupid or ignorant or biased. The idea of democratizing research is designed precisely to address such exclusion; yet it is difficult to see how to make it compatible with recognizing the authority of genuine experts.

Related to this is the problem that John Stuart Mill called "the tyranny of the majority." Mill was concerned that ideas not be suppressed because a majority found them offensive or threatening to conventional views, especially moral, political, or religious views. The idea of democratizing research faces the dangers that majorities might suppress research projects that promise to challenge accepted ideas, or that they might approve research that exploits the weakness of some populations. This is obviously a problem for feminist research, which investigates questions that are often unpopular by means that are sometimes unorthodox.

To interpret free inquiry in terms of democratic inquiry is to point toward a research ideal that is as vague and riven with tensions as its parent ideal of political democracy. Realizing in practice the ideal of democratic research requires mediating many tensions—among openness to dissent, respect for expertise, and the need for criticism to be informed; between unimpeded investigation and public accountability; and between full disclosure and responsibility to research subjects. The challenge is to figure out how all those with a legitimate stake in research and with relevant expertise may have a voice and have that voice heard. Perhaps different voices would participate at different stages of research, such as deciding on initial projects, deciding on techniques for gathering evidence, deciding how to interpret the evidence, deciding when to stop doing research, and deciding how the results be presented and used.

In the end, fully democratized research processes can occur only in societies with a fully democratic infrastructure. This requires that members of diverse populations, especially historically underrepresented groups including women, have equal access to professional specializations so that they may become full members of communities of qualified experts. In many societies, this might require affirmative action in the short term; in the long term, it might require transforming educational systems. Democratizing research also requires transparency in government-funded research projects and accountability on the part of corporate research. Democratizing research is likely not only to improve the epistemic trustworthiness of research conclusions but also to increase the probability of producing knowledge that is unbiased and ethically conducted and that serves the larger social interest.

Patricia Maguire

Feminist Participatory Research

... This [reading] focuses on participatory research, one alternative paradigm approach to social science and educational research. Participatory research offers a way to openly demonstrate solidarity with oppressed and disempowered people through our work as researchers. In addition to recognizing many forms of knowledge, participatory research insists on an alternative position regarding the purpose of knowledge creation. The purpose of participatory research is not merely to describe and interpret social reality, but to radically change it. Furthermore, the intent is to transform reality "with" rather than "for" oppressed people. Participatory research places human self-determination, emancipation, and personal and social transformation as the central goals of social science....

DEFINING PARTICIPATORY RESEARCH

Participatory research combines three activities: (1) investigation, (2) education, and (3) action. It is a method of social investigation of problems, involving participation of oppressed and ordinary people in problem posing and solving. It is an educational process for the researcher and participants, who analyze the structural causes of named problems through collective discussion and interaction. Finally, it is a way for researchers and oppressed people to join in solidarity to take collective action, both short and long term, for radical social change. Locally determined and controlled action is a planned consequence of inquiry (Hall, 1979, 1981; Participatory Research Network, 1982).

The direct link between research and action is perhaps the most unique aspect of participatory research. Combining the creation of knowledge about social reality with concrete action on reality removes the traditional research dichotomy between knowing and doing (Tandon, 1981b; Hall, 1981). Participatory research aims at three types of change, including the following:

- development of critical consciousness of both researcher and participants;
- improvement of the lives of those involved in the research process; and
- transformation of fundamental societal structures and relationships.

The investigation, education, and action components of participatory research are collective processes. The investigative component begins with collective problem posing. Ideally, a community group, working with a researcher, names existing problems which they want to eliminate or change. These existing community problems become the basis for research (Hall, 1981). Together they try to understand why and how the problem exists, particularly focusing on what Park calls the "human-made" nature of the problem (1978b:24). By looking at the why's and how's of the problem, the group investigates the concrete and complex social reality in which they live but may not thoroughly understand.

Collective inquiry builds group ownership of information as people move from being mere objects to acting as subjects of their own research process. Research is demystified by involving people in deciding what to investigate, what questions to ask, how to gather information, and how to organize and use information (PR Network, 1982:38).

Participatory research includes an educational component to assist people to further develop skills in collecting, analyzing, and utilizing information. The educational process is potentially liberating as it provides a way for people to develop an increasingly critical understanding of social problems, their underlying causes, and possibilities for overcoming them (PR Network, 1982:1).

By learning through doing, people strengthen their awareness of, and belief in, their abilities and resources for organizing (Brown and Tandon, 1983)…. The important point is that those involved in the production of knowledge are involved in the decision making regarding its use and application to their everyday lives.

Collective investigation, education, and action are important to the rehumanizing goal of participatory research. By treating people as objects to be counted, surveyed, predicted, and controlled, traditional research mirrors oppressive social conditions which cause ordinary people to relinquish their capacity to make real choices and to be cut out of meaningful decision making. The collective processes of participatory research help rebuild people's capacity to be creative actors on the world.

The three-pronged participatory research process is more than a new set of techniques. It is a systematic approach to radical social transformation grounded in an alternative paradigm world view. The ideological foundation of participatory research is in open opposition to the underpinnings of dominant social science research. The core issue in participatory research is power. The objectives of participatory research include the transformation of power structures and relationships as well as the empowerment of oppressed people. Transformation not only requires a critical understanding of current and historical social realities, but it is also a vision of what a just and loving society should be (Horton, 1981; Park, 1978a).

ORIGINS OF PARTICIPATORY RESEARCH

Participatory research has emerged from and has been influenced by other movements which share a vision of society without domination.... Participatory research emerged from the concrete experience of such people coming face to face with the politics of their work and concluding that Freire's (1970) observation was right: domination is the fundamental theme of our epoch and liberation is the goal.

The emergence of participatory research can be linked to the following three trends:

- radical and reformist reconceptualizations of international economic development assistance;
- the reframing of adult education as an empowering alternative to traditional educational approaches; and
- an ongoing debate within the social sciences, challenging the dominant social science paradigm. (Hall, 1979; Tandon, 1981b; Horton, 1981; Vio Grossi, Martinic, Tapia, and Pascal, 1983)

ALTERNATIVE CRITIQUES OF INTERNATIONAL DEVELOPMENT

In the 1960s and 1970s, the failed policies of more than a quarter century of international development assistance came under scrutiny by both the development industry and its critics. Despite development efforts, the absolute number and percentage of the world's people living in oppressive poverty continue to increase daily. In fact, such poverty is increasingly visible in the industrialized "first world" (Tandon, 1981b). Tandon observed that frustrated development policy makers and administrators "called for something new." That something new included a search by the development assistance community for ways to bring the poor more rapidly into full participation in development decisions, processes, and benefits.

... Dependency theorists pointed out that unequal relationships of international trade and investment between the technically advanced and third world nations set up dominant-dependency relationships (Kindervatter, 1979).... Because of the inequitable patterns of capitalist accumulation, "development in one part of the world is premised on and has generated underdevelopment in another" (Brydon-Miller, 1984:16).... Schemes aimed at integrating marginal people into development leave intact the very economic, political, and social structures which support the maintenance of poverty (Heatley, 1979; Vio Grossi et al., 1983). Rather than promote ordinary and oppressed people's increased participation in unaltered systems of domination, the critics call for radical transformation of systems and relationships based on domination....

ADULT EDUCATION AS A SOURCE OF PARTICIPATORY RESEARCH

During this same period, both in the Third World and in the West, adult educators were also questioning traditional practices. Criticizing mainstream international development assistance, spokesmen for Third World adult educators challenged traditional education which nurtures social relationships based on dominance (Freire, 1970, 1981; Nyerere, 1969).[1] Among this group, Paulo Freire has had a strong influence. Freire emphasized the importance of critical consciousness or "concientizacao" for social change. To develop critical consciousness is to learn to perceive economic, political, and social contradictions and take action to change oppressive elements of reality (Freire, 1970).

Within the southern United States, as early as the 1930s, Myles Horton and those at Highlander Center had recognized adult education as a powerful vehicle for social change (Adams, 1975). The Highlander Folk School began working with poor Appalachian mountain people to use education as a tool to question and challenge an unjust society, particularly in the areas of labor and civil rights.... For them education is another vehicle for transforming people and unjust social structures.[2]

Another small group of adult educators which continues to have a prominent place in participatory research, particularly as practitioners, is the Participatory Research Network, sponsored in 1977 by the International Council for Adult Education. Participants in the network are united by dissatisfaction with the existing social order, their commitment to change social inequities in partnership with poor and marginal peoples, and their commitment to utilize education and research approaches which actively involve local people (Participatory Research Network, 1982:3).

A well known participatory researcher, Bud Hall has been influential in bringing knowledge about participatory research practices to adult educators (1975).... After being involved with two survey research projects, Hall concluded that traditional research methods were inconsistent with the principles of adult education. Adult education is built on a philosophy and set of techniques which treat adult learners as "whole people participating actively in the world" (Hall, 1975:28). Yet adult education researchers were using methods which treated adults as passive objects, incapable of active involvement in the research process.

...

As we have seen, participatory research builds on critiques of the domination inherent in mainstream development, education, and the social sciences. Taken individually, the premises of participatory research are not unique. Rather, as Horton pointed out, participatory research is unique in integrating the premises into a systematic approach to social change (1981:1).

UNDERLYING ASSUMPTIONS

Participatory research assumes that there is a political nature to all we do; all of our work has implications for the distribution of power in society. Given this assumption, there can be no neutral or value-free social science. Participatory research requires that researchers be clear about where they choose to stand regarding the daily struggles of oppressed people (Horton, 1981).

Participatory research begins with the premise that knowledge has become the single most important basis of power and control (Tandon, 1981b). Furthermore, one particular form of knowledge, technical or "scientific," has become the only legitimate form. Knowledge production has become a lucrative business. It is, in fact, a monopolized industry with knowledge itself as the commodity (Hall, 1979; Tandon, 1981b).

Given this framework, ordinary people are rarely considered knowledgeable, in the scientific sense, or capable of knowing about their own reality. They are excluded from the increasingly more specialized research industry, barred by requirements of the "scientific method," and by intimidating concepts and jargon, money, time, skills, and experience. In addition to being excluded from meaningful participation in knowledge creation processes, oppressed and ordinary people are subjected to research processes which treat them as objects and things. Hence, traditional research processes are often alienating and dehumanizing. Decisions which ultimately shape the lives of the poor and even the middle class are increasingly made by experts.... Strict adherence to the procedures of the dominant research model becomes more important than actual social problems.

Experts' assessment of common people's inability to "know" becomes a self-fulfilling prophecy. Taught to believe they cannot adequately understand their own lives, and deprived of participation in inquiry processes which might enhance their understanding, ordinary people simply stop trying....

This "ordinary person" is not only the illiterate or the poor. Thousands of people in the most industrialized nations are immobilized by these myths. Building on the work of Lukacs (1971), Shor noted: "As a result of this mystery, poor and middle class alike often put their energy into beating rather than changing a system which they assume is beyond their compre-hension or control" (Shor, 1980).

In a vicious cycle, people do often lack the information, skills, and experience to criti-cally understand and analyze the social structures and relations which shape their powerlessness (Ellis, 1983; Tandon, 1981b). Their lack of information and preoccupation with daily survival interfere with their understanding of how power structures work and affect their lives (Tandon, 1981b). Therefore, the oppressed often share the oppressors' viewpoint, blaming themselves for their own poverty and powerlessness....

One of the greatest obstacles to creating a more just world is the power of the dominant hegemony, "the ideological oppression which shapes the way in which people think" (Participa-tory Research Network, 1982:43).

Herein lies a dilemma for the participatory researcher. To purposefully embark on a research approach that promotes oppressed people's empowerment as an explicit goal requires a belief that people need empowerment, or conversely, that people are oppressed and powerless. Likewise, it requires a belief that this research approach can make a contribution to social change. A participatory researcher must find a balance between assuming that oppressed people fully understand their own oppression and the researcher does not, or conversely, that the researcher fully understands the truth about people's oppression, and they do not.

Participatory researchers caution against either dichotomy: "They know, I don't know." or "They don't know, I know." Instead, participatory research offers a partnership: *We both know some things; neither of us knows everything. Working together we will both know more, and we will both learn more about how to know.* Participatory research requires that both the researcher and researched be open to personal transformation and conscientization....

Participatory research assumes that the oppressors' power is, in part, derived from their control of both the process and products of knowledge creation. Dominant groups also have the power to shape what is considered "common knowledge." For example, many battered women believe the myth perpetuated by abusers and many societal institutions that the violence women experience is somehow their own fault. Women, we are told, provoke men's abusive behavior. That myth is supported by hundreds of messages about women's "irrational behavior" and inferior status. The entertainment and pornography industries, both male controlled, lend credence to the belief that "women enjoy violence." That line of thinking asks, "Why else do women stay in abusive relationships?" Important questions, such as "Why do men brutalize women in love relationships?" and, "How does society support such violence?" are ignored. The ability to shape both common and scientific knowledge is a source of power for dominant social groups.

In order to produce and share more critical knowledge, participatory researchers abandon the dominant research tenets of detachment and unilateral control of the research process and products. When the objects of research are considered incapable of understanding their lives and reality and the researchers are considered capable of separating knowing from feeling, the detachment of researchers from the researched seems logical. However, when you start with other assumptions about people, detachment hinders rather than helps the research process.

Participatory research assumes that ordinary people, provided with tools and opportuni-ties, are capable of critical reflection and analysis. Given this premise, establishing reciprocal, empathic adult relationships between the researcher and the researched no longer endangers knowledge creation. Instead, it improves the possibility of jointly creating a more critical understanding of a given reality.

The principle of shared power is central to participatory research. Power sharing begins with a shift in the most basic power relationship in research, the relationship between the researcher and the research participants. Participatory research is structured to shift the power and control of decision making and decision taking increasingly into the hands of the participants.

Involving research subjects as partners in the entire research process also increases the potential to distribute the benefits of the research process more equitably. When the objects of research become subjects and partners, they benefit not only from the opportunity to learn about and understand their own reality, but also by sharing directly in subsequent policy and program decision making and control.

    … Participatory research assumes that returning the power of knowledge production and use to ordinary and oppressed people will contribute to the creation of a more accurate and critical reflection of social reality, the liberation of human creative potential, and to the mobilization of human resources to solve social problems (Hall, 1975).

    …

PHASES AND GUIDELINES FOR CONDUCTING PARTICIPATORY RESEARCH

There are numerous models within the literature for conducting participatory research (Marshall, 1981; Le Boterf, 1983; Fernandes and Tandon, 1981; Park, 1978a). Each model is usually presented as one possible approach among many, carefully avoiding the claim that there is or should be only one way to do participatory research. Cautions are made that in each case, the actual model must evolve out of and in response to the unique conditions and context of the specific situation (Le Boterf, 1983; Vio Grossi, Martinic, Tapia, and Pascal, 1983).

    While noting the impossibility of constructing a generalized participatory research model, Vio Grossi, Martinic, Tapia, and Pascal (1983) identified five phases common to actual participatory research projects. Likewise, Hall (1975, 1981) has identified principles or guidelines for conducting participatory research. This [reading] integrates many of Hall's guidelines into the five phases identified by Vio Grossi et al. (1983)….

Phase 1: Organization of the Project and Knowledge of the Working Area

The initial phase includes gathering and analyzing existing information about the research area and about the central problems faced by people. A project usually focuses on a particular group of exploited or oppressed people, for example, laborers, immigrants, indigenous people, or women. This phase may occur prior to entry into an area as well as during the initial stage in the community. The phase includes establishing relationships with community organizations, leaders, and institutions. At this point, the researchers either invite particular organizations to participate in the project or respond to a community request. A key guideline is that the research problem should originate in the community (Hall, 1975, 1981).

Phase 2: Definition of Generating Problematics

In this phase, numerous techniques and processes are used to enable both researchers and participants to identify and understand participants' perceptions of their most significant problems. Problem-posing continues as a dialogue over time; each phase takes the researchers and participants to a deeper and more critical understanding of reality as perceived and experienced by both participants and the researcher.

Phase 3: Objectivization and Problematization

The third phase attempts to link participants' individual interpretations of problems to the broader context, including the structural conditions of social reality. As noted, ordinary and oppressed people often lack the skills and information for a critical analysis of their situation. Collective educational activities can be important in this phase to help participants further examine their interpretations as well as to identify and to discuss the broader causes of their problems. By the end of this phase, the researchers and participants have compiled the questions and themes which will be investigated. Note that in each phase, participants are increasingly more involved in controlling decision making and taking in the project. Likewise, each phase is itself an educational experience that helps participants and researchers increase their understanding of problem solving and commitment to it. Each phase strengths the participants' awareness of their own resources and abilities for mobilization and action.

Phase 4: Researching Social Reality and Analyzing Collected Information

Having defined the main problem themes and posed related questions, the researchers and participants should ideally design a process to investigate specific problems together. Participants can be involved to varying degrees and through various methods in information gathering, classification, analysis, and conclusion building depending on their training and the design of the project. In this phase, participants develop their own theories and solutions to problems (Hall, 1975). However, for new knowledge to increase people's power, it should be applied to creative strategies and action for social transformation.

Phase 5: Definition of Action Projects

Finally, researchers and participants decide on what actions to take to address the problems that they have collectively defined and investigated. In this way, both the process and products of research can be of direct and immediate benefit to those involved. Ordinary and oppressed people move from being objects to being the subjects and beneficiaries of research. Likewise, researchers move from being "detached extractors of information" to involved activists (Park, 1978a:9).

DIFFICULTIES AND LIMITATIONS OF PARTICIPATORY RESEARCH

Advocates of participatory research make no pretense that this alternative approach will, by itself, create "the revolution." ...

While endorsing participatory research as one approach that can make a contribution to the long-haul struggle to create a just world, most advocates acknowledge impediments and limitations. The Participatory Research Network declared that its members "do not underestimate the obstacles to effective social change" (1982:4). ... Others caution that participatory research is neither the long awaited miracle solution nor an overnight magic (Horton, 1981; Kanhare, 1982). However, participatory researchers must avoid the tendency to imply that their style of research is the only research approach that can contribute to social transformation.

An exhaustive analysis of the difficulties and limitations of engaging in participatory research is beyond the scope of this work. However, a discussion of several of these drawbacks will be discussed and will suggest topics for exploration in greater depth.

One difficulty is that participatory research makes great demands on researchers. The researcher's role is expanded to include educator and activist and in this role the researcher is expected to take a value position and act accordingly (Horton, 1981). The participatory researcher is also called upon to transfer organizational, technical, and analytical skills to participants. This transfer of skills is not easy to accomplish (Participatory Research Network, 1982). It requires commitment, teaching skill, and the ability to set up a project structure and processes to facilitate the transfer. Furthermore, the researcher must have access to financial and institutional resources.

... Ideally, participatory research is initiated at the request of a community group which is involved in the entire research process. Realistically, participatory research projects are more likely to be initiated by outside researchers. Given this, transfer of project control from researchers to participants is difficult. Under what circumstances is the greatest transfer of project control most likely?

Although the research problem should originate in the community, the literature is vague about how the research problem makes itself known (Horton, 1981). The literature does note numerous problems with identifying, establishing, and building relationships with community-based groups that represent the oppressed and powerless. Park (1978b) noted that although a community may have "feelings" about problems requiring attention, it rarely articulates those feelings as "topics for investigation." There may not even be a group to voice the collective opinion of oppressed sectors as the oppressed "do not readily form groups ... to do research to better their lives" (Marshall, 1981:3). The "oppressed" or "the people" are not an undifferentiated, homogenous mass. Therefore, even within popular people's organizations, the most oppressed still remain underrepresented and powerless....

Organizations and leaders who act as advocates for different sectors of the oppressed may have little actual commitment to power sharing, community-based participation, or democratic organizational structures and procedures. Instead such leadership may attempt to use participatory research projects to enhance their own power base (Vio Grossi, 1982b; Colletta, 1982).

These difficulties and limitations revolve around the issue of people's organizations. On the one hand, the importance of organizations to oppressed people's mobilization and participation in development efforts is well supported by rural development research (Uphoff, 1979; Korten, 1980). Likewise, Horton (1981) claims that participatory research requires some organizational entity. On the other hand, the most oppressed are precisely the least likely to have already developed their own advocacy organizations. For this reason, Tandon (1981b) noted that creation of an organization of "have-nots" may be an outcome of participatory research projects....

Vio Grossi (1981) observed that there is no inherent guarantee that the practice of participatory research results in the actual increase of power among oppressed people. Power has a material base, which may include financial and organizational resources. Without a material base, increased knowledge may be insufficient for increased power and action....

People require both the will and the resources to participate and act collectively (Elden, 1981). The development and enhancement of popular organizations may contribute to the long-term continuation of project benefits for participants. More attention should be given to the conditions which enhance possibilities for mobilization either short-term or sustained over the long haul.

In regard to the difficulties involved in accepting outside support for participatory research projects, the Participatory Research Network warned, "It is a strategic choice to use institutional resources for work aimed at social change" (1982:43). The choice is not between acceptance and refusal of institutional resources. Participatory research simply cannot take place without some combination of institutional resources, human, financial, and material....

One of the most underrated limitations on participatory research is simply time. While researchers may be able to invest their total work time in a participatory research project, participants continue their regular life activities. How much time is required of local people to participate in a project? Likewise, what kind of time commitment can the researcher(s) make to an area? One time consuming aspect of participatory research is establishing the community contacts and relationships necessary to link up with a group for the project or to be requested to do research by a community group. Building trust takes time. Fordham, Poulton, and Randle wrote of the New Communities Project: "Our first task, therefore, was not to do anything, but spend six months listening to local people, talking with them, finding out what might be possible and deciding on the things to which people might respond" (1982:133).

The time frame of a project is related to the possible emancipatory outcomes and to the transfer of project control from researchers to participants. Short cutting the educational activities may minimize the empowering outcomes of participatory research. Mduma wrote of the Tanzanian Bwakira Grain Storage Project: "... time limitations meant that the outside team could not always wait for the level of group consciousness to rise to a certain level of understanding about a particular problem before moving on" (1982:203).

Likewise, inadequate project time was blamed for limited outcome from the Jipemoyo project....

Many participatory research projects conclude that a common result of time constraints is a less radical or less critical analysis and vision for action (Horton, 1981; Mustafa, 1982a).

...

NOTES

1. The use of the term "spokesmen" is intentional. See Gayfer (1980) and Yanz (1986) for a discussion of male domination of international adult education policy making and advocacy groups.

2. For discussion of education for empowerment and social change, see Kindervatter, 1979; Adams, 1975; Wren, 1977.

· · ·

... This [reading] continues the assessment of the Former Battered Women's Support Group Project using the framework for feminist participatory research which was developed out of a critical review of the literature and the early phases of the field study. In this way, theory and practice inform each other. Conclusions are drawn regarding feminist participatory research. The [reading] ends with recommendations for the further development of feminist participatory research (FPR).

ASSESSMENT OF THE PROJECT USING THE FRAMEWORK

Critique of Social Science Research

While the project did begin from a critique of positivism, the feminist and joint critique emerged from the interaction between the field experience and the literature review....

Central Place for Gender in the Agenda of Participatory Research Issues

Gender had a central place in the literature review, field study, and overall theoretical base of the support group project. The degree to which this particular project helps raise the issue of gender and androcentrism within other participatory research projects and the larger participatory research community ... will depend on dissemination and publication of the case study results within the various participatory research networks.

Central Place for Feminism in Participatory Research Theoretical Debates

Feminism had a central place in this project.... Again, the degree to which the project helps feminism to move into a more central place within participatory research theoretical debates remains to be determined.... The theoretical base of the study draws heavily on critical theory in addition to feminism. Thus, the study provides one example of the potential for integrating other theories into feminism as a basis for participatory research.

None of the project participants identified themselves as feminists, nor did I ever ask the group members whether or not they considered themselves feminists. However, as noted in a previous chapter, many women were exploring an analysis of male violence congruent with an explicitly feminist analysis.

Explicit Attention to Gender Issues in Each Phase of the Participatory Research Project

One of the strengths of the project was consideration of gender issues in each phase. More attention was given to gender issues regarding women than men. This is primarily a result of an all-women project.

In the first phase (gathering and analyzing information about the project area) attention was given to how problems differed for community men and women, as well as for native and non-native people.... Similarly, area attention to woman-battering has focused more heavily on the problems and resources for abused women rather than problems and resources for male abusers. This is partially a reflection of the "blaming the victim" mentality which considers battering the woman's problem and subtly absolves men of responsibility for their abusive and violent behavior. It also reflects the limitations of the area resources and expertise to provide appropriate and innovative programs for abusers.

In the second and third phases of the project, during which the participants and the researcher attempted to develop increasingly deeper and more critical understanding of participants' problems, more attention could have been given to an analysis of the relationship between patriarchy and former battered women's problems. Attention was given to group members analysis of male violence against women, but this happened primarily during individual interviews and was not adequately dealt with throughout the project.

Although the project did not significantly increase members' understanding of a structural analysis of sexism, classism, or racism, the project did increase women's awareness and understanding of how male domination was manifested in their immediate lives.... In terms of how they benefited from the group or what members viewed as the group's major accomplishments, many women observed that they had gained a greater appreciation of women's strengths and their own ability to live without dependency upon men.

...

Similarly, while members did not gain a sophisticated structural economic analysis, some members began to explore connections between economic factors and their problems as women. For example, in the final interview, one woman noted that she was going to seek counseling at the community mental health center. However, she wanted to find a counselor who understood the economic situation of mothers receiving public assistance....

In the second phase (defining problems and generative themes) I thought that in addition to gender, the connection between race and the problems women experienced upon leaving the shelter should be explored. The majority of support group members were Navajo. My perception of the project area was that racism was connected with many of the problems which the women faced. In an initial attempt to focus on how women's problems were affected by, or differed by, race or culture, I asked numerous questions in the individual interviews. Typically, most of the women, regardless of race or culture, denied any connection between racism or cultural discrimination and their problems or problems experienced by other battered women. Instead, women implied that class rather than race contributed to women's differing experience of post-shelter life....

Several of the Navajo women explored connections between the discrimination and changing roles experienced by Navajo men and women and male violence against Navajo women. One Navajo mother of four children explained:

> The Navajo male has been dominant over women for quite some time.... It's changing, at least within our community. That's the way I see it. Women are the ones who are providing. There's just a number of jobs that are available to men out in the community, not something that is promising for them, just temporary jobs. There is a lot of domestic violence. I think it's frustration. Women that are providing do get battered every now and then. Men are still trying to hold on to that superior role their father held. And the changing role of women, it's like force, women are forced to do it. And men are not taking it well.

Racism and cultural discrimination were not adequately examined within the group.... Women examined racial and cultural differences in safe contexts, for example, in relation to their experience of spirituality and religion. Similarly, we did not explore racism or cultural bias between group members. This is due, in part, to my facilitation choices based on the continued resistance I got to raising issues related to racism or cultural discrimination. The group may not have felt enough trust to discuss these issues. The fact that I am an Anglo may have affected women's willingness to respond to questions and comments exploring racism.

During phases four and five, in which participants created a support group, investigated various individual, collective, and agency problems, and took a variety of small actions, gender issues were central. For example, participants paid close attention to the effect of child care responsibilities on women's ability to participate in the project.... Members were concerned that women's child care responsibilities and the lack of monetary resources for women on public assistance should not become obstacles to anyone's involvement. Meetings were scheduled to accommodate some women's "double day" responsibilities of work both within and outside the home. Social time was built into meetings because isolation was a problem for many women who had no private transportation, spent long hours alone with young children, and had few social activities outside the home.

Some attention was given to members' inexperience and lack of confidence with group discussion. More attention might have been given to the relationship between being battered and lacking confidence in talking in a group....

Consideration could also be given to the relationship between culture and group participation. The two Anglo women appeared more at ease and more skillful at group discussion, even when they were in the minority in the group. Most of the Navajo women stated in the follow-up interviews that they wanted to participate more frequently in discussions and that they benefited from participation. More structured facilitation and periodic reflection on our group process may have encouraged more equal participation.

When asked to contribute to the BFS decision of whether or not to allow male on-call volunteers, gender was the primary issue considered by group members. Women were not against the use of male volunteers in other agency roles, rather, they were against male volunteers conducting intake duties with recently abused women. Their reasons came out of their direct experience as battered women. Interestingly enough, Board members also considered gender in this discussion. However, lacking direct experience as hurt, confused, and scared battered women seeking entrance to a safe and secret shelter, several Board members were more concerned with the issue of sexual discrimination if men were not allowed to be intake volunteers. Thus, how gender is taken into consideration is dependent upon many factors, including direct life experience.

Attention to How Men and Women Benefit from Project

All support group project members were women. In this case, any benefit to men, either to those in relationships with project members, or men in general in the project area, would be secondary and speculative. Several members noted that their growth and development through the project affected their relationships with men....

During the initial interviews, several women noted that there should be more area resources for abusers who are willing to work on changing their violent behavior. Members suggested additional counseling services and a support group for abusers. Nationwide, a growing number of men's counseling programs are reporting success in decreasing and changing men's violent behavior in intimate relationships. All-male abuser groups promote learning nonsexist, nonviolent behaviors and attitudes (Brisson, 1982, Emerge, n.d.; Brygger, Long, and Morse, 1982; SANE news, 1983).

Both the group and myself lacked the resources to tackle programs for abusers. However, one potential long-term outcome of follow-up programs for women who leave the shelter might be the impetus for BFS to team up with other community resources to initiate programs for abusers. Many women do not want to end their relationships, they simply want the violence in the relationship to stop. They might eventually advocate for programs for their abusive partners.

Attention to Gender Language

I have attempted to be specific about gender when writing and speaking. The case study language clearly indicates that this particular participatory research focused on former battered women. In the introduction a rationale was provided for referring, in the context of this project, to batterers or abusers as male and abuse victims as female.

Attention to Composition of the Project Team

… Perhaps my familiarity with area battered women and many project members prior to the interviews was as important as my gender. When project members generated a list of reasons why they were not in favor of male volunteers, many women indicated that they would not be comfortable talking to a man about the abuse they experienced. I did not ask all the women how they might have felt about working with a male researcher….

Overall Project Evaluation Attention to Gender

Gender is a central focus of this evaluation….

Track and Review Project with Gender in Mind

Because the project involved only women, no direct comparison can be made within the project between problems identified by men and women…. [I]n this case, women named problems related to isolation and loneliness, finances, parenting, education, employment, and lack of self-confidence resulting from the battering that they experienced. In particular, women explored these problems in the context of surviving and ending abusive relationships.

   … An overall strength of the project was attention to issues specific to … this group of women. Attention to how issues affected, and were relevant to, project women was a result of the underlying theoretical base of the project, an inclusive feminism which embraced women's diversity.

OBSERVATIONS ON FEMINIST PARTICIPATORY RESEARCH

As it stands, participatory research is built on a critique of positivism which often ignores and, hence repeats, many of the androcentric aspects of dominant social science research. Without recognition of, and attention to, its male biases, participatory research cannot be truly emancipatory for all people. By combining feminist research's critique of androcentrism with participatory research's critique of positivism, a feminist participatory research provides a powerful approach to knowledge creation for social and personal transformation.

   Most participatory research projects begin with the researcher's rather than participants' commitment to an alternative approach to social science research. A secondary goal of participatory research or feminist participatory research may be to increase participants' critical understanding and analysis of social science research…. Even without a detailed analysis of research practices, participants can develop a more critical social analysis. In this case, it was possible to conduct feminist participatory research with participants who were neither explicitly committed to feminism nor to alternative paradigm social science research, and yet, increase their consciousness regarding gender oppression.

… An inclusive feminism acknowledges the diversities and the commonalities of women's experiences. Feminism can offer participatory research a broader, more inclusive analysis of all forms of oppression.

The challenge for feminist participatory research is to simultaneously put gender, class, and race or culture at the center of its issues agenda. It is important to recognize the commonalities and diversities of people's experience when all these factors are kept in focus. For example, attention to cultural appropriateness and sensitivity must be balanced with attention to who speaks for and represents a particular cultural viewpoint. When acting as a spokesperson for a specific culture, what gender and class interests are represented? There is danger in assuming homogeneity in any gender, class, race or cultural grouping.

Feminist participatory research would encourage attention to the differences and similarities of perceptions of issues among women and men. For example, feminist participatory research would pay as much attention to how machismo affects men in a project as to how it affects women.…

Because of limited resources, many participatory research projects will continue to focus more explicitly on one gender than another. Perhaps no single project can successfully juggle simultaneous attention to injustices based on gender, class, race, and culture. Regardless, project evaluations should specify how men and women, whether included or excluded from the project, were affected by the project, even if this requires declaring that one gender did not reap any immediate or direct benefits. Likewise, project evaluations should declare whether or not community men may gain power at the expense of community women. The only way for women to gain more power is to share in the power and privilege that men already enjoy.

… Generic gender language easily obscures who was actually involved in, and benefited by, a project. Challenging androcentric language is critical to challenging androcentric power structures, assumptions, and values because language helps shape our viewpoint.

Although project staffing and case study reports should pay attention to the composition of the research team, this is not to imply that only female staff are best suited to work with women participants or male staff with men. In fact, in most instances, the most effective staff may be the most diverse. Limitations and strengths of a research team based on gender, class, and race should be included in staffing decision making and planning. Of course, other factors, such as areas of expertise and relevant experience, would also be considered in staffing decisions.… Projects should take a close look at the sexual division of labor and power among project staff members. An approach to knowledge creation can hardly be emancipatory if staff experience differing levels of privilege and power based on gender. All participatory researchers may have to assess their willingness to take a public stand against male oppression of women.

The participatory research community should devote extensive and explicit attention to reviewing the collection of past participatory research projects with gender in mind. To date, how has participatory research challenged patriarchy? Since men and women appear to consistently choose different problems and oppressive systems to investigate and act on, what does this mean for participatory research as a tool for radical social and personal transformation? … Explanations such as Reason and Rowan's "We just didn't think about it" (1981) are no longer adequate.

CONCLUSION

… The framework responds to the need to shift participatory research away from its male center to equally include women's perspectives, issues, and insights. In actuality, feminist participatory research increases the emancipatory potential of participatory research for both men and women by constructing a participatory research which challenges all forms of oppression, not merely those experienced among men.

The suggested framework is presented as a place to begin dialogue within both feminist and participatory research communities rather than as a finished product. The framework provides considerations for all participatory researchers to include in planning, conducting, and evaluating a project. Based on the individual and collective experience of more participatory and feminist researchers, of course, the framework should be further examined and modified.

The Former Battered Women's Support Group Project has demonstrated that it is possible to utilize the framework with nonfeminist identified women of different colors, cultures, and classes. Because the framework was utilized in an all-women project, it remains to be determined how the framework might be applied to an all-male project. The framework did help project members and myself explore the oppression women experience as women. It should also help men explore the privilege they enjoy as men and the roles they play in the oppression of women.... [F]eminist participatory research does not put gender, class, color, or culture analysis in competition but rather in cooperation.

... Feminist participatory research challenges participatory researchers to evaluate what personal and public stance we are willing to take on all forms of oppression. Feminist participatory research challenges us to build an approach to knowledge creation which seeks to explore and change all forms of oppression, not only those experienced among men.... This study does not maintain that participatory research, feminist or otherwise, is the only tool for social change, nor that it is the only possible approach to knowledge creation for social justice. Feminist participatory research simply provides one more tool in the long struggle for social and personal transformation.

RECOMMENDATIONS

To further develop feminist participatory research, several recommendations are offered.

1. *Participatory researchers must further familiarize and educate ourselves about feminist theories and practices.* Participatory researchers, both male and female, must critically examine our own position on male domination and women's oppression. It is important to initiate greater dialogue regarding the tensions between cultural traditions of gender oppression and women's liberation, particularly when cultural traditions are evoked to defend injustice and degradation based on gender. Across cultures we must consider who is defining what is culturally relevant and appropriate. Do women have an equal voice in this? Are there instances in which participatory researchers are willing to defend or ignore gender oppression because of cultural traditions?

I maintain that feminist participatory research can be respectfully conducted across cultures when local women have an equitable voice and power in participatory research projects. To further develop feminist participatory research in a variety of cultural settings project staff should give serious attention to the considerations outlined in the feminist participatory research framework. In particular, this requires listening to how women in a specific setting define their unique problems, needs, and strengths. It requires listening to local women's own brand of feminism.

2. *Participatory researchers must expand the circle of colleagues with whom we share and debate our research theories and practices.* This will require participatory researchers to aggressively seek out opportunities to attend a broader variety of community-based and professional conferences and to present papers at them, as well as conduct workshops and facilitate discussions. In particular, participatory researchers will have to increase dialogue and exchange with the feminist research community and the more grassroots feminist activist community. My reading of both feminist and participatory research literature indicates that there has been little formal exchange. Both groups are still largely uninformed about the other's work. Perhaps a series of

regional conferences sponsored and initiated by the various worldwide participatory research networks would be a bold step toward instituting dialogue on what feminist and participatory researchers can learn together.

3. *Participatory researchers must challenge each other to give serious attention to the feminist participatory research framework in project publications and case study reports.* Editors of participatory research publications can have important impact by requiring articles to address the questions raised in the framework. Similarly, participatory researchers should initiate dialogue to continue to modify and apply the framework. Initially, even if actual projects do not change in any significant way, at least the information available on projects will change....

4. *Participatory research project team members must challenge each other to include the feminist participatory research framework in project planning, implementation, and evaluation.* In particular, we need experience utilizing the framework in all-men projects. I maintain that men, both as researchers and as participants, can conduct feminist participatory research. However, the premise requires testing through actual field projects.

Participatory research emerged in part from people like ourselves struggling with the contradictions of our work, including our research practices and our politics. What are the implications of our work for the redistribution or consolidation of power? Whose problems do we try to solve through our work? Which systems of oppression do we openly seek to transform? Feminist participatory research expands our challenge to create a world in which women have a central role and voice in determining what that transformed world will include. Feminist participatory research challenges us to refuse to allow participatory research to become yet another male monopoly.

REFERENCES

Adams, Frank, with Myles Horton. 1975. *Unearthing Seeds of Fire: The Idea of Highlander.* Winston Salem, NJ: John F. Blair.

Brisson, Norman. 1982. "Helping Men Who Batter Women." *Public Welfare* (Spring): 29–34.

Brown, David L., and Rajesh Tandon. 1983. "Ideology and Political Economy of Inquiry: Action Research and Participatory Research." *Journal of Applied Behavioral Science* 19: 227–294.

Brydon-Miller, Mary L. 1984. Accessibility Self-Advocacy at an Independent Living Center: A Participatory Research Approach. Unpublished Ph.D. diss., University of Massachusetts at Amherst.

Brygger, Mary Pat, Don Long, and Joseph Morse. 1982. "Working with Men Who Batter: A Discussion Paper." Presented in Southern California Coalition of Battered Women/National Coalition Against Domestic Violence meeting materials.

Colletta, Nat. 1982. "Participatory Research or Pretense?" In B. Hall, A. Gillette, and R. Tandon, eds., *Creating Knowledge: A Monopoly?* pp. 87–100. New Delhi: Society for Participatory Research in Asia.

Elden, Max. 1981. "Sharing the Research Work: Participative Research and Its Role Demands." In P. Reason and R. Rowan, eds., *Human Inquiry: A Sourcebook of New Paradigm Research,* pp. 253–266. New York: John Wiley and Sons.

Ellis, Patricia. 1983. *Participatory Research: An Integral Art of the Developmental Process.* St. Michael, Barbados: WAND Unit.

Emerge. n.d. "Getting Rid of the Excuses Men Use for Abusing Women." Boston, MA: Emerge.

Fernandes, W., and Rajesh Tandon, eds. 1981. *Participatory Research and Evaluation: Experiments in Research as a Process of Liberation.* New Delhi: Indian Social Institute.

Fordham, Paul, Geoff Poulton, and Lawrence Randle. 1982. "Research in the New Communities Project." In B. Hall, A. Gillette, and R. Tandon, eds., *Creating Knowledge: A Monopoly?* pp. 127–152. New Delhi: Society for Participatory Research in Asia.

Freire, Paulo. 1970. *Pedagogy of the Oppressed.* New York: Seabury Press.

———. 1981. *Education for Critical Consciousness.* New York: Continuum.

Gayfer, Margaret. 1980. "Women Speaking and Learning for Ourselves." *Convergence:* 1–13.

Hall, Bud. 1975. "Participatory Research: An Approach for Change." *Convergence:* 24–32.

———. 1979. "Participatory Research: Breaking the Academic Monopoly." In J. Niemi, ed., *Viewpoints on Adult Education,* pp. 43–69. Northern Illinois University Press.

———. 1981. "Participatory Research, Popular Knowledge, and Power: A Personal Reflection." *Convergence* 3: 6–19.

Heatley, Rachel. 1979. *Poverty and Power.* London: Zed Books.

Horton, Billy. 1981. "On the Potential of Participatory Research: An Evaluation of a Regional Experiment." Paper presented at the annual meeting of the Society for the Study of Social Problems, August, Toronto, Ontario.

Kanhari, Vijay. 1982. "India: Tribal Women Organize." In *Participatory Research: An Introduction,* pp. 35–36. New Delhi: Society for Participatory Research in Asia.

Kindervatter, Suzanne. 1979. *Nonformal Education as an Empowering Process.* Amherst: University of Massachusetts Center for International Education.

Korten, David. 1980. "Community Organization and Rural Development: A Learning Approach." *Public Administration Review* 40, no. 5 (September–October): 1–32.

Le Boterf, Guy. 1983. "Reformulating Participatory Research." *Assignment Children* 63: 167–192.

Lukacs, George. 1971. *History and Class Consciousness.* Cambridge: Massachusetts Institute of Technology Press.

Marshall, J. P. 1981. "Participatory Research: A Model for Initiating Problem-Solving Education in the Community." Paper presented at the annual meeting of the American Sociological Association for the Study of Social Problems, August, Toronto, Ontario.

Mduma, E. K. 1982. "Appropriate Technology for Grain Storage at Bwakira Chini Village." In Y. Kassam and K. Mustafa, eds., *Participatory Research: An Emerging Alternative Methodology in Social Science Research,* pp. 198–213. New Delhi: Society for Participatory Research in Asia.

Mustafa, Kemal. 1982. "Tanzania: Jipemoyo Project—Role of Culture in Development." In *Participatory Research: An Introduction,* pp. 30–33. New Delhi: Society for Participatory Research in Asia.

Nyerere, Julius. 1969. "Education for Self-Reliance." *Convergence* 3, no. 1: 3–7.

Park, Peter. 1978a. "Social Research and Radical Change." Paper presented at the 9th World Congress of Sociology, August, Uppsala, Sweden.

———. 1978b. *Principles for Conducting Community-Based Research.* Amherst: University of Massachusetts Department of Sociology.

Participatory Research Network. 1982. *Participatory Research: An Introduction.* PRN Series no. 3. New Delhi: Society for Participatory Research in Asia.

Reason, Peter, and John Rowan, eds. 1981. *Human Inquiry: A Sourcebook of New Paradigm Research.* New York: John Wiley and Sons.

SANE News. 1982. "Profile of a Program for Batterers: Batterers Anonymous." *SANE News* 2, no. 4: 6–7.

Shor, Ira. 1980. *Critical Teaching and Everyday Life.* Boston: South End Press.

Tandon, Rajesh. 1981b. "Participatory Research in the Empowerment of People." *Convergence* 14, no. 3: 20–27.

Uphoff, Norman, J. Cohen, and A. Goldsmith. 1979. *Feasibility and Application of Rural Development Participation: A State of the Art Paper.* Ithaca, NY: Cornell University Rural Development Committee.

Vio Grossi, Francisco. 1981. "Sociopolitical Implications of Participatory Research." *Convergence* 3: 43–51.

Vio Grossi, Francisco, Sergio Martinic, Gonzalo Tapia, and Ines Pascal. 1983. *Participatory Research: Theoretical Frameworks, Methods, and Techniques.* International Council for Adult Education.

Wren, Brian. 1977. *Education for Justice.* New York: Orbis.

Yanz, Linda. 1986. *ICAE Women's Program Newsletter* (February–March). Presented at the International Council for Adult Education Assembly, Buenos Aires, Argentina.

Vandana Shiva

Democratizing Biology: Reinventing Biology from a Feminist, Ecological, and Third World Perspective

WHY BIOLOGY NEEDS TO BE DEMOCRATIZED

The dominant paradigm of biology is in urgent need of reinvention and democratization because it is inherently undemocratic. There are three aspects to this. In the first place, it is socially undemocratic. The dominant paradigm casts patterns of human social behavior as biologically determined, thus ignoring the ways in which they are in reality outcomes of social prejudice and bias on the basis of race, class, and gender. Notions that human behavior is the product of biological determinism make such prejudice immune to democratic questioning and transformation, thus perpetuating social and economic inequalities.

Second, biology is the basis of all food production systems that are intimately linked to survival and to women's work and knowledge in the Third World. All of these are threatened by reductionist biology, particularly in the form of genetic engineering. The reinvention of biology is therefore also an economic imperative so that alternative production systems which are more socially just and ecologically sustainable have a chance to flourish.

Third, the dominant approach to studying biology is undemocratic with respect to non-human species. It is based on the metaphor of "man's empire over inferior creatures" rather than the metaphor of "the democracy of all life." It therefore contributes to a "war against species," manipulating them without limits if they are economically useful and pushing them to extinction if they are not. It also erodes biodiversity, leaving us materially impoverished. Last but not least, intellectual property rights in the area of life forms that are constructed on the basis of a reductionist biology deepen the exclusion of other knowledge systems.

The democratization of biology requires that culturally and socially determined behaviors and characteristics are removed from the domain of biological determinism. This in turn makes it an imperative that excluded groups such as women and Third World communities have a role in reinventing biology on democratic principles. Democratizing biology from the perspective of the democracy of all life requires that we reinvent biology to account better for the intrinsic worth and self-organizing capacities of all living organisms.

The democratization of biology involves the recovery of pluralism of knowledge traditions, both within the modern Western traditions and within ancient time-tested, non-Western traditions of agriculture and health care. Democratizing biology requires that the latest application of biology, genetic engineering, be evaluated in the context of alternatives; it also needs to be evaluated in the context of empirical evidence that is undermining the basic tenets of genetic determinism and the assumption of immutable, unchanging genes. Democratizing biology, in addition, involves coherence and honesty both in the "owning" of benefits and the "owning" of risks of genetic engineering. There is therefore a need to have a coherent theory of "novelty" in the areas of intellectual property rights (which deal with ownership of benefits) and biosafety (which deal with the "owning" of risks and hazards).

...

THE UNDEMOCRATIC PARADIGM OF BIOLOGICAL DETERMINISM

The dominant paradigm of biology has been an imperialist one. Biological difference between human and nonhuman species, between white and colored peoples, and between men and women has been seen as reason and justification for the rule of the white man over nature, women, and all nonwhite races. Not only is the dominant biology based on these three exclusions, the exclusions themselves are interwoven and interlinked. And the exclusions are shaped by and in turn shape the mode of knowing and thinking about the world. It is these multiple and complex relationships between science, gender, and ecological survival that I want to explore.

Feminist critiques of dominant science emerged from analysis by feminist scientists, who showed how biology as a science was constructed on the basis of the gender biases of patriarchy, and these biased social constructions were then used to justify women's continued oppression.[1]

Central to the patriarchal construction of biology was the association of activity and creativity with the male and passivity with the female. Furthermore, this construction was based on an artificial mind-body dichotomy, a dichotomy which was also seen as gendered. These distortions have led to the equation of "biology" with lack of mind and intelligence, and intelligence as something outside biological organisms. The world was thus split into "thinking humans" and "vegetating other species." The relationship of domination of humans over other species and of white men over other humans is based on and justified through the myth of the disembodied mind.

The Enlightenment was also a period in which human beings became seen as separate from other species. The ecological separation from the earth body went hand-in-hand with the epistemological separation from the human body. The human body was treated as "nature"; the disembodied mind alone was a truly human faculty....

This is in total contrast to other cultures of knowledge which do not split the mind from the body. The Western patriarchal conceptualization of biology was based on robbing intelligence from organisms if they were female or nonhuman. Intelligence and "higher" faculties, for the production of "culture" and "science," were kept as a monopoly of men, particularly European men. By being robbed of their intelligence and minds, women, like Third World peoples, have been treated as not fully human. They have in fact been seen as closer to nature while godlike men have the exclusive capacity for creation of culture.

The treatment of other species mirrors the treatment meted out to the "others" of the human species.... Out of these multiple exclusions mutually exclusive dualities are carved:

> Nature is opposed to culture
> Human is opposed to nature
> Human is opposed to animal
> Man is opposed to woman
> Mind is opposed to body
> Science is opposed to superstitions.

In most non-Western cultures, all species have been seen as part of an earth family. We have called it Vasudhaiva Kutumbkam in India. For native Americans, "kinship with all creatures of the earth, sky, and water was a real and active principle."[3] ... These non-Western perceptions have been viewed as a block in establishing "man's empire" over other species in the interactions of European men with other cultures in the process of colonization.

...

Modern Western science and technology have in fact been the continuation, not a break, with the Judeo-Christian myth of creation, according to which all species were made for man's use. The worldview within which Western science is practiced is based on imperialism, not democracy....

In Genesis, Eve (woman) created sin by forcing Adam (man) to eat the forbidden fruit. This story of "original sin" still underlies the dominant paradigm of biology. It is, for example, the metaphor in such popularizations of modern biology as Matt Ridley's *Red Queen*[7] and Richard Dawkins's *Selfish Gene*[8] and *The Blind Watchmaker.*[9]

The exclusion of all women and of men from non-Western cultures from the category "human" continues as biological determinism is articulated at newer and deeper levels. Non-Western men and all women are the "others" among the human species who have been excluded from the human family, just as the nonhuman species have been excluded from the earth family. . . .

Furthermore, the assumption of superiority of white men over other humans and other species has justified violence to and extinction of nonhuman species and non-Western cultures. Violence in human society has often been justified on the grounds that some humans are closer to "nature" and other species, and hence not fully human.

BIOLOGY AND THE THIRD WORLD

The Western worldview has sanctified European man as being made in the image and likeness of God. The Christian theology of man as the master of all species justified the domination over, and even the decimation of, all life that happened to be nonwhite and nonmale. St. Augustine said that "man but *not* woman was made in the image and likeness of God." And all non-Europeans were, of course, not in God's likeness because they were colored and in every way so different from the colonizers. . . .

Whenever Europeans "discovered" the native people of America, Africa, or Asia, they projected upon them the identity of savages who needed redemption by a superior race. Even slavery was justified on these cosmological grounds. It was considered wise that Africans should be carried into slavery, since they were carried, at the same time, out of an "endless night of savage barbarism" into the embrace of a "superior civilization."[11] All brutality was moralized on the basis of this assumed superiority and the exclusive status of European men as fully human.

The decimation of original peoples everywhere was justified morally on the grounds that indigenous people were not really human. They were part of the fauna. . . . Being animals, the original Australians and Americans, the Africans and Asians, possessed no rights as humans. They could therefore be ignored as people and exterminated. . . . European men were thus able to see their invasions as "discovery," piracy and theft as "trade," and extermination and enslavement as their "civilizing mission."

Since Columbus arrived in North America, the indigenous populations continue to be decimated, largely on the grounds of their not being treated as fully human. . . . The original inhabitants, who had populated the land for thousands of years, were decimated after the arrival of Europeans in America. From a total population of 72 million in 1492, their population declined to about 4 million in a few centuries. Their land was conquered and colonized, their resources raped and destroyed. The worldview of man's empire over lesser creatures rendered each act of invasion into other people's land as "discovery": in America in 1492, in Australia in 1788, in Africa and Asia through the past 500 years of colonization.

. . . In Africa, an official of the Belgian Commission, reporting in 1919, reached the conclusion that the population of the Belgian Congo has been reduced by half since the beginning of the European occupation in the 1880s.

In Africa, depopulation was an obvious effect of the slave trade, which involved the deportation and death of several tens of millions of Africans over three or four centuries. The rate of mortality among slaves taken from Africa to the Americas was so high that whole "slave populations" had to be replaced every few years. The long-sustained destruction of African people is set forth in the German imperial records. "I know these African tribes," wrote Von Trotha, the general entrusted with the task of putting down the Herero and Nama in South

Africa.... "They respect nothing but force. To exercise this force with brute terror and even with ferocity was and is my policy.... Only by sowing in this way can anything new be grown, anything that is stable."[14]

In 1904 it was estimated that there were 80,000 Herero and 20,000 Nama. In 1911, the estimates showed 15,130 Herero and 9,871 Nama remaining alive. Nearly 75,000 of them had paid the price for a "new" order based on the domination of the Europeans, who regarded themselves as naturally superior to the Africans and could use the most brutal forms of oppression and exploitation for their civilizing mission.

Western science continues to turn non-Western peoples into less than human objects of scientific inquiry. For example, U.S. scientists have started a Human Genome Diversity Project to collect human DNA samples from indigenous communities around the world. The economic opportunity to collect and the push to preserve human genetic diversity has been fired by the development of new biotechnologies and the formation of the Human Genome Organization (abbreviated HUGO). Medical science has long been aware that there is not just one human genetic map. Each ethnic community may have a slightly different genetic composition. Some of the differences and mutations could someday prove to be invaluable to medicine.

Officials of the Human Genome Diversity Project estimate that an initial five-year sweep of relatively accessible populations will cost $35 million and will allow sampling from 10,000 to 15,000 human specimens. At an average total cost of $2,300 per sample, the project will spend more money gathering the blood of indigenous peoples than the per capita GNP of any of the world's poorest 110 countries.

...

In the draft report of the Human Genome Diversity Project, preservation is the dominant theme, and there is an assumption that many or most of the human populations are inevitably going to disappear. The project's emphasis on preservation and its insensitivity to indigenous peoples is best exhibited by the term used to describe indigenous communities that have been targeted for human DNA sampling: "isolates of historic interest" (IHIs).

Sometimes the interest is more than historical. It is also directly economic, as illustrated in the case of the patent claim WO 9208784 A1 lodged by the U.S. secretary of commerce for the human T-lymphotropic virus type 2, drawn from the "immortalized" DNA of a twenty-six-year-old Guami Indian woman from Panama. The original blood sample is cryogenically preserved at the American Type Culture Collection in Rockville, Maryland. Under citizen pressure, the secretary of commerce was forced to withdraw the patent claim. However, no ethical or legal framework exists to prevent such patenting in the future. Meanwhile, similar patents have been claimed for indigenous communities from Papua New Guinea and the Solomon Islands.

The use of other peoples as raw material is one of the aspects of an imperialistic science of biology. Other aspects include the targeting of Third World women for population control and the treatment of Third World biodiversity and Third World biological knowledge as raw material for the economic empires of northern corporations in the age of biology....

WOMEN'S INDIGENOUS KNOWLEDGE AND THE CONSERVATION OF BIODIVERSITY

The links between gender and diversity are many. The construction of women as the "second sex" is linked to the same inability to cope with difference as the development paradigm that leads to the displacement and extinction of diversity in the biological world. In the patriarchal worldview, man is the measure of all value and there is no room for diversity—only hierarchy. Woman, being different, is treated as unequal and inferior. Nature's diversity ... gets value only through economic exploitation for commercial gain. Within a commercial value framework, diversity thus is seen as a problem, a deficiency. Destruction of diversity and the creation of monocultures becomes an imperative for capitalist patriarchy.

The marginalization of women and the destruction of biodiversity go hand-in-hand. Diversity is the price paid in the patriarchal model of progress which pushes inexorably toward monocultures, uniformity, and homogeneity. In the perverted logic of progress, even conservation suffers. Agricultural "development" continues to work toward the erasure of diversity, while the same global interests that destroy biodiversity urge the Third World to conserve it. This separation of production and consumption, with "production" being based on uniformity and "conservation" desperately attempting to preserve diversity, guarantees that biodiversity will not be protected. It can only be protected by making diversity the basis, the foundation, the logic, of the technology and economics of production.

The logic of diversity is best derived from biodiversity and from women's links to it. It helps look at dominant structures from below, from the ground of diversity. From this ground, monocultures are not productive, they are unproductive; and the knowledge that produces monocultures is not sophisticated, it is primitive.

Diversity is, in many ways, the basis of women's politics and the politics of ecology. Gender politics is, to a large extent, a politics of difference. Ecopolitics, too, arises from the fact that nature is varied and different, while industrial commodities and processes are uniform and homogeneous.

The two politics of diversity converge in a significant way when women and biodiversity meet in fields and forests, in arid regions and wetlands. Diversity is the principle of women's work and knowledge. It is the reason that women's knowledge and work have been discounted in the patriarchal calculus. Yet it is also the matrix from which an alternative calculus of "productivity" and "skills" can be built, one that respects diversity instead of destroying it.

In Third World economies, many communities depend on biological resources for their sustenance and well-being. In these societies, biodiversity is simultaneously a means of production and an object of consumption. It is the survival base that has to be conserved. Sustainability of livelihoods is ultimately connected to the conservation and sustainable use of biological resources in all their diversity.

However, biodiversity-based technologies of tribal and peasant societies have been viewed as backward and primitive, and have been displaced by technologies which use biological resources in such a way that they destroy diversity and people's livelihoods. There is a general misconception that diversity-based production systems are low-productivity systems. However, the high productivity of uniform and homogeneous systems is a contextual and theoretically constructed category, based on taking only one-dimensional yield and output into account … [and is] therefore not based on a neutral, scientific measure, but [is] biased toward the commercial interests for whom maximizing of one-dimensional output is an economic imperative.

This push toward uniformity, however, undermines the diversity of biological systems which form the production system. It also undermines the livelihoods of the people whose work is associated with diverse and multiple-use systems of forestry, agriculture, and animal husbandry.

As an example, in the state of Kerala, which derives its name from the coconut palm, coconut is cultivated in a multistoried, high-intensity cropping system along with betel and pepper vines, bananas, tapioca, drukstick, papaya, jackfruit, mango, and vegetables. Compared to an annual labor requirement of 157 person-days per year in a monoculture of coconut palm, the mixed cropping system increases employment to 960 person-days per year. In the dryland farming systems of the Deccan, the shift from mixed cropping of millets with pulses and oilseeds to eucalyptus monocultures has led to a loss of employment of 250 person-days per year.

When labor is scarce and costly, labor-displacing technologies are productive and efficient. When labor is abundant, labor displacement is unproductive because it leads to poverty, dispossession, and destruction of livelihoods. In Third World situations, sustainability has therefore to be achieved at two levels simultaneously—natural resources and livelihoods. Biodiversity conservation has to be linked to the conservation of livelihoods derived from biodiversity.

In India, agriculture employs 70 percent of the working population and about 84 percent of all economically active women.[15] ... According to Vir Singh's assessment, in the Indian Himalaya a pair of bullocks work for 1,064 hours, a man for 1,212 hours, and a woman for 3,418 hours a year on a one-hectare farm. Thus a woman works longer than men and farm animals combined![17]

... Joan Mencher's studies in the Palghat region of Kerala reveal that apart from ploughing, which is exclusively men's work, women have a predominant role in all other processes. On the basis of this study, it is estimated that more than two-thirds of the labor input is female.[19] ... A detailed study by Jain and Chand in three villages each in Rajasthan and West Bengal, covering 127 households over twelve months, highlights the fact that women in the age group nineteen to seventy spend longer hours than do men in a variety of activities.[21]

Women's work and livelihoods in subsistence agriculture are based on multiple use and management of biomass for fodder, fertilizer, food, and fuel. The collection of fodder from the forest is part of the process of transferring fertility for crop production and managing soil and water stability. The work of the women engaged in such activity tends to be discounted and made invisible for all sectors.[22] When these allied activities which are ecologically and economically critical are taken into account, agriculture is revealed as the major occupation of "working" women in rural India. The majority of women in India are not simply "housewives" but farmers.[23]

Women's work and knowledge is central to biodiversity conservation and utilization because women work between "sectors" and perform multiple tasks. Women have remained invisible as farmers in spite of their contribution to farming, as people fail to see their work in agriculture. Their production tends not to be recorded by economists as "work" or as "production" because it falls outside the so-called production boundary. These problems of data collection on agricultural work arise not because too few women work but because too many women have to do too much work. There is a conceptual inability of statisticians and researchers to define women's work inside and outside the house (and farming is usually part of both). This recognition of what is and is not labor is exacerbated by the great volume of work that women do. It is also related to the fact that although women work to sustain their families and communities, most of their work is not measured in wages.

Women's work is also invisible because women are concentrated outside market-related or remunerated work and are normally engaged in multiple tasks. Time allocation studies, which do not depend on an a priori definition of work, reflect more closely the multiplicity of tasks undertaken and the seasonal, even daily, movement in and out of the conventional labor force which characterizes the livelihood strategy for most rural women. Studies with a gender perspective which are now being published prove that women in India are major producers of food in terms of value, volume, and hours worked.

In the production and preparation of plant foods, women need skills and knowledge. To prepare seeds they need to know about germination requirements, seed preparation, and soil choice. Seed preparation requires visual discrimination, fine motor coordination, and sensitivity to humidity levels and weather conditions. To sow and strike seeds one needs to know about seasons, climate, plant requirements, weather conditions, microclimatic factors, soil enrichment; sowing seeds requires physical dexterity and strength. To care for plants properly, one needs information about the nature of plant diseases, pruning, staking, water supplies, companion planting, predators, sequences, growing seasons, and soil maintenance. Plant propagation also requires persistence and patience, physical strength, and attention to plant needs. Harvesting a crop requires judgments in relation to weather, labor, and grading, and knowledge about preserving, immediate use, and propagation.

Women's knowledge has been the mainstay of the indigenous dairy industry. Dairying, as managed by women in rural India, embodies practices and logic rather different from those contained in the dairy science imparted at institutions of formal education in India, since the latter is essentially an import from Europe and North America. Women have been experts in the breeding and feeding of farm animals, which include not just cows and buffaloes but also pigs, chickens, ducks, and goats.

In forestry, too, women's knowledge is crucial to the use of biomass for feed and fertilizer. Knowledge of the feed value of different fodder species, of the fuel value of firewood types, food products, and species is essential to agriculture-related forestry in which women are predominantly active. In low-input agriculture, fertility is transferred from the forest and farm trees to the field by women's work, either directly or via animals.

It is in the "in-between" spaces ... that women's work and knowledge in agriculture are uniquely found, and it is through these linkages that ecological stability and sustainability and productivity under resource-scarce conditions are maintained. The invisibility of women's work and knowledge arises from the gender bias which has a blind spot for realistic assessment of women's contributions. It is also rooted in the sectoral, fragmented, and reductionist approach to development, which treats forests, livestock, and crops as independent of each other.

The focus of the "green revolution" has been to increase grain yields of rice and wheat by techniques such as dwarfing, monocultures, and multicropping. For an Indian woman farmer, rice is not only food, it is also a source of fodder for cattle and straw for thatch. High-yield varieties (HYVs) can increase women's work. The destruction of biological diversity undermines women's diverse contributions to agriculture by eroding biological sources of food, fodder, fertilizer, fuel, and fiber. The shift from local varieties and local indigenous crop improvement strategies can also take away women's control over seeds and genetic resources. Women have been the seed custodians since time immemorial, and it is their knowledge and skills which should be the basis of all crop improvement strategies.

Women have been the custodians of biodiversity in most cultures. They have been selectors and preservers of seed. However, like all other aspects of women's work and knowledge, their role in development and conservation of biodiversity has been represented as nonwork and nonknowledge. Their labor and expertise has been defined into nature, even though it is based on sophisticated cultural and scientific practices.... Women's role in the conservation of biodiversity, however, differs from the dominant patriarchal notions of biodiversity conservation in a number of ways.

The recent concern with biodiversity at the global level has grown as a result of the erosion of diversity due to the expansion of large-scale monoculture-based production in agriculture and the vulnerability associated with it. However, the fragmentation of farming systems which was linked to the spread of monocultures continues to be the guiding paradigm for biodiversity conservation. Each element of the farm ecosystem is viewed in isolation, and conservation of diversity is seen as an arithmetic exercise of collecting variety.

In contrast, biodiversity in the traditional Indian setting is a relational category in which each element gets its characteristics and value through its relationships with other elements. Biodiversity is ecologically and culturally embedded. Diversity is reproduced and conserved through the reproduction and conservation of culture in festivals and rituals. Besides being a celebration of the renewal of life, these festivals are the platform for carrying out subtle tests for seed selection and propagation. These tests are not treated as scientific by the dominant worldview because they are not embedded in the culture of the lab and the experimental plot; *they* are carried out not by men in lab coats but by village women....

Women have been the selectors and custodians of seed. When they conserve seed, they conserve diversity; and when they conserve diversity, they conserve a balance and harmony. *Navdanya*, or nine seeds, are the symbol of this renewal of diversity and balance, not just of the plant world but also of the social world. It is this complex, relational web which gives meaning to biodiversity in Indian culture and has been the basis of the conservation of that diversity over millennia.

Women's work in organic agriculture also supports the work of decomposers and soil builders which inhabit the soil. It is based on partnership with other species.... Soils treated with farmyard manure have from two to two-and-a-half times as many earthworms as untreated soils. Farmyard manure encourages the buildup of earthworms through increasing their food supply, whether they feed directly on it or on the microorganisms it supports. Earthworms contribute to soil fertility by maintaining soil structure, aeration, and drainage and by breaking down organic matter and incorporating it into the soil....

The little earthworm working invisibly in the soil is actually the tractor and fertilizer factory and dam combined.... Yet the earthworm was never seen as a worker in "scientific" agriculture.[25] The woman peasant who works invisibly with the earthworm in building soil fertility has also not been seen as doing "productive" work or providing an "input" to the food economy. We need to look beyond the mentality that tells us that fertility is "bought" from fertilizer companies; we need to look beyond the fertilizer factory for maintaining soil fertility; and we need to recover the work of women and peasants who work with nature, not against it. In regions of India which have not yet been colonized by the green revolution, women peasants continue to work as soil builders rather than soil predators, and it is from these remaining pockets of natural farming that the ecological struggles to protect nature are emerging.

However, these sophisticated systems of agriculture which used biological diversity to provide internal inputs for pest control, fertility renewal, and soil and water conservation were displaced by the chemical-industrial model from the West, financed by aid and pushed by planning from international agencies like the World Bank under the label of the green revolution.

At the technological level, the instrumental and functionalist approach to nonhuman species tends to lead to the extinction of those species which capitalist patriarchy does not value. Distortion and mutilation in the name of "improvement" is likely to be the fate of those species that are found useful. In either case, entire communities of species become victims of imperialism. In this way, the so-called green revolution led to the displacement of thousands of varieties of crops and seeds. Wheat, maize, and rice were treated as the only crops of "value." To increase their commodity value, these crops were engineered to become dwarf varieties so that they could take up more chemical fertilizers. The engineered crops were vulnerable to pests and disease, so they needed more pesticides and fungicides.

... Biotechnology can be expected to increase the reliance of farmers on purchased inputs even as it accelerates the process of polarization. It will even increase the use of chemicals instead of decreasing it. The dominant focus of research in genetic engineering is not on fertilizer-free and pest-free crops but on pesticide- and herbicide-resistant varieties. For the seed and chemical multinational companies, this might make commercial sense, since it is cheaper to adapt the plant to the chemical than to adapt the chemical to the plant....

Like green revolution technologies, biotechnology in agriculture can become an instrument for dispossessing the farmer of seed as a means of production. The relocation of seed production from the farm to the corporate laboratory relocates power and value between the North and South and between corporations and farmers. It is estimated that the elimination of homegrown seed would dramatically increase the farmers' dependence on biotechnology industries by about $6 billion annually.[27]

... "Improvement" of a selected characteristic in a plant also constitutes a selection against other characteristics which are useful to nature, or for local consumption. "Improvement" **is** not a class- or gender-neutral concept. Improvement of partitioning efficiency is based on the enhancement of the yield of the desired product at the expense of unwanted plant parts. The desired product is, however, not the same for rich people and poor people, or rich countries and poor countries; nor is efficiency. On the input side, richer people and richer countries are short of labor, and poorer people and poorer countries are short of capital and land. Most agricultural development, however, increases capital input while displacing labor, thus destroying livelihoods. On the output side, which parts of a farming system or a plant will be treated as "unwanted" depends on what class and gender one is. What is unwanted for the better off may be the wanted part for the poor. The plants or plant parts which serve the poor are usually the ones whose supply is squeezed by the normal priorities of improvement in response to commercial forces.

The destruction of people's livelihood and sustenance goes hand-in-hand with the erosion of biological resources and their capacity to fulfill diverse human needs while regenerating and renewing themselves.... Both people and nature are impoverished; their needs are no longer met by the one-dimensional production systems which replace biologically rich and diverse ecosystems and put added burdens on remaining pockets of biodiversity that could satisfy these needs.... Protection of biodiversity can only be ensured by regenerating diversity as a basis of production in agriculture, forestry, and animal husbandry....

There are two conflicting paradigms on biodiversity, and from them emerge different paradigms of biology. The first paradigm is held by communities whose survival and sustenance is linked to local biodiversity utilization and conservation. The second is held by commercial interests whose profits are linked to utilization of global biodiversity for production of inputs into large-scale homogeneous, uniform, centralized, and global production systems. For local indigenous communities, conserving biodiversity means to conserve the integrity of ecosystems and species, the rights to their resources and knowledge, and their production systems based on biodiversity. For commercial interests, ... biodiversity in itself has no value. It is merely "raw material" to provide "components" for the genetic engineering industry. This leads to a reductionist paradigm of biology and production based on biodiversity destruction, since local production systems based on diversity are displaced by production based on uniformity. The reductionist paradigm of biology leads to the paradigm of genetic engineering for production and reproduction. It is also closely associated with the treatment of living organisms as manufactured commodities, as "products of the mind," needing "intellectual property protection."

INTELLECTUAL PROPERTY RIGHTS AND INTELLECTUAL IMPERIALISM

Even as feminists, environmentalists, and Third World scientists reshape our ideas of knowledge, the Cartesian and Baconian project of the disembodied mind as the model knower and control and domination as the goal of knowledge continues. Intellectual property rights (IPR) as related to biological organisms are the ultimate expressions of the Cartesian mind-body split and of knowledge as invasion to establish "man's empire over lesser creatures." In intellectual property rights, the legacies of Descartes, Locke, and Hobbes meet to create an antinature view of "creation." *Creation* here does not refer to the rich diversity of life but to the products of "godlike" acts of one group of humans. And through this distorted definition of creation, this group claims ownership of life in all its diversity.

The freedom that transnational corporations are claiming through intellectual property rights protection in the GATT agreement is the freedom that European colonizers have claimed since 1492, when Columbus set the precedent of treating the license to conquer non-European peoples as a natural right of European men.... The colonizers' freedom was built on the enslavement and subjugation of the people with original rights to the land. This violent takeover was rendered "natural" by defining the colonized people into nature, thus denying them their humanity and freedom.

Locke's treatise on property[29] effectively legitimized this same process of theft and robbery during the enclosure movement in Europe. Locke clearly articulates capitalism's freedom to build on the freedom to steal; he states that property is created by removing resources from nature through mixing them with labor. But this labor is not physical labor, but labor in its "spiritual" form as manifested in the control of capital. According to Locke, only capital can add value to appropriated nature, and hence only those who own capital have the natural right to own natural resources, a right that supersedes the common rights of others with prior claims. Capital is thus defined as a source of freedom, but this freedom is based on the denial of freedom to the land, forests, rivers, and biodiversity that capital claims as its own. Because property obtained through privatization of commons is equated with freedom, those commoners laying claim to it are perceived to be depriving the owner of the capital of freedom.

Thus peasants and tribals who demand the return of their rights and access to resources are regarded as thieves.

Within the ambit of IPRs, the Lockean concept of property merges with the Cartesian concept of knowledge to give shape to a perverted world which appears "natural" in the eyes of capitalist patriarchy. During the scientific revolution, Descartes fashioned a new intellectual world order in which mind and body were deemed to be totally separate, and only the male European mind was considered capable of complete intellectual transcendence of the body.... The application of IPRs to agriculture is the ultimate denial of the intellectual creativity and contribution of Third World peasants, women and men who have saved and used seed over millennia.

The implication of a worldview that assumes the possession of an intellect to be limited to only one class of human beings is that they are entitled to claim all products of intellectual labor as their private property, even when they have appropriated it from others—the Third World. Intellectual property rights and patents on life are the ultimate expression of capitalist patriarchy's impulse to control all that is living and free.

Corporations have patented naturally occurring microorganisms. Merck has a patent on soil samples from Mount Kilimanjaro in Kenya for production of an antihypertensive and a patent for soil from Mexico for production of testosterone.... Corporations have patented the biopesticide and medicinal products from neem *(Azadirichta indica),* though Indian women in every village and every household have been processing and using neem products for crop and grain protection and as medicine for centuries.[31]

In cases where patent claims are not based on natural products or prior knowledge of non-Western cultures but on genetically modified organisms, they are still false. In the case of plants that are not genetically engineered, patents given for medical and agricultural uses are often based on a theft of knowledge from non-Western cultures that use nonreductionist modes of knowing....

A shift to a postreductionist paradigm of biology that recognizes that biological organisms are complex and that ways of knowing their properties can be plural would undermine the epistemological basis of IPRs for life forms. In the area of IPRs and life forms, the issue is not merely *who* will own life but *whether* life can be owned. IPRs are therefore an issue not just of ownership but also of ethics.

REINVENTING BIOLOGY, REINVENTING CREATIVITY

Reinventing biology to include concern and respect for all species and all humans requires other reinventions. Knowledge systems which view humans as members of an earth family locate creativity in understanding the relationships between different organisms. This generates different ways of knowing and different claims to knowledge. Third World, feminist, and environmental approaches to science are converging in a reinvention of biology based on the recognition of creativity across cultures.

Third World, non-Western scientific traditions and feminist perspectives have sought to evolve noninvasive modes to know other organisms which are seen as live, not dead, matter.... [The] Western scientific method [studies] biological organisms as if they were dead matter and confirms that assumption with its invasive and destructive methods of experimentation.

Mae Wan Ho has called this the "cataclysmic violence of homogenisation."[34] She, like Bose, is working toward a biology that allows organisms to inform.... The reinvention of biology is inspired by a convergence of non-Western scientific traditions and feminist approaches to science, exemplified so powerfully in Barbara McClintock's "feeling for the organism" and Rachel Carson's "listening to nature."[35]

The dominant paradigm of biology excludes knowledge in which organisms are treated as subjects, not mere objects of manipulation. In the genetic engineering revolution phase, species are being even further manipulated to serve the distorted and narrow ends of a small class of humans. Plants are being engineered to become poison factories, cows are being engineered to produce human protein in their milk, pigs are being engineered with human genes governing growth. Carp, catfish, and trout have also been engineered with a number of genes from humans, cattle, and rats to increase their growth. Mammals are being genetically engineered to secrete valuable pharmaceuticals in their milk.... Living organisms are being reduced to mechanical systems to be manipulated at will....

And while scientists play god with living organisms, they want no questions asked about the ethical and ecological implications of their "god tricks." Experts at fragmenting life take on the arrogant stance of being experts at everything.... Besides excluding people from decisions of public concern, the new technologies have also worked out the exclusion of ethical concern which reinforces "man's empire over lesser creatures."

All life is precious. It is equally precious to the rich and the poor, to white and black, to men and women. Universalization of the protection of life is an ethical imperative. On the other hand, private property and private profits are culturally and socioeconomically legitimized constructs holding only for some groups. They do not hold for all societies and all cultures. Laws for the protection of private property rights, especially as related to life forms, cannot and should not be imposed globally. They need to be restrained.

Double standards also exist in the shift from private gain to social responsibility for environmental costs. When the patenting of life is at issue, arguments from "novelty" are used. Novelty requires that the subject matter of a patent be new, that it be the result of an inventive step, and not something existing in nature. On the other hand, when it comes to legislative safeguards, the argument shifts to "similarity," to establishing that biotechnology products and genetically engineered organisms differ little from parent organisms.

What counts as "nature" is constructed differently in patriarchal systems, depending on whether it is rights or responsibilities which have to be owned. When property rights to life forms are claimed, it is on the basis of them being new, novel, not occurring in nature. However, when environmentalists state that being "not natural," genetically modified organisms will have special ecological impacts, which need to be known and assessed, and for which the "owners" need to take responsibility, the argument is that they are not new or unnatural. These organisms are "natural," and hence safe. The issue of biosafety is therefore treated as unnecessary.[39] Thus when biological organisms are to be owned, they are treated as not natural; when the responsibility for consequences of releasing genetically modified organisms is to be owned, they are treated as natural. These shifting constructions of "natural" show that the science that claims the highest levels of objectivity is actually very subjective and opportunistic in its approach to nature.

The inconsistency in the construction of the natural is well illustrated in the case of the manufacture of genetically engineered human proteins for infant formula. Gen Pharm, a biotechnology company, is the owner of the world's first transgenic dairy bull, called Herman. Herman was bioengineered by company scientists while an embryo to carry a human gene for producing milk with a human protein. This milk is now to be used for making infant formula.

The engineered gene and the organism of which it is a part are treated as nonnatural when it comes to ownership of Herman and his offspring. However, when the issue is safety of the infant formula containing this bioengineered ingredient extracted from the udders of Herman's offspring, the same company says, "We're making these proteins exactly the way they're made in nature." Gen Pharm's chief executive officer, Jonathan MacQuitty, would have us believe that infant formula made from human protein bioengineered in the milk of transgenic dairy cattle is human milk: "Human milk is the gold standard, and formula companies have added more and more [human elements] over the past twenty years." Cows, women, and children are merely instruments for commodity production and profit maximization in this perspective.[40]

...

However, this kind of opportunistic biology, in which species are manipulated arbitrarily for profits, is not inevitable. In its place we could have democratized biology in which diversity is recognized as the very basis of life and is treated as a reason for celebration rather than a reason for exploitation and in which ordinary citizens have a say in biotechnology policy.

Democratizing biology involves recognition of the intrinsic value of all life forms and their inherent ability and right to survival, independent of gender, race, and species differences. It also involves the recognition of the rights of all citizens in determining how we relate to diverse species. Through such democratization we could create sciences that respect all "others," and include all "others." In a democratized biology, knowledge of different cultures and groups has equal standing, and no arbitrary assumptions are made about the creative and self-organizational capacities of nonhuman species or about the expertise and ignorance of technocrats and citizens. The colonization of other species, other cultures, and all societies has threatened both biological and cultural diversity. The democratization of biology offers an opportunity to undo these colonizations and to create possibilities for the flourishing of diversity in nature and in our minds.

NOTES

1. Lynda Birke, *Women, Feminism and Biology* (Brighton: Wheatsheaf Books, 1986); Evelyn Fox Keller, *Reflections on Gender and Science* (New Haven, Conn.: Yale University Press, 1985); Sandra Harding and Jean F. O'Barr, *Sex and Scientific Inquiry* (Chicago: University of Chicago Press, 1987); Ruth Bleier, *Science and Gender* (New York: Pergamon Press, 1984); Ruth Hubbard, *The Politics of Women's Biology* (New Brunswick, N.J.: Rutgers University Press, 1990).

. . .

3. Chief Luther Standing Bear, quoted in *Touch the Earth,* compiled by T. C. McLuhan (London: Abacus, 1982), p. 6.

. . .

7. Matt Ridley, *The Red Queen* (Harmondsworth: Penguin Books, 1993).

8. Richard Dawkins, *The Selfish Gene* (Oxford: Oxford University Press, 1976).

9. Richard Dawkins, *The Blind Watchmaker* (Harmondsworth: Penguin Books, 1988).

. . .

11. Basil Davidson, *Africa in History* (New York: Collier Books, 1974).

. . .

14. Davidson, *Africa in History,* pp. 178–179.

15. Vandana Shiva, "Most Farmers in India Are Women," FAO, Delhi, 1991, p. 1.

. . .

17. Vir Singh, "Hills of Hardship," *Hindustan Times Weekly,* Delhi, January 18, 1987.

. . .

19. Joan Mencher, "Women's Work and Poverty: Women's Contribution to Household Maintenance in Two Regions of South India, in *A Home Divided: Women and Income Control in the Third World,* ed. D. H. Dwyer and J. Bruce (Palo Alto, Calif.: Stanford University Press, 1987).

. . .

21. Devaki Jain and Malini Chand Seth, "Domestic Work: Its Implications for Enumeration of Workers," in Saradamoni (ed.), *Women, Work, and Society,* Indian Statistical Institute, Delhi, 1985.

22. Vandana Shiva, *Staying Alive: Women, Ecology, and Development* (London: Zed Books, 1988).

23. Vandana Shiva, "Women's Knowledge and Work in Mountain Agriculture," paper presented at Conference on Women in Mountain Development, ICIMOD, Kathmandu, 1988.

. . .

25. J. E. Satchel, *Earthworm Ecology* (London: Chapman and Hall, 1983).

. . .

27. J. Kloppenburg, *First the Seed* (Cambridge: Cambridge University Press, 1988).

. . .

29. John Locke, *Two Treatises of Government,* Peter Caslett (ed.) (Cambridge: Cambridge University Press, 1967).

...

31. Vandana Shiva and Radha Holla Bhar, "Intellectual Piracy and the Neem Patents," Research Foundation for Science, Technology, and Natural Resource Policy, Dehra Dun, 1993.

...

34. Mae Wan Ho, "The Physics of Biology," unpublished manuscript, 1992.

35. See Evelyn Fox Keller, *A Feeling for the Organism: The Life and Work of Barbara McClintock* (New York: Freeman, 1983).

...

39. UNEP, Report of Panel IV, Expert Group on Biosafety, Nairobi, Kenya, 1993.

40. Rural Advancement Fund International Communique, June 1993, Ontario, Canada.

...

Jan Bootinand for the Global Alliance Against Traffic in Women

Feminist Participatory Action Research in the Mekong Region

... In the Mekong subregion, the socioeconomic and political changes that have taken place in countries like Cambodia and Vietnam in the past decades have been accompanied by greater mobility of people internally as well as across borders. Experience from a country like Thailand has shown that the movement of people, particularly women, into various types of labor and service sectors, including marriage, has been increasingly accompanied by deception, coercion, and exploitation.

The Research and Action Project on Trafficking in Women in the Mekong Region—in short, the RA Project[1]—was a response to the growing concern over the increasing number of women who had been "trafficked" in Cambodia and Vietnam in the late 1980s and early 1990s. At that time, there was a general lack of reliable data on the trafficking situation as well as a lack of appropriate strategies to provide support to affected women. The main objectives of the RA Project were to document the situation of trafficking in women in Cambodia and Vietnam and to develop appropriate strategies to address the problems and support the women concerned. The methodology employed was one of action research with a feminist and participatory approach.... The project was divided into two phases: a research phase and an action phase. It was implemented by four partner organizations: the Cambodian Women's Development Agency (CWDA) in Cambodia, the Youth Research Institute (YRI) based in Hanoi for the work in Northern Vietnam, the Women's Union of Ho Chi Minh City, and Tay Ninh Women's Union in Southern Vietnam. The Global Alliance Against Traffic in Women (GAATW), based in Bangkok, Thailand, acted as a coordinating agency, providing assistance and facilitating the project.... [T]his four-year-long project (1997–2001) brought about a number of tangible positive outcomes.

...

THE IDEA OF TRAFFICKING: AN EVOLVING DISCUSSION

The conceptual understanding of the issue of trafficking is perhaps one of the most important factors that influenced the RA Project. However, when the project was conceived in 1995–1996, there was no internationally agreed definition of trafficking in persons. For the project partner in Cambodia, the concept of trafficking was understood in the context of a human rights violation, connected to the growth in prostitution. For the project partners in Vietnam, trafficking was perceived as related to women being forced or deceived into prostitution or into becoming wives of foreign men. While the perception of the issue by the project partners may reflect the actual trend of trafficking phenomena at that time, it must be recognized that the understanding of the trafficking issue by project partners—particularly those in Vietnam—also followed the legal concept of trafficking in each country. This understanding was largely based on the historical understanding of trafficking in international law that focused on the recruitment and movement of women across borders for the purpose of prostitution.[2] ... Thus, despite the absence of an internationally agreed upon definition, trafficking was often associated with the crime of harboring or facilitating prostitution....

To set a common conceptual framework for the research, GAATW as the coordinating agency shared an analysis of the issues of migration, trafficking, and prostitution based on the research experience in Thailand (Foundation For Women 1996).... Terms such as trafficker, brothel owner, pimp, matchmaker/recruiter, buyer, and prostitute/sex worker were used to imply a trafficking case although it was not always clear that there were situations of deception, coercion, or exploitation taking place. For example, there was generally no or little distinction made between voluntary migration and trafficking. As there seemed to be a lack of a clear understanding of what constituted trafficking, GAATW provided a two-part definition that was used in the International Report Project on Trafficking in Women in 1997.[3]

The researchers were also cautioned that although the term trafficking was often used to describe situations of illegal migration and/or situations of women going into prostitution, they needed to recognize that each of these phenomena was separate, although they may be interrelated....

In the last few years, discussion on the definition of trafficking, and measures to combat it, has been progressing at the international level. The Special Rapporteur on Violence Against Women commented in her report to the UN Commission on Human Rights during its 56th session in April 2000, that definition of trafficking should focus on forced-labor and slavery-like practices rather than narrowly focusing on prostitution or sexual exploitation (Coomaraswamy 2000)....

COMPLEX REALITIES

Recognizing that the scope of trafficking in women included more than just forced prostitution or sexual exploitation, GAATW encouraged the project partners in Vietnam and Cambodia to look beyond the original research scope.... During the first phase, researchers in Cambodia found many cases of trafficking of women for forced labor or for begging in Thailand.[4] In Vietnam, the discussion and understanding of the issue were more complex because the implementing agencies had to operate within the existing legal framework and the official perception of the trafficking issue in the country. In this regard, it was also more difficult to expand the scope of the research here and it was particularly clear in Vietnam during the course of the project that the official perception of the trafficking issue influenced the research process and the nature of the research findings....

The conceptual conflation between trafficking in women and prostitution that was employed had some impact on the quality and character of data collected. This was particularly the case with the initial research in Southern Vietnam, in which much of the findings only described the situation of women who had to resort to prostitution because of their difficult circumstances or that of their family.... This was perhaps because of the focus on prostitution rather than on elements of trafficking. The Northern Vietnam research team also discussed living and working conditions of prostitutes as those of trafficked women, without making any distinction between the two groups.

The conflation between trafficking and illegal migration, which was consistent with the official line in Vietnam, also had an impact upon the quality of the research findings and analysis presented in the reports.... The researchers included data on women sent back by the Chinese authorities, those who had gone away and lost contact with their families, and those who did not give official notification to, nor receive permission from, local authorities before migrating. No distinction was made between these different groups. Researchers obtained these figures mostly from local authorities, the border police, or the local Women's Union and cited them in the report without further explanation. Cross-checking with local authorities by GAATW during a monitoring visit clarified the detail of these figures. Moreover, at the beginning of the project, it was difficult for the researchers to gain support for women returnees from the local authority.... This was because local authorities viewed trafficking and illegal migration only as a matter of law and order, in line with the country's legal framework. Most of the women and their families did not approach local authorities for help because they were afraid of punishment.

In rural Northern Vietnam, the general community attitude toward migration, especially to China, did not seem to be a positive one. Thus, researchers encountered some resistance from community people when they tried to set up women's groups to support returnees from China....

In spite of these complications and the fact that trafficking and prostitution were conflated—and that illegal migration was an ongoing issue—some changes in the perception were noted on both individual and organizational levels. In the context of Northern Vietnam, the researchers were instrumental in engaging in discussion with local authorities concerning the latter's view on the status of returnees. Instead of seeing them as criminals, the local authorities gradually developed an understanding about the situation of women who had been cheated and had to leave the country illegally. In the later stage of the project, this shift in perception resulted in the involvement of local authorities in the provision of support to the women returnees and their families, as well as to the women's support groups that had been formed. Similarly, more openness and a change in perception about trafficking were developed during the project in Southern Vietnam....

METHODOLOGY: FEMINIST PARTICIPATORY ACTION RESEARCH (FPAR)

The project framework was one of action research with a feminist and participatory approach, which would give women a voice and a chance to improve their living conditions (or to address their situation) through taking actions themselves. The research methodology included both quantitative and qualitative techniques. Questionnaire surveys were carried out during the project extension period on the situation of Vietnamese women marrying foreigners. Secondary information was also collected from published reports and newspapers. However, the project relied mostly on primary data gathered from interviews with women and other informants. The concepts of participation, participatory action research, and feminist research as understood by GAATW for the RA Project are summarized below.[5]

Participation

Participation is a powerful but slippery concept. Within the context of development projects it may mean anything from having people contribute to the project with cash or labor, to involving them in planning and decisions, or taking part in research and evaluation of projects. Clearly this last type of involvement means that people are able to share ideas about problems and possible solutions. The participants are seen as "insiders"—they ... actively codetermine every phase of the research process. Through this form of research the participants' knowledge and experiences are valued and their confidence in their ability to analyze their situation themselves is enhanced.

Another very important aspect of participatory research is the involvement of participants as a group, not just as individuals. By encouraging participants to share information and analyze problems among themselves, it is possible to develop an even clearer view on the issues being studied. In this way, the research process can function as a conscientization process. The importance of working with groups of participants, rather than with individuals only, is reflected in the methods specifically developed for participatory research. Almost all of these methods, or techniques, have been adopted to be used in group discussions. Such techniques are also useful in social science research....

Participatory Action Research

The purpose of participatory research is not only to describe and interpret social reality in a more reliable way, but to radically change it as well. Moreover, it aims to transform reality *with* rather than *for* oppressed people. This is the concept of "partnership approaches." Participatory action research combines three activities: investigation, evaluation, and action. The link between research and action is the most important aspect—when people are directly involved in an analysis of their situation, it follows that they want to find solutions to the problems they have identified.... By taking action, the participants and the researcher can work together to change the existing social structures.

An important aspect of action research is its cyclic nature: it starts with studying, learning, and analyzing the situation and problems. From this emerges planning of possible solutions, and then action is taken. The result of the action is then evaluated, a new analysis of the changed situation is made, new planning with new action follows, and so on.... This type of research is supposed to break down the distinction between the "knowers" (researchers, scholars, experts) and "not-knowers" (peasants, women, poor people; in short, all those who are "subjects" of research).

Participatory action research contrasts sharply with the conventional model of research, in which participants are treated mostly as passive subjects only, and sometimes as receivers of the results. It is not always recognized that this still unconventional type of research can also enhance the validity of the findings. Causal inferences about the behavior of people are likely to be more valid and able to be acted upon when the people themselves take part in developing and testing them. Clearly, participatory action research not only requires considerable skills of the researcher in using participatory techniques as indicated above, but also open-mindedness and a pleasant manner with the participants. Her attitude and her role are different from those of a "traditional" researcher—she not only gathers information, but also clarifies, stimulates, supports, and assists. Her work will always include a transfer of organizational, technical, and analytical skills from the researcher to the participants.

Feminist Research

The most important premises which govern this research can be summarized as follows:

- a focus on the lives, the opinions, and the experiences of women; this includes women's relations with children and men;
- a focus on possibilities for changes in thinking and behavior, in order to fight against

oppression and exploitation and to improve living conditions and interpersonal relationships;

- to abandon the conventional idea that knowledge is something that exists by itself
and for itself, free of the scientist or researcher and his or her background and environment (sex, culture, language, position, etc.);
- knowledge should be accessible to everyone, not only to the researcher or the scientific community.

Comparing these premises with the principles of participatory research and action research
described above, it becomes clear that there is a considerable overlap in basic thinking for all
three research modes. Feminist research is mainly different in its main focus on women, and in
rejecting any male bias or androcentrism in research. . . . It is believed that looking at the world
through the eyes of women and studying women's experiences will adjust the male-biased view
on reality which is still not uncommon in the social sciences.

An important aim of feminist research is to understand the extent, the dimensions, the
forms, and the causes of exploitation and oppression of women. Then, it is also thought important to study the means through which women may already challenge systems and institutions
which limit their choices. Oppression is an extraordinarily complex process in which women
(and people in general) are not necessarily totally powerless, in that they may utilize a range of
resources—verbal, interactional, and others—as forms of everyday resistance.

Because feminism is committed to changing the conditions of exploitation and
oppression, a large section of feminist research focuses on possibilities for such changes.
This requires new methodologies and new approaches in doing research, as have been
developed in the participatory and action research approaches. Central in these approaches
are, firstly, sharing of data and findings with participants, and secondly, using the research
as a means toward conscientization, for both the women participants and for the researcher.
A heightened awareness, and enhanced skills to analyze their situation, will then encourage and empower the women to take action, to find solutions to their problems, and to
change their lives. . . .

Another important requirement in conventional social science is that researchers must
be objective—their personal ideas are not supposed to color the research. Feminist scholars
point to the impossibility and even the undesirability of this view. Researchers should not only
look at their own "hidden" values on moral issues, but take a clear stand in reciprocity and
solidarity with the participants in their research. It is also generally agreed that it is preferable
that women researchers should be working with women participants. Female researchers usually have an advantage over males in communicating with other women; in addition they may
share a set of common experiences with other women and therefore be able to identify with
their situations and problems.

. . .

THE FPAR METHODOLOGY IN ACTION

. . .

The application of FPAR was challenging in the particular sociopolitical contexts of
Cambodia and Vietnam. Specifically, these contexts determine the structure of the society and
the degree of openness and control within that society. Such factors influence the freedom to
which a research methodology can be applied in that situation and the success of its outcome.
Moreover, the sensitive nature of the issue of trafficking in these countries and confusion over
the understanding of what it involved further complicated the application of FPAR (see earlier
discussion). . . .

Cambodia

In Cambodia, data collection was done in the first phase of the project in order for researchers to have an understanding of the situation and problems of trafficking. This period was also an important time for the researchers to establish contact with research participants and community people. All of the researchers were either local social or development workers.... The researchers reported some difficulties in talking to local people in the villages due to the situation of political unrest during the time of the research (CWDA 1997).... Furthermore, security of the researchers and of the women they talked to was of concern since the trafficking network was connected to some powerful people including some in the armed forces. As for interviews with sex workers, some researchers also found it difficult to talk in detail to the women in brothels because of the close watch kept by the brothel owners. After the process of data collection, the researchers arranged for meetings to share and discuss research findings with the women concerned, i.e., those in the villages and brothels.

In the villages, sharing of research findings, namely the situation of trafficked women from the villages, led to discussion on causes of the problems and actions that needed to be taken to address them. Consequently, information-sharing groups were formed to monitor what was happening to women locally. Subsequent activities that developed in the communities, including literacy classes, a reading room, and income-generating activities, can be seen as responses to some of the problems identified—i.e., low literacy rate and high levels of poverty. Although the focus on and participation of women were central in all activities initiated, the impact of this approach could also be seen at the family and community level in terms of increased gender awareness. In most of the project villages, the number of domestic violence cases has reportedly declined.

Researchers also tried to arrange such sharing sessions with sex workers in the brothel areas.... [R]esearchers were able to negotiate with brothel owners to allow some of the sex workers to gather for one or two hours during the days when they were not working.... This sharing and discussion among sex workers in the Toul Kork area led to the formation of the Cambodian Prostitute Union.

In this way, the application of FPAR in the project in Cambodia contributed to the conscientization of women sex workers to demand their rights. In the villages, the use of FPAR also contributed to the empowerment of women to address some common problems....

Vietnam

... Unlike the Cambodian researchers, however, in Northern Vietnam the researchers were not locals of the project communities.... Initially, the researchers relied on assistance from local authorities in providing information on the situation in the villages and in identifying research participants. In order to get to know the research participants in the communities, researchers stayed in or near the villages for 10–14 days at a time. The researchers felt that, despite some difficulties, the process was successful in helping them to gain the trust of the women and that the information obtained was accurate and useful in understanding the situation of trafficking and the conditions that the women faced.

For Southern Vietnam, the research team contacted women who had engaged in sex work (those returned from "reeducation" centers), or families with daughters working in prostitution.... When making a visit to the women and interviewing them, the researchers offered a small amount of money to the women or their family as a token of appreciation for their time. According to the researchers, this gesture was necessary because most of the women were in difficult economic situations.

In the project in Vietnam, the process after the completion of the research phase was somewhat different than in Cambodia. Sharing of research findings with the research participants did not happen in the first step as in the Cambodian project. In Vietnam, the focus at the beginning of the second phase was on the formation of women's groups. Researchers and project staff invited potential participants (returnees, mothers of trafficked women, high-risk women) to a meeting and to join the group. They informed the women of the objectives of the group including the aim of helping one another both financially and personally. Researchers also told the women that they would be entitled to take a loan from the project....

For the project in Northern Vietnam, the observation regarding the formation of women's groups was made based on the fact that many women refused or were hesitant to join the groups at the invitation of the researchers. In the researchers' view, this was because the women were busy making a living and also because they had inferiority complexes and therefore were not open to and avoided the researchers. However, looking at it from the women's perspective, some of them were afraid that the researchers were making investigations in order to arrest them (YRI 2000, 211). There was also a negative perception about the women's groups that would be formed. Some parents remarked that if they let their unmarried daughter join the group of "social evil" women, then the daughter would "lose her honor." ...

For the project in Southern Vietnam, the process of bringing women together to form groups was similar to that in Northern Vietnam. However, the VWU was already running a number of programs, including some credit schemes, skills training, and HIV/AIDS and health education. The researchers and project staff already had contact with many women, including former prostitutes, those still working in prostitution, and women in difficult circumstances who were identified as high-risk women. Many of those women were invited to come together and form a group of "women in especially difficult circumstances" and told that they would be eligible to take out a loan from the project and participate in other activities.... Nevertheless, there was a new element in the work of both research teams, i.e., the use of participatory techniques.... Women who joined in the group were encouraged to share and discuss their situation and problems. Together, they also tried to identify some possible ways to address the problems.

Whilst the major activities of the women's groups that were formed during this RA Project were similar among the groups in Northern and Southern Vietnam, the impact and the outcomes were somewhat different. Most evidently, there seemed to be more cohesion and the sense of bonding among members of the women's groups in Northern Vietnam. This was an interesting outcome considering the difficulties and ambiguity in the initial process of group formation. After the women agreed to join the groups, the process of sharing of experiences among the group members helped create a positive impact on the empowerment of the women....

A number of factors may have contributed to the different dynamics found between the women's groups in Northern Vietnam and Southern Vietnam. The first is the different geographical context of the project sites and the various basic livelihood strategies of the women in project areas. Most of the women in the project area in rural Northern Vietnam had land for housing and basic cultivation. In comparison, the women in Southern Vietnam lived in the city in squatter areas and were trying to make a living from petty trading.... Moreover, life in the countryside moved at a slower pace while poor women in the city struggled to make a daily living. These situations had some impact on the women's ability to participate in the women's groups.

Second, the backgrounds of the members of the women's groups in Northern Vietnam and Southern Vietnam were different. Amongst the general public, there appeared to be less stigma attached to women who had been trafficked to China than those who had worked in prostitution.... While trafficked women were seen as being cheated or deceived, many people saw those who engaged in prostitution as being "greedy," "lazy," or "wanting easy money." It was generally believed too that former prostitutes needed to be "rehabilitated." ...

Third, the researchers and project staff in the Northern Vietnam and Southern Vietnam teams had different experiences. Prior to the implementation of the RA Project, project

staff and researchers from VWU had their own "top-down" approach to working with the women. The old style of interaction with women was still observed, especially during the initial period of the project. It was not very easy for the VWU staff to understand and practice the bottom-up approach that was introduced in the RA Project. To do this, they had to learn to trust and respect the women and to listen to their views. The women themselves were also perhaps used to interacting with the VWU staff in a more reserved manner....
On the contrary, the researchers from the YRI did not have experience working with a community at the grassroots level. In this respect, it was perhaps easier for them to embrace the participatory and bottom-up approach and apply it in the work with the women's groups once they had been formed. Participation and the open sharing among the women certainly had positive impact on group dynamics.

REFLECTIONS ON THE FPAR METHODOLOGY

To a large extent, the application of feminist participatory action in the project was influenced by the sociopolitical context of the countries in which it was run, especially in Vietnam. In this regard, preparation for the project that took into account the country's sociopolitical context was essential. Similarly, providing orientation and training for researchers and project staff on FPAR and the conceptual understanding of trafficking was crucial for the effective implementation of the project....

The use of economic incentive to attract women to join the group, as in Vietnam, may be thought to be inappropriate or in conflict with the concepts of real participation and empowerment. However, once the groups formed, women became involved and participated in sharing and discussion as well as in other activities. The changes that were seen amongst women in the groups, particularly in Northern Vietnam, included an increased confidence to take action to improve their situation and an increased ability to support one another. This can be considered as an empowerment. Even among the women in the groups in Southern Vietnam, one could observe changes during the course of the project. One criticism of the project in Southern Vietnam could be that it focused mostly on providing economic support to the women. However, it should be mentioned that for many women, the ability to generate income could be an empowering process. Some women said that they felt more confident and that their families saw them as more capable when they had a loan to start a small business. For other women, more earning capacity meant more decision-making power for them....

The use of feminist participatory action research in a project like this can have different impacts on different people involved in the project. For the women, it allowed their voices to be heard and their needs and problems addressed. For the researchers, FPAR meant learning to listen to and to respect and trust the women as participants of the project. They learned to work *with* rather than working *for* the women and the process became *bottom up* instead of *top down*....

For members of GAATW, coordinating this project was a rewarding and challenging experience. We felt that our role in facilitating the learning and understanding of the issue of trafficking and the sharing of ideas and experiences on participatory approach was positive. Nevertheless, we also realized that while the key premises and the methodology of feminist research in combination with participatory action research can offer an excellent base for the research on trafficking in women, the actual implementation of the methodology was not always easy and the results may not be the most desirable. Experience from the project shows that there is a need to be flexible in developing responses to the problems identified, particularly at the policy level. Such flexibility depends greatly on the country's political system and the existence of local nongovernmental organization/civil groups that are able to challenge state policies. An important lesson learned from the project is that while policy responses may be more rigid and slow to change (especially in a country like Vietnam), some changes can be seen at the individual and local levels. In such a case, action at the grassroots level can bring about tangible positive outcomes....

REFLECTIONS ON THE MAIN RESEARCH FINDINGS

One important issue that a number of research projects on trafficking, including the RA Project, seek to identify is the cause and contributing factors to trafficking. In the findings and discussion in the project reports from both Northern and Southern Vietnam, poverty and lack of education were identified as important causal factors.[6] For Northern Vietnam it was concluded that "poverty and hunger constitute a socioeconomic basis for the formation and development of social evils including trafficking in women" (YRI 2000, 55)....

A problem with linking poverty and trafficking is that the actual context of trafficking is simplified. In addition, statistics of trafficked women as given by the authorities were questionable. "Trafficked" women were largely identified as those who had left home without official reporting or those who had been "pushed back" from China because of their undocumented status. An important pattern observed in Northern Vietnam, although not always clearly formulated as such in the final research report, was that women were moving in order to look for ways to earn a living. However, because they lacked information about travel and contacts at the proposed destinations, or because of a general lack of experience, many of the women relied on friends or strangers to facilitate their movement and many times they were cheated. In this regard, poverty may well be just one of the causes of female migration while other factors make these women vulnerable to deceit and exploitation during the travel process and at the destination....

For Southern Vietnam, the research indicated that a percentage of the women interviewed during the first phase of the project entered prostitution due to poverty and indebtedness. In this regard, poverty was one reason for women to resort to prostitution as a means of living, or in order to get out of a difficult economic situation. Nevertheless, it is important to note that poor women are placed in especially difficult circumstances because they have very limited access to assistance from the state....

For Cambodia, poverty was referred to as one of the main factors pushing women and girls into leaving home. The majority of the interviewees stated that they left home because of the promise of a job or because they were looking for work or additional income in order to improve the family's plight or social status. In this regard, there seems to be a clear indication of the desire of women and girls to improve their life and their family's situation through migration.

The research findings from both Vietnam and Cambodia indicated that many women chose migration as a means of escaping domestic violence, boring or abusive marriages, or relationship problems.... While these underlying causes need further research and analysis, they have often been explained under headings such as failed love affairs or broken marriages. Such terminology appears again to have negative connotations for women, reflecting the attitude of society at large toward them.... However, it should be noted that not all women were compelled to migrate by difficult circumstances. Findings by the implementing agencies showed that there were also a number of women coming from well-to-do families who still made the decision to migrate for some adventure.

A low level of education has often been cited as a contributing factor to women being trafficked.... It is important to note here that the low level of education referred to in the Vietnamese context was a primary school level of education. Among the women interviewed, very few were illiterate. However, the majority of them only had a primary school level of education.[8] In contrast, the majority of girls and women interviewed in Cambodia were illiterate, as they had no school education at all.

Lack of or minimal formal education alone may not be the most important factor contributing to the vulnerability of women to deception, or to lack of choices in life. The research in Northern Vietnam indicated that a lack of information and services ... in poor rural areas prevented many women from being aware about trafficking; hence they were easily deceived. Indeed, in most of the cases interviewed, the women had never left the village before they were cheated. Lack of experience made them dependent on friends/neighbors who may want to take advantage of them. It should be noted, however, that even when informed about the risk of being trafficked, many women still took the chance, since staying in their villages was not always a good alternative.

Education may provide access to a better opportunity. However, one needs to question the kind of education and skills that really give that option. Having literacy skills is certainly an advantage which helps the women in many situations. For example, a sex worker in Cambodia was under debt bondage because she had signed a false contract with brothel owners without being able to read it. In another case, literacy skills saved a Vietnamese woman who had been forced to marry a man in China, since she was able to write to her friend to ask for help. Nevertheless, simply being able to read and write does not seem to be adequate in giving access to better life conditions, especially in Vietnam where the standard of education is relatively high. However, in a country like Cambodia where the education level is low among the general population, literacy may be a very important factor in assisting women in gaining access to better opportunities. In any case, what is necessary is education to empower women. It is probable that providing access to a combination of formal education and appropriate vocational and life skills training could assist in reducing the vulnerability of women and girls to being trafficked. The impact of the level of education in preventing trafficking requires further study.

LESSONS LEARNED

The Research and Action Project on Trafficking in Women in the Mekong Region (Cambodia and Vietnam) that was implemented during 1997–2000 was probably the first of its kind. The project set out to achieve many objectives, including the generation of reliable information on the situation of trafficking in women in Cambodia and Vietnam. It aimed as well to develop strategies, both at a local and policy level, to address the problem of trafficking....

An important lesson learned from the project is that while changes at the policy level may be more difficult and slow to take effect, actions can happen more quickly at the individual and local levels. In such cases, initiatives at the grassroots level can bring about tangible, positive outcomes. The RA Project with its specific methodology contributed positively to strengthening individual and community support of women returnees as well as empowering women. This was particularly evident in the project outcomes seen in Northern Vietnam and Cambodia. Furthermore, the formation of the Cambodian Prostitute Union (CPU) can be seen as action by an "affected" grassroots group to challenge policies and practices that violate and discriminate against women in prostitution.

The RA Project provided an important learning ground for the implementing agencies in the understanding and application of feminist research and participatory methodology. While the use of the FPAR concept and methodology in a project like this was considered innovative, particularly in Vietnam, the implementing agencies felt that this new approach brought about many positive results. Nevertheless, experience from the RA Project has also pointed to the need for further validation and consolidation of the use of FPAR in the context of trafficking in women.[9] Finally, the project was essentially about the lives of women in particular contexts and circumstances. These are women who have lived and are still living. Their lives are real and their voices need to be listened to. The Global Alliance Against Traffic in Women concluded that research with and for women must continue in order that the types of violations of women's human rights that were uncovered through this project can be successfully challenged.

NOTES

1. The basic framework of the RA Project was based on a project—"The Research and Action Project on Trafficking in Women in Thailand" (RATW)—that was an action-oriented research project carried out by the Foundation For Women (FFW). This project was designed to develop a reliable database about trafficking in women in Thailand and to define workable strategies to fight this problem. When the results of the RATW Project were presented during the International Workshop on Migration and Traffic in Women held in Chiang Mai, Thailand, in October 1994, participants from Vietnam and Cambodia expressed their concern over the emerging problems of trafficking in their countries. They also expressed a strong interest in, and a need to, carry out a similar project to the RATW in their own countries. This was the inception of the RA Project.

2. The 1949 Convention did not give a definition of trafficking but described punishable acts related to prostitution.

3. This report was coordinated by GAATW and the Foundation Against Trafficking in Women (STV) and created the following definitions: (1) Trafficking in Women: "All acts involved in the recruitment and/or transportation of women by means of violence or threat of violence, abuse of authority or dominant position, debt bondage or other forms of coercion." (2) Forced Labor and Slavery-like Practices: "The extraction of work or services from any woman or the appropriation of the legal identity and/or physical person of any woman by means of violence or threat of violence, abuse of authority or dominant position, debt bondage or other forms of coercion." See Marjan Wijers and Lin Lap-Chew, *Trafficking in Women, Forced Labor and Slavery-Like Practices in Marriage, Domestic Labor and Prostitution* (Utrecht: STV, 1997).

4. However, information regarding other forms of trafficking was not discussed in detail in the CWDA report.

5. This section relies on a preliminary paper written by Mary Boesveld for an internal GAATW discussion on the research methodology. The paper was revised in collaboration with Jan Bootinand. See Mary Boesveld and Jan Bootinand, "Practicing Feminist Participatory Research Methodologies." *GAATW Newsletter* no. 11 (January 1999):14–17.

6. In Vietnam, Kelly and Le (1999) comment that description of root causes of trafficking becomes rhetoric with the focus on "poverty," "lack of education," and "doi moi." While this may be rhetorical description, the examination and analysis of these factors by implementing agencies contribute to further understanding of the complexity and contextuality of the root causes of trafficking.

. . .

8. 50.9 percent in Southern Vietnam and 57 percent (30 of the 57 interviewees) in Northern Vietnam had less than 6 years' education.

9. A separate review and evaluation of the project was conducted, and a sharing of this review with external audience was organized in December 2001. During this external sharing, the three implementing agencies also made their presentations on process and outcome of the project as seen in their own context.

REFERENCES

Boesveld, Mary, and Jan Bootinand. "Practicing Feminist Participatory Research Methodologies." *GAATW Newsletter* no. 11 (January 1999):14–17.

Coomaraswamy, Radhika. "Integration of the Human Rights of Women and the Gender Perspective: Report of the Special Rapporteur on Violence Against Women, Its Causes and Consequences." Submitted in accordance with Commission on Human Rights resolution 199/44, E/CN.4/2000/68.

CWDA (Cambodian Women's Development Agency). "Report." 1997.

Foundation For Women. "Final Report of the Research and Action Project on Traffic in Women." Bangkok: Foundation For Women, July 1996.

GAATW (Global Alliance Against Traffic in Women). "The Research and Action (RA) Project on Trafficking in Women in the Mekong Region." Bangkok: Global Alliance Against Traffic in Women, 2002.

Kelly, Paula Frances, and Duong Bach Le. "Trafficking in Humans From and Within Vietnam." 1999.

VWU (Vietnam Women's Union). "The Research and Action Project on Traffic in Women in Ho Chi Minh City and Areas of the South." Ho Chi Minh City: Vietnam Women's Union, 1997.

Wijers, Marjan, and Lin Lap-Chew. *Trafficking in Women, Forced Labor and Slavery-Like Practices in Marriage, Domestic Labor and Prostitution.* Utrecht: STV, 1997.

YRI (Youth Research Institute). *Prevention of Trafficking in Women in Vietnam.* Hanoi: Labour and Social Affairs Publishing House, 2000.

13
Feminist Ethics in Research

We have seen that feminist research is defined by its commitment to producing knowledge likely to be useful in opposing the many varieties of gender injustice. It seeks to create knowledge that is not infected by gender and related biases and so does not lend itself to rationalizing the subordination of women and others subjected to oppressive constructions of masculinities and femininities. Feminist research should not only be unbiased but also be guided by feminist ethical principles, which should inform the selection and design of research programs, strategies for gathering and interpreting evidence, and decisions for publishing or otherwise acting on the results. This chapter identifies a few of the dilemmas faced by researchers who seek to apply their feminist ethical commitments in the practice of their research.

INSTITUTIONAL AND INDIVIDUAL ETHICS

Past traditions of Western research have often been marked by cruelty and abuse. Innumerable animals have been vivisected, justified by Cartesian assurances that animals had no more sensitivity than machines, and the name of one animal species, guinea pig, has become almost synonymous with research object. In the name of research, archaeological sites have been destroyed and human remains treated disrespectfully. Human research subjects have been drawn primarily from populations unable to withhold and therefore to give consent: slaves, prisoners, soldiers, orphans, people with disabilities perceived as "idiots," and citizens of nations under occupation. Although some abusive research has always been conducted, research in the nineteenth and early twentieth centuries expanded enormously, and so more harm was done in the name of expanding knowledge.

Following World War II and inspired by the horrors of so-called Nazi science, which had some parallels in other Western countries, new efforts were made to set ethical constraints on the conduct of research. These efforts were manifest at international, national, and institutional levels. The Nuremberg Code was established immediately after World War II, and in 1954 the World Medical Association passed the Declaration of Helsinki, since revised on several occasions. In the United States, government agencies such as the National Institute of Health and the National Science Foundation have developed codes of ethics, and a federal Office for Human Research Protections has been established. Nongovernmental organizations, such as the Alliance for Human Research Protection, exist to promote ethical research, and most research disciplines, especially in the social and biomedical sciences, have their own professional codes of ethics. All these codes are designed to address concerns such as safety, dignity, cultural respect, privacy, and consent that is genuinely informed and uncoerced. In research institutions, institutional review boards, along with animal and human research committees, monitor how the codes are applied in practice.

This web of codes and committees constitutes the public ethical framework within which most contemporary researchers conduct their work. The establishment of these codes and committees signals a welcome move toward democratization and public accountability, although the codes can never anticipate all the ethical questions likely to be raised by researchers. Feminist commitments pose special challenges for researchers, and some examples are offered below.

SOME ETHICAL CONCERNS FOR FEMINIST RESEARCHERS

Most feminist scholars recognize that research is more than the disinterested pursuit of "objective" knowledge, that investigations and outcomes are always value-laden and never morally or politically neutral. All researchers must confront decisions concerning the sorts of research projects to which they are willing to devote their life energies, but these questions often emerge with special intensity for feminists. For instance, feminists ask whether it is compatible with feminist principles to engage in space research, military research, or cosmetic research. They question how researchers' concerns for feminist ethics may be balanced with their wish for a secure income or the need to support dependents.

Standpoint and other approaches to methodology recommend that research should begin from the problems of the marginalized, who are often disadvantaged by gender as well as other factors. But how should we select among so many groups and/or determine their problems? Should we research only our "own" group, however we identify that, in order to avoid intrusion into the lives of "others"? Will focusing on our own group mean that our reputations as researchers become stereotyped and limit our future work and influence?

Issues of accountability are especially difficult. To whom are feminist researchers accountable? To our research subjects? To some broader "women's" community? To those who pay for our research, institutions or taxpayers? To ourselves? Or only to the advancement of knowledge? Questions of accountability intersect with questions of loyalty. How can we balance loyalty to disadvantaged groups with other values? Some research may be used to dishonor heroes such as Martin Luther King Jr. and Rigoberta Menchú Tum. Researching past practices of human sacrifice or present practices of drug use, domestic violence, rape, female genital mutilation, or gang activity may discredit the communities where those practices occur or have occurred. Should feminist researchers refrain from such investigations? When, if ever, is research an act of betrayal?

Feminists are often concerned that the consequences of research may be harmful in ways that go beyond those considered by official agencies. For instance, they may be concerned about the consequences of revealing information that reinforces negative stereotypes, about exploiting the ignorance or poverty of members of disadvantaged social groups, and about deepening the silence of those who are already marginalized and excluded. Feminist awareness of these dangers influences their selection of research projects.

Many research projects are undertaken on groups whose members are unlikely to be among the primary beneficiaries of that research. Especially notorious is the long-standing research practice of testing pharmaceuticals on poor populations in developing countries. Are such research projects compatible with feminist principles? After all, they may provide a chance at recovery to people who would otherwise lack any treatment at all. Should feminist participation depend on estimating such probabilities as the likelihood of the subjects' benefiting from the experimental drug, the size of the possible benefit, and the length of time the benefit might last? Is research, like politics, a practice in which it is very difficult to maintain clean hands?

Research projects are inseparable from the methods used to conduct them, and feminist ethical principles clearly have bearing on which methods are selected. Is it important for feminist researchers to use collaborative methods? If so, with whom should we collaborate and why? Does respect for the subjectivity of research participants as fully human agents require feminists to use participatory methods? Should research subjects be compensated for their time, either by monetary payment or by academic credit?

Some feminist researchers oppose animal vivisection (Birke and Hubbard 1995). Other feminists are concerned about researchers' responsibility to cultural artifacts and human remains. Questions about the treatment of human research subjects are especially pressing. What does it mean to treat research subjects respectfully and not to harm them? What does it mean for them to give informed and uncoerced consent?

Relevant to the question of informed consent is the question of full disclosure by the researcher. Although deception of research subjects is ordinarily condemned, it may be permitted in some circumstances. But what are those circumstances, and when, if ever, may deception be used by feminist researchers? Disclosing one's research purposes may make it more difficult to access information. Is it ever permissible to deceive members of a community to which one has gained entry only through one's own membership? Is it easier for feminists to justify the use of deceit in researching antifeminist or racist groups such as the Klu Klux Klan? One kind of deception feminist researchers may consider is withholding information about one's feminist commitments; this may involve conforming to styles of self-presentation that will be approved by research subjects or refraining from challenging comments that disparage some group. Feminist researchers must reflect carefully upon how the disclosure of their feminist commitments is likely to affect their research subjects, their own reputation, their work, and its reception.

Reflexivity is often recommended as a methodological practice for feminist researchers, who are advised to consider how their questions, methods, and conclusions are affected by their own positionality. However, reflection on researchers' positionality should consider not only its epistemic but also its moral implications. How should the costs and benefits of the research to the researchers as well as to the research subjects be weighed? These questions are especially acute for insider-outsider researchers. In translating their own communities to the larger world, do researchers risk being co-opted? Do they become colonizers of their own communities? How can researchers avoid "othering" the communities they are investigating, and how are they aligning themselves vis-à-vis those communities?

Ethical values also pertain to the presentation of feminist research. How can feminist researchers balance recognition of research subjects' agency and the constraints on that agency, of oppressors' humanity as well as their cruelty? Should research findings be taken back to the relevant communities for approval? If so, can researchers claim authorship? What if the communities, or some members, disapprove of the research findings? How can responsibility to research participants or to particular communities be balanced with responsibility to larger communities?

A final set of questions concerns the uses that feminist researchers may make of their work. Should they utilize their research to assist their research subjects, perhaps intervening by giving them information or urging them to take some course of action? Should researchers become advocates? How can this be achieved without silencing their research subjects? How can researchers avoid becoming positioned as rescuers? Is it really possible to fulfill simultaneously the roles of scholar, activist, and citizen?

IS REFLECTION ON ETHICS ONLY A CONSTRAINT ON RESEARCH OR CAN IT ALSO ADD VALUE?

Considering ethical questions such as those mentioned above is usually difficult, sometimes painful, and occasionally paralyzing. Nevertheless, just as democratizing research is likely to improve its epistemic trustworthiness as well as its potential for emancipation, so too our research may benefit when our methodology is guided by ethical considerations. Inclusiveness is a central theme in most of the ethical questions raised above, and feminist methodology is especially concerned to address hitherto neglected problems, hear hitherto silenced voices, and promote universal rather than narrow sectional interests. Attention to ethical concerns of safety, dignity, diversity, and responsibility not only is important for its own sake but may also yield new perspectives and valuable information.

ETHICS, METHODOLOGY, AND REFLECTIVE EQUILIBRIUM

The ethical principles informing good feminist research practice need not be exclusively feminist; they may also be shared with other progressive, critical, or emancipatory social movements and research inquiries. However, feminist research ethics are distinguished by their special concern for generating knowledge useful in ending the subordination of those oppressed by gender constructions. Feminist principles of ethical research are likely to include respect for research subjects, especially members of subordinated and marginalized groups, concern for their dignity and safety, and concern for the researchers' own integrity.

Ethical principles are always general and can never replace ethical reflection on specific cases; however, they can point us in the right general direction. Similarly, study of specific cases can sensitize us to general issues. In considering the ethical issues that arise in connection with specific research projects, researchers must endeavor to balance feminist principles of ethical research practice with the exigencies of particular research projects.

The readings in this chapter offer both specific case studies and guidelines regarding some of the above questions. Naheed Islam discusses the responsibilities of a researcher who is also a member of a minority community; should she reveal information that reflects badly on the community, specifically its racism? Barrie Thorne raises questions of informed consent and its relationship to systems of power. Linda Alcoff considers the problems and benefits of speaking for others, in the context of power disparities among researchers and research subjects. This sensitivity to the ways in which research practices are related to social power is one of the defining features of feminist reflections on the ethics of methodology.

REFERENCE

Birke, Lynda, and Ruth Hubbard. 1995. *Reinventing Biology: Respect for Life and the Creation of Knowledge.* Bloomington: Indiana University Press.

BARRIE THORNE
"You Still Takin' Notes?": Fieldwork and Problems of Informed Consent

It has long been acknowledged that the openings of field research—gaining access, entree and rapport, and developing a workable relationship with those one wants to study—involve serious ethical questions.... Old debates have assumed new, more urgent form, and the question of *who* should make ethical determinations has become a heated topic in response to new federal regulations governing social research.[1]

Implemented by granting agencies and university review boards as a condition for funding or sponsoring research, HEW regulations for "Protection of Human Subjects" have begun to affect research practices and the terms of ethical discussions. According to the guidelines, review boards are initially to examine proposed research projects to decide if human subjects are at risk: "If it is decided that risk is involved, the review must further determine whether the risks are outweighed by any benefit that might come to the subject or by the importance of the knowledge to be gained, that the rights and welfare of the subjects will be adequately protected, that legally effective informed consent will be obtained, and that research will be reviewed at timely intervals" (Bond, 1978: 149).

This [reading] is focused on only one part of the regulations, the requirement that researchers must obtain "legally effective informed consent" from those they study.... Using the federal regulations as a starting point, I will explore some of the practical difficulties involved in implementing informed consent within the contexts of participant-observation. I will then return to assumptions involved in the doctrine of informed consent—especially the premise of abstract individualism and the neglect of social stratification and the uses of knowledge—and I will argue that discussions of ethics and fieldwork should involve a critique, as well as serious consideration, of informed consent.

THE "PROTECTION OF HUMAN SUBJECTS" REGULATIONS AND THEIR APPLICABILITY TO FIELDWORK

The notion of informed consent, as spelled out in the federal regulations, was originally designed to protect patients from abuses by medical researchers.... According to the regulations, informed consent means "the knowing consent of an individual or his legally authorized representative, so situated as to be able to exercise free power of choice without undue inducement or any element of force, fraud, deceit, duress, or other forms of constraint or coercion" (Annas *et al.,* 1977: 291). The regulations specify basic elements of information necessary to such consent: "fair explanation" of the purpose of the research and the procedures to be followed; a description of risks and benefits which might reasonably be expected; an offer to answer any inquiries concerning the procedures; and instruction that the person is free to withdraw consent and discontinue participation in the project at any time.

As Wax (1977) and Cassell (1978) have argued, the federal regulations are based on a biomedical, experimental model of research, and there is some question about their suitability as guidelines for ethnographic research. In fieldwork the risks are less dramatic than, say, in medical intervention; the benefits, too, are less striking than they might be in biomedical research—and both risks and benefits (especially long-term ones) are often difficult to assess, especially at the beginning of a field study. Fieldworkers have less control over the research setting than do experimentalists; in the immediate research situation, the gap of power between researcher and subject is less than in experiments, and the flow of interaction is broader and more reciprocal and open-ended. Finally, the new federal regulations, especially when they are translated into highly standardized activities, such as asking each member of a setting to sign a consent form before one even begins observing, seem overly legalistic, formalized, and intrusive in the more fluid context of field research.

Beyond the fact that the new government regulations are cut from a pattern which doesn't quite fit the practices of fieldwork, there are serious questions, which I will not pursue here, concerning the government's intrusion into the processes of social research.[2] The requirement that one obtain signed consent forms from everyone one studies may violate anonymity and actually create risks for some groups of subjects. In the end, the procedures may result in meaningless rituals rather than improving the ethics of field research.

However, the notion of informed consent *is* relevant to the ethics of fieldwork. Although it has important limitations, as I will later argue, the ethical perspective embodied in the notion of informed consent can help illuminate the array of research "bargains"—as Everett Hughes (1974) describes the often shifting connections between the observer and the observed—which have been struck in the course of field research.

THE COMPONENTS OF INFORMED CONSENT

The notion of informed consent helps put into focus specific strands in the relationships between fieldworkers and those they study. According to the regulations, informed consent is consent which is *knowledgeable,* exercised in a situation of *voluntary* choice, made by individuals who are *competent* or able to choose freely. As Freedman (1975) suggests, the legal requirement of informed consent embodies a "substantial requirement of morality," anchored in the Kantian categorical imperative, the belief that all individuals have a right to be treated as persons rather than objects, and to have their autonomy and dignity respected (also see Cassell, 1980).

The federal regulations mix both utilitarian and Kantian lines of reasoning. A utilitarian calculation of risks and benefits is required when review boards determine whether the regulations are applicable to a proposed research project, and when they determine if the subjects' rights seem adequately protected. Once granted approval, the researcher is required to inform the subjects of both risks and benefits entailed in the research. The principle of informed consent—based on Kantian assumptions—is included to protect individual rights against researchers' claims of broad social need or benefit (e.g., "the public's right to know"; "the development of science") which are often included in utilitarian calculations (Soble, 1978)....

The three dimensions of informed consent—knowledgeability, voluntary and competent choice—are merely starting points, since it is unclear just how much information needs to be imparted or present for consent to be knowledgeable, or how to know exactly when a given choice is sufficiently voluntary and responsible (Kelman, 1972: 1002). Furthermore, as the guidelines suggest, as risks increase, so does the importance of informed consent, because the actions taken by the researcher thereby become more fateful and the abrogation of rights more serious.

As many have noted, to understand the meaning of informed consent in the context of fieldwork requires going beyond abstract formulations to explore particular situations—and the fieldwork literature contains a large array. I will discuss two of the components of informed consent—knowledgeable and voluntary choice[3]—with reference to some of the specific situations and vicissitudes which fieldworkers have encountered.

WHEN IS CONSENT INFORMED? HOW MUCH INFORMATION SHOULD BE GIVEN?

The new regulations imply that uninformed consent is "tantamount to no consent at all" (Freedman, 1975), that researchers are obligated to disclose whatever information potential subjects would need to make an intelligent decision about participating in a study....

Erikson (1967) and Kelman (1972) have summarized the ethical objections to studies which involve deliberate misrepresentation of identities: such deception is intentionally dishonest, violating the trust basic to all social relationships; it invades privacy, denying subjects a chance to weigh possible risks and to determine what they want to reveal; special harms (e.g., stress if the fraud is uncovered or even suspected) may follow from acts of total deception, which also diminish the general public climate of trust toward sociology....

Erikson has identified a domain which many fieldworkers agree constitutes unethical conduct. As I will later elaborate, some kinds of disguised research may be defended on other ethical grounds, but from the Kantian perspective of informed consent, deliberate deception is unethical—and rests at a polar extreme from fully informed consent.

Although one can identify extremes, the actual dividing line between informed and uninformed remains unclear. Roth (1962: 283) has argued that "all social research is secret in some ways and to some degree—we never tell the subjects everything." One major reason for this, which Wax (1977) has emphasized, is that fieldworkers usually enter the field with an open-ended sense of purpose; they tend to work inductively and may shift interests and outlooks as the research proceeds; practical exigencies may force extensive change of plans. The very flexibility which is often cited as a major strength of field research poses obstacles for implementing a tight notion of informed consent, especially at the start of a research project.

And yet, do fieldworkers generally even *try* to fully share what they do know of their research goals, frameworks, methods, patterns of sponsorship, and expected reporting? I believe the answer is no; fieldworkers are rarely as honest and forthcoming with information as they could be. Barnes (1963) has noted that when they explain research to informants, ethnographers often stress the most innocuous aspects of their studies.... Self-introductions are bound up with efforts to gain access, and that practical motive, weighted heavily by investments of time, money and career, tends to squeeze honesty to the side.

Reviewing ethnographies to examine modes of self-introduction (when they are mentioned at all), I have been struck by the widespread use of partial truths. Gathering data for *Asylums*, Goffman spent a year doing fieldwork in a large mental hospital. According to the book's preface he told the hospital administrators something of his purpose, but with the patients—whose daily experiences were the focus of his study—Goffman assumed the role of an assistant to the athletic director, "when pressed, avowing to be a student of recreation and community life" (1971: ix).

When he was a participant-observer in the West End of Boston, Gans (1962) told community residents that he was "doing a recent history of the area," mainly surveying the institutions, organizations and the redevelopment process in the neighborhood. Gans mentioned, but did not emphasize, his interest in observing the everyday life of residents, and he did not tell them that he attended social gatherings "in the dual role of guest and observer" (1962: 344). Gans writes that with hindsight and additional fieldwork experience in another community, he came to believe he could have been more open about his research role....

The practical problem of gaining access to the groups they want to study has led investigators to provide vague and even misleading initial statements of identity and purpose. Another part of the problem—less within the control of fieldworkers—is that identities are a negotiated matter and even the most forthright observers cannot fully determine what they will be taken to be. When she studied the Thrashing Buffalo Indians, R. Wax (1971: 369) discovered that she was "variously taken for a teacher, an FBI investigator, a social worker, a professional cowgirl, a Wave recruiter and a communist agitator." ... [S]ince one may discover such misconceptions long after they have circulated, they may be difficult to correct....

When I did fieldwork among 4th and 5th grade school children, they sometimes took me to be a teacher's aide or a "yard duty" (playground supervisor). I tried to clarify that I had no formal role of authority in the school, partly because I wanted to get close to the children's world as it emerges when unconfined by adults. When I tried to explain to the children what I was up to with my constant roaming and busy scribbling, I often felt frustrated. For a while I explained that I was interested in "understanding the way children behave," until a boy said defensively "I didn't do nuthin'," and I realized the disciplinary connotations of the word "behavior." Gaps in understanding due to differential experiential worlds may hamper a researcher's ability to provide informed consent.

A More Complete Telling?

In developing relations in the field, how open can and should participant-observers be? The answer, of course, depends in large part upon context. One's ability to provide an informative and accurate form of self-identification varies with the group one is studying. As will later be argued (a line of argument not suggested by the notion of informed consent), the type of knowledge sought, and the nature of the group being studied ... may also have ethical bearing on choices about how to identify oneself.

There is another consideration: what sorts of information will individuals need in order to make a meaningful decision about participating? The federal regulations offer a listing suited for experiments: a description of risks and benefits, an offer to answer questions about the procedure, and instruction that the person is free to discontinue participation at any time. The list seems less pertinent in the looser and lengthier "research designs" of ethnography.

Subjects may, with good reason, want to know one's analytic framework since starting assumptions may pose long-term risks for a group. As Cassell (1978) has suggested, frameworks which reaffirm a "blaming the victim" or a "deficiency" approach to oppressed segments of society may affect public policy and reinforce existing inequalities. When I proposed to study the draft resistance movement, one of the leaders questioned me to see if I regarded resisters as "deviants"; he considered sociological conceptualizations of deviance to be politically and intellectually objectionable and wanted (understandably, in my view) to protect the movement from that sort of definition.

Patterns of sponsorship are also of no small import when one has a larger political understanding of the locations and potential uses of knowledge; Stephenson (1978) provides frightening documentation of secret CIA sponsorship of his study of Hungarian refugees, who, he notes, would probably "not have been so candid in the interviews," had they known the funding source. In some situations, researchers' naivete is small defense against the risk to which they may be putting the subjects. Especially in studying vulnerable groups, we have an obligation to try to understand, and to share with those we study, the political and social contexts of our projects.

These types of information bear on the long-range harms and benefits of social research. The day-to-day process of doing fieldwork may also entail felt harms. People aware of a fieldworker's general purpose and presence often do not realize what the methodology entails: making daily and detailed written records of ongoing behavior. I realize more fully now than I did at the time that my cumulative fieldnotes on the draft resistance movement were a potential source of jeopardy for participants who acted on the margins of the law and were the target of government surveillance. My field notes could easily have been stolen and used to document group and individual activities (although I changed names in my notes, the contexts would have facilitated identification). The notes, of course, were subject to subpoena, and although I vowed to burn them, were I subpoenaed, that intent didn't vitiate the fact that my daily research acts created risks for others—and risks not under *their* control.

In some settings the special kind of witnessing which is the essence of most fieldwork—the detached and analytic perspective, the gathering and recording of concrete detail to be sifted into analytic reports which will circulate to outsiders—may feel like a particular violation (Hughes, 1971: 505). Groups demanding extreme commitment and partisanship may not want the presence of an avowed neutral.... The opportunity to exercise informed consent seems to vary by *setting*, which may not be defensible on any ethical grounds. (Although disguised research may be more justifiable in fleeting encounters and public settings—where the stakes are low and people are already on guard—than in intensive, private sorts of settings.)

How and When Should One Inform?

The new HEW regulations have the effect of standardizing the initial phases of social research; getting a signed consent form has become an opening ritual. Some institutional review committees require ethnographers as well as experimentalists to obtain signed consent forms as a condition for obtaining funds or using the university's name.[6] Bortner (1979) documents such a case in a field study of a juvenile court. The review committee in her university stipulated that she had to obtain written informed consent from all those she observed. She asked court officials to sign consent forms, and then asked the presiding officer to read a statement as each juvenile came for a hearing. The statement identified her as a researcher, promised that she would not record or disclose individual identities, requested permission for her to remain, and appraised them of their right to order her departure at any point in the proceedings. Bortner not only experienced this procedure as a great nuisance (as, she reports, did the court officials), but also had doubts about whether the resulting consent was fully informed and voluntary.

The setting Bortner studied—a courtroom—is more in the spirit of the HEW legalistic opening ritual than are most fieldwork situations. Mann's (1976) description of how she gained access to observe in a bar is at another extreme. She was already a waitress before she decided to study the setting; the mode of interaction between bartenders and waitresses was one of joking and constant banter, with a tacit rule to avoid serious discourse. Mann informed the other employees (but not, apparently, bar patrons) of her research identity after she had been gathering data for some time; and she did so not by speaking to each person individually, providing them detailed information and a chance to refuse to participate (which is another dimension involved in the new regulations about informing), but by letting word about her activities get through the grapevine. She used a more direct explanation only near the end of her research, when she had developed good rapport with the other employees in the bar, and even then, she found her low status as a female prevented serious discussion of the topic. A great deal—the nature of the setting, the sequence of her research involvement, the way she was regarded—sets this fieldwork endeavor apart from the model for informing and asking consent which is embodied in the federal regulations. It may be worthwhile to ask if she *could* have come closer to the ideal of informed consent.

Mann's approach to gaining access is more typical of field studies than is Bortner's. Ethnographers do not tend to give extensive information to each person they observe, nor do they usually offer them an explicit moment of choice, telling them they have a right to decline participation or to withdraw from being studied at any time. Fieldworkers tend to assume that if their presence is tolerated, if they aren't told to leave, consent has been granted.... I want to call attention to the gap—partly anchored in the practical exigencies of research in natural settings—between customary fieldwork practice and the model embodied in the federal regulations.

Should Informed Consent Be Renewed?

Experiments and interviews are bounded events of short duration. Fieldwork, however, is a longer-term venture, sometimes extending to several years. Ethnographers try to become a part of ongoing daily worlds, and their lives intertwine with the lives of those they study much more fully and complexly than is the case with other types of research. Relationships between observer and observed emerge and change over time, and there may also be changes in the setting, organization or group being studied. Such changes may warrant a new, explicit effort to communicate one's purpose and one's methods as a researcher, and to ask for a renewed granting of consent. Cohen (1976) was sensitive to this situation when she did fieldwork with the American Indian Movement. As the movement shifted from a local to a national context and as its participants changed, she reassessed her relationship to the group, believing (although the leaders apparently didn't feel this way) that the consent the original group had given extended only to that original situation. She assessed the risks and dangers at the new stage of movement activity, and decided not to continue her research, partly for ethical reasons.

To meet the ethical requirement that consent should be informed, researchers may need to reassess their activity and provide fresh communications along the way. Informed consent may need renewing through another kind of effort: reminding those one is studying about the research purpose, if it seems to have slipped from awareness. This problem is not as acute in experiments or formal interviews, where the relationship of researcher and subject is highly segmentalized and limited, and where the situation—presence in a laboratory, or a short-term encounter defined as an interview—provides a steady reminder that research is in progress.

In contrast, fieldworkers often have what Chrisman (1976) calls "multiple identities." In addition to being observers, they may have a work role (Mann was a waitress; Goffman, a recreation director); they may be a committed member of a group (as I was in the draft resistance movement); they may share ethnic identity where that is a salient quality of participants (as Chrisman did with the Danish Americans he observed); they may—to return to an earlier point—*be taken to be* any number of things. And—most complicated and painful of all—fieldworkers may become good friends with those they are observing. Having other connections and modes of relating can be a source of access, acceptance and trust, and may provide ways of giving something back to those one has studied....

But many-stranded relationships also pose ambiguities. They make it easier for one's subjects to forget they are subjects, to think of the researcher *only* as a friend, movement member or coworker. This is especially true if one's social categories—age, sex, culture, ethnicity—don't visibly mark one as an outsider, as open note-taking or tape-recording tend to do. Fieldworkers often do not try to prevent this forgetting of the research purpose; the trust and acceptance feel good; information is more readily forthcoming. It is not a case of total deception because they indeed may be what they are taken to be—but they are also more. If the observed forget about the research activity—for example, if they give information with the understanding they are talking *only* to a friend or coworker and the information then goes into fieldnotes—is that ethical behavior? Many fieldworkers apparently feel it is not....

Part of the difficulty in these many-stranded relationships is that pressure against informed consent may come from subjects as well as from the fieldworker. Millman (1975: 619) has observed that it may be easier for everyone concerned if the researcher acts like part of the group; flaunting "mental outsidership" is interpersonally disruptive.

The Kantian idea that people should not be treated as objects suggests they should know they are being studied, and should be able to withhold information they don't want made into grist for the researcher's mill. A utilitarian calculus of harms and benefits also suggests people should be told when they are being studied, for the research role changes the horizon of consequences for the information conveyed. The information would not otherwise be systematically recorded, nor find its way to outside audiences.

IS THE CONSENT VOLUNTARY?

The notion of informed consent contains an image of a moment of individual, free choice—an occasion when a potential subject decides if she or he wishes to participate, understanding what participation would entail (especially possible risks), and without "intervention of any overt or indirect element of force, fraud, deceit, duress, overreaching, or other ulterior form of constraint or coercion" (Annas *et al.,* 1971: 291). This is the ideal, but given the complex conditions of the real world, we are left with the usual sort of sticky question: at what point is the consent sufficiently voluntary?

If one is recruiting subjects for an experiment, a survey or an interview, one must ask them to do something special: to come to one's lab and follow instructions, to fill out a questionnaire, to answer questions. The methods themselves provide points of choice, and asking subjects to sign a consent form can be fitted fairly easily into the opening phases of research. In contrast, participant-observers don't recruit individual subjects. They go to natural settings and tend to work their way in slowly, developing contacts, building trust, carving out a workable social position. The beginnings, as R. Wax (1971) has beautifully illustrated, are often fraught with false starts and difficulties, especially if the fieldwork is in a different culture. Participant-observers hope their subjects will continue their usual activities as if the observer weren't there.... Hence, the method of participant-observation does not in itself lead to moments of announcement and choice, unless one must formally request access to a setting, is asked to justify one's presence, or asks subjects for interviews.

In some situations there is such rapid turnover of participants (as in the draft resistance office, where new people continually came in for information) that it would be impossible to gain consent from every individual one might observe. In addition, the nature of the situation may be at odds with the action of providing formal choice points, as in the bar setting which Mann (1976) describes.

There is an added obstacle to realizing the ideal of informed consent.... Ethnographers seek access to natural groupings—communities, institutions, work groups, associations, social movements—and the organization of these groupings may have a strong and unavoidable effect on how much information each individual receives about the study, on whether or not consent is specifically requested, and on how truly voluntary an individual's consent might be.

Gatekeepers or potential sponsors are more likely to be told about the research project and to realize they have a right to say no, than are group members not in these positions. To gain access to a prison, one must get formal consent from prison authorities, but not necessarily from prisoners.... To be sure, gaining acceptance from captive populations (prisoners, patients, students) requires additional effort, and fieldworkers often take great care to try to separate themselves from the official lines of authority, especially if they want to study the subordinated groups (Becker, 1970). But there is still stratification of ability and opportunity to extract information about the study, to negotiate conditions, and to formally deny consent.

When I wanted to observe in an elementary school, I first approached the principal who asked knowledgeable questions about my background, purpose and method, and who set conditions: I was not to disrupt the classroom activities and take up their time, and I was to share my findings. I had similar entry discussions with the classroom teacher. The teacher introduced me to the children simply by name, and—I confess a bit ruefully now that I've been persuaded of the ethical importance of a fuller sense of informed consent, especially when one is studying relatively powerless groups—it never occurred to me to provide an initial explanation of my presence to the children, nor to ask them if they would consent to being observed....

Patterns of sponsorship and introduction affect the voluntary quality of individual choices to participate in field research. A powerful sponsor who vouches for a fieldworker may, in effect, abrogate the rights of other individuals in a setting to decide if the research should go on. Whyte (1955) gained access to a streetcorner gang through the sponsorship of Doc, who turned out to be the gang leader. If the gang members' bowling scores tended to be lower than Doc's (with game performance following social status—one of Whyte's findings), isn't it also possible that the other gang members felt constrained to accept Whyte's presence because Doc had agreed to it? Liebow describes the slow and often unpredictable route he took towards acceptance in a male streetcorner world in an urban black community. After he had hung out for four months, accepted and vouched for by a number of the men, he reports that "at least two men did not trust me or like me, but by then I was too strongly entrenched for them to challenge successfully my right to be there, even had they chosen to do so" (1967: 269). Did the situation deny those two men the right of voluntary consent? And what if some members of the gang wanted to be studied, while others did not—whose choice should prevail?

Even when consent forms are used, the organization of the immediate situation can diminish subjects' sense of choice. The juveniles and parents whom Bortner (1979) observed in a courtroom were each asked to sign a consent form, and told they had rights to refuse her presence, but their acceptance (in all but 2 of 250 hearings) was influenced, she believed, by their knowledge that court officials had already granted permission for her to observe. Situational rules—e.g., constraints to be polite and not to make the sort of scene which expelling a researcher might require[7]—may hamper the voluntary quality of a subject's participation. Furthermore, if a fieldworker was already present in the setting, as an employee, a group member or a resident, *before* undertaking the study (or at least revealing the research role), those observed may also feel less choice about letting the researcher stay on and observe.

THE ASSUMPTIONS OF INFORMED CONSENT: WHAT ETHICAL ISSUES ARE NEGLECTED?

Thus far I have described the obstacles to informed consent as *practical* difficulties. The last general point—that the contours of the natural groups and settings of field research run against the individual model of informed consent—leads to broader ethical questions. I have emphasized (as I believe the doctrine of informed consent tends to do) the right of individuals to say, "No," to being researched. But is there also a right to say, "Yes?"[8] What if a group of prisoners or mental patients want their situation studied and made public, but the wardens or the hospital administrators, fearful of exposure, refuse a researcher's request for access to the institution? If it made unjust conditions known so they might be remedied, such a study could be justified on ethical grounds, but if researchers had to disguise their purpose to conduct the study, they would violate the ethical principle of informed consent. The abstract, universal and individualistic assumptions of informed consent limit its ability to help resolve this sort of ethical dilemma. The doctrine of informed consent does not take account of ethical dimensions of the knowledge a researcher may seek. Informed consent applies to individuals, each of whom is to be treated the same, and ignores social structure and deep-seated differences of power.

Is Everyone Equally Deserving of Informed Consent?

Informed consent is asserted as a universal right, and the federal regulations apply to all potential subjects. But the regulations were instituted because some groups of subjects lack power relative to researchers and hence have less capacity to freely choose to participate.... As Kelman persuasively argues, ethical problems arise "because of the fact that, and to the extent that, the individuals, groups, and communities that provide data for social research are deficient in power relative to the other participants in the research process" (1972: 989). Patients, who are dependent upon doctors, may not feel able to say, "No," to medical research; other vulnerable groups, like children and mental patients, and subordinated populations (deviants, ethnic minorities, prisoners, students) may need special protection against possible exploitation by researchers. The requirement of informed consent is most easily justified with reference to relatively powerless groups, as a way of giving them a sense of countervailing power in research situations where they may feel coerced.

In itself, the universal principle of informed consent does not distinguish between the powerful and the powerless, but it offers some protection to the powerless simply by extending a right to be left alone which the powerful have always claimed for themselves.[9] It has often been observed that to be powerful is to be able to guard one's interests, to protect one's self from unwanted intrusions. The literature of the social sciences bears out this fact: the bulk of research has been on the less powerful, to whom researchers have greater access; only recently have ethnographers begun to urge the importance of studying up.

Elite groups are less in need of the protection granted by the principle of informed consent. They may also *warrant* less protection. In a much cited essay, Rainwater and Pittman argue that when the powerful are publicly accountable figures—government officials, police officers, physicians, college teachers—the public has a right to know what they are up to. Social scientists, they argue, have an obligation to generate information which will help further public accountability "in a society whose complexity makes it easier for people to avoid responsibilities" (1967: 365)....

In trying to further public accountability, Rainwater and Pittman argue that researchers may need to avoid promising confidentiality. They do not discuss whether disguised research is ethical in such circumstances, but others (e.g., Galliher, 1973; Christie, 1976) have argued that it might be. Galliher argues that ethical principles like informed consent ostensibly protect individuals, but also serve to protect powerful groups; they neglect the organization as a unit of analysis, and fail "to hold actors accountable in their organizational and occupational roles" (1973: 96). He calls for discussion of "whether only people in their roles as private citizens are to be protected, or if this protection also extends to actors filling roles in government and business."

The ethical dimensions of knowledge may qualify the principle of informed consent not only in situations of public accountability, but also in situations where behavior is so reprehensible or immoral that it warrants exposing. Fichter and Kolb suggest that if those studied have, in effect, renounced membership in a moral community by "choosing modes of action which violate ... basic values of dignity and worth" (1953: 549), rights to privacy may not apply. They offer the example of individuals like Hitler or Stalin, and groups like "Murder Incorporated" and the Ku Klux Klan, whose activities deserve to be reported in full detail. Fichter and Kolb also emphasize the great responsibility entailed in judging people or groups to be outside the moral community, and they warn against making the decision lightly, especially when "unpopular" groups are involved.

This warning points to difficult ethical judgments. But the element of judgment, in a concrete situation, is always crucial to considerations of ethics. While the principle of informed consent in some ways seems appealing because it is absolute and hence apparently an ideal for all circumstances, that is precisely one of its limitations. In its abstract individualism, the vision is narrow; it ignores historical and social contexts and questions about the purposes of knowledge. By itself, the doctrine of informed consent does not do full justice to the complexity of the ethical judgments fieldworkers confront.

There is danger that contemporary discussions of the ethics of social research will follow primarily along the lines set forth in the new federal regulations. While the doctrine of informed consent is central, it is not exhaustive, and we should not let it blind us to important questions about the responsibilities of social scientists and the ethical uses of knowledge in contemporary society.

NOTES

1. The traditional autonomy which fieldworkers have claimed to study what they want in the ways they choose and to make their own judgments about ethics has also been challenged by groups of subjects who—like patients disenchanted with the medical profession—are less acquiescent than in the past to the conditions set by researchers. Groups of blacks, Native Americans, and other minorities, and members of protest movements have begun to claim the right to review research proposals and to negotiate conditions; sometimes they have refused to be studied at all. Another challenge to the right fieldworkers claim to define the terms of their research has come from within the ranks of social scientists. Advocates of "action anthropology" (Lurie, 1973), "advocacy anthropology" (Schensul and Schensul, 1978), and "participatory research" (Cain, 1977) seek to develop more cooperative arrangements between researchers and the communities or groups to which they are attached, to work "with" or "for" rather than "on" a particular group (Jacobs, 1974). These movements have all emerged in research settings where the subjects are economically, socially and politically disadvantaged.

2. This paper deals only tangentially with emerging legal control of the relationship of researchers and subjects of research. It should be emphasized that many matters which used to be handled as more or less private ethical decisions are increasingly subject to official, including legal, sanctions and controls.

3. I will not deal with the third component of informed consent—the requirement that the consenting individual be competent, able to comprehend the information and to make a reasonable decision—partly because it has practical bearing only in fieldwork among children and the mentally ill. (Although, as John Kitsuse has pointed out to me, the more general question of how much subjects understand, of how they interpret and make sense of the researcher's presence, also bears on questions of whether consent is "competent.") It should be noted that for research involving children and institutionalized mental patients, government regulations specify that permission of parents or guardians must be obtained, as well as the assent of the child or the mental patient. In the case of children, such assent is required after the age of 7, although at any age the child's objection to nontherapeutic research is binding. In the case of mental patients, the individual's assent to participation must be secured if the consent committee judges that "he or she has sufficient mental capacity to understand what is proposed and to express an opinion as to his or her participation" (Annas *et al.,* 1977: 322).

...

6. According to Cassell (1978), citing information from William C. Sturtevant of the American Anthropological Association, institutional review boards interpret the federal regulations in varying ways: prestigious private universities tend to exempt ethnographic research from institutional review, with some routinely finding that ethnography constitutes no risk (so informed consent is not made an issue). Smaller, less prestigious institutions tend to apply the regulations with great literalness to fieldwork.

7. See an anonymous note in *The American Sociologist* (vol. 13, Aug., 1978) from a sociologist who describes the situational constraints s/he felt to continue as a respondent in an interview which s/he found offensive.

8. I am grateful to Howard Becker for drawing this question to my attention.

9. As Richard Colvard (1967: 341) has suggested, informed consent is closely tied to the right to privacy, a broad right to be left alone and free from intrusion in one's personal life. Legal conflicts

between the rights to privacy and free speech are pertinent to the ethical dilemmas bound up with informed consent.

REFERENCES

Annas, George J., Leonard H. Glantz and Barbara F. Katz. 1977. *Informed consent to human experimentation: The subject's dilemma.* Cambridge: Ballinger.

Barnes, J. A. 1963. Some ethical problems in field work. *British Journal of Sociology* 14:118–134.

Becker, Howard S. 1970. *Sociological work: Methods and substance.* Chicago: Aldine.

Becker, Howard S. 1971. Problems in the publication of field studies, pp. 267–284 in *Reflections on Community Studies,* ed. Arthur J. Vidich, Joseph Bensman, and Maurice R. Stein. New York: Harper Torch Book.

Bond, Kathleen. 1978. Confidentiality and the protection of human subjects in social science research: A report on recent developments. *The American Sociologist* 13:144–152.

Bortner, Peg. 1979. *The dilemma of human subjects regulations and research within the juvenile court.* Unpublished paper, Sociology Department, Washington University, St. Louis, Missouri.

Cain, Bonnie J. 1977. *Participatory research: Research with historic consciousness.* Participatory Research Project Working Paper No. 3 (24 Prince Albert, Toronto, Ontario, Canada M5 1B2).

Cassell, Joan. 1978. Risk and benefit to subjects of fieldwork. *American Sociologist* 13:134–143.

Cassell, Joan. 1980. Ethical principles for conducting fieldwork. *American Anthropologist* (in press).

Chrisman, Noel J. 1976. Secret societies: The ethics of urban fieldwork, pp. 135–147 in *Ethics and Anthropology: Dilemmas in Fieldwork,* ed. Michael A. Rynkiewich and James P. Spradley. New York: John Wiley and Sons.

Christie, Robert M. 1976. Comment on conflict methodology: A protagonist position. *Sociological Quarterly* 17:513–519.

Cohen, Fay. 1976. The American Indian movement and the anthropologist: Issues and implications of consent, pp. 81–94 in *Ethics and Anthropology: Dilemmas in Fieldwork,* ed. Michael A. Rynkiewich and James P. Spradley. New York: John Wiley and Sons.

Colvard, Richard. 1967. Interaction and identification in reporting field research: A critical reconsideration of protective procedures, pp. 319–358 in *Ethics, Politics and Social Research,* ed. Gideon Sjoberg. Cambridge: Schenkman.

Davis, Fred. 1960. Comment on "Initial Interaction of Newcomers in Alcoholics Anonymous." *Social Problems* 8:364–365.

Erikson, Kai T. 1967. A comment on disguised observation in sociology. *Social Problems* 14:366–373.

Festinger, Leon et al. 1956. *When prophecy fails.* New York: Harper and Row.

Fichter, Joseph H. and William L. Kolb. 1953. Ethical limitations on sociological reporting. *American Sociological Review* 18:455–550.

Freedman, Benjamin. 1975. A moral theory of informed consent. *Hastings Center Report* 5:32–39.

Galliher, John F. 1973. The protection of human subjects: A reexamination of the professional code of ethics. *The American Sociologist* 8:93–100.

Gans, Herbert J. 1962. *The urban villagers: Group and class in the life of Italian-Americans.* New York: Free Press.

Gans, Herbert J. 1968. The participant-observer as a human being: Observations on the personal aspects of fieldwork, pp. 300–317 in *Institutions and the Person,* ed. H. S. Becker et al. Chicago: Aldine.

Glazer, Myron. 1972. *The research adventure: Promise and problems of fieldwork.* New York: Random House.

Goffman, Erving. 1971. *Asylums.* New York: Anchor Books.

Gusfield, Joseph. 1955. Fieldwork reciprocities in studying a social movement. *Human Organization* 14:29–33.

Harrell-Bond, Barbara. 1976. Studying elites: Some special problems, pp. 123–134 in *Ethics and Anthropology: Dilemmas in Fieldwork,* ed. Michael A. Rynkiewich and James P. Spradley. New York: John Wiley and Sons.

Hughes, Everett C. 1971. *The sociological eye: Selected papers.* Chicago: Aldine.

Hughes, Everett C. 1974. Who studies whom? *Human Organization* 33:327–334.

Humphreys, Laud. 1970. *Tearoom trade: Impersonal sex in public places.* Chicago: Aldine.

Jacobs, Sue-Ellen. 1974. Action and advocacy anthropology. *Human Organization* 33:209–215.

Kelman, Herbert C. 1972. The rights of the subject in social research: An analysis in terms of relative power and legitimacy. *American Psychologist* 27:989–1016.

Liebow, Elliot. 1967. *Tally's corner.* Boston: Little, Brown.

Lofland, John F. 1966. *Doomsday cult: A study of conversion, proselytization and maintenance of faith.* Englewood Cliffs, N.J.: Prentice-Hall.

Lofland, John F. and Robert A. Lejeune. 1960. Initial interaction of newcomers in Alcoholics Anonymous: A field experiment in class symbols and socialization. *Social Problems* 8:102–111.

Lurie, Nancy Osterich. 1973. Action anthropology and the American Indian, pp. 4–14 in *Anthropology and the American Indian: Report of a Symposium.* San Francisco: Indian Historian Press.

Mann, Brenda J. 1976. The ethics of fieldwork in an urban bar, pp. 55–109 in *Ethics and Anthropology: Dilemmas in Fieldwork,* ed. Michael A. Rynkiewich and James P. Spradley. New York: John Wiley and Sons.

Millman, Marcia. 1975. Review of R. Fox and J. P. Swazey "The Courage to Fail: A Social View of Organ Transplants and Dialysis." *Contemporary Sociology* 4:617–619.

Nader, Laura. 1969. Up the anthropologist—Perspectives gained from studying up, pp. 284–311 in *Reinventing Anthropology,* ed. Dell Hymes. New York: Random House.

Rainwater, Lee and David J. Pittman. 1967. Ethical problems in studying a politically sensitive and deviant community. *Social Problems* 14:357–366.

Riesman, David and Jeanne Watson. 1967. The sociability project: A chronicle of frustration and achievement, pp. 270–371 in *Sociologists at Work,* ed. P. E. Hammond. Garden City: Anchor Books.

Roth, Julius. 1962. Comments on "Secret Observation." *Social Problems* 9:283–284.

Roy, Donald F. 1965. The role of the researcher in the study of social conflict. *Human Organization* 24:262–271.

Schensul, Stephen L. and Jean J. Schensul. 1978. Advocacy and applied anthropology, pp. 121–165 in *Social Scientists as Advocates,* ed. George Weber and George McCall. Views from the Applied Disciplines. Beverly Hills: Sage.

Soble, Alan. 1978. Deception in social science research: Is informed consent possible? *Hastings Center Report* 8:40–46.

Stephenson, Richard M. 1978. The CIA and the professor: A personal account. *The American Sociologist* 13:128–133.

Thorne, Barrie. 1979. Political activist as participant observer: Conflicts of commitment in the study of the resistance movement of the 1960's. *Symbolic Interaction* 2:73–88.

Von Hoffman, Nicholas, Irving Louis Horowitz and Lee Rainwater. 1970. Comment—an exchange: Sociological snoopers and journalistic moralizers. *TransAction* (May):4–8.

Wax, Murray L. 1977. On fieldworkers and those exposed to fieldwork: Federal regulations and moral issues. *Human Organization* 36:321–328.

Wax, Rosalie. 1971. *Doing fieldwork: Warnings and advice.* Chicago: University of Chicago Press.

Whyte, William F. 1955. *Street corner society.* Chicago: University of Chicago Press.

Naheed Islam

Research as an Act of Betrayal: Researching Race in an Asian Community in Los Angeles

As a Bangladeshi-American antiracist researcher working in the Bangladeshi immigrant community in Los Angeles, I had to negotiate two contradictory locations. Because of my Bangladeshi origins—my ethnicity/nationality—the academic community viewed me as an insider within my research community. However, the community questioned my insider status. Critical to this dynamic was my research topic. In this chapter I employ a *transnational* frame to explore how, when, and where "race" and "racism" entered the discourses of the Bangladeshi immigrants I interviewed in Los Angeles. I also examine how the discursive practices I detected (located within their ideological and material contexts) sustained antiblack and Latino racism while resisting racial hierarchies that positioned Bangladeshi-Americans as "not white" in the U.S. national context.

. . .

In their critique of positivist research methods feminists have demonstrated that researchers interpret, define, and therefore construct reality (Collins 1991; Reinharz 1992). But this constructivist perspective has been slow to change research on race and immigrant communities. Social scientists are only just beginning to acknowledge that research methodologies within the sociology subfields of race and ethnicity have been shaped by dominant discourses on race that have excluded more recent ethnic groups like South Asian immigrants.

. . .

In the sociological literature, immigrant communities are discussed in the context of three distinct concerns, namely, immigration, ethnicity, and race. The literature on immigration (Portes and Rumbaut 1990) uses an assimilationist model, examining how immigrants adjust to life in the United States. Ethnicity is seen as a resilient identity that shapes the immigrant experience. The ethnicity literature focuses on the culture of immigrants to explain differences between groups. . . .

Recent discussions on immigrant groups have been informed by a reshaped ethnicity framework. The continued primacy of ethnic identity, community (Chang and Leong 1994; Park 1997), and entrepreneurship (Light and Bonacich 1988) are used to analyze a group's location within the economy. Economic processes, the labor market, and class are considered more fundamental than race (Bonacich 1980; Wilson 1978). However, while ethnicity constructs group identity, group boundary, and social relationships, an analysis limited to ethnicity masks how race operates in the United States. This framework avoids an analysis of the structural and ideological underpinnings of racial inequality.

. . . Asians are among the fastest growing new actors entering the stage (Espiritu 1997). These new actors are racialized within the structural, discursive, and ideological spheres. The state plays a role in controlling their labor by delineating the boundaries of race and the citizenship/immigration processes. . . . In general, racialized group relations have been analyzed in relation to studies of blacks and whites (Gordon 1964; Jordon 1977; Essed 1991). A few scholars have explored the position of Latinos (Rodriguez 1991; Almaguer 1994; Gutierrez 1995). With the exception of Loewen (1971), scholarship about and by Asian and South Asian Americans has mostly focused on the areas of literary studies (Chin et al. 1974; Kim 1982) and history (Melendy 1981; Takaki 1987, 1989; Jensen 1988; Okihiro 1994).

This project attempts to address these gaps by examining the impact of South Asian immigration on racial formation in Los Angeles. Furthermore, it analyzes how relations are racialized between ethnic minority groups and ultimately how racist ideology is reproduced, maintained, and transformed. I argue that the experiences of Bangladeshis are linked to their racialization and to their racialized relationships with blacks, Latinos, other Asians, and whites in Los Angeles. It is also related to their understanding of "Americanness" and the U.S. racial categories imposed on them and the grounds on which they contest them.

OUTER BOUNDARIES: RESEARCH DESIGN

. . . My research examines a relatively new and growing immigrant community, that of the Bangladeshis in Los Angeles. I employed a three-pronged approach consisting of interviews, participant observation, and review of documents regarding the history of racial claims made by South Asians in the legal arena.

During the summer of 1993, I interviewed fourteen Bangladeshi women and four men. . . . I used a snowball method, asking each interviewee to introduce me to a few other Bangladeshis, to select the initial sample. Through these interviews I identified different segments of the community and initiated contact for the next stage of research.

Between 1993 and 1995, I spent eight months in Los Angeles. My initial survey located two distinct class-segregated communities. The first was a working-class community[2] in downtown Los Angeles, while the second was composed of professionals, including middle- to upper-middle-class immigrants.... I talked to at least a hundred people informally in various social and community gatherings and at their workplaces whenever possible.

I conducted sixty taped interviews, each lasting between two and four hours. I interviewed most people at least twice. The interviews had two sections. The first was a series of general questions regarding a person's date of migration, socioeconomic background, immigration status, and the box[4] he or she filled when asked his or her race. Then I used open-ended, semistructured interviews to analyze the everyday discourse of race, racism, self, and other in different spheres of immigrant life (Essed 1991; Twine, Warren, and Fernandiz 1991; Twine 1998).... Open-ended questions allowed me to analyze how they structured discourses on race and how they defined *race* and *racism,* to identify disruptions and continuity in their narratives, and to see what kinds of situations brought out racialized narratives. This process maximized "discovery and description."[5]

... I also reviewed the popular Bengali-American newspaper *Thikana* over a two-year period, to examine discussions of racialized experiences in the United States. A review of the history of legal racial classifications of Indians, Bangladeshis, and South Asians[6] in the United States was also made to examine the contestation and transformation of racial categories by Bangladeshis and South Asians at the state level. Multiple methods were thus used to achieve a triangulation method in order to link the micro and macro processes of racialized identity construction and to examine racialized experiences.

LANGUAGE AND TRANSNATIONAL CONSTRAINTS

There is no word for race in Bengali. My interviews were conducted primarily in Bengali, the official language of Bangladesh.... This linguistic gap is indicative of the differences in the concepts of race and its contents in Bangladesh, the United States, and transnational communities.[7] Middle- to working-class interviewees did not typically respond to direct questions regarding... what their "racial" identity was. Yet when asked about their experiences in the United States, racialized discourse became critical to their narratives. In conversation, *American* was equated with "white" Anglo-Americans and blacks, white being the norm. They translated some English terms into Bengali. Thus, European-Americans or whites were called *shada* (white) and black Americans were called *kallu* (black). They also used the English terms *negro, black, red Indian,* and *Native American.* People of Spanish-speaking backgrounds were referred to as Mexican or Spanish rather than Latino, Chicano, or Hispanic.

Interviewees had several responses to questions about racism and racial discrimination. A few had had no experience of racism or anti-immigrant sentiment. This may have been because they did not experience it, did not conceptualize it as such, or did not wish to share it with me. But most men and women provided many examples of what I viewed as a form of racial discrimination or racism. They offered three types of narratives. First, in some narratives they described being discriminated against because they were "foreign"; second, some narratives had an implicit element of racism, as when someone pointed to their "nonwhite" status; and third, some were explicitly racist.

"Foreign and American" is a racialized oppositional construction (Espiritu 1997) used to exclude racial minorities.... I view the claims to antiforeign and nonwhite status as interrelated forms of racialized exclusion. But these are also distinct narratives in which the interviewees do not *name* their experience as racism. Respondents usually shared these narratives with me during discussions about their everyday lives and problems rather than in response to direct questions about racism. Therefore, it is critical that researchers explore descriptive life histories. Such a method uncovers the conceptual framework of respondents, which is different from the one the researcher employs.

For a researcher working in immigrant communities, questions about race can be particularly tricky. The categories of race are not stable or static in any context (Omi and Winant 1986; Root 1992; Davis 1993; Twine 1996; Warren and Twine 1997).[8] But this is especially true when we deal with *transnational* notions of race, for racial concepts do not travel easily across national contexts or translate across languages and conceptual frameworks (Rodriguez 1991; Marable 1993). First, the very notion of "race" needs to be problematized and explored for its content. Second, narratives need to be examined for the immigrants' unique and multiple notions of race and racism, and to identify where and how these notions reside in the narrative. Third, one must recognize the critical problems posed when one analyzes the experiences of immigrant communities solely within a nationality/ethnicity framework. Immigrant groups are racialized in specific ways in the post–civil rights United States. As they develop and/or acquire a racialized identity in relation to other racial groups, their location within the United States can transform their notions of "race" and Americanness. A researcher therefore needs to develop strategies to highlight and contextualize indigenous, postcolonial, *and* U.S. systems of racialization in immigrant narratives.

ME AND MY COMMUNITY: CONFRONTING OUTSIDER WITHIN STATUS

I concur with Patricia Hill Collins (1991) and extend her analysis to include a Bangladeshi-American researcher. As an outsider in the U.S. academic community I can provide a unique perspective about the experience of Bangladeshi immigrants. But I also question the construction of community boundaries, asking who and what constitute belonging to a community. There are many axes of difference and commonality between me and "my community." Growing up in Bangladesh and interacting with Bangladeshi-American communities gave me an insight into some of the differences across gender, class, ethnic, religious, linguistic, cultural, and national lines that I would have to negotiate. . . . These negotiations interacted with my research interest to produce particular dilemmas. Maxine Baca Zinn . . . argues that minority scholars can generate questions that are different and that they face less distrust, hostility, and exclusion from minority communities (Andersen 1993: 41). I did face less hostility in some areas and could ask many questions about race and racism that "outside" scholars cannot do. But as an insider I also faced specific sites of hostility and dilemmas because of my class, gender position, the questions I asked, and the research product I have presented to the "outside" world.

I am a sociologist of upper-middle-class[9] Bangladeshi Muslim origin. I have lived in Bangladesh and the United States for almost equal lengths of time. My parents live in Bangladesh, while I have established a home in Oakland, California. This transnational experience shapes my communities and sense of belonging. . . . This multiplicity of belongings raises the question, am I conducting research in my "own" community when I do research in the Bangladeshi community in Los Angeles? What are the contours of this belonging or exclusion?

CONTOURS OF BELONGING/EXCLUSION

Most of my colleagues in the U.S. academy view me as an "insider" in my research community. However, the essentialized categories of nationality and ethnicity mask the complexities of "community" and its transnational boundaries. We are not automatically considered insiders in our respective ethnic communities. And both insider and outsider status hold specific meaning and consequences. Whenever I entered an interview session, I was interviewed first. . . . The most common questions were about my father's occupation, my parents' region of origin, my marital status, my role as a cook and homemaker, and my plans for motherhood. These questions were a means of evaluating my relationship to the individual members of the community and specific gendered constructions of community boundaries.

As South Asian feminist scholars have documented, in the early twentieth century, a nationalist discourse about "woman" became critical to the struggle against British imperialism in the region (Liddle and Joshi 1986; Banerjee 1989). The interaction between imperialism and nationalism created a binary opposition between world and home, Western(ized) and Eastern(deshi or national) (Chatterjee 1989).[10] Women were defined as belonging within the home and as symbols of tradition and upholders of the moral order (Liddle and Joshi 1986; Chatterjee 1989).[11] Nationalism reified middle-class women as the norm and reinscribed their role in the domestic sphere. Their sexuality and labor were controlled through marriage (Hartman 1981; Liddle and Joshi 1986). But middle- and upper-class women could avoid housework by purchasing the labor of working-class men and women. The ideal South Asian woman was also partially constructed against the notion of "Western" women. Western was defined as white and viewed in terms of the good woman–bad woman dichotomy (Jayawardena 1995). Good women are those who maintain gender hierarchy, while bad women are sexually immoral and licentious. South Asian women were/are scrutinized for signs of Westernness which was/is symbolized by their clothing and other markers.[12] In light of this nationalist discourse, the questions asked of me by members of the Los Angeles Bangladeshi community can be understood as an evaluation of my place within the class, gender, and race-specific notions of Bangladeshness and Westernness.[13]

An acquaintance invited me to a social gathering which was described as a young bicultural group. I dressed in jeans and a jacket. When I arrived, I found that all the women were wearing saris. For a large part of the evening I spoke to the only non-Bangladeshi woman in the room.... After the party one of the women informed me that I was being talked about. I was seen to have been acting white and wanting to be white.

My short hair, and the way I walked and talked, all inscribed me as outside the dominant nationalist definition of Bangladeshness. While I always tried to answer questions truthfully, I also policed how I presented myself....

My *marital* status and housework skills helped me establish relationships with married women and gain respectability. Since my husband had not accompanied me to Los Angeles, I brought up his name occasionally to remind people that I was married. It provided me with a "legitimate" relationship with male members of the community....

Nevertheless, I had a very difficult time setting up interviews with men, particularly when they were single.[19] ... I was repeatedly warned by members of the community that if I went to a man's house alone my reputation would be tarnished and my safety would be at stake. I tried to meet some men in cafés. But most men were uncomfortable sharing a meal or tea with a woman in a public space. Such encounters were also charged with sexual innuendo.... I used my professional researcher status to distance and shield myself from the sexual advances of men.

While being a female interviewer created particular challenges, my gendered class background gave me privileges that were also problematic. A male interviewee explained ... [that] he had been unable to find a good job in Bangladesh because he was not related to any wealthy people.... It was in Bangladesh that the upper class had treated him poorly. While he shared this story with me he also reminded me that I was a part of the group that had treated him with disrespect.

...

Throughout our discussion he maintained an idealized image of the United States. Later, when I interviewed his wife this narrative was disrupted. She explained that they had moved from Texas because they had gotten tired of the harassment they faced and wanted a new start. When her husband walked home from work a group of white men would routinely throw beer cans at him and shout profanities.[20] She said he always kept walking and never reported these incidents to anyone.... Perhaps my class and gender position had foreclosed discussions of experiences he considered humiliating. He also wished to portray an idealized place in which he could maintain his pride and dignity....

My class, gender, and bicultural identity all shaped my relationship to members of the community. I had to survey my own presentation constantly to remain inscribed within community boundaries.... While my insider status provided me with unique insights and access, it also created particular dilemmas.

ASSUMED, SHARED RACISM

Most of the time I was considered a racial insider. During interviews people felt very comfortable making vehemently racist statements against blacks and Latinos because it was assumed that I would share these views. Most people freely made statements, in public and private, which were particularly virulent against black Americans. Blacks are commonly called *kallus* (blackies) in Bengali.... The comments ranged from claims that blacks ruined property values, that they were thieves, to the general assumption that they were an inferior group of people. Blacks were considered naturally savage and delinquent. This inferiority was seen to be proven by their enslavement. Patricia Hill Collins has called these "controlling images" (Collins 1990). Such images are used by the political and economic elite to naturalize racism, sexism, and poverty. Immigrant groups who face specific controlling images can also reproduce controlling images of their own about groups such as blacks, thus participating in the maintenance of a racial hierarchy.

... One day I struck up a conversation with a Bangladeshi man, Shahed, who was working in a parking lot. Within the first ten minutes he identified the main source of his problems as black Americans. He said vehemently, "I hate blacks. Black people are my worst enemy. Even if someone slapped me I would forgive them, but I would never forgive a black. I will always hate blacks, they are my worst enemy in this country." He said he constantly distanced himself from blacks to gain dignity in the United States (see Warren and Twine 1997).... Our "foreign" language had created a private space even in a public arena. This shared language created an insular and permissive space for such conversation.

... I began to ponder my response and its place in my research. Should I challenge these views? To what extent and in what form would I respond to such comments within and outside the interviews?

INTERVIEWEE RESPONSES

Striking Back

... As an "insider" I recognized that skin color is a very sensitive issue in the Bangladeshi community. White and fair skin signify beauty and power. There is an intricate color hierarchy, in which darker-skinned people are called dirty and fairer ones are called clean. Being very dark automatically means one is ugly. It is considered rude to point to the darkness of one's skin color unless the person being referred to is absent. When people want to speak about someone who has dark skin they always say, *"even though* s/he is black ... (they have a sweet face or ...)."

... I have found that while people would deny that they had ever been mistaken for a black person, they would turn around and say that I could easily pass for black. These interactions carried two kinds of meaning. The first response was what I call *striking back*. They were insulted by what they considered my insinuation about their skin color and that they may pass for the "idea" of black in America. They were retaliating by calling me black. Noting skin color and/or associating it with blacks was a way of telling me that I was not fair skinned (superior) myself. I was the one who could pass for black, not the other way around.... Therefore, as a researcher I had to negotiate my own insider knowledge about the connotations and sensitivity around skin color and decide how and when to call attention to it. Just as my insider status gave me access to particular discourses, it also made others difficult to explore.

From my exposure to different Bangladeshi communities, I was familiar with racist attitudes toward U.S. blacks. But I was not prepared for the extent to which it was a part of everyday life and conversation. This "discovery" forced me to recognize all the times when I had listened to similar comments and ignored them or had been silent in its presence. I had focused on the experiences I shared with other Bangladeshis.... This commonality gave me access and entry into the Bangladeshi community in Los Angeles.

But as I entered the community as a researcher, I contemplated the price for my inclusion in "my community." If I challenged antiblack comments I could be silenced by being ignored and made invisible. The hostility generated by my questions could easily shut me out of critical parts of the community and my research interest. But if I were to remain silent I would be participating in perpetuating racist discourse. Since I had been reminded that I could be symbolically expelled from the community if I associated members of the community or myself with the category "black," the price for my entry and inclusion was my silence.

Marking Ethnicity

The second response to my question regarding racial identity was to *mark ethnicity*. Bangladeshis tacitly recognize that they can easily be coded as black and Latino in the United States. They point to their ethnic markers as a way of distancing their own bodies from blacks. They create a racialized discourse about the ways in which they are culturally and physically distinct from blacks and Latinos. These distinctions are class- and gender-specific. Blacks and Latinos, particularly of the working class, are seen to be promiscuous and immoral. In the U.S. context, the gendered anticolonial definitions of Western as white are expanded to include working-class white, black, and Latina women. "Their" women's immorality is marked by their choice of clothing, body language, associations with men outside the family, and consumption of alcohol. Therefore, an idealized Bangladeshi woman cannot and does not do any of these things.... This process of marking ethnicity also demonstrated how the boundaries of ethnicity are constructed against specific racialized images. Therefore, ethnicized and racialized discourses are intertwined.

PRESENTING THE COMMUNITY: CONTAINING BOUNDARIES

An immigrant community redefines the boundaries of "community" when there is a sudden and dramatic shift in geography and socioeconomic and political context. This shift can lead to intense struggles over representation and contestation by groups to control the boundaries of community in the new social order. The following are excerpts from some interviews that highlight the slippery terrain of these boundaries and the way race, class, and gender shape them in the U.S. context. These contestations occurred in three arenas, through attempts to exclude the stories of earlier immigrants because of their racial affiliations and social location, which marked some members of the same national group as racial outsiders, and marked me as a racial other. These stories illustrate how immigrant communities redraw community boundaries in a system where bodies are racially marked and where racial signification is linked to power and status in the larger society (Islam in press).

Those Racially Other Bangladeshis

The markers of nationality and ethnicity are considered primary in researching immigrant communities in the United States. Yet no national and/or ethnic community is homogeneous. And in the context of the U.S. racial order, not all groups in such communities occupy the same racial location. For example, in Bangladesh the Hill Peoples of the south are marked by their clothing and language and by the Animist, Buddhist, and Hindu religions. Although seen as Bangladeshi citizens, they are second class (Tripura 1992). They are socially and politically repressed through the military and by an ideology of ethnic and religious inferiority. When Bangladeshi immigrants construct a new community in the United States, they try to create it on the basis of old boundaries and new contexts. While Hill People and lowland Bengali Muslim immigrants do have some connections, they are limited to individual contacts. The relationships and markers of exclusion and inclusion between the two groups are further complicated by the racialized terrain of American society.

I met two Hill People immigrants in Los Angeles by a mixture of luck and my own insider identity.... They informed me that in the United States they are viewed as East Asian. Their associations through temple, family, and friendship in combination with physical markers had shaped this racialization.

...

Hill People and tribes and other ethnic and religious minorities in Bangladesh are excluded from the boundaries of Bengali/Bangladeshi identity. These ethnic identities have carried over to the immigrant landscape. But the immigrant space also helps pry open assumed categories and transposes new lenses—a racialized lens. After the interviews with Opu and Shefal I asked Non–Hill Peoples from Bangladesh how Hill Peoples were viewed in the community. A few people said that while they "admitted" that Hill Peoples were Bangladeshi, they did not see them as part of the Bangladeshi community....

Racial categories are not stable and may be transformed upon migration. Groups whose exclusion from the dominant Bangladeshi communities may have been based on religious and ethnic differences can take on a racial meaning in the United States.... When community boundaries are reconstructed in a new national context, a homogenized, contained and deliberately exclusive version of a community will be produced. Scholars must therefore be conscious of the contestation and transformation of racial categories by immigrant communities in the United States.

Mixed Marriages and Early Immigrant History

During my research I uncovered evidence of early Bangladeshi immigration (1900–1945),[23] most of it by poor male merchant marines who overstayed their shore leaves. They faced segregation, antimiscegenation laws, and were employed at low-wage agricultural and service jobs. They married black and Mexican-American women and became integrated into multiracial communities. The men who married black women faced some social distancing from those who married Mexican women. All these immigrants have died. The next group of immigrants (1945–1975) consisted of students and middle-class male professionals who brought back wives from Bangladesh. I tried to trace the lives of the early immigrants to document their racialized location and track how and if it changed for later immigrants who possessed more resources.

Mr. Mir, a middle-class immigrant, immigrated to the U.S. in the 1950s. While he distinguished his class background from the merchant marines, his current socioeconomic position in the United States did not differ significantly. He knew the earlier merchant marine immigrants and attempted to restrict the representations of community history by excluding the stories of the widows of these immigrants and their children.... So he directed and tried to control the boundaries of my research. While he was willing to talk to me he refused a formal interview and tried to block my efforts to contact the black and Mexican-American spouses. He also spread the word to other older immigrants and asked them to deny me interviews.

I had talked to Mr. Sheikh who came in the 1950s and knew the earlier immigrants. He had initially promised an interview. But when I called back to set up a time I faced questions and barriers and eventually a refusal to be interviewed because of my interest in earlier immigrants. He claimed that this was not a legitimate arena of inquiry.... Then he decided to tell me how to conduct my research. He said, why do you need to talk to people, why don't you just send off a survey questionnaire? That would be a lot better. When I tried to answer his questions, he reminded me that he spoke from a position of authority as he was an older male and had studied "pure science." ... Mr. Sheikh used his "authority" as an older male to discipline and silence me.[24] This group of immigrants had decided that Mexican-American and black spouses were not legitimate purveyors of community history, though they had created the space in their homes for the community to meet and build itself up. The children of mixed black, Mexican, and Bangladeshi heritage were not seen as being "inside" the community. Although patriarchy inscribes children as the father's "property," in this instance the children were associated with their mother's "race." They were not considered a part of the Bangladeshi community.[25]

The reason why the older immigrants were trying to "shelter" this part of the community's history had to do with the racial and class positions of the early immigrants. Most of the initial immigrants came from poor backgrounds and wanted to escape their lower status. Some came from middle-class backgrounds and found themselves unable to maintain their class status in the United States. And they faced a racially divided world in which they saw themselves as being at the bottom. They were excluded from citizenship, delegated to the worst agricultural jobs, not allowed to buy land or to work in most jobs (Jensen 1988), and were forced to live in segregated neighborhoods as did blacks, Asians, Latinos (and other racial minorities), based on their "race." . . .

Most of the early immigrants told me what I should write about the later immigrants who are professionals, have been economically successful, and have had more "dignified" histories. Show the good face of the community, they instructed. Men who were poor and/or had married black and Mexican women were not the good face and neither were their families. Efforts were also under way to systematically eliminate or contain the stories of women and the working class. Only middle- and upper-class, legal immigrants deemed economically successful were worthy of representing Bangladeshis. Therefore, the legitimate storytellers were assigned by class, gender, and racial position, association, and history.

This attempt to contain a community's representation is reflected in the desire of segments of that community to maintain a model minority image (Espiritu 1997; Okihiro 1994). This image is constructed against the image of blacks who are seen to have failed due to their inability to take advantage of the American Dream. This dream serves as a "controlling image" repressing both Asian Americans and blacks (Espiritu 1997), while justifying the racial hierarchy. France Winddance Twine theorizes, in the context of her research in Brazil, that silences that do not challenge racism maintain white supremacy. Many professional Bangladeshis (and other Asians) reproduce and maintain this racial hierarchy by accepting and perpetuating the model minority myth. By challenging the border patrols of representation and unpacking the racialized narratives in the framework of domination and resistance, Bangladeshi and Asian American scholars can attempt to break this silence and challenge racial hierarchies.

The Researcher as Translator and Betrayer

I spent many hours with interviewees who recounted stories of their own degradation as nonwhites and foreigners in U.S. society. They described facing intense forms of racism and exclusion. Bangladeshis viewed themselves as under attack from the U.S. state which restricted their immigration and rights, and from "Americans"[26] (defined as whites and blacks) and East Asians (at times defined as white) in their everyday lives. They described incidents that were daily reminders of their low social status. They claimed that both blacks and whites reminded them that even if they gained official citizenship they would not be included in the cultural representations of an "American." They would always be seen as "foreigners" and asked where they were really from. Middle-class Bangladeshis reported that they confronted the glass ceiling in the workplace and other forms of exclusion. Working-class Bangladeshis reported frequent incidents of physical violence and threat of violence or verbal abuse from Americans. They described verbal racialized violence and humiliation from whites, blacks, and East Asians. They did not mention Latinos in this context.[27] Thus, faced with the idea of permanent exclusion from the U.S. national community and multiple forms of discrimination, they felt besieged as well.

People in the community saw my research project as an opportunity to document their community history for the next generation, to present themselves to the larger (white) American community, to voice their grievances, and to fulfill my personal and academic interests. They documented their life stories and own racialized oppression while reproducing a racist ideology about "other" racial minorities. Some wished to present an idealized model minority image of the community that necessitated severing any relationship to blacks and Latinos. As a researcher parts of the community expected me to censor and skew my presentation to meet these interests....

Given this context, a Bangladeshi scholar documenting the experiences of her "own" community faces a critical responsibility. By outlining the contours of the racial ideology of Bangladeshi immigrants I risk being viewed as a traitor within my ethnic community. My very insider status allowed me to participate in and overhear conversations that routinely included racist views. The price of my inclusion in the community was to leave racist discourses uncontested. Should I reveal this "dirty laundry" once I have completed my research? By doing so, will I be distancing myself from and claiming to be better than the rest of "my community"? The history and experiences of the Bangladeshi community in the United States are yet undocumented. Should its introduction be "overshadowed" by the racist discourse the community reproduces? How should I represent a marginalized community within and through my work?

A Bangladeshi community is a part of my community. But I challenge the notion of an essentialized national and/or ethnic community. The Bangladeshi immigrant communities themselves reconstruct community boundaries within the racialized context of the United States. Those who do not fit the dominant interests of the community and its idealized image are excluded. If a part of that exclusion is based on one's antiracist politics then I claim my own belonging within a different political community.

As bell hooks reminds us, third world nationals (within and outside the U.S.) can illuminate their own oppression yet be silent about the position of those of African descent:

> We often forget that many third world nationals bring to this country the same kind of contempt and disrespect for blackness that is most frequently associated with white western imperialism. While it is true that many third world nationals who live in Britain and the United States develop through theoretical and concrete experience knowledge of how they are diminished by white western racism, that does not always lead them to interrogate the way in which they enter a racialized hierarchy where in the eyes of whites they automatically have a greater status and privilege than individuals of African descent. (1990: 93–94)

CONCLUSION

My research reemphasized my own need to interrogate everyday narratives since racism is deeply embedded in everyday language, and in ways of knowing and living. If I sanitize and silence parts of my research that challenge the Bangladeshi community's image of itself and its role in perpetuating racism, I betray my commitment to struggle against racism. Describing the process by which Bangladeshis reproduce racism and racist ideologies need not negate a presentation of the oppression Bangladeshis themselves face, and vice versa. Silencing either may he viewed as an act of betrayal. Scholars facing such dilemmas may choose to remain silent about how minority communities can participate in and reproduce racist ideologies. Ultimately such silences subvert an analysis and understanding of how racism operates and how racialized systems of domination and inequality are maintained. Therefore, such silences are a betrayal of antiracist politics.

NOTES

...

2.   ... I define them as working class because of their current class position in the United States, not because of their middle-class or upper-middle-class origins in Bangladesh.

...

4. France Winndance Twine asked interviewees how they self-identified racially when forced to choose from among the identity boxes on federal and other official forms. This enabled her to analyze the construction of racial identity and racial consciousness among young adults who had one black and one nonblack (Asian, white, Latino) parent in the post–civil rights United States. See Twine, Warren, and Fernandiz 1991; and Twine 1996.

5. From Janice Raymond, *The Transsexual Empire: The Making of the She-Male* (Boston: Beacon Press, 1976), quoted in Reinharz 1992.

6. Bangladesh was a part of India until 1947 and of Pakistan until 1971. Therefore, Bangladeshis appear in historical documents as Indian and Pakistani citizens. Recent scholarship in the United States has placed Bangladeshis within a South Asian category (Islam 1993). Therefore all these categories are applicable to Bangladeshi immigrants.

7. Some did not speak English at all. This difference in language skills usually reflected class background. People from upper-class or middle-class backgrounds were much more likely to speak English fluently. Depending on people's language skills, I also used Bengali and English interchangeably in some interviews. I later translated and transcribed all the interviews into English.

8. Scholarship on the construction of the U.S. categories referred to as black and white has illuminated the social construction of race. People of ambiguous racial ancestry who self-identify as "mixed race" or multiracial have always posed a challenge to the naturalness of these racial categories and boundaries.

9. My life history encompasses a few shifts in class position. I have moved from middle-class to upper-middle-class status through my parents' upward mobility and my own marriage.

10. *Deshi* is a Bengali and Urdu/Hindi word meaning "of one's own country."

11. Chatterjee notes that Indians could utilize science and technology in the outside world but at home their "true identity" was to be maintained. Within the home the man was also the ruler, a role denied him in the public world by the colonizer. "In the world, imitation of and adaptation to western norms was a necessity; at home they were tantamount to annihilation of one's very identity" (1989: 239).

12. Class and Westernness are often intertwined. Upper-class women are more likely to be viewed as Western.

13. I will be using the terms Bangladeshness and Westernness to signify dominant discourses of nationality and inclusion developed within a South Asian anticolonial context.

...

19. Many immigrant men are forced to live without their families. Men come as primary migrants and are unable to bring their families to the United States due to immigration restrictions and financial instability. There are also many unmarried men between the ages of twenty and thirty.

20. She did not tell me exactly what these men had said. She said she could not bring herself to speak such words. But she described them as being against foreigners.

...

23. There has been mention of a few early Bangladeshi immigrants in documents on South Asian–American history (Jensen 1988; Melendy 1981). But my research is the first to document the life stories of Bangladeshis arriving between 1910 and 1960.

24. Anthropologist Dorinne Kondo addresses similar problems, describing how she was viewed as a subordinated daughter/woman, rather than a competent researcher, by older men in the Japanese community (Kondo 1986).

25. During my visits to Bangladesh since this research I have noticed children of mixed race and how they are perceived there. Children born to Bangladeshi mothers or fathers are treated as Bangladeshi. Families do often joke that these children are "foreign." But second-generation Bangladeshi-Americans both of whose parents are Bangladeshi are also referred to as foreign, referring to their culture rather than their race.

26. Though inscribing blacks within the "American" category is fraught with silences about their exclusion and oppression, Bangladeshi immigrants view blacks as the "other" Americans. While whites are the "norm," blacks are seen to have successfully claimed their status as "Americans" in a way that Asian and Latino groups have not been able to.

27.   Bangladeshis may view upper-class Latinos as whites since they partly define *white* by skin color. Working-class and brown-skinned Latinos are viewed as "illegal," "alien," and inscribed outside the construction of the category "American."

REFERENCES

Allen, Theodore. 1994. *The Invention of the White Race.* New York: Verso.

Almaguer, Tomas. 1994. *Racial Fault Lines: The Historical Origins of White Supremacy in California.* Berkeley: University of California Press.

Andersen, Margaret L. 1993. "Studying across Difference: Race, Class, and Gender in Qualitative Research." In *Race and Ethnicity in Research Methods,* edited by John Stanfield and Dennis M. Rutledge. Newbury Park, Calif.: Sage.

Banerjee, Sumanta. 1989. "Marginalization of Women's Popular Culture in Nineteenth Century Bengal." In *Recasting Women: Essays in Colonial History,* edited by Kumkum Sangari and Sudesh Vaid. New Delhi: Kali for Women.

Blauner, Robert. 1972. *Racial Oppression in America.* Berkeley: University of California Press.

Bonacich, Edna. 1972. "A Theory of Ethnic Antagonism: The Split Labor Market." *American Sociological Review* 37: 547–59.

———. 1973. "A Theory of Middleman Minorities." *American Sociological Review* 38: 583–94.

———. 1980. "Class Approaches to Ethnicity and Race." *Insurgent Sociologist* 10 (2): 9–23.

Chan, Sucheng. 1991a. *Asian Americans: An Interpretive History.* Boston: Twayne Publishers.

———. 1991b. *Asian Californians.* San Francisco: MTL/Boyd and Fraser.

Chang, Edward T., and Russell Leong, eds. 1994. *Los Angeles—Struggles toward Multiethnic Community.* Seattle: University of Washington Press.

Chatterjee, Partha. 1989. "The Nationalist Resolution of the Women's Question." In *Recasting Women: Essays in Colonial History,* edited by Kumkum Sangari and Sudesh Vaid. New Delhi: Kali for Women.

Chin, Frank, Jeffery Chan, Lawson F. Inada, and Shawn Hsu Wong, eds. 1974. *An Anthology of Asian American Writers.* Washington, D.C.: Howard University Press.

Collins, Patricia Hill. 1990. *Black Feminist Thought: Knowledge, Consciousness, and the Politics of Empowerment.* New York: Routledge.

———. 1991. "Learning from the Outsider Within: The Sociological Significance of Black Feminist Thought." In *Beyond Methodology: Feminist Scholarship as Lived Research,* edited by Mary Margaret Fonow and Judith A. Cook, pp. 35–59. Bloomington: Indiana University Press.

Davis, James. F. 1993. *Who Is Black? One Nation's Definition.* University Park: Pennsylvania State University Press.

Espiritu, Yen Le. 1997. *Asian American Women and Men.* Thousand Oaks, Calif.: Sage.

Essed, Philomena. 1991. *Understanding Everyday Racism: An Interdisciplinary Theory* (Sage Series on Race and Ethnic Relations, vol. 2). Newbury Park, Calif.: Sage.

Fisher, Maxine P. 1980. *The Indians of New York City: A Study of Immigrants from India.* New Delhi: Heritage Publishers.

Frankenberg, Ruth. 1993. *White Women, Race Matters: The Social Construction of Whiteness.* Minneapolis: University of Minnesota Press.

Glazer, Nathan, and Daniel P. Moynihan. 1963. *Beyond the Melting Pot.* Cambridge: M.I.T. Press.

Goffman, Erving. 1959. *The Presentation of Self in Everyday Life.* New York: Anchor Books.

Gordon, Milton. 1964. *Assimilation in American Life: The Role of Race, Religion, and National Origins.* New York: Oxford University Press.

Gutierrez, David G. 1995. *Walls and Mirrors: Mexican Americans, Mexican Immigrants, and the Politics of Ethnicity.* Berkeley: University of California Press.

Hartman, Heidi. 1981. "The Unhappy Marriage of Marxism and Feminism: Towards a More Progressive Union." In *Women and Revolution,* edited by Lydia Sargent. London: Pluto.

hooks, bell. 1981. *Ain't I a Woman: Black Women and Feminism.* Boston: South End Press.

———. 1990. *Yearning: Race, Gender, and Cultural Politics.* Boston: South End Press.

Ignatiev, Noel. 1995. *How the Irish Became White.* New York: Routledge.

Islam, Naheed. 1993. "In the Belly of the Multicultural Beast I Am Named South Asian." In *Our Feet Walk the Sky: Women of the South Asian Diaspora,* edited by the Women of South Asian Descent Collective. San Francisco: Aunt Lute.

————. In press. "Race Markers Transgressors: Mapping a Racial Kaleidoscope within an (Im)migrant Landscape." In *American Encounters,* edited by Rajini Srikanth, Roshni Rustomji-Kerns, and Leny Strobel. Boston: Rowman and Littlefield.

Jayawardena, Kumari. 1995. *The White Woman's Other Burden: Western Women and South Asia during British Rule.* New York: Routledge.

Jensen, Joan M. 1988. *Passage from India: Asian Indian Immigrants in North America.* New Haven: Yale University Press.

Jibou, Robert M. 1988. *Ethnicity and Assimilation: Blacks, Chinese, Filipinos, Japanese, Koreans, Mexicans, Vietnamese, and Whites.* Albany: State University of New York Press.

Jordon, Winthrop D. 1977. *White over Black: American Attitudes towards the Negro, 1550–1812.* New York: Norton.

Kim, Elaine H. 1982. *Asian American Literature: An Introduction to the Writings and Their Social Context.* Philadelphia: Temple University Press.

Kondo, Dorinne K. 1986. "Dissolution and Reconstruction of Self: Implications for Anthropological Epistemology." In *Cultural Anthropology* 1 (1): 74–88.

Liddle, Joanna, and Rama Joshi. 1986. *Daughters of Independence: Gender, Caste and Class in India.* New Brunswick, N.J.: Rutgers University Press.

Light, Ivan, and Edna Bonacich. 1988. *Immigrant Entrepreneurs: Koreans in Los Angeles.* Berkeley: University of California Press.

Loewen, James W. 1971. *The Mississippi Chinese: Between Black and White.* Prospect Heights, Ill.: Waveland Press.

López, Ian F. Haney. 1996. *White by Law: The Legal Construction of Race.* New York: New York University Press.

Lowe, Lisa. 1996. *Immigrant Acts: Asian American Cultural Politics.* Durham: Duke University Press.

Marable, Manning. 1993. "Beyond Racial Identity Politics: Towards a Liberation Theory for Multicultural Democracy." *Race and Class* 35 (1): 113–30.

Mazumdar, Sucheta. 1989. "Race and Racism: South Asians in the United States." In *Frontiers of Asian American Studies.* Pullman: Washington State University Press.

Melendy, H. Brett. 1981. *Asians in America: Fillipinos, Koreans, and East Indians.* New York: Hippocrene Press.

Min, Pyong Gap. 1996. *Caught in the Middle: Korean Merchants in America's Multiethnic Cities.* Berkeley: University of California Press.

Okihiro, Gary Y. 1994. *Margins and Mainstreams: Asians in American History and Culture.* Seattle: University of Washington Press.

Omi, Michael, and Howard Winant. 1986. *Racial Formation in the United States: From the 1960s to the 1990s.* New York: Routledge.

Ong, Paul, Edna Bonacich, and Lucie Cheng. 1994. *The New Asian Immigration in Los Angeles and Global Restructuring.* Philadelphia: Temple University Press.

Park, Kyeyoung. 1997. *The Korean American Dream: Immigrants and Small Business in New York City.* Ithaca: Cornell University Press.

Park, Robert E. 1950. *Race and Culture.* Glencoe, Ill.: Free Press.

Portes, Alejandro, and Ruben G. Rumbaut. 1990. *Immigrant America: A Portrait.* Berkeley: University of California Press.

Reinharz, Shulamit. 1992. *Feminist Methods in Social Research.* New York: Oxford University Press.

Rodriguez, Clara E. 1991. *Puerto Ricans: Born in the U.S.A.* Boulder, Colo.: Westview Press. Originally published in 1989.

Roediger, David. 1991. *The Wages of Whiteness: Race and the Making of the American Working Class.* New York: Verso.

Root, Maria P. 1992. *Racially Mixed People in America.* Newbury Park, Calif.: Sage.

Stanfield, John H., and M. Dennis Rutledge, eds. 1993. *Race and Ethnicity in Research Methods.* Newbury Park, Calif.: Sage.

Takaki, Ronald, ed. 1987. *From Different Shores: Perspectives on Race and Ethnicity in America.* New York: Oxford University Press.

————. 1989. *Strangers from a Different Shore: A History of Asian Americans.* Boston: Little, Brown.

Tripura, Prashanta. 1992. "The Colonial Foundation of Pahari Ethnicity." *Journal of Social Studies* 58 (October): 1–16. Dhaka: Centre for Social Studies.

Twine, France Winddance. 1996. "Brown-Skinned White Girls: Class, Culture, and the Construction of White Identity in Suburban Communities." *Gender, Place, and Culture* 3 (2): 205–24.

————. 1998. *Racism in a Racial Democracy: The Maintenance of White Supremacy in Brazil.* New Brunswick, N.J.: Rutgers University Press.

Twine, France Winddance, Jonathan W. Warren, and Francisco Fernandiz. 1991. *Just Black? Multiracial Identity.* New York: Filmmakers Library.

Waldinger, Roger. 1996. "When the Melting Pot Boils Over: The Irish, Jews, Blacks, and Koreans of New York." In *The Bubbling Cauldron,* edited by Michael Peter Smith and Joe R. Feagin. Minneapolis: University of Minnesota Press.

Warren, Jonathan, and France Winddance Twine. 1997. "Whites, the New Minority? Non-Blacks and the Ever-Expanding Boundaries of Whiteness." *Journal of Black Studies* 28 (2): 200–218.

Waters, Mary C. 1990. *Ethnic Options: Choosing Identities in America.* Berkeley: University of California Press.

Wilson, William Julius. 1978. *The Declining Significance of Race.* Chicago: University of Chicago Press.

Wong, Sau-Ling Cynthia. 1993. *Reading Asian American Literature: From Necessity to Extravagance.* Princeton: Princeton University Press.

LINDA ALCOFF
The Problem of Speaking for Others

Consider the following true stories:

1. Anne Cameron, a very gifted white Canadian author, writes several semifictional accounts of the lives of Native Canadian women. She writes them in first person and assumes a Native identity. At the 1988 International Feminist Book Fair in Montreal a group of Native Canadian writers decided to ask Cameron to, in their words, "move over" on the grounds that her writings are disempowering for Native authors. She agrees.[1]

2. After the 1989 elections in Panama are overturned by Manuel Noriega, President Bush of the United States declares in a public address that Noriega's actions constitute an "outrageous fraud" and that "the voice of the Panamanian people has spoken." "The Panamanian people," he tells us, "want democracy and not tyranny, and want Noriega out." He proceeds to plan the invasion of Panama.

These examples demonstrate some of the current practices and discussions around speaking for others in our society. As a type of discursive practice, speaking for others has come under increasing criticism.... There is a strong, albeit contested, current within feminism which holds that speaking for others is arrogant, vain, unethical, and politically illegitimate.... In her important paper, "Dyke Methods," Joyce Trebilcot ... renounces for herself the practice of speaking for others within a lesbian feminist community and argues further that she "will not try to get other wimmin to accept my beliefs in place of their own" on the grounds that to do so would be to practice a kind of discursive coercion and even a violence (1).[2] In anthropology there is also much discussion going on about whether it is possible to adequately or justifiably speak for others....

The recognition that there is a problem in speaking for others has arisen from two sources. First, there is a growing recognition that where one speaks from affects the meaning and truth of what one says, and thus that one cannot assume an ability to transcend one's location. In other words, a speaker's location (which I take here to refer to their social location or social identity) has an epistemically significant impact on that speaker's claims and can serve either to authorize or disauthorize one's speech. The creation of women's studies and African-American studies departments was founded on this very belief: that both the study of and the advocacy for the oppressed must come to be done principally by the oppressed themselves.... The unspoken premise here is simply that a speaker's location is epistemically salient....

The second source involves a recognition that, not only is location epistemically salient, but certain privileged locations are discursively dangerous.[4] In particular, the practice of privileged persons speaking for or on behalf of less privileged persons has actually resulted (in many cases) in increasing or reinforcing the oppression of the group spoken for....

As philosophers and social theorists ... we must begin to ask ourselves whether this is a legitimate authority. Is the discursive practice of speaking for others ever a valid practice, and, if so, what are the criteria for validity? In particular, is it ever valid to speak for others who are unlike me or who are less privileged than me?

We might try to delimit this problem as only arising when a more privileged person speaks for a less privileged one. In this case, we might say that I should only speak for groups of which I am a member. But this does not tell us how groups themselves should be delimited. For example, can a white woman speak for all women simply by virtue of being a woman? If not, how narrowly should we draw the categories? ... The criterion of group identity leaves many unanswered questions for a person such as myself, since I have membership in many conflicting groups but my membership in all of them is problematic. On what basis can we justify a decision to demarcate groups and define membership in one way rather than another? No easy solution to this problem can be found by simply restricting the practice of speaking for others to speaking for groups of which one is a member.

Moreover, adopting the position that one should only speak for oneself raises similarly problematic questions. For example, we might ask, if I don't speak for those less privileged than myself, am I abandoning my political responsibility to speak out against oppression, a responsibility incurred by the very fact of my privilege? If I should not speak for others, should I restrict myself to following their lead uncritically? ...

The answers to these questions will certainly differ significantly depending on who is asking them.... So the question arises as to whether all instances of speaking for others should be condemned and, if not, where the line of demarcation should be drawn.

In order to answer these questions we need to become clearer on the epistemological and metaphysical issues that are involved in the articulation of the problem of speaking for others.... But first I need to explain further my framing of the problem.

In the examples used above, there may appear to be a conflation between the issue of speaking for others and the issue of speaking about others. This conflation was intentional on my part. There is an ambiguity in the two phrases: when one is speaking for others one may be describing their situation and thus also speaking about them. In fact, it may be impossible to speak for others without simultaneously conferring information about them. Similarly, when one is speaking about others, or simply trying to describe their situation or some aspect of it, one may also be speaking in place of them, that is, speaking for them. One may be speaking about others as an advocate or a messenger if the persons cannot speak for themselves. Thus I would maintain that if the practice of speaking for others is problematic, so too must be the practice of speaking about others, since it is difficult to distinguish speaking about from speaking for in all cases.[7] Moreover, if we accept the premise stated above that a speaker's location has an epistemically significant impact on that speaker's claims, then both the practice of speaking for and of speaking about raise similar issues. I will try to focus my remarks in this paper on the practice of speaking for others, but it will be impossible to keep this practice neatly disentangled from the practice of speaking about.

If "speaking about" is also involved here, however, the entire edifice of the "crisis of representation" must be connected as well. In both the practice of speaking for as well as the practice of speaking about others, I am engaging in the act of representing the other's needs, goals, situation, and in fact, who they are. I am representing them as such and such, or in poststructuralist terms, I am participating in the construction of their subject-positions. This act of representation cannot be understood as founded on an act of discovery wherein I discover their true selves and then simply relate my discovery. I will take it as a given that such representations are in every case mediated and the product of interpretation (which is connected to the claim that a speaker's location has epistemic salience). And it is precisely because of the mediated character of all representations that some persons have rejected on political as well as epistemic grounds the legitimacy of speaking for others.

And once we pose it as a problem of representation, we see that not only are speaking for and speaking about analytically close, so too are the practices of speaking for others and speaking for myself. For, in speaking for myself, I am also representing myself in a certain way, as occupying a specific subject-position, having certain characteristics and not others, and so on. In speaking for myself, I (momentarily) create my self just as much as when I speak for others I create their selves—in the sense that I create a public, discursive self, which will in most cases have an effect on the self experienced as interiority. The point is that a kind of representation occurs in all cases of speaking for, whether I am speaking for myself or for others, that this representation is never a simple act of discovery, and that it will most likely have an impact on the individual so represented.

Although clearly, then, the issue of speaking for others is connected to the issue of representation generally, the former I see as a very specific subset of the latter....

There is another sense of representation that may seem also vitally connected here: political representation.... Elected representatives have a special kind of authorization to speak for their constituents, and one might wonder whether such authorization dissolves the problems associated with speaking for others and therefore should perhaps serve as a model solution for the problem. I would answer both yes and no. Elected representatives do have a kind of authorization to speak for others, and we may even expand this to include less formal instances in which someone is authorized by the person(s) spoken for to speak on their behalf.... However, the procurement of such authorization does not render null and void all attendant problems with speaking for others. One is still interpreting the other's situation and wishes (unless perhaps one simply reads a written text they have supplied), and so one is still creating for them a self in the presence of others. Moreover, the power to confer such authorization, and to have power over the designated representative, is rarely present in the instances where one is being spoken for. Intellectual work has certainly not been guided by the mandate to get permission from those whom one is speaking for and about, and it is safe to say that most political representatives have not been strictly guided by the need to get such authorization either. The point here is that the model of political representation cannot be used in all instances of speaking for others, though it may prove instructive when we attempt to formulate responses to the problem.

Finally, the ... problem is a social one, the options available to us are socially constructed, and the practices we engage in cannot be understood as simply the results of autonomous individual choice. Yet to simply replace the "I" with a "we" does not solve this problem because the "we" is also a product of mediating forces and, in a certain sense, is also a fictional construct. Yet, to replace both "I" and "we" with a passive voice that erases agency results in an erasure of responsibility and accountability for one's speech, an erasure I would strenuously argue against (there is too little responsibility-taking already in Western practice!). Further, I would argue that when we sit down to write, or get up to speak, we experience ourselves as making choices.... On the one hand, a theory that explains this experience as involving autonomous choices would be false and ideological, but on the other hand, if we do not acknowledge the activity of choice and the experience of individual doubt, we are denying a reality of our experiential lives.[8] So, despite its inadequacies, I have decided in this article to use the "I" (and in some cases the "we") in articulating this set of problems.

The possibility of speaking for others bears crucially on the possibility of political effectivity. Both collective action and coalitions would seem to require the possibility of speaking for.... Yet, Trebilcot has renounced for herself the act of speaking for others, and the danger of speaking for others has caused many people to question its validity. I want to explore what is at stake in rejecting or validating this as a discursive practice. But first, we must become clearer on the epistemological and metaphysical claims that are implicit in the articulation of the problem.

I

A plethora of sources have argued in this century that the neutrality of the theorizer can no longer, can never again, be sustained, even for a moment.... Who is speaking to whom turns out to be as important for meaning and truth as what is said; in fact what is said turns out to change according to who is speaking and who is listening. Following Foucault, I will call these "rituals of speaking" to identify discursive practices of speaking or writing that involve not only the text or utterance but their position within a social space including the persons involved in, acting upon, and/or affected by the words. Two elements within these rituals will deserve our attention: the positionality or location of the speaker and the discursive context. We can take the latter to refer to the connections and relations of involvement between the utterance/text and other utterances and texts as well as the material practices in the relevant environment, which should not be confused with an environment spatially adjacent to the particular discursive event.

Rituals of speaking are constitutive of meaning, the meaning of the words spoken as well as the meaning of the event. This claim requires us to shift the ontology of meaning from its location in a text or utterance to ... a space that includes the text or utterance but that also includes the discursive context.... [Thus] meaning must be understood as plural and shifting.... Not only what is emphasized, noticed, and how it is understood will be affected by the location of both speaker and hearer, but the truth-value or epistemic status will also be affected.

For example, in many situations when a woman speaks the presumption is against her; when a man speaks he is usually taken seriously.... The rituals of speaking that involve the location of speaker and listeners affect whether a claim is taken as a true, well-reasoned, compelling argument, or a significant idea. Thus, how what is said gets heard depends on who says it, and who says it will affect the style and language in which it is stated, which will in turn affect its perceived significance (for specific hearers)....

This point might be conceded by those who admit to the political mutability of interpretation, but they might continue to maintain that truth is a different matter altogether. And they would be right that the establishment of location's effect on meaning and even on whether something is taken as true within a particular discursive context does not entail that the "actual" truth of the claim is contingent upon its context. However, this objection presupposes a particular conception of truth, one in which the truth of a statement can be distinguished from its interpretation and its acceptance. This concept of truth would make truth by definition independent of the speakers' or listeners' embodied and perspectival location (except in the trivial case of a speaker's indexical statements, e.g., "I am now sitting down").

Thus, the question of whether location bears simply on what is taken to be true or what is really true, and whether such a distinction can he upheld, involves the very difficult problem of the meaning of truth. In the history of Western philosophy, there have existed multiple, competing definitions and ontologies of truth: correspondent, idealist, pragmatist, coherentist, and consensual notions. The dominant view has been that truth represents a relationship of correspondence between a proposition and an extradiscursive reality. In this view, truth is about a realm completely independent of human action and expresses things "as they are in themselves," that is, free of human interpretation.

Arguably since Kant, more obviously since Hegel, it has been widely accepted that an understanding of truth which requires it to be free of human interpretation leads inexorably to skepticism, since it makes truth inaccessible by definition. This creates an impetus to reconfigure the ontology of truth, or its locus, from a place outside human interpretation to one within it....

For example, in a coherentist account of truth, ... truth is defined as an emergent property of what is essentially a discursive situation, when there is a specific form of integration between various elements. Such a view has no necessary relationship to idealism. In terms of the topic of this paper, the social location of the speaker can be said to bear on truth to the extent that it bears on the full meaning of any speech act....

Let me return now to the formulation of the problem of speaking for others. There are two premises implied by the articulation of the problem, and unpacking these should advance our understanding of the issues involved.

> Premise 1: The "ritual of speaking" in which an utterance is located, always bears on meaning and truth such that there is no possibility of rendering positionality, location, or context irrelevant to content.

The phrase "bears on" here should indicate some variable amount of influence short of determination or fixing.

One important implication of this first premise is that we can no longer determine the validity of a given instance of speaking for others simply by asking whether or not the speaker has done sufficient research to justify his or her claims. Adequate research will be a necessary but insufficient criterion of evaluation....

> Premise 2: Certain contexts and locations are allied with structures of oppression, and certain others are allied with resistance to oppression. Therefore all are not politically equal, and, given that politics is connected to truth, all are not epistemically equal.

The claim here that "politics is connected to truth" follows necessarily from premise 1. Rituals of speaking are politically constituted by power relations of domination, exploitation, and subordination. Who is speaking, who is spoken of, and who listens is a result, as well as an act, of political struggle. Simply put, the discursive context is a political arena. To the extent that this context bears on meaning, and meaning is in some sense the object of truth, we cannot make an epistemic evaluation of the claim without simultaneously assessing the politics of the situation.

According to the first premise, though we cannot maintain a neutral voice we may at least all claim the right and legitimacy to speak. But the second premise disauthorizes some voices on grounds which are simultaneously political and epistemic.

The conjunction of premises 1 and 2 suggests that the speaker loses some portion of his or her control over the meaning and truth of his or her utterance. Given that the context of hearers is partially determinant, the speaker is not the master or mistress of the situation. Speakers may seek to regain control here by taking into account the context of their speech, but they can never know everything about this context and with written and electronic communication it is becoming increasingly difficult to know anything at all about the context of reception.

This loss of control may be taken by some speakers to mean that no speaker can be held accountable for their discursive actions. However, a partial loss of control does not entail a complete loss of accountability. Clearly, the problematic of speaking for has at its center a concern with accountability and responsibility. Acknowledging the problem of speaking for others cannot result in eliminating a speaker's accountability.

  ...

II

The first response [to the problem of speaking for] I will consider is to argue that the formulation of the problem with speaking for others involves a retrograde, metaphysically insupportable essentialism that assumes one can read the truth and meaning of what one says straight from the discursive context. This response I will call the "charge of reductionism" response, because it argues that a sort of reductionist theory of justification (or evaluation) is entailed by premises 1 and 2. Such a reductionist theory might, for example, reduce evaluation to a political assessment of the speaker's location, where that location is seen as an insurmountable essence that fixes one, as if one's feet are superglued to a spot on the sidewalk.

...

I, too, would reject reductionist theories of justification and essentialist accounts of what it means to have a location. To say that location bears on meaning and truth is not the same as saying that location determines meaning and truth. And location is not a fixed essence absolutely authorizing one's speech in the way that God's favor absolutely authorized the speech of Moses. Location and positionality should not be conceived as one-dimensional or static, but as multiple and with varying degrees of mobility.[10] What it means, then, to speak from or within a group and/or a location is immensely complex. To the extent that location is not a fixed essence, and to the extent that there is an uneasy, underdetermined, and contested relationship between location on the one hand and meaning and truth on the other, we cannot reduce evaluation of meaning and truth to a simple identification of the speaker's location.

Neither premise 1 nor premise 2 entails reductionism or essentialism. They argue for the relevance of location, not its singular power of determination. Since they do not specify how we are to understand the concept of location, it can certainly be given a nonessentialist meaning.

... [A] second response which I will call the "retreat" response has been popular among some sections of the U.S. feminist movement. This response is simply to retreat from all practices of speaking for and assert that one can only know one's own narrow individual experience and one's "own truth" and can never make claims beyond this. This response is motivated in part by the desire to recognize difference without organizing these differences into hierarchies.

Now, sometimes I think this is the proper response to the problem of speaking for others, depending on who is making it. We certainly want to encourage a more receptive listening on the part of the discursively privileged and discourage presumptuous and oppressive practices of speaking for. But a retreat from speaking for will not result in an increase in receptive listening in all cases; it may result merely in a retreat into a narcissistic yuppie lifestyle in which a privileged person takes no responsibility for her society whatsoever....

However, opting for the retreat response is not always a thinly veiled excuse to avoid political work and indulge one's own desires. Sometimes it is the result of a desire to engage in political work without engaging in what might be called discursive imperialism.

The major problem with such a retreat is that it significantly undercuts the possibility of political effectivity. There are numerous examples of the practice of speaking for that have been politically efficacious in advancing the needs of those spoken for, but I think the example of Menchú is particularly instructive. Menchú is a Quiché Indian born and raised in Guatemala. (I use the term "Indian" to follow R. M.'s choice of words.) Her family suffered the same fate of intense exploitation by the landowners and the government faced by nearly all Guatemalan Indians—a life in which, as of this writing, death by malnutrition and insecticide poisoning is a common occurrence.... Her father and mother were brutally tortured and murdered by the army, as was her brother. Menchú made a decision to learn Spanish, travel to other countries to tell people about the massacres, and, in so doing, try to stop the genocide.

In her autobiographical book Menchú opens with the claim that her story is "not only my life, it's also the testimony of ... all poor Guatemalans. My personal experience is the reality of a whole people" (1). Thus, throughout the book she asserts that she is speaking not only for her family and her community of Quiché Indians, but for all of the 33 other Indian communities of Guatemala, who speak different languages and have different customs and beliefs than the Quiché. She explains their situation with force and eloquence, and decisively refutes any "hierarchy of civilizations" view that would render her agrarian culture as inferior and therefore responsible for its own destruction....

Menchú's words have helped publicize the situation in Guatemala, raise money for the revolution, and bring pressure against the Guatemalan and U.S. governments who have committed the massacres in collusion. The point of this example is not to argue that for Menchú there is no problem of speaking for others. She herself is very aware of the dangers and instructively recounts how this problem was addressed in the revolutionary movement of the Indians....

Yet instead of retreating from speaking for others, Menchú and her compañeros devised methods to decrease the dangers. And despite the significant and complex differences between the many Indian communities in Guatemala, she has not flinched from the opportunity to speak on behalf of all of them.

Trebilcot's version of the retreat response needs to be looked at separately because she agrees that an absolute prohibition of speaking for would undermine political effectiveness. She applies her prohibition against the practice only within a lesbian feminist community. So it might be argued that the retreat from speaking for others can be maintained without sacrificing political effectivity if it is restricted to particular discursive spaces. Why might one advocate such a retreat? ... Given that interpretations and meanings are discursive constructions made by embodied speakers, Trebilcot worries that attempting to persuade or speak for another will cut off that person's ability or willingness to engage in the constructive act of developing meaning. Since no embodied speaker can produce more than a partial account, everyone's account needs to be encouraged (that is, within a specified community ...).

There is much in Trebilcot's discussion with which I agree. I certainly agree that in some instances speaking for others constitutes violence and should be stopped. But there remains a problem with the view that, even within a restricted, supportive community, the practice of speaking for others can be abandoned.

This problem is that Trebilcot's position, as well as a more general retreat position, presumes ... that one can retreat into one's discrete location and make claims entirely and singularly based on that location that do not range over others, that one can disentangle oneself from the implicating networks between one's discursive practices and others' locations, situations, and practices.... But there is no neutral place to stand free and clear in which one's words do not prescriptively affect or mediate the experience of others, nor is there a way to decisively demarcate a boundary between one's location and all others. Even a complete retreat from speech is of course not neutral since it allows the continued dominance of current discourses and acts by omission to reinforce their dominance.

As my practices are made possible by events spatially far from my body so too my own practices make possible or impossible practices of others. The declaration that I "speak only for myself" has the sole effect of allowing me to avoid responsibility and accountability for my effects on others; it cannot literally erase those effects.

Let me offer an illustration of this. The feminist movement in the United States has spawned many kinds of support groups for women with various needs: rape victims, incest survivors, battered wives, and so forth, and some of these groups have been structured around the view that each survivor must come to her own "truth," which ranges only over oneself and has no bearing on others. Thus, one woman's experience of sexual assault, its effect on her and her interpretation of it, should not be taken as a universal generalization to which others must subsume or conform their experience. This view works only up to a point.... [While] it represents real progress beyond the homogeneous, universalizing approach that sets out one road for all to follow, ... it is an illusion to think that, even in the safe space of a support group, a member of the group can, for example, trivialize brother-sister incest as "sex play" without profoundly harming someone else in the group.... Even if the speaker offers a dozen caveats about her views as restricted to her location, she will still affect the other woman's ability to conceptualize and interpret her experience and her response to it. And this is simply because we cannot neatly separate off our mediating praxis that interprets and constructs our experiences from the praxis of others....

Thus, the attempt to avoid the problematic of speaking for by retreating into an individualist realm is based on an illusion.... It is an illusion that I can separate from others to such an extent that I can avoid affecting them. This may be the intention of my speech, and even its meaning if we take that to be the formal entailments of the sentences, but it will not be the effect of the speech, and therefore cannot capture the speech in its reality as a discursive practice. When I "speak for myself" I am participating in the creation and reproduction of discourses through which my own and other selves are constituted.

A further problem with the retreat response is that it may be motivated by a desire to find a method or practice immune from criticism. If I speak only for myself it may appear that I am immune from criticism because I am not making any claims that describe others or prescribe actions for them. If I am only speaking for myself I have no responsibility for being true to your experience or needs.

But surely it is both morally and politically objectionable to structure one's actions around the desire to avoid criticism, especially if this outweighs other questions of effectivity. In some cases perhaps the motivation is not so much to avoid criticism as to avoid errors, and the person believes that the only way to avoid errors is to avoid all speaking for others. . . .

A final response to the problem that I will consider occurs in Gayatri Chakravorty Spivak's rich essay "Can the Subaltern Speak?" In Spivak's essay, the central issue is an essentialist, authentic conception of the self and of experience. She criticizes the "self-abnegating intellectual" pose that Foucault and Deleuze adopt when they reject speaking for others on the grounds that it assumes the oppressed can transparently represent their own true interests. According to Spivak, Foucault and Deleuze's position serves only to conceal the actual authorizing power of the retreating intellectuals, who in their very retreat help to consolidate a particular conception of experience (as transparent and self-knowing). Thus, to promote listening to as opposed to speaking for essentializes the oppressed as nonideologically constructed subjects. But Spivak is also critical of speaking for others: that engages in dangerous representations. In the end Spivak prefers a "speaking to," in which the intellectual neither abnegates his or her discursive role nor presumes an authenticity of the oppressed but still allows for the possibility that the oppressed will produce a "countersentence" that can then suggest a new historical narrative.

This response is the one with which I have the most agreement. We should strive to create wherever possible the conditions for dialogue and the practice of speaking with and to rather than speaking for others. If the dangers of speaking for others result from the possibility of misrepresentation, expanding one's own authority and privilege, and a generally imperialist speaking ritual, then speaking with and to can lessen these dangers.

Often the possibility of dialogue is left unexplored or inadequately pursued by more privileged persons. Spaces in which it may seem as if it is impossible to engage in dialogic encounters need to be transformed in order to do so. . . .

Spivak's arguments, however, suggest that the simple solution is not for the oppressed or less privileged to be able to speak for themselves, since their speech will not necessarily be either liberatory or reflective of their "true interests," if such exist. I would agree with her here, yet it can still be argued, as I think she herself concludes, that ignoring the subaltern's or oppressed person's speech is "to continue the imperialist project" (298). But if a privileging of the oppressed's speech cannot be made on the grounds that its content will necessarily be liberatory, it can be made on the grounds of the very act of speaking itself. Speaking constitutes a subject that challenges and subverts the opposition between the knowing agent and the object of knowledge, an opposition that is key in the reproduction of imperialist modes of discourse. The problem with speaking for others exists in the very structure of discursive practice, no matter its content, and therefore it is this structure itself that needs alteration.

However, while there is much theoretical and practical work to be done to develop such alternatives, the practice of speaking for others remains the best possibility in some existing situations. An absolute retreat weakens political effectivity, is based on a metaphysical illusion, and often effects only an obscuring of the intellectual's power. Therefore, in the remainder of this paper I will ask, how can we lessen the dangers of speaking for?

III

In rejecting a general retreat from speaking for, I am not advocating a return to an un-self-conscious appropriation of the other, but rather that anyone who speaks for others should only do so out of a concrete analysis of the particular power relations and discursive effects involved. I want to develop this point through elucidating four sets of interrogatory practices that are meant to help evaluate possible and actual instances of speaking for. In list form they may appear to resemble an algorithm, as if we could plug in an instance of speaking for and factor out an analysis and evaluation. However, they are meant only to suggest a list of the questions that should be asked concerning any such discursive practice....

1. The impetus to speak must be carefully analyzed and, in many cases, ... fought against. This may seem an odd way to begin discussing how to speak for, but the point is that the impetus to *always* be the speaker and to speak in all situations must be seen for what it is: a desire for mastery and domination. If one's immediate impulse is to teach rather than listen to a less-privileged speaker, one should resist that impulse long enough to interrogate it carefully. Some of us have been taught that by right of having the dominant gender, class, race, letters after our name, or some other criterion we are more likely to have the truth. Others have been taught the opposite, and will speak haltingly, with apologies, if they speak at all.[12]

At the same time, we have to acknowledge that the very decision to "move over" or retreat can occur only from a position of privilege. Those who are not in a position of speaking at all cannot retreat from an action they do not employ. Moreover, making the decision for oneself whether to retreat is an extension or application of privilege, not an abdication of it. Still, it is sometimes called for.

2. We must also interrogate the bearing of our location and context on what it is we are saying, and this should be an explicit part of every serious discursive practice we engage in. Constructing hypotheses about the possible connections between our location and our words is one way to begin. This procedure would be most successful if engaged in collectively with others, by which aspects of our location less highlighted in our own minds might be revealed to us.[13]

One deformed way in which this is too often carried out is when speakers offer up in the spirit of "honesty" autobiographical information about themselves usually at the beginning of their discourse as a kind of disclaimer. This is meant to acknowledge their own understanding that they are speaking from a specified, embodied location without pretense to a transcendental truth. But as Maria Lugones and others have forcefully argued, such an act serves no good end when it is used as a disclaimer against one's ignorance or errors and is made without critical interrogation of the bearing of such an autobiography on what is about to be said. It leaves for the listeners all the real work that needs to be done.... Simple unanalyzed disclaimers do not improve on this familiar situation and may even make it worse to the extent that by offering such information the speaker may feel even more authorized to speak and be accorded more authority by his peers.

3. Speaking should always carry with it an accountability and responsibility for what one says. To whom one is accountable is a political/epistemological choice contestable, contingent, and, as Donna Haraway says, constructed through the process of discursive action. What this entails in practice is a serious and sincere commitment to remain open to criticism and to attempt actively, attentively, and sensitively to "hear" (understand) the criticism. A quick impulse to reject criticism must make one wary.

4. Here is my central point. In order to evaluate attempts to speak for others in particular instances, we need to analyze the probable or actual effects of the words on the discursive and material context. One cannot simply look at the location of the speaker or her credentials to speak, nor can one look merely at the propositional content of the speech; one must also look at where the speech goes and what it does there.

Looking merely at the content of a set of claims without looking at effects of the claims cannot produce an adequate or even meaningful evaluation of them, partly because the notion of content separate from effects does not hold up. The content of the claim, or its meaning, emerges in interaction between words and hearers within a very specific historical situation. Given this, we have to pay careful attention to the discursive arrangement in order to understand the full meaning of any given discursive event. For example, in a situation where a well-meaning First World person is speaking for a person or group in the Third World, the very discursive arrangement may reinscribe the "hierarchy of civilizations" view where the United States lands squarely at the top. This effect occurs because the speaker is positioned as authoritative and empowered, is the knowledgeable subject, while the group in the Third World is reduced, merely because of the structure of the speaking practice, to an object and victim that must be championed from afar, thus disempowered. Though the speaker may be trying to materially improve the situation of some lesser-privileged group, the effect of her discourse is to reinforce racist, imperialist conceptions and perhaps also to further silence the lesser-privileged group's own ability to speak and be heard.[14] This shows us why it is so important to reconceptualize discourse, as Foucault recommends, as an *event*, which includes speaker, words, hearers, location, language, and so on.

All such evaluations produced in this way will ... obtain for a very specific location and cannot be taken as universal. This simply follows from the fact that the evaluations will be based on the specific elements of historical discursive context, location of speakers and hearers, and so forth. When any of these elements is changed, a new evaluation is called for.

Let me illustrate this by applying it to the examples I gave at the beginning. In the case of ... President Bush, when [he] claims that Noriega is a corrupt dictator who stands in the way of democracy in Panama, he repeats a claim that has been made almost word for word by the Opposition movement in Panama. Yet the effects of the two statements are vastly different because the full meaning of the claim changes radically depending on who states it. When the president of the United States stands before the world passing judgment on a Third World government, and criticizing it on the basis of corruption and a lack of democracy, the full meaning of this statement, as opposed to the Opposition's, is to reinforce the prominent Anglo view that Latin American corruption is the primary cause of the region's poverty and lack of democracy, that the United States is on the side of democracy in the region, and that the United States condemns corruption and tyranny. Thus, the effect of the president's speaking for Latin America is to reconsolidate U.S. imperialism by obscuring its true role in the region in torturing and murdering hundreds and thousands of people who have tried to bring democratic and progressive governments into existence. And this will continue to be its effect unless and until he radically alters U.S. foreign policy and admits its history of international mass murder.

CONCLUSION

This issue is complicated by the variable way in which the importance of the source, or location of the author, can be understood. In one view, the author of a text is its "owner" and "originator" credited with creating its ideas and with being their authoritative interpreter. In another view, the original speaker or writer is no more privileged than any other person who articulates those views; and in fact the "author" cannot be identified in a strict sense because the concept of author is an ideological construction many abstractions removed from the way in which ideas emerge and become material forces.[15] Now, does this latter position mean that the source or locatedness of the author is irrelevant?

It need not entail this conclusion, though it might in some formulations. We can deprivilege the "original" author and reconceptualize ideas as traversing (almost) freely in a discursive space, available from many locations, and without a clearly identifiable originary track, and yet retain our sense that source remains relevant to effect. Our meta-theory of authorship does not preclude the material reality that in discursive spaces there is a speaker or writer credited as the author of their utterances ... or that the term feminism itself has been and is associated with a

Western origin. These associations have an effect, an effect of producing distrust on the part of some Third World nationalists, an effect of reinscribing semiconscious imperialist attitudes on the part of some First World feminists. These are not the only possible effects, and some of the effects may not be pernicious, but all the effects must be taken into account when evaluating the discourse of "patriarchy." I don't wish to imply here that I believe the term "patriarchy" should be rejected, or that the responses of hearers must be accepted without argument, but if we ignore the real effects and concentrate only on "content" (as if these could be separated), our evaluation will be seriously inadequate.

The emphasis on effects should not imply, therefore, that an examination of the speaker's location is any less crucial. This latter examination might be (and has been) called doing a genealogy. In this sense a genealogy involves asking how a position or view is mediated and constituted through and within the conjunction and conflict of historical, cultural, economic, psychological, and sexual practices. But it seems to me that the importance of the source of a view, and the importance of doing a genealogy, should be subsumed within an overall analysis of effects, making the central question what the effects are of the view on material and discursive practices through which it traverses and the particular configuration of power relations emergent from these. Source is relevant only to the extent that it has an impact on effect. . . .

In conclusion, I would stress that the practice of speaking for others is often born of a desire for mastery, to privilege oneself as the one who more correctly understands the truth about another's situation or as one who can champion a just cause and thus achieve glory and praise. And the effect of the practice of speaking for others is often, though not always, erasure and a reinscription of sexual, national, and other kinds of hierarchies. I hope that this analysis will contribute to rather than diminish the important discussion going on today about how to develop strategies for a more equitable, just distribution of the ability to speak and be heard. . . .

We must ask further questions about its effects, questions that amount to the following: will it enable the empowerment of oppressed peoples?

NOTES

1. See Maracle, 9–10.

2. Trebilcot is explaining here her own reasoning for rejecting these practices, but she is not advocating that other women join her in this. Thus, her argument does not fall into a self-referential incoherence.

. . .

4. To be privileged here will mean to be in a more favorable, mobile, and dominant position vis-à-vis the structures of power/knowledge in a society. Thus privilege carries with it presumption in one's favor when one speaks. Certain races, nationalities, genders, sexualities, and classes confer privilege, but a single individual (perhaps most individuals) may enjoy privilege with respect to some parts of their identity and a lack of privilege with respect to others. Therefore, privilege must always be indexed to specific relationships as well as to specific locations.

. . .

7. For example, if it is the case that no "descriptive" discourse is normative- or value-free, then no discourse is free of some kind of advocacy, and all speaking about will involve speaking for someone, ones, or something.

8. Another distinction that might be made is between different material practices of speaking for: giving a speech, writing an essay or book, making a movie or TV program, as well as hearing, reading, watching and so on. I will not address the possible differences that arise from these different practices, and will address myself to the (fictional) "generic" practice of speaking for.

. . .

10. See my "Cultural Feminism versus Post-Structuralism." For more discussions on the multidimensionality of social identity, see Lugones and Anzaldúa.

. . .

12. See Said, 219, on this point, where he shows how the "dialogue" between Western anthropology and colonized people ha[s] been nonreciprocal, and supports the need for the Westerners to begin to *stop talking.*

13. See again Said, 212, where he encourages in particular the self-interrogation of privileged speakers.

14. How one evaluates a particular effect is left open; number 4 in my list argues simply that effects must always be taken into account.

15. I like the way Susan Bordo makes this point. In speaking about theories or ideas that gain prominence, she says: "all cultural formations ... (are) complexly constructed out of diverse elements— intellectual, psychological, institutional, and sociological. Arising not from monolithic design but from an interplay of factors and forces, it is best understood not as a discrete, definable position which can be adopted or rejected, but as an emerging coherence which is being fed by a variety of currents, sometimes overlapping, sometimes quite distinct" (135). If ideas arise in such a configuration of forces, does it make sense to ask for an author?

REFERENCES

Alcoff, Linda. "Cultural Feminism versus Post-Structuralism: The Identity Crisis in Feminist Theory." *Signs* 13.3 (Spring 1988): 405–36.

Anzaldúa, Gloria. *Borderlands: La Frontera.* San Francisco: Spinsters Ink/Aunt Lute Book Company, 1987.

Bordo, Susan. "Feminism, Postmodernism, and Gender-Skepticism." *Feminism/Postmodernism.* Ed. Linda Nicholson. New York: Routledge, 1989. 133–56.

Christian, Barbara. "The Race for Theory." *Cultural Critique* 6 (Spring 1987): 51–63.

Clifford, James. "On Ethnographic Authority." *Representations* 1.2: 118–46.

Clifford, James and George E. Marcus, eds. *Writing Culture: The Poetics and Politics of Ethnography.* Berkeley: U of California P, 1986.

Deleuze, Gilles and Michel Foucault. "Intellectuals and Power." *Language, Counter-Memory, Practice.* Ed. Donald Bouchard. Trans. Donald Bouchard and Sherry Simon. Ithaca: Cornell UP, 1977. 205–17.

Gates, Henry Louis, Jr. "Authority, (White) Power and the (Black) Critic: It's All Greek to Me." *Cultural Critique* 7 (Fall 1987): 19–46.

Lugones, Maria. "Playfulness, 'World'-Travelling, and Loving Perception." *Hypatia* 2.2: 3–19.

Lugones, Maria and Elizabeth Spelman. "Have We Got a Theory for You! Cultural Imperialism, Feminist Theory and the Demand for the Women's Voice." *Women and Values: Readings in Recent Feminist Philosophy.* Ed. Marilyn Pearsall. Belmont, CA: Wadsworth Publishing, 1986. 19–31.

Maracle, Lee. "Moving Over." *Trivia* 14 (Spring 1989): 9–12.

Marcus, George E. and Michael Fischer, eds. *Anthropology as Cultural Critique.* Chicago: U of Chicago P, 1986.

Menchú, Rigoberta. *I ... Rigoberta Menchú.* Ed. Elisabeth Burgos-Debray. Trans. Ann Wright. London: Verso, 1984.

Rabinow, Paul. "Discourse and Power: On the Limits of Ethnographic Texts." *Dialectical Anthropology* 10.1 and 2 (July 1985): 1–14.

Said, Edward W. "Representing the Colonized: Anthropology's Interlocutors." *Critical Inquiry* 15.2 (Winter 1989): 205–25.

Spivak, Gayatri. "Can the Subaltern Speak?" *Marxism and Interpretation of Culture.* Ed. Cary Nelson and Lawrence Grossberg. Urbana: U of Illinois P, 1988. 271–313.

Trebilcot, Joyce. "Dyke Methods." *Hypatia* 3.2 (Summer 1988): 1–13.

Trinh T. Minh-ha. *Woman, Native, Other: Writing Postcoloniality and Feminism.* Bloomington: Indiana UP, 1989.

Wilson, Judith. "Down to the Crossroads: The Art of Alison Saar." *Third Text* 10 (Spring 1990): 36.

Index

Credits

Mary Belenky, Blythe McVicker Clinchy, Nancy Rule Goldberger, and Jill Mattuck Tarule, "Procedural Knowledge: Separate and Connected Knowing," in *Women's Ways of Knowing: The Development of Self, Voice, and Mind,* 2d ed. (New York: Basic Books, 1997), pp. 100–130. Reprinted by permission.

Patricia Hill Collins, "Black Feminist Epistemology," in *Black Feminist Thought: Knowledge, Consciousness, and the Politics of Empowerment,* 2nd ed. (New York: Routledge, 2000), pp. 251–272. Copyright © 2000 Routledge. Reproduced by permission of Routledge, a division of Taylor and Francis Group.

Nancy Tuana, "Revaluing Science: Starting from the Practices of Women," in Lynn Hankinson Nelson and Jack Nelson, eds., *Feminism, Science, and the Philosophy of Science* (Dordrecht, The Netherlands, Kluwer Academic, 1997), pp. 17–35. Reprinted by permission of Springer Science and Business Media.

Joan W. Scott, "Experience," in Judith Butler and Joan W. Scott, eds., *Feminists Theorize the Political* (New York: Routledge, 1992), pp. 22–40. Copyright © 1992 Routledge. Reproduced by permission of Routledge, a division of Taylor and Francis Group.

Renée T. White, "Talking about Sex and HIV: Conceptualizing a New Sociology of Experience," in Kim Marie Vaz, ed., *Oral Narrative Research with Black Women* (Thousand Oaks, CA: Sage Publications, 1997), pp. 99–118. Copyright © 1997 Sage Publications. Reprinted by permission of Sage Publications.

Lorraine Code, "Incredulity, Experientialism, and the Politics of Knowledge," in *Rhetorical Spaces: Essays on (Gendered) Locations* (New York: Routledge, 1995), pp. 58–82. Copyright © 1995 Routledge. Reproduced by permission of Routledge, a division of Taylor and Francis Group.

Patricia Hill Collins, "Learning from the Outsider Within: The Social Significance of Black Feminist Thought," *Social Problems* 13, no. 6 (December 1986): 14–32. Reprinted by permission of the University of California Press.

Maria Mies, "The Need for a New Vision: The Subsistence Perspective," in Maria Mies and Vandana Shiva, *Ecofeminism* (London: Zed Books, 1993), pp. 297–324. Reprinted by permission of Zed Books.

Sandra Harding, "Borderlands Epistemologies," in Sandra Harding, *Is Science Multicultural? Postcolonialisms, Feminism, and Epistemologies* (Bloomington: Indiana University Press, 1998), pp. 146–164. Reprinted by permission of Indiana University Press.

Donna Haraway, "Situated Knowledges: The Science Question in Feminism and the Privilege of Partial Perspective" was originally published in *Feminist Studies* 14, no. 3 (Fall 1988): 575–599. Reprinted by permission of the publisher.

Nancy Fraser and Linda J. Nicholson, "Social Criticism without Philosophy: An Encounter between Feminism and Postmodernism," *Communication* 10 (1988): 345–366. Reprinted by permission of the authors.

Anne Opie, "Qualitative Research, Appropriation of the 'Other' and Empowerment," *Feminist Review* 40 (Spring 1992): 52–69. Reprinted by permission of the author.

Alison M. Jaggar, "Love and Knowledge: Emotion in Feminist Epistemology," *Inquiry* 32 (1989): 151–176. Reprinted by permission of Taylor and Francis.

Helen E. Longino, "Values and Objectivity," in *Science as Social Knowledge: Values and Objectivity in Scientific Inquiry* (Princeton, NJ: Princeton University Press, 1990), pp. 62–82. Copyright © 1990 Princeton University Press. Reprinted by permission of Princeton University Press.

Naomi Scheman, "Epistemology Resuscitated: Objectivity as Trustworthiness," in Nancy Tuana and Sandra Morgen, eds., *Engendering Rationalities* (Albany: State University of New York Press, 2001), pp. 23–54. Reprinted by permission of SUNY Press.

Patricia Maguire, "Adjusting the Lens: Participatory Research" and "A Feminist Participatory Research Framework," in Patricia Maguire, *Doing Participatory Research* (Amherst, MA: Center for International Education, 1987), pp. 28–47 and 200–215. Reprinted by permission of the Center for International Education.

Vandana Shiva, "Democratizing Biology: Reinventing Biology from a Feminist, Ecological, and Third World Perspective," in Lynda Birke and Ruth Hubbard, *Reinventing Biology: Respect for Life and the Creation of Knowledge* (Bloomington: Indiana University Press, 1995), pp. 50–71. Reprinted by permission of Indiana University Press.

Barrie Thorne, "You Still Takin' Notes?" Fieldwork and Problems of Informed Consent," *Social Problems* 27, no. 3 (February 1980): 284–297. Reprinted by permission of University of California Press.

Naheed Islam, "Research as an Act of Betrayal: Researching Race in an Asian Community in Los Angeles," in France Winddance Twine and Jonathan W. Warren, eds., *Racing Research, Researching Race: Methodological Dilemmas in Critical Race Studies* (New York: New York University Press, 2000), pp. 35–66. Reprinted by permission of New York University Press.

Linda Alcoff, "The Problem of Speaking for Others," *Cultural Critique* (Winter 1991–1992): 5–32. Reprinted by permission of the University of Minnesota Press.